# Contents

List of Tables                                                    v

Acknowledgments                                                 vii

Map of Europe in 1815                                          viii

Map of Europe in 1914                                            ix

Introduction                                                     xi


Part One
TECHNIQUES OF POLITICAL REPRESSION
IN NINETEENTH-CENTURY EUROPE                                      1

1    SUFFRAGE DISCRIMINATION IN NINETEENTH-CENTURY
     EUROPE                                                       3
     Suffrage Discrimination for Lower Legislative
     Chambers                                                    8
     Suffrage Discrimination for Upper Legislative
     Chambers                                                   25
     Suffrage Discrimination in Local Elections                 29

2    RESTRICTIONS ON FREEDOM OF EXPRESSION AND
     ORGANIZATION                                               34
     Repression of the Press in Nineteenth-Century Europe       34
     Restrictions on Freedom of Assembly and Association        47
     Restrictions on Labor Unions and Strikes                   55
     The Use of Official Violence Against Dissidents            63
     "Dirty Tricks": Secret Police, Mail Opening, and
     Agents Provocateurs                                        69
     Restrictions on Academic Freedom                           74

3    THE VICTIMS OF REPRESSION:
     POLITICAL PRISONERS AND EXILES                             80

Part Two
A HISTORY OF POLITICAL REPRESSION
IN NINETEENTH-CENTURY EUROPE                              89

4    THE AGE OF REPRESSION AND REVOLUTION,
     1815-1850                                            91
     The Economic and Social Structure of Europe,
     1815-1850                                            91
     The European Political Structure and Political
     Mood in 1815                                         102
     Unrest and Rigidity During the Restoration,
     1815-1830                                            109
     The Revolutions of 1830-1832 and their Aftermath     144
     The Revival of Political Dissent, 1840-1846          170
     On the Eve of Revolution, 1846-1847                  180
     The Revolutionary Wave of 1848-1849                  185

5    THE AGE OF REPRESSION AND RECONSTRUCTION,
     1850-1870                                            193
     The Economic and Social Structure of Europe,
     1850-1870                                            193
     A Decade of Reaction, 1850-1858                      200
     The Revival of Dissent and the Reconstruction
     of Europe, 1859-1870                                 215

6    THE AGE OF REPRESSION AND REFORM, 1870-1914          240
     The Economic and Social Structure of Europe,
     1870-1914                                            240
     General Patterns of Repression and Reform,
     1870-1914                                            247
     Regional Differentiation, Repression and Reform,
     1870-1914                                            256


Part Three
SUMMARY AND CONCLUSIONS                                   331

7    POLITICAL REPRESSION IN NINETEENTH-CENTURY
     EUROPE                                               333
     The Impact of Political Repression in
     Nineteenth-Century Europe                            333
     Trends in Nineteenth-Century European Political
     Repression                                          344
     An Afterthought                                      350

     References                                           353

     Index                                                377

# Tables

| 1.1 | Percentage of Total Population Enfranchised for Lower Legislative Chambers in Europe, 1815-1915 | 4 |
| 1.2 | Suffrage Statistics for the Italian Lower Legislative Chamber, 1861-1913 | 9 |
| 1.3 | Suffrage Statistics for the Spanish Lower Legislative Chamber, 1812-1910 | 14 |
| 1.4 | Percentage of Total Population Enfranchised in European Local Elections, 1830-1914 | 30 |
| 1.5 | Voter Distribution in 3-Class Voting Systems in European Cities, 1870-1912 | 32 |
| 2.1 | Repression of the Press in Europe, 1815-1914 | 35 |
| 2.2 | Restrictions on Trade Unions and Strikes in Nineteenth-Century Europe | 56 |
| 2.3 | Incidents in Which 25 or more Civilians Were Killed by Official Forces in Europe, 1815-1914 | 65 |
| 2.4 | Some Noted Persons Fired from Academic Positions for Political Reasons in Europe, 1815-1914 | 76 |
| 5.1 | European Historical Statistics, 1850 and 1870 | 195 |
| 6.1 | European Historical Statistics, 1870 and 1910 | 241 |

# Acknowledgments

I am deeply indebted to Oakland University and to a number of its employees and departments for providing essential assistance that made the preparation and publication of this book possible. Most of all, I am grateful for the invaluable and indispensable assistance of Anne Lalas, editorial associate of the College of Arts and Sciences of Oakland University, who supervised the final typing of the manuscript, read and edited the entire book, and in innumerable ways played a vital role in all decisions involved with style, design and layout of the book. Mrs. Lalas's assistance was not only crucial to the preparation of the final manuscript, but was rendered with great efficiency, patience, enthusiasm and cheerfulness. I am also indebted to the Office of the Dean, College of Arts and Sciences at Oakland University, and to the Department of Political Science for generously allowing me to take two years off from my teaching duties to complete the research and writing of the manuscript, and to the Department of Political Science, the Office of the Provost and the Office of Research Services for providing critical financial assistance. The actual typing of the final manuscript was done primarily, and with great speed and efficiency, by Beth Huffman. She was assisted by Anne Ahearn and Lora Ratliff. In addition to the individuals and offices associated with Oakland University, I am deeply indebted to Peter Stearns, Professor of History and Editor of the Journal of Social History at Carnegie-Mellon University in Pittsburgh, for his enormous encouragement and help throughout the more than five years involved in the preparation of this book. Professor Stearns graciously read hundreds of pages of manuscript and unfailingly provided quick and helpful comments that have improved the final work immeasurably. Needless to say, I alone bear final responsibility for whatever errors and deficiencies remain--and would greatly appreciate their being brought to my attention.

Scattered portions of this book draw on material that appeared previously as "Political Repression and Political Development" in Comparative Social Research, vol. 4 (1981) and as "Freedom of the Press in Europe, 1815-1914," in Journalism Monographs, no. 80 (February 1983). I am most grateful for permission to borrow from these publications.

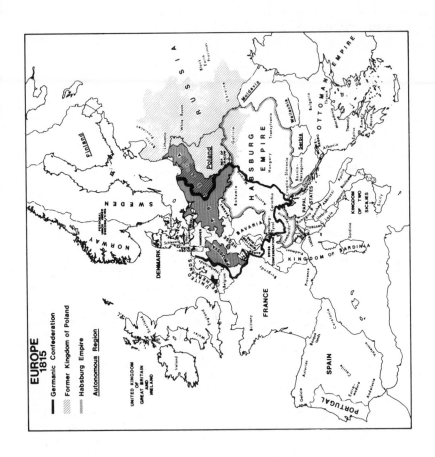

EUROPE
1815

— Germanic Confederation
⫶ Former Kingdom of Poland
⫶ Habsburg Empire
Autonomous Region

UNITED KINGDOM
OF
GREAT BRITAIN
AND
IRELAND

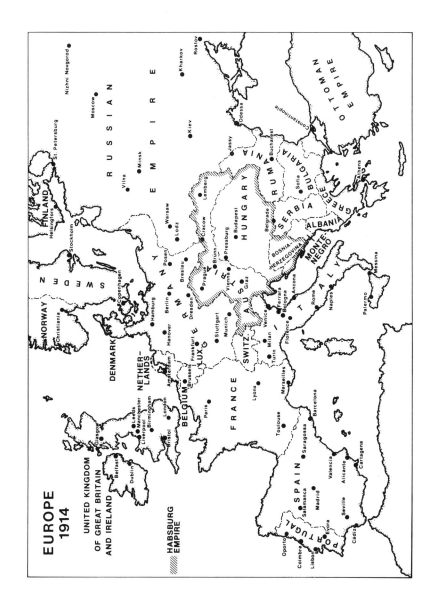

**EUROPE 1914**

UNITED KINGDOM
OF GREAT BRITAIN
AND IRELAND

HABSBURG
EMPIRE

NORWAY

SWEDEN

FINLAND
Helsingfors

St. Petersburg

Christiania

Stockholm

Nizhni Novgorod

Moscow

RUSSIAN EMPIRE

Minsk

Vilna

Kiev

Kharkov

Rostov

DENMARK

Copenhagen

Hamburg

Berlin

Posen

Warsaw

Lodz

NETHER-
LANDS

Amsterdam

GERMANY

Hanover

Breslau

Dresden

Cracow

Lemberg

Jassy

RUMANIA

Bucharest

Sofia

BULGARIA

Odessa

OTTOMAN EMPIRE

Constantinople

BELGIUM

Brussels

LUX.

Frankfurt

Stuttgart

Prague

Brünn

Pressburg

Budapest

HUNGARY

Belgrade

SERBIA

BOSNIA

HERZEGOVINA

MONTE-
NEGRO

ALBANIA

GREECE

Athens

Glasgow

Belfast

Dublin

Leeds

Manchester

Liverpool

Bristol

Birmingham

London

Paris

FRANCE

Munich

Vienna

Graz

AUSTRIA

SWITZ.

Turin

Milan

Venice

Ferrara

Bologna

Ancona

ITALY

Florence

Rome

Naples

Messina

Palermo

Lyons

Marseilles

Toulouse

Barcelona

Saragossa

Valencia

Alicante

Cartagena

SPAIN

Madrid

Salamanca

Seville

Cádiz

PORTUGAL

Lisbon

Coimbra

Oporto

Évora

# Introduction

The primary purpose of this book is to bring together in one convenient volume material related to the subject of political repression in nineteenth-century Europe. Although reference to this topic is made in many general and specialized studies of the period, there currently exists no single source that covers the entire Continent over the time span included herein. Many studies exist that focus on other subjects that affected all of Europe during the nineteenth century--for example, urbanization, industrialization and nationalism--yet the topic of restrictions on political liberty and popular struggles against such restrictions has been curiously neglected, save for specialized treatment of individual countries and/or relatively short time periods. Thus, the reader interested in obtaining an overview of this subject has been forced to consult literally hundreds of books and articles.

This book seeks to be of use to both the specialist in European social and political history and the interested layperson. A considerable amount of general background information is included. Most specialists will be familiar with it, but the average lay reader should find it useful in putting material on political repression into a broader context. Of course, in any study dealing with approximately twenty countries over a one-hundred-year period, it is frequently necessary to reduce, in the words of the great British historian E. J. Hobsbawm, extremely important information "to a paragraph or two, a line, a passing mention or a mere nuance of treatment" where it is not omitted altogether (1979: xiv).

## Some Definitions

I have defined "Europe" to encompass all of the countries of that continent, including the sometimes neglected smaller nations. Far too often, studies of "Europe" turn out to be at most about Great Britain, France, Italy, Germany, Russia and the Habsburg Empire, even though in 1900 75 million Europeans lived in Scandinavia, Ireland, Switzerland, the Low Countries, the Balkans and Iberia.

I have defined the nineteenth century as the period between the defeat of Napoleon at Waterloo (1815) and the outbreak of World War I

(1914). Obviously this period, technically, does not include all of the nineteenth century and includes part of the twentieth century. However, it has become a historical convention to refer to these one hundred years as the nineteenth century; and since the approach of this book is to treat political repression and the struggles against it as a part of the general process of European modernization, this periodization is an appropriate one. These one hundred years marked a crucial transition period between Europe of the "old order" preceding the French Revolution and modern European society. This periodization also seemed particularly appropriate because the 1815-1914 era in Europe is in many ways quite analogous to the contemporary era in the "developing" world. Most of the current problems faced by the countries of Latin America, Asia and Africa today are the same problems that Europe encountered in the nineteenth century: the adjustment of societies to the impact of such developments as massive population growth, rapid industrialization and urbanization, revolutions in transportation and communication, and especially the emergence of formerly "invisible," poverty-striken masses, who are increasingly aware, educated and politicized and demand improvements in their political and social rights. Although it is not a pleasant fact to recall, most nineteenth-century European regimes responded to rising lower-class demands for reforms and political power in the same repressive manner which many present-day Third World regimes do.

Except in a few isolated instances--for example, the suppressions of the 1871 Paris Commune and of the 1907 Rumanian peasant rebellion--nineteenth-century European political repression did not involve mass executions or killings, and nineteenth-century European regimes rarely if ever engaged in random killings simply to create a climate of terror. Therefore, the analogy that is suggested between nineteenth-century Europe and current events in the developing world should not be interpreted to suggest that such recent experiences as the mass slaughters and "disappearances" in Cambodia, Uganda, Argentina, Guatamala and elsewhere are typical of nineteenth-century Europe. On the other hand, nineteenth-century European political repression was often sufficiently intense to destroy opposition groups or drive them underground for years or decades, and certainly there is nothing inherent in "western civilization" that grants immunity from mass slaughter, as the twentieth century in Europe conclusively demonstrates.

In my book Political Repression in Modern America I devoted several pages to a discussion of a definition of political repression: "Political repression consists of government action which grossly discriminates against persons or organizations viewed as presenting a fundamental challenge to existing power relationships or key governmental policies, because of their perceived political beliefs" (1978: xvi). Admittedly, this definition is not entirely adequate, since it is not specific enough to allow an absolute determination as to whether or not all possibly politically repressive acts fall within its confines. However, after having studied the subject of political repression for about ten years, I have concluded that this definition is about as specific as it can be, because the variety of ways in which political repression can be implemented defy even the most expert lexicographer. From a practical standpoint, the types of political repression especially focussed on in this book are relatively straightforward, involving the denial of liberties, such as freedom of the press, speech, assembly and association, and the right to vote, either generally or for certain segments of populations whose particular beliefs are undesirable according to the perception of the political authorities. Political repression, in this perspective, can be peaceful and "legal" as well as violent and "illegal." An example of perfectly peaceful and legal repression that was of incalculable import in nineteenth-century Europe was the enfranchisement for most or all of the period in almost every country of only the wealthiest segments of the population, for fear that, if the poor were allowed to vote, there might be a "legal" social and political revolution.

## The Methodology and Plan of the Book

Because of the enormous amount of material available that in some way touches on the subject of nineteenth-century European political repression, it was necessary to limit the scope of my research. To quote Hobsbawm again, "An enormous amount has already been written about the nineteenth century, and every year adds to the height and bulk of the mountain ranges which darken the historical sky ... the quantity of information which must be absorbed is far too great for even the most erudite and encyclopedic scholar" (1979: xiii-xiv). In order to cope with this historical mass, I generally restricted my reading to secondary sources published in English since about 1940, although even so this left thousands of sources to consult, not all of which could be read. In order to avoid flooding the book with footnotes, I have used citations only when material is directly quoted or statistical material is used in tables. However, following the selected list of sources at the end of the book is an analytical guide that indicates which sources were relied upon most heavily for various subjects.

The book is divided into three major parts. In the first part, there is a summary, with numerous examples taken from all of the European countries, of the major techniques used to repress political dissent throughout the nineteenth century and also of means by which dissidents attempted to evade such repression. The following techniques are discussed in this part of the book, roughly in order of their overall importance in affecting nineteenth-century European history and as contemporary political issues: suffrage restrictions, limitations on freedom of the press, assembly, and association, restrictions on trade unions and strikes, the use of violence and secret police techniques against dissidents, and restrictions on academic freedom. I have also included in this part of the book a discussion of the victims of political repression: political prisoners and exiles.

In the second part of the book, I have attempted to construct a chronological history of political repression in nineteenth-century

Europe, set in a general context of social and political history. Within this part of the book, I refer frequently to specific techniques of political repression, usually without detailed elaboration, on the assumption that the reader has already perused the first part of the book. However, some readers may find it more congenial to read the second part of the book first, and they can probably do so without serious difficulty. The chronological history is divided into three major time periods: 1815-50, 1850-70, 1870-1914. The major dividing lines within the 1815-1914 period are the suppression of the European revolutions of 1848-49 and the Franco-Prussian War (1870) and its side-effect, the Paris Commune of 1871. These divisions are fairly standard in European historiography because they coincide with more general benchmarks in European social and political history. They suit my purposes also. In a rough sense, during the 1815-50 period, the "old order" remained relatively intact, and in most countries almost all political opposition and groups outside the traditional ruling clerical-aristocratic-monarchial coalition were met with repression. The 1850-70 period in many European countries marked a general industrialization "takeoff" period, and one in which the upper middle class was accepted into the governing coalition, although lower-class attempts to influence politics still met mostly with repression. During the 1870-1914 period, in most countries repression became less intense and the lower classes were finally able to organize and obtain varying degrees of political influence.

Within these three major time divisions, I have organized the material somewhat differently, depending upon what seemed the most effective and efficient way to present it. For the period between 1815 and 1870 I have made chronological subdivisions (1815-30, 1830-39, 1840-49, 1850-58, 1859-1870), and in most cases within these sub-divisions European countries are grouped together to the extent they experienced similar developments. I have subdivided the 1870-1914 period by regions of Europe (northwestern, central, and eastern and southern) that experienced similar developments, and within those divisions each country is discussed over the entire 45-year period. In short, the primary subdivision between 1815 and 1870 is by time, and the primary subdivision between 1870 and 1914 is by region.

The reason for this difference in approach within the chronology is quite simple. Most European countries were affected to some degree during the 1815-70 period by certain events relevant to political repression, such as the 1819-21, 1830-2 and 1848-9 periods of widespread unrest, which tended to create similar patterns of response across the Continent. In particular, the major continental European regions--France, Germany, Russia, Italy, and the Habsburg Empire--all exhibited roughly similar trends in terms of heightened or decreased repression on a cyclical basis within the 1815-70 period. In the other European countries, a similar, although generally less intense pattern was exhibited. Therefore, a subdivision by time, and within that by region--usually between the major continental territories and the other European countries--seemed to be the most sensible approach to the 1815-70 period. After 1870, with the major exception of the 1871 Paris Commune, there were relatively few events that triggered similar responses relevant to political repression across the Continent. Instead, the response of European countries to political dissent after 1870 became increasingly differentiated by region. In general, the northwestern countries, which were the most economically advanced regions, became increasingly democratic after 1870, the eastern and southern countries--which were also the most backwards economically--tended to respond to dissent almost exclusively with repression, while the central European countries were "in between" both in economic development and in responses to dissent. Since the differentiated response to protest after 1870 appears to have been closely related to general differences in economic and social development, it seemed to make sense to discard the all-European time subdivision used previously as an organizing approach and shift to a regional analysis. Skillful use of the index will allow the reader to construct a coherent chronological account of any particular country during the entire period covered in the book. For a quick refresher in nineteenth-century European political geography the maps on pages viii and ix should prove helpful.

In the final part of the book, I have briefly summarized the most important information contained in the preceding sections and have tried to analyze the long- and short-term importance of political repression in the nineteenth century for European historical development during that century and afterwards. In short, my argument is that political repression and the struggle against it was one of the great themes of nineteenth-century Europe, helping to shape fundamental aspects of European political development and in some cases leaving historical legacies that continue to effect European society and politics even today. I also suggest that, unfortunately, political repression seems to be a "normal" part of the process of political modernization, and that, particularly given the advanced military technologies supplied so readily to the developing countries by today's "advanced" nations, it is likely to be a major theme in the news for a long time to come.

Part One

# Techniques of Political Repression in Nineteenth-Century Europe

Chapter 1

# Suffrage Discrimination in Nineteenth-Century Europe

Universal suffrage, according to Danish Prime Minister Jacob Estrup (1875-94), a conservative landowner, was the "greatest folly in this otherwise so abundantly foolish age." It would add, he stated, to "liberalism, radicalism, socialism and anarchism" and ultimately to the "collapse of everything we have learned, to respect and love" (Woodhouse 1974: 203). Similarly, François Guizot, the conservative premier of France (1847-8) termed universal suffrage "absurd." Under such a system, he said, "Every living creature would be granted political rights" (Fejto 1973: 77). Conservative legislator Robert Lowe, in opposing a proposed expansion of the suffrage in the United Kingdom in 1866, declared, "It is the order of Providence that men should be unequal, and it is ... the wisdom of the State to make its institutions conform to that order" (Smith 1966: 81).

Such sentiments were by no means confined to European conservatives during the nineteenth century. Until late in the century, most European "liberals," who demanded extension of the suffrage to encompass the middle and professional classes, were among the most ardent foes of enfranchising the poor. Thus, the Whig (liberal) historian and parliamentarian Thomas Macaulay declared in 1842 that universal suffrage would be "fatal to the purposes for which government exists" and was "utterly incompatible with the existence of civilization" (Arnstein 1971: 32). The writer and social critic Thomas Carlyle termed universal suffrage the "Devil-appointed way" to count heads, one that would equate "Judas Iscariot to Jesus Christ" (Smith 1966: 242). Odilon Barrot, a leader of the liberal opposition to the Guizot regime in France, declared:

> "Vox populi, vox Dei," which gives to a majority the infallibility of God is the most dangerous and the most despotic absurdity that has ever emerged from a human brain. If you want to ruin a state, give it universal suffrage (Fasel 1970: 21).

In fact, as Table 1.1 indicates, the great majority of European countries adopted highly discriminatory suffrage systems for lower

Table 1.1:  Percentage of Total Population Enfranchised
for Lower Legislative Chambers  in Europe, 1815-1915

| | Austria | Belgium | Bulgaria | Denmark | Finland | France | Germany | Greece | Hungary | Italy |
|---|---|---|---|---|---|---|---|---|---|---|
| 1815 | 0 | 1.4 | – | 0 | (7) | 0.3 | | – | 1 | – |
| 1820 | 0 | 1.4 | – | 0 | (7) | 0.3 | | – | 1 | – |
| 1825 | 0 | 1.4 | – | 0 | (7) | 0.3 | | – | 1 | – |
| 1830 | 0 | 1.1 | – | 0 | (7) | 0.5 | | 0 | 1 | – |
| 1835 | 0 | 1.1 | – | 0 | (7) | 0.5 | | 0 | 1 | – |
| 1840 | 0 | 1.1 | – | 0 | (7) | 0.6 | | 0 | 1 | – |
| 1845 | 0 | 1.1 | – | 0 | (6) | 0.7 | | 23 | 1 | – |
| 1850 | 0 | 1.8 | – | 15 | (6) | 20 | | 23 | 0 | – |
| 1855 | 0 | 1.8 | – | 15 | (6) | 25 | | 23 | 0 | – |
| 1860 | 0 | 2.0 | – | 15 | (6) | 25 | | 23 | 0 | 1.7 |
| 1865 | 5.9 | 2.2 | – | 15 | (6) | 25 | | 23 | 6.1 | 2.0 |
| 1870 | 5.9 | 2.2 | – | 15 | (6) | 26 | | 23 | 6.5 | 2.0 |
| 1875 | 6 | 2.2 | – | 15 | (6) | 27 | 19 | 23 | 5.1 | 2.1 |
| 1880 | 5.9 | 2.2 | (22) | 16 | (6) | 27 | 20 | 23 | 5.2 | 2.2 |
| 1885 | 7.2 | 2.2 | (22) | 16 | (6) | 28 | 20 | 23 | 5.4 | 8 |
| 1890 | 7.2 | 2.2 | (22) | 16 | (5) | 29 | 21 | 23 | 6.3 | 9.1 |
| 1895 | 7.2 | 22 | (22) | 16 | (5) | 29 | 21 | 23 | 5.6 | 6.7 |
| 1900 | 19 | 22 | (22) | 17 | (5) | 29 | 21 | 23 | 6.1 | 6.9 |
| 1905 | 20 | 22 | 22 | 17 | 4.5 | 29 | 21 | 23 | 6 | 7.5 |
| 1910 | 21 | 23 | 23 | 17 | 45 | 29 | 22 | 23 | 6.2 | 8.3 |
| 1915 | 21 | 23 | 25 | 18 | 45 | 29 | 22 | 23 | 7.7 | 23.2 |

Explanations for  Table  1.1:  A  dash  (–)  indicates  this
country did  not  exist  as  a geopolitical  entity  at  the  time.
A zero (0) indicates the lack of a popularly elected national
legislative  assembly.   Data  enclosed  in  parentheses  are
estimated based on the provisions of electoral laws and/or
known data for other dates.  All other data are precise
calculations  or  interpolations  within  known  data.   Had
universal manhood suffrage been in effect, 20-25 per cent of
the   total   population   of   each   country   would   have   been
enfranchised;   universal   adult   suffrage   would   have
enfranchised 40-50 per cent of each country's population.
The figures for Denmark after 1910, Finland after 1905 and
Norway after 1905 reflect total or partial enfranchisement of
women.   In Germany before 1870 and in Switzerland before 1850
the  confederation  legislatures  were  elected  by  state  or
cantonal governments, which themselves were elected on widely
varying franchises.  The data for Belgium before 1830 and for

| | Netherlands | Norway | Portugal | Rumania | Russia | Serbia | Spain | Sweden | Switzerland | United Kingdom |
|------|------|------|------|------|------|------|------|------|------|------|
| 1815 | 3.9 | 10 | 0 | 0 | 0 | 0 | 0 | (10) | | 2.5 |
| 1820 | 3.9 | 10 | 0 | 0 | 0 | 0 | (20) | (10) | | 2.5 |
| 1825 | 3.7 | 9.1 | 0 | 0 | 0 | 0 | 0 | (9) | | 2.5 |
| 1830 | 3.5 | 8.5 | 0 | (2) | 0 | 0 | 0 | 9 | | 2.1 |
| 1835 | 3.4 | 8.3 | (15) | (2) | 0 | 0 | 0.1 | 8 | | 3.2 |
| 1840 | 3.3 | 8.1 | (10) | (2) | 0 | 0 | 3.4 | 7 | | 3.4 |
| 1845 | 3.1 | 8 | .7 | (2) | 0 | 0 | 0.8 | 7 | | 3.6 |
| 1850 | 2.5 | 8 | .7 | 0 | 0 | 0 | 1.1 | 6 | 22 | 4 |
| 1855 | 2.7 | 7.8 | 9 | 0 | 0 | 0 | 4.6 | 5 | 22 | 4.3 |
| 1860 | 2.7 | 7.8 | 9 | 0.1 | 0 | 0 | 1.0 | 6 | 22 | 4.5 |
| 1865 | 2.7 | 7.5 | 9 | (15) | 0 | 0 | 2.7 | 5.9 | 22 | 4.4 |
| 1870 | 2.9 | 7.5 | 9 | (15) | 0 | (20) | 24 | 5.6 | 22 | 8 |
| 1875 | 2.9 | 7.5 | 9 | (15) | 0 | (20) | 24 | 5.8 | 22 | 8.7 |
| 1880 | 3.0 | 7.6 | 14 | (15) | 0 | (20) | 5.1 | 6 | 23 | 8.7 |
| 1885 | 3.0 | 9.4 | 18 | (15) | 0 | (20) | 4.7 | 6 | 23 | 8.7 |
| 1890 | 6.5 | 9.8 | 18 | (15) | 0 | (20) | 24 | 6 | 22 | 16 |
| 1895 | 6.2 | 11 | 10 | (15) | 0 | (20) | 24 | 6.2 | 22 | 16 |
| 1900 | 11 | 20 | 10 | (15) | 0 | (20) | 24 | 7 | 22 | 16 |
| 1905 | 14 | 20 | 10 | 16 | (20) | 23 | 24 | 8.1 | 22 | 18 |
| 1910 | 14 | 33 | 12 | 16 | (15) | 23 | 24 | 19 | 22 | 18 |
| 1915 | 16 | 45 | 8 | 16 | (15) | 23 | 24 | 20 | 23 | 18 |

Hungary before 1870 are for provincial legislatures; until 1830 Belgium was part of the United Netherlands along with the Dutch Netherlands, and before 1867 Hungary was an integral part of Austria. Finland was under Russian sovereignty but had its own legislature throughout the 1815-1914 period. Norway was united with Sweden through allegiance to the Swedish king, although autonomous in domestic affairs, until 1905. Belgium (1893-1919), Austria (1861-1907), Rumania (1866-1917), and Russia (1905-1917) all used class-weighted voting systems (see text for explanation).

Major sources: Mackie and Rose 1974; Rokkan and Meyriat 1969; Anderson and Anderson 1967: 320; Garver 1978: 349; Rokkan 1967; Wandwycz 1974: 318; Rothschild 1959: 44; Dedijer 1974: 379; Payne 1973: 474, 543; Seton-Watson 1934: 357; Seton-Watson 1972: 467; Kent 1937: 26; Neufeld 1961: 524; Walker 1973.

legislative chambers for most or all of the 1815-1915 period. Universal male suffrage (which is what was meant when universal suffrage was discussed) at age 21 would have enfranchised about 25 per cent of the European population during the nineteenth century, while universal adult (including female) suffrage would have given the vote to about 50 per cent of the population. Female suffrage at the national level was not granted by any European country before 1915 save Finland (after 1906) and Norway (after 1907). While disenfranchisement of women reflected a general discrimination against rich and poor females alike, disenfranchisement of men was based clearly on class. As late as 1880, as a result of class-biased suffrage systems, less than 10 per cent of the total population was enfranchised in Austria, Belgium, Finland, Hungary, Italy, the Netherlands, Norway, Russia, Spain, Sweden, and the United Kingdom.

The clear purpose of the class-biased suffrage systems that prevailed in most European countries for all or part of the nineteenth century was to protect the wealth and power of the dominant elements of European society. This purpose was rarely articulated as directly as Macaulay's warning that the "populace" would use political power to "plunder every man in the kingdom who had a good coat on his back and a good roof over his head" (Langer 1969: 55). Instead, disenfranchisement of the poor, or the extra-weighting of the votes of the wealthy if the poor were enfranchised, was usually justified by more lofty and less obviously self-interested principles. The primary justification, repeated over and over again by both conservatives and liberals, was that wealth and property were signs of intelligence and ability, and that it was only reasonable to entrust the control of state policies to those who had demonstrated their qualifications by material well-being. Since, according to this argument, any talented person was capable of acquiring wealth, the denial of universal suffrage did not discriminate against poverty, but against ignorance, sloth and general incapacity. Thus, "enrichissez-vous" (get rich) was the solution made famous by Guizot for those who complained they could not vote under the French laws that disenfranchised over 99 per cent of the population before 1848.

The thesis that wealth and property were the best indicators of electoral ability was so frequently espoused that Spanish liberals noted in the prologue to their 1837 electoral law--which disenfranchised 98 per cent of the population--that "in all the nations of Europe which have proceeded us in the ways of representative government, private property has been considered the only proper indication of electoral capacity" (Marichal 1977: 105). In blunter terms, a member of the Spanish legislature told that body in 1845 that poverty was a "sign of stupidity" (Carr 1966: 237), and Italian Prime Minister Francesco Crispi (1887-91, 1893-6) told his parliament that the common people were "corrupted by ignorance, gnawed by envy and ingratitude, and should not be allowed any say in politics" (Smith 1959: 175). Francisco Romero Robledo, who became notorious for his election rigging as minister of the interior in late nineteenth-century Spain, told the Spanish legislature in 1876:

I have fought universal suffrage all my life because I consider it to be an instrument of tyranny and an enemy of liberty. Suffrage is not an independent right but a political function that demands conditions of capacity and most Spaniards do not have sufficient culture or intelligence to understand the public interest when they deposit their slip of paper in the electoral urn (Kern 1974: 38).

Supplementing the argument that wealth per se was a sign of electoral capacity was a related and sometimes intertwined argument that the wealthy had more of a stake in and made more of a contribution to society, and therefore were more deserving of a say in determining governmental policy. Thus, the Prussian aristocrat Baron Adolf Senfft von Pilsach declared:

I cannot consider it just and reasonable that a simple working man has as much voice as his employer who hires hundreds or thousands like him, gives them bread and feeds their families (Hamerow 1974: 211-12).

When a class-weighted voting system was introduced in Prussia in 1849, the Prussian ministry defended it as allowing the "several classes of the people that proportional influence corresponding to their actual importance in the life of the state" (Anderson and Anderson 1967: 307). When a similar system was introduced for local elections in Russia in 1864, the government noted that voting was based on the principle that "participation in the conduct of local affairs should be proportionate to everyone's economic interest" (Mosse 1962: 79).

Another argument used to justify restricting or biasing the suffrage in favor of the wealthy was that those with money were most qualified to determine public policy because only they had enough leisure to carefully consider affairs of state. Thus, the leading French Restoration liberal-radical Benjamin Constant declared:

Those whom poverty keeps in eternal dependence and who are condemned to daily work are no more enlightened on public affairs than children. ... Property alone, by giving sufficient leisure, renders a man capable of exercising his political rights (Artz 1929: 206).

A final argument used by those opposing a broad suffrage was that the wealthy would pursue a "disinterested" approach to politics since their affluence allowed them to ignore their own interests, while the poor would always be influenced by their need to obtain more money and would always pursue selfish policies. This argument sounds ludicrous today, since the basic purpose of class-biased suffrage systems was precisely to preserve the existing structure of power and wealth, an aim hardly disinterested from the standpoint of those who benefitted from that structure. Nevertheless, it was made frequently and perhaps even innocently by those whose vision was so clouded by upper-class bias that to them such a system was normal and anything else was clouded by selfish interests. Thus, one of the great British aristocrats, Lord Robert Cecil, who as the Marquis of Salisbury served three times as prime minister (1885-6, 1886-92, 1895-1902), argued that only by preserving political power for the wealthy would politics "not be defiled by the taint of sordid greed." Under a democratic suffrage, he maintained, "passion is not the exception but the rule," with power entrusted to those whose minds "are unused to thought and undisciplined to study." Under such a system, he argued, "the rich would pay all the taxes and the poor make all the laws" (Tuchman 1967: 11).

## Suffrage Discrimination for Lower Legislative Chambers

The most common device for excluding the poor from voting for lower legislative chambers was to make the franchise dependent upon a minimum amount of income, a minimum amount of property, and/or the payment of a minimum amount of direct tax based on property or income. Thus, under the French constitution of 1814-30, to vote one had to pay 300 francs ($60) per year in direct taxes, a requirement that reduced the electorate to less than 100,000 (about 0.3 per cent) in a population of about 30 million. Following the July 1830 revolution in France--partly sparked by the attempt of King Charles X (1824-30) to reduce the suffrage to about 25,000--the franchise was slightly liberalized. Under the 1830 constitution, which remained in effect until universal male suffrage was introduced in 1848, the direct tax requirement was reduced to 200 francs per year, thus enfranchising in 1842 about 220,000 people in a population of 34 million.

More or less similar systems were the norm for most European countries during all or most of the nineteenth century. Thus, in Belgium, the suffrage under the electoral law of March 1831 depended upon a direct tax payment requirement that enfranchised fewer than 50,000 Belgians (about 1 per cent) in a population of 4 million in 1831. In 1848, the tax requirement was liberalized, increasing the eligible Belgian electorate to about 80,000 in a population of 4.5 million. The 1848 law remained in effect until 1893, when Belgium adopted a system of universal male suffrage with extra votes for the wealthy and highly educated.

Uniquely among European countries, Italy from 1860 to 1912 required adult males to be literate and to pay a minimum direct tax in order to vote. The Italian system was somewhat mitigated by waiver of the tax payment requirement for those demonstrating a certain level of education, which in 1882 was lowered to four years of primary schooling. Before that year, only about 2 per cent of the Italian population could vote, and even afterwards the suffrage was restricted to less than 10 per cent of the citizenry (see Table 1.2). The literacy/education/tax-payment barrier proved especially pernicious in its discrimination against southern Italy, the poorest area of the country, which received little attention from the Italian government partly because so few of its inhabitants could cast ballots. Thus, in 1871, 46 per cent of all adults in northern Italy were literate, compared with only 16 per cent of adult southern Italians. Universal male suffrage was finally introduced in Italy in 1912.

Table 1.2 Suffrage Statistics for the Italian Lower Legislative Chamber, 1861-1913

| Date | Italian Population | Enfranchised Voters | % of Total Population Eligible to Vote |
|------|--------------------|--------------------|--------------------------------------|
| 1861 | 25,017,000 | 418,696 | 1.7 |
| 1865 | | 504,263 | 2.0 |
| 1867 | | 498,208 | 1.9 |
| 1870 | | 530,018 | 2.0 |
| 1871 | 26,801,000 | | |
| 1874 | | 571,939 | 2.1 |
| 1876 | | 605,007 | 2.2 |
| 1880 | | 621,896 | 2.2 |
| 1881 | 28,450,000 | | |
| 1882 | | 2,017,829 | 6.9 |
| 1886 | | 2,420,327 | 8.1 |
| 1890 | 30,300,000 | 2,752,658 | 9.1 |
| 1892 | | 2,934,445 | 9.4 |
| 1895 | | 2,120,185 | 6.7 |
| 1897 | | 2,120,909 | 6.6 |
| 1900 | | 2,248,509 | 6.9 |
| 1901 | 32,475,000 | | |
| 1904 | | 2,541,327 | 7.5 |
| 1909 | | 2,930,473 | 8.3 |
| 1911 | 34,671,000 | | |
| 1913 | | 8,443,205 | 23.2 |

Sources: Neufeld 1961: 524; Mitchell 1978: 5.

In addition to Italy, several other countries waived normal tax, income, or property requirements for those holding certain educational degrees or, in some cases, holding certain official positions and middle-class occupations. Norway was especially liberal in this regard, enfranchising after 1814 all government officials as well as citizens licensed as merchants and artisans. Spain after 1836 and Hungary after 1865 enfranchised a wide variety of persons following middle-class and professional occupations (known as capacidades in Spain and honoratiores in Hungary). Among those thus enfranchised in

Hungary regardless of wealth were scholars, surgeons, artists, lawyers, engineers, teachers, and ministers. The attempt by these and several other countries to give extra weight to or at least to enfranchise all "responsible" citizens regardless of wealth--with the hope of thus eliminating from the ranks of the disaffected the most educated and articulate segments of the population, while still short-weighting or disenfranchising the rabble--gave rise to some electoral laws of staggering complexity. Thus, the Dutch electoral reform of 1896, which doubled the electorate by enfranchising 12 per cent of the population, provided that adult Dutch males could obtain the suffrage by: 1) paying one or more direct taxes at specified levels; 2) demonstrating they were householders or lodgers paying a minimum rent; 3) demonstrating they owned or rented boats of over 24 tons capacity; 4) demonstrating they earned an annual wage of about $115; 5) possessing a savings account of about $20 or owning about $40 in government bonds; or 6) passing a recognized examination qualifying for certain offices or employment or giving the right to work in specified professions. That even these seemingly liberal qualifications excluded about half of all Dutch male adults clearly demonstrated the poverty of the population.

A similarly convoluted franchise law introduced in Russia in 1907 led one American academic to conclude, "Even the educated man could not find his place in this complicated system; the uneducated man was quite lost" (Anderson and Anderson 1967: 336). The official Hungarian government organ conceded that Hungary's 1874 electoral law--which reduced the suffrage from 900,000 to 700,000--was so complex that "the confusion of Babel has really been erected into law" (Seton-Watson 1934: 402). In 1912, there existed in the United Kingdom, according to electoral expert J.A. Pease, 11 distinct ways of qualifying for the franchise, with a total of 19 different variations altogether. Pease told the House of Commons in June 1912, "The intricacy of our franchise law is without parallel in the history of the civilized world" (Blewitt 1965: 30).

The most extraordinary class-biased suffrage systems in nineteenth-century Europe were those that gave extra votes to the wealthy and/or well educated (plural voting systems) or that separated citizens into voting categories by class criteria and extra-weighted upper-class votes (variously known as class, curial or estate voting systems). The Belgian plural voting system of 1893, in effect until equal and universal male suffrage was adopted in 1919 (along with limited female suffrage), enfranchised 1,354,891 Belgians (21 per cent of the population) compared with the previous tax-based system that gave the suffrage to 136,775. However, while all 25-year-old males were enfranchised in 1893, wealthy Belgians received a second vote. Those with a higher education, regardless of wealth, received two extra votes. No one could cast more than three votes. In 1893 under this system 850,000 Belgians had one vote; 290,000 voted twice; and 220,000 cast three votes. Thus, the 510,000 Belgians with plural votes, with a total of 1.24 million votes, could outpoll the remaining 850,000 Belgians. Plural voting was also allowed in the United Kingdom throughout the 1815-1914 period, in France between 1820 and 1830, in the lower two houses of the Swedish and Finnish diets (until 1866 and 1906, respectively), and in Russia between 1905 and 1907. Plural voting was also allowed on a trivial scale in Austria between 1861 and 1896, and on a wide scale there between 1896 and 1907.

About 7 per cent of the electorate in the United Kingdom--those meeting more than one franchise requirement or meeting property requirements in more than one constituency--cast plural votes in 1911, and in some cases individuals cast dozens of votes. Thus, the London Daily News of December 20, 1910, noted that a man "may own 20 small stables in 20 constituencies and he exercises 20 votes" (Blewitt 1965: 45). About 40 per cent of Austrian males cast two votes under the electoral system of 1896-1907. Under the French system of 1820-30, 90,000 Frenchmen elected 258 parliamentary deputies, while the richest 25 per cent of these electors cast a second vote and elected an additional 172 deputies.

Plural voting was defended by the same arguments used to justify other forms of class-based suffrage discrimination. Thus, Sir William Anson, a leading conservative constitutional lawyer, asked the British House of Commons in 1912, "Is the man who is too illiterate to read his ballot paper, who is too imprudent to support his children, to be placed on the same footing as the man who by industry and capacity has acquired a substantial interest in more than one constituency?" (Blewitt 1965: 45).

While plural voting systems explicitly and directly placed extra weight on the votes of the well-to-do and/or well educated, class, curial or estate voting systems did so indirectly by separating voters by class criteria into categories and assigning disproportionate numbers of legislative deputies to the upper-class voters. Under these systems, all voters cast only one ballot, but some ballots counted much more than others. Such systems were used in Prussia (1849-1918), Rumania (1866-1917), Austria (1861-1907), Russia (1905-17), Finland (from medieval times until 1906) and Sweden (from medieval times until 1866).

Perhaps the simplest of these systems was the three-class voting scheme imposed by royal decree of Prussian King Frederick William IV (1840-1858) in 1849, after the legislative body elected under his previously decreed universal, equal manhood suffrage of 1848 displeased him. Under the provisions of the May 30, 1849 decree-law, about 80 per cent of all adult males qualified to vote. However, the wealthiest voters, those who collectively paid one-third of direct taxes, were entitled to elect one-third of the electors, who then elected deputies to the lower legislative chamber. Middle income voters, those who collectively paid another third of direct taxes, also elected one-third of the electors, while those too poor to pay taxes and those who collectively paid the final third of taxes elected another one-third of the electors. This system, which stayed in effect for Prussian state elections after Prussia became part of the German Empire in 1871, allowed the approximately 85 per cent of the electorate in the third class to be out-voted two to one by the 15 per cent who comprised the upper two classes. Thus, in 1908, of every 10,000 people eligible to vote in Prussia, 382 voted in the first class, 1,386 in the second, and 8,232 in the third. In 2,200 of the 29,000 Prussian electoral districts, a single voter constituted the entire first class in 1908, as in the case of the arms magnate Krupp in Essen! Since the electors chosen by the three classes in each district met together collectively to choose legislators, the lower-class electors could be completely shut out in the final election process. Thus, the three-class system produced ludicrous results, such as in the 1903 state elections, when the Social Democratic and conservative parties each gained 19 per cent of the popular vote, but the conservatives obtained 143 legislative seats and the socialists none.

This system drastically decreased voter interest among the Prussian lower classes, who knew their ballots counted very little. Voter turnouts in the Prussian state elections were twice as high in the first as in the third class. While only about 30-35 per cent of the eligible Prussian electorate voted in the state elections, with its indirect, unequal and public voting, 70 per cent of the same electorate voted in German national elections, which had direct, equal and secret balloting.

Under the Rumanian system of 1866, as slightly modified in 1884, all adult male taxpayers (about 16 per cent of the population in 1905) were enfranchised. However, the electorate was divided into three "colleges" or curia. The first college, including persons with income of 1,200 lei ($500) or more, had 15,973 voters in 1905, or 1.5 per cent of the total electorate, but elected 41 per cent of the lower legislative chamber. The second college, including urban residents who paid 20 lei or more in direct taxes, as well as those with a primary education, following certain middle-class professions or having retired from military or civil service positions, comprised 34,742 persons in 1905. This group, constituting 3.5 per cent of the electorate, chose 38 per cent of the legislature. The other 95 per cent of the electorate, including all other taxpayers, constituted the third college and chose the remaining 21 per cent of the legislature. Thus, the votes cast in the first college counted more than twice as much as those in the second college and about 130 times as much as a third college vote.

Under the Russian electoral system of 1905 (similar to the Austrian system of 1861-1907), voters were divided into four categories or curia: landowners, urban residents, peasants, and industrial workers. Voters in each category voted for electors who then chose representatives to the lower legislative chamber (duma). By arbitrarily fixing the ratio of electors to voters in each curia, a system was devised in which 2,000 landowners chose one elector, as did 7,000 townsmen, 30,000 peasants, and 90,000 workers. Thus, one vote in the first curia was equal to 3.5 in the second, 15 in the third and 45 in the fourth. In 1907, this system was illegally changed by decree to create an even more reactionary system. Urban residents were divided into two sub-categories on the basis of wealth, with the result that one elector now was chosen by 230 landowners, 1,000 wealthy urban residents, 15,000 members of the urban lower middle class, 60,000 peasants or 125,000 industrial workers. Thus, one landowner's vote in the first curia now equalled over four votes in the wealthy half of the urban curia, 65 votes in the poorer half of the urban curia, 260 peasants' votes or 543 workers' votes. Under the 1907 system, 200,000 large landowners chose about 50 per cent of all electors, while the other 150 million Russians were represented by the other 50 per cent.

The four-estates system used in Finland until 1906 and Sweden until 1866 were identical, deriving from Sweden's rule over Finland until 1809. Finland was conquered by Russia in that year, but the Finnish diet was allowed to function along traditional lines under Russian rule (although it was never convened between 1809 and 1863). Both Finland and Sweden had a four-house parliament, with separate houses or estates for the nobility, clergy, burghers (wealthy townsmen) and independent peasantry. In both countries, adult male heads of each noble family were automatically represented in the estate of the nobility. The highest ranking clergy automatically sat in the second house, while the lower ranking clergy elected representatives to that estate. Urban residents following certain professions or meeting certain income requirements voted for the burghers' estate. Only independent farmers could vote for the peasants' estate, thus excluding the large and growing number of tenant farmers and agricultural laborers in both countries. In the last unreformed Swedish diet, in 1866, about 235,000 Swedes were enfranchised (about 6 per cent of the population), while in the last unreformed Finnish diet, that of 1906, only 127,000 (5 per cent) could vote. Since each of the four estates had equal power, the system gave the approximately 3 per cent of the population in each country that was represented in the upper three estates three times as much power as the 97 per cent of the population that was either completely unrepresented or voted in the fourth estate. Thus, in Finland around 1900 the 150 or so noble families had representation equivalent to the 1,083 enfranchised clericals, the 23,469 eligible burghers, and the 102,184 enfranchised peasants.

Although, as Table 1.1 clearly indicates, the general trend in nineteenth-century Europe was expansion of the suffrage, many countries actually reduced the percentage of the population enfranchised, or lessened the weight accorded to lower-class voters at one time or another during the 1815-1914 period. Such "negative reforms" occurred in the United Kingdom (1829), Belgium (1830), France (1850), the Netherlands (1850), Rumania (1866), Sweden (1866), Hungary (1874), Italy (1894), Russia (1907) and Portugal (1842, 1895, and 1913). The all-time champion in this area was undoubtedly Spain where the franchise was reduced in 1814, 1823, 1845, 1856, and 1876 (see Table 1.3).

## Indirect Voting, Open Ballots, and High Minimum Age Requirements

Besides the exclusion or short-weighting of the votes of the poor, a number of other devices were used in nineteenth-century Europe to

Table 1.3:   Suffrage Statistics for the
Spanish Lower Legislative Chamber,
1812–1910

| Date | Spanish Population | Enfranchised Voters | % of Total Population Eligible to Vote |
|---|---|---|---|
| 1812 | | | c. 20 |
| 1814 | | | 0 |
| 1820 | | | c. 20 |
| 1822 | 11,661,865 | | c. 20 |
| 1824 | | | 0 |
| 1834 | 12,162,172 | 18,000 | 0.15 |
| 1836 | | 65,067 | 0.52 |
| 1837 | | 257,984 | 1.7 |
| 1839 | | 342,559 | 2.78 |
| 1840 | | 423,787 | 3.44 |
| 1843 | | c. 600,000 | c. 4 |
| 1846 | | 97,100 | 0.79 |
| 1850 | | 121,770 | 1.11 |
| 1854 | | 694,110 | 4.6 |
| 1856 | | c.1,000,000 | c. 6.5 |
| 1857 | 15,464,340 | 147,000 | 0.95 |
| 1858 | | 157,931 | 1.02 |
| 1860 | 15,673,481 | | |
| 1863 | | 179,413 | 1.14 |
| 1864 | | 144,291 | 1.06 |
| 1865 | | 418,271 | 2.67 |
| 1867 | | 396,863 | 2.38 |
| 1869 | | 3,801,071 | 24.3 |
| 1871 | 16,794,970 | 4,030,792 | 24 |
| 1873 | | 4,551,436 | 27.1 |
| 1876 | 16,623,384 | 3,989,612 | 24 |
| 1877 | 16,634,345 | | |
| 1879 | | 846,961 | 5.1 |
| 1881 | | 846,961 | 5.1 |
| 1884 | 17,254,764 | 808,243 | 4.7 |
| 1887 | 17,549,600 | | |
| 1897 | 18,108,610 | | |
| 1900 | 18,594,000 | | |
| 1907 | | 4,479,114 | 23.7 |
| 1910 | 19,994,600 | 4,650,000 | 23.3 |

Sources:   Harrison 1978: 23; Payne 1973: 474; Marichal 1977:
266; Kiernan 1966: 95, 192.

limit lower-class influence in the election of lower legislative chambers. Indirect voting, in which ballots were cast not for legislative deputies, but for electors who in turn selected representatives to parliament, was used in many countries. Among them were the Netherlands and Switzerland from 1815 to 1848, Norway from 1815 to 1906, Prussia from 1849 to 1918, Russia from 1905 to 1917, France from 1815 to 1817, Austria from 1861 to 1873, Portugal for most of the period from 1834 to 1852, and, in the lower curial elections, Rumania (1866-1917), Austria (1873-1907), Sweden (until 1866) and Finland (until 1906). It was generally--and correctly--believed that imposing an intermediate stage in the electoral process would make it more likely that only well-known and "respectable" candidates would be ultimately selected. Thus, in the Russian district assemblies (uiezd zemtvos) elected in 1865-7, there were 42 per cent nobles, 38 per cent peasants, 11 per cent merchants and 7 per cent members of priestly families, while in the provincial assemblies (zemtvos), elected by the uiezd zemtvos, the corresponding percentages were 74, 11, 11 and 4. That indirect elections were especially designed to filter out potentially "dangerous" candidates from the lower classes is evident from the fact that only lower colleges or curiae voted indirectly in Rumania, Austria, Finland and Sweden. In the Russian electoral system, most voters went through only one indirect electoral stage, while the lower classes went through multiple indirect stages.

Another technique used in a number of European countries to discourage the election of "unreliable" candidates was the use of "open" balloting, usually by oral voting or a show of hands. Open balloting greatly facilitated the use of pressure and manipulation by governmental officials and local elites, especially in rural areas of Ireland, Hungary, Prussia and Austrian Galicia, where landlords continued to exercise a semi-feudal domination over the peasantry until well into the twentieth century. Open balloting was used in Hungary and Prussia as late as 1914, while the secret ballot was introduced quite late in the 1815-1914 period in the United Kingdom (1872), Belgium (1877), Serbia (1879), Norway (1885), Denmark (1901), and Austria (1906). In France, the ballot was theoretically secret but in practice privacy was not protected until after 1900. Particularly during the 1815-30 period, any French voter who insisted on concealing his ballot immediately branded himself an opponent of the government, and in any case the number of eligible voters was so small that handwriting could often be recognized. The crown-appointed head of one electoral college in France wrote to the Minister of the Interior in 1824: "All the voters cast open ballots in my presence ... the most horrible liberals wrote their choice under my gaze in favor of the royalist candidates" (Sauvigny 1966: 297). In rural areas of Europe where the open ballot was used voters were often forced to state their preferences in front of their employers or local elites who served as election judges or observers. "By forcing him to repeat the name of his preference several times, members of the local elite ... let the voter understand that his first choice met with disapproval and that insistence upon it would lead to reprisals" (Anderson and Anderson 1967: 342).

Open threats were sometimes made to influence voting in such situations. Thus, one landlord in Prussian Silesia announced during the critical 1863 election that those who voted against "the disposition and will of his Majesty and his ministers" would

> if they are workers in the forest or on the estates be dismissed, and that the same procedure shall be followed in the brickworks, the peat banks, and the factory for ovenware and pottery; that the supervisory personnel of the forest, the estate, the garden, the mill, the bakery and the sawmill shall be given notice; that final accounts shall be settled with handicraftsmen, ... as well as with the merchants who sell them anything; furthermore those who have rented a dwelling or leased farm or forest land shall be given notice as soon as the contractual obligation ends (Hamerow 1974: 299-300).

Those who defended the open ballot argued that voters should be willing to defend their choices publicly--ignoring the economic vulnerability of the lower classes--and that only the open ballot would insure that voters be exposed to "proper" influences. Thus, the preface to a ludicrous electoral "reform" bill proposed by the Hungarian government to parliament in 1908, which retained the open ballot, argued that secret voting "everywhere conflicts with the views, the customs and the moral feelings of society ... it weakens the true moral principle that it is every man's duty to have the courage to express his opinion freely" (Seton-Watson 1911: 31). The Prussian political observer Theodor von Bernhardi argued:

> The proper influence of social position, of education and of higher insight and intelligence ceases under secret voting and in its place comes the improper influence of the basest political agitation. ... We will then not be the ones who will lead the great uneducated mass. It will be the worst individuals, the most dangerous elements of civil society who will then gain an entirely incalculable influence (Hamerow 1974: 294).

Another device used to keep down the number of "undesirable" votes and voters was the specification of artificially high minimum age requirements for the suffrage in many nineteenth-century European countries. The most common minimum voting age was 25 (in effect during most or all of the century in Norway, Belgium, Spain, Italy, Rumania, Germany and Russia), although most males began working full-time in their early teens and average life expectancy was less than 40 in 1850 and only 45 as late as 1900. Maintaining such high voting ages tended to increase conservative chances during elections because voters generally became more conservative with age and because the lower classes died much younger than the upper classes, with the result that the higher the age requirement for voting, the lower the percentage of the poor still alive and able to cast ballots (assuming they were not otherwise disenfranchised). Because conditions were generally much healthier in non-urban than in urban areas, high age requirements also tended to benefit rural areas, which were generally more conservative than the cities.

The impact of high minimum age requirements in disenfranchising the poor can be clearly seen in age data for nineteenth-century urban workers. In 1841, 82 per cent of 2,017 tobacco workers in Bremen, Germany were 25 years old or younger, and 61 per cent were 20 or younger. Among 108,000 Moscow factory workers in 1902, only 43 per cent were 30 or more, while about 40 per cent were below the age of 25. When the Spanish voting age was lowered from 25 to 21 in 1873, the number of eligible voters increased by over 500,000 (13 per cent).

Legislators in nineteenth-century Europe seem to have recognized that raising the voting age disproportionately decreased the percentage of the poor enfranchised to vote. Thus, in Sweden, wealth-based suffrage requirements for voting for the lower chamber were relaxed in 1909, but the age requirement was raised from 21 to 24 as a clear compensating measure. Similar events occurred in the Netherlands (1897) and Hungary (1913), and, for upper legislative houses, in Belgium (1893) and Denmark (1915).

Restrictions on Eligibility for Service in Lower Legislative Chambers

Aside from restrictions and repressive techniques designed to discourage "unreliable" voting, many European countries also attempted to discourage "unreliable" candidates for legislative office during the nineteenth century. Techniques to this end were the failure to pay legislative deputies in several major European countries, and the imposition of age and wealth requirements on legislative candidates above those required to vote. While most of the minor European countries early provided pay for lower legislative deputies (for example the Netherlands in 1815, Norway in 1814, Belgium in 1831 and Denmark in 1849), the record of the major countries in this area was extremely poor. Deputies were not paid in France until 1852, in Germany until 1906, in Italy until 1911 and in the United Kingdom until 1912. Spanish deputies remained unpaid throughout the period. This lack of payment was deliberate and perceived as a form of discrimination by the lower classes since it made independent wealth a requirement to serve in legislative office. Thus, one of the six demands of the Chartist movement that flourished in the United Kingdom between 1835 and 1848 was for payment of deputies. When the British House of Lords, in the Osborne Judgment of 1909, disallowed the trade union practice of contributing funds to members of parliament as a substitute for legislative pay, the resultant uproar not only led to provision of such pay in 1911, but also to greatly strengthening the newly born Labour party. Prussian Prime Minister Otto von Bismarck (1862-90, and German chancellor, 1871-90) bitterly and successfully opposed legislative pay when the constitution of the North German Confederation, the precursor of the German Empire, was drawn up in 1867. He declared, "Per diem allowances for legislators are a remuneration to the educated proletariat for the purpose of the vocational practice of demagogy" (Hamerow 1972: 332).

Age and wealth requirements to serve in lower legislative chambers higher than those required to obtain the suffrage was another widely used technique designed to encourage conservative tendencies among legislators. Higher age requirements were imposed in many countries, including, at various times, France, Hungary, Italy, Greece, Serbia, Sweden and the Netherlands. Higher wealth requirements were imposed for part or all of the nineteenth century in France, Portugal, the United Kingdom, Spain, Rumania, Serbia, and many of the German states. In some cases, the wealth requirements were devastatingly high and eliminated huge percentages of the population. Eligibility requirements of the 1817 French electoral law were so high that only 16,000 Frenchmen (less than 0.1 per cent) out of 30 million qualified. After the requirement was "liberalized" in 1830, fewer than 50,000 were eligible. In Portugal, under the 1842 constitution, only 4,500 (0.1 per cent) of the population of 3.4 million qualified. The tiny German state of Nassau, with a population of about 100,000 in 1815, "had such high property requirements that in one election no eligible candidates could be found in 12 of the 20 electoral districts, while in the entire state there were only 70 men qualified to be candidates" (Sheehan 1978: 10).


Gerrymandering and Electoral Corruption
Gross gerrymandering was another technique designed to hold down the impact of "undesirable" voters. Gerrymandering took different forms, reflecting the particular constellation of elite interests in different countries. In the Scandinavian countries, urban areas were generally overrepresented in the legislatures, reflecting the influence of bureaucratic-mercantile interests. Thus, in Sweden, under the 1866 electoral reform, one member of the lower chamber represented 40,000 rural inhabitants, but only 6,000 citizens of small towns and 10,000 inhabitants of large cities. Overrepresentation of urban areas was especially notorious in Norway, where the so-called bondeparagrafen of the 1814 constitution guaranteed urban areas one-third representation in the Storting, although 90 per cent of the population was rural. The bondeparagrafen, along with the system of indirect voting used in Norway until 1906, reflected the general disdain and fear held by the dominant bureaucratic-official class for the peasantry.

In Austria, "electoral geometry" also grossly overrepresented urban areas and interests, in this case to assure that political dominance would remain in the hands of the disproportionately urbanized German elements rather than the overwhelmingly rural Slavic areas. Under the 1907 Austrian electoral reform, which specifically allocated legislative seats by nationality, Germans, with

36 per cent of the population, received 45 per cent of the mandates, while the Slavic groups, constituting 60 per cent of the population, obtained only 50 per cent of the legislative seats. In the United Kingdom, failure to reapportion the House of Commons significantly until 1885 left rapidly growing and reformist-oriented industrialized areas grossly underrepresented, while scores of "rotten boroughs" (depopulated constituencies) were controlled by large landowners who were able to manipulate the votes of their personal or economic dependents in a reliably conservative direction.

Failure to reapportion the German Reichstag between 1871 and 1914 also resulted in severe discrimination against the rapidly growing industrial areas, which tended to support socialist and liberal parties, and vast overrepresentation of the stagnant or declining small towns and rural areas that supported conservatives. Around 1900, constituency sizes ranged from 9,500 for a Reichstag seat from Schaumburg-Lippe to 247,000 for Berlin-Treptow. In the 1907 election, the Social Democratic party won only 43 Reichstag seats with 3.25 million votes, while two conservative parties gained 85 seats with 1.56 million votes.

Gerrymandering had perhaps the greatest significance in Hungary, where skillful drawing of electoral boundaries together with gross corruption and fraud maintained governments in power for decades after 1865 that were probably opposed by a majority of the enfranchised population. Although a basic element of government policy in Hungary was discrimination against non-Magyar nationalities, such as Slovaks and Rumanians, most Magyar elements in the country viewed the regime as insufficiently militant in demanding greater freedom from Austria under the 1867 settlement that gave Hungary domestic autonomy, but placed foreign policy, defense and some financial matters under joint Austro-Hungarian control. Since most of the Magyar population opposed the government, the only way in which ruling elites in Hungary could maintain power was to cluster huge numbers of Magyar votes in a small number of constituencies, thus limiting the impact of their vote, while vastly overrepresenting non-Magyar areas. While these areas also tended towards opposition to the government, the small number of voters per constituency and the open ballot used in Hungary lent itself to easy intimidation of non-Magyars, directed by Magyar officials who owed their jobs to the government. This system was consecrated in the 1877 electoral reapportionment act, which redistributed districts so that "opposition regions" often represented seventy-five times as many voters as "government regions." Nine representatives, for example, were allocated to the 80,000 voters of Budapest, while in heavily non-Magyar Transylvania 9,000 voters were allocated 74 seats. Bizarrely shaped electoral districts reminded one scholar of the "most difficult Chinese puzzles of our childhood" (Seton-Watson 1911: 8).

Many nineteenth-century European governments relied upon techniques far more corrupt than gerrymandering to insure that electoral results turned out "correctly." Elections were massively fixed by methods ranging from bribery, threats, and falsification to outright terrorism on a systematic and institutionalized basis in Bulgaria, Greece (until about 1875), Hungary, Italy, Portugal, Rumania, Serbia (until 1903) and Spain. In reading scholarly histories of all of these countries, one encounters time and again phrases such as "it was the government which made the election, not the election the government" (Smith 1959: 200), and elections "always returned an overwhelming majority for the government in power" (Eidelberg 1974: 18). Electoral manipulation was so extensive in these countries that voting results often showed ludicrous shifts from election to election if a new government conducted the balloting. Thus, the Bulgarian parliament (Sobranie) dissolved in 1908 contained 150 liberals and 6 members of Alexander Malinov's Democratic party. When Malinov was called to power by Bulgarian Czar Ferdinand in that year, elections controlled by his party produced a Sobranie with 166 Democrats and no liberals. In 1911, Ferdinand called to power a coalition of Nationalists and Progessive Liberals, who managed elections in which the Democrats fell to four seats while the ruling coalition returned 159 deputies. Severe electoral corruption, although usually considerably less blatant than it was in Iberia, the Balkans, Hungary and Italy, was also common in France, Prussia, Austria and the United Kingdom until the last quarter of the nineteenth century, and in Russia after the inauguration of elections there in 1906. Switzerland also saw a considerable amount of electoral chicanery, especially before 1848, although it was not in the same league with any of the aforementioned countries. Elections in Scandinavia and the Low Countries were generally free from corrupt practices.

Governmental manipulation of elections was made easier by the high degree of bureaucratic centralization that prevailed in the countries of Latin and eastern Europe, including Spain, France, Italy, Russia and the Balkans. Centralization greatly facilitated coordinated governmental electoral corruption, particularly when severe suffrage restrictions created small electorates that were highly visible and vulnerable, especially since many voters depended upon governmental patronage or favors of some sort. In France, 85 per cent of the deputies were elected by fewer than 400 votes in 1846. Under the 1845 Spanish constitution, there was an average of less than 300 voters per constituency, and in some cases half or more of the electorate "was composed of government and municipal employees or those on government pensions" (Carr 1966: 213). In Italy until 1882 the average number of votes needed to elect a deputy was 500, while in Hungary in 1901 about two-thirds of all deputies were elected by less than 1,000 votes. In the United Kingdom (where power was relatively decentralized) before 1832 about half of the House of Commons was elected from constituencies with fewer than 250 voters, who were often highly vulnerable to pressure from local elites. Many of these "rotten borough" constituencies were literally bought and sold by rich landowners. Sir Robert Peel (prime minister 1834-35, 1841-46) was given his seat in the House of Commons at Cashel in County Tipperary, Ireland, as a present from his father on his twenty-first birthday, while the famous constituency of the elder William Pitt at Old Sarum did not contain a single inhabitant!

In some countries, the science of election fraud was so advanced that a special vocabulary developed to describe various corrupt techniques. Thus, in 1891, the great Italian sociologist Vilfredo Pareto noted in his nation's elections:

> It is called the blocco when the whole contents of the voting urns are changed, or the pastetta when one changes only a part of them. There is still no word for when absent people and even the dead are made to vote, though one will soon appear when this usage becomes general (Smith 1959: 220).

The Spanish had a name for it--the lazaros technique, named after the man whom Jesus brought back to life. "On one occasion, a whole cemetery, 700 strong, gave their vote, and it was edifying to see that though they had been illiterate in their lifetime, they had all learned to write in the grave" (Brenan 1964: 5-6). Another technique used in Spain was known as actas en blanco, when members of the election committee would certify that they had counted the votes but "left the column of results blank for the Civil Governor to fill in as he pleased later" (Brenan 1964: 6).

Spain seems to have developed the most pervasive and systematic use of electoral fraud, although Hungary provided close competition. Spain "was not a parlimentary system with abuses; the abuses were the system" (Carr 1966: 367). One Spanish precinct that had 124 voters in 1918 returned 9,015 votes for the official candidate! After 1875, the two major Spanish parties, the Conservatives and the Liberals, agreed to take turns governing and fixing elections, thus giving each a chance at the governmental gravy while avoiding the need for the violent revolts that had plagued Spanish politics before 1875. Since both parties represented the same upper middle-upper class constituencies, the so-called turno pacifico ("peaceful rotation") spared each the need even to pretend to concern themselves with the problems of the masses of the population. It was normal under the turno pacifico for the party that "made" the election to allow leaders of the other party to be returned to parliament along with a reasonable contingent of their followers to maintain good feelings.

The key mechanism of the Spanish system was the cacique, or local political boss, who was guaranteed control of patronage and power in his locality by the central government in exchange for the proper electoral returns. The cacique obtained votes for the government by such techniques as parcelling out jobs, adjusting taxes, exempting men from the draft, and settling various local disputes on behalf of those who pledged their votes. Since for the cacique to operate effectively he had to control the local governments and courts, "every electoral contest was preceded by a massive change of mayors and local judges" (Carr 1980: 11). If the usual means of pressure or bribery failed, opposition voters could be excluded from the electoral rolls and government backers would cast ballots several times. The lazaros or actas en blanco techniques might also be used. Although before 1900 the Spanish system was so iron-clad that election results were sometimes published in the press before ballots were cast, after the turn of the century it became increasingly difficult to manipulate elections in the rapidly growing and relatively sophisticated urban areas (where so-called votos verdad, or "true votes," were cast). Therefore, the system became almost completely dependent upon massive faking of rural ballots. The two dominant parties frequently resorted to gerrymanders that overcame the problem of the votos verdad by combining rural and urban areas in the same voting district so that the manipulated rural ballots would be decisive.

Fake two-party systems essentially identical to that in Spain functioned also in Portugal and Rumania. In Bulgaria, under Prince Ferdinand (1887-1918, czar after 1908) elections were also totally controlled by the government, but Ferdinand encouraged the development of numerous parties to allow him better to preserve his own power by playing the parties off against each other. As the contemporary British historian R. W. Seton-Watson noted:

> The secret of Ferdinand's power has lain in his skill in calculating the psychological moment for driving each batch of swine from the trough of power. ... There was always a waiting list for the post of premier, and whenever Ferdinand had had enough of one politician and his following he merely had to turn to a rival group and entrust it with the "making" of an election and a majority (quoted in Stavrianos 1963: 43).

The Serbian system was similarly manipulated, although with considerably less success, by the kings Milan Obrenović (1868-89) and his son Alexander (1889-1903). Until about 1875, Greek elections were especially distinguished by the use of government-paid bands of thugs who resorted to outright terrorism to intimidate voters. Such methods were especially notorious under the premiership of John Kolettis (1844-7). One election official recalled later that "at the time of Kolettis ... even murders and forgeries and all other crimes were ordered, the only requirement being that they achieve an electoral victory" (Kousoulas 1974: 28).

The Italian and Hungarian regimes, after 1875, were characterized by dominance by a single amorphous party, which through a combination of absorption and co-option of opposition groups (known in Italy as trasformismo) and outright electoral fraud succeeded in monopolizing political power continuously (save in Hungary between 1905 and 1910). The Italian system used patronage, bribery, physical intimidation, threats against government employees and sometimes outright terrorism and murder. These techniques were especially applied in the backwards southern region of Italy and reached their culmination during the ministries of Giovanni Giolitti (1892-3, 1903-1905, 1906-1909, 1911-14), dubbed by one of his opponents il ministro della mala vita ("the minister of the underworld").

Opposition voters in the south were sometimes arrested on trumped-up charges the day before the elections; criminals could be released from prison to use their influence on behalf of the official candidate ... and names of opponents might be erased from lists on the spurious plea of illiteracy. Government servants--under which category came schoolmasters, university teachers, magistrates and railroadmen--might be threatened with loss of employment or removal to some inhospitable post on the islands ... blotting paper was issued to voters which had to be returned showing the name of the favored candidate upon it; banknotes were torn in two and given half before and half after voting; ... electoral lists included fictitious names, sometimes gathered from tombstones in the town cemetery (Smith 1959: 200, 221).

In Hungary, in order to reduce the vote turnout and facilitate manipulation in non-Magyar areas, polling booths were often located tens of miles away from voters in areas without railroads. Bridges would be closed and all horses placed under "veterinary supervision" on the day of elections.

The minutes and the entire proceedings of the election are conducted in Magyar and the slightest slip in that language often serves as an excuse for disqualifying [non-Magyars]. A standard trick of the officials is to refuse to recognize electors with whom they are personally acquainted and thus let them lose their vote for lack of identification. A still worse trick--and by no means uncommon--is to allow unqualified persons to vote in the name of dead electors whose names have been intentionally left upon the register (Seton-Watson 1911: 16).

Opposition candidates in Hungary were frequently arrested or physically barred from appearing in their constituencies, and known opposition voters were blocked from attempting to reach the polls by concentrations of troops. Hungarian elections also often featured physical attacks by troops upon dissident voters, with frequent high casualties. Thus, about 100 people were killed or wounded in the 1896 elections, 25 casualties were reported in 1901, and there were a dozen killed in 1910. The British ambassador in Vienna noted in the 1870s that reports from the Hungarian elections "have all the character of bulletins from the field of battle" (May 1968: 85). Although in general Austrian elections were free of such terroristic tactics, this was not the case in Galicia, where the Polish upper classes used techniques of electoral corruption and intimidation against the Ruthenian (Ukrainian) peasantry that "left their Hungarian counterparts in the shade" (Macartney 1969: 677). Over 40 people were killed or wounded in the 1894 elections in Galicia, while during the 1911 elections in the village of Drohobycz "a volley was loosed upon the electorate which resulted in 27 deaths and 84 serious injuries in order that the reign of the Polish Szlachta [nobility] should be maintained over the Ruthenian peasants" (Jaszi 1966: 146).

In France, the "making" of elections was notorious during the Restoration (1815-30), the July Monarchy (1830-48) and the Second Empire (1851-70). Aside from the usual patronage and threats, France saw some highly unusual techniques of electoral manipulation. It was common for the government in Restoration France to reduce the taxes of known opponents of the regime so they could not qualify for the suffrage; before the 1820 elections, for example, 14,500 voters (of a total electorate of only 85,000) were suddenly disenfranchised by this technique. Ineligible voters known to support the government were placed on the electoral rolls, while qualified opposition voters would be "accidentally" omitted. To prevent appeals against exclusions, the electoral lists would sometimes be posted at the last moment, at night, in random order or in a remote place high up on a wall where they could be read only with the use of a ladder. French elections throughout the 1815-70 period featured "official candidates" who received all sorts of assistance from government officials, including the expenditure of public funds. French public employees were quite openly instructed by government ministers to apply pressure on behalf of the "official candidates." Thus, in 1824 the French minister of justice informed government officials:

> The government gives out jobs only to those who will serve and support it. .... If the official refuses to perform the services expected of him, he betrays his trust and voluntarily breaks the agreement concerning the objective or the conditions of his job. The government no longer owes anything to anyone who does not in turn fulfill his obligation (Sauvigny 1966: 296).

Electoral fraud and manipulation did not always succeed. Despite severe administrative pressure, for example, opposition parties triumphed in the French elections of 1827, 1830 and 1877, the Prussian elections of 1862 and 1863, the Serbian election of 1883, the Russian elections of 1906 and early 1907, the Croatian elections of 1908 and 1911 and the Bulgarian election of 1913. However, governmental parties never lost a single election between 1860 and 1913 in Rumania, Italy, Spain and Portugal.

## Legislative Dissolution and Electoral Coups d'Etat

A final repressive electoral technique used in nineteenth-century Europe was legislative dissolution--i.e., simply setting aside election results that did not please the government and calling new elections. The dissolution power that most European monarchs could use at their discretion was perfectly legal and usually implemented without force (although not always, as in the use of troops to dissolve the Austrian and Prussian assemblies of 1848 and the Hungarian and Russian legislatures in 1906). Therefore it may seem odd to include this technique as an example of political repression. However, in practice legislative dissolution could be and often was used simply to void arbitrarily entire election results and therefore was even more repressive than any of the techniques previously discussed. During the famous "constitutional conflict" in Prussia in the early 1860s, King William I (1861-88, and German emperor, 1871-88) dissolved the Prussian Landtag in 1861, 1862, and 1863 before finally resorting to rule without reference to that body. An amazingly similar conflict erupted in Denmark about ten years later, where the lower house of the Danish parliament was dissolved about ten times between 1876 and 1894 and the government finally resorted to rule by decree. King Victor Emmanuel II of Piedmont (1849-61, and king of Italy, 1861-1878) dissolved the legislature there twice in 1849 before he was able to obtain a docile majority, and there were multiple dissolutions also in Saxony (1848-9), Württemberg (1848-50), the Netherlands (1866-8), and Croatia (1908-12). There were repeated dissolutions in Austria between 1861 and 1879, as Emperor Franz Joseph (1848-1916) kept changing his domestic and foreign policies and required similarly changing legislatures to keep pace with him. In Finland, the diet was dissolved by the Russian czar almost every year between 1907 and 1913.

In countries where governmental control of elections was highly efficient, as in Iberia and the Balkans, the monarch's dissolution power meant he alone could singlehandedly decide when and how power shifted from one party or faction to another. In Spain, Portugal and Rumania, where systems of rotating power between two essentially identical parties were well established by the last quarter of the nineteenth century, such decisions were often reached by monarchs in consultation with party leaders. But in Bulgaria, Serbia (until 1903) and Greece (until about 1875) the dissolution power was used to keep all political factions dependent upon the monarchs' whims.

In a number of cases, legislative dissolution was combined with arbitrary decrees changing the electoral laws, as monarchs attempted to rid themselves of unfriendly legislatures once and for all by what amounted to electoral coups d'état. Such events occurred in Russia in 1907, and in Prussia and a number of other German states, including Saxony and Württemberg, in the wake of the 1848 revolutions. The attempt by Charles X of France to effect such an electoral coup d'état (along with other repressive measures including a decree imposing press censorship) directly provoked the French revolution of July 1830. The dissolution power was not arbitrarily used or abused in many European countries. Few or no instances of such abuses occurred in the United Kingdom, the Low Countries, Scandinavia (save in Denmark as noted above), Italy, or, after about 1880, Greece.

## *Suffrage Discrimination for Upper Legislative Chambers*

Most discussions of suffrage discrimination in nineteenth-century Europe concentrate exclusively upon lower legislative chambers, but this is a serious error, since during the period most upper legislative chambers had powers equivalent to those of the lower chambers. (In a few countries, such as Bulgaria, Serbia, Greece [after 1864] and Finland [after 1906] the legislatures were unicameral.) Austria, Hungary, Italy, the United Kingdom, France (until 1870), Sweden (until 1866), Finland (until 1906), Greece (until 1864), the Netherlands (until 1848), Portugal (with brief exceptions until 1911) and Spain (with brief exceptions) all had upper chambers based solely on the nobility and/or persons appointed by the king or obtaining their seats ex officio. These bodies were completely non-elective, and usually represented no more than 1 or 2 per cent of the population. In most of these chambers, the monarch had unlimited appointment powers, so the upper house could be "packed" or threatened with packing if it obstructed legislation favored by the monarch, or simply if the king wished to reward his friends with prestigious titles. Such packing was notorious in Restoration France, where the number of peers increased from 210 to 384 between 1815 and 1830, as well as in Portugal, Italy and Austria. In Portugal, packing occurred so frequently that a special term, fornada (a baking or ovenful) was applied. Sixty new Portuguese peers were baked in three separate fornadas in 1879-81 alone. In Italy, where the cognate term infornata was used, membership in the upper house leaped from 270 to 390 between 1873 and 1892, while membership in the Austrian Herrenhaus jumped from 92 to 153 between 1873 and 1898. In the United Kingdom, the threat of packing, which would have diluted the power of incumbent peers, was enough to force through major constitutional reforms and avert serious crises in 1832 and 1911. In Hungary, where the power of packing (known as the pairschub, from the French word for peer and the German word for shift) was first obtained by the government in 1885, the House of Lords avoided the need for its use by deferring to the lower house when threatening noises were made.

In Germany, the Netherlands (after 1848), Sweden (after 1866), Switzerland (after 1848), and Portugal (after 1911), the upper chambers were elected indirectly by lower governmental bodies. In Belgium after 1893 half the members of the upper house were popularly elected and half were chosen by provincial governments. In Denmark after 1866 a combination of popular election and royal appointment was used, while in France after 1870 the selection process was made by lower-chamber deputies and local governmental officials. In Russia, half the members of the upper house were chosen by the czar, and half by an extrmely narrow electorate, consisting of a relative handful of church officials, academics, businessmen, nobles and great lords. In Norway, the upper house was chosen by the lower house from among its own membership. Of all the European countries, only Rumania (after 1866), Belgium (between 1831 and 1893), and Denmark (from 1849 to 1866) had upper houses completely elected by direct popular election.

Wherever upper houses were completely or partially elective, whether directly through popular elections or indirectly by elected governmental bodies, the suffrage and/or eligibility requirements were invariably extremely restrictive (save in Switzerland after 1848,

France after 1870, and Denmark between 1849 and 1866). In Rumania, although about 15 per cent of the population voted for the lower house, only 24,571 people (less than half of 1 per cent of the population) could vote for the upper house in 1905. In Belgium, the same franchise that restricted the lower-house suffrage to 2 per cent of the population was used for the upper chamber (senate) until 1893. Aften then, the same type of plural voting system used for the chamber of deputies was used to elect half of the senate, although the voting age for the senate was raised to 30 and retained at 25 for the deputies. In 1904-1905, 1.3 million Belgians could vote for the senate, but since 251,994 cast three votes and 335,194 had two votes, they could outpoll the 727,132 voters who cast only one ballot. After 1893, the other half of the Belgian senate was elected by provincial governments that were elected by the same voters entitled to vote directly for the senate, save for a plural vote maximum of four rather than three.

In Denmark, while the upper house (Landsting) was elected on the same quasi-universal manhood suffrage used to choose the lower house (Folketing) from 1849 until 1866, after 1866 the franchise and composition of the Landsting was drastically revised to reduce popular influence. In that year, the king was empowered to appoint almost 20 per cent of the Landsting, with the remaining members to be elected indirectly by electoral colleges, half of whom were chosen by all those enfranchised for the Folketing, with the other half elected only by the wealthiest taxpayers. This system gave control of half of the electoral colleges to about 1,000 great landowners and a few thousand wealthy urban merchants and businessmen. Thus, in Copenhagen in 1906, 2,148 wealthy taxpayers with a minimum taxable income of 4,000 kroner ($1,000) voted for half of the electors, while 33,918 voters chose the other half.

In Sweden, members of the upper house were chosen after 1866 by local governmental bodies, for whom the income-based suffrage was wider than for the lower chamber. Thus, in 1871, 460,000 Swedes (11 per cent of the population) could vote for the upper house, compared with 236,000 (5.6 per cent) enfranchised for the lower house. However, this wider franchise was completely vitiated by the Swedish system of plural voting in local elections. Although after 1869 plural votes in urban districts in local elections were limited to a maximum of 100 votes, or 2 per cent of the total ballots cast, until 1900 plural votes, figured in direct proportion to taxes paid, were completely unlimited in local rural elections, so that in some areas one person cast 90 per cent or more of the total vote. After 1900, plural votes in rural districts were limited to 5,000 per voter (!!) or 10 per cent of the total district vote. After the 1907-1909 electoral reforms, plural votes in urban or rural local elections were limited to 40 votes per person, but equal and universal adult suffrage was introduced in Sweden for such elections only in 1918. Around 1900, the elections of nearly 10 per cent of the 2,386 Swedish election districts were controlled by three voters or fewer, and less than 1 per cent of the total population controlled the composition of the Swedish upper house. Under the system of local plural balloting poor Swedes responded by not voting. Thus, in Stockholm in 1872, fewer than one out of 1,000 eligibles in the lowest tax bracket voted, compared with 26 per cent in the highest bracket. These wholesale abstentions magnified the political inequality between the poorest and wealthiest voters in Stockholm from 100:1 to 26,000:1.

Aside from highly class-biased suffrage restrictions whereby upper legislative chambers were elected, a conservative cast was further ensured by the general lack of pay for legislators--for example, members of the Belgian and Swedish lower chambers were paid, but members of the upper house were not--and by extremely high age and wealth requirements for prospective members. Age requirements for the upper chambers were generally considerably higher than for lower chambers. Thus under the Belgian (1831), Piedmont (1848), Danish (1849), Rumanian (1866) and French (1884) constitutions or electoral laws, deputies could serve at age 25 in lower chambers but had to be at least 40 to serve in upper chambers. The wealth requirements imposed for service in some of the elective upper chambers--notably those in Sweden, Belgium, the Netherlands and Rumania--can only be described as staggering. In the Netherlands until 1887 members of the upper house had to come from the wealthiest 0.03 per cent of the population, making only about 1,000 Dutchmen eligible. In Belgium until 1893, when qualifications were slightly lowered, senate members had to pay about 1,000 florins in direct taxes, at a time when the suffrage requirement of paying 20 florins in direct taxes to vote excluded 98 per cent of the population. Only 6,100 Swedes qualified to sit in the Swedish upper chamber around 1870, of whom 4,350 lived in Stockholm. The Swedish wealth qualifications were slightly lowered in 1909, but not abolished entirely until 1933. In Rumania around 1900, members of the upper house had to have an assured annual income of 9,400 lei (about $1,900) although only about 10,000 Rumanians had an income of even 2,000 lei. In France, a conservative bias was built into the structure of the upper house by a provision in the 1875 electoral law that guaranteed gross overrepresentation of rural areas. Each commune, no matter what its population, was granted at least one vote in the indirect elections for the senate conducted by local legislative bodies. Thus, the rural communes near Marseilles, with a total population of 250,000, cast 313 votes for the senate, while Marseilles itself, with nearly a million inhabitants, cast only 24 votes.

The gross disparities in the composition of upper and lower legislative chambers flowing from their differing origins led to severe turmoil between the houses in several European countries. After the 1866 constitutional revision in Denmark, the composition of the two Danish chambers became so dissimilar that the government was paralyzed, leading to a semidictatorship based solely on the upper house between 1876 and 1901, when the king finally accepted the principle of parliamentary responsibility based on the lower house. A similar conflict between the two Swedish houses lasted until the suffrage for the upper chamber was reformed in 1918. In the United

Kingdom, the House of Lords repeatedly vetoed legislation passed by the House of Commons when liberal governments were in power after 1850, especially measures threatening class privileges, such as tax reform and abolition of plural votes. In Russia, the upper house vetoed virtually all progressive legislation passed by the lower house throughout the 1905-17 period, including even bills sponsored by Czar Nicholas II for universal primary education and religious toleration, thereby earning the nickname "the graveyard of Duma legislation" (Charques 1965: 184).

Conflicts between the two houses generally did not arise where the monarch was willing to pack the upper house (e.g., Austria, Italy, Portugal), where both houses were chosen by essentially similar systems (e.g., Switzerland and Norway, where relatively democratic systems were used, and Rumania and Belgium, where highly class-biased systems were used for both houses) or where constitutional development led the upper house to defer usually to the lower house (e.g., for the most part in the Netherlands).

## Suffrage Discrimination in Local Elections

Most countries adopted a similar approach in developing suffrage laws for local elections (including village, city, county, provincial and district balloting, if such existed) as were used for national legislative elections. Countries that introduced universal manhood suffrage relatively early on the national level, such as Switzerland, Greece, and Bulgaria, usually used the same procedure early for local elections. (Germany, which adopted universal manhood suffrage for national elections in 1871 but which featured highly discriminatory voting schemes in most state and local elections, is a notable exception.) Countries with relatively straightforward wealth-based national suffrage systems, such as the Netherlands, Italy, and Norway, used similar schemes for local elections. Countries, such as Belgium, Austria, Prussia, and Russia, with a penchant for complicated suffrage provisions (e.g., plural and class voting) introduced similar methods for local voting. In some countries, such as the Netherlands and Norway, national and local suffrage systems were completely identical throughout most or all of the 1815-1914 period. In other cases, there were slight variations. For example, in Belgium, the local suffrage was made more liberal than the national suffrage in 1871 and 1883, so that by 1892 only 2 per cent of the population could vote at the national level, but 7 per cent could vote in local elections and 9 per cent in provincial. In 1893-95 the Belgian suffrage was liberalized at all levels, but more so at the national level, so that 23 per cent of the population in 1912 could cast up to three votes in national elections, while 18 per cent could cast up to four votes in local elections and 20 per cent up to four in provincial.

In many European local elections, especially before 1890, the percentage of the population enfranchised was extremely low. Thus, in 1830 only 141 residents of Cologne could vote in a population of

Table 1.4:  Percentage of Total Population
Enfranchised in European Local Elections, 1830-1914

| Date | Location | % | Date | Location | % |
|------|----------|---|------|----------|---|
| 1830 | Cologne | 0.2 | 1880 | Norway | 7 |
| 1830 | Liverpool | 3 | 1880 | Netherlands | 3 |
| 1830 | Portsmouth | 0.2 | 1884 | Moscow | 2.6 |
| 1830 | Plymouth | 0.6 | 1888 | Belgium | 8 |
| 1831 | Exeter | 6 | 1889 | Italy | 11 |
| 1835 | Spain | 4 | 1890 | Graz | 7 |
| 1837 | Liverpool | 3 | 1890 | Moscow | 2.6 |
| 1837 | Portsmouth | 2.6 | 1890 | St. Petersburg | 2.1 |
| 1837 | Toulouse | 3.3 | 1891 | Vienna | 5.8 |
| 1840 | Netherlands | 3 | 1892 | Cologne | 8.8 |
| 1840 | Norway | 8 | 1892 | Sweden | 14.3 |
| 1840 | Copenhagen | 1.7 | 1892 | Moscow | 0.9 |
| 1841 | Denmark | 2 | 1892 | St. Petersburg | 0.6 |
| 1841 | Birmingham | 3 | 1895 | Belgium | 18 |
| 1841 | Leeds | 9 | 1898 | Italy | 9 |
| 1846 | St. Petersburg | 1.2 | 1900 | St. Petersburg | 1 |
| 1847 | Hamburg | 1.1 | 1900 | Copenhagen | 12 |
| 1850 | Switzerland | 25 | 1900 | Denmark | 15 |
| 1851 | Birmingham | 3 | 1902 | Breslau | 6 |
| 1851 | Leeds | 9 | 1902 | Leipzig | 6 |
| 1860 | Norway | 7 | 1903 | Cologne | 12 |
| 1860 | Belgium | 2 | 1905 | Netherlands | 14 |
| 1860 | Spain | 5 | 1905 | Italy | 10 |
| 1860 | Netherlands | 3 | 1908 | Denmark | 30 |
| 1861 | Graz | 3.6 | 1910 | Norway | 45 |
| 1861 | Vienna | 3.8 | 1910 | Moscow | 0.5 |
| 1864 | Leipzig | 7 | 1910 | Kiev | 0.8 |
| 1865 | Greece | 25 | 1910 | Kazan | 0.8 |
| 1865 | Italy | 4 | 1912 | London | 12 |
| 1871 | Birmingham | 18 | 1912 | Berlin | 17 |
| 1871 | Leeds | 19 | 1913 | Vienna | 17 |
| 1871 | Sweden | 11 | 1913 | Prague | 7.8 |
| 1873 | St. Petersburg | 2.7 | 1914 | Hanover | 5 |

Major Sources:  Hubbard 1970: 38, 43; Hennock 1973: 12;
Seton-Watson 1967: 662; Munro 1913: 132, 216, 230;
Keith-Lucas 1952: 60; Miller 1968: 186-87; Bater 1976:
356-60; Dawson 1914: 63-66; Hanchett 1976: 93, 101; Lafferty
1971: 133; Fried 1963: 128.

65,000 and 5,000 citizens of Liverpool were enfranchised out of 165,000 residents. Two thousand citizens of Copenhagen could vote in a population of 120,000 in 1840, while six years later 6,000 inhabitants of St. Petersburg could vote in a population of 485,000. In the 1860s, only 18,000 Viennese could vote in a population of 476,000 and fewer than 6,000 out of 80,000 residents of Leipzig could vote. As late as 1910, fewer than 20,000 citizens of Moscow and St. Petersburg could vote in local elections, although both cities were inhabited by about 1.5 million people (see Table 1.4 for additional data).

Where national elections were consistently rigged, as in Iberia and the Balkans, the same prevailed at the local level; indeed, such repressive measures were often applied in an even more intense manner by local elites and ensured grossly undemocratic local government. In general, in highly agrarian areas of Europe characterized by large landed estates and mass poverty and illiteracy, such as the southern parts of Spain, Italy and Portugal, eastern Germany, Hungary, Rumania and Russia, local governmental power was either formally entrusted to or informally dominated by semifeudalistic landowner cliques who manipulated and intimidated the rural masses through their economic power, education and ties to other ruling elements in their countries. These large landlords formed a key part of their countries' ruling coalitions, and used their economic and political power to shamelessly distort local government tax, spending and other policies. "A survey of Calabria [southern Italy] in 1910 found in one commune 83 usurpations of the common land, two of them by brothers of the mayor, 17 by his first cousins, two by his nephews, and a dozen more by communal councilors and their friends" (Smith 1959: 237).

Aside from the plural suffrage systems previously described for Sweden and Belgium, the most unusual local franchise laws were those of Germany, Austria, Hungary, Russia, and Denmark. The Prussian three-class voting system used in local elections was like that used on the Prussian state level, except that the poorest 10-15 per cent of the population was completely disenfranchised at the local level, voting was direct rather than indirect and one-half of all city councilmen were required to be resident homeowners; thus, in Berlin, for example, in 1908 only 9,000 persons (about 0.5 per cent of the population) could qualify for half the council seats. In 114 Prussian towns studied around 1910, it was discovered that 8,600 voters (1.3 per cent of all electors) fell in the highest tax class and elected one-third of all city councillors, while another 48,000 (7 per cent) and 629,360 (91.7 per cent) fell in the second and third class respectively, and exercised equivalent power (see Table 1.5 for data on specific cities in Prussia and elsewhere using the three-class system). In Berlin in 1912 a voter in the first class wielded power equivalent to that of 34 second-class voters and 378 third-class voters. Under this system, in some cases the first class consisted of a single voter, and the death or departure of a single wealthy person might drastically change the voting structure. Thus, at Essen, when the last member of the Krupp family died, the first voting class increased from 4 to 600 persons. A number

Table 1.5: Voter Distribution in 3-Class Voting Systems in European Cities, 1870-1914

| Date | City | Class I Voters Number | Class I Voters % of All Voters | Class II Voters Number | Class II Voters % of All Voters | Class III Voters Number | Class III Voters % of All Voters | Total Voters | % of Total Population |
|------|------|------|------|------|------|------|------|------|------|
| 1870 | Graz | 843 | 20 | 1,284 | 31 | 2,001 | 48 | 4,128 | 5.1 |
| 1873 | St. Petersburg | 224 | 1 | 887 | 5 | 17,479 | 94 | 18,590 | 2.7 |
| 1884 | Moscow | 222 | 1 | 1,360 | 7 | 18,315 | 92 | 19,892 | 2.6 |
| 1890 | Graz | 1,924 | 24 | 2,924 | 37 | 3,057 | 39 | 7,905 | 7.1 |
| 1891 | Berlin | 3,555 | 1 | 18,030 | 7 | 239,132 | 92 | 260,717 | 16.5 |
| 1891 | Vienna | 5,409 | 7 | 23,236 | 28 | 51,570 | 65 | 80,215 | 5.8 |
| 1900 | Essen | 3 | 0.015 | 401 | 2 | 18,991 | 98 | 19,295 | 16 |
| 1902 | Leipzig | 1,487 | 5 | 4,430 | 15 | 24,463 | 81 | 30,380 | 6 |
| 1903 | Cologne | 511 | 1 | 5,659 | 12 | 41,321 | 87 | 47,491 | 12 |
| 1903 | Berlin | 1,857 | 0.5 | 29,711 | 9 | 317,537 | 91 | 349,105 | 18 |
| 1910 | Graz | 2,596 | 19 | 4,634 | 34 | 6,386 | 47 | 13,616 | 8.9 |
| 1912 | Berlin | 936 | 0.2 | 32,096 | 8 | 353,704 | 92 | 360,717 | 16.5 |

Sources: Hubbard 1970:26, 38; Bater 1976: 356; Hanchett 1976: 101; Munro 1913: 132; Dawson 1914:66.

of other German states used variations of the Prussian system in local elections, such as the five-class system used in several cities in Saxony after 1890 and the reservation of certain elective posts for the most wealthy citizens of Hesse.

The Prussian three-class system (first used in the Prussian Rhineland in 1845 and then applied throughout the country in 1850) was also used in Austrian local elections after 1852 and Russian city elections between 1870 and 1892. In Austria, those who paid no taxes were disenfranchised in most cities, while those who together paid one-sixth of local taxes automatically sat on local city councils (see Table 1.5 for data on specific Austrian cities). In 1900, all adult males in Vienna who had resided in the city for three years, regardless of taxpaying status, were placed in a fourth voting class, comprising 228,000 people, who elected 20 city councillors, while the 60,000 voters in the original three classes collectively elected 46 councillors. In Russia, the three-class system introduced in 1870 for 423 cities excluded those who did not pay taxes and did not own a home, thus reducing the suffrage to less than 1 per cent in most towns. In 1892, the three-class system was abolished in Russia, but wealth requirements for voting were drastically raised, reducing the number enfranchised in St. Petersburg from 21,176 to 7,152 in a population of about one million. In rural areas of Russia, a system of class voting was established in 1864, with separate curia for landowners, townsmen and peasants. Under this system, the landowners, who constituted about 1 per cent of the population, obtained about 40 per cent of the seats in the district assemblies (uiezd zemtvos) and about 75 per cent of the seats in the provincial zemtvos, which were elected by the uiezd zemtvos. Austrian provincial diets were elected on a similarly biased four-curia system for all or most of the 1861-1914 period. Thus, in Galicia, a deputy to the provincial diet elected from the curia of the great landowners represented 52 electors, and a deputy elected from the chambers of commerce curia represented 39 electors, but deputies in the urban and rural curias represented 2,264 and 8,764 electors respectively. Under the Austrian provincial diet scheme, the vast majority of the poor were completely disenfranchised.

In Hungary, after 1867 half of county and local officials were elective (by a fairly broad franchise of all taxpayers in rural villages and small towns but only by the 6 per cent or so enfranchised for national elections in counties and large cities). The other half of local and city councils consisted of the largest taxpayers only, who gained their seats automatically. In Denmark, local elections dating from 1837 enfranchised less than 1 per cent of the population in rural areas, about 2 per cent in Copenhagen, and 7 per cent in six other major cities. In 1855, the local suffrage throughout Denmark was expanded to include all those enfranchised for the Folketing (lower chamber)—about 15 per cent of the population—but these voters elected only half of city and provincial councils while the 20 per cent of the tax payers who paid the highest taxes elected the other half. In 1908 the privilege of the large taxpayers was abolished.

# Chapter 2

# Restrictions on Freedom of Expression and Organization

*Repression of the Press in Nineteenth-Century Europe*

Conservative elites in nineteenth-century Europe were, in general, as opposed to freedom of the press as they were to universal suffrage. Metternich, who sponsored the infamous Carlsbad Decrees of 1819, which gagged the German press for the following 30 years, termed liberty of the press a "scourge" and the "most urgent evil" of his time (Talmon 1967: 35; Emerson 1968: 116). Shortly before King Charles X of France attempted to impose prior press censorship in that country in 1830, thereby helping to set off a revolution that overthrew him, he received a report from his ministers that claimed the press had been by nature, at all times "only an instrument of disorder and sedition" (Rader 1973: 222). Viscount Sidmouth, home secretary during the reactionary English ministry of Lord Liverpool (1812-22), termed the press the "most malignant and formidable enemy to the constitution to which it owed its freedom" (Aspinall 1949: 42).

Conservatives complained that the press spread lies and led the masses to believe themselves competent to deal with matters of public affairs that they did not and could not understand. Moreover, the conservatives feared that press freedom would lead to increasing public demands for political power, which, like universal suffrage, would only threaten the public good--as well as the conservatives' own power and privileges. Napoleon I once candidly declared, "If I allowed a free press, I would not be in power for another three months" (Olson 1966: 156). Lord Ellenborough, a British conservative, in defending a proposal introduced in parliament in 1819 designed to tax the radical working class press out of existence, declared that the "pauper press" had become

> an utter stranger to truth, and only sent forth a continual stream of falsehoods and malignity. ... The mischief arising from them in the deception and delusion practised upon the lowest classes by means of the grossest and most malignant falsehoods, was such that it threatened the most material

Table 2.1: Repression of the Press in Europe, 1815-1914

| Country | Constitutional or Legal Ban Ending Prior Press Censorship | End of Severe Administration of Press Restrictions | End of Special Press Taxes (where applied) |
|---|---|---|---|
| Austria | 1867 | never before 1914 | 1899 |
| Belgium | 1830 | 1830 | 1848 |
| Bulgaria | 1879 | sporadic until 1914 | |
| Denmark | 1849 | 1846 | |
| France | 1830 | 1881 | 1881 |
| Germany (Prussia before 1870) | 1849 | never before 1914 | 1874 |
| Hungary | 1867 | never before 1914 | |
| Italy (Sardinia before 1870) | 1848 | c. 1900 | |
| Netherlands | 1815 | c. 1848 | 1869 |
| Norway | 1814 | 1814 | |
| Portugal | 1834 | 1852 | |
| Rumania | 1866 | 1866 | |
| Russia | 1865 (partial)/1905 | never before 1914 | |
| Serbia | 1869 | 1903 | |
| Spain | 1837 | 1883 | |
| Sweden | 1809 | 1838 | |
| Switzerland | 1848 | c. 1830 | |
| United Kingdom | 1695 | c. 1830 | 1861 |

injuries to the best interests of the country unless some means were devised of stemming its torrent (Aspinall 1949: 58).

Occasionally the remedy proposed by European conservatives for curbing press abuses was drastic indeed. Thus, Friedrich Gentz, Metternich's secretary, wrote in 1819, "As a preventive measure against the abuses of the press, absolutely nothing should be printed for years. ... With this maxim as a rule we should in short time get back to God and the truth" (Artz 1963: 67). The Spanish dictator Ramon Narváez, who dominated affairs in his country for much of the mid-nineteenth century, declared, "It is not enough to pick up the copies of the newspapers--you have to kill the newspapermen" (Payne 1967: 24).

Although freedom of the press was dreaded by most conservatives, demands for such freedom were a major cry of political dissidents wherever press restrictions were maintained in ninteenth-century Europe. Before 1850, middle-class liberals made freedom of the press, expansion of the suffrage, and the introduction of constitutional government their key demands wherever such were lacking. In most European countries, press regulations were eased enough by about 1870 to allow moderates and liberals to express themselves, but radicals and socialists frequently continued to face repression and to make demands for press freedom a major grievance.

Liberals and radicals often deified press freedom in terms as exaggerated as those conservatives used to condemn it. Thus, eighteenth-century British philosopher David Hume, referring to the capacity of public opinion to thwart evil ambitions on the part of the monarchy, saw nothing "so effectual to this purpose as the liberty of the press by which all the learning, wit and genius of the nation may be employed on the side of freedom and everyone be animated to its defence" (Ruud 1979: 522). British advocates of complete freedom of the press during struggles against newspaper taxes during the 1830s declared that press liberty would bring about the "liberation of the whole human race" and the disappearance forever of "internal discord, commotion and strife" (Wiener 1969: 120). A French writer termed press freedom "the entire constitution. ... the guardian of manners, the protector against injustice. Nothing is lost as long as it exists" (Anderson and Anderson 1967: 253).


## Techniques of Repression of the Press

The development of the modern printing press and the development of press repression were virtually simultaneous. By 1600, licensing and censorship systems for printed matters were universal throughout Europe, and violations of repressive press laws subjected printers and journalists accused of sedition, heresy or treason to death in many countries, including Spain, France, Austria, Germany, England, and some of the Swiss cantons. Thus, in 1664, John Twyn, an English printer convicted of treason, was hanged, cut down while still alive, and then emasculated, disemboweled, quartered and beheaded.

Previously existing controls were drastically tightened in most European countries with the outbreak of the French Revolution. In several countries, including Spain and Russia, virtually all news about the Revolution was banned from the press and all French publications were barred from importation. Empress Catherine the Great of Russia, declaring that it was "absolutely necessary to exterminate everything French, down to the name" (Yarmolinsky 1962: 21) barred the import of all objects of French origin, including works of art, while her successor, Emperor Paul I, barred the importation of all printed matter from anywhere, including musical scores. In Austria, all reading rooms and lending libraries were shut down in 1798-99, and in 1801 censorship was extended to include mottoes on fans, snuff boxes, musical instruments and toys.

Meaningful freedom of the press in Europe in 1815 existed only in Norway. A few other countries--including the United Kingdom, Sweden and the United Netherlands--had technically abolished prior censorship, but even in these countries various administrative techniques and post-publication prosecutions were used to reduce press freedom severely. As late as 1850, meaningful press freedom existed only in the Low Countries, Scandinavia and the United Kingdom. By 1914, major restrictions on press freedom still continued in Russia, Germany, Hungary, and, to a slightly lesser extent, in Austria (see Table 2.1).

Where severe restrictions on press freedom existed, newspapers were often reduced to complete blandness and usually could not cover public affairs in any meaningful way. An English visitor to Spain in 1820 noted that the papers there contained nothing but reports of the weather and "accounts of miracles wrought by different Virgins, lives of holy friars and sainted nuns, romances of marvelous conversions, libels against Jews, heretics and Freemasons, and histories of apparitions" (Artz 1963: 134-35). The great Czech historian František Palacký complained in 1830, "I do not know how it will end when we cannot write about anything except cook-books and prayer-books, fairy-tales and charades" (Zacek 1970: 99), while the Saxon journalist Robert Blum complained in the 1840s, "We must write pure nonsense or not be published at all" (Newman 1974: 46). A French journalist, commenting on the German press in 1841, remarked, "If an American indian had had the opportunity to read such a paper for the first time, he would have come to the conclusion that German life consisted of hunting and eating" (Fetscher 1980: 380).

Regulation of the press was the subject of great attention and much legislation in nineteenth-century Europe. Between 1810 and 1883, there were at least 15 major press laws and decrees issued in Spain, while the French press law of 1881 replaced 42 laws containing 325 separate clauses that had been passed during the previous 75 years. Repressive techniques used in nineteenth-century Europe to control the press can be divided into two major categories: 1) direct forms of repression, designed either to prevent undesirable material from ever being printed (prior censorship) or to punish those responsible for such material that did appear in print (punitive or post-publication censorship); and 2) indirect repression, which did not specifically outlaw or punish particular journalists or published material but was designed to discourage the poor from publishing or buying newspapers by imposing financial constraints upon the press. Frequently direct and indirect means of press regulation existed in the same country simultaneously.

Direct repression of the press: Prior censorship and licensing. The focus of the greatest discontent over press repression in the pre-1848 period was on systems of prior censorship and licensing that were used in the overwhelming majority of European nations. Where press licensing was required, it was illegal to publish a newspaper or other printed matter without first obtaining a permit from the authorities. Thus the regime ensured that only "reliable" individuals engaged in publishing. Where prior censorship was imposed, material could not be set in type without being approved by the authorities. Together, systems of licensing and prior censorship were designed to ensure that only non-objectionable persons would be in the printing business and that the particular material they published would be scrutinized to ensure that nothing "harmful" slipped through. Licensed printers who showed signs of "unreliability" could have their licenses withdrawn and objectionable material could be excluded before it ever appeared in print.

As can be seen in Table 2.1, prior censorship was gradually abolished during the nineteenth century, and by 1914 no European country maintained such a system. In most countries, licensing systems died along with prior censorship systems, but this was not always the case. Thus, prior censorship was barred, but licensing was required under the Prussian press law of 1851, the 1852 French law, the 1867 Austrian law, and the 1879 Spanish law.

By far the most notorious prior censorship systems in nineteenth-century Europe were those in pre-1860 Austria and pre-1905 Russia. The Austrian censorship banned 5,000 books during the 1835-48 period, including works of Rousseau, Spinoza, Goethe and Schiller, and even extended to inscriptions for gravestones, memorial cards, badges, cuff links and tobacco boxes. In Russia, in 1897 the catalog of forbidden or expurgated foreign works alone included 7,500 French and German titles. Among the authors banned at one time or another in Russia were Diderot, Hobbes, Jefferson, Stendhal, Balzac and Hugo, and the particular titles banned included Hawthorne's Scarlet Letter, Peter Parley's Juvenile Tales for Boys and Girls, and a book in French on Physiology and Hygiene of the Beard and Mustache. The pre-1848 prior censorship systems in Germany and Italy were also often extremely harsh. In 1835, for example, the German Confederation diet banned the entire literary school known as "Young Germany," which was headed by the towering writers Ludwig Börne and Heinrich Heine.

Direct repression of the press: Post-publication (punitive) censorship. While prior censorship systems were special targets of liberals' opprobrium, systems of post-publication retribution, sometimes known as punitive censorship, often proved just as threatening to press freedom. Every European country maintained some laws that provided punishment for alleged abuses of the press even after prior censorship and licensing systems were abolished. In Russia, Austria, Hungary and Germany, these systems of punitive censorship were so severe that press freedom never existed in any meaningful form as late as 1914. In some cases, punitive censorship systems were administered by methods that made them practically identical to prior censorship schemes. Thus, under the systems established in France in 1822, Russia in 1865, Austria in 1867, and Germany in 1874, copies of "non-censored" newspapers had to be submitted to the authorities either just before or simultaneous with the final printing process for distribution. This allowed the authorities, if they spotted undesirable material, to seize the press run before any significant distribution occurred. Realistically, the only difference between punitive censorship and prior censorship schemes was that under prior censorship the censors usually got the blame if something slipped through, and the publisher did not lose money when already printed material was seized, while under punitive censorship systems the publisher risked both huge financial losses and administrative or judicial sanctions.

The massive press repression that frequently occurred in regimes that had abolished prior censorship clearly demonstrates that press freedom was by no means synonymous with an end to such procedures. In Germany for example, where press censorship was explicitly forbidden in the 1874 press law, over 3,200 prosecutions were brought between 1874 and 1890, and under the anti-socialist law of 1878-90 1,229 different publications were suppressed by administrative measures. Over 600 prosecutions for "lèse-majesté" (criticism of the emperor) alone were brought throughout Germany in 1894; in the city of Düsseldorf during the 1890s, socialist editors were prosecuted 144 times and sentenced to a total of six years in jail for a variety of press law violations. In France, where prior censorship was barred after 1830, there were 520 press prosecutions in Paris alone between 1830 and 1834. Between December 1848 and December 1850 in France, 185 republican newspapers in 177 cities faced press charges that succeeded in forcing over 40 papers out of business. During an 1877 constitutional crisis in France, over 2,500 press prosecutions were brought during a seven-month period. In Austria, where prior censorship ended in the 1860s, over 2,000 newspapers were prosecuted between 1877 and 1880. In Russia, where all prior censorship was abolished in 1905, a total of 4,386 administrative penalties were imposed on periodicals between 1905 and 1910, and nearly 1,000 newspapers were suppressed during the same period. Of the 645 issues of the Bolshevik newspaper Pravda published between April 1912 and July 1914, 155 were confiscated and 36 drew fines.

In most European countries, including both those with prior and those with punitive censorship systems, journalists were constantly faced with vague provisions and inconsistent enforcement. They seldom knew what was and was not legal to print. The post-1815

Austrian censorship in Lombardy-Venetia barred any writing that "offended against the rules of style and purity" (King 1912: 55), while the Russian censorship decree of 1826 banned writing that violated the "rules and purity of the Russian language" or was "full of grammatical errors" (Seton-Watson 1967: 251). The French press law of 1822 authorized suppression of newspapers when the overall "tone" in a "series of articles constitutes an attack upon public peace, the respect due the religion of the state or other religions legally recognized in France, the authority of the King, the stability of constitutional institutions, the inviolability of the sale of national property and the peaceful possession thereof" (Stewart 1968: 137). The 1822 Spanish press law banned writings that "spread rules or doctrines or ... refer to acts dedicated to exciting rebellion or disturbing the public peace, even though they may be disguised as allegories of imaginary persons or countries or of past times, or as dreams or fictions or anything similar" (Schulte 1968: 142). An 1863 Russian censorship directive banned materials that "contradict the fundamental ideas of our state structure and root conditions of public order" (Balmuth 1979: 13).

Sometimes the confusion and vagueness of repressive press laws and decrees shone clearly through official statements. Thus, the Austrian censorship decree of 1810 declared:

> In the future no ray of light, wherever it should appear should be disregarded and unrecognized in the monarchy. Nor should it be robbed of any useful result. But the heart and head of the immature are to be protected cautiously from the poisonous aspirations of the self-seeking seducers and from the dangerous illusions of crazed heads (Emerson 1968: 29).

Even the censors could often not determine what they should or should not allow, with the result that material rejected by one censor was sometimes allowed by another and censors who allowed material that turned out to be displeasing to the authorities might lose their jobs or even be jailed. One Russian censor who was detained briefly in 1842 in such an instance requested the secret police chief to tell Czar Nicholas I "how difficult it is to be a censor. We really do not know what is demanded of us. ... We are never safe and can never fulfill our obligations" (Monas 1961: 180-81). Austrian intellectuals who appealed for an end to prior censorship there in 1845 complained, "The writer is judged by norms which he does not know and is condemned without being heard and without being able to defend himself" (Anderson and Anderson 1967: 263).

The French dramatist Pierre Beaumarchais satirized such press regulations in pre-revolutionary France when he put the following words in the mouth of the hero of The Marriage of Figaro (1784):

> They all tell me that if in my writings I mention neither the government, nor public worship, nor politics, nor morals, nor people in office, nor influential corporations, nor the opera,

nor the other theatres, nor any one who has ought to do with anything, I may print everything freely, subject to the approval of two or three censors (Hohenberg 1971: 72).

Seventy years later, another French writer, Maxime du Camp, complained that before writing a word under the regime of Napoleon III, "you had to turn your pen around seven times between your fingers, since before the courts you could sin by thought, by word, by action or by omission" (Spencer 1956: 27).

Indirect repression of the press: Caution money and special taxes. A number of nineteenth-century European countries supplemented direct prior or punitive censorship of objectionable material with "indirect" forms of press controls, involving the requirement that publishers pay security bonds or "caution money" and that newspapers pay special taxes. The caution money requirement was intended to ensure that only the relatively wealthy could publish newspapers, while the purpose of special press taxes was to ensure that only the relatively wealthy could buy them. Since neither type of requirement directly restricted particular material, they amounted to indirect attempts to restrict the circulation of "undesirable" printed matter.

The security bond or caution money requirement involved the mandatory deposit of specified sums of money with governmental officials before it was legal to publish a periodical. Supposedly its purpose was to ensure payment of fines in case of future transgressions of press laws, but its real purpose was unquestionably to prevent the poor from publishing newspapers. Caution money was required for part or all of the nineteenth century in at least Austria, Hungary, Spain, Germany, France and Russia. The requirement seems to have been especially significant in France--where one scholar notes the amount required fluctuated "in inverse ratio to the liberality of the regime and also to the degree of security it felt it enjoyed" (Hemmings 1971: 53)--and in Spain. In France, the caution money requirement was first introduced in 1819. It was lowered in 1828 and again in 1830, raised in 1835, abolished in 1848, reinstated in 1849, raised in 1852, abolished in 1870, reinstated once more in 1871, and finally terminated for good in 1881. At their heights, the required caution money fees for Parisian and Madrid dailies were respectively $20,000 in 1835 and $18,000 in 1857.

Special taxes were imposed on the press in nineteenth-century Europe in at least Belgium, Austria, the Netherlands, France, Germany and England (see Table 2.1). They were designed, as the preamble to an 1819 stamp tax bill in the United Kingdom explained forthrightly, to "restrain the small publications which issue from the Press in great numbers and at a low price" (Aspinall 1949: 9) by making them too expensive for the poor to buy. Although such taxes most commonly took the form of a stamp tax that had to be paid on each newspaper sold, in some cases special taxes were also imposed on newspaper advertisements or on paper, all of which were similarly reflected in increased purchase prices. As one British newspaper vendor charged with illegally selling newspapers without having paid the stamp tax told a court in 1831, the purpose of such taxes was to keep the poor "from getting information" and "from knowing their rights" (Wiener 1969: 117).

### The Impact of Press Repression in Nineteenth-Century Europe

Press repression unquestionably was effective in reducing the amount of published material in nineteenth-century Europe, and especially the publication and circulation of opposition writings. In the Habsburg Empire, for example, the number of periodicals jumped from 184 in 1847 to 368 in 1848 when press controls were ended as a result of the 1848 revolution. The post-1848 reaction reduced the number of Austrian periodicals to 128 by 1856, but an easing of controls after 1856 led to a tripling of periodicals published by 1862. Following a further easing of controls in the 1860s the number of periodicals published in the Austrian half of the Habsburg Empire alone jumped to 1,378 by 1882, and after caution deposits and stamp taxes were abolished in the 1890s the number reached 5,534 by 1912. Similar data could be cited for many other European countries, with an invariable growth of newspapers and newspaper circulation under liberal press laws, and a contraction in the press with the imposition of harsh controls. Thus, in France, Napoleon I reduced the number of Parisian newspapers from 72 to 4 through harsh repression between 1799 and 1811, but the end of press controls brought about by the 1848 revolution there led to an explosion of new papers and a quadrupling of newspaper circulation in Paris. Harsh repression under the regime of Napoleon III reduced the number of political journals in the French provinces from 420 in 1851 to 260 by 1865; subsequently the passage of a liberal press law in 1881 fostered an increase in the number of provincial dailies from 114 to 280 between 1880 and 1885.

Special press taxes had an enormous impact upon nineteenth-century newspaper circulation. In Great Britain, annual newspaper circulation jumped from 25.5 million to over 53 million during the two years following a drastic lowering of the stamp tax in 1836. Until the final abolition of the British stamp, paper and advertising taxes in 1855-61, not a single daily newspaper was published outside of London; afterwards they developed in a flood, with the total number of papers in the United Kingdom rising from 795 in 1856 to 1,450 in 1871. In the Netherlands, where a crushing stamp and advertising tax swallowed up over 50 per cent of gross newspaper revenues and increased prices as much as 10 cents per copy, the number of daily newspapers jumped in one year from 9 to 14 after the measures were abolished in 1869.

Thousands of journalists were fined and/or jailed as a result of press repression, and thousands more censored themselves to avoid prosecution. The great Austrian dramatist Franz Grillparzer lamented, "Despotism has destroyed my literary life," (Seton-Watson 1965: 165) while the Russian literary giant Alexander Pushkin moaned in a letter to his wife, "Only the devil could have thought of having me born in Russia with a mind and talent" (Monas 1961: 244).

A complete list of the prominent nineteenth-century Europeans who were jailed for their writings would be very long indeed. Among them were the English journalists William Cobbett and Richard Carlile, the French caricaturist Honoré Daumier, Swedish socialist leaders August Palm and Hjalmar Branting (later Swedish prime minister), Serbian radical leader and later prime minister Nicholas Pasic, Austrian socialist leader Victor Adler (jailed eight different times for his writings), Dutch socialist leader Domela Niuwenhuis (jailed for eight months in 1887 for writing that the Dutch king had made "little of his job" [Kendall 1975: 248]), Hungarian socialist leader Leo Frankel, German socialist leaders Wilhelm and Karl Liebknecht, anarchist writer Prince Peter Kropotkin and Hungarian nationalist leader Louis Kossuth. Karl Marx was expelled from France, Belgium and Prussia for his writings, while the great French anarchist philosopher Pierre-Joseph Proudhon was repeatedly prosecuted in his homeland for his writings on such charges as "exciting hatred and outrage against the king's government" and "reproduction in bad faith of false news likely to disturb the public peace" (Woodcock 1972: 66, 216).

## Resistance to Repression of the Press in Nineteenth-Century Europe

Although press repression in nineteenth-century Europe severely cramped discussion of public affairs and led to the persecution of thousands of journalists, the best efforts of governments to control the press were never entirely effective. Throughout the century, journalists and citizens conspired, often with considerable success, to evade press regulations by legal technicalities, evasions and outright defiance. Even the most repressive regimes--Metternich's Austria and Czarist Russia--were never able to stop completely the tide of journalistic and popular resistance.

Resistance to press repression took two major forms: 1) legal means of resistance, including the use of "Aesopian language" and various technical means of evading press regulations; and 2) illegal means of resistance, including clandestine publishing and the smuggling of illegal materials. The use of so-called "Aesopian language" (to use the term that gained wide currency in Russia) was universal in regimes that had repressive press laws. It consisted simply of making political points without ever using language direct enough to run afoul of press laws. Political criticism was often disguised as literary or social commentary, and remarks about the political regime in which the publication appeared would on the surface pretend to be about another country. Thus, political messages that could not be expressed directly were expressed through the use of allusion. And as Stendhal wrote of Italians, "If you are dealing with a race which is at once dissatisfied and witty, everything soon becomes an 'allusion' " (Martin 1969: 219). It was virtually impossible to prevent such material from appearing in the press without entirely suppressing the printed word, and even the most repressive governments were almost helpless in the face of such techniques. Thus, V. K. Plehve, the reactionary minister of the interior in Russia before his assassination in 1904, is reported to have asked one prominent radical, "Why do you want freedom of the press when even without it you are a master of saying between the lines all that you wish to say?" (Seton-Watson 1967: 481). Historian Bertram Wolfe has elaborated some of the specific techniques of "Aesopian language" used in Russia:

> Since direct political discussion was prohibited, all literature tended to become a criticism of Russian life, and literary criticism but another form of social criticism. ... If the censor forbade explicit statement, he was skillfully eluded by indirection--by innocent seeming tales of other lands or times, by complicated parables, animal fables, double meanings, overtones, by investing apparently trivial events with the pent-up energies possessing the writer, so that the reader became compelled to dwell upon them until their hidden meanings became manifest. Men found means of conveying a criticism of the regime through a statistical monograph on German agriculture, through the study of a sovereign four centuries dead, the review of a Norwegian play, the analysis of some evil in the Prussian or some virtue in the British state (1964: 36).

One especially common type of "Aesopian language" was to hide criticism of a particular regime behind supposed criticism of a foreign country. The great Czech journalist Karl Havlíček became famous for his discussions of British mistreatment of Ireland in his newspaper Prazke Noviny, which everyone in Bohemia knew were really about Austrian denial of Czech national rights. It was especially common for writers in Austrian-dominated Italy to refer to past French and Spanish domination of their homeland when Austria was really meant. Thus, it is reported that in Florence when the French minister became indignant during a play about a Sicilian revolt against French rule in 1282, the Austrian minister told him, "Don't take it badly; the envelope is addressed to you but the contents are for me" (Hearder 1963: 131). In Serbia, the satirist Radoje Domanović became a sensation for his tales of "Stradija," a mythical country famous "for its swine and tomfooleries in which ministers played musical chairs while police spared the voters the trouble of choosing candidates to parliament" (Petrovich 1976: 488).

Another legal means of resistance to press repression was the employment of technical evasions of press regulations. Thus, until 1819, the British stamp tax could be evaded by publishing newspapers in a format that technically fell outside the legal definition of "newspaper." After William Cobbett, publisher of the Political Register was forced to pay the tax by the 1819 law, circulation fell from 50,000 to 400 per week. In some countries, suppression of a newspaper could be evaded by starting up the same paper again with the same staff but with a slightly different name. In Sweden, Lars Johan Hierta's Aftonbladet went through 23 minor name changes before King Charles John finally gave up prosecuting it in 1838. The Bolshevik newspaper Pravda (Truth) was repeatedly suppressed but kept reappearing under titles such as Workers Truth and Labor

Truth before it was suppressed for good in 1914 in its eighth reincarnation. The Carlsbad Decrees of 1819, which required prior censorship of all publications in Germany of 320 pages or less (designed to stem the tide of cheap radical tracts), were evaded by printers who used the largest possible type and the smallest possible page so that even short works would exceed that length. French publishers evaded the 1820 press law, which provided censorship for periodicals only (i.e., material published under the same title at regular intervals) by printing material banned by the censorship in irregularly published pamphlets under such titles as "censorship rejects."

In a number of countries, including France, Russia and Germany, where press laws required that newspapers name a "responsible editor" who would be liable for all published material that contravened press laws, it became common to name non-essential volunteers to serve in that position who would be willing to go to jail while the real editors went about their business. Thus, in 1913 the Russian police noted that the "responsible editor" for Pravda was usually an "unintelligent individual who does not take part in the work of the paper and who is often, ... absolutely illiterate" (Bassow 1954: 60). A sign was often posted in the Pravda office, reading, "No editors needed." Even the requirement that newspapers be submitted simultaneously with publication for possible confiscation in some regimes that had eliminated prior censorship could be evaded. Thus, the Russian law of 1905 required that the first three copies of any newspaper be submitted to the Committee on Press Affairs, but did not specify how long it might take to deliver them. The editors of Pravda, published in St. Petersburg after 1912, entrusted the task of daily deliveries of the first three copies to:

> 70-year old Matvej, the plant watchman, whose advanced years and slow gait guaranteed that the trip across the city to the Committee's office would indeed be a time-consuming one. Matvej left the Pravda plant around 3 a.m. and usually took one and one-half to two hours to reach his destination. After delivering the papers, the old man remained in the office, ostensibly to rest but really in order to keep a close watch on the inspector. ... If, after reading Pravda, the inspector turned to another newspaper, Matvej returned at a leisurely pace to the plant on foot, but if the inspector telephoned the Third Police District, which included Pravda's plant, Matvej flew out of the room, hailed a droshky and raced back. Watchers stationed around the plant waited for his return and when they saw him coming around the corner at full speed, ... the alarm was passed and everyone started working feverishly. ... By the time the police arrived, most of the papers were gone. Only a few were left behind for the sake of "protocol" (Bassow 1954: 51-52).

In a number of European cities, literate members of the working class overcame the high prices of newspapers caused by press taxes (and other factors) by banding together to share newspapers or subscribing to public reading rooms where individuals who paid a small fee could gain access to a wide variety of publications. As one scholar notes, "Working people clubbing together for subscriptions and collective reading formed the very basis of the new working-class culture in places like Lyon, Berlin and Birmingham" (Gillis 1977: 219). Thus, in England, reading rooms competed for working-class customers by subscribing to large numbers of periodicals and boasting of their other comforts and conveniences. One Manchester reading room claimed in a March 1833 advertisement that it purchased 96 newspapers, including the "most able and popular publications of the day, whether political, literary or scientific," and promised in addition a "wholesome and exhilirating beverage at a small expense, instead of the noxious and intoxicating stuff usually supplied at the ale-house," all to be consumed "in a comfortable and genteel apartment, in the evening brilliantly lit with gas" (Aspinall 1949: 26).

Legal resistance to press repression was accompanied in many countries by illegal resistance, particularly the publishing of clandestine periodicals and the smuggling of forbidden materials into countries. Clandestine publishing probably was most widespread in Russia, where the intensity of the repression forced radicals to develop highly ingenious methods of defiance. Thus, the Bolsheviks set up a quite literally "underground" press in Baku, which printed over a million copies of periodicals and leaflets during the 1900-1910 period. Smuggling was very widespread in nineteenth-century Europe. Giuseppe Mazzini's newspaper Young Italy was smuggled into Italy from France inside barrels of pumice stone, boxes of fish and false-bottomed trunks. Vladimir Jovanović's Liberty was smuggled into Serbia from Geneva in ordinary envelopes after being printed on extremely thin paper, while Lenin's newspaper, Iskra, was printed in tiny characters on thin cigarette paper and smuggled into Russia from Germany and Switzerland. In probably the most sophisticated smuggling operation of nineteenth-century Europe, the German Social Democrats, under the direction of "Red Postmaster" Julius Motteler, smuggled 10,000 copies a week of Sozialdemokrat into Germany after the paper was forced out of the country by the anti-Socialist law of 1878-90. In Great Britain, publishers widely defied the stamp taxes in the 1830-36 period by simply refusing to pay it. During those years they published an estimated 500 periodicals, with a peak circulation of 100,000 a week, without paying the tax. The "war of the unstamped" played a major role in convincing parliament to reduce the tax greatly in 1836.

The "war of the unstamped" in England, the publication of clandestine papers, the smuggling of illegal materials, and the use of such legal evasions as "Aesopian language" all depended to a large degree upon widespread popular support and understanding. Thousands of ordinary Europeans joined with journalists and publishers in both risking retaliation and resisting the law in the cause of freedom of the press. One English seller of unstamped newspapers declared in 1835:

> Were I to give over selling the Unstamped, my customers
> declare that they will get them of some other person; as
> they were determined to have an Untaxed Newspaper, even
> if they subscribed among themselves to purchase the
> material for printing, for cheap knowledge they would have
> (Wiener 1969: 116).

## Restrictions on Freedom of Assembly and Association

Virtually every European country placed severe restrictions on
freedom of political assembly and association during part or all of the
1815-1914 era. Before 1848, the dominant rural character and low
level of mass politicization in most European countries combined to
make restrictions on freedom of assembly and association of relatively
minor significance to most of the European population. However,
beginning with the 1848 revolutions, demands for such freedoms on an
unrestricted basis were made with increasing frequency. Despite
these growing demands and a rapidly increasing politicization of the
burgeoning urban lower classes, socialist political activity, a major
target of continuing restrictions, remained effectively outlawed or
severely constrained until 1880 in France, 1890 in Germany and
Austria, 1900 in Italy and until 1914 in Hungary and Russia. As late as
1914, only the United Kingdom, France, Scandinavia, Switzerland, the
Low Countries, Italy, Greece and Serbia enjoyed meaningful freedom
of assembly and association. In Germany, Austria, Hungary, Russia,
Iberia, Rumania and Bulgaria such freedoms were either still subjected
to severe legal restrictions or, even if secure in law, were subject to
frequent abridgment in practice.

Before 1848 almost every European state imposed highly
restrictive statutory or administrative restrictions on freedom of
assembly and association. The major exceptions were Great Britain
(where freedom of petition had been won in 1689, although in practice
assembly and association were often obstructed during the pre-1848
period during times of high social unrest); Belgium (which guaranteed
such freedoms in the landmark liberal constitution of 1830); and
Switzerland (where free assembly and association were among the
major demands won in many of the cantonal revolutions of 1830).

Elsewhere, most European countries maintained harsh restrictions
on such activity, either through explicit legislation or under the
tradition of Roman Law, which regarded voluntary association for any
purpose as suspect and required such groups to obtain governmental
authorization to be regarded as legal. The Prussian law code issued in
1794 spelled out such restrictions, barring all associations whose
purposes and activities were deemed "contrary to the general peace,
security and order" (Anderson and Anderson 1967: 202). All political
gatherings and associations were banned throughout Germany by the
German Confederation diet in 1832 in the aftermath of uprisings in a
number of German states in 1830. In Austria during the early

nineteenth century the formation of virtually all groups, including charitable and learned societies, had to be approved by the government. "The term 'association' was stretched so widely that permission had to be obtained even for a dance employing an orchestra of more than two instruments" (Macartney 1969: 165). In France, a provision of the 1810 penal code (which remained in effect until 1901) required governmental approval for the formation of any organization of over 20 people concerned with "religious, literary, political or other matters" (Dupeux 1976: 143). King Ferdinand I of the Two Sicilies (1759-1825) refused to sanction even the formation of societies for improving the mulberry bush or lighting towns with gas, on the grounds that "associations are hurtful to the state, for they enlighten the people and spread Liberal ideas" (King 1912: 39).

During the 1848 revolutions, the demand for freedom of assembly and association was raised across Europe from France to the Danubian Principalities. In most areas where violent outbreaks occurred, including France, Austria, Italy, Germany and Wallachia, this demand was temporarily won in 1848. Scores of organizations suddenly emerged, and usually just as suddenly collapsed or were shut down when freedom of assembly and association was withdrawn with suppression of the revolts.

Although the political gains of the 1848 revolutions quickly evaporated in most countries, permanent constitutional protection for freedom of assembly and association was obtained in Piedmont (1848—extended to the rest of Italy after 1859), the Netherlands (1848), Switzerland (1848) and Denmark (1849). Subsequent constitutional or legal guarantees were granted in Rumania (1866), Austria (1867), Spain (1876), Bulgaria (1879), Serbia (1881), France (1901), Russia (1906), Portugal (1911) and Greece (1911). Hungary, almost uniquely, never recognized freedom of assembly and association even in principle, and the requirement that every proposed organization and meeting receive official approval, imposed by ministerial decree, was administered in a highly arbitrary manner, especially when minority nationalities and socialists sought permission. Thus, even an attempt to form a singing society in the Slovak town of Tiszolcz was repeatedly blocked, and one meeting of rural laborers was forbidden by police in 1898 on the grounds that "it does not seem suitable that the workmen should concern themselves with questions which offer no advantage to them, or should be roused to excitement in public assemblies." A meeting planned by Slovaks in 1907 to demand suffrage reform was blocked partly because it was allegedly not made clear whether the franchise demands desired were to be "exercised in the territory of the Hungarian State or that of another State" (Seton-Watson 1972: 282).

Although illegal meetings were dispersed everywhere in Europe before freedom of assembly and association was granted, the repeated use of mounted troops, whips and sabres to disrupt brutally such assemblies distinguished Russia from the other European nations. To cite one dramatic example, a peaceful meeting of 1,500 students in a large hall at Nizhny Novgorod (Gorky) on December 29, 1904 called to urge the granting of a constitution was invaded by 100 mounted police wielding bared sabres. "Resistance was offered with sticks and chairs, but the floor caved in almost immediately with many injuries on both sides" (Emmons 1977: 61).

Even after freedom of assembly and association was recognized in principle, many European countries, especially in southern, central and eastern Europe, continued to impose various restrictions upon such activities in practice or suspended constitutional guarantees wholesale during periods of high political tension. Many countries retained provisions authorizing administrative or judicial dissolution of associations and public assemblies for extremely vague reasons, such as pursuing "illegal" goals or threatening "public security," as in the Danish constitutional provision of 1849, the Dutch law of 1855, the Swedish decree of 1864, the Austrian law of 1867, the Bulgarian constitutional provision of 1879, the Italian law of 1886 and the Russian decree of 1906. In Germany, Austria and Russia, numerous additional restrictions were imposed and were often administered in a severe manner. Thus, a public lecture on "tuberculosis and its social causes" was forbidden in Russia in 1906, and in 1912 a Russian official halted a lecture on "nationality" by the noted historian Paul Miliukov after Miliukov noted that nationalism had become a "banner of the liberal movement" (Thurston 1980: 337). The general tenor of the Austrian and German restrictions has been synthesized in one scholarly account:

> An official agency must receive a copy of the agenda of a meeting and statutes and all publications of an association; it must be supplied with the names ... of the members, ... and of the persons attending the assembly or belonging to the association; it must be notified ... in advance of each assembly. ... The law ... prohibited either children under 18 or women or both from attending certain kinds of meetings or belonging to certain associations. It forebade all assemblies in the open air without previous official consent and it asserted the right for at least one policeman or other official to be present at an assembly; these officials were empowered to close the meeting if speakers strayed from the agenda or the meeting considered matters outside its jurisdiction as stated in the statutes or in the event of any infraction of law and order. The law prohibited an association from having branches in the state or nation and required that associations be locally organized (Anderson and Anderson 1967: 279).

In most of the countries of southern, central, and eastern Europe, constitutional or statutory guarantees of freedom of assembly and association were simply swept aside by the passage of exceptional legislation or the declaration of states of emergency during periods of tension. Thus, special anti-socialist legislation in Germany effectively outlawed the Social Democratic party between 1878 and 1890, and was used to ban 2,167 associations and publications. In Austria, constitutional guarantees were repeatedly suspended in Bohemia to crush Czech nationalist agitation, and special anti-anarchist measures made it impossible for socialists and trade unions to function in the Habsburg Empire in the 1880s. In Italy, constitutional guarantees were repeatedly revoked or ignored between 1860 and 1900, making it impossible for socialist groups to function until the latter date. In response to violent disorders that were brutally repressed in Italy in 1893-94 and 1898, hundreds of newspapers, trade unions, socialist groups and Catholic organizations were arbitrarily dissolved. Constitutional guarantees were also frequently suspended in Spain, Bulgaria and Serbia (before 1903), while in Russia the 1906 guarantees of free assembly and association were disregarded more than they were observed.

Restrictions on freedom of assembly and association unquestionably severely hampered the organization and growth of dissident groups in nineteenth-century Europe. This was demonstrated graphically with the eruption and then deflation of hundreds of political organizations during the 1848 revolutions and the subsequent repression, a pattern later repeated during the Spanish revolution of 1868-74 and the Russian 1905 revolution. Even aside from such revolutionary situations when normal governmental controls disintegrated, restrictions on freedom of assembly and association were never entirely effective. Wherever a significant urban middle and lower class existed and was forbidden to engage in political activity, clandestine or semi-clandestine organizations existed, at least to some extent, even under the most repressive regimes as in czarist Russia and Germany during the 1878-90 anti-socialist laws. One favorite device of clandestine political groups in Russia was to organize meetings in secluded outdoor locations:

> In order to organize a forest meeting a special group was formed in the [dissident] organization, which was very familiar with the area, ... knew all the paths and trails in the woods. Two weeks before the meeting, this group would go to the forest and find a suitable place ... it was usually in a deep valley, surrounded by small and large hills. They would make signs on the paths so that it would be easier to find them later (Mendelsohn 1970: 138).

A somewhat opposite technique was used in Bulgaria in 1891 during the founding meeting of the Bulgarian Socialist party. About 20 party members successfully eluded discovery by meeting near Turnovo during patriotic commemorations of an 1868 battle against the Turks, which attracted such large crowds that the socialists went unnoticed. Clandestine political meetings were held in private homes in many countries, and especially in France, in cafés and public inns where all regular patrons were well known (to avoid police infiltration).

Sometimes police bans on meetings and organizations were defied outright or evaded by the use of technicalities. Especially after 1900, illegal anti-government protest demonstrations were staged with considerable frequency in Russia--and were often brutally attacked by mounted Cossacks. In Germany, when police in Berlin banned a demonstration demanding suffrage reforms in Prussia that was scheduled for March 6, 1910, socialist sponsors of the demonstration announced a "suffrage promenade" (Wahlrechtsspaziergang) instead, to be held at Treptow Park. When police cut off all trolley and subway service to Treptow and surrounded the park, 150,000 people converged on the Tiergarten Park instead, upon clandestinely circulated instructions from socialist leaders. In Ireland, when British authorities sought to crush the Catholic Association, an organization devoted to repealing the ban on Catholics serving as members of parliament, by outlawing in 1825 all Irish political societies that had a longer duration than 14 days, Association leader Daniel O'Connell evaded the law by forming the "New Catholic Association," a "non-political" organization, which carried on as before. O'Connell warned against further attempts to outlaw the movement:

> If they pass an act preventing three men from meeting to discuss Catholic affairs, we will take off our gloves and hold up our hands in the street, declaring that we are not speaking on Catholic affairs. ... If they prevent us from speaking at our meals, we will proclaim a fast day and in prayer we shall talk of Catholic politics. ... If they prevent us from talking politics, why we will whistle or sing them (Reynolds 1954: 28).

Sixty years later, British efforts to ban meetings held to organize rent boycotts in Ireland were sometimes evaded by making it difficult for police to arrest the speakers by having them address crowds from "hotel windows, from moving wagons and from boats anchored off a lake shore," leading one frustrated official to suggest that police "use tricycles to capture offenders" (Curtis 1963: 209-10).

Another common means of evading restrictions on assembly and association was the use of ostensibly non-political (and therefore usually tolerated) occasions or organizations as "fronts" for political activity. Thus, during the periods leading up to the 1848 French revolution and the 1905 revolution in Russia, the general ban on political meetings was evaded by the holding of ostensibly non-political "banquets," which in fact were used as forums for criticism of the government. The pre-1905 Russian banquets, for example, were "officially" commemorations of the fortieth anniversary of the 1865 judicial reforms or marked such anniversaries as the founding of the Medico-Surgical Academy in St. Petersburg or the sesquicentennial of the opening of the University of Moscow. "Almost any anniversary provided the excuse for a banquet; and a banquet, the opportunity for long and impassioned anti-regime speeches and strongly worded resolutions" (Harcave 1970: 59).

In Denmark, where political organizations were not authorized before 1848, such organizations as the Copenhagen Fire Insurance

Company, the Students' Society, the Liberal Reading Club and especially the Society for the Correct Application of the Freedom of the Press functioned as political forums. Nationalist political groups in Switzerland before 1830, in Germany before 1860 and in Italy before 1848 functioned under the cloak of rifle societies, literary clubs and scientific and scholarly organizations. Thus, in Italy during the 1839-1847 period, yearly scientific congresses helped to increase the sense of common nationality among the professional middle classes, and an agricultural society formed in Sardinia in 1842 quickly became heavily politicized--"if they began with talking of cabbages, it was not long before they were talking of kings" (Whyte 1965: 48). Czech nationalists in Bohemia expressed their aspirations during the 1840-80 period by raising funds for construction of a Czech National Theatre Building and the organization of cultural, economic and gymnastics groups, especially the gymnastic society Sokol. Pre-1905 dissent in Russia was channeled through such groups as the Russian Writers Union, the Imperial Free Economic Society and the Moscow Law Society, and such meetings as that of the Tenth Congress of Natural Scientists and Doctors at St. Petersburg in 1901, the Moscow Teachers Congress of 1902 and the All-Russian Husbandry Exhibition at Kharkov in 1903. The Third Congress of Activists in the Field of Technical Education, which attracted over 3,000 delegates to its St. Petersburg gathering in January 1904, was so open in its anti-government activities that the police closed it down and arrested the major radical speakers (earlier, the Moscow Law Society had been shut down in 1899 and the St. Petersburg Writers Union was closed in 1901). In France, during the Second Empire of Napoleon III members of the French Academy expressed their opposition to the regime by electing known opposition figures to their ranks. Between 1852 and 1870, 25 of 32 elections to the academy were strongly influenced by political reasons, and the list of those elected read like a "catalogue of the leading opponents of the regime" (Reichert 1963: 32). In 1864 the Serbian government temporarily shut down virtually its only opposition forum, the Society of Serbian letters, after the society adopted a similar tactic—the election of leading European liberals, such as Garibaldi, as honorary members.

In Germany, during the 1878-90 period when the anti-socialist law was in effect:

> Front organizations were created in the form of singing clubs, smoking societies, scientific study groups or gymnastic associations. As soon as one of these could be determined to socialistic and was banned, the police complained, it would reappear as a new organization with a new name. ... Red flags mysteriously appeared atop towers, telegraph poles and factory smokestacks. Secret meetings were held in forests or small villages near large cities, while others were open picnics attended by hundreds of persons wearing red ribbons or carrying flowers. Funerals of party leaders became political demonstrations; the police

estimated that 20,000 of the Hamburg faithful turned out in August 1879 for the most impressive one, that of former Reichstag deputy August Gelb (Snell 1976: 203).

German workingmen's choral societies were a particularly popular form of socialist "front group" during the period of the anti-socialist laws. Such groups found it easy to preserve their camouflage by setting the words to workers' songs "with a view to parody, to other well-known tunes, including such hymns of national and military fervour as Die Wacht am Rhein. The result was that in the event of a police visit the singers could simply switch over to the 'official version' " (Dowe 1978: 276).

"Political funerals" were a common form of evading restrictions on public assemblies and political meetings in many Euopean countries aside from Germany. Even the most repressive governments were generally reluctant to interfere with such manifestations—or in some cases were unable to respond quickly enough to word-of-mouth campaigns that organized such demonstrations, sometimes for relatively obscure figures, at short notice. Among the most notable "political funerals" were the great nationalist demonstrations in Bohemia in 1847 and 1856 for Czech linguist Joseph Jungman and Czech journalist Karl Havlíček respectively; the April 1860 burial of a student killed by police during Budapest demonstrations for Hungarian autonomy from Austria (the burial attracted 40,000 people); the January 1881 service for French revolutionary August Blanqui, attended by 100,000; the October 20, 1905 funeral in Moscow for Nikolai Bauman, a murdered Bolshevik, which drew 200,000; and the September 1907 service for Spanish anarchist Fermin Salvochea, attended by 50,000. Perhaps the most unique political funeral of nineteenth-century Europe occurred in late 1819 near Preston, England, when thousands of people turned out for the burial of "orator" Henry Hunt's horse, "Bob." The funeral was held shortly after the "Peterloo Massacre," in which scores of people had been killed and injured when troops arrested Hunt and disrupted a peaceful mass rally held to demand suffrage reform.

In a few cases, political funerals had major political significance. In June 1832, a Paris funeral for General Lamarque, a popular liberal figure, developed into a serious insurrectionary outburst that was put down at the cost of 150 lives. The inflammation of feelings that led to the Polish insurrection of 1863 was to a considerable extent fed by a series of political funerals and historical commemorations. Political funerals were especially common in France, and during 1849-52 and 1866-69 a wave of such manifestations expressed popular opposition to the authoritarian regime of Louis Napoleon. A total of 61 political funerals in 1850-51 were reported in the departments of Vaucluse and Hérault alone. The French minister of police was so alarmed by the wave of political funerals in 1852 that a letter was dispatched to the prefect in Lille warning against an excessive leniency toward such manifestations:

While the government is disposed to allow full latitude to

> meetings which form under the inspiration of familial affection or relations of friendship it must be attentive to preventing this sort of profanation which grasps as a pretext the mortal remains of someone unknown to the crowd to simulate a respect which is only a lie and to make a political demonstration which does not fool anyone. The best means to prevent them is to forbid too large a meeting at the mortuary, to break up any meeting which has the character of a mob, to forbid entrance to the cemetery of too many people who are unknown to the family and to forbid any type of oration (Tamason 1980: 25).

Even such restrictions could be foiled, however. Thus, when authorities at Lyon barred more than 300 persons from funerals, precisely that number showed up for the formal ceremony for a worker, but tens of thousands more followed the casket through the streets or watched the procession.

Two other methods of evading restrictions on organized political activity in nineteenth-century Europe were generally confined to areas such as Austrian-ruled Hungary, Bohemia and northern Italy, where nationalist resistance was an important component of the struggle for political liberty. These were the wearing of certain dress styles and the use of social boycotts (a form of negative demonstration) as a means of protest. Magyar national dress was used to express demands for autonomy in Hungary, while Italian patriots in Austrian-ruled Lombardy, during the period leading up to the March 1848 revolution in Milan, were even more inventive:

> One day all patriots appeared with their hat bands buckled in front. When the [Austrian] bureaucracy caught on and passed an ordinance forbidding it, the same gentlemen came out the next day with the beaver fur of their hats brushed against the nap, the next another unusual fashion, and then another (Robertson 1960: 139).

Social boycotts of Austrian officials in Lombardy-Venetia, Bohemia, and Hungary were another form of protest. The La Scala opera house in Milan was often empty save for white-coated Austrian military officials during the pre-1848 period. At Pavia, in Lombardy, the Austrian commander was so rattled by an organized boycott of the local theatre during the severe post-1848 reaction that he declared, "If anybody by criminal political obstinacy should persist in not frequenting the theatre, such conduct should be regarded as the silent demonstration of a criminal disposition which merited to be sought out and punished" (Martin 1969: 394). When Austrian Emperor Franz Joseph visited Lombardy-Venetia in 1856-57, he was greeted by silent crowds in Venice and shuttered houses in Milan, and ceremonial balls planned for his tour had to be cancelled when Italian women made it clear that they would not dance with Austrian officers. The leading Milanese newspaper Il Crepuscolo ("twilight," a clear reference to the character of the Austrian regime) was suppressed for refusing to mention the imperial visit, in keeping with its long-standing policy of never referring to Austrian affairs. Similar social boycotts of Austrian officials were carried out on a large scale in Hungary during the 1850-60 decade of reaction, while Czechs studiously boycotted the December 1908 celebrations of the sixtieth anniversary of Franz Joseph's accession to the throne. During the emperor's visit to Prague in that year, little paper sticks termed "hole na prochazku" (literally, walking sticks, but also meaning sticks to beat Prochazka, the Czech nickname for Franz Joseph) were sold.

A final example of the ingenuity displayed by nineteenth-century Europeans in holding unauthorized organized displays of opposition activity occurred in France on May 17, 1866 when Emperor Napoleon III attended a theatre performance at the Odéon. As the Emperor was about to depart in his carriage, several sewage disposal vehicles rolled into the square outside the theatre. "They were immediately surrounded by about 100 cheering students, waving their hats and shouting long life to the Emperor, a demonstration carried out with complete solemnity" (Williams 1969: 8).

## Restrictions on Labor Unions and Strikes

Labor unions and strikes were illegal for part or all of the nineteenth century in every major European country (see Table 2.2.). Even after formal legal restrictions on trade union activity were eased, labor organizations and strikes in many European countries were subjected to continued harassment and persecution that either nullified or considerably curtailed such activities. For all practical purposes, therefore, as late as 1890, among all of the European countries where a reasonably sized urban industrial labor force existed (i.e., excluding the Balkans), only the United Kingdom, France, Switzerland, the Low Countries, and the Scandinavian lands afforded meaningful freedom to union activities. Labor organizations were tolerated, often under severe constraints, only after 1890 in Germany and Austria, after 1900 in Italy and, for all practical purposes, never before World War I in Spain, Portugal, Hungary and Russia.

In many of the European countries, restrictions on trade unions and strikes pre-dated the French Revolution. Thus, a French royal edict of 1539 forbade "all craftsmen to form brotherhoods or unions, large or small, for any purpose whatever" (Rice 1970: 49). An English statute of 1548 made it illegal for workers to "conspire, convenant or promise together . . . that they shall not make or do their works but at a certain price or rate or shall not enterprize or take upon them to finish that another hath begun . . . or shall not work but at certain hours and times" (Wedderburn 1965: 216).

While conservative politicians--as well as employers--clearly regarded trade unions as subversive conspiracies directed against the interests of the state and the public good, the articulate elements within the working class viewed the right to form trade unions

Table 2.2:  Restrictions on Trade Unions and
Strikes in Nineteenth-Century Europe[a]

| Country | Imposition of Bans on Trade Unions and Strikes | Formal Legalization of Trade Unions and Strikes | End of Severe Harassment of Trade Unions and Strikes |
|---|---|---|---|
| Austria | 1731/1852/1859 | 1867/1870 | c. 1890 |
| Belgium | 1831 (& under earlier Dutch and French rule) | 1866 | relaxed after 1866, but considerable harassment thereafter also |
| Denmark | 1734/1800/1823 | 1849 | c. 1890 |
| France | 1791 (& earlier) | 1864/1884 | relaxed after 1884, but considerable harassment thereafter also |
| Germany | 1731/1845 (Prussia) | 1869 | relaxed after 1890, but considerable harassment thereafter also |
| Hungary | 1852/1859 | 1872/1884 | never before 1914 |
| Italy | outlawed in all Italian states, save possibly Piedmont before 1859 | 1859/1889 | very substantial easing after 1900, although frequent resort to violence continued |
| Netherlands | 1815 (& before under Fr. rule) | 1872 | 1872 |
| Portugal | 1852 | 1910 | never before 1914 |
| Russia | 1845/1874 | 1906 | never before 1914 |
| Spain | 1844/1857/1874 | 1868/1876/1881/1887 | never before 1914 |
| Sweden | 1739/1770 | 1846/1864/1885 | c. 1890 |
| U.K. | 1799-1800 (& earlier) | 1824 | c. 1875 |

[a]Norway, Switzerland and the Balkans (except for Greece) never formally outlawed organized labor activity before 1914, although in the case of the Balkans this largely reflected the lack of a large urban industrial workforce.  Rumania for example, outlawed strikes in 1920.

(frequently termed the right of association) as the only way to protect their interests. Thus, one working-class newspaper in Lyon, France, declared in 1834 that, while "poverty gives birth to crimes, association kills poverty. Let us push on toward association; the people will become moral, the people will become happy." A semi-clandestine Lyon workers group declared at about the same time:

> If we remain isolated, scattered, we are feeble, we will be easily defeated and will submit to the law of the masters; if we remain divided, cut off from one another, if we do not agree among ourselves, we will be obliged to surrender ourselves to the discretion of our bourgeois. There must hence be a bond that unites us, an intelligence that governs us, there must be an association (Sewell 1980: 216).

Similarly, the first working class newspaper published in Toulouse, France, the Voice of the People, declared in February 1847:

> Unemployment, inequitable taxes, clerical education and all abuses have occurred because the children of the people, isolated and without ties, do not think to associate. If workers came together and organized in a truly fraternal manner, nothing would be able to stop them. Union is our greatest need (Aminzade 1981: 75).

Despite the numerous restrictions on trade unions and strikes, even before the French Revolution such activities were not unknown, even though they were often suppressed with great harshness. For example, a series of strikes by Vienna artisans in the early eighteenth century was ended by the introduction of martial law and the execution of two labor leaders in 1722. A rebellion at the Demidov iron-works in the Russian Urals in 1760 was broken by the jailing of 300 workers, and strikes in Lyon in 1786 were suppressed when mounted police fired into a crowd and two leaders were publicly executed. Major strikes at Breslau in April 1793 were crushed when about 350 strikers were arrested and 37 were shot to death by troops.

During the nineteenth century, in those countries where strikes and unions were illegal, such activity continued to be met frequently with arrests, troops, and considerable brutality, although the response varied from country to country and from time to time. Dutch and Portuguese authorities were frequently fairly tolerant of illegal labor activities, but in Russia, Belgium and Spain, police and arrests were the almost invariable response to such behavior. In France, repression of illegal labor activities was often intense during strike waves and periods of high political tensions, but fairly tolerant during other periods. "Intermittently the [French] workers were permitted to organize, only to have the police come down upon them later. Tolerance alternated with prosecutions, fines and jailings" (Lorwin 1954: 5).

The basic French anti-labor law was the Le Chapelier Act of 1791 and the anti-coalition provisions of the 1810 penal code (which were also applied to Belgium and the Netherlands under Napoleonic rule, remaining in effect in those countries until 1866 and 1872, respectively). The Le Chapelier law declared that gatherings of workers "directed against the free exercise of industry and work" were to be considered "riotous" and to be "dispersed by force and punished with all the severity which the law permits" (Kendall 1975: 13). The 1810 penal code outlawed any "coalition on the part of the workingmen to cease work at the same time, to forbid work in a shop, to prevent the coming or leaving before or after certain hours, and in general, to suspend, hinder or make dear labor" (Levine 1914: 23). Although coalitions among employers to force wages down "unjustly and abusively" were also outlawed, the maximum jail term in such cases was one month, compared to a maximum of up to five years for strike organizers and three months for ordinary strikers. Between 1825 and the legalization of strikes in France in 1864, about 14,000 Frenchmen were prosecuted for strike activity, of whom 150 were jailed for a year or more, and over 9,000 received shorter jail terms. Prosecution was especially intense during the massive strike wave of 1840, when almost 500 were jailed, and during the first years of Louis Napoleon's Second Empire, when over 2,000 were imprisoned between 1852 and 1855. In Toulouse, 22 out of 28 strikes reported between 1830 and 1864 led to prosecutions, a proportion probably typical of France as a whole.

Many European countries supplemented their basic restrictions on unions and strikes with additional regulations that severely curtailed workers' freedoms. In England, the so-called Master and Servant acts dating back to 1351 subjected workers who failed to meet their obligations to employers to criminal penalties, but employers who breached agreements with employees were subjected only to civil proceedings. Although strikes were legalized in England in 1824, the Master and Servant acts were frequently used by judges to threaten striking workers with jail unless they returned to work. In 1854, over 3,000 English workers were jailed for leaving or neglecting their work. In 1872, even after the 1867 Master and Servant Act eliminated criminal penalties for workers in breach of contracts save in cases of "aggravated misconduct," over 17,000 workers were prosecuted and over 10,000 convicted under Master and Servant acts legislation. In France, basic legislation outlawing strikes and unions was supplemented with laws passed in 1803 that allowed courts to accept an employer's word in wage disputes, while requiring evidence from workers to support their claims, and that required all workers to carry an identification booklet (livret) in which employers noted their terms of service and conduct. Livret-type requirements were also imposed at various times in the nineteenth century in Saxony, Spain, and Belgium. In Belgium and France, where the livret remained on the books until 1883 and 1890 respectively, workers who could not produce a booklet attesting that they had met all debts and other obligations to past employers were legally barred from further employment and subject to arrest for vagrancy.

In Sweden, under various laws dating back to medieval times and updated in 1833, workers were barred from changing employment save at a brief period during each year, and those unable to show they had a source of income for "protection" (laga försvar) could be prosecuted for being "unprotected" (försvarslösa) and then drafted or assigned to compulsory service in a state institution. This provision, which remained in force in Sweden until 1885 (and was law in Finland, dating back from the period of Swedish rule, until 1883) was used to prosecute and threaten strikers, although striking per se was not illegal in Sweden after 1864. Prosecution for försvarslösa was one of the techniques used to break the first great strike in Swedish history, in the Sundsvall lumber industry in 1879. In 1884, there were 4,131 försvarslösa prosecutions (most of which undoubtedly did not involve strikers).

Even after trade unions and strikes were legalized, in many nineteenth-century European countries legal provisions or exclusions were maintained that could be used to limit labor activities severely, or arbitrary harassment of union activity was continued without any real legal basis. Thus, in Austria, although unions and strikes were legalized in 1870, leaders of a December 1869 workers demonstration that was largely responsible for the easing of restrictions were arrested and convicted of high treason. Unions were repeatedly dissolved on flimsy legal pretexts in Austria during the 1870s, while a harsh "anti-anarchist" decree imposed in 1884 made it virtually impossible for unions to function openly until it expired in 1891. In Hungary, unions and strikes were technically legalized by laws passed in 1872 and 1884, but the attitude of the government was more accurately characterized by the minister of the interior's remarks to a delegation of workers in 1875: "Are you industrial workers? If so, then work industriously. You do not have to bother with anything else. You need no associations and if you mix into politics, I will teach you a lesson you will never forget" (Janos 1982: 163). Between 1878 and 1904 provisions of the Hungarian penal code outlawed "gatherings for the purpose of extracting wages" and "violent arguments for the furtherance of wage claims." Unions were legally required to be non-political, and until 1899 the government refused to recognize nationwide labor organizations. Laws passed in 1898 and 1907 completely outlawed labor organizations among Hungarian agricultural workers, who far outnumbered urban industrial workers. The 1898 law, officially designed to "secure the undisturbed execution of agricultural labor contracts," but commonly known as the "Slavery Law," not only barred agricultural unions and strikes, but even made it illegal to "address, attend or hire a hall for meetings with a view to organizing a union" (May 1968: 373). Rural laborers were obliged to sign work contracts whose breach subjected them to two months in jail and forcible return to work. The "Second Slavery Law" of 1907, officially titled an act to "prevent abuses to the laborer and to improve his social and economic conditions," reinforced the ban on agricultural strikes and unions, and barred workers from leaving their place of employment or receiving outside visitors without the permission of their landlords.

Although unions and strikes were legalized in Germany in 1869, in

Prussia and some of the other German states certain categories of laborers, such as agricultural and railway workers, household servants, and seamen, were denied the right to join unions. Between 1878 and 1890 all socialist unions in Germany, which had an estimated membership of 50,000 in 1878, were suppressed (as were many non-socialist unions) under the anti-socialist law in effect during those years. In Italy, unions were tacitly legalized in 1889, but they were dissolved throughout the country under states of emergency declared during localized outbreaks of violence during the 1890s and could not really function effectively until after 1900. In Spain and Russia, where unions were legalized respectively in 1881 and 1906, they were subjected to repeated waves of severe repression and could not function with any assurance of toleration before 1914. The 1906 Russian decree legalizing unions was filled with restrictions and loopholes, including a provision authorizing police to close any such organization that seemed to threaten "public safety and calm or to take a clearly immoral direction" (Thurston 1980: 324). The legalization of strikes in both Portugal and Greece in 1910 seems to have led to a significant increase in repressive activity directed against unions, although this may have largely reflected the sudden jump in labor activity. Perfectly legal railroad strikes in Italy (1902), Hungary (1904), Bulgaria (1907), France (1910), and Spain (1912) were crushed when the governments in those countries conscripted striking workers and placed them under military discipline and the threat of court martial.

Even Denmark, which compared with most European countries was highly tolerant of trade union activities, subjected its emerging labor movement to considerable harassment during the 1870-90 period, although the legal status of unions and strikes was unquestioned after 1849. The Danish section of the First International was outlawed and its leaders jailed in the early 1870s, and until about 1890 the police and courts showed considerable hostility to unions. In some cases the proclamation of strikes and boycotts, the publication of names of strikebreakers and even picketing was treated as illegal. Socialist newspaper editors who denounced such actions by the authorities often found themselves behind bars.

In virtually every European country, after strikes and unions were legalized, legislation was retained that outlawed, often in highly vague terms, the use of violence or coercion during labor disputes. The widely hated Åkarp law of 1899 in Sweden made even peaceful picketing or peaceful molestation of strikebreakers punishable by up to two years in jail. Paragraph 153 of the German industrial code, which authorized prison terms of up to three months for the use of "physical force, threats, insults or oaths," was used by some German judges to jail workers merely for calling another a strikebreaker or even shouting "pfui" during labor disputes. Similarly vague legislation passed in Belgium in 1866 was used to jail almost 1,900 workers and convict almost 3,000 others between 1898 and 1920. Following a violent strike in Belgium in 1886, put down by troops at the cost of about a dozen lives, Edouard Anseele, one of the founders of the

Belgian socialist party, was jailed for six months for urging soldiers' mothers to implore their sons not to shoot down strikers. Provisions of the 1884 French law legalizing unions that required registration of the names of labor officials and other formalities were used to harass the labor movement. Thus, in 1889 a Bordeaux court dissolved the local bakers' union for having admitted three restauranteurs as honorary members, and 33 Paris unions were dissolved in 1893 for failure to deposit their rules with the authorities in accord with the 1884 law. French legislation of 1864 and 1884 outlawing the use of violence to support strikes or interfere with the freedom to work was used in many cases to jail strikers, sometimes merely for staring at or pointing to strikebreakers. Almost 900 were fined or jailed under such provisions between 1864 and 1870, and hundreds were jailed on vague charges of "intimidation" during several strikes in the 1900-14 period.

British legislation of 1825 that outlawed "threats or intimidation," "molesting," and "obstruction" in labor disputes was interpreted by courts to outlaw peaceful picketing, and in at least one 1871 case was used to convict some women who said "bah" to strikebreakers. Although peaceful picketing was seemingly explicitly legalized in an 1875 law, a British court decision in 1896, handed down by a judge who declared, "You cannot make a strike effective without doing more than is lawful" (Wedderburn 1965: 233), concluded that such activity was in violation of common law. Yet another law had to be passed in 1906 before peaceful picketing was clearly recognized as legal in the United Kingdom.

Worker-originated violence was by no means a complete fantasy in the minds of conservative legislatures. Sometimes it reached serious dimensions, as in the Belgian strikes of 1886, the uprising by textile workers in Lille, France, in 1903, the Welsh dock, mine, and railroad strikes of 1910-11, the German Ruhr coalminers' strike of 1912, and some of the Greek and Portuguese strikes of 1910-14. Some European labor leaders openly advocated the commission of acts of violence and sabotage, especially in the French syndicalist movement of the 1900-10 period. But on the whole, such advocates were a tiny minority of labor leaders, and violence during labor disputes was surprisingly rare. In Italy, which had one of the most violent labor histories in Europe, only 11 per cent of the strikes between 1894 and 1903 experienced violent episodes. In Germany, fewer than 75 out of 31,000 strikes between 1891 and 1913 were violent, and in France, out of about 20,000 strikes between 1890 and 1914 "only 300 to 400 produced any violence beyond the scale of minor pushing and shoving" (Tilly, Tilly and Tilly 1975: 249). During the French railroad strike of 1910, one of the most violent in European history, over 1,400 incidents of sabotage were reported, but most were relatively minor, including almost 1200 cases involving cutting of telegraph and telephone wires. The more serious incidents involved 11 attempted bombings and 82 attempted train derailments.

Governmental persecution unquestionably delayed and hindered the emergence of the labor movement in nineteenth-century Europe, but never succeeded in completely crushing labor organization in those countries where a significant number of urban industrial workers existed. That repression did hinder the development of the labor movement is clear both from the thousands of arrests already enumerated, and also from statistics on union membership and strike activity before and after the easing of labor restrictions in various countries. In France, for example, it is estimated that in 1884, the year trade unions were finally legalized, there were about 70 unions with 70,000 members. Ten years later, almost 2,200 unions existed in France with a membership of over 400,000. In Germany, membership in socialist unions jumped from 140,000 to 680,000 between 1889 and 1899, following expiration of the anti-socialist law in 1890. In Italy, where strikes and unions were effectively illegal until 1900, the average number of strikes per year jumped from 611 to over 900 between 1895-99 and 1900-1904, while union membership increased from under 150,000 to almost 700,000 between 1900 and 1904. In Russia, where trade unions were outlawed before 1906, almost 250,000 workers joined unions within a year of their legalization.

Repressive legislation and law enforcement was never completely able to suppress organized labor activity wherever a social base for such existed. Clandestine unions and strikes were more or less continuous, even during periods of illegality, in France and England after 1815, in the Barcelona textile industry after about 1840, in Germany during the 1878-90 anti-socialist law, and in urban industrial centers of Russia after about 1880, to mention the most notable examples. During the 1830-47 era, there were over 300 illegal strikes in France and 20 such walkouts in Germany. About 50,000 workers struck in Barcelona in July 1855 to demand legalization of unions. In Russia, almost 1,600 illegal strikes were recorded between 1895 and 1904, while in Portugal 25,000 workers illegally struck in the decade before strikes were legalized in 1910.

Although for obvious reasons the history of the clandestine unions that were responsible for many of the illegal strikes is difficult to piece together, it is known that in some countries, such as France, Belgium, and Germany, unions were able survive by masking their activity behind legal "fronts." Frequently such "front" groups were mutual aid societies (workers' groups organized to provide sickness, unemployment and death benefits), which most governments tolerated since they reduced public relief expenditures. In Marseilles, France, for example, some form of organized trade union activity, usually disguised as a mutual aid society, existed in 43 trades in the 1840s, including all but four of the skilled trades with 100 or more employees, and in several of the smaller trades as well. In the case of the tanners' "mutual aid society" in Marseilles, a successful strike in 1834 forced employers to grant a significant wage increase and to promise not to hire in the future any tanner who was not a member of the group. In 1855, a Marseilles police official, having uncovered the secret statutes of the tanners' group, declared that the organization "hid behind a veil of mutual aid" but was in fact a "permanent coalition" (i.e., trade union) and that it was a matter of "public notoriety that nearly all the so-called benevolent societies are nothing but trade associations, in each of which regulations are created that are often contrary to the general interest" (Sewell 1980: 172, 177). Similarly, the public prosecutor in Toulouse, France, which housed 96 mutual aid societies benefitting over one-third of the working class in 1862, informed his superiors in 1865:

> I must once again point out the danger posed by working class trade associations, which under the cover of mutual aid, have organized the trades, subjected workers to rigorously enforced clandestine regulations, and often placed employers at the mercy of their workers. These numerous associations have treasuries which, in the event of a work stoppage, can serve to support a strike (Aminzade 1981: 74).

In Russia, clandestine unions often met in taverns, street corners, or forests on the outskirts of towns. The vigorous Jewish artisan labor movement in the Pale of Russia (the area of western Russia where Jews were allowed to live) was especially inventive in evading repressive czarist labor laws. Illegal libraries with detailed lending regulations were established in the major cities of the Pale for workers' edification; and clandestine lectures, assemblies, and plays were organized and presented. Special streets, known as birzhes, were the focal points for labor organizing. "When a 'birzhe' was overrun with police spies, it was simply moved to another location" (Mendelsohn 1970: 69).

Before leaving the subject of governmental discrimination against the nineteenth-century European labor movement, it should be noted that, especially after about 1880, governments in some countries—notably France, Germany, Britain, and Denmark—sponsored labor arbitration boards, officials, and/or courts that sometimes intervened on behalf of workers and strikers. Despite the long history of antagonism between French governments and workers, for example, strikers frequently sought to obtain intervention from French arbitration officials after strikes were legalized in 1884. Thus, French working-class militants were "able to curse the state from one side of their mouth and plead for its intervention in their affairs from the other" (Shorter and Tilly 1974: 33). In the German town of Düsseldorf, about 700 to 800 workers a year brought cases before the worker-employer mediation courts (Gewerbegerichten) during the 1890s, and almost half won some redress; however, the courts excluded many cases from their jurisdiction and often failed to enforce settlements.


## The Use of Official Violence Against Dissidents

The use of brutal and frequently deadly violence against strikes, demonstrations, and other manifestations of popular dissatisfaction was a frequent response of governments in nineteenth-century Europe. In hundreds of incidents, civilian demonstrators, strikers and rioters were killed during encounters with troops and police between 1815 and 1914, and in at least 20 such clashes 25 or more civilians died (see Table 2.3). In many incidents, violence erupted before governments resorted to the use of deadly force, but in many others protests were completely peaceful until troops and police opened fire or otherwise attacked demonstrators. As one historian has noted:

> A large proportion of the European disturbances ... turned violent at exactly the moment when the authorities intervened to stop an illegal but nonviolent action. This is typical of violent strikes and demonstrations. Furthermore, the great bulk of the killing and wounding in those same disturbances was done by troops or police rather than by insurgents or demonstrators. The demonstrators, on the other hand, did the bulk of the damage to property (Tilly 1969: 42).

In most cases, the use of repressive force was effective in suppressing unrest, at least in the short run. For example at Fourmies, a textile center in the department of the Nord in France, a deadly fusillade put an end to disturbances arising from strikes on May Day 1891. Scuffles broke out in the morning, and demonstrators were arrested for urging others to join them. Over a thousand protesters who had gathered in the central square in the afternoon to demand release of those arrested were then ordered to disperse. When the crowd refused, mounted police launched an indiscriminate assault on the gathering. The protesters responded with stones, and troops then opened fire, killing nine and wounding scores of others. In Hamburg, Germany, general rioting developed on January 17, 1906 after police tried to prevent over 30,000 marchers who were protesting a proposed reactionary revision of the local suffrage law from converging on the town hall. Police put down the disorders with extreme brutality, killing two men with sabre blows and injuring many more. Subsequently the Hamburg police arrested everyone they found who was wearing bandages or who had been treated in local hospitals for sabre wounds "on the assumption that anyone hit by a police sabre must have been committing a crime" (Evans 1979: 15). Fifty people were tried in connection with the Hamburg disorders after languishing three months in jail, and a number of them received five- to ten-month jail terms.

While such techniques and other less brutal forms of repression usually quelled demonstrations and disturbances, in a number of instances violent repression of peaceful demonstrations directly provoked revolutionary outbursts or greatly intensified an atmosphere of conflict that led up to such uprisings. The clearest example is the Russian revolution of 1905, a direct response to the slaughter of peaceful demonstrators in St. Petersburg on January 9, 1905.

Table 2.3: Incidents (other than those arising from revolutionary outbreaks) in Which 25 or More Civilians Were Killed by Official Forces in Europe, 1815–1914

| Date | Location | Type of Incident | Deaths | Source |
|---|---|---|---|---|
| 6/1844 | Prussian Silesia | Labor riots | 35 | Reichard 1969: 31 |
| 2/23/1848 | Paris, France | Anti-govt. demonstrations | c.40 | Duveau 1968: 29 |
| 3/18–20/1848 | Stockholm, Sweden | Anti-govt. rioting | 30 | Derry 1979: 224 |
| 4/1848 | Rouen, France | Election riots | 59 | Price 1972: 143 |
| 8/23/1848 | Vienna, Austria | Labor riots | 30 | Noyes 1966: 259 |
| 4/8/1861 | Bezdna, Russia | Peasant demonstrations | 41 | Ulam 1977: 83 |
| 9/21–22/1864 | Turin, Italy | Anti-govt. rioting | 197 | Martin 1969: 670 |
| 12/1868–2/1869 | Italy | Anti-tax riots | 257 | Neufeld 1961: 167–74 |
| 7/25–26/1866 | Amsterdam, Neth. | Anti-police riots | 26 | Kossmann, 1978: 316 |
| 5/6–10, 1892 | Lodz, Rus. Poland | Labor riots | 46 | Leslie 1980: 57 |
| 1893 | Sicily | Strikes, demonstrations, | 92 | Tannenbaum 1976: 293–4 |
| 1896 | Hungary | Election disorders | 32 | Seton-Watson 1911: 10 |
| 1897 | Bosnjaci, Croatia | Election disorders | 28 | Gazi 1973: 200 |
| 1898 | Milan, Italy | Anti-government rioting | 80 | Smith 1959: 192 |
| 1897–98 | Hungary | Agrarian strikes | 51 | Pamlényi 1975: 379 |
| 3–5/1900 | northeast Bulgaria | Anti-tax demonstrations | 94 | Bell 1977: 43–46 |
| 3/1903 | Zlatoust, Russia | Strikes | 69 | Crankshaw 1976: 315 |
| 1904 | Alesd,Transylvania | Peasant demonstrations | 33 | Otetea 1970: 432 |
| 1/9/1905 | St. Petersburg Russia | Anti-govt. demonstrations | 130+ | Sablinsky 1976: 266 |
| 3/1910 | Kileler and Larissa, Greece | Peasant demonstrations | 27 | Papacosma 1977: 143 |
| 1911 | Drohobycz, Austrian Galicia | Election disorders | 27 | Jaszi 1966: 146 |
| 4/4/1912 | Lena Goldfields, Russia | Strike | 170 | Kochan 1966: 154 |

They had sought to march on the royal palace with petitions demanding social reforms and civil liberties, including a political amnesty, and freedom of speech, press and assembly. They were also demanding a constituent assembly elected by secret, universal and equal suffrage, which was termed "our chief request" and "the only means of healing our painful wounds" (Harcave 1970: 287). According to official figures, 130 people were killed and 300 were injured on "Bloody Sunday," although unofficial accounts suggest that over 4,500 casualties were inflicted. In November 1831 a violent uprising by striking textile workers in Lyon, France erupted when troops attempted to block a march into the city. They shot eight workers to death in a crowd that had hurled stones at them. The February 1848 revolution in France originated in agitation and demonstrations following the government's attempt to ban a "political banquet," a previously tolerated opposition device used to evade the ban on political meetings. On the evening of February 23, 1848, what began as a protest demonstration became a revolutionary outburst, when in the so-called Massacre of the Boulevard des Capucins, troops fired on marchers, killing or wounding about 80 people. Enraged Parisians paraded the bodies of the dead through the city during the night, and by morning over a million paving stones and 4,000 felled trees had been utilized to construct over 1,500 barricades.

Festering tensions between police and troops and the citizenry greatly contributed to the atmosphere that led up to several others of the 1848 revolutions. In Milan, for example, then the capital of Austrian-controlled Lombardy, the growing resentment of the Austrian military was greatly intensified in early January 1848 by an incident known as "I Lutti di Lombardia" (the mournings of Lombardy). On January 3, after the citizenry began boycotting tobacco to deprive the Habsburg treasury of its tobacco tax, Austrian soldiers began parading the streets with two or more cigars in their mouths, blowing smoke into the faces of the Milanese. Insulting calls of "porchi tedeschi" (German pigs) and scuffles inevitably followed, whereupon the soldiers brutally attacked unarmed people with swords and bayonets, killing five and seriously wounding 60 others. On March 18, 1848 revolution erupted in Milan after news was received of the March 13 uprising in Vienna, which was in turn touched off by the news from Paris and the killing of five Viennese protesters by troops who opened up on a rioting crowd. By 1848, the military in Vienna were so detested "that the mere sight of a soldier's uniform was a red rag to the people" (Macartney 1969: 329).

Similar hatred for the military was a major factor in the 1848 revolution in Berlin. The Prussian military had long been noted for their harsh behavior, which included the "massive and brutal use" of the practice of "riding into crowds and of striking with the broad side of the blade, and even with the cutting edge, a speciality of the Gendarmerie in Berlin" (Ludtke 1979: 207). Thus, seven people were killed during labor riots at Aachen in August 1830, and harsh measures were also taken at Cologne in 1830, in Münster in 1837 and in Berlin in September 1830 (the "tailors' revolution"), August 1835 (the "fireworks revolution") and April 1847 (the "potato revolution"). Thirty-five people were killed by Prussian troops in suppressing the Silesian weavers uprising of June 1844, an event whose impact upon German public opinion has been compared by one historian to "that of the 'Peterloo' massacre of 1819 in the mind of the English public" (Rohr 1963: 65). Also in 1844, the "whole city of Königsberg was aroused when a young lieutenant named Leithold accused a local barrister of lèse-majesté, called him out and killed him in a duel" (Craig 1964: 90). In August 1846, after citizens taunted troops during an annual Cologne festival, a number of civilians were sliced up by military swords and one worker was killed, arousing great anger. News of the Parisian and Viennese revolutions in early 1848 touched off a series of public meetings, demonstrations and bloody clashes with troops in Berlin beginning on March 13. On every day between March 13 and March 16, troops brutally dispersed peaceful, although frequently taunting crowds, with two people killed by a fusillade on the latter date. By then, "the entire hatred of the populace of Berlin was concentrated on the military machine that had shoved them off the streets and given them insolent orders for so many years" (Robertson 1960: 117). Finally, on March 18, following a series of political concessions by King Frederick William IV, what started out as a day of general rejoicing ended in a popular uprising after a huge crowd that gathered outside the royal palace to render thanks to the king was dispersed by troops with drawn swords and a general panic was set off when two soldiers' rifles discharged, perhaps because of jostling by the crowd.

Although occasional instances of excesses by police and troops can be uncovered in nearly every European country at one time or another during the 1815-1914 period, the problem of excessive and arbitrary use of force by law enforcement bodies was most persistent and serious in Russia, Hungary, Germany (especially Prussia), Italy, Spain, France, Ireland, and Belgium. In Russia, peaceful and non-peaceful protests and strikes were dispersed, frequently with great brutality, by troops and the hated mounted Cossacks as a matter of course. Between 1891 and 1904, troops were called out an astounding total of 944 times to suppress protests and strikes in Russia. As noted previously, the "Bloody Sunday" massacre of January 9, 1905, touched off the 1905 revolution, while the Lena Goldfields massacre of April 4, 1912, during which 170 people were killed, sparked a massive wave of strikes and disorders that convulsed Russia for the following two years. The atmosphere leading up to the 1905 revolution was greatly exacerbated by the violent dispersal of a mass demonstration on March 4, 1901 at Kazan Square, St. Petersburg by Cossacks and police wielding sabres and whips who dispersed thousands of peaceful demonstrators. About 60 people, including the revered poet N. F. Annenskiy, were injured, and about 1,500 were arrested, many of them students who were detained for three weeks and then expelled from the university and city of St. Petersburg. The Kazan Square affair attracted especial attention because of writer Maxim Gorky's account of the event, the "Song of the Stormy Petrol," which was hectographed in millions of copies and became something of a revolutionary ballad with its warning, "The storm! Wait! Soon it will burst" (Salisbury 1977: 78).

In France, troops summarily executed about 3,000 people after a workers' uprising in June 1848 was suppressed, and another 20,000 or more after the Paris Commune of 1871 was put down. Even after labor unions were legalized in France in 1884, police and troops were promiscuously dispatched to virtually all major and some minor strikes, and clashes with workers were frequent. Large mining and dock strikes in France were usually patrolled by one soldier for every two or three strikers, while even a small strike of 150 weavers in the department of the Nord in 1903 attracted 55 police. Between 1906 and 1908, about 20 workers were killed and almost 700 injured in French labor disputes.

In Hungary and Spain, the rural police forces were noted for both their unusual and intimidating costumes and their brutal behavior. The rural police in Hungary "roamed the villages and fields, usually in pairs, ... and always with bayonetted rifle on shoulder, ready to hit or stab or shoot as required. They put the fear of God into the peasants" (Ignotus 1972: 79). An estimated 51 people were killed and 114 wounded in clashes arising from agrarian strikes in Hungary in 1897-98. In Spain the rural police, known as the Civil Guard, were forbidden to intermarry or associate on friendly terms with local inhabitants. According to Gerald Brenan's classic account, "every Civil Guard became a recruiting office for anarchism, ... Again and again mild riots and demonstrations have become dangerous because the Civil Guard could not keep their fingers off their triggers" (1964: 156-57). Equally hated were the special anti-anarchist police established in Barcelona, the Brigada Social, which was notorious for torturing prisoners and their murky relationship with terrorist bands and shady informants.

In Germany and Belgium, one historian notes, strikes were often marked by "calvalry charges against strike meetings and ... bloody use of sabers on the unprotected heads of strikers" (Stearns 1971: 14). Another historian characterizes the Belgian military as resorting to "persistent, outrageous and quite unnecessarily lethal violence" against strikers and demonstrators (Kendall 1975: 217). In Ireland, the frequently brutal behavior of the Protestant-dominated constabulary against the Catholic peasantry engendered great hatred and led to endemic clashes. Between 1826 and 1834, when such violence reached one of its greatest peaks, almost 150 people, including 25 police, lost their lives. The brutal use of deadly force by troops and police in Italy was unmatched in Europe save for Russia. Almost 700 people were killed during clashes with Italian troops in 1864, 1868-9, 1893, 1898 and 1901-1904. Strikes were repeatedly triggered between 1904 and 1914 in Italy by the killing of demonstrators.

## *"Dirty Tricks": Secret Police, Mail Opening, and* Agents Provocateurs

The use of secret police agencies to infiltrate and in some cases disrupt or provoke opposition groups--a technique that came to be known in the United States as "dirty tricks" in the wake of the 1970s Watergate scandal--was widespread in nineteenth-century Europe. The exact scope and significance of such activities will probably remain forever enshrouded in mystery; it seems likely that the very inability to obtain comprehensive and confirmed information on much of the material related to this subject has lent itself to exaggerations of their importance, except perhaps in Austria and Russia.

Secret police techniques were by no means unknown before the nineteenth century. Thus, a Parisian police official reportedly boasted to King Louis XV around 1750 that "when three people chat in the street, one of them is my man" (Monas 1961: 6), while the mission of the secret police in Austria in 1790 was described in one document as the discovery of "all persons who are or might be dangerous to the state [and of] any discontent arising among the people, all dangerous thoughts and especially any incipient rebellion and to nip these in the bud" (Doyle 1978: 249). Secret police operations expanded to hitherto unknown dimensions during the nineteenth century by governments that feared, especially in the immediate post-1815 period, the existence of secret revolutionary societies and a recurrence of the "French disease" of 1789. The height of secret police operations was reached during the extremely repressive period between 1815 and 1860, when restrictions on voting, assembly, association, unions and the press were so severe in most European countries that opposition groups were forced into conspiratorial activities. "Extended activity of the secret police forms one of the most characteristic features of the period after Waterloo; the archives of every European capital contain hundreds of dossiers of their reports. ... The records of the police in every country contained detailed information about all important persons" (Artz 1963: 6). After restrictions on the suffrage and civil liberties were lifted in most countries around 1860, the scope and significance of the secret police declined, save in the remaining highly repressive regimes such as Russia. Since most opposition groups conducted their affairs openly and used legalitarian tactics once such avenues became possible, the need for secret police surveillance and countermeasures declined.

The Austrian secret police were the most notorious during the 1815-60 period. Secret police operations in the Habsburg realm had been drastically expanded in response to the threat posed by the French Revolution and the uncovering of a supposed "Jacobin Conspiracy" in 1794, which led to the executions of nine people on extremely flimsy evidence. Huge numbers of informants--especially in such occupations as servants, prostitutes, waiters and doormen--were hired to report to the police on the activities and conversations of Austrians, and an extremely effective shroud of intimidation was lowered over the Austrian public that was not significantly lifted until after 1860. As early as 1794, the young composer Beethoven wrote from Vienna, "One doesn't dare lift his voice here, otherwise the police find lodging for you" (Emerson 1968: 24). Eight years later, a visitor to Vienna commented:

> You can visit public places for months without hearing a single word about politics, so strict is the watch maintained over orthodoxy in both state and church. In all the coffee-houses, there reigns such a reverent silence that you might think high mass was being celebrated where no one dares to breathe (Wangerman 1973: 184).

An Austrian who wrote his memoirs in 1884 recalled that when he left his home in the early 1820s his father warned him:

> Keep out of any conversation on politics and the organization of the state; even among close friends keep completely silent on these matters. ... Don't even joke about matters of government. If something seems questionable or even wrong, then trust that your lack of insight has given you a mistaken point of view (Emerson 1968: 100).

One of the most effective techniques used by the Austrian secret police--and their counterparts in every other major European country in the immediate post-1815 period--was the clandestine opening of private mail. Every major Austrian post office had mail-opening departments, known as Logen, attached to them. The function of the Logen was the secret opening, copying, and then resealing of mail sent to persons of interest. In Vienna a special Secret Cipher Chancery (Geheime Ziffenkanzlei) was maintained to read and decipher correspondence written in code. It was generally known in Austria that mail was opened, so many Habsburg subjects took great care in what they wrote. Thus, the great Czech historian František Palacký apologized to a friend in 1855 for writing so seldom, nothing that "whenever I feel like writing I am seized by rage" that "what I send you from a fervent heart should be sniffed [by]_____ in human likeness [to] see if it smells according to their regulations" (Zaeck 1970: 111).

The fruits of the Austrian mail interception and secret police surveillance were delivered daily to Emperor Francis I (1792-1835) and his foreign minister, Metternich. It is said that Francis's daily "Morgenplaisir" ("morning pleasure") consisted of hours spent reading through these reports, while Metternich enjoyed dropping tidbits gleaned from secret police findings during conversations with foreign diplomats in order to cultivate an aura of omnipotence and omniscience. Metternich boasted to a friend in 1817 that Austria had developed a police force "on a scale far outstripping anything that has existed before," and told the French minister in Turin, "You see in me the chief Minister of Police in Europe. I keep an eye on everything.

My contacts are such that nothing escapes me" (Sauvigny 1962: 105). In 1832, Friedrich Gentz, Metternich's secretary, in a letter to a friend sent by diplomatic courier to avoid the mails, wrote, "You must realize that the mistrust towards one and all, the espionage against one's own confidants and the opening of all letters without exception has here reached heights for which there can scarcely be a parallel in all history" (Musulin 1975: 253).

The Russian secret police, known during the reign of Nicholas I (1825-55) as the Third Section, were only slightly less notorious than those of Austria. Nicholas directed his police to oversee virtually all aspects of Russian society, especially the activities of intellectuals, foreigners, dissenters and any other possible threats to the regime. The official charge to the Third Section, drafted personally by Nicholas, included the gathering of "information concerning all events, without exception" (Monas 1961: 63). The organization was given the power to arrest and exile "suspicious or dangerous persons" without trials or charges. Although full-time Third Section employees only numbered about 40, their net spread throughout Russia via an extensive informant organization. Many of these informants deliberately supplied the Third Section with false or exaggerated information to increase their own importance. Eventually the Third Section took to punishing some of them and staging weekly burnings of their reports.

The activities of the Austrian and Russian secret police during the 1815-60 period were the most extensive in Europe, but all of the other major countries, including especially France, Germany, and the United Kingdom, carried out similar surveillance activities in a scaled-down form. In the United Kingdom, there was a great scandal in 1844 when it was revealed that Home Secretary James Graham had directed the Post Office to intercept the mail of the exiled Italian revolutionary Giuseppe Mazzini and supplied the information thus obtained to Austria. Many Britons took to marking their envelopes "Not to be Grahamed," while Punch published a series of "anti-Graham wafers" to be attached to mail, bearing messages, such as "Nothing particular inside" imprinted across a profile of Graham's head (Smith 1970: 198). Parliamentary inquiry revealed that every home secretary had authorized the opening of mail in specific cases since parliament had legalized the practice in 1711 and that during the early 1840s Graham had had the mail of leading political dissidents in Great Britain, including one member of parliament and a leader of the moderate middle class anti-Corn Law movement, opened. Despite the 1844 uproar, the authority of British officials to open private mail was not revoked, although it was used much more sparingly thereafter.

After about 1860, the significance of secret police activity declined markedly save in those countries, such as Russia, France under Napoleon III, and Germany during the 1878-90 anti-socialist laws, where restrictions on political activity forced opposition groups underground. These regimes not only continued to make extensive use of secret police for domestic surveillance, but also sent agents abroad to spy on political opponents living in exile. Thus, in 1870 the French secret police had over 60 agents stationed abroad, while the foreign section of the Russian secret police (known as the Zagranichnaia Agentura or Foreign Agency), founded in 1885, employed about 70 detectives and informants.

The activities of the Zagranichnaia Agentura were so blatant that they often aroused great anger and trepidation among Russian political exiles. Thus, the Russian anarchist theoretician Peter Kropotkin, who had escaped from a czarist prison, claimed in his memoirs that during his period in exile in France during the 1880s, "Flocks, literally flocks of Russian spies besieged the house seeking admission under all possible pretexts, or simply tramping in pairs, trios and quartettes in front of the house" (Kimball 1973: 53). Another Russian political exile, a man by the name of Sibiryakov, ended up in an English mental hospital in the 1870s after developing an acute case of paranoia. He imagined that scores of Russian secret police were following him all over Europe, and to his dismay "discovered" also that all of his hospital doctors and nurses, with one exception, were personal agents of the Russian ambassador in London.

As was the case with domestically employed secret police agents, those employed abroad varied greatly in their efficiency and accuracy. Thus, one historian who carefully studied the daily reports, totalling thousands in all, dispatched by the six or seven French secret police assigned to oversee the 3,500 refugees from the 1871 suppression of the Paris Commune who fled to England concluded, "One agent would give vent to what were, in retrospect, the most extreme and violent fantasies; another would provide cogent and detailed accounts which accord with and illuminate information available from other sources" (Martinez 1982: 100).

Perhaps related to the apparent inability or unwillingness of European governments to train and control their operatives adequately is one dark and usually murky strain that periodically emerged throughout the nineteenth century: the secret police official as agent provocateur. The profession of secret police agent or informant frequently attracted persons of unstable or violent vent, and in any case such persons who infiltrated clandestine opposition groups generally felt constrained to become active participants to maintain their credibility. It is often difficult to determine the exact role of such persons, to distinguish between "participation" and "manipulation" or "incitement" and to determine whether or not clearly provocative police activities were the work of individual agents or the result of state policy. In any case, there are scattered cases in which secret police agents in many different countries took a leadership role in fomenting violence or other forms of opposition to European regimes. Thus, in Austrian-ruled Lombardy, a revolutionary plot broken up with about 100 arrests in 1855 was organized by a police spy, Giuseppe Bideschini, who had successfully insisted that all plans be put in writing. In 1889, the Belgian government was severely discredited when it was discovered that a police agent had furnished dynamite used in a violent strike the previous year. In Spain, there was a great scandal in 1907 when a man named Juan Rull was arrested and it was revealed that he had organized the planting of a series of bombs while in the pay of the police. Apparently Rull was collecting money for providing spurious information about the bombing "perpetrators." In Germany, the secret police fostered a small anarchist-terrorist movement in the 1880s, apparently in hopes of discrediting the outlawed but peacefully oriented socialist movement; in one instance a police agent paid the travel expenses of an anarchist who was involved in an unsuccessful attempt to assassinate the emperor, and in other cases police officials, at the least, knew about planned terrorist actions in advance, but did nothing to stop them. In France, a plot uncovered in 1869 to kill Emperor Napoleon III was reported to the police by an informant who told them about the activities of a man named Guérin who was manufacturing bombs. After the regime was overthrown in 1870, it was discovered that the informant and Guérin were one and the same! In 1880 the French police established a militant anarchist newspaper in Paris, La Revolution Sociale, edited by one of its own agents. Around 1905 a leading trade union militant in France named Métivier, who was arrested for instigating strikes, was paid two salaries while in jail—one by the police and one by his union.

Undoubtedly the role of agents provocateurs in Russia between 1900 and 1914 far exceeded their importance in any other country or time in Europe between 1815 and 1914, and in fact it makes the scattered instances reported in other countries seem relatively trivial by comparison. The most fantastic case was that of Yevno Azef, who between 1903 and 1908 simultaneously served as a secret police agent and as head of the terrorist section of the Social Revolutionary party, a militant and violence-oriented opposition group. In many cases Azef betrayed his revolutionary comrades to the secret police, but in others he planned in minute detail and successfully supervised terrorist acts, including the assassination of his own superior, Minister of the Interior Plehve in 1904, and that of the czar's brother, the Grand Duke Sergei in 1905. In 1911, another Social Revolutionary police agent, Dmitri Bogrov, assassinated Russian Prime Minister Peter Stolypin. Bogrov's role as an agent was hushed up, and he was secretly tried and executed within 24 hours. Although the evidence is not entirely conclusive, it strongly suggests that Bogrov murdered Stolypin "with the connivance of high police officials" who used Bogrov to "eliminate a Premier who was hated in palace circles but who had proved difficult to remove in other ways" (Hosking 1973: 148).

Russian secret police infiltration of the highest levels of the Bolshevik (radical-revolutionary) wing of the Social Democratic party opposition reached extraordinary levels during the 1910-14 period. "The agents ascended quickly in the Party heirarchy by the simple expedient of arranging the arrest of incumbents, persons who suspected them and others who stood in their way" (Wolfe 1964: 540). Thus, two police agents were on the editorial board of the Bolshevik newspaper Pravda when it began publishing in 1912, and the leader of the Bolshevik organization in Moscow in 1910 was an agent. Another agent, Roman Malinovsky, was a member of the Bolshevik Central Committee and the chief spokesmen for the Bolsheviks in the Russian legislature (duma) until the police exposed him in 1914. Malinovsky carried out the policy of both the Bolshevik leader, Lenin, and the police, which was to deepen the split between the Bolshevik and Menshevik factions of the Social Democrats (favored by the police as weakening the opposition and by Lenin as fostering his consolidation of control over the Bolsheviks). Thus, when Malinovsky ran for the duma in 1912 both the Bolsheviks and the police worked with great energy to gain his election--the police, in fact, more or less guaranteed this by arresting the leading rival candidates. While serving in the duma as a Bolshevik deputy, Malinovsky arranged for the arrest of a number of leading Bolsheviks, including Stalin, published fiery denunciations of the Mensheviks in Pravda--which by 1913 had a police agent as editor-in-chief--and delivered speeches in the legislature that were virtually co-written by Lenin and the police. At one point Malinovsky served as treasurer of Pravda and turned over to the police lists of contributors to the paper while raising funds for it and personally contributing sums furnished by the police. These monies were recovered by fines levied by the authorities, "in one case a fine of 500 rubles for an article written by none other than Duma deputy Malinovsky" (Wolfe 1964: 548). As one former top-ranking czarist official noted, by the eve of World War I, it was almost impossible to determine in Russia "where the secret police agents stopped and the revolutionaries began" (Zuckerman 1977: 205).

## Restrictions on Academic Freedom

Virtually all European governments maintained controls over their education systems during the nineteenth century to ensure that "subversive" ideas and instructors did not infiltrate them. This was especially the case in Germany, Russia, and the Habsburg Empire, where for part or most of the nineteenth century students were forbidden to study abroad, student associations were not allowed or were strictly regulated, and minute scrutiny was maintained over teacher hiring and the school curriculum. Thus, in 1819, the Prussian government called upon all of the German states to rid their universities of "teachers who have obviously demonstrated their incapacity to fill their offices by demonstrable deviation from their duty, or transgressing against the limits of their profession, or misusing their proper influence on the young, or spreading harmful theories inimical to public order and peace or destructive to existing political institutions" (McClelland 1980: 218-19). Austrian Emperor Francis I told a delegation of school masters in 1821, "I have no use for scholars, but only for good citizens. It is up to you to mold our youth in this sense. Who serves me must teach what I order; who cannot do this or comes along with new ideas, can leave or I shall get rid of him" (May 1963: 79). Under Francis, educational controls were so strict that even the titles of books that professors took out from libraries were scrutinized by the authorities. In Russia, the already-tight restrictions on education were drastically tightened in the aftermath of the 1848 European revolutions (which did not spread to Russia). Students were required to wear uniforms and have their hair cut in a certain style, and they were barred from visiting coffeehouses or reading foreign newspapers. The study of the constitutional law of those European powers "that had been shaken internally to their foundations by uprisings and riots" was barred from university study, as was the discipline of philosophy "in view of the scandalous development of this science by contemporary German scholars" (Alston 1969: 40). Minister of Education Shirinsky-Shikmatov pointed out that in any case, "The value of philosophy is unproved, but harmful effects from it are possible" (Seton-Watson 1967: 277). In Germany, Emperor William II ordered Prussian school teachers in 1889 to help combat the "spread of socialist and communist ideas" and to show pupils "how constantly during the present century the wages and living conditions of the working class have improved under the guiding care of the Prussian kings" (Snell 1976: 249).

Hundreds of instructors were fired for political reasons from teaching positions in European schools during the nineteenth centry. Many of these victims of political repression were extremely well known at the time of their firing, or became so afterward, including prime ministers of France, Rumania and Serbia, two presidents of Spain and a Nobel Prize-winning Italian poet. In some cases, as in those of the eminent historians George Gervinus, Jules Michelet and Edgar Quinet, the same professor was fired twice for political reasons (see Table 2.4). In many other cases, eminently qualified scholars decided not to seek university employment (e.g., Karl Marx) or were barred from positions because of political considerations. For example, the noted Danish literary critic Georg Brandes was blocked from appointment to the University of Copenhagen for 30 years until the Danish political situation changed in 1901, and the leading sociologist Robert Michel had to seek a position in Italy after he was kept from a post at the University of Marburg in Germany. The famous revisionist theologian David Strauss was prevented from taking a position at the University of Zurich in 1839 when 10,000 armed peasants marched on the government of Zurich canton in protest over Strauss's appointment and forced it to resign.

In a number of cases, political firings of well-known professors or other forms of political repression in educational policy attracted enormous public attention and became major grievances among students and middle-class liberals. Perhaps the most notorious case of political firings came in the German state of Hanover in 1837. The despicable new king, Ernst Augustus--one London newspaper wrote he had committed every crime in his life except suicide--dismissed seven eminent professors at the University of Göttingen, including the Grimm brothers and the famous historians Gervinus and Friedrich Dahlmann, when they opposed his arbitrary abolition of the liberal 1833 constitution. Ernst Augustus dismissed their protests, declaring, "Professors and whores can always be had for money" (Professoren und Huren sind immer für Geld zu haben [Reichard 1969: 26]), to which Dahlmann responded:

Table 2.4: Some Noted Persons Fired from Academic
Positions for Political Reasons in Europe, 1815–1914

| Year | Name | Institution/Location | Discipline/Contribution | Source |
|------|------|----------------------|-------------------------|--------|
| 1819 | Friedrich List | Univ. of Tübingen (Württemberg) | Economics | Holborn 1969: 20 |
| 1820 | Ernst Moritz Arndt | Univ. of Bonn (Prussia) | History | Lees 1974: 195 |
| 1820 | Bernhard Bolzano | Univ. of Prague (Austria) | Philosophy/Math | Seton-Watson1965:179 |
| 1821 | Victor Cousin | Sorbonne (Paris) | Philosophy | Sauvigny 1966: 407 |
| 1822 | Francois Guizot | Sorbonne (Paris) | History (Fr. premier 1840-48) | Moody 1978: 24 |
| 1823 | A. I. Arwidsson | Univ. of Turku (Finland) | Finn. nationalist | Juttikala 1962: 202 |
| 1824 | Joachim Lelewel | Univ. of Wilno (Russian Poland) | History | Wandycyz 1974: 86 |
| 1827 | Abel Villemain | Sorbonne (Paris) | Lit. criticism | Sauvigny 1966: 407 |
| 1832 | Karl Welcker | Univ. of Freiburg (Baden) | Political theory | Rohr 1963: 113 |
| 1832 | Karl von Rotteck | Univ. of Freiburg (Baden) | Political theory | Snell 1976: 36 |
| 1837 | J. and W. Grimm | Univ. of Göttingen (Hanover) | Folklore | Holborn 1969: 28 |
| 1837 | Friedrich Dahlmann | Univ. of Göttingen (Hanover) | History | Holborn 1969: 28 |
| 1837 | Wilhelm Weber | Univ. of Göttingen (Hanover) | Physics | Holborn 1969: 28 |
| 1837 | George Gervinus | Univ. of Göttingen (Hanover) | History | Holborn 1969: 28 |
| 1839 | Johan Snellman | Univ. of Turku (Finland) | Finn. nationalist | Wuorinen 1965: 155 |
| 1841 | Karl Welcker | Univ. of Freiburg (Baden) | Political theory | Rohr 1963: 113 |
| 1842 | H. von Fallersleben | Univ. of Breslau (Prussia) | Poetry | Stadelmann 1975: 40 |
| 1843 | M. Kogălniceanu | Mihilena Academy (Moldavia) | History (Rum. premier 1863-65) | Seton-Watson1934:217 |
| 1844 | Adam Mickiewicz | Collège de France (Paris) | Poetry | Langer 1969: 250 |
| 1845 | Edgar Quinet | Collège de France (Paris) | History | Gallaher 1980: 14 |
| 1845 | Friedrich Vischer | Univ. of Tübingen (Württemberg) | Philosophy | Lees 1974: 209 |

| Year | Name | Institution/Location | Discipline/Position | Source |
|---|---|---|---|---|
| 1848 | Jules Michelet | Collège de France (Paris) | History | Gallaher 1980: 15 |
| 1850 | Lorenz von Stein | Univ. of Kiel (Denmark) | Econ./Sociology | Lees 1974: 108 |
| 1850 | Theodore Mommsen | Univ. of Leipzig (Saxony) | History | Bazillon 1978: 83 |
| 1851 | Jules Michelet | Collège de France (Paris) | History | Merriman 1978: 125 |
| 1852 | Edgar Quinet | Collège de France (Paris) | History | Moody 1978: 59 |
| 1853 | George Gervinus | Univ. of Heidelberg (Baden) | History | Lees 1974: 200 |
| 1853 | Karl Biedermann | Univ. of Leipzig (Saxony) | History | Lees 1974: 196 |
| 1864 | Emilio Castelar | Univ. of Madrid (Spain) | History (Sp. president 1873-74) | Herr 1971: 104 |
| 1864 | Vladimir Jovanović | Belgrade Lyceum (Serbia) | Politics | Stokes 1975: 66 |
| 1865 | Djuro Daničic | Belgrade Lyceum (Serbia) | Philology | Petrovich 1976: 351 |
| 1863 | Ernest Renan | Collège de France (Paris) | History | Thompson 1967: 242 |
| 1867 | Giosuè Carducci | Univ. of Bologna (Italy) | Poetry | Smith 1959: 68 |
| 1873 | Nikola Pašić | Belgrade Academy (Serbia) | Politics (Serb. premier 1904-19) | Dragnich 1974: 13 |
| 1875 | Nicholas Salmerón | Univ. of Madrid (Spain) | Philosophy (Sp. president 1873) | Herr 1971: 124 |
| 1876 | F. G. de los Riòs | Univ. of Madrid (Spain) | Education Reform | Herr 1971: 124 |
| 1879 | Heinrich Friedjung | Univ. of Vienna (Austria) | History | McGrath 1974: 74 |
| 1890 | Dmitri Mendeleyev | Univ. of St. Petersburg (Russia) | Chemistry | Crankshaw 1976: 301 |
| 1895 | Paul Miliukov | Univ. of Moscow (Russia) | History-Politics | Charques 1965: 105 |

Must I now teach that the supreme principle of the state is that whatever pleases those in power is law? As a man of honor I would rather give up teaching altogether than sell to my audience as truth that which is a lie and deceit (Pinson 1954: 60).

The so-called Göttingen Seven immediately became liberal martyrs in Germany. Student demonstrations at Göttingen were put down by troops, while "Göttingen Associations" sprang up throughout Germany to raise money for the Seven until they could find other positions.

Another academic cause célèbre in Germany erupted in the late 1890s when the Prussian Ministry of Education unsuccessfully demanded that a young socialist physics lecturer at the University of Berlin be dismissed by the faculty, although there was no evidence that his political beliefs had affected his teaching. Emperor William II personally intervened, declaring in 1897, "I tolerate no socialists among ... teachers in the royal institutions of higher education" (Snell 1976: 243). Finally the lecturer, Leo Arons, was dismissed when the Prussian legislature passed a special law (the so-called Lex Arons of 1899) that declared that the "deliberate promotion of Social Democratic purposes is incompatible with a teaching post in a royal university" (Craig 1980: 202). A Spanish case that attracted immense attention was the 1864 firing of Emilio Castelar, a University of Madrid professor dismissed for his criticism of Queen Isabel II. Student demonstrations protesting the affair were dispersed in central Madrid by troops who killed nine and wounded 100 in the so-called hecatomb of St. Daniel's Night (April 10, 1865).

The Castelar affair was one of the major events leading to the 1868 Spanish Revolution that overthrew the Isabeline regime. In several other cases, student resentment over political firings of instructors and other political controls also helped to spark revolutions. For example, the February 1848 revolution in France was partly triggered by student resentment over educational controls, and especially the firing of immensely popular historian Jules Michelet in January 1848. In Austria, the 1848 insurrection grew directly out of demonstrations called by students at the University of Vienna to demand academic freedom and civil liberties, and students organized in the "academic legion" played a leading role in the subsequent direction of the revolution.

In Russia, students were at the forefront after 1855 in the opposition movement. They repeatedly rioted and demonstrated to protest the suffocating restrictions on their activities, and almost invariably an upsurge in student dissent presaged a general rise in opposition activity. Thus, the unrest that culminated in the 1905 revolution was foreshadowed in a massive increase in student dissent in the late nineteenth and early twentieth centuries. In early February 1899, rowdy student demonstrators at the University of St. Petersburg were brutally attacked by mounted police. Afterwards, 25,000 students at 30 universities and institutions of higher learning struck, shutting down the entire system of higher education. Students were further antagonized by July 1899 regulations that ordered the expulsion and conscription of student activists, and by the conscription of 200 students at the University of Kiev who demonstrated in 1900 to protest this decree. When Minister of Education N. P. Bogolepov was assassinated on February 14, 1901 students throughout Russia demonstrated in celebration. A series of student demonstrations in late 1910 demanding abolition of capital punishment foreboded another upsurge in Russian opposition after the crushing of the 1905 revolution. Minister of Education L. A. Kasso responded to the demonstrations with expulsions and arrests of over 3,000 students and forbade all student associations and meetings, in violation of the university autonomy that had been granted in 1905 and generally respected since then. All institutions of higher education in St. Petersburg and Moscow struck in protest for the entire spring term of 1911. When several top officials of Moscow University resigned from their positions to protest Kasso's policies, they were fired from their university chairs, whereupon 100 faculty members resigned, including the noted historians Vasily Klyuchevsky and Paul Vinogradov.

Chapter 3

The Victims of Repression: Political Prisoners and Exiles

Hundreds of thousands--perhaps even millions--of people who lived in
Europe during the 1815-1914 period suffered severe penalties for their
political beliefs, for peaceful if often illegal activities, such as strikes
and demonstrations, and for violent resistance to regimes that offered
no meaningful peaceful avenues for protest. Every major European
country had special jails or designated places of exile for political
prisoners, and the most notorious of these were infamous throughout
Europe. The Austrian fortress-prison at Spielberg, near Brno (Brünn)
in Moravia, was immortalized by the Italian dramatic poet Silvio
Pellico, in his book Le mie prigioni (My prisons), an account of his
eight-year stay there after his arrest for anti-Austrian plotting in
Lombardy in 1820. Le mie prigioni, published in 1832, created a
sensation in Europe. Other jails used for political prisoners in the
Habsburg monarchy, especially in the aftermath of the 1848
revolutions, were located at Kufstein, Josephstadt, Olmütz (Olomouc),
Munkacs (Mukachevo), Komarom, and Theresienstadt (which was later
the site of a Nazi concentration camp). In France, the leading prison
for non-violent political offenders was the extremely benign
Sainte-Pélagie in Paris, but those implicated in the June 1848 workers'
uprising, resistance to the December 1851 coup d'état of Louis
Napoleon, and the 1871 Paris Commune were shipped off to terrible
prison camps in the French colonies of Guyana, Algeria, and New
Caledonia. In Russia, the most notorious political prisons were located
at the Saint Peter and Paul Fortress in St. Petersburg and the
Schlüsselberg prison 25 miles away from the capital, but there were
many others, such as the Butyrka and Taganka prisons in Moscow. In
addition, hundreds of thousands of political prisoners, recalcitrant
serfs, petty criminals, and others who displeased czarist officials were
condemned to long periods of internal exile in Siberia or other remote
areas of Russia. According to one tally, 680,000 Russians were
deported to Siberia between 1823 and 1881 alone. In the United
Kingdom, over 150,000 convicts were transported to Australia between
1787 and 1868, including 3,600 persons involved in politically
motivated (and usually violent) activities.

In Spain, the fortress-prison of Montjuich overlooking Barcelona became a symbol of tyranny when brutal tortures of anarchist prisoners there in the 1890s were exposed in the book Les Inquisiteurs de l'Espagne, published by one of the victims, Tarrida del Marmol. Mass meetings were held to protest the Spanish tortures in London and elsewhere in Europe. One of the victims of Montjuich was paraded around Europe, demonstrating that "his toe-nails had been pulled out, his body was a mass of cuts and stripes and his sexual organs had been burned" (Brenan 1964: 169). Other Spanish political prisoners were packed off to colonies, such as the Philippines and Spanish Sahara. Authorities in the Kingdom of the Two Sicilies (before it was absorbed into Italy in 1860) and in Italy (after 1860) frequently deported political dissidents, often without trial, to the islands off the southern Italian coast, a tradition continued by Mussolini. In his 1851 exposé of conditions in the Two Sicilies, Two Letters to Lord Aberdeen on the State Prosecutions of the Neapolitan Government, British politician William Gladstone made a profound impression upon liberal Europe. Especially poignant was the case of Carlo Poerio, a respected lawyer and minister of education during the short-lived revolutionary government of 1848, who was sentenced in 1851 to 24 years in irons on the basis of perjured and forged evidence. When Gladstone visited Poerio at the island prison of Nisida, the latter was sick, exhausted, and perpetually chained to another convict.

Aside from Europeans who were jailed or involuntarily exiled for their political beliefs or activities, other scores of thousands fled into exile because they feared retribution or could no longer endure the regimes of their homelands. Every failed revolution and every repressive regime produced such exiles, while the more tolerant European governments, such as Switzerland, Belgium, and especially the United Kingdom, housed thousands of political refugees. The great age of political refugees was between 1820 and 1860, resulting from the severe repression characteristic of many European governments and especially from the repressive aftermaths of the revolutionary outbursts of 1820, 1830, and 1848. The failed revolutions of 1848 produced the single largest crop of political exiles, including an estimated 100,000 from the Italian states alone as well as additional thousands from France, the Habsburg monarchy, Germany, and the Danubian Principalities.

Perhaps the most famous flight of political refugees followed the collapse of the Polish revolt against Russian rule in 1830-31. An estimated 10,000 Poles, including many leading intellectuals, government officials and landholders became part of what was soon known as the "Great Emigration." The cause of Poland became a major rallying cry for liberals and radicals throughout Europe because of the brutal nature of Russian policy in Poland after 1830 and the constant and skillful propaganda activity of many of the exiles. The greatest of the Polish propagandists was the noted exiled poet Adam Mickiewicz, who in his writings, such as the 1832 poem The Books of the Polish Nation and of the Polish Pilgrims, developed the theme that Poland was the Christ of the nations, chosen by God as a martyr to expiate the sins of other nations and bring about a new era of justice and brotherly love on earth. Largely through the agitation of Mickiewicz and other emigré Poles, the "Poles were seen as the children of light who fought the champion of darkness [Russia], as the defenders of civilised Europe who had entered the lists against the barbarism of Asia" (Weisser 1975: 49).

Aside from Mickiewicz, among the most famous political refugees were Heinrich Heine, the German lyric poet and journalist, who spent most of his life in Paris; the French writer Victor Hugo, who lived many years as an exile in England and Belgium; and a trio of revolutionary leaders who spent much of their lives in exile in London: the German Karl Marx, the Hungarian Louis Kossuth, and the Italian Giuseppe Mazzini. Kossuth, who perfected his English while jailed for press offenses in Hungary in the 1830s and led the futile 1848-9 Hungarian revolution against Austrian rule, mesmerized audiences in the United States and England during triumphant tours in the early 1850s with his eloquent speeches. In England alone, over 100 books and several thousand articles were published about Kossuth. Marx was expelled for his political beliefs and writings from Prussia, Belgium, and France in the 1840s. His most famous work, The Communist Manifesto, was commissioned by an organization of German political exiles living in London, the League of the Just (Bund der Gerechten), which changed its name in 1847 to the Communist League.

European diplomatic relations were frequently strained during the nineteenth century by demands made by the home governments of political refugees that those countries that gave them asylum either expel them or curb their alleged (and often very real) political activities aimed at discrediting or overthrowing their native regimes. Thus, in September 1849, Russia and Austria broke diplomatic relations with Turkey when the Ottoman government refused to extradite Hungarian and Polish refugees who had fought in the 1848-9 Hungarian revolution: the peace of Europe was severely threatened when Britain and France sent warships into Turkish waters to oppose the Russo-Austrian demands. Sardinia broke relations with Austria in 1853 when the Habsburg regime, in violation of treaty obligations, sequestered the property of political refugees from Austrian-controlled Lombardy-Venetia in the aftermath of an attempted revolt in Lombardy allegedly instigated by Sardinian-based exiles. Belgium and Switzerland were repeatedly subjected to severe and often successful pressure to expel prominent refugees by France, Austria, and Germany. Belgium's King Leopold I, whose country faced bitter complaints from France after accepting about 7,000 refugees following Louis Napoleon's 1851 coup, noted the exposed situation of small countries faced with the complaints of a larger power in a letter to his niece, Queen Victoria of England:

We are here in the awkward position of persons in hot climates, who find themselves in company, for instance in their beds, with a snake; they must not move because that irritates the creature, but they can hardly remain as they are without a fair chance of [being] bitten (Helmreich 1976: 90).

Britain was in a far stronger position than Belgium or Switzerland to resist demands to expel political refugees and maintained a position of free asylum for political exiles of all persuasions throughout the nineteenth century. After the 1848 revolutions, conservatives, such as the deposed French King Louis Philippe and the ousted Foreign Minister Clemens von Metternich of Austria, and radicals, such as Kossuth and Mazzini, found refuge in England. This policy was a matter of considerable pride among Britons. Thus, the Times of London stated in February 1853:

> Every civilized people on the face of the earth must be fully aware that this country is the asylum of nations, and that it will defend the asylum to the last ounce of its treasure and last drop of its blood. There is no point whatever on which we are prouder and more resolute (Porter 1979: 7).

In March 1872, in response to a Spanish diplomatic note urging that refugees from the Paris Commune of 1871 be barred from asylum, the British government declared that under British law, "all foreigners have an absolute right to enter the country and to remain" and that aliens had the same right as British citizens to be "punished only for offenses against the law" (Braunthal I, 1967: 163).

Other European governments were often deeply angered by the British policy. Thus Belgian King Leopold wrote to Queen Victoria in June 1853 that the general impression in Europe was that "in England a sort of menagerie of Kossuths, Mazzinis ... etc., is kept to be let occasionally loose on the continent to render its quiet and prosperity impossible" (Thompson 1967: 178). In 1858, after a bomb attempt by the Italian radical Felice Orsini on the life of French Emperor Napoleon III was found to have been plotted in England, French demands for a curb on political exiles led to a major crisis in Anglo-French relations and even the threat of war. Although Napoleon was able to use the Orsini affair to bully Belgium and Sardinia into crackdowns on press criticism of him, French threats led only to anger in Britain. One of Orsini's co-plotters was acquitted in the British courts despite his obvious guilt, and the House of Commons brought down the government of Lord Palmerston when it refused his request for a small and meaningless gesture in the French direction.

Life in exile was difficult for most political refugees. Although some of the most prominent exiles, such as Kossuth and Mazzini, were able to live reasonably well, most suffered from loneliness, a sense of isolation in a strange land and, often, from bitter poverty. Even Marx lived for many years in London in the most degrading poverty. Thus, during the 1850s, a Prussian police spy reported the following after gaining access to Marx's apartment:

> He lives in one of the worst and cheapest neighborhoods in

London. He occupies two rooms. There is not one clean or decent piece of furniture in either room, everything is broken, tattered and torn, with thick dust over everything. ... Manuscripts, books, and newspapers lie beside the children's toys, bits and pieces from his wife's sewing basket, cups with broken rims, dirty spoons, knives, forks, lamps, an inkpot, tumblers, pipes, tobacco ash--all piled up on the same table. On entering the room smoke and tobacco fumes make your eyes water to such an extent that at first you seem to be groping about in a cavern--until you get used to it and manage to make out certain objects in the haze. Sitting down is a dangerous business. Here is a chair with only three legs, there another which happens to be whole, on which the children are playing at cooking. That is the one that is offered to the visitor, but the children's cooking is not removed, and if you sit down you risk a pair of trousers. But all these things do not in the least embarrass Marx or his wife. You are received in the most friendly way and are cordially offered pipes, tobacco and whatever else there may happen to be. Presently a clever and interesting conversation arises which repays for all the domestic deficiencies and this makes the discomfort bearable (Berlin 1959: 180).

Especially in London, the exiles tended to cluster in their own communities, such as the areas around Soho and Leicester squares, and to frequent their own clubs, shops and cafes. Many of them lived mostly in the past. Thus, Alexander Herzen, the uncrowned king of the Russian exile community in London during the 1850s, wrote in his memoirs:

They point to one event, the end of some event, they think about it, they go back to it. Meeting the same men, the same groups--in five or six months, in two or three years—one feels terrified: the same arguments are still going on, the same personalities, the same recriminations, only the furrows drawn by poverty and privation are deeper, jackets and overcoats are shabbier; there are more grey hairs, and everything about them is older and bonier and even more gloomy ... and still the same things being said over and over again (Binkley 1963: 135).

Many of the exile communities, above all the Poles and Russians, were notorious for internal political divisions over personalities and/or the best theoretical approach to take to gain the hoped-for revolution. One bewildered newspaper reporter at an 1839 London meeting concerned with Poland wrote that when someone proposed that a major Benkiowski take the chair, this proved the signal "for an explosion of frantic fury on the part of a portion of the crowd ... blows were dealt most energetically and indiscriminately, and a hundred voices, hoarse with rage, all shouting at once, rendered the scene as exciting as it was unaccountable." The reporter could not determine the cause of the commotion, even after all parties had "bumped and bellowed themselves into exhaustion" but concluded "it seemed to stem from the fact that some Poles did not like Major Benkiowski" (Weisser 1975: 118-19). In Switzerland, where an enormous Russian colony developed after about 1880--in 1907 Russians constituted over one-third of total Swiss university enrollment--their reputation for unusual hours and raging quarrels was so great that it was common to see advertisements reading, "Roomers wanted, no Russians" (Wolfe 1964: 38).

Although hundreds of thousands of Europeans suffered real hardships as a result of their political beliefs and politically motivated actions, it would be quite misleading to suggest that the governments of nineteenth-century Europe operated with the kind of brutality and efficiency associated with twentieth-century totalitarianism. Austrian socialist leader Victor Adler's characterization of the Habsburg monarchy in the late nineteenth century as "an absolutism tempered by slovenliness" (Ein Absolutismus gemildert durch Schlamperei [Jaszi 1966: 165]) could be applied to many of the regimes. This was above all true of czarist Russia, which was both the most repressive and most inefficient regime among the major nations. Thus, although it is quite true, as one historian has noted, that the list of Russian political prisoners and exiles reads like a "who's who of Russia's great men and women" (Wolfe 1964: 205), it is also the case that the list of escapees from Russian prisons and Siberian exile is almost as distinguished. Between 1878 and 1887 alone, over 160 exiles or jailed political prisoners escaped. Among the most notable escapees were the anarchist writers and activists Michael Bakunin and Prince Peter Kropotkin, radical writers Peter Lavrov and Peter Tkachev, terrorist leader Gregory Gershuni, and socialist activists Leo Jogiches (Rosa Luxemburg's lover), Felix Dzierzynski (later head of the Soviet secret police) and Josef Pilsudski (later prime minister of Poland). Joseph Stalin and Leon Trotsky both escaped czarist custody twice, while one of Stalin's associates escaped no fewer than five times! Escapes sometimes occurred in other countries also, although less frequently. Among the most remarkable were the escape of Louis Napoleon Bonaparte (the future Emperor Napoleon III) from the fortress of Ham in 1846, six years after his incarceration for an abortive attempt to overthrow King Louis Philippe; the escape of the Italian revolutionary Orsini from the Austrian jail at Mantua in Lombardy in March 1856; and the escape by boat of the Italian anarchist Errico Malatesta from the island prison of Lampedusa in 1899, where he had been incarcerated for "seditious association."

In a number of highly charged political cases European governments were unable to obtain convictions. Perhaps the most famous case was that of Vera Zasulich, a Russian revolutionary acquitted by a jury of the attempted assassination of General Feodor Trepov, the St. Petersburg police chief, in 1878, although she was obviously guilty of the crime. General opposition to the Italian government was similarly manifested in a series of acquittals of anarchists who were clearly implicated in attempts to organize rebellions at Bologna in 1874 and Benevento in 1877. The unpopularity of the French government in the early 1830s was shown when Parisian juries elected acquittal in 332 out of 520 press prosecutions brought between 1830 and 1834. Karl Marx, French anarchist theoretician Pierre-Joseph Proudhon and German labor leader Ferdinand Lasalle were all acquitted in the 1840s in cases based purely on speech or press offenses.

Political prisoners who were convicted and sentenced to jail or exile did not always suffer terrible conditions. The jocularly named "Pavillion des Princes" section of the Sainte-Pélagie prison in Paris, used for non-violent political offenders, such as journalists, was notoriously lax. Prisoners were allowed to receive visitors, hold boisterous parties with outside guests, write, obtain books, order food from restaurants, and even leave a few nights a week on the honor system for such pressing duties as attending the theatre. It was common for journalists expecting to be prosecuted to reserve their favorite cell there, and since they were allowed to pursue their vocation from jail, "it was a preposterous but normal procedure for prisoners to be brought before the courts and charged with fresh press offenses that had been committed while they were still in prison" (Spencer 1956: 36). Proudhon, who married and became a father during his prison stay at Sainte-Pélagie, wrote in a letter to a friend in October 1849:

> Here in Ste. Pélagie, I am as well off as one can possibly be in prison. Even in the Rue Mazarin when I was a deputy [Proudhon was a member of parliament when he was jailed for his writing] I was not so well lodged. I eat the prison bread, which is good; I take the midday soup, with meat twice a week and without on the other five days, and anything else I want I can get sent in from the restaurant. The authorities provide a wine at 12 sous a litre which is better than the wine merchant would sell at one franc fifty. I receive my visitors in my own room, and I have obtained permission to have newspapers and pamphlets. ... My desire is, in spite of the annoyance of prison and the physical and moral inconvenience which goes with it, to remain where I am for 18 months (Jackson 1962: 78).

While imprisoned at what he called the "University of Ham," Louis Napoleon enjoyed similarly benevolent treatment, including conjugal visits with his mistress, games of whist with the prison commandant and the opportunity to do a considerable amount of writing. In the United Kingdom, the Irish nationalist leader Daniel O'Connell, jailed for sedition in 1844 at Richmond prison, was given the use of the warden's house for himself and his family, and received so many visitors while incarcerated that a large tent had to be erected so he could receive them all. German socialist leader August Bebel, who spent over four years in at least five different jails for speech and press violations, spent much of his time gardening, writing, and reading books like Marx's Capital and Engel's Conditions of the Working Class in England. Although gaunt and in poor health when he entered jail in July 1872 (for criticizing Prussian policies during the Franco-Prussian War of 1870), Bebel was described a few months later by fellow convict and socialist leader Wilhelm Liebknecht: "Bebel is getting fat!" Bebel himself wrote shortly after his release in April 1875, "I have definitely recovered my health in prison; yet three years ago I was in a deplorable condition" (Maehl 1980: 100).

Even in Russia, conditions for many non-violent political prisoners were often surprisingly lax. Trotsky described his jail cell at the notorious Peter and Paul Prison as "perfect for intellectual work" (Kochan 1966: 140). He received all the books he required, including Capital, smuggled articles he wrote out through his lawyers, and received twice-weekly visits from Natalia Ivanovna, who falsely claimed to be his legal wife. Trotsky assured her that it was a pleasure to work in his quiet jail cell "without any danger of being arrested" (Wolfe 1964: 334). During his four years in jail and Siberian exile, Lenin had no difficulty in obtaining hundreds of books and journals, many of which were mailed to him in Siberia from distant libraries. Visitors and mail arrived unhindered, and his future wife, Krupskaya, was allowed to join him, after she was also sentenced to Siberian exile, on condition they marry immediately.

Lenin completed all the research and writing for his first major book, The Development of Capitalism in Russia, while in jail and in exile, and he published it under a false name without interference from czarist officials who were quite aware of the author's identity. Other works produced in Russian jails included Nicholas Chernyshevsky's revolutionary classic, What is to be Done? and Lavrov's Historical Letters. Writing completed in prisons elsewhere included German socialist leader Bebel's History of Women and Socialism, Italian radical Francesco Guerrazzi's The Siege of Florence, Louis Napoleon's The Extinction of Pauperism, and three books by Proudhon.

In some instances, the imprisonment of political dissidents backfired on governments, creating only martyrs and greater publicity for opposition spokesmen. Shortly before abdicating in 1889, King Milan Obrenović of Serbia complained bitterly in a letter to German Emperor William II that "every individual who comes out of prison becomes a popular political personality whom everyone likes and respects" (Dragnich 1978: 79). The great poet Pierre Béranger was lionized by French society after being jailed twice for his writings during the Restoration, while a jail term during Napoleon III's reign in France became such a mark of distinction for writers that when the opposition journalist Lucien Prévost-Paradol was showered with congratulatory letters upon being elected to the French Academy in 1866 it is reported that his concierge "asked him shyly if he was being sent to jail" (Hemmings 1971: 66). In a number of cases, jailed opposition figures were elected to legislative assemblies either because of or in spite of their incarceration. For example, the great Czech journalist Karel Havliček was elected to the Austrian constituent assembly of 1848 from five different districts shortly after being jailed for press offenses in July 1848. Henri Rochefort, perhaps the leading opposition journalist under Napoleon III, was elected to parliament in November 1869 shortly after being arrested; he campaigned on the slogan, "Vote for Rochefort because the government doesn't want him" (Edwards 1977: 34). The Irish revolutionary leader O'Donovan Rossa was elected to the British parliament in 1869 while residing in Millbank Jail (the election was disallowed) while the German socialist Bebel was twice elected to the Reichstag while under arrest for sedition in 1872. French socialist leader Paul Lafargue, Karl Marx's son-in-law, was elected to the French legislature shortly after receiving a one-year jail term for allegedly inciting a riot (which transpired three weeks after Lafargue's supposedly inflammatory speech!) in which French troops shot to death ten unarmed workers.

In one famous Swedish case, Captain Anders Lindeberg, editor of the Stockholmposten, was convicted of treason in 1834 for implying that King Charles John might need to be deposed. Lindeberg was sentenced to death by decapitation as the law required in treason cases, but the king mitigated the sentence to three years in jail. When Lindeberg insisted upon his right to be beheaded and refused to take advantage of the government's attempts to encourage him to escape from jail, the king, in desperation, issued a general amnesty to all "political prisoners awaiting execution." When this still failed to convince Lindeberg to leave jail (he was the only such prisoner), the government finally locked him out of his cell one day when he was taking a walk in the prison courtyard. In Greece, a previously obscure politician, Charilaos Tricoupis, became famous overnight after he was jailed for publishing an attack on King George I in 1874. Shortly afterward, the king called upon him to become prime minister, and Tricoupis subsequently served seven times in that capacity.

# Part Two

# A History of Political Repression in Nineteenth-Century Europe

Chapter 4

# The Age of Repression and Revolution, 1815-1850

*The Economic and Social Structure of Europe, 1815-1850*

Most of the basic socio-economic aspects of the ancien regime (i.e., the pre-1789 order) in Europe remained intact during the first half of the nineteenth century. The daily lives of most Europeans, in fact, differed little from what they had been 100, 200 or even 600 years before. From a modern perspective, Europe between 1815 and 1850 was an extremely poor and backwards continent. Although, during this period, urbanization, industrialization, and literacy, among other indexes of modernization, increased at an unprecedented rate, in 1850 almost 90 per cent of the population lived in rural areas or small towns of under 20,000 people; about 70 per cent of the labor force was employed in agriculture; and less than half of the adult population was literate (see Table 5.1).

Except in England, the Netherlands and a few other scattered areas where significant agricultural modernization had begun, the peasantry farmed with the same tools and same inefficient techniques--such as letting one-third or more of the land lay fallow each year--that had been used for hundreds or even thousands of years. "The face of rural Europe looked much as it had in the Middle Ages, the farm animals were not of better quality, and the yields from the fields, were at best, not significantly higher" (Blum 1978: 154). The most backwards area of Europe by far was the Balkans, which had been under Turkish rule for hundreds of years and had been completely cut off from economic, social and technological developments occurring elsewhere in the Continent. In Serbia, for example, around 1830, there were no law codes, virtually no roads, no doctors, no banks, no currency and almost universal illiteracy.

Of the European population as a whole during the 1815-50 period, approximately one-third lived below the level of subsistence and "on the brink of starvation" (Langer 1969: 182), one-third lived at subsistence level but had no reserve for periods of unemployment or high food prices, and one-third could afford some luxuries and had some financial reserves. The bottom two-thirds of the population ate almost exclusively foods made from cereal grains, such as bread and porridge, supplemented with potatoes and maize. Meat was eaten by this segment of the population only a few times a year on special holidays; fruit was almost never consumed; and vegetables, save for peas and beans, were a rarity. Urban workers and peasants who lacked enough land to grow their own sustenance spent as much as 75 per cent or more of their income on food, although in times of scarcity the cost of food alone could swallow up a family's total income. Life expectancy in Europe during the period was about 30-35 years, only a few years longer than in the Middle Ages, and 20-25 years less than present life expectancy in the developing world. Over 20 per cent of all children born alive did not survive their first birthday, and about the same percentage died before the age of 20. Perhaps 15 per cent of peasant women died in childbirth.

Comparative statistics strongly suggest that in overall terms conditions were probably better in rural areas than in urban centers and that everywhere the lower classes paid for their poverty by especially shortened life spans and poor health. In rural Swedish areas between 1841 and 1850, the annual mortality rate was 10.7 per 1,000 population, while in urban areas the rate was 28.7; and in Stockholm, the largest Swedish city, the figure was 38.1. In Manchester, the average age of death in the 1840s was 22, while in the English agricultural town of Kendal, Westmoreland, people lived to an average age of 36. In France around 1840, 40 per cent of potential draft recruits from rural areas were rejected for health reasons, while the rejection rate was as high as 90 per cent from industrialized urban areas. In the 1840s, mortality rates in the poorest sections of Paris were over twice the rate in wealthy areas, while in the industrial town of Lille, France, 21 per cent of the children of the bourgeoisie died before the age of five, but over 50 per cent of workers' children were dead by that age. In Barcelona, estimated life expectancy for a poor male was less than 20 years in 1837-47, while the wealthy classes had an average life span of 34 years. In the 1840s in Manchester, the average age at death among professional persons, the gentry and their families was 38, but mechanics, laborers and their families had an average age of 17 at death. Quite literally, then, as the English rural laborers sang, "If life was a thing that money could buy, the rich would live and the poor might die" (Hobsbawm 1962: 248).

Although the threat of famine and epidemic disease gradually lessened in most of Europe after 1700, these ancient scourges continued to haunt the daily thoughts of most inhabitants of the Continent. Rural Europe experienced famine to some degree of severity about once every four years in the eighteenth century. While famine was less frequent after 1815, large areas of the Continent were afflicted and tens of thousands starved to death in 1816-17 and 1846-7. Regional famines occurred somewhere every year. Typhus, yellow fever, tuberculosis, cholera and, in southeastern Europe, the plague, were major scourges to which the poor were especially vulnerable because of poor nutrition and bad sanitary facilities and practices. As historian Louis Chevalier has noted, the disproportionate toll of the poor by the great cholera epidemics of

1830-7 and 1848-51 "made precise the biological foundation of class antagonism" (McGrew 1960: 65). Altogether about 2 million people died during these catastrophic epidemics, including about 250,000 each in Russia and Hungary and 100,000 each in Spain and France in the 1830-7 period alone. The 1848-51 cholera epidemic killed a million Russians and 60,000 in the United Kingdom. Almost invariably, when cholera outbreaks occurred, rumors were widely circulated and believed among the poor that the disease had been deliberately caused by the rich to wipe them out. Such rumors, together with the general panic created by the outbreaks, led to severe riots during epidemics in Russia (1830-1), Hungary (1831), France (1832), Spain (1834), and Sicily (1837).

Aside from the constant threat of hunger and disease, the lives of early nineteenth-century Europeans were highly constrained by the difficulties of transportation and communication, which until the slow spread of railroad and telegraph networks after 1830 had not advanced in thousands of years beyond animal-drawn conveyance on land and the barge or sailship on water. Although reasonably good road networks were built by 1850 in the most advanced countries, such as Great Britain and France, in the most backwards areas of Europe, such as much of Iberia, the Balkans, Scandinavia and Russia, roads were virtually non-existent, making even travel by stagecoach impossible and leaving horseback and foot power as the only alternatives. To cover the 300 miles from London to Edinburgh (which had taken 10 days around 1750) required only 48 hours, but it took over four days to cover the 100 miles from Palermo to Messina in Sicily, and three to five days to travel 80 miles by horseback or oxcart in Serbia. When Sir Robert Peel was called back from an Italian holiday to become British prime minister in 1834, his journey was no speedier than that of Roman couriers 1,600 years earlier. The building of the Transiberian Railroad in Russia in 1891-1905 reduced the time required for a trip from Moscow to the Pacific Ocean from a year to eight days.

Travel and trade in Europe were further hindered by the proliferation of customs barriers and the profusion of local weights, measures, and currencies, which reached ludicrous dimensions in Germany, Italy, and the Swiss Confederation. In Switzerland, there were 400 different internal tolls and tariffs--28 in the 30 miles between Ragaz and Rapperwil--60 different solid measures, 81 liquid measures, and 11 different currencies with over 300 separate coins.

Transportation difficulties together with frequent crop failures combined to create wild gyrations in food prices from region to region in the same year and from year to year in the same region. Local famines amidst bountiful harvest elsewhere in the same country were common. Thus, in the French department of Ille-et-Vilaine, in December 1827 the average price of a hectoliter of wheat was 14.18 francs ($2.84), while in the Vaucluse the price was 30.95 francs ($6.19). A sack of rye selling for 6-8 rubles ($27-$35) in south-central Russia in 1835 sold for up to 30 rubles ($140) in the northwestern province of Pskov.

## Population Growth

Probably the most significant development in European society between 1815 and 1850 was the continued extraordinarily rapid pace of population growth. Between 1600 and 1700, the European population had grown extremely slowly--as it had for centuries--rising from about 100 to about 114 million. However, between 1700 and 1815, another 100 million Europeans were added to the population. Between 1815 and 1850 the population jumped another 25 per cent, reaching about 266 million by the latter date, or almost two and one half times the level of 1700! This incredible population increase seems to have resulted above all from rising food supplies after 1700, which resulted largely from the expansion of land under cultivation and the introduction of the potato and maize, both of which provided a better yield of caloric food per acre than did other crops.

Unfortunately, the evidence clearly suggests that the expanded production of food did not result in an increase in the standard of living or a decrease in the cost of food. Rather, its main impact seems to have been in supporting a dramatic increase in the size of the population that was living at subsistence and below-subsistence levels. Previously, many at these levels would not have survived to child-bearing years. Most of the population increase occurred in rural areas, where it led to a tremendous jump in the number of serfs, landless day laborers, and farmers with tiny plots ("dwarf farmers").

The rising pressure of population on land and food supplies boosted rents and food prices, while the increased labor supply depressed agricultural and industrial wages. Increasing numbers of peasants were left entirely without land or without enough land to support themselves, and the number of urban and rural inhabitants unable to find work increased considerably. In England, where landless laborers outnumbered landed peasants by two to one as early as 1690, the former almost doubled during the following 140 years, because of the population increase and the widespread enclosures of former common lands, carried out by large estate owners, and subsequent evictions. Peasant households in Saxony (Germany) with enough land to support themselves declined from 39 per cent in 1750 to 22 per cent in 1843, while dwarf farmers and landless peasants in Hungary, almost unknown in 1700, increased to 47 per cent of all peasants in 1828 and 60 per cent in 1848. In rural Belgian Flanders, per capita grain consumption declined about 50 per cent between 1710 and 1820, while in Antwerp rents jumped 135 per cent between 1780 and 1850 and per capita consumption of grain, meat, and salted fish declined 20, 22, and 49 per cent, respectively.

In Sweden, the percentage of landless or dwarf farmers, estimated at about 20 per cent of the population in 1750, increased to nearly 40 per cent by 1850, while in Norway, this group increased by over 50 per cent from 1801 to 1855 when it reached about 25 per cent of the total population. Rural overcrowding reached critical dimensions during the 1815-50 period in southwestern Germany and above all in Ireland, where the population increased from 6.8 to 8.1 million between 1821 and 1841. According to an 1836 government report, about 585,000

Irishmen, with 1.8 million dependents, were unemployed for at least seven months a year in the mid-1830s.


## Urbanization, Industrialization, and Literacy

The rapid population growth of the first half of the nineteenth century was accompanied by increases in urbanization, industrialization, and literacy, which, especially in Great Britain, France, Belgium, western Germany and a few other scattered regions, were historically unprecedented, although modest in a post-1850 perspective. Thus, between 1815 and 1850, the total population of European cities of 100,000 or more and 20,000 or more both doubled, reaching about 12 million and 30 million respectively. Yet the 1850 populations of such cities still comprised only about 5 and 12 per cent, respectively of the total European population; 20 per cent or more of total national populations lived in cities of 20,000 or more by that date only in the Netherlands and Great Britain (see Table 5.1).

Although industrialization made great progress during the 1815-50 period, its overall impact on European society was quite limited. In 1850, 25 per cent or more of the labor force was employed in industry only in Great Britain, France and Belgium (see Table 5.1) and except in Great Britain agricultural workers far outnumbered industrial workers everywhere in Europe. In 1850, Great Britain had over 40 per cent of all European railroad track, produced more coal and pig iron, and consumed more raw cotton than the rest of Europe combined.

Most European industry during the period—and indeed throughout the nineteenth century—continued to involve urban artisans and craftsmen working in small shops, and rural dwellers working at home (known as domestic workers). Even in Great Britain, factory workers in 1850 constituted less than 10 per cent of the population and were equalled by the number of traditional craftsmen and artisans. Elsewhere, less than 5 per cent of the total population worked in factories. For example, in Hungary, only 20,000 employees in a population of 11 million worked in factories in the 1840s. In most European countries, organized working class protest throughout the nineteenth century was led by urban artisans and craftsmen, although their conditions were often better than those of agricultural laborers, factory workers, and the unemployed and unskilled. This reflected the fact that many artisans and craftsmen had a long history of non-politically oriented fraternal organization and also had the community roots, leisure time and education that facilitated organized protest, factors that were generally lacking among other, poorer, working class elements. Another factor that fostered protest especially among the artisans was their correct perception that the rise of long-distance trade and mechanized factories, the growth of sweated competition that accompanied population increase, and the rise of industrialists and merchant capitalists who were gaining increasing influence over the European economy were devaluing their status, skills, and independence by depriving them of their prior ability to control markets, prices, and work conditions. Thus, during the 1848 revolutions it was primarily artisans, such as masons, carpenters, and tailors who fought on the barricades, rather than the factory workers or the masses of the unemployed and unskilled.

Improvements in the European literacy rate in the 1815-50 period occurred primarily in central and northwestern Europe. It was only in these regions that serious attempts were made by state, church, or voluntary organizations to provide mass education, with the result that in the most literate countries, such as Germany and Switzerland, 80 per cent of adults could read and write by 1850. In southern and eastern Europe literacy rates were still well below 25 per cent by that date (see Table 5.1). At most only elementary school education was tuition-free, and even this in a mere handful of countries. Thus, only the middle and upper classes could give their children the type of education that offered the prospect of obtaining prestigious and well-paying positions and advancing in social status.

Wherever generally accessible educational instruction existed during the 1815-50 period, governmental and/or clerical authorities insured that all material critical of the status quo was excluded. The curriculum offered to the lower classes was generally limited solely to religion and the basics of reading and writing. European elites argued that providing more knowledge than this for elements of the population destined for menial positions would be fruitless and pointless. Thus, one Danish publicist warned against education that would deprive the poor of that "certain degree of stupidity and insensitiveness" that "alone can render their condition supportable" and deprive them of whatever degree of happiness they had, which would "cease as soon as [they] should begin to think" (Blum 1978: 47). Similarly, an 1803 Prussian decree declared, "The children of the working class are to read the catechism, Bible and Hymn Book; to fear and love God and act accordingly; to honor authority. Whoever attempts to stuff them with more than this, sets himself a useless and thankless task" (Snell 1976: 15). Danish King Frederick VI declared in 1833, "The peasant should learn reading, and writing and arithmetic; he should learn his duty toward God, himself and others and no more. Otherwise he gets notions into his head" (Hovde 1943: 600). Russian Czar Nicholas I's secret police chief summed up the underlying fear the ruling classes had of providing education to the poor with a candor that bordered on naivety: "One should not be too hasty with education, since it is hardly desirable that the common people should be lifted, in the range of their understanding, to the same level as their monarch, since this would undoubtedly lead to a weakening of monarchial power" (Monas 1961: 93). Similarly, Metternich's secretary, Friedrich Gentz, explained to the British reformer Robert Owen, "We do not by any means desire the great masses to become wealthy and independent, for how could we govern them?" (Collin 1964: 278).


The Rural and Urban Lower Classes
The urban and rural poor lived in a world apart from that of the middle

and upper classes. Benjamin Disraeli, the future prime minister of the United Kingdom penned in his 1845 novel Sybil a passage that became famous, describing England as:

> Two nations between whom there is no intercourse and no sympathy; who are ignorant of each other's habits, thoughts and feelings, as if they were dwellers in different zones, or inhabitants of different planets, who are formed by a different breeding, are fed by a different food, are ordered by different manners and are not governed by the same laws (Gillis 1977: 185).

The majority of the rural and urban population of Europe lived in extremely bad conditions during the first half of the nineteenth century. Most peasants were serfs, landless laborers, tenant farmers, sharecroppers, domestic servants, or holders of land too small to support them. In the so-called "servile lands" of eastern Europe (eastern Germany, most of the Habsburg Empire, Russia, and the Danubian Principalities of Moldavia and Wallachia--the core of modern Rumania), the nobility was either the only class allowed to own land (as in Hungary) or had monopolized this right for so long (in Russia until 1801 and in Prussia until 1808) that they held virtually all privately owned land. The vast majority of the peasants, or serfs, in these areas, held only usufructuary rights (i.e., the right to use but not ownership) to portions of the nobles' estates. In payment for such rights, the serfs were usually required to work a certain number of days per week on non-usufructuary land owned by the nobles and purely for the lord's benefit. Although varying from region to region, usually three to four days a week of such services were obligatory, sometimes increasing to six days a week at harvest (and thus forcing the serfs to work their usufructuary land at night and on Sundays). By 1815, the serfs could, except in Russia, theoretically leave their land without the lord's permission so long as they had fulfilled their obligations. In reality, the peasants were generally so enmeshed in a tangle of legal and monetary obligations to the lord that for all practical purposes they were bound to the soil.

Although the most onerous burden was the labor service, numerous other obligations were extracted, some for usufructuary privileges, others for the lord's performance of judicial and police functions on his estates, others in recognition of the lord's superior personal status, and still others for reasons lost in the mist of history. The total of the serfs' obligation was bewildering in their variety and staggering in their burden. Napoleonic officials abolished 1,395 clearly distinguished feudal rights and privileges in Naples and Sicily, while as late as 1840 the serfs in the Austrian province of Moravia owed a total of over 240 separate obligations; in nearby Carniola the peasants escaped with only 123. These obligations levied such high charges that most east European serfs were forced to seek additional sources of income, such as cottage industry, to borrow money at usurious rates from their landlords, or to absorb the deficit by slow starvation. With rising population and demands for east European grain after 1700, peasant usufructuary lands diminished per capita while the lords increased their demands. The total burden in Transylvania increased an estimated 400 to 1,000 per cent during the eighteenth century while labor service obligations in White Russia, Lithuania and the Danubian Principalities increased 1.5 to 3 times in the period after 1750.

One of the most ludicrous obligations of the serfs to the nobles was the compensation in cash or equivalent for the nobles' exercise of police and judicial powers on their estates, including the right to fine and beat peasants and even to judge legal disputes involving the peasants' obligations to them! In Poland until 1768 lords had the right to kill their serfs, while in Russia after 1760 they were entitled to buy, sell, mortgage or give away their serfs, as well as to conscript them into the army or exile recalcitrants to Siberia. Russian serfs could not leave their estates, marry or learn a new profession without the lord's permission. As Empress Catherine the Great (1762-96) explained in a letter, "Landowners do whatever seems good to them on their estate, except inflict capital punishment; that is forbidden" (Wood 1964: 22). Even where independent courts existed in eastern Europe, as they did in some areas for serious cases or some landlord-peasant disputes, the outcome was usually loaded against the serfs. As one rich Russian landlord explained to a French traveller in the 1840s, "How can you expect the peasant to obtain justice, when he only gives [the judge] an egg, while we give a silver ruble?" (Blum 1978: 90).

Although some independent peasant freeholders (i.e., persons not owing servile dues and labor services) existed in eastern Europe, they were very few. Even in the non-servile lands, where the peasants were free to live where they wished and either owned their land outright, worked estates in return for wages, or rented land in return for payment in kind or money, the majority of the peasantry were completely landless or did not own or rent enough land to support themselves. Landless laborers predominated in the United Kingdom, Iberia, and southern Italy. In Spain, for example, about 50 per cent of the rural labor force was completely landless; 30 per cent rented land; and only 20 per cent were landowners. Masses of Spanish day workers (jornaleros) lived in conditions of dreadful poverty in southern and western Spain and were only able to find work a few months a year. Sweden was one of the few countries where peasants owned a majority of the land (53 per cent in 1815, compared to 33 per cent held by the .39 per cent of the population that was noble and 15 per cent held by the crown) and a majority of peasants (about 75 per cent in 1815) were classified as independent.

Although agricultural conditions were not good anywhere, they were relatively best in Scandinavia, Switzerland, the Low Countries, France and portions of western Germany and nothern Spain and Italy. Conditions were the worst in the servile lands of eastern Europe, in those areas of non-servile Europe dominated by landless laborers, and in those areas of the Balkans still under Ottoman control. In Ottoman Turkey, a previously relatively benevolent system of land tenure had disintegrated after 1600 and public security had disappeared as Turkish soldiers and officials battled for the right to control regions of the empire, many of which completely escaped the supervision of Constantinople. Large areas of the Turkish Balkans, as well as some of the other worst regions, such as Ireland and the southern parts of Spain and Italy, were frequently controlled during the 1815-50 period by bands of brigands composed of peasants who fled into the hills and forests to escape intolerable conditions. In the Balkans, the brigands became popular heroes, lionized in countless songs and legends as the Ottoman regime increasingly disintegrated.

In addition to brigandage, massive peasant rebellions were not unusual in the servile lands of eastern and central Europe and in the Balkans during the immediate pre-1815 period. For example, there were major revolts in Hungary in 1751, 1753, 1755, 1763-6, and 1784, several of which involved more than 10,000 serfs. In Russia, an estimated 3 million peasants murdered over 3,000 nobles and almost overthrew the regime during the Pugachev uprising of 1773-5, and in 1796-7 there were 278 separate serf outbreaks (mostly minor) in central Russia alone. Other massive peasant outbreaks occurred in Bohemia in 1775, in Saxony in 1790, in Prussian Silesia in 1793 and 1798, and throughout much of the Balkans between 1804 and 1815. Even more common than violent outbreaks in the servile lands of eastern and central Europe were peasant work slowdowns and passive resistance in the performance of feudal obligations. As one Russian serf told the agrarian reformer Alexander Radischev (who was exiled to Siberia for his writings in 1790), "No matter how hard you work for the master, no one will thank you for it" (Doyle 1968: 16). In both Russia proper and Russian-controlled Poland, the saying "to work as you work on the desmesne [the lord's land]" became a peasant phrase for laziness (Leslie 1956: 62).

As conditions worsened and populations grew in rural areas, hundreds of thousands of Europeans migrated to cities during the 1815-50 period, often arriving with virtually no skills and no money. European cities were thus inundated with paupers, petty criminals, prostitutes, and other elements that made up a "floating population" of about 15 to 30 per cent of the total urban citizenry that was without any means of support or was dependent upon charity, begging, and occasional menial employment. Many of the rapidly growing cities were completely unprepared and unequipped to cope with the population explosion in terms of housing, sanitary capacity or social services. Thus, the population of Vienna jumped 45 per cent between 1827 and 1847, but housing supply increased by only 11 per cent, and in Paris the 34 per cent population increase between 1831 and 1846 far outstripped the 22 per cent increase in housing stock. Many lower-class families lived in single rooms in urban areas, and it was not uncommon for two or more families to share a room. For example, of nearly 6,000 families visited in Bristol, England in the late 1830s, 47 per cent either lived in one room or shared a room with another family. A government commission in St. Petersburg found 3,776 workers who were visited in the 1840s living in 199 residences, or an average of 19 workers per apartment. As pressure on housing supply increased, rents soared. In Paris, for example, rents jumped 25 per cent between 1812 and 1827. Every major European city had notorious slum districts, inhabited largely by the destitute, e.g., St. Giles in London, Little Ireland in Manchester, the Voigtland in Berlin and the Lyon suburbs of Saint-Georges and Croix-Rousse. Friedrich Engels described one of the worst Manchester slums in 1844:

> Heaps of refuse, offal and sickening filth are everywhere interspersed with pools of stagnant liquid. The atmosphere is polluted by the stench and is darkened by the thick smoke of a dozen factory chimneys. A horde of ragged women and children swarm about the streets and they are just as dirty as the pigs which wallow on the heaps of garbage and in the pools of filth (Weisser 1981: 144).

Even for employed urban workers, conditions were often extremely bad. The average industrial work day was 12-15 hours, with about 1 1/2 hours off for rest and meals. Discipline in the new mechanized factories was extremely strict, with drastic fines levied on workers who came to work a few minutes late or for such "offenses" as laughing, talking, or whistling on the job. Frequently, factory workers were paid by the "truck system," in which they were given coupons good for purchases only at management-owned stores where shoddy goods were sold at inflated prices. Wages were generally so low for semi- and unskilled factory labor that wives and children were forced to work also, usually for 25-50 per cent of wages paid to men. It was not unusual for children as young as six years old to work full-time for pittance salaries. In the English cotton industry in the 1830s, an estimated 42 per cent of all employees were women, and children under the age of 13. Periodic economic depressions and mass unemployment made the lives of urban workers even more miserable than usual. During such periods, which affected Great Britain in 1826-32, 1837-42 and 1846-9, it was not uncommon for 60 per cent of urban workers to be unemployed. For example, in the textile center of Bolton, during the catastrophic 1842 depression 3,062 men worked in the mills, compared to 8,124 in 1836, and only 16 bricklayers were employed compared to 120 six years before.

## The Upper and Middle Classes

Although conditions for the vast majority of the European population were, to put it mildly, not conducive to good health or long life, a tiny fraction of the European population lived extremely well. About 5,000 great landed aristocrats were fabulously wealthy and dominated European society, politics, culture, and economics. With minor exceptions, such as Switzerland, Norway, the Dutch Netherlands, and the Balkans (except for the Danubian Principalities) where the nobility was weak or non-existent, these magnates virtually monopolized the upper levels of political office and held landed wealth vastly disproportionate to their numbers.

Around 1815, a few hundred aristocratic families owned 25 per cent of all the land in England and Wales, and a similar number of landed magnates owned about one-third of the Habsburg Empire. Five families owned 15 per cent of Hungary, while about 15 to 20 families owned over one-third of the land in the Danubian Principalities. The Danish and Swedish nobilities, each of which constituted less than 1 per cent of the population of its country, owned about one-third of their nations' lands, while the Spanish nobility, about 5 per cent of the population, owned over half of their country. Similar concentrations of landholdings were found in Ireland, eastern Germany, the southern parts of Portugal and Italy, and Russia. Thus, almost half of Prussian Silesia was owned by 54 proprietors with holdings of over 2,500 acres each, while about 30 per cent of the 10 million or so serfs owned privately in Russia belonged to 2,300 great landlords. Russian Count D. N. Sheremetev owned 1.9 million acres and about 300,000 serfs. The largest Hungarian landowner, Prince Paul Esterházy, owned about 10 million acres, on which 700,000 peasants (6.5 per cent of the population of Hungary) lived.

The gulf between the fabulously wealthy aristocracy, which constituted well under 1 per cent of the European population, and the great mass of urban and rural laborers was somewhat bridged by the lesser nobility, a small number of relatively well-to-do peasants and skilled artisans and industrial workers, and a variegated urban middle class of shopkeepers, civil servants and the professional classes. In general, explicitly political discontent during the 1815-50 period was largely concentrated among the urban middle classes, who collectively constituted about 10 per cent of the European population (slightly more in the more industrialized and urbanized regions and considerably less in most other areas). Although the middle class shared with the upper classes a deep-seated fear of the "dark masses" below, they shared with the poor during the period a growing dissatisfaction with the existing state of affairs. Although members of the middle class gained access to a share of power in the United Kingdom, France, Belgium, Spain, Portugal, and Switzerland during the period, in most European countries political power remained an effective monopoly in the hands of the monarchs and the old landed nobility. Even in the United Kingdom, where a landmark electoral reform in 1832 admitted the upper middle class to the franchise, 64 of 81 cabinet ministers in 1832-66 were nobles, and the nobility continued to monopolize the House of Lords and control about half of the House of Commons. As late as 1842 in Prussia, nobles occupied 9 of 11 ministries, 29 of 30 ambassadorships, 20 of 28 provincial governorships and 7,264 of 9,434 officer positions in the army.

The middle class deeply resented their exclusion from political power in most European countries and the restrictions on suffrage, press, and associational freedom that made it difficult or impossible for them to voice their views and try to make their influence felt. While the grievances of the artisan element and the even more distressed rural and urban underclass were primarily economic, the middle classes wanted above all recognition, a chance to gain governmental jobs and power, an end to barriers and regulations that restricted trade and industry, and the abolition of petty police harassment and restrictions on suffrage, speech, press, and assembly. Middle-class discontent was especially marked among urban professional elements, such as journalists, teachers, lawyers, physicians, and civil servants who grew rapidly in numbers, especially after 1840, as the rise of urbanization, trade, and industrialization was accompanied by major expansions in the size of government bureaucracies and in demands for professional services. Despite their fears of a lower-class uprising that might threaten the rights of property, these discontented middle-class elements found themselves almost forced by the rigidity of most European regimes into a tacit coalition with the lower classes--especially the more organized, educated and articulate artisan elements--who also harbored grievances against the status quo, even though the proposed solutions and hopes for the future of these disparate elements radically differed.

The lower classes wanted above all economic relief and security, while the middle classes wanted respect, status, and political representation. The existing regimes denied to both groups their concrete immediate desires. By also denying to those two highly disparate groups their more abstract desires for greater personal and political freedom, the ruling elites offered at least one common rallying point for them. When the 1848 revolutions erupted across Europe, the single common demand made by all protesting groups was for an end to political repression. "It was the absence of liberty which in one form or another was most deeply resented by the people of Europe and led them to take up arms" (Droz 1967: 248). Only when the revolutions temporarily triumphed did a deep rift between the lower and middle classes become obvious, and this split played a crucial role in allowing the old ruling classes to return to power. But the folly of alienating the growing and increasingly powerful industrial and professional middle classes became apparent to the traditional elites, so that the post-1848 period saw a growing alliance between these elites and the rising middle classes against the lower classes in place of the tacit pre-1848 coalition of the lower and middle classes against the old regime.

## The European Political Structure and Political Mood in 1815

The dominant form of government in Europe in 1815 was absolute monarchy, defined as rule by a hereditary sovereign unrestricted by the bounds of either a written constitution or a national representative assembly. By this definition, absolute monarchs ruled in the Russian, Habsburg and Ottoman empires, Denmark, Spain, Portugal, all of the 10 or so Italian states and the vast majority of the almost 40 German states, including Prussia, Baden, Bavaria, Hanover, and Saxony. In some of these countries, including Prussia, Austria, and Russia, local representative assemblies did exist, but they were generally completely insignificant. Thus, in the Habsburg Empire, the traditional provincial diets or estates had been reduced to purely ceremonial importance everywhere except Hungary by 1815. Emperor Francis I (1792-1835) declared, "I have my estates and if they go too far I snap my fingers at them and send them home" (Artz 1963: 137).

Yet the extent of royal power in the absolutist states can easily be exaggerated. While many of the absolute monarchs claimed a mandate from heaven, when they ruled upon the earth they depended heavily on the support or at least acquiescence of their nobilities and bureaucracies (which in Prussia, Russia, and in some other states were practically synonymous). Almost everywhere in absolutist Europe, monarchs and nobles reached a tacit agreement in which the crown agreed to let the nobles rule over their peasants without interference, and in return the nobility agreed to support royal policies in foreign, military, and national affairs. The monarchs also rewarded the upper reaches of the nobility by allowing them to dominate the most prestigious and lucrative positions at court, in the civil service, in the military, and in the diplomatic corps.

The non-absolutist states of Europe in 1815 included the United Kingdom of Great Britain and Ireland, France, the United Netherlands (Belgium and the Dutch Netherlands, joined together at the Congress of Vienna), the Swiss Confederation, the German city-states of Hamburg, Lubeck, Frankfurt and Bremen, a few of the German kingdoms, duchies, etc. (notably Württemberg and Mecklenburg) and the Kingdom of Norway and Sweden (each domestically autonomous but united under the Swedish crown). Save for the German city-states and the cantons of the Swiss Confederation, which were republics, all of these countries were monarchies; however, their rulers were limited by the existence of representative assemblies and usually also by written constitutions. Except for six rural and mostly Catholic Swiss cantons (Uri, Schwyz, Unterwalden, Zug, Glarus and Appenzell), which had traditionally been governed by the Landsgemeinde, an annual assembly of all free citizens, the Swiss cantons and German city states were governed by either self-perpetuating closed oligarchies or legislative bodies elected by highly restrictive suffrages. Even the Swiss Landsgemeinde cantons restricted full citizenship rights to certain privileged districts, giving 20,000 voters control over more than 300,000 persons deprived of suffrage rights. In the constitutional monarchies, the system of government in the United Netherlands, France, and Sweden gave overwhelming power to the king. Thus in Sweden, under the 1809 constitution drawn up by the parliament (riksdag) after the autocratic King Gustav IV (1792-1809) was deposed, the monarch had an absolute veto and appointed all ministers and other executive officials. Under the United Netherlands constitution of 1815 (the grondwet), King William I (1813-40) appointed ministers, was empowered to declare war, make peace, and conclude treaties, and could control a large proportion of the nation's finances without reference to parliament. King William boasted, "I can reign without ministers. It is I alone who govern and am responsible" (Wood 1964: 33).

Of the European constitutional monarchies, significant power was wielded by legislatures in 1815 only in Norway and the United Kingdom. Norway had declared its independence in April 1814 rather than accepting a transfer from Danish to Swedish rule, which had been provided for in the 1814 Treaty of Kiel. Rejection of the Kiel treaty reflected the general hostility held by the Norwegian Danish-speaking bureaucracy toward Sweden, Denmark's traditional rival, and a general fear that Norway would be swallowed up in an amalgamation with a nation three times as populous, more advanced economically and with a powerful nobility, whose orientation was in conflict with the relatively equalitarian cast of Norwegian society. After Swedish and Russian troops invaded Norway in mid-1814 to uphold the Kiel treaty, Norwegian officials agreed to accept a personal union only with the Swedish crown. Swedish King Charles XIV John in turn accepted the extremely liberal Norwegian constitution adopted at Eidsvoll in April, thus agreeing to Norwegian autonomy and a constitutional system in which he was allowed only a suspensive veto over legislation. Furthermore, the crown could not dissolve the legislature (storting); freedom of speech and press were guaranteed; and future additions to the already weak ranks of the Norwegian nobility were barred. Although two-thirds of Norway was owned by the peasantry and about half of them were enfranchised under the liberal Eidsvoll suffrage, they were too disorganized, uneducated and deferential to challenge the entrenched power of the urban Danish-speaking mercantile-bureaucratic elite, which was reflected immediately in the storting. As one Norwegian historian notes, the "bureaucracy continued to rule after 1814, in the name of the constitution, as they had done before 1814 in the name of the [Danish] absolute monarch" (Hovde 1943: 512).

In the United Kingdom, the modern system of parliamentary responsibility had not been completely established in 1815 and the crown still retained significant formal powers, including the right to appoint ministers, dissolve the lower legislative chamber (House of Commons) and make unlimited appointments to the upper chamber (House of Lords). However, in practice the king normally accepted the wishes of the leader of the largest party in the Commons. Other formal royal powers, such as the right to veto legislation, had withered away from disuse. King Charles X of France (1824-30) remarked, "I would prefer to saw wood than to be king under the conditions of the kings of England" (Sauvigny 1966: 269). Real power in the United Kingdom was wielded by the high aristocracy, a few hundred great landed nobles who owned about 25 per cent of England and Wales, monopolized the House of Lords, and dominated the House of Commons, the two political parties (Whigs and Tories), the cabinet, and the upper levels of the military, the church and the foreign service. Although the civil liberties of the British population were better protected than in any other European country, except perhaps Norway, a highly restrictive suffrage, legal bans on unions and strikes, and taxes that priced newspapers out of the reach of the lower classes left the upper classes with a monopoly of political power, as in 1752 when the novelist Henry Fielding defined "No Body" as "all the people in Great Britain except about 1,200" (Webb 1969: 14). Popular disorders were one of the few outlets for expressing lower-class grievances, and they occurred often enough so that one historian has described the political system as "aristocracy tempered by rioting" (Webb 1969: 29).

Civil Liberties and Political Justice in 1815
Civil liberties were highly restricted almost everywhere in Europe in 1815, including both absolutist and constitutional regimes. In the absolutist countries, there was no suffrage or legislative assembly at the national level, and among the constitutional regimes, less than 5 per cent of the population was enfranchised in the United Kingdom, France, and the United Netherlands, as well as in most of the non-Landsgemeinde Swiss cantons and the German city-states and constitutional monarchies. In Sweden and Norway, about 10 per cent of the population was enfranchised, but in Sweden a tiny fraction of the population controlled three of the four legislative houses. Norway had the only reasonably free press in Europe in 1815. The press in the United Kingdom, the United Netherlands, Sweden, and Denmark was also free from prior censorship but subjected to such severe and often arbitrary post-publication sanctions that significant dissent was extremely risky. Elsewhere, especially in Spain, Italy, the Habsburg Empire, Russia, and most of the German states, the press was subjected to rigorous prior censorship. Trade unions and strikes were illegal in all the major countries, and freedom of assembly and association was recognized in principle only in the United Kingdom, although even there it tended to be honored only when it would be ineffective, and suspended during periods of lower-class unrest.

Almost everywhere in Europe, the exclusion of the lower classes from political power was especially reflected in extremely discriminatory taxation and conscription policies. In most countries, the European nobility was either exempted entirely from taxation or given enormous tax preferences, with the result that the lower classes bore the overwhelming burden of taxes, which were generally heavily levied on essential consumption items like salt and bread. Similarly, in most countries the lower classes bore the burden of conscription, since the wealthier classes were either formally exempt or could buy their way out if they were drafted. Thus, in Spain, throughout the nineteenth century anyone who was rich enough to pay a redemption bounty (redencion a metalica) could avoid military service, while others could obtain "legal exemption," with the result that 33,000 out of 97,000 Spaniards drafted by lot in 1862 escaped induction. In most European countries, tax and conscription systems were reformed only after 1870, often shortly after the suffrage was expanded to include the middle and lower classes.

The judicial system in most European countries was barely emerging from medievalism in 1815. Most countries used torture as a matter of course in judicial proceedings until late in the eighteenth century. In a number of countries, including Spain, Portugal, France, and Switzerland, alleged witches were occasionally burned at the stake or otherwise executed as late as the second half of that century. Thus, in Spain, where the activities of the Inquisition resulted in the execution of about 3,000 alleged heretics between 1480 and 1780, one of the last victims was burned in 1781 "for having carnal converse with the devil and laying eggs that had prophecies written on them" (Brenan 1964: 205).

The alleged crimes of political rebels and economically motivated crimes of the poor were treated with extraordinary harshness in many countries in 1815. In the United Kingdom, there were 220 offenses for which the death penalty could be imposed, including pickpocketing, stealing five shillings from a shop, sheep stealing, forgery, and even "injuring Westminster Bridge or impersonating out-pensioners of Chelsea Hospital" (Thomson 1950: 17).

Especially harsh punishments were reserved for political rebels. The official punishment for treason in the United Kingdom in 1800--which was defined as including such offenses as "imagining the death of the king"--was as follows: "Traitors were drawn to the scaffold on a hurdle; after being hanged by the neck, they were cut down while still alive, disemboweled, and forced to watch their entrails burned before their faces; then they were decapitated and their bodies quartered, the heads and quarters were then exposed to the public view in some conspicuous place" (Ingraham 1979: 57). While after 1815 this punishment was modified and never carried out to its full extent, similarly gruesome executions were retained on the statute books in other countries and were implemented in Spain, southern Italy, Hungary, and the Balkans during the 1820s.

Public disturbances were often put down with great ferocity during the period leading up to 1815. Thus, in 1740, 50 prisoners protesting a cut in their bread rations were shot to death in France, while 42 draft protesters were killed in England in 1761. The massive anti-Catholic Gordon Riots of 1780 in London did not result in a single death at the hands of protesters, but were suppressed at the cost of 285 deaths among the rioters and followed by 25 hangings. Several hundred people were killed in the suppression of riots in Paris in April 1789, while the famous storming of the Bastille in July 1789 was largely sparked by the firing of troops into a crowd, which killed or wounded 150.


The European Political Mood in 1815

The European political mood in 1815 was a mixture of exhaustion, frustration and fear. For most Europeans, exhaustion was probably dominant. The defeat of Napoleon at Waterloo on June 18, 1815 brought to an end 23 years of almost continuous warfare that in its wake left severe physical destruction, economic dislocation, a heavy cost in lives and money, and a general disruption of normal existence. Under these circumstances, the great majority of the European population seems to have been quite content in 1815 to witness the dismantling of the Napoleonic Empire and the restoration of the political and socioeconomic structure of pre-1789 Europe. The most fervent wish was probably for a return of peace and order. Although the serfs of eastern Europe, the free peasantry of western Europe, and the lower urban classes throughout the Continent enjoyed no significant improvement in their status, for the most part they were too ignorant, disorganized, and preoccupied with basic survival to pose a threat to the restored regimes.

However, for a small, but often strategically placed segment of the European population, the dominant emotion was frustration. The disintegration of the Napoleonic Empire after 1810 and the decisions of the victorious powers at the 1814-15 Congress of Vienna led to a restoration of deposed kings and regimes in Iberia, Switzerland, France, most of the Italian states, and the more significant of the German states, while in the United Kingdom, Scandinavia, Russia, and the Habsburg Empire the old regimes had never been toppled and continued to function much as before. Everywhere, political liberals complained about the lack of constitutionalism in absolutist regimes, the restricted suffrage in non-absolutist regimes, the stifling press controls, the restrictions on freedom of assembly and association, and the swarms of secret police and bureaucratic regulations that seemed to oversee all aspects of life. The major focal points of discontent were usually among university students, merchants, professionals, intellectuals and younger military officers. In Norway, Belgium, Italy, Germany, and Poland, nationalistic grievances were as or more important than complaints about civil liberties among these elements. The transfer of Norway from Danish to Swedish rule and of Belgium from Austrian to Dutch rule led to great anger among such sectors of the Norwegian and Belgian populations, as did the continued division of Italy and Germany into numerous states and the continued partition of Poland into Russian, Austrian, and Prussian spheres among these elements of the Italian, German, and Polish populations.

To escape restrictions on political organization, malcontents often expressed themselves and sought to organize opposition in secret societies, such as the Freemasons in Spain and Portugal, a nationalistic-constitutionalist group known as the Carbonari (charcoal-burners) in Italy, and the Philike Hetairia among Greeks in the Balkans. In general, political discontent in 1815 was serious only where a large urban middle and lower class existed and had long been exposed to radical political currents, as in France and Great Britain, and in regions where repression and governmental incompetence combined to antagonize large segments of the population, as in Iberia, Ireland, the Balkans, the Papal States, and the Two Sicilies.

For the tiny fraction of the European population that constituted the ruling order in 1815, the dominant emotion was neither exhaustion nor frustration, but fear that the ideologies and disorders spawned by the French Revolution would return to haunt Europe again. Liberalism and nationalism, the catchwords of the opponents of the Vienna settlement, were the chief villains from the standpoint of the European ruling orders, threatening to bring the restored European order tumbling down once again. The leading opponents of liberalism and nationalism in Europe in 1815 were Emperor Francis I (1792-1835) of the Habsburg Empire and his faithful foreign minister Prince Klemens von Metternich (1809-1848).

Since the Habsburg Empire was both an absolute monarchy and a multi-national state, liberalism and nationalism each posed a mortal threat to the regime. "My realm resembles a worm-eaten house," Francis once told a Russian diplomat. "If one part is removed, one cannot tell how much will fall" (May 1968: 22). Francis's philosophy was summed up in one of his favorite sayings, "One has to sleep on this" (Ginsborg 1979: 5) and in his will, in which he instructed his successor to "Govern and change nothing" (Artz 1963: 238). Francis's fear of change was almost total and virtually pathological. When an official submitted a plan for railway construction to him in the 1830s he responded, "No, no, I will have nothing to do with it, lest the revolution might come into the country" (Jaszi 1966: 80). Francis's attitude toward internal change in the Habsburg Empire and Metternich's corresponding attitude towards any challenge to the international political settlement reached at Vienna took on extraordinary importance during the three decades after 1815 because the Empire dominated Germany and Italy as well as the Habsburg lands. Since France was too weak after 1815 to challenge the Vienna settlement and the kings of Prussia and Russia either agreed with or were dominated by Metternich, especially after 1819, almost all of continental Europe was guided by the Francine-Metternichian approach. The essence of this approach was to seek to head off expressions of dissent in advance by rigid censorship, an extensive secret police system, and strict controls over education and public assemblies and association. If such measures failed to stifle dissent, then swift and harsh repression was to be implemented. Thus, Metternich stated the ultimate solution for discontent in Italy was a "forest of bayonets" (Ginsborg 1979: 9) and once remarked:

> It is only necessary to place four energetic men, who know what they want and are agreed on the manner of carrying out their wishes, in the four corners of Europe. Let them raise their voices and their arms at the same moment and the whole agitation vanishes like so much smoke (Artz 1963: 6).

Especially in the Catholic countries of southern and central Europe (Iberia, France, the Habsburg Monarchy, the Italian states, and many of the German states), the royal families and their noble allies ruled with the strong support of the clergy. In these countries the Catholic hierarchies often exercised significant control over the censorship and almost all educational institutions, and they preached support of the ruling authorities in return for strong state support for the Church. A number of Catholic laymen, such as Count Joseph de Maistre of Savoy, preached what might be termed the Restoration philosophy, or perhaps theology--a hazy and heavily romanticized version of traditional society, in which the collaboration of church and state was seen as the only means of maintaining an "organic" and natural society based on the supremacy of the inherently superior orders, i.e., the clergy, the nobility, and the monarchy. These thinkers, like the secular Restoration rulers, were obsessed with the need to maintain social hierarchies, threatened by the ideologies of the French Revolution, so that "social order" would be upheld, and with it the traditional privileges and wealth of the ruling classes. Repression and fear were seen by them as the ultimate basis of an ordered society. Thus, de Maistre wrote:

> All greatness, all power, all order depend upon the executioner. He is the tie that binds society together. Take away this incomprehensible force and at that very moment order is suspended by chaos, thrones fall and states disappear (Artz 1963: 73).

## Unrest and Rigidity During the Restoration, 1815-1830

The most striking characteristic of European politics between 1815 and 1830, a period generally known as the Restoration, was the lack of any significant domestic political change in the regimes, except in the Balkans. In the Habsburg Empire, Scandinavia, and the Dutch Netherlands, the Restoration was marked by almost complete political apathy, resulting from a combination of exhaustion and repression. In Switzerland and Belgium, opposition to the regimes mounted after 1815 but did not become significant until the late 1820s. The other European regions (the United Kingdom, France, Italy, Germany, Russia, and Iberia) followed a common pattern during the Restoration. Discontent with the regimes in these regions grew after 1815, although except in the United Kingdom, France, and southern Italy organized expressions of discontent were largely restricted to the urban middle classes and/or segments within the military. In all of these regions save Russia, discontent climaxed between 1819 and 1821 in scattered outbreaks of violence (the United Kingdom, France, and Germany) or in temporarily successful military-led revolts with constitutionalist aims (Spain, Portugal, the Two Sicilies, Sardinia). In the United Kingdom, France, and Germany the outbreaks were relatively trivial--except in Ireland--and in each case their main impact was to trigger harsh repressive crackdowns that crushed dissent or drove it underground. The Italian revolutions of 1820-1 were crushed by Austrian military intervention in early 1821, authorized by joint decision of Austria, Prussia, and Russia, while the Spanish revolution of 1820 was defeated by similarly authorized French intervention in 1823. The collapse of the Spanish revolt triggered a right-wing counterrevolution that overturned the revolutionary regime in Portugal, also in 1823. The defeat of the Italian and Iberian revolts led to repression in those regions far harsher than the contemporaneous reactions in the United Kingdom, France and Germany, reflecting both the more ruthless natures of the restored regimes in Italy and Iberia as well as the more serious natures of the unrest.

Since the general European unrest of 1819-21 also spurred a tightening of controls in the Habsburg Empire and Russia, despite the lack of any significant disturbances in those regions, by the early 1820s all of the major European countries were in the grip of a harsh reaction, which, except in Russia, stilled virtually all political dissent for almost a decade. Pressure from the conservative powers also forced Switzerland to clamp down on its press and expel political refugees after 1823 and led to a crackdown also in the tiny Polish Republic of Cracow, which had been granted independence by the Congress of Vienna in 1815 largely because neither Austria nor Russia would agree to let the other control it. Although Cracow had a relatively liberal constitution, it functioned under the supervision of resident representatives of Austria, Russia, and Prussia, who exercised a joint protectorate over the republic. The major center of liberalism in the republic was the University of Cracow, which originally enjoyed virtual autonomy. In 1821 and 1823 pressure from the three powers drastically curbed the autonomy of the university, and in 1826 a Russian official was made curator of the university. Perhaps symptomatic of Russia's general backwardness and also of the inefficiency of repression and everything else in that country, the climax of the post-1815 discontent came there in 1825, five years later than elsewhere, when a ludicrous insurrectionary attempt took place, promptly collapsed, and was followed by the usual crackdown.

Significant political change during the Restoration came only in the Balkans. In Serbia, an insurrection that erupted in early 1815 succeeded in gaining semi-autonomy from Turkey, which was steadily expanded over the next 15 years. In the Danubian Principalities, an uprising in 1821 led the Turks to give the native nobility increased control, setting aside a century of domination by Greeks acting under Turkish control. In Greece, an anti-Turkish uprising in 1821 succeeded in gaining complete independence by 1830, largely because of intervention by the European powers.

The Greek Revolution and its ultimate success were major factors in the revival or increase of discontent noticeable in a number of European countries in the later 1820s. Liberals and nationalists identified the Greek struggle with their own, viewing the rebels through decidedly rose-colored glasses as reincarnated ancient Athenians now fighting for national rights, liberty, and Christian western civilization against the barbaric infidel hordes of Asia. Pro-Greek sentiment (philhellenism) became an instrument for the general expression of liberal-nationalistic ideas, especially since "at a time when it was impossible to cry 'Long Live Liberty!' those who were disaffected were quick to see the advantages of shouting 'Long live the Greeks!' " (Artz 1963: 208). Philhellenes throughout Europe gathered money and supplies to send to Greece and several thousand even went there to aid in the fight against Turkey. Literary giants such as Hugo,

Shelley, Chateaubriand, and Byron devoted their talents to publicizing the Greek cause. Shelley wrote:

> We are all Greeks. Our laws, our literature, our religion, our arts have their roots in Greece. But for Greece. ... we might still have been savages or idolators (St. Clair 1972: 54).

## The Disturbed Regions of Restoration Europe

France. Despite the granting of a constitutional charter by King Louis XVIII in June 1814, upon the first abdication of Napoleon, large segments of the middle and lower classes had no love or loyalty for the Bourbon dynasty and feared that the flock of highly reactionary nobles who returned to France would be satisfied with no less than a complete overturning of the gains of the French Revolution, including a return of lands confiscated from the Church and nobility and subsequently purchased by the peasants and bourgeoisie. There was also much dissatisfaction over the ludicrously restricted suffrage and the imposition of prior censorship in August 1814 in apparent violation of the charter. By seeking to appease the old nobility with appointments and displays of royal favor, Louis only whetted their appetite, while further angering those who feared a restoration of the ancien regime and were antagonized by the growing influence of the Catholic church, the restoration of an extravagant royal court and the continuation of excise taxes whose repeal had been earlier promised.

When Napoleon escaped from Elba and returned to France in March 1815, the French army deserted Louis and the restored Bourbon regime collapsed. After Napoleon's defeat at Waterloo on June 18, 1815, Louis was quite literally restored "in the baggage wagons of the foreigners" (Brogan 1963: 14). The "Hundred Days" of Napoleon's return to power bitterly inflamed public passions and killed any chance that the second French restoration would be marked by a spirit of reconciliation. Upon the defeat at Waterloo, a so-called "white terror" erupted in southern France. Bands of royalists acting without governmental authority, but without any interference either, murdered over 200 persons accused of Jacobin or Bonapartist loyalties, jailed several thousand others, and forced many thousands more into hiding. In mid-August, as the "white terror" was petering out, 48,000 voters (0.16 per cent of the population) elected a lower legislative chamber of extremely reactionary composition, dubbed by King Louis the Chambre Introuvable (meaning something like the "unmatchable" chamber). Together with a House of Peers that had been purged of Bonapartists and was newly packed with 94 members, the Chambre Introuvable instituted what became known as the "legal terror." Marshal Ney, a hero of the revolutionary wars who had defected to Napoleon during the Hundred Days, was tried for treason by the House of Peers (after refusing to take advantage of opportunities to escape) and executed, along with about 15 other high Napoleonic officials. In October and November laws were passed providing for the temporary arrest and detention without trial or judicial review of persons suspected of plotting against state security. Any speech or writing, including the Marseillaise, deemed as menacing to the royal family or capable of weakening its authority was made illegal. Display of the revolutionary tricolor flag and cries such as "Long live the Emperor" were also outlawed. A law passed in December provided that political crimes could be tried by special military provost courts without juries or the right to appeal. During the period between July 1815 and June 1816, about 50,000 to 60,000 persons were purged from governmental positions—about one-third of the entire civil service—and about 6,000 were convicted for political offenses before regular courts, some on charges, such as "having worn a tricolor emblem in his hat ... in the marketplace" (Resnick 1966: 111). By December 1816, another 3,400 people had been arrested or were being held under house arrest without trial. By early 1818 the provost courts had heard 2,280 cases. Only 237 of these cases involved purely political acts, such as seditious speech and writing; most arose from a wave of food riots in 1816-17 that accompanied the grain shortage and high prices of that period. The most serious disturbances of 1816-17, quasi-insurrections at Grenoble in mid-1816 and at Lyon in June, 1817, resulted in 28 executions and over 20 sentences of transportation abroad.

The general direction of the French government after the Chambre Introuvable was dissolved in September 1816 was towards a policy of reconciliation, partly because of pressure from the European powers, who feared the post-1815 repression would provoke serious unrest. The newly elected chamber proved far more moderate, partly because of considerable governmental electoral pressure. As repression eased after 1816, liberal strength in the Chamber of Deputies increased with each annual election of one-fifth of the total membership. These gains, and especially the liberal victories in 36 of the 55 seats filled in the elections of late 1819, deeply alarmed French conservatives, and led the king's favorite, Elie Decazes, who had directed the reconciliation policy, to prepare a revision in the electoral law to forestall further gains by the left when the French political situation was completely transformed on February 12, 1820. On that date the Duke of Berry, son of the king's younger brother and, at the time, the last of the royal line, was assassinated by a madman. The reactionaries blamed Decazes's tolerance of the opposition for the murder, and a drastic shift to the right ensued in French politics. Decazes was forced out, press censorship and detention without trial were reimposed on a temporary basis, many opposition papers that had sprung up with the ending of censorship in 1819 were forced to close, and a new electoral law in June 1820 gave an extra vote to the wealthiest 25 per cent of the electorate. In preparation for the November 1820 elections the government reduced the taxes of over 14,000 opposition voters (in a total electorate of less than 100,000) to disenfranchise them.

These measures, which ensured a reactionary triumph in the elections—over 60 per cent of the lower chamber chosen in November 1820 was noble, well above even the Chambre Introuvable of 1816—along with the example of the 1820-1 revolutions in Italy and

Iberia, drove the left opposition into conspiratorial plotting. According to educated guesses, perhaps 40,000 to 60,000 Frenchmen joined a secret society, the Charbonnerie Française--based on the Italian Carbonari--in the years immediately after 1820. They organized for suffrage expansion, constitutional reform, and in some cases a violent overthrow of the regime. A dozen or so Charbonnerie plots, most of which never got off the ground, were broken up in 1821-2, resulting in 11 executions, including those of the so-called four sergeants of La Rochelle, who became martyrs to the left for their refusal to answer questions about the Charbonnerie. Until his death in 1824, Louis drifted in an increasingly reactionary direction, influenced by the beautiful young Madame du Cayla, who, under the sway of the reactionaries, took advantage of her charms to brainwash him. A harsh new measure to repress the press was passed in 1822, and clerical influence in education increased drastically, leading to the firing of several liberal professors including the future prime minister François Guizot.

Louis's brother and successor, Charles X (1824-30), was a dedicated reactionary whose rule quickly assumed an ultra-conservative tone. Liberals were deeply alienated by the growing clerical control over education, the 1825 law that authorized the death penalty for the profanation of sacred religious vessels and the granting of compensation to émigré nobles who lost land during the French Revolution. Following liberal victories in the 1827 elections, Charles adopted a more conciliatory policy, but he switched directions again in 1829, appointing a new ministry headed by Prince Jules de Polignac, one of the most notorious reactionaries in France, who could not possibly gain majority support in the Chamber of Deputies. As liberals gained in strength and organization, Polignac unleashed a major campaign against the opposition press, bringing about 80 prosecutions within a year. Many of the cases ended with acquittals, while others only produced martyrs, as in the case of the six-year sentence meted out to the great liberal poet Pierre Béranger for two of his recent songs, which were "memorized and sung by thousands throughout France" (Rader 1973: 193).

In mid-1830, Charles dissolved the Chamber of Deputies, two months after he had been rebuked by that body for his policies by a vote of 221 to 181. Despite severe administrative pressure, in the new elections of July 1830, 202 of those who had voted for the rebuke were re-elected, and the opposition won a total of 264 of the 428 seats. On July 26, Charles issued the "July Ordinances," which decreed prior press censorship, dissolved the newly elected Chamber, and reduced the electorate to the wealthiest 25 per cent of those previously enfranchised. No military preparations were made to deal with any possible resistance, and Charles went off to hunt at his Rambouillet estate. The Paris prefect of police assured the ministry, "No matter what you do, the people of Paris will not stir. Go ahead boldly, I'll stake my head on Paris, I'll see to her" (Sauvigny 1966: 411).

The United Kingdom. The United Kingdom was one of the most

politically disturbed regions of Europe in 1815. In Great Britain, one of the most urbanized and by far the most industrialized European region, a combination of severe economic distress among the lower classes along with a high level of mass politicization and an anachronistic political system that confined political power to a tiny fraction of the population fostered considerable popular unrest. Unrest was even more widespread and severe in Ireland, one of the most backwards regions in Europe, where massive population growth and land hunger reduced large segments of the peasantry to abject misery and produced widespread brigandage and terrorism.

In Great Britain, agitation for parliamentary reform among the urban lower classes revived after 1814. It had been smashed by extremely severe repression between 1793 and 1800, which included suspension of freedom of assembly and the writ of habeas corpus, the imposition of press censorship, treason trials in response to completely peaceful political agitation, and the outlawing of all trade unions. Tension arising from the renewed demands for parliamentary reform was agravated by the economic disruptions caused by the Napoleonic Wars. Many workers were reduced to desperation, especially after 1810. A wave of machine-breaking ("Luddism") among textile workers beginning in 1811 led in January 1813 to 19 executions. In 1816, a severe wave of food riots, labor disorders, machine breaking, and incendiarism erupted, resulting in 12 more executions and 12 sentences of transportation to Australia for terms ranging up to life. The parliamentary reform campaign also reached major dimensions in 1816. Over 500,000 signatures were appended to petitions calling for such measures as universal male suffrage and the secret ballot, and tens of thousands attended meetings demanding such reforms. The extremely conservative Tory administration of Lord Liverpool (1812-27) chose to view the reform movement as an insurrectionary conspiracy, partly because of sensational and misleading reports of government informers and agents provocateurs. However, except for a tiny handful of extremists, those involved in the movement were dedicated to legal reform through parliamentary channels. Nonetheless, the Tory interpretation was greatly reinforced in December 1816 when, at the end of a mass meeting for parliamentary reform attended by thousands at Spa Fields near London, a handful of participants looted and attacked food stores and gunsmith shops.

In early 1817, parliament established two secret committees to investigate the unrest. The committees produced highly alarmist reports that warned, with no evidence other than the reports of an agent provocateur named John Castle, of plans for an impending general insurrection. Based on these reports, parliament suspended the writ of habeas corpus and outlawed all public meetings and societies not licensed by government officials. "One magistrate refused to sanction a minerological society on the pretext that the study of such a subject led to atheism" (Artz 1963: 122). A series of trials of alleged rioters and conspirators followed, along with a wave of press prosecutions—42 in 1817—and the detention of about 35 people without trial before habeas corpus was restored in January

1818. The repression, along with a good harvest in 1817, succeeded in quieting things down or driving discontent underground, although there were two further incidents before the 1816-7 scare died down. On March 10, 1817, as parliament was acting on the bill to outlaw unlicensed meetings, thousands gathered in Manchester to march to London in support of parliamentary reform. The event, known as the "blanket march" for plans to carry blankets during the long trek to London, was disrupted by troops and special constables before it could begin. Large numbers of blanket marchers were arrested but were later freed without trial. The final episode of the 1816-17 period of unrest involved two weak insurrectionary attempts by separate bands of a few hundred men at Pentrich and Huddersfield on the night of June 8, 1817. The risings quickly collapsed. Three leaders of the Pentrich rising were executed, and another 14 were transported to Australia for life, although the Huddersfield conspirators escaped without punishment. Ironically, the government was probably more discredited by the Pentrich affair than were the rebels, when it was revealed that a government agent, W. J. Richards (known as "Oliver the spy") had played a key role in the rising.

Discontent grew again in Great Britain after mid-1818. There was a poor harvest that year, and repression had eased with the restoration of habeas corpus and the expiration of the 1817 legislation that banned unlicensed public meetings. The Lancashire textile industry was rocked by a wave of strikes in the second half of 1818 and the parliamentary reform movement enjoyed a strong revival in 1819. Huge crowds turned out once more to attend parliamentary reform meetings—over 20,000, for example, at Birmingham on July 12. The British elite became increasingly fearful, especially since some of the meetings featured inflammatory rhetoric and some working-class leaders had a habit of trying to instill discipline by sponsoring unarmed but military-style marching and drilling. On August 16, 1819, the reform campaign was scheduled to climax with a mass meeting at St. Peter's Field in Manchester, to be addressed by Henry Hunt, a well-known speaker. As Hunt began to address a completely peaceful crowd of over 50,000 people—the largest mass meeting in British history—the local authorities, who had made no attempts to block the assemblage, sent in mounted yeomanry and troops to arrest him. The densely packed crowds and the police forces panicked; about 15 people in the crowd were killed and 400 injured by being trampled or slashed by sabres. There were no serious injuries among the troops. When the crowds had been dispersed, an eyewitness reported that the entire field was covered with discarded "caps, bonnets, hats, shawls and shoes. ... Several mounds of human beings still remained where they had fallen, crushed down and smothered" (Marlow 1971, 153). Five leaders of the demonstration, including Hunt, were convicted of unlawful assembly, and Hunt received a jail term of 2 1/2 years.

In response to what soon became known as the "Battle of Peterloo," the British parliament in December 1819 passed the so-called "Six Acts," which, among other things, restricted public meetings to those called by public officials, suppressed the radical pamphlet press by subjecting it to the heavy stamp tax that had previously been evaded through technicalities, and imposed new penalties for the publication of blasphemous and seditious libels. Together with another spate of press prosecutions--96 in 1819--the Six Acts, most of which were soon repealed, succeeded in crushing the radical press and movement for a decade. Among the press prosecutions was the notorious three-year jail term given to printer Richard Carlile for publishing the works of Thomas Paine.

With virtually all legal channels for redress of grievances closed in Great Britain, the only recourse for those radicals not terrified into silence or apathy was conspiracy. In February 1820, the plot of a small band of hotheads to murder the Liverpool cabinet and overthrow the government was uncovered, leading to five executions and five sentences of transportation to Australia. Like the 1817 Pentrich affair, a government agent provocateur was highly involved in this incident, known as the "Cato Street Conspiracy." A few months later, two small armed bands, numbering fewer than 100 people, sought to turn a general strike in Glasgow into a general uprising on the night of April 5/6. One group clashed with a band of soldiers in the "Battle of Bonnymuir" before the rebellion was quashed. Three leaders of the rising were executed, and 19 were transported to Australia. The "Battle of Bonnymuir" was the last gasp of the 1815-20 protest movement, not only because of the repression but also because of the generally good economic conditions that prevailed between 1820 and late 1825. The general easing of tension and return of economic prosperity fostered a slight liberalization of the Liverpool government in the mid-1820s. The death penalty was removed for about 100 offenses; trade barriers were eased; and the Test and Corporation Act, which technically (although not actually) prevented Protestant dissenters from holding public office, was repealed. In 1824 the reformer Francis Place was even able to convince parliament to repeal the Combination laws, which outlawed trade unions and strikes, by arguing that the laws only fostered discontent and violence among workers. The 1824 law passed with little discussion or attention amidst a general political quiet. However, an outbreak of strikes immediately thereafter, some of which were violent, led to a new law in 1825 that did not revoke the legalization of unions and strikes but imposed so many restrictions on labor activities that almost any effective action risked prosecution.

In Ireland, severe economic distress among the Catholic peasantry erupted into major agrarian disorders in 1813, and by 1815 large parts of central and southwestern Ireland were effectively under the control of bands of armed peasants. Although about 80 per cent of the Irish population were Catholic descendants of the ancient inhabitants of the island, about 90 per cent of Ireland was owned in 1815 by about 6,000 Protestant landlords (the "Protestant Ascendancy") who dominated the island and whose ancestors had been given land by British kings during Britain's gradual assertion of military control after 1500. In 1815, Irish Catholics still suffered from lingering legal barriers, de facto discrimination in wide areas of life and the bitter memories of the notorious penal laws of the seventeenth and eighteenth centuries and the ferocious suppression of the Irish rebellion of 1798, during which almost 30,000 people (not all Catholic) had been killed. Most of the penal laws, which had sought to destroy the Irish Catholic church and denied Catholics the right to vote, hold office, purchase property, establish schools, bear arms or even own a horse worth over five pounds, had either fallen into disuse or been repealed by 1815. For example, Catholics were enfranchised according to the same highly restrictive suffrage as non-Catholics in 1793. However, Catholic tenant farmers were often unable to cast independent ballots because of pressure from Protestant landlords in public ballot elections, still had to pay a tithe to support the Church of England (Anglican), and were still barred from serving in parliament or in hundreds of other high-level positions. Moreover, Protestants filled 95 per cent of the Irish governmental posts to which Catholics could legally aspire, and controlled the judicial and law enforcement agencies.

The major grievance of the 90 per cent of the Irish Catholic population that lived in rural areas concerned agricultural conditions, which had drastically deteriorated as a result of the phenomenal rise of the Irish population from about 2.5 million to almost 7 million between 1770 and 1820. Tenant farms were subdivided into mere scraps of land. Tens of thousands of people were reduced to the status of landless laborers. Agricultural wages were depressed, and rents skyrocketed. After 1760, Irish peasants began protesting their conditions by organizing secret societies with such names as the Whiteboys, Ribbonmen, Caravats, and Rockites, which used terrorist tactics, including cattle-maiming, destruction of crops, arson, beatings and murder, to punish landlords and their agents, tithe collectors, and in many cases other Catholics who rented land or took jobs formerly held by local residents who had been evicted or fired. Most British politicians had little knowledge or understanding of Irish conditions and held deep-seated anti-Catholic prejudices. Therefore, they attributed the constant disorders in Ireland to an inherent savagery in the Irish character. Thus, in 1813, Robert Peel, the chief secretary for Ireland, wrote to Prime Minister Lord Liverpool (1812-27) that the disturbances resulted from "that natural predilection for outrage and a lawless life which I believe nothing can control" (Broeker 1970: 20). Over 50 years later, Queen Victoria wrote that the Irish "are really shocking, abominable people--not like any other civilized nation" (Curtis 1963: 13).

In 1814, in response to the disorders that had erupted on a wide scale in 1813, the British parliament passed the Insurrection Act. It authorized the suspension of trial by jury in areas found to be in "disturbed" conditions. Persons could be transported to Australia for seven years for possessing weapons, administering secret oaths, or even being found outside their homes after sunset and before sunrise. Although the disorders were controlled by 1816 and the Insurrection Act lapsed in 1818, serious agrarian outbreaks flared again after 1819, and until 1823 large parts of Ireland were again controlled by terrorist bands. The Insurrection Act was revived between 1822 and 1825, and repression was implemented with greater harshness than previously. Between about 1820 and 1826, a total of almost 400 Irishmen were executed under various legal provisions, and another 400 were transported to Australia as the result of almost 4,000 prosecutions brought under the Insurrection Act. In many cases people were transported to Australia solely for having been away from their homes at night, including 26 Limerick men dispatched on one ship. Among them was one man with a wife and six children, who, according to his own account, had been ordered by a magistrate to put his name up on his door and being illiterate "had gone to a neighbor's house to have him write it for him" (Rude 1978: 105).

While agrarian disorders declined after 1823, a new popular movement arose soon thereafter in the form of the Catholic Association, led by the Irish lawyer Daniel O'Connell. The main aim of the Association was for "Catholic Emancipation," or the repeal of certain oaths required to be sworn in order to hold high public office, including seats in parliament, which excluded Catholics from such positions. Although the prospect of holding such offices was meaningful only for the small Irish Catholic middle class, repeal of the oath became a general symbol to the degraded Irish peasantry of the struggle against the Protestant Ascendancy that had oppressed them for centuries. About three million peasants joined the Catholic Association by paying a penny per month in the so-called Catholic Rent, which was usually collected at church under clerical supervision. For the first time, the Irish Catholic peasantry, previously either sunken in apathy or engaged in anarchic terrorism, was mobilized into a disciplined and effective political force and given a sense of pride in themselves and their religion. One Protestant nobleman reported to British officials in 1827, "I must say that I never saw such a change in the Mind of any body of People as has been effected ... in this country" (Palmer 1977: 11).

By 1825, alarm in Great Britain over the Catholic Association became so great that parliament attempted to destroy the organization by outlawing all Irish political societies that had been in existence more than 14 days. However, O'Connell circumvented the law by forming the "New Catholic Association," a "non-political" organization that carried on much as before. In 1826 the Catholic Association showed its power when Catholic smallholders and renters, traditionally under the control of the great landlords, elected pro-Emancipation candidates to the House of Commons in four counties, including Waterford, where the Beresford family, which had controlled the seat for generations, was defeated. In mid-1828 O'Connell himself was elected to parliament for County Clare, defeating an Irish Protestant landlord and member of the British cabinet. The election of O'Connell brought the growing tension in Ireland to a head. As a Catholic he could not be seated in parliament; but to deny him his seat was widely seen as an invitation to open insurrection in Ireland. After massive demonstrations by tens of thousands of Irish Catholic peasants and the stationing of 60,000 troops in Ireland and on the west coast of Great Britain, the Tory government of the Duke of Wellington (1828-30) gained the reluctant consent of King George IV (1820-30) to introduce a Catholic emancipation bill. At the same time the bill was passed by parliament in April 1829, the New Catholic Association was outlawed and Irish suffrage requirements were drastically increased, thereby reducing the franchise from about 100,000 to under 50,000 in Ireland. The Catholic peasantry had won the battle for Catholic emancipation for the middle class, but had lost their own right to vote.

In Great Britain, opposition groups were inspired by the success of the Catholic Emancipation movement, which together with the change in the Irish franchise dispelled the myth that the electoral system was sacrosanct. The 1829 endorsement of Catholic emancipation by the Wellington ministry also split the Tory party, thus cracking the solid Tory opposition to reform. In December 1829, the Birmingham Political Union for the Protection of Public Rights was organized, kicking off what turned out to be a new and successful chapter in the long struggle for parliamentary reform.

Italy and Germany. In Italy and Germany, the mostly urban and middle class nationalists and liberals who dreamed of united and constitutional countries were bitterly disappointed at the return to authoritarian rule and territorial fragmentation confirmed by the Vienna settlement of 1815. Although Napoleon had consolidated the 11 major states of pre-1789 Italy into only three divisions, the Congress of Vienna established eight major states in Italy, thus ensuring that the peninsula remained, in Metternich's famous phrase, "A group of independent states linked only by a common geographical expression" (Sigman 1973: 164). Further, the previously strong Austrian influence in Italy was increased by the Vienna agreement to the point where Italy virtually became a satellite region of the Habsburgs. Lombardy and the former Republic of Venice were placed under direct Austrian rule, while cadet members of the Habsburg dynasty were made sovereigns of the duchies of Tuscany, Parma, and Modena. Austrian family ties in Italy were supplemented by treaties with the Kingdom of the Two Sicilies and Tuscany, in which those countries agreed to render military aid to Austria and not to change their forms of government without consulting Austria. Austria also exerted influence over Italy by means of the 60,000 or so troops that were stationed permanently in Lombardy-Venetia, and by the garrisons that were maintained under treaties at Piacenza in the Duchy of Parma and at Comacchio and Ferrara in the Papal States.

In Germany, the Congress of Vienna made no attempt to resurrect the old Holy Roman Empire, which had been divided into over 300 separate free cities and secular and ecclesiastical states, plus almost 1,500 minute independent territories ruled over by the Imperial Free Knights. However, German nationalists--as well as mapmakers--were disappointed that the new German Confederation still contained 39 separate states, 20 of which contained fewer than 100,000 people. Germans who hoped for a strong and united nation were further disappointed at the lack of any effective structure to coordinate activities among the 39 states. Although a German Confederation diet under the presidency of Austria was established at Frankfurt, with representatives from each of the states, it had little power and to the extent it functioned at all served largely as an "annex of the Chancellery in Vienna" (Dill 1961: 89), aiding Metternich's attempts to stifle all signs of liberalism or nationalism in Germany. In general, the restored Italian and German regimes were not brutal or vicious, and in a few cases, such as Parma, Lucca, and Tuscany in Italy, and Saxe-Weimar in Germany, the rulers were generally honest and supportive of progress in education and economics. However, all of the Italian states and almost all of the German states were absolutist, and most of them seemed determined to set the clock back at least 100 years.

In Germany, nationalist-liberal sentiment was largely confined to university students who became imbued with patriotic fervor during the resistance to Napoleon, to urbanized western German areas contiguous to France and thus particularly susceptible to French revolutionary impulses, and to businessmen and intellectuals who regarded the petty German states as a barrier to free commerce and free thought. The German peasantry—about 75 per cent of the population—had little political knowledge or interest, and were used to centuries of authoritarian rule by petty despots. As German poet and journalist Heinrich Heine noted, "In those days, crowns sat firmly on the princes' heads, and at night they just drew their night caps over them, while the people slept peacefully at their feet" (Artz 1963: 137).

German liberal hopes were fastened upon a provision of the 1815 Federal Act that created the German Confederation. Endorsed by the Congress of Vienna, it declared that each German state should establish eine landstandische Verfassung ("a constitution based upon estates"). However, the meaning of this phrase was highly ambiguous, and since no time limit was set for establishing such constitutional regimes, the liberals were soon to discover, in the phrase of journalist Joseph Görres, that all that had been established was "an unlimited right of expectation" (Passant 1962: 16). Liberal disappointment over the continuation of absolutist government was especially keen among the middle classes in Prussia, where King Frederick William III (1797-1840) failed to honor his repeated pledges to institute constitutional government and, in general, after the defeat of Napoleon, abandoned the reform course of the 1807-14 period that had been designed to enlist popular support against the French.

In Italy, oppositon to the restored regimes was considerably more widespread than in Germany. Although explicitly liberal and nationalist sentiment was restricted to a relatively narrow group of urban middle-class Italians, the grossly incompetent nature of the regimes in the Papal States and the Two Sicilies, which together contained half of the peninsula's 20 million people, created a far broader general sense of alienation. The regimes in these two states were so corrupt, backwards, and inefficient that it is difficult to say whether they were badly misgoverned or not governed at all. Both were teeming with beggars and brigands, and the lower classes lived in conditions of appalling degradation. In the Papal States, Pope Pius VII (1800-23) was dominated by a fanatically reactionary faction known as the zelanti. The pre-1789 regime of total clerical domination, including the Inquisition, was restored. Jews were forced back into the Roman ghetto, and progressive French innovations, such as a modern law code, vaccinations, street lighting, and uniform weights and measures, were repealed. Little had changed since the late eighteenth century, when Goethe wrote that conditions in the Papal States were so bad the cities there "seem to stand only because the earth is unwilling to swallow them up" (Martin 1969: 65).

In the Kingdom of the Two Sicilies the restored king, Ferdinand I (1759-1825), formerly known as Ferdinand IV of Naples and Ferdinand III of Sicily, thoroughly antagonized the upper and middle classes in Sicily by abrogating the considerable autonomy the island had had since its union with the crown of Naples in 1735. He abolished the 1812 Sicilian constitution and the centuries-old Sicilian parliament. Ferdinand also ignored his pledge to establish a constitutional regime for the entire kingdom and restored nobles and clerics to their former positions while shunting aside many who had either served the French regime or led the fight against it. Although the king's chief minister, Antonio Canosa, declared "the first servant of the crown should be the executioner" (Artz 1963: 144), the most notable characteristic of the regime was not brutality but its gross corruption and complete inability to ensure either security or justice to the population.

Elsewhere in Italy, there was a smoldering anger over the policies of the strict and bigoted Duke Francis IV of Modena (1814-46), who censored even love letters in the mails. In Austrian-ruled Lombardy-Venetia, the Austrian policy of staffing top bureaucratic posts with Germans and referring all major decisions to Vienna aroused anger, as did the presence of German troops, whose foreign mannerisms were culturally jarring to the easy-going Italians. Although the regime in the Kingdom of Sardinia was efficient and honest, it was completely under the domination of reactionary aristocratic-clerical forces. The future Italian prime minister Camilio Cavour described the country as an "intellectual hell" (Packe 1957: 9) and the capital at Turin as "half barracks, half cloister" (Holt 1971: 36). Among the first actions of the restored King Victor Emmanuel I (1802-21) were the cancellation of all laws (except for new taxes) passed during French rule, including the French abolition of feudal dues and ecclesiastic courts; the uprooting of French plants from the botanical gardens; the removal of French furniture from the royal palaces; and discouragement of the use of French-built roads.

Opposition in Italy was organized in a variety of secret societies that honeycombed the peninsula, of which the most important was the Carbonari, a Masonic offshoot that combined vague concepts of Christian idealism, liberalism, constitutionalism, and nationalism. The Carbonari had tens of thousands of adherents and was especially strong in the Two Sicilies, where it operated almost as a state within a state. The first Carbonari-planned insurrection, at Macerata in the Papal States in June 1817, turned into a complete fiasco when most of the conspirators failed to show up at the appointed place, and the few who did quickly dispersed upon hearing gunshots--which had been fired by one of their own men. Large numbers of arrests followed, and 10 persons were sentenced to life in jail, with another 20 sent to the galleys for five years or more.

In contrast to the Macerata fiasco, the Carbonari were deeply involved in a successful revolution in the Two Sicilies in July 1820, which forced King Ferdinand to accept the liberal 1812 Spanish constitution. Metternich regarded this development, which came shortly after flurries of unrest in France, Germany, and Great Britain, and a few months after the Spanish revolution of January 1820, as a threat to Austrian domination over Italy and ultimately to the integrity of the Habsburg Empire. In late October 1820 Russia, Austria, and Prussia met at Troppau (Opava) in Austrian Silesia to discuss the Neapolitan developments (Britain and France sent observers to the conference who were not empowered to take any action). On November 19, 1820 the three eastern powers issued a declaration, known as the Troppau Protocol, that asserted that when revolutionary changes of government threatened other European states, "the powers bind themselves, by peaceful means, or if need be by arms, to bring back the guilty state" into a position of "legal order and stability" (Artz 1963: 164-5). At a subsequent conference at Laibach (Ljubljana) in Austrian Carniola in January 1821, the three powers authorized Austria to suppress the Neapolitan revolt forcibly. Austrian troops subsequently smashed the Neapolitan army at Rieti on March 7, 1821, but the departure of Habsburg forces from Lombardy-Venetia to deal with the Neapolitan revolt triggered a military revolt with constitutional and anti-Austrian designs in Sardinia. On April 8, Austrian and anti-constitutionalist Sardinian troops defeated the revolutionary forces.

In Germany, opposition to the restoration was weaker and more quickly and easily scotched than in Italy. The opposition first aroused alarm in Metternich and other conservatives as the result of a gathering of about 500 members of the Burschenschaften, an organization of students with vague liberal, nationalist, and Christian ideals, at the Wartburg Castle in Saxe-Weimar on October 18, 1817, the anniversary of the Battle of Leipzig and the tercentenary of the beginning of the Reformation. The students sang some patriotic songs, and they engaged in demonstrations of "beery teen-age nationalism" (Dill 1961: 90). After the formal celebration was over, a small group of students gathered around a bonfire and burned slips of paper inscribed with the names of reactionary authors, as well as other hated symbols of reaction and censorship, such as a corporal's cane and a policeman's pigtail. This childish, totally insignificant event was magnified by German conservatives into something akin to the storming of the Bastille. Continuing demands in Hesse-Darmstadt and elsewhere that the constitutional promises of 1815 be implemented set conservative nerves further on edge as did demands for greater democracy made by members of the diets in states where constitutions had been proclaimed. Between 1814 and 1820, 13 of the 39 German states did grant constitutions—notably Baden (1818), Bavaria (1818), and Württemberg (1819)—but the two dominant states, Prussia and Austria, were not among them. Where constitutions were granted, they were established (except in Württemberg) by unilateral royal decree, greatly restricted the powers granted to legislative assemblies, and (except in Baden, where near-universal male suffrage was established for the lower house) had extremely high requirements both for voting and sitting as deputies. Thus, in Bavaria, less than 2 per cent of the population could vote for the lower chamber, and only 0.3 per cent could serve in the legislature.

On March 23, 1819, Metternich was handed an ideal excuse for repression when in Mannheim Karl Sand, a disturbed theological student, murdered August von Kotzebue, a reactionary playwright and journalist known to be in the pay of Russian Czar Alexander I. Kotzebue was a figure of little significance, but given Sand's association with the Burschenschaften and Kotzebue's attacks on the student movement in his newspaper, Literarisches Wochenblatt, the incident provided such ideal grist for Metternich that he almost chortled over the murder. In letters written in April 1819, Metternich referred to the "excellent Sand" and wrote "my concern is to turn the affair to good account" (Eyck 1955: 38; Simon 1955: 139).

Aside from the hanging of Sand in 1820, the upshot was that Metternich was able to convince Prussian King Frederick William III to co-sponsor with Austria a drastic crackdown on the German press and universities. Since the other German states were also caught up in the general panic, Austria and Prussia were able to jam through the Confederation diet on September 20, 1819, the so-called Carlsbad Decrees, which imposed nationwide censorship of all printed material under 320 pages, established strict supervision of all German universities, and established a special investigating commission at Mainz to investigate the "origins and manifold ramifications of the revolutionary plots and demagogical associations directed against the existing constitutions" (Ingraham 1979: 88).

The course of developments in Germany and Italy in the 1820s was more or less parallel. In Germany, what became known as the "demagogue hunt" followed passage of the Carlsbad Decrees, during which liberal professors and students were harassed, dismissed, frightened into exile, and, in over 100 cases instigated by the Mainz Commission between 1819 and 1827, prosecuted by various German states, leading to 66 convictions and jail terms. Among those arrested in the "demagogue hunt" was Ludwig Jahn, a well-known nationalist and physical culture enthusiast who had been influential in the resistance to Napoleon and in the founding of the Burschenschaften. The political exiles of the immediate post-1819 period included Francis Lieber, later to become a major American political philosopher, and the great economist Friedrich List, who was fired from his post at the University of Tübingen in Württemberg. Although the Carlsbad Decrees were not rigidly enforced in all of the German states, they effectively terminated organized public reform agitation for the next ten years. Meanwhile, under the influence of Metternich and the demagogue scare, Frederick William abandoned his constitutional promises in 1819 and purged most of the remaining liberals from his government. In 1820, the German Confederation adopted new rules that further restricted the powers of the state legislatures (where they existed). Gentz, Metternich's secretary, gloated over what he termed the "greatest retrograde movement that has taken place in Europe since 1789" (Collins 1964: 291). In 1824, there were mass arrests of surviving Burschenschaften members and in that same year Metternich convinced the Confederation diet to extend indefinitely the previously temporary Carlsbad Decrees. Despite these measures, some underground chapters of the Burschenschaften survived and their activities stepped up when repression eased slightly towards the end of the 1820s.

In Italy, the collapse of the 1820-1 Neapolitan and Sardinian revolts triggered a wave of reaction. Austrian-directed secret police activity intensified throughout Italy to the point that, as the satiric poet Giuseppe Giusti noted, Italians "ate Austria in their bread" (King 1912: 115). Austrian troops remained in Sardinia until 1823 and in the Two Sicilies--where they chewed up 70 per cent of the country's total revenues for their support--until 1827. In Naples, suspected liberals were massively purged from the clergy and civil service, hundreds were arrested and suspected Carbonari members were publicly whipped in the streets. The corrupt and inefficient nature of the regime did not change, leading Metternich to complain in 1821 that King Ferdinand "still imagines that the throne is an easy chair in which to sprawl and fall asleep" (Martin 1969: 203). Conditions remained the same under Ferdinand's successor, King Francis I (1825-30), who declared, "The man who pays for a post wants to keep it and is loyal" (King 1912: 88). An 1828 rising at Cilento in the Two Sicilies was crushed with great ferocity. Its leaders were decapitated and their heads were paraded from village to village in iron cages by a colonel who received from a grateful King Francis a large pension and the title of Marquis.

In Sardinia, in the aftermath of the 1821 revolt, 19 officers were executed, 21 were sent to the galleys or jails, 54 were sentenced to death in abstentia, and over 200 were dismissed from the military or reduced in rank. In Sardinia, Modena, and Lombardy-Venetia, membership in secret societies was outlawed. Hundreds of suspects were jailed or banished in the Papal States in 1821 without trials or charges, and there was also a wave of arrests in Modena in 1820-1, after which prisoners were forced by torture and intimidation into making false confessions. Many Modenese were given long sentences to the galleys and jails, and one young priest was executed in October 1822, five months after the hated chief of the Modenese secret police, Besini, was assassinated. In Lombardy-Venetia, an abortive plan for a coordinated revolt with Sardinia was uncovered in 1820. A wave of arrests followed and at least 15 people were sentenced to death, although the penalties were commuted to long jail terms.

In the Papal States, Pope Leo XII (1823-29) proved to be even more reactionary than Pius VII. The papal police ordered special surveillance of what one police document termed "the class called thinkers" (King 1912: 78), and the authorities fought against the Carbonari with their own organization, the Sanfedisti or Centurions, whose ranks included thugs and criminal gangs. In Umbria, Romagna, and the Marches running battles verging on civil war were fought between the Sanfedisti and Carbonari, marked by assassinations and endless vendettas by both sides. The problem was most chronic at Ravenna, where the reactionary Cardinal Agostino Rivarola established a special court in 1825 in an attempt to smash the Carbonari. The court quickly sentenced 7 men to death, 6 to life in prison, 109 to varying terms of forced labor, jail or exile, and 286 to special police supervision. An attempt to assassinate Rivarola went askew, and the wrong man died, whereupon a number of suspects were hanged after a summary trial and their bodies were left to rot on the gallows as an example to others.

Iberia. The relative harmony of Portuguese and Spanish society was irrevocably shattered by the French revolutionary wars, which left behind deep internal divisions that were to keep the peninsula in turmoil for decades after 1815. In both countries, absolute monarchy during the pre-1789 period had rested on a coalition between the nobility, clergy, and crown. Although both countries were overwhelmingly rural and agrarian, the slow growth of domestic industry and the rapid growth of trade with Iberia's Latin American colonies during the eighteenth century had fostered a considerable increase in the urban middle class strata. Segments of the upper crust of the merchant and professional community proved highly responsive to the French revolutionary calls for significant social reforms, and especially for curbing the power of the ruling coalition elements. As a result of the chaos and economic dislocation created by the French conquest of Iberia in 1807-1808 and subsequent years of guerrilla warfare, the authority of the Church, nobility, and crown were undermined in both Spain and Portugal. Monarchical authority was particularly eroded by the disreputable behavior of Spanish King Charles IV (1788-1808), including his flight from Madrid when French troops entered there in March 1808, and by the parallel flight of the Portuguese royal family to Brazil after the 1807 French occupation there.

In Spain, violent riots erupted to protest Charles's flight, forcing him to abdicate in favor of his son Ferdinand VII (1808-1833). When Napoleon forced Ferdinand to abdicate and held him captive in France, popular resistance to French rule erupted spontaneously. Juntas of resistance led by local notables sprang up throughout Spain in the name of Ferdinand to organize guerrilla resistance and also to head off the possibility of a democratic social revolution directed against themselves. Partly under the pressure of middle class merchants and businessmen who demanded a resurrection of the once-powerful cortes (legislature), the highly conservative central junta issued a call for elections by universal household suffrage to elect a constitutional cortes in 1810. The cortes, which convened in

Cadiz in late 1810, had a markedly liberal-radical complexion, and in 1812 produced a constitution with a similar cast. The constitution established a unicameral legislature endowed with broad powers and elected by universal household suffrage. Sovereignty was declared to reside in the nation and the king was given a suspensive veto only. Freedom of the press was guaranteed, and feudal and clerical jurisdictions were abolished, as were the Inquisition and aristocratic control of local governments, although no attempt was made to redistribute land or address lower class social grievances. After his release by Napoleon following the withdrawal of French troops from Spain in mid-1813, Ferdinand swore allegiance to the 1812 constitution, but on May 4, 1814 he suddenly declared the document void and announced the restoration of absolutism after receiving assurances of support from some reactionary army officers and about 100 royalist deputies. Deputies and others associated with the constitution were arrested wholesale, and 12,000 persons were sentenced without trial to perpetual banishment in a single decree. Seignorial jurisdictions, the Inquisition, and a rigorous press censorship were all restored, and an extensive secret police system was organized.

Meanwhile, in Portugal, the anger caused by the 1807 flight to Brazil of King John VI (regent for the insane Maria I, 1792-1816, king 1816-26) increased when John failed to return after the French departure in 1811. Portugal was left under the control of an English general, William Beresford, who was named field general and commander-in-chief of the Portuguese army and who ruled the country in the king's absence until 1820. British officers were introduced into the Portuguese army, and the country was gradually turned into "an English protectorate and a Brazilian colony" (Oliveira 1976: I, 429). Beresford continued the ferocious persecution of liberals that had been initiated before the departure of the royal family by police chief Pina Manique (1780-1803).

In both Spain and Portugal, middle-class anger over the repressive nature of the Restoration regimes was compounded by the general incompetence of the Fernandine and Beresford governments, especially their inability to cope with the disastrous economic conditions that resulted from wartime devastation and the loss of much of the lucrative Latin American trade. There was also considerable disgruntlement among military officers who felt they had been inadequately rewarded for their resistance activities, with the result that the clandestine Masonic lodges that became the locus of the Iberian liberal opposition included a high percentage of army men. Growing disaffection was reflected in military plots and uprisings in Portugal in 1817 and in Spain in 1814, 1815, 1816, and 1817. They all proved futile, and most were followed by executions, with the most severe reprisals in Portugal, where 12 insurgents were executed after the 1817 plot.

Finally, in 1820 military risings aimed primarily at obtaining the introduction of constitutional government succeeded in both countries. King Ferdinand agreed to re-adopt the 1812 Spanish constitution in March 1820, while a Portuguese constituent assembly adopted a constitution there in 1822. The Portuguese suffrage was limited to literate males, but otherwise the constitution there was largely based on the liberal Spanish document. Since neither regime made any attempt to redistribute land or address the problems of the rural masses and both had alienated the traditional ruling classes, the revolutionary governments rested on fragile ground. Their weak position was compounded by internal splits within the new regimes. "Liberal" and "radical" factions emerged in each country. They had some ideological, class, and occupational bases, but largely seem to have represented an early emergence of the competition for government employment (known in Spain as empleomania), which was to become a major curse of nineteenth-century Iberian politics.

While Portuguese developments between 1820 and 1823 remained relatively peaceful, with King John VI agreeing to return from Brazil and serve as constitutional monarch, Spanish politics were chaotic. From 1820 to 1822, moderates controlled the regime, but they were undercut by the intrigues of the radicals, who frequently resorted to street riots to pressure the government, by reactionary and traditionalist forces in the field, and by King Ferdinand's constant plotting to regain his lost powers. By late 1822, large portions of northern Spain were in the hands of royalist bands, and the country was in the throes of anarchy and civil war. The agony of the Spanish revolution ended in April 1823, when 100,000 French troops, acting under the aegis of the conservative European powers who met in late 1822 at Verona, invaded and restored Ferdinand to absolute power.

The events in Spain triggered a military counterrevolution in Portugal in May 1823 supported by King John VI. The 1822 constitution was abolished, but John indicated his intention to draw up a new constitution to establish a limited monarchy. The followers of John's ultra-conservative son Miguel were outraged by this promise, and their revolt in April 1824 was thwarted only by opposition from the European powers, who viewed the move as a threat to the principle of legitimacy. The death of King John in 1826 left succession to the crown unsettled between Miguel, who was supported by John's reactionary wife Carlota Joaquina, and their other son, Pedro, the relatively liberal Emperor of Brazil (whose independence was recognized by Portugal in 1825). While Pedro was technically the royal heir, there was great opposition in Brazil and Portugal to uniting the two countries under a single monarch.

Pedro attempted to reach a compromise settlement in 1826 by promulgating a conservative constitutional charter that established an appointed upper legislative chamber and a lower chamber elected on a restricted franchise. The charter reserved substantial powers, including an absolute veto, for the king. Pedro disavowed any further claim to the Portuguese throne in favor of his seven-year-old daughter Maria de Gloria, upon condition of her taking an oath to the charter. Miguel, Maria's 24-year-old uncle, was to be regent until her majority in 1837 on condition that he marry his niece and uphold the charter. Widespread insurrections that sought to proclaim Miguel absolute monarch were put down only with the help of 5,000 British troops;

Miguel himself, then living in Austria, swore to accept Pedro's conditions. However, upon his return to Portugal in February 1828, Miguel immediately began behaving as an absolute monarch in violation of his pledge. The charter was abolished, liberals were purged, and feudal rights that had been abolished after the 1820 revolution were restored. Newly opened schools were closed and their teachers persecuted for allegedly liberal sympathies. In June 1828 the medieval Portuguese cortes was convoked, complete with rigged elections, to anoint Miguel absolute king. These events triggered an abortive liberal rising in mid-1828, which ended with over 5,000 rebels fleeing the country. A ferocious reign of repression was Miguel's response to the rising. About 14,000 people were arrested and dozens of murders and executions were carried out.

In Spain, the reaction that followed the restoration of King Ferdinand VII to absolute power was so savage that even the French king and Russian czar protested (although King Louis XVIII also agreed to keep 45,000 troops in Spain until 1828). Although Ferdinand had promised a complete amnesty, thousands of liberals were jailed, hundreds were executed and about 10,000 liberals fled into exile. The period of Ferdinand's restored absolutist rule from 1823 to 1833, known in Spanish liberal tradition as the "shameful decade," was a time of almost unrelieved reaction, led by Minister of Justice Francisco Calomarde. Not only was the 1812 constitution abolished, but all of the liberal reforms (save for the abolition of the Inquisition) were rescinded and the flourishing press of 1820-3 was suppressed, reducing the number of periodicals in Madrid from 45 in 1822 to 4 by 1824. The general intellectual climate is illustrated by the address of the University of Cervera to the king, which began, "Far from us the dangerous novelty of thinking" (Atkinson 1960: 271).

Despite the savage repression, Ferdinand faced opposition from ultra-reactionary forces supporting his brother and heir apparent Carlos. The Carlists, or Apostólicos, demanded re-institution of the Inquisition, an even more total extirpation of liberalism than Ferdinand had carried out, and in general a return to something like the sixteenth century, in which Spain would be under total feudal-clerical domination and the traditional local provincial privileges would be maintained intact. In 1827 a major peasant revolt under Apostólico influence in western Catalonia was put down with great ferocity and followed by 300 executions. Since Carlos had been expected to succeed to the throne upon the death of the childless king, the Apostólicos were deeply angered when Ferdinand married for the fourth time in December 1829 and by the 1830 pregnancy of his wife (and niece) María Cristina, which re-opened the succession issue.

Russia. Russian discontent in the post-1815 period was most widespread among liberal noble army officers who had been exposed to modern currents during their service in the Napoleonic Wars in western Europe. They had returned to Russia with a sense of shame at Russian backwardness and steady disillusionment over the failure of

Czar Alexander I (1801-25) to implement significant reforms. As Prince Volkonsky wrote in his memoirs:

> The campaigns in 1812-14 brought Europe nearer to us, made us familiar with its form of state, its public institutions, the rights of its people. By contrast with our own state, the laughably limited rights which our own people possessed, the despotism of our regime first became truly present in our heart and understanding (Kochan 1963: 143).

This sense of shame was only compounded by Alexander's failure to fulfill his early reputation and signs of liberalism. Although shortly after taking office upon the murder of his father, Czar Paul I, in 1801 Alexander had eased controls on the press and foreign travel, freed about 12,000 persons jailed or exiled, and greatly expanded the Russian university system, the two key bulwarks of autocratic and feudal rule in Russia, the lack of a constitution and national legislature, and the brutal institution of serfdom, were left untouched. Until his regime took a decidedly reactionary turn in 1820, Alexander seems to have been torn between his abstract desires for significant liberal reform in Russia, and his concrete fears of diminishing his own power and antagonizing the upper levels of the nobility. Thus, he toyed with proposals for constitutional reform and easing the burden of the serfs, but he never implemented any significant change. After relying heavily upon a liberal advisor, Michael Speransky, for several years, he had Speransky arrested and exiled without trial in 1812 as the result of demands by influential nobles. Perhaps the best summary of Alexander's attitude was ventured by his friend, the Polish Prince Adam Czartoryski, who declared, "He would willingly have agreed that every man should be free, on the condition that the whole world gladly do his bidding" (Yarmolinsky 1962: 26).

Following Speransky's dismissal, Alexander's domestic policies took on an increasingly conservative tone, although they became decidedly reactionary only after the general outbreak of unrest in Europe in 1819-21, including the murder of his agent Kotzebue in Germany in 1819 and a minor incident in the Semyonovsky Regiment of Imperial Guards--the czar's favorite--in St. Petersburg in October 1820. The Semyonovksy incident involved a relatively minor protest over the brutal behavior of a commanding officer and had no political overtones, but in the context of the 1820-1 revolutions Alexander interpreted the affair as part of the alleged international revolutionary conspiracy of secret societies that Metternich was always talking about.

The growing tendency towards reaction in Russia after 1812, and especially after 1820, is generally associated with the name of Count Alexis Arakchevyev, a conservative landowner who was given free reign over most Russian internal affairs. Arakchevyev was a brutal martinet, who, on his own estates, commanded all married female serfs to bear a child every year. His equally brutal mistress was hacked to death during a serf revolt in 1825. Arakchevyev was especially associated with the notorious "military colonies." The military colonies were originated by Alexander in 1810, and were designed with benevolent and liberal purposes. The basic idea was to allow men who were drafted into the army to live with their families in newly established farming communities when they were not on active service. Thus, families would no longer be separated, and through farming and other activities the military would pay for itself instead of draining the treasury. By 1820, about one-third of the standing army was established in the colonies, which were well-funded and provided with educational, sanitary, and other facilities that made living conditions far superior to those of the typical serf village. However, the colonies were administered with the gross corruption and inefficiency typical of Russian bureaucratic life, and every aspect of daily existence in the colonies, including time of awakening and sleep, marriage, and childbearing, were regulated by strict military discipline. Frequent revolts were crushed with severe measures. The so-called arakchevyevshina, as the 1815-25 period is known to Russian history, was also marked by an increasingly reactionary and obscurantist educational policy, associated with Prince Alexander Golitsyn, who was appointed minister of education in 1816. After the European events of 1819-21, Russians were barred from studying at four German universities, and there were major purges and crackdowns at the universities of Kazan, Kharkov, and St. Petersburg. Mikhail Magnitskii, the reactionary curator at the University of Kazan, ordered mathematics teachers to point out that the triangle was symbolic of the Christian Trinity and warned that the "evil spirit of the times, the spirit of free thought" must be stopped (Flynn, 1971: 610). The censorship was drastically tightened, so much so that even an article by Magnitskii attacking constitutionalism was rejected, on the grounds that no discussion of constitutions was needed in Russia, either pro or con.

After 1816, disappointed Russian liberals began to form private discussion groups to air their grievances, which centered on their desires for constitutional government in Russia and an end to serfdom. Alexander's failure to grant a constitution was especially resented since he had accepted constitutional rule in Russian-controlled Poland and Finland, and had supported constitutionalism in Germany and France. As the reaction deepened in Russia, especially after an 1822 decree banning all secret societies, the liberals were driven into greater radicalism and clandestineness. By 1825, two underground groups, one centered in the north at St. Petersburg and the other in the south at Tulchin, the headquarters of the second army, were planning a revolutionary overthrow of the government. Both were extremely narrowly based, being almost exclusively made up of military officers and members of the lesser nobility, leading the military governor of Moscow in the 1820s to comment drolly, "Ordinarily it is the shoemakers who make revolutions to become great lords, but in Russia it is the great lords who want to become shoemakers" (Kochan 1963: 143).

The conspirators originally planned to revolt in May 1826 but moved up their scheme when Alexander suddenly died in November 1825, leaving the imperial succession in a state of confusion. The legitimate heir, Grand Duke Constantine, had secretly renounced the throne, while the heir-apparent, Grand Duke Nicholas, hesitated before asserting his rights. The so-called Decembrist revolt that followed (named for its occurrence in December 1825) was a total fiasco. Leaders of the northern group of conspirators convinced 3,000 troops in St. Petersburg to assemble on the Senate Square and refuse to take an oath to Nicholas. Most of the troops had no idea of the real aims of the Decembrist leaders, but regarded Nicholas as a usurper. The rebel leaders made no attempt at any military action, and after a few hours Nicholas had loyal troops open fire on the mutineers with cannon. They killed 60 or 70 and dispersed the rest. In the south, a revolt of about 800 men was suppressed with little difficulty. Nicholas personally supervised the subsequent interrogation of the Decembrists, which led to 5 executions, 31 sentences of Siberian exile at hard labor for life, and over 200 lighter penalties. The hangings were bungled by an inexperienced executioner before they were completed--symptomatic of Russian efficiency. It is reported that one of the victims declared, "I am happy that I shall die twice for my country" (Yarmolinsky 1962: 61). Although a few minor conspiracies were broken up in the next few years, the Decembrist movement was the last serious--if one can call it that--revolutionary movement in Russia for 40 years.

In Russian-controlled Poland, the lands seized from Poland in 1772, 1793, and 1795, known as the western guberniias and populated mostly by Lithuanians, Byelorussians, and Ukrainians, continued to be administered after 1815 as an integral part of the Russian Empire. However, the Polish ethnic lands formerly controlled by Austria and Prussia but ceded to Russia at the Congress of Vienna were organized as an autonomous kingdom, known officially as the Kingdom of Poland and informally as Congress Poland. In 1815, Czar Alexander issued to Congress Poland a markedly liberal constitution, which guaranteed freedom of speech and press and established a two-house legislature with a lower chamber elected by about 3 per cent of the population, a suffrage more generous than that in contemporary France and the United Kingdom. Poland was granted the right to its own army, citizenship, religion, administrative personnel, and language. The czar, in his capacity as King of Poland, appointed all ministers and could legislate by decree, although the budget and all important legislation were supposed to be submitted to the Polish legislature.

If the 1815 Polish constitution had been honored, the regime would have been among the most liberal in Europe, in contrast to the conditions under which Poles in Austria and Prussia lived. In fact, however, the Polish constitution was repeatedly violated by Russian authorities. Thus, censorship was introduced in Poland in 1819, and members of the Polish diet who criticized Alexander in 1820 were barred from further attendance. As Russian controls tightened on Poland, including a ban on secret societies in 1821 and a purge of the University of Wilno in 1823, Polish army officers and members of the intelligentsia and lesser gentry who dreamed of an independent Poland

and bitterly resented the separation of the western guberniias from Congress Poland turned to conspiratorial plotting. This plotting continued despite arrests in Congress Poland in the aftermath of the Decembrist uprising. By the late 1820s, most politically aware Poles were in opposition to the regime. The rallying points of the opposition were defense of the Polish constitution and the independence of the Polish parliament, and an end to the Russian censorship and secret police.

Finland, taken by Russia from Sweden in 1808-1809, had a constitutional arrangement much like Congress Poland's. It remained quiet during the 1815-30 period and indeed up until Russia's 1809 pledge to respect Finnish autonomy was violated in 1899. The 1809 agreement included Russian respect of Finland's laws, religions, rights, and institutions as established under the previous semi-absolutist Swedish constitution of 1789. Since Finland had formerly been an integral part of Sweden--the Finnish diet had not met as a separate institution since 1676--it actually enjoyed increased self-government under Russian control during the next 90 years. While ultimate authority resided in the czar as Grand Duke of Finland, in practice day-to-day affairs were handled by the Finnish senate, consisting of Finns appointed by the czar. Although the Finnish diet was not convened after 1809 until 1863, effective power in Finland continued to be exercised, as before, by Swedish-speaking nobles and bureaucrats.

The Balkans. Discontent in the Balkans was largely in response to the catastrophic decline in the quality of the Ottoman administration after about 1600. Aside from the general collapse of law and order and the rapacious demands of local soldiers and officials, many Balkan Christians resented being subjected to the control of people they regarded as religious infidels. Numerous forms of discriminatory measures, such as the ban against non-Moslems riding horses or bearing arms and the requirement that Christians wear distinctive dress and pay a special tax, were also bitterly resented.

The growing anger of the Balkan peasantry was reflected in the massive growth of brigandage after 1700, as well as increasingly frequent uprisings. Among a series of peasant revolts that erupted between 1800 and 1810, the most serious broke out in Serbia, where Turkish troops, or janissaries, had inaugurated a reign of terror and pillage, culminating in the massacre of scores of Serb notables in early 1804. The massacre triggered a peasant rebellion involving about 30,000 Serbs. Although the uprising originated as a movement directed only against the abuses of the janissaries and for the restoration of autonomous rights that had been briefly granted Serbia in the 1790s, it gradually developed into a movement for complete independence. In July 1813 Turkish forces regained their control of Serbia and unleashed a massive reign of terror, including numerous murders of adult males and enslavement of women and children. A new revolt in September 1814 was quickly suppressed and followed by another round of several hundred grisly tortures and murders, in violation of a promised amnesty. Yet another rebellion broke out in

April 1815, under the leadership of Miloš Obrenović, one of the leaders of the 1804 rising. The insurrection ended six months later when Turkey agreed to make major concessions after several Serbian victories, partly because Miloš pledged his loyalty to the sultan and partly because the end of the Napoleonic wars threatened to bring the intervention of Russia, Turkey's bitterest foe, on behalf of Serbia. In November 1815 Turkey agreed to recognize Miloš as supreme Serbian leader and to grant substantial internal autonomy.

For the next 24 years, Miloš ruled as probably the most arbitrary and absolutist sovereign in Europe. He established a highly centralized administration in violation of long-standing Serbian traditions of strong local government, decided the most minute aspects of state policy, personally controlled all trade and not infrequently murdered his perceived or potential rivals. Thus, in 1817 Miloš arranged for the murder of the main leader of the 1804 revolt, George Petrović, known as Karageorge, thereby beginning a bitter hatred, which was to plague the country for the next 100 years, between the Obrenović and Karageorgević claimants to the Serbian throne. Some of Miloš's rivals were executed after public trials, while others were murdered in the middle of the night "by accident" under such flimsy pretexts as "rifles having gone off by mistake" (Dedijer 1974: 280). Miloš completely commingled his own funds with public monies and plundered the state treasury to such an extent that by 1837 his personal income amounted to 17 per cent of Serbia's total income. The government was administered as an extension of Miloš's own household and was generally based on a combination of whim and terror. All major local officials and judges, most of whom were illiterate, were appointed and paid by Miloš, and he supplemented their activities by judging criminal cases personally and ordering such punishments as amputations of hands or ears. Miloš's greatest positive contribution to Serbia was that through an adept combination of negotiation, bribery and intimidation, he was gradually able to curtail Turkish power and oust Turkish landlords from Serbia, so that the quasi-autonomy granted in 1815 was transformed into a real autonomy even before the Turks formally conceded this in February 1830. Further, Miloš ensured that a class of great landlords did not supplant the collapse of the Turkish landed class, instead sponsoring the creation of a system based on free land tenure and small family farms.

The exhaustion of Serbia in 1815 after a decade of warfare and the general gratitude to Miloš for his successful leadership against the Turks kept down serious discontent with his authoritarianism in the years immediately afterwards. However, an opposition gradually arose that was especially strong among Serbians who had risen to local prominence before or during the insurrections, and who resented Miloš's monopoly of power and control over all trade. In 1821 a minor revolt was easily put down, but in 1825 a rebellion involving 5,000 dissidents lasted 10 days. The revolt, known as Djak's Rebellion, was aimed at socioeconomic reforms, and above all an end to Miloš's arbitrary rule. The ninth of 15 demands issued by a popular assembly that met at Topola on February 1, 1825 read:

Lord, the people have become sore afraid, and both great and small are in fear of sudden death. Whoever speaks such words, you can cut him down and now all have become afraid so that neither the guilty nor the just can come before you, and this has driven us all into the woods, for a chopped off head makes a terrible wound (Petrovich 1976: 117).

Miloš put down the revolt by sending troops to attack the Topola assembly. Following a brutal dispersal and massacre at Topola, the leader of the revolt was shot and an orgy of killings, beatings, and plundering ensued. In 1826, another uprising broke out, which was again put down with murders, beatings and jailings.

As the Serbian revolt progressed during the 1804-15 period, there was also a marked growth of unrest among the Greeks, which partly reflected a situation of deteriorating security and the increasing land hunger of the peasantry. Although most Greek peasants had no sense of nationalism--they still called themselves "Romans" from the days of Roman rule--they were fully prepared to revolt against the existing system when a secret society known as the Philike Hetairia (Society of Friends) organized a rising in 1821. The Philike Hetairia was organized by a group of Greek merchants in Odessa (Russia) in 1814. It reflected the rise of a true form of modern Greek nationalism after about 1780 among Greek merchants and sailors who came into contact with and were highly influenced by western developments, including the ideologies of the French Revolution.

In the Danubian Principalities of Wallachia and Moldavia, and to a much lesser extent in Bulgaria, where nationalistic stirrings were extremely faint in 1815, anti-Turkish feelings in 1815 were accompanied by strong anti-Greek feelings. After the seventeenth century, the Ottoman regime relied increasingly upon influential Greek families in Constantinople (known as Phanariot Greeks or Phanariots after the Phanar, or lighthouse, district where they lived) to fill positions of great importance. The Phanariots were more skilled in foreign languages, trade, and diplomacy than the Turks. They regularly filled such offices as dragoman of the fleet (undersecretary of the navy), dominated the heirarchy of the Greek Orthodox church, and after 1710, regularly purchased from Turkish officials the lucrative positions of hospodars, or princes, of Moldavia and Wallachia, which had formerly been filled by native Rumanian boyars (great landlords). Since the Greek Orthodox church was the dominant organ of culture and self-government in the Christian communities of the Balkans, the Phanariots' monopoly of top church positions led to Greek domination of culture and education in Bulgaria and Rumania as well as in Greece itself (this was true to a much lesser extent in Serbia, where the Serbian Orthodox church was allowed to remain autonomous between 1557 and 1766). Thus, as nationalistic sentiment grew in Rumania and Bulgaria, Greek cultural and linguistic domination became as much an object of hatred as was Turkish political and economic oppression.

Although the Danubian Principalities, unlike the rest of the Balkans, never were placed under direct Turkish rule and were officially autonomous tributary provinces of the Ottoman Empire, Turkish control over Rumanian exports and over the appointment of hospodars had reduced Moldavia and Wallachia to puppet states by 1815. The regime of the Phanariot hospodars after 1710 led to a drastic rise in corruption and extortionate taxation in the principalities. In order to recover the bribe money with which they purchased their positions from the Turks before another Phanariot offered an even higher price and replaced them, the hospodars resorted to drastic increases in financial demands made upon the boyars, who in turn passed these on to the peasants. One hospodar, Constantine Hangerli, it was reported, told demonstrators protesting a huge tax increase, "Pay the taxes and you won't be killed" (Seton-Watson 1934: 158), before he was himself killed by order of the Turkish sultan--a fate that befell several other hospodars. Another Phanariot hospodar, Ion Caragea, is credited with the stupendous feat of increasing taxation eightfold during his unusually long seven-year term; his name is memorialized in the Rumanian proverb that speaks of "stealing as in the days of Caragea" (Seton-Watson 1934: 193). By 1815, the Rumanian peasants were on the verge of revolt against the boyars, the hospodars and the Turks, while the boyars were increasingly determined to regain the right to oppress the peasantry on their own terms without having to bow and scrape to the Greeks. In the meantime, as one observer who travelled to Moldavia in the 1780s noted, the Rumanian peasants were "slaves of a man [the boyar] who trembles before the slave [the hospodars] of the Porte [Constantinople]" (Seton-Watson 1934: 128).

In 1821, revolts erupted in the principalities and Greece. In January, a peasant uprising broke out in Wallachia, shortly before a planned Hetairia-sponsored invasion of the principalities by Greeks and other volunteers living in Russia who hoped to trigger a Balkan-wide revolt that would lead to a revival of a Byzantine-type empire in southeastern Europe under Greek political and cultural hegemony. The Wallachian revolt was led by Tudor Vladimeriscu, a man of peasant origin who had gained wealth and prominence. He had been in contact with a group of Rumanian boyars who had been cooperating with the Hetairia leaders, but when he led a revolt of about 5,000 peasants his declared target was not the Turks but instead Greek Phanariot-Rumanian boyar rule and oppression of the peasantry in the principalities. Thus, the rebels attacked boyar estates and monasteries and burned feudal account books.

About a month after the Vladimeriscu rebellion, the Hetairia invasion of the principalities was launched by Alexander Ypsilantis, the son of a former hospodar and a major general in the Russian army. Russian Czar Alexander I immediately denounced the Ypsilantis invasion, and since under treaty arrangements Russian consent was needed before Turkey could send troops into the principalities, Alexander's action meant the death knell for the Hetairia in Rumania. Vladimeriscu abandoned any thought of supporting Ypsilantis, moderated his anti-boyar stand, and after entering into negotiations with moderate boyars, jointly appealed to the Turks for an end to Phanariot rule in the principalities. Vladimeriscu's sudden about-face alienated many of his peasant followers, while Ypsilantis, infuriated over what he regarded as a betrayal, had Vladimeriscu kidnapped and murdered. The peasant movement thereupon collapsed, while Turkish troops entered the principalities, savagely destroyed Ypsilantis's army and engaged in wholesale plunder and repression. This seeming fiasco had major consequences for both the principalities and for Greece. The Turks, recognizing the growing Rumanian hatred for the Phanariot regime, agreed to appoint native boyars to serve as princes in Wallachia and Moldavia beginning in July 1822. A rapid disintegration of Greek cultural, educational, and linguistic domination in the principalities ensued. And although the Ypsilantis invasion was a disaster for Greek influence in Rumania, it touched off a massive peasant uprising in Greece itself that led to the establishment of an independent Greek state after nine years of warfare.

The Greek revolution was marked by savage atrocities on both sides, among them the Turkish execution of 80 Greek Orthodox bishops—including the hanging of the patriarch in his sacred vestments on the gate of the patriarchate in Constantinople on Easter Sunday 1821—the Greek butchery of 10,000 Turkish men, women and children at Tripolitsa in October 1821, marked by truly medieval scenes of torture and mutilation, and the massacre and enslavement of thousands of Greek residents of the island of Chios in 1822, an event made famous by the paintings of Delacroix. In 1827, after six years of warfare and severe internal factionalization among the Greeks, and two years after an apparently decisive intervention by Egyptian troops allied with the Turks, the Greeks appeared on the brink of defeat when intervention by the European powers saved them. The European intervention after six years of inaction owed little to the Philhellenic agitation. Instead it reflected British fears that continued disorders in Greece and a strong Turkish presence there would disrupt Mediterranean commerce. It also reflected mutual distrust between France, Britain, and Russia as to each others' intentions. The defeat of the Egyptian fleet by the combined fleets of the three European powers at Navarino Bay in 1827 and the subsequent defeat of Turkey by Russia in a brief war in 1828-29 resulted in the 1829 Russo-Turkish Treaty of Adrianople and the 1830 London Protocol, signed by France, Russia, and the United Kingdom. In the Adrianople treaty, Turkey agreed to recognize the autonomy of Serbia and the Danubian Principalities, which amounted to a fait accompli in the case of Serbia, but to acceptance of Russian hegemony in the principalities since Russian troops were to remain there pending payment of an indemnity by Turkey. In the London Protocol, the three powers declared Greece an independent and monarchical state under their guarantee. The powers immediately began searching for a foreign king to impose upon the Greeks—a decision reached without Greek consultation or consent.

The Quiet Realms of Restoration Europe
The Habsburg Empire. Except to a limited extent among the Magyar nobles of Hungary, the Habsburg Empire was almost completely devoid of political life during the Restoration. Emperor Francis was haunted--to a degree that can only be described as pathological--by the fear that the demons of the French Revolution would emerge again if any free thought or social change was allowed in his realm. A high official in the Emperor's inner circle noted, "Believe me, he who has to serve for any time in the immediate entourage of the Emperor must become a philosopher or an intriguer or an ox in order to endure it." Another official replied, "Of those three most people hold to the juste milieu, namely intrigue" (Seton-Watson 1965: 164).

The Habsburg secret police was virtually the only element in the regime that displayed any energy or efficiency, and its well-publicized penetration into all aspects of public life completely paralyzed all political discussion. As one high-ranking Austrian nobleman wrote in a book published in Germany and smuggled into Austria, the attitude of the Habsburg authorities was that

> Men should be merry, should become drunk, should tell obscene jokes, or at best should establish a cotton factory or read the theater paper ... but all interests concerning their community, their province, their state, the most important question of the epoch, however much they affect their purse and their whole existence, they should politely leave alone in order not to incommode the governing gentlemen (Jaszi 1966: 77).

In response to the unrest in Germany in 1817-19, political controls were tightened even beyond the already stifling levels of 1815. When it was discovered that a few student organizations parallel to the Burschenschaften existed in Austrian university towns, a grand inquisition was launched against professors and a number of them were fired, including the eminent philosopher and mathematician Bernard Bolzano, who lost his position at the University of Prague. Surveillance of professors and education in general soon reached absurd lengths, and the censorship became so strict that one serious medical work was forbidden for containing a passing reference to the poor state of the roads in the province of Carinthia.

Yet the regime was not a brutal one, and most of its repressive energies were directed towards prevention of dissent rather than punishment. Thus, while the Austrian mails were notoriously surveilled, intercepted letters were used for intelligence rather than prosecutory purposes and "a man might have his doings and sayings reported for years and yet live quite unmolested" (Macartney 1969: 164). Indeed, in the Habsburg Empire, the police state par excellence of the Restoration, there was not a single political trial of an Austrian subject in the Germanic or Bohemian lands between 1815 and 1835 (although this was largely a tribute to the secret police's effectiveness in intimidating dissenters into silence).

The Germanic subjects of the empire, about 25 per cent of the total population, were politically silent during the Restoration, as were the seven different Slavic ethnic-linguistic groups (40 per cent of the population) and the Italians and Rumanians (about 10 per cent each). Despite the favored position enjoyed in the empire by the German language and German-speaking administrators, signs of life among the Slavs were almost entirely confined to the cultural-linguistic sphere and posed no apparent political threat, aside from some muted passive resistance among the Polish nobles of Galicia. The most advanced Slavic cultural-linguistic movement, that of the Bohemian Czechs, was expressed through organizations such as the Royal Bohemian Society of Sciences and the Society of the Bohemian Museum. During the Restoration, Czech nationalism had barely advanced, however, beyond the perhaps apochryphal meeting in Prague in the late eighteenth century at which a pioneering Czech is reported to have remarked among fellow nationalists, "If the ceiling were to fall on us now, that would be the end of the national revival" (Taylor 1976: 29).

The weakness of the non-Magyar nationalities in 1815 temporarily masked the danger posed to the Habsburg Empire by its multinational character and lack of any real sense of organic unity. The Empire had been put together by the Habsburg dynasty over hundreds of years through inheritance, diplomacy, marriages, and wars. Each province retained to a considerable degree its own language, religion, customs, and sense of historic identity, so the Empire resembled a "vast family estate, in which the separate regions simply owed a personal allegiance to the Emperor" (Wood 1964: 31). For most of the population, the views expressed by a Tyrolese in the eighteenth century still held true:

> What does it concern the people of the Tyrol what happens in Bohemia, Moravia, and other countries? ... It is a matter of pure accident that their prince also happens to rule over other countries (Blanning 1970: 73).

This attitude did not disturb Emperor Francis, who saw no threat in the general lack of strong attachments to the empire among its many people, but instead an opportunity for "divide and rule" politics. He told the French ambassador:

> My people are strange to each other and that is all right. They do not get the same sickness at the same time. ... The one does not understand the other and one hates the other ... From their antipathy will be born order and from the mutual hatreds general peace (Jaszi 1966: 82).

The only significant signs of discontent in the empire during the Restoration came from the Magyar nobility of Hungary. When the Hungarian diet elected a Habsburg king for the first time in 1526, it did so on condition that Hungarian privileges and autonomy would be respected, including the famous Golden Bull of 1222, in which the Magyar nobility had extracted from King Andreas II complete immunity from taxes and the right to resist improper royal actions. In 1678-81 and 1703-11 major nationalist rebellions erupted in Hungary, and the brink of rebellion was reached again in 1790 in response to alleged Habsburg infringements of Hungarian rights. Although the revolts were put down with military force in each case, Habsburg monarchs were forced repeatedly to repledge their respect for Hungarian autonomy--in 1687, 1723, 1740, 1791, and 1792. Nonetheless, between 1812 and 1815 Emperor Francis repeatedly imposed taxes and military levies on Hungary by royal decree, in violation of the Hungarian constitution, which required the Hungarian diet to approve such measures, and for 13 years after 1812 he refused to convene the diet, in violation of his coronation pledge of 1792. Francis's imposition of military levies in 1820-2 to support suppression of the Italian revolts without consulting--or indeed convening--the diet led to wide-spread resistance from the Hungarian county administrations, which were responsible for furnishing recruits. When the use of royal commissioners from Vienna and a display of force failed to gain complete compliance, Francis yielded and convened the diet for the first time in 13 years in September 1825. Having systematically violated the Hungarian constitution and his own coronation oath, Francis, sensing the growing anger of the Magyar nobility, issued a quasi-apology to the diet and promised to henceforth abide by Hungary's laws.

The Low Countries. In the United Netherlands (formed when the Congress of Vienna transferred Belgium from the Habsburg Empire to the Dutch Netherlands), there was little sign of Dutch opposition during the 1815-30 period to King William's increasing authoritarianism, marked by frequent rule by decree and a virtual ignoring of parliament. However, in Belgium there was considerable and growing resentment over Dutch rule, which went beyond urban areas to encompass significant segments of the Catholic rural population. Belgian grievances over the enforced union festered over language and religion (Belgium was French in culture and Catholic in religion, while the Netherlands used the Dutch language and was Calvinist). Other grievances flowed from King William's gross favoring of Dutch over Belgian appointees to administrative and military positions and the fact that both halves of the new country were given equal representation in the lower legislative chamber and expected to assume equal shares of the national debt, although the Belgian population was 50 per cent greater than that of the Netherlands and the pre-1815 Dutch debt was twelve times that of the Belgian provinces. One clear sign of things to come was the rejection of William's proposed constitution (grondwet) by an assembly of Belgian notables by a vote of 796-527 in 1815. Undaunted, William counted as positive 126 negative votes that had been cast on religious grounds, as well as abstentions and absentees, and announced that the grondwet had been approved. The Belgians immediately coined the term "Dutch arithmetic" to characterize the king's action (Eyck 1959: 52).

In the Dutch Netherlands, the general mood was marked by apathy and demoralization, reflecting the psychological and economic crisis caused by the steady Dutch decline from the seventeenth century "Golden Age," when the Netherlands had been the leading commercial power in Europe, and by the humiliation of 20 years of French domination and manipulation. The Dutch mercantile elite, which had long dominated society and politics in the Netherlands, was quite content to dream about the past--the slogan of the day was "als vanouds" (as of old)--ignore the degrading poverty of the masses, and trust in the authoritarian-paternalistic rule of King William I, who was expected to protect them against the threat of being overwhelmed by Belgium's language, religion, industry, and numbers.

Until 1828, factional differences greatly hampered the Belgian opposition movement. Belgian elites were deeply divided between a group of liberal urban-based industrial entrepreneurs, whose influence grew with the very rapid industrialization experienced in Belgium during the Restoration, and a group of conservative rural-based Catholic prelates and landed nobles. Although King William strongly encouraged the spread of both industry and education in Belgium, the liberals were alienated by his restrictions on the press, while the conservatives were outraged by his attempts to supplant and regulate the Catholic schools. In 1828, the continued prosecution of the liberal press and discrimination against Catholic schools led the basically anti-clerical Belgian liberals and the basically anti-liberal Belgian Catholics to unite around the slogans of freedom of education (i.e., the right of Catholics to control their own schools) and freedom of the press. Growing demands were also heard for Belgian autonomy and the need to curb King William's power. In 1829 the lower house of the United Netherlands parliament was flooded with petitions signed by 40,000 Belgians supporting the demands of the Catholic-liberal union. In November 1829, the leading opposition figure, Louis de Potter, editor of the liberal newspaper Courrier des Pays-Bas was given an 18-month jail term after publishing a scathing attack on the regime. During the next few months, over 350,000 Belgians, mostly in rural Flanders, took part in a renewed and massive church-organized petition campaign. "By putting their signatures--or--as in thousands of cases--just a cross under the petitions" they "manifested their desire to free the press which they could not read, the schools which they did not attend and a language which they did not understand" (Kossmann 1978: 149). In April 1830, tensions increased again when Potter and three other prominent journalists were sent into exile.

Switzerland. Discontent in Switzerland centered among urban liberals who opposed the highly restricted suffrage and political controls of the restored cantonal regimes, and among rural inhabitants who opposed the discrimination against non-urban areas built into the political structure of many of the urban cantons. Thus, in Zurich canton,

10,000 townsmen were given 130 representatives on the governing council, while the 200,000 rural residents had only 82; and in Basel canton 15,000 inhabitants of the capital received 90 representatives, while the 30,000 rustics had only 60 deputies. Under the influence of the conservative Restoration atmosphere and the constant snooping of Metternich, the Swiss Federal diet and the cantonal diets met in secret; freedom of press and assembly was highly restricted; and in some cantons, extremely archaic legal codes, some of which authorized the use of torture, were resurrected. The extremely weak structure of the Swiss Confederation also annoyed some liberals, as the central diet was relatively toothless and there was no common Swiss citizenship, freedom of settlement, or commercial regulations.

Following the repression of unrest in Germany and Italy in 1819-21, Switzerland came under attack from the conservative powers for exercising its traditional policy of granting asylum to political refugees from those and other lands. In 1822 the Congress of Verona--which authorized the French suppression of the Spanish revolution--authorized Metternich to demand on behalf of the French, Austrian, Prussian and Russian governments that the Swiss take firm steps against the refugees. Faced with a barrage of threats from Metternich, the Swiss Federal diet, fearing military intervention, passed the "Press and Aliens Conclusum" of 1823, which enforced upon the cantons a strict censorship of news about foreign countries and required that all aliens be granted specific permission to live in Switzerland by cantonal authorities. Subsequently, many of the more vocal refugees fled the country.

Swiss liberals and nationalists were deeply humiliated by the 1823 crackdown. By the last few years of the 1820s, Switzerland was in the grips of a general mood demanding political reform, aimed first at political liberalization and ultimately at creating a much stronger and unified country no longer subject to foreign dictation. As a result of the growing pressures for reform, the press was admitted to legislative meetings in Geneva and Vaud after 1828; in 1829 the Swiss Federal diet allowed the 1823 Conclusum to lapse and press censorship was abolished in Zurich and Appenzell. Minor liberal reforms were passed in other cantons, while in Ticino a bloodless popular revolution in 1829 led to adoption of a new liberal constitution on July 4, 1830. When the national shooting match--a major occasion for the expression of reform sentiment--met at Berne in July 1830 "there was thunder in the air" in Switzerland, and the news of revolution in France on July 27 "fell like a thunderbolt" (Bonjour 1952: 251).

Scandinavia. Politics in Scandinavia was muted and conservative during the 1815-30 period, aside from signs of Norwegian nationalistic dissatisfaction with the Swedish union. Calm was especially pervasive in Denmark, where one historian has noted, "One might almost say there was no politics" (Hovde 1943: 511) during the period. Danish society, demoralized by the loss of Norway to Sweden in 1814 and the economic dislocations engendered by the Napoleonic Wars, tended to rally around King Frederick VI (1808-39), whose rule was entirely absolutist and quite conservative but generally well-meaning and benevolent. According to the dramatist Thomas Overskou, "Only one feeling really united high and low alike, both sexes and all ages: respect for the king" (Jones 1970: 59).

Frederick governed Denmark with the aid of an appointed bureaucracy that had little independent power. The power of the traditional landed nobility had been greatly diminished since absolutism had been introduced in 1660, but their substantial landholdings made them a potentially strong political force if the power of the king were to be eroded. Frederick's conservative inclination was reinforced in 1817 when inmates of two Copenhagen prisons simultaneously revolted. The insurrection was put down by troops and followed by 14 executions and 40 floggings, along with other brutal punishments. Despite the lack of any real opposition, even peaceful dissidents faced harsh treatment. Thus, an obscure cleric who agitated for constitutional reform was sentenced to death--later commuted to over 20 years in jail--in 1821, and in 1826 another cleric, N. F. S. Gruntvig, later to become famous as the founder of the Danish folk high school movement, was fined for his theological writings and barred from preaching.

In Sweden, the forceful personality of King Charles John, a former French official and soldier who had served Napoleon and never bothered to learn Swedish or Norwegian, dominated the political scene. Charles John made it clear that he did not look kindly upon being crossed--"Opposition, c'est conspiration" was one of his better known statements (Anderson 1955: 323). Highly suspicious by nature and paranoid about possible efforts of adherents of the former Vasa dynasty to reclaim the throne, the king fought any signs of "conspiration" by buying off the nobility with jobs and money, organizing a secret police force along Napoleonic lines and silencing the opposition press. Although the 1809 constitution eliminated the former noble monopoly on high civil service positions, the king placated the thousand or so Swedish noble families by filling top positions almost exclusively from among them and by appointing solely nobles to his cabinet until 1828. For all practical purposes, Sweden under Charles John, like the United Netherlands under William I, was ruled very much as an absolute monarchy despite its constitutional trappings. A slow growth of opposition to his authoritarian rule was easily kept under control during the 1820s. The opposition press was checked by the king's frequent exercise of his authority under the 1812 press law that allowed him to administratively suppress newspapers found to be "imperilling the public safety." In a few cases, critics of the king were tried for treason, including C. H. Anckarsvärd, a member of the Riksdag Estate of the Nobility and leader of the parliamentary opposition, who was acquitted on charges that resulted from his harsh attacks on government financial policy in 1823. Most of the scattered opposition that did exist was focussed on alleged excessive government expenditures and other narrow financial issues.

In Norway, the general disdain held by the ruling mercantile-bureaucratic elite for the peasantry was reinforced in 1818 when a group of peasants sought to march peacefully on Christiania (Oslo) to demand a return to the absolute monarchical form of government they had known under Danish rule, which they associated with lower taxes. The peasant march was broken up with almost 300 arrests, and their leader, Halvor Hoel, was denied the right to take his elected storting seat on the flimsy grounds that he had been indicted in a criminal case, even though he had been subsequently acquitted by the highest court.

While many Norwegian peasants clearly preferred a stronger monarchy, the ruling elements who dominated the storting spent most of their energies in resisting attempts by Swedish King Charles John to increase his powers under the Norwegian constitution. In 1821 a major crisis blew up between the storting and Charles John over the legislature's determination to abolish the Norwegian nobility and its reluctance to ratify an agreement negotiated between the king and Denmark that committed Norway to pay one-eighth of the Danish debt that had accumulated while Norway was under Danish sovereignty. When the storting continued to resist ratifying the debt agreement and also seemed on the verge of passing a bill that would abolish the nobility, Charles John sent a circular note to the European powers in June 1821 suggesting he might change the Norwegian constitution to increase royal powers. He also sent the storting a note urging them not to abolish the nobility since, given the high state of social tension in Europe, it was "reasonable to believe that so decisive a step ... would attract a great deal of attention in other lands" (Hovde 1943: 514). The storting finally agreed to ratify the debt measure in 1821, but passed the measure abolishing the nobility. Widespread Norwegian fears of a royal coup were reinforced when the king assembled 6,000 troops near Christiania in July 1821 and sent a Swedish naval squadron into waters near the capital. Although no military action was taken, Charles John subsequently submitted to the storting 13 proposed amendments to the Norwegian constitution. The amendments would have drastically increased his authority, for example, providing him with an absolute instead of a suspensive veto and authorizing him to re-establish a hereditary nobility. Every one of the king's proposals was unanimously rejected at the 1824 storting session, although the king was to reintroduce all of them to no avail at every storting session until his death in 1844.

Following another threatened but unconsummated royal coup in 1828, an 1829 incident reinforced the growing Norwegian sense of nationhood. From 1824 on, the Norwegians celebrated the May 17 anniversary of Norway's 1814 constitution, in preference to the November 4 anniversary of the 1815 union with Sweden. Despite Charles John's well-known disapproval, on May 17, 1829 small private celebrations were held by university students. Late that evening, crowds milled about peacefully in Christiania's marketplace, partly to watch the arrival of a paddle steamer and partly to see if any excitement would result from the anniversary celebrations. Troops were sent in to clear the marketplace when the crowd disobeyed an order to disperse. Not a shot was fired, there was no serious violence or injuries, and not even a window was broken. However, a subsequent official inquiry, in which over 300 witnesses were called "served to build up the 'Battle of the Marketplace' as a kind of Peterloo" (Derry 1973: 64). Subsequent tolerance of the May 17 celebrations made the 1829 affair a landmark in the growth of Norwegian nationalism.

## *The Revolutions of 1830-1832 and Their Aftermath, 1830-1839*

The European revolutionary wave of 1830-2 was far more widespread and broadly based than the earlier period of unrest in 1819-21 but less extensive in geographical scope and popular support than the great revolutionary wave of 1848-9. The 1830-2 unrest had violent repercussions with overt political significance in France, Germany, Russian Poland, Belgium, Italy, Great Britain, Switzerland, and Iberia. While nationalistic sentiment played a major role in the disturbances in Poland, Belgium, Italy, and Switzerland, a major force behind the outbreaks everywhere was the demand for civil liberties and constitutional government (where it did not exist). Expansion of the suffrage was also a key demand in the disorders in Great Britain, France, and Switzerland. While the 1820-1 revolutions were largely carried out by middle-class army officers, in most cases the 1830-2 disturbances enlisted considerable middle-class civilian support; and in some cases, including France, Great Britain, Belgium, and Switzerland there was also considerable participation by working-class elements, especially in urban areas. That the 1830-2 disorders did not enlist the massive lower-class backing later evident in the 1848-9 revolutions partly demonstrated the lesser degree of lower-class politicization in 1830-2. It also reflected that by 1830 urbanization and industrialization had not yet created the large urban working class that was to emerge by 1848.

Even in those countries that were not directly affected by disturbances in 1830-2, the unrest of the period had significant repercussions. In short, in all of the major regions of continental Europe (France, Italy, Germany, Russia, the Habsburg Empire), the disturbances ultimately led to an intensification of repression that virtually silenced dissent in those areas until 1840 or after. However, in the United Kingdom and the minor countries of continental Europe, the disorders generally led to moderate, but still significant, constitutional or other reforms that facilitated growing popular participation and dissent in the post-1830 period.

### The Major Continental European Regions, 1830-1839
Although the Habsburg Empire and Russia (save for Poland) experienced no violent episodes in 1830-2 save for disorders related to cholera epidemics, the disturbances elsewhere in Europe triggered a severe tightening of repressive controls there. This was also the outcome of the revolutionary outbursts in France, Italy, and Germany.

Thus, in all of the major continental regions, the 1830-2 disorders led to a renewed repressive crackdown. The subsequent enforced political silence, like that of the post-1820 period, lasted in most of the regions for about a decade. Although technically the 1830 revolution in France is considered to have been a success, unlike the disorders in Poland, Italy, and Germany, its limited effectiveness was symbolized by the intense repression of the post-1830 period and the fact that the suffrage was expanded as a result of the revolution only from 0.3 to 0.5 per cent of the population.

The fears of the reactionary European powers in the wake of the 1830 revolts were clearly reflected in the September 1833 Austro-Russian Convention of Münchengrätz, joined shortly thereafter by Prussia, which asserted the right of any sovereign threatened by revolt to call upon the signatories for help. Metternich chortled, "So long as the union of the three monarchs lasts there will be a chance of safety in the world!" (Artz 1963: 289) The new pope, Gregory XVI (1831-46), lent his moral authority to the repressive inclinations of the reactionary powers. In the aftermath of the 1830 Polish revolt he told the Polish Catholic clergy they should preach "obedience and submission" to Russia. Shortly after, in the August 1832 encyclical Mirari Vos, he referred to liberty of the press as "that deadly freedom" and warned that "states have perished from this single evil, unrestrained freedom of thought, freedom of speech and the love of novelties" (Hales 1966: 287; May 1963: 110).

Joint Austrian, Russian, and Prussian interests in keeping Poland partitioned and Polish nationalism under control operated as a highly tangible concern that bolstered the alliance of the eastern autocracies. The tiny Republic of Cracow, which harbored refugees from the partitioned Polish lands and was a hotbed of Polish nationalism, became a victim of the fears of the eastern powers after 1830, as it had in the wake of the disturbances of 1819-21 in Europe. In 1832, Russian troops briefly occupied Cracow. In 1833, the three powers purged liberals from the Cracovian government and stripped the University of Cracow of its remaining shreds of authority. In 1834, supreme authority in the republic was vested in the resident representatives of the three powers. In early 1836, Austrian troops began a five-year occupation of Cracow after members of the large Polish refugee community there killed a Russian police agent named Behrens. Over 1,000 refugees were expelled within a few weeks of the Austrian occupation, and a wave of political purges and repression were set in train. Even visiting cards and epitaphs were subject to censorship. Gulliver's Travels and Robinson Crusoe were banned and "from Hamlet was purged the Soliloquoy on Death" (Kieniewicz 1947: 76).

France. The "July Ordinances" proclaimed by King Charles X on July 26, 1830 touched off three days of violent street fighting in Paris that led to Charles's abdication and the overthrow of the Bourbon monarchy. When the news arrived in Vienna, Metternich reportedly collapsed at his desk, moaning, "My whole life's work is destroyed!"

(Macartney 1969: 233). The opposite reaction was registered by European radicals, such as the expatriate German Heinrich Heine, who wrote that when he heard the news his soul was kindled into a "wild glow" and that each newspaper item he read from Paris was a "sunbeam, wrapped in printed paper" (Artz 1963: 277).

Louis Philippe of the House of Orléans (the younger branch of the Bourbons), who had a reputation as a moderate liberal, was proclaimed "King of the French, by the grace of God and the Will of the nation" by the legislative assembly that Charles X had attempted to dissolve. The assembly promulgated a new constitution that declared press censorship and the hereditary peerage abolished and replaced the formerly hereditary upper legislative chamber with a body that consisted of lifetime, royally appointed members. The revolutionary tricolor and the Marseillaise, both of which had been banned for 15 years, were allowed once more. However, in the most crucial decision of the legislative assembly, the electoral law of April 1831 expanded the suffrage of the lower legislative house (Chamber of Deputies) only from about 95,000 Frenchmen to about 167,000. Legislative eligibility remained highly restricted, so that only about 25,000 qualified to run for election to the chamber. The subsequent narrowness, shortsightedness, and repressiveness of the new regime, known as the July Monarchy, were directly related to this highly restrictive franchise, and eventually led to another revolution in February 1848.

The most pressing problem in France in mid-1830 and throughout the July Monarchy was the plight of the lower classes, whose conditions had worsened during post-1826 economic difficulties and remained highly precarious throughout the 1830-48 period. Their situation was probably considerably better than in many European countries, but the legacy of the 1789 and 1830 revolutions created much more highly politicized lower classes in France than elsewhere (except perhaps in Great Britain). Workers were not only disenfranchised, but they could not strike or form trade unions, and no serious attempt was made to restrict the growing abuses of the emerging factory system. "The workers must realize that their only salvation lies in patient resignation to their lot," (Fejto 1973: 26) was the only answer proffered by Prime Minister Casimir-Périer (1831-2), whose appointment by King Louis Phillippe in March 1831 signalled a clear decision by the king to back the repressively oriented faction known as the "Party of Resistance" over the desires of the "Party of Movement" faction to support social reform and revolutionary movements abroad.

The 1830 revolutions in France and elsewhere in Europe disrupted international markets and frightened businessmen. As entrepreneurs and merchants made extensive withdrawals of investments and orders, economic conditions in France worsened after the July Revolution and did not recover until after 1832. The 1830-4 period was filled with working-class strikes, riots, and demonstrations focussed on political and economic grievances. On four occasions, the disturbances reached serious dimensions. In mid-February 1831, following a memorial mass for the Duke of Berry, assassinated 10 years earlier, Paris was rocked by severe anti-clerical rioting, during which crowds sacked the archbishop's palace and the Church of Saint-Germain-l'Auxerrois. In November 1831, the severely distressed Lyon silk weavers rose up and held their city for ten days, proclaiming their determination to "live free working or die fighting," after troops who had been stoned by a crowd shot to death eight weavers. The rising was put down by 20,000 troops at a cost of 600 military and civilian casualties. In June 1832, amidst a terrible cholera epidemic, which carried off Prime Minister Casimir-Périer and 100,000 other Frenchmen, the funeral of General Lamarque, a Napoleonic hero, touched off an uprising that was put down at the cost of about 150 killed and 500 wounded. In Lyon in April 1834, the silk weavers revolted again, in response to the prosecution of the leaders of an earlier strike, to the impending passage of a law that would further restrict freedom of association, and to attempts by police to suppress the distribution of republican handbills. About 300 people were killed in six days of fighting, during which troops fired over 250,000 musket shots and over 1,700 artillery rounds. The April insurrection in Lyon touched off minor disorders in nine other cities. In Paris, a half-hearted attempt to raise barricades was crushed with ferocious brutality, including the notorious incident in the Rue Transnonain (renamed the Rue Beauborg in 1851) immortalized in a famous lithograph by Honoré Daumier, in which troops indiscriminately slaughtered about ten residents of a house from which gunfire was thought to have come. Altogether, 2,318 Frenchmen were arrested for the 1834 rising, including many republican leaders and many people who had been swept up in mass arrests in the Latin Quarter of Paris. All the patrons of one cafe on the Rue des Mathurins-Saint-Jacques, for instance, were arrested. Only 163 people were eventually prosecuted. About 90 of those got 20-year jail terms, and another 18 were transported to French penal colonies. In celebration of the marriage of Louis Philippe's eldest son, in 1837 they were amnestied.

The reaction of the July Monarchy to strikes, demonstrations, and uprisings provoked by economic misery and the lack of any peaceful channels for the disenfranchised to express themselves was almost exclusively fear and repression rather than any serious attempts at social and political amelioration. Troops were frequently used to break strikes, and over 1000 strikers were jailed in 1830-4. Over 500 press prosecutions were brought in Paris alone in 1830-4, but juries acquitted over 60 per cent of the time. The 1834 Law on Associations, which helped touch off the Lyon rising, outlawed unauthorized associations consisting of over 20 persons, even if they were divided into separate groups of less than 20 each; it was designed to suppress republican and other groups that sought to circumvent the 1810 law that outlawed unauthorized societies of over 20 people by forming affiliated sub-sections. Shortly before its passage a group of workers in Lyon who later helped lead the uprising declared:

> Considering as a general thesis that association is a natural right for all men, that it is the source of all progress ...

> Considering in particular that the association of laborers is a necessity of our age, that it is a condition of existence ... in consequence the Mutualists protest the liberticidal law on associations and declare that they will never bow their heads under this arbitrary yoke and that their meetings will never be suspended. Relying on the most inviolable right they will resist with all their energy which characterizes free men (Sewell 1980: 217).

In September 1835 new severely repressive measures were enacted following a gruesome assassination attempt on Louis Philippe that killed 18 Parisians. The so-called September Laws, enacted under the slogan, "Legality will kill us," have been characterized by one historian as so draconian that they amounted to a "change of regime" (Talmon 1967: 74). The September Laws drastically increased newpaper caution deposits—forcing the immediate closure of 30 journals—and banned the publication of any drawing, engraving, or emblem and the production of any play without prior governmental approval. They outlawed "insulting of the king," holding the king responsible for governmental acts, attacking the "principle or form of the government" and "expressing the wish, the hope or the threat of the destruction of the constitutional monarchial order" (Beik 1965: 146-7). Even the word "republican" was outlawed. After 1835 it was impossible to organize legally or agitate for any significant change in the nature of the regime. Dissent was silenced or driven underground. Attempted coups by Napoleon's nephew, Louis Napoleon Bonaparte, in 1836 and 1840, were complete fiascos, and an attempted uprising in May 1839 by an underground group in Paris was fully infiltrated by the police and proved a debacle.

Germany. The July 1830 revolution in France immediately touched off riots and demonstrations in about 10 of the German states. The generally urban disorders focussed on demands for constitutional government and political liberalization. In Brunswick, crowds stoned the mad and brutal Duke Charles (1815-30), burned down his palace and forced him to abdicate in favor of his younger brother, William I (1831-84), who granted a constitution. The rulers of Hesse-Cassel, Hanover, and Saxony were also forced to grant constitutions or liberalize existing documents. The general liberal tide was also reflected in elections in Bavaria, Württemberg and Baden, and the Burschenschaften surfaced again, with greater boldness and strength than ever. In 1831, the Bavarian parliament forced King Ludwig I (1825-48) to dismiss his interior minister and to withdraw the repressive press decree the minister had countersigned by threatening to withhold the budget. In early 1832, the Baden diet forced the granting of complete press freedom there by similar threats.

The rising tide of nationalist sentiment in Germany was fueled in the spring of 1832 by the migration of several thousand refugees from the failed Polish Revolution of 1830-1. They were hailed by German liberals and nationalists as defenders of liberty and western civilization against Russian barbarism, feted at numerous banquets, supplied with substantial sums of money and lionized in scores of poems and songs, known as Polenlieder. To avoid the ban on political parties, a series of liberal and radical "banquets" and "festivals" were held in various parts of Germany to demand further reforms. The greatest of these was the mass meeting of about 20,000 Germans at Hambach (the Hambacher Fest) in the Bavarian Palatinate on May 27, 1832, sponsored by the Press and Fatherland Society, an organization formed in early 1832 by two radical journalists, Philipp Seibenpfeiffer and Johann Wirth, to promote press freedom and a united German republic. The Hambacher Fest was completely peaceful, featuring beer-drinking, patriotic songs and denunciations of the repressive policies of the Confederation diet and the German states.

Metternich had been forced to devote his attention to stamping out revolution in Italy in 1831 and early 1832, but the Hambacher Fest and growing unrest in Germany caused him and the rulers of many of the German states increasing anxiety. In early 1832, the Confederation diet, acting under the 1819 Carlsbad Decrees, ordered the suppression of several newspapers published in Bavaria and Württemberg, including those of Siebenpfeiffer and Wirth. The Bavarian government banned the Press and Fatherland Society shortly after its organization, and following the Hambacher Fest sent troops into the Palatinate to enforce martial law. Siebenpfeiffer and Wirth were given two-year jail terms, and scores of other radicals fled Germany. In June and July 1832 the Confederation diet, under strong Austro-Prussian pressure, passed the so-called Six Acts and Ten Articles, which collectively obligated German rulers to uphold the monarchial principle, curbed the state diets' powers, further restricted the press, and banned political associations, popular demonstrations and festivals, the wearing of political badges or colors, the flying of political flags and the planting of liberty trees.

The repressive crackdown of 1832 led a small group of radicals, mostly instructors and students affiliated with the Burschenschaften at Heidelberg and nearby universities, to turn to conspiratorial plotting. On April 3, 1833 about 50 insurgents occupied several public buildings in Frankfurt as part of a plot to seize the Confederation diet in hopes of setting off a general German revolution. There was no public response to the so-called Wachensturm ("storming of the guardhouse") revolt, which was easily suppressed and followed by a new wave of repression. About 1,800 people, including 1,200 Burschenschaften members, were rounded up in mass arrests. Eleven Frankfurt revolutionaries were given life sentences and others implicated in the rising got long jail terms. The Prussian government sentenced 39 Burschenschaften members to death--later commuted to life imprisonment--and another 150 to long-term or life jail terms. "The secret interrogations, the solitary confinement, the prolonged starvation, the deprivation of sleep and the physical punishment made political persecution a terrible and unforgettable experience and brought the governments, especially the Prussian, into deepest ill repute" (Langer 1969: 112).

Repressive controls continued to tighten in Germany after 1833. Thus, the Confederation diet prohibited German students from attending suspect Swiss universities at Zurich and Bern, forbade journeymen from going to countries "in which associations and meetings exist openly aimed at endangering and destroying public order" (Noyes 1966: 50) and outlawed the entire literary school known as Young Germany, on the grounds it attacked religion in a "most insolent manner," "demeaned" existing social relationships, and disturbed all "manners and morality" (Werner 1977: 165). The resurrected Central Investigating Committee of Carlsbad days compiled a list of 2,140 politically suspect individuals between 1833 and 1842. The gains of 1830 were reversed everywhere except in Baden, Württemberg, and Saxony, where a few traces of liberalism remained. In Hesse-Cassel, the 1830 constitution was undermined by the brutal and sadistic Prince Regent Federick William and his hated minister Hans Hassenplug, while Professor Sylvester Jordan of the University of Marburg, who had authored the document, was dismissed from his post. Bavarian King Ludwig I and his reactionary minister, Karl von Abel, grew increasingly repressive. Metternich crowed that his system had proved "triumphantly fireproof" (Bruun 1960: 43).

The apex of the post-1830 repression was reached in 1837 in Hanover, where the new king, Ernst Augustus (1837-51)--described by one German historian as a man who found a "certain delight in disturbing the peace, denying justice, stamping out happiness and mocking at the modest and weak" (Valentin 1940: 110-11)--revoked the liberal constitution of 1833 and fired seven leading members of the University of Göttingen who protested his action. Another cause célèbre was the 1837 Prussian jailing of the archbishop of Cologne for refusing to carry out Prussian policy on mixed marriages that conflicted with papal directives.

Italy. The July Revolution greatly encouraged Italian conspirators, especially since French officials repeatedly made public statements that suggested that the new government would not tolerate outside intervention in Italy (thus hinting that Austrian intervention against risings in the peninsula would lead to a French military response). Acting under this delusion, Carbonari exiles in France and two Modenese patriots, Ciro Menotti and Enrico Misley, planned revolts for Modena, Parma, and the Papal States in hopes of forming a unified constitutional regime in central Italy. Misley and Menotti counted on support from the reactionary and treacherous Duke Francis IV of Modena, in return for supporting his well-known ambitions for territorial aggrandizement. Francis, who had discussed the plot with Misley and Menotti, apparently without entirely committing himself, betrayed the conspirators at the last moment, surrounding Menotti's house in Modena on the evening of February 3, 1831 and arresting the leading rebels. Nonetheless, the rising broke out as scheduled in outlying parts of Modena, then spread to Parma and throughout the Papal States, except in Rome and a few nearby cities. The major demand of the revolts was for constitutional government, and, in the Papal States, lay participation in government.

The newly elected pope, Gregory XVI (1831-46), and the deposed rulers of Modena and Parma requested Austrian aid. Austrian troops restored them to their thrones while France stood by--partly because of Russian and Prussian threats to support Austria if France intervened in Italy. Duke Francis burned all compromising documents and had Menotti hanged before he issued a limited amnesty decree in October 1831. Pope Gregory withdrew the amnesty he had promised to entice the surrender of 38 prominent rebels, and many of them were jailed by the Austrians for nine months in Venice and then exiled by the papal regime. Hundreds of others compromised in the risings fled into exile. Austrian troops withdrew from the Papal States in July 1831 under French pressure, after Pope Gregory promised to accept some reforms urged upon him by the European powers. However, the papal regime soon sabotaged the reforms and returned to its usual misgoverning ways, leading to new uprisings in the Romagna. Austrian and papal troops were sent into Bologna in early 1832 to put down the revolt, and as a counter-balance France occupied Ancona. The Papal States remained under this joint occupation until 1838.

The collapse of the 1831-2 insurrections and the general crackdown that followed brought about the final demise of the Carbonari. A new generation of Italian revolutionaries emerged after 1830 under the leadership of Giuseppe Mazzini, a Genoese who had been exiled for life from Sardinia in 1831 for urging King Charles Albert (1831-49) to proclaim a constitution and lead a crusade for Italian unity. From his exile bases in France, Switzerland, and ultimately England, Mazzini turned his enormous energies to the creation of and propagandizing for a new revolutionary organization, Young Italy. Although the repressive conditions of Italian life forced Young Italy to adopt the same conspiratorial techniques fostered by the Carbonari, unlike the latter group Young Italy used the press to proclaim its aim--the creation of a unified and independent Italian republic.

Mazzini was enormously successful as a propagandist, but he was far less successful in his pragmatic revolutionary attempts. His repeated conspiratorial plotting, which obsessed him until his death in 1872, invariably ended in total fiasco and led to the deaths and arrests of scores of men. Mazzini's first major plot, an attempt to organize a military conspiracy in Piedmont, was uncovered in mid-1833 when two soldiers loudly accused each other of telling their common female friend too much about the scheme. Subsequent investigations led to about 100 arrests, 14 executions and the complete destruction of the widespread Young Italy network in Piedmont. Mazzini, who was sentenced to death in absentia, immediately began planning another revolt, which called for Italian exiles and volunteers to invade Piedmont from Switzerland and simultaneously stage a rising in Genoa after arriving from Marseilles by boat. This plot collapsed in complete confusion in early 1834 with arrests in Genoa and the dissolution of the invading army from Switzerland before any significant action was taken. Another crackdown followed in Italy, with arrests of members of Young Italy in Tuscany, Naples, and Lombardy-Venetia.

The 1835-9 period was characterized by a continuation of rule by reactionary absolutist princes, supported by the censorship and secret police. The Papal States did not allow railroads for fear of subversives who might enter. The Two Sicilies did not allow trains to operate at night and tunnels were not used because of the perceived moral consequences of darkened railway cars. The long pattern of papal misrule, corruption and near-anarchy intensified under Pope Gregory XVI. The Italian writer Massimo d'Azeglio wrote, "If you ask a youth in Romagna if he has been in prison, he replies, 'I am hardly a man or I should'" (King 1912: 143). The British historian Thomas Macauley, visiting Rome in 1838, commented:

> The states of the Pope are, I suppose, the worst governed in the civilized world; and the imbecility of the police, the venality of the public servants, the desolation of the country and the wretchedness of the people force themselves upon the observation of the most heedless travellers (Thompson 1967: 105).

To combat continuing unrest in the Romagna and Marches, the papal government continued to enlist bands of irregular ruffians, known as the Centurions, who numbered an estimated 50,000. The Centurions waged guerrilla warfare against liberals while enjoying complete immunity from prosecution themselves. The archbishop of Imola, later to become Pope Pius IX, complained to his superiors that at least 20,000 citizens under his jurisdiction were under sentence for political offenses, that the Centurions included undisciplined and criminal elements and that the police commissioner was "one of those Papalini who are fanatics to the point of folly and would like to see 15 people hanged every hour" (Hales 1954: 275).

The Russian Empire. The repressive inclinations of Czar Nicholas I, already stoked by the 1825 Decembrist revolt, were greatly fueled by the 1830 revolutions in Europe, a November 1830 uprising in Poland and cholera riots in Russia in 1830-1. The Polish uprising was the product of conspiracies in the Polish army and among student groups that reflected general dissatisfaction with Russian rule and repression among the gentry and urban classes. It was touched off by reports that the Russians were about to arrest conspirators. In Warsaw and the former Polish provinces of Lithuania, the revolt took on a genuinely popular character, but the failure of the middle-class and gentry leadership of the rising to offer the peasantry meaningful reforms, divisions within the ranks of the leadership, and the failure of the western countries to come to Poland's aid doomed the movement.

As the revolution collapsed, about 9,000 Poles, including the nation's intellectual elite, fled the country, while the Russian government instituted a campaign of severe repression and Russification. Reprisals were especially intense in the formerly Polish-controlled provinces of western Russia that had not been part of the Congress Kingdom (the western guberniias), where the rebels were regarded as traitorous Russian subjects rather than Poles. The guberniias were exempted from the amnesty (excluding leaders of the revolt) applied to the Congress Kingdom in November 1831, and in order to reduce Polish influence there about 54,000 members of the lesser gentry were deprived of their noble status and deported to eastern and southern Russia. The Polish language was eliminated from administrative use in the guberniias in favor of Russian, the University of Wilno was closed and centers of Polish culture were harassed or dismantled. In the Congress Kingdom, the 1815 constitution was suspended and the Polish parliament and army were abolished. Military rule was maintained in Congress Poland for 24 years, institutions of higher learning were shut down, and many library and museum collections were transported to Russia proper. Almost 1,150 persons who fled the Congress Kingdom were sentenced to death in abstentia and the property of 2,300 exiles was seized.

In Russia proper, the 1830-1 cholera epidemic killed over 250,000 people and sparked serious riots in Tambov, Saratov, and Kursk provinces, in St. Petersburg, and in the Novgorod province military colonies. As in almost simultaneous cholera riots in Hungary, the disorders were sparked by brutal, ineffective and stifling quarantine regulations, as well as by rumors of poison plots. Czar Nicholas had the units considered most responsible for the Novgorod disorders marched to St. Petersburg, where they were subjected to public beatings. "Birches, rods and the knout were all employed; more than 2500 men were bloodied and beaten, and 129 lay dead when justice's orgy was finally finished" (McGrew 1965: 121). Shortly thereafter a decision was made to phase out the military colonies, although the process took 25 years to complete.

After 1830, Nicholas's long rule, which lasted another 25 years, increasingly froze Russia into an intellectual, social, and political Siberia like Francis's Austria. One popular historian has exaggerated only slightly by writing that "except in purely chronological terms, nothing happened over a span of nearly 30 years" (Crankshaw 1976: 43-4). One czarist civil servant commented toward the end of Nicholas's rule, "The main failing of the reign of Nicholas Pavlovich was that it was all a mistake" (Crankshaw 1976: 44). Nicholas was obsessively insecure and fearful of subversion, factors that combined with his rigid and authoritarian personality and his military mania led him to desire to control everything in Russian life. He constantly appeared in military dress, personally designed army uniforms down to the ribbons and buttons and never tired of military parades and reviews. In 1839 he had the Battle of Borodino of the Napoleonic wars re-enacted on the site, with 150,000 soldiers dragooned to play out their roles. One observer of Nicholine Russia commented, "Fish swam in the water, birds sang in the forest because they were permitted to do so by the authorities" (Riasanovsky 1969: 221). On one occasion Nicholas read a report ending with the word "progress," and stormed, "Progress! What Progress? That word shall be struck from out of the official vocabulary" (Fejto 1973: 395). On another occasion, after a marriage had been annulled, Nicholas announced, "This young lady shall be considered a virgin" (Riasanovsky 1969: 199).

Restrictions on foreign travel and the press were drastically tightened after 1830, and the powers of the notorious Third Section—the secret police—were expanded. Intellectuals and writers suffered constant harassment. One author, Peter Chaadayev, was personally declared insane by Nicholas and subjected to a temporary form of house arrest after his Philosophical Letters, which had circulated clandestinely for years in manuscript, slipped through the censorship and was published in 1836. The literary critic Viassarion Belinsky was expelled from the University of Moscow in 1831 for writing a story attacking serfdom, and his very name was banned from the press. Alexander Herzen, later the leading intellectual émigré of Nicholine Russia, was banished to a remote province in 1834 for organizing a student group that discussed utopian socialism; he was branded by the Third Section "a daring free thinker, extremely dangerous" (Langer 1969: 159-60). Nicholas's minister of education, the reactionary Count Serge Uvarov (1832-49), told one of his assistants, "Russian literature should be abolished ... then I will at least sleep undisturbed" (Monas 1961: 181).

The Habsburg Empire. The Habsburg Empire was little affected by the events of 1830, save for a "little coffee-house talk and the appearance of a few mildly pink literary effusions" (Macartney 1978: 57). In Hungary, the only real trouble spot in the Empire, there was considerable sympathy for the Poles by Magyar nobles who identified their own struggle against German-Austrian domination with the Poles' fight against Russia. However, the major impact of the 1830 Polish revolt upon Hungary came from the spreading of the Russian cholera epidemic over the Polish-Hungarian frontier by fleeing Polish soldiers. The devasting epidemic killed over 230,000 Hungarians and triggered a massive peasant uprising in the most-affected northern counties. The uprising reflected long-standing peasant grievances as well as harsh and inefficient quarantine regulations and the usual rumors that the upper class was deliberately carrying out a poison plot to kill off the poor. An estimated 45,000 peasants, joined by some petty nobles, attacked and burned the mansions of the landed magnates and barbarously murdered a number of nobles, officials, priests and Jews. Retaliation was swift and brutal. Fifteen peasants were killed by troops in one encounter; 119 executions were carried out; and there were hundreds of jailings, including 700 imprisonments in Zemplen County.

The already stifling political controls were further tightened in the Habsburg Empire as a result of the events of 1830. Thus, Austrian students were barred from studying at foreign universities. Emperor Francis told a top aide in 1831, "I won't have any innovations. ... This is no time for reforms. The people, as it were, are badly wounded. One must avoid irritating these wounds by touching them" (Seton-Watson 1965: 170). The most disastrous result of Francis's rigid conservatism was his decision that, to uphold the principle of legitimacy, his eldest son Ferdinand should succeed him, even though Ferdinand was feeble-minded to the point of idiocy. Of Emperor Ferdinand (1835-48), the Russian Empress wrote, "Good heavens, I had heard much of him, of his puny, wizened figure, his great head devoid of any expression save stupidity, but the reality transcends all descriptions" (Valentin 1940: 14). One top bureaucrat termed the Austrian regime after 1835 an "absolute monarchy without a monarch" (Seton-Watson 1965: 179). Power in Austria after Francis's death in 1835 fell into the hands of a State Conference consisting of Metternich, Count Anton Kolowrat and Archduke Ludwig, Francis's least distinguished brother. Under this troika, the Austrian administration became increasingly paralyzed since Metternich and Kolowrat hated each other. Kolowrat wrote that Metternich viewed himself as someone who "all his life has never been wrong, has foreseen everything and still foresees everything that happened and didn't happen. In a word, I can't get on with him" (Seton-Watson 1965: 181).

Although Ferdinand—popularly known as "Nandle der Trottel" (Dottled Ferdy)—began his reign with an extensive amnesty for political prisoners that benefitted many Italians, the basic character of the regime remained a centralized and bureaucratic police state. The only vigorous actions of the State Conference in the 1835-9 period were attempts to crush Polish conspiracies in Galicia and the resurgent Hungarian nationalist movement. Polish underground groups in Galicia were repeatedly broken up as they sought to foster peasant uprisings, and hundreds of Poles were jailed in the former Carmelite headquarters in Lemberg (Lvov) or at the fortresses at Spielberg and Kufstein. In Hungary, the period after the 1831 peasant revolt witnessed a marked increase in nationalist sentiment and a growing feeling among influential sectors of the gentry and small professional class that Hungary needed major social reforms to modernize and strengthen the country. After the modestly reformist 1832-6 Hungarian "long diet" adjourned, the Habsburg government filled key government posts in Hungary with reactionary officials and arrested Louis Kossuth, a diet member who had become well known through his widely circulated accounts of proceedings of the diet and the Hungarian county assemblies mailed in violation of Austrian press laws and the long-standing tradition of secrecy that enveloped governmental proceedings. At about the same time as Kossuth's arrest in May 1837 for disloyalty and treason, four young Hungarian jurists were arrested for treason, and Baron Miklos Wesselényi, leader of the opposition in the Transylvanian diet, was charged with sedition and treason. Kossuth and Wesselényi were given three-year jail terms; one of the jurists, Ladislas Lovassy, got ten years; two others got light sentences; and the fourth, a government agent provocateur, was released immediately despite a ten-year jail sentence. Kossuth became a national martyr as the result of his widely publicized trial. There was also great indignation over the long sentence given Lovassy, who went insane in prison.

## The United Kingdom and the Minor Continental States, 1830-1839

In contrast to the failure of the 1830-2 disturbances to foster political liberalization in the major continental regions, in the United Kingdom and the minor continental states they generally led to or facilitated significant turning points in liberal constitutional development (although with the major exception of Switzerland the reforms were generally moderate and failed to encompass the lower classes). In the United Kingdom, the disorders elsewhere considerably fueled popular agitation that led to a landmark, if highly restricted, expansion of the suffrage. In Scandinavia, the disturbances led to the first crack in the regime of total absolutism that had ruled in Denmark for 170 years, spurred the organization of the Norwegian peasantry, and greatly encouraged liberal forces in Sweden. In Switzerland, the 1830 disturbances gained striking democratic reforms in about half of the cantons, while in Belgium independence was won from the Dutch and a constitution with extensive civil liberties protections, albeit a highly restricted suffrage, was adopted. In Iberia, the disorders elsewhere in Europe helped to encourage liberal forces that eventually bested absolutism in both Spain and Portugal by 1834, although the triumphant Iberian constitutionalists were soon torn apart by internal dissension that kept the peninsula in a state of constant turmoil. In most of these countries, the regimes of the 1830s were still conservative and often repressive, but in general some dissent was tolerated, if not encouraged, and repression was far less harsh and pervasive than in the major continental states.

The Balkans were at most only slightly affected by the 1830-2 disorders elsewhere in Europe, but the post-1830 period there witnessed trends roughly similar to those experienced by the other minor continental states. Thus, in Serbia and Greece there was rising discontent after 1830 with the systems of absolutism that prevailed, while in Bulgaria and the Danubian Principalities there was growing opposition to Turkish and Russian domination, respectively.


## The United Kingdom.

The entire decade of the 1830s was a period of severe unrest in Great Britain, as was the 1830-3 period in Ireland. The marked increase in dissent in the United Kingdom in the early part of the decade was due partly to the French example and partly to the severe depression of 1827-32 in Great Britain and continued economic distress in Ireland, including crop failures in 1829 and 1832. The Irish peasantry, who had lost their suffrage in gaining Catholic emancipation for the middle class in 1829, returned their attention afterwards to their fundamental grievances--high rents, lack of security against evictions and compulsory tithe payments to support the hated Church of England. In 1830-3 there was a resurgence of traditional rural violence fostered by secret societies and supported by small farmers. There was also a simultaneous but organizationally unrelated non-violent campaign against tithe payments led by larger farmers and Catholic priests.

The basic technique of the 1830-3 "Tithe War" was the use of non-violent resistance and ostracism directed against those who tried to collect the tithe or agreed to pay it. Since any combination advocating tithe abolition was illegal, organizational meetings were held under the guise of hurling matches, and anti-tithe agitation was carried on at meetings called for other purposes. The campaign was extraordinarily successful: in 1833 Church tithe agents collected less than 2 per cent of the money owed. One military officer in County Kilkenny noted that when tithe enforcement was at issue, "the Population of Every Grade appears as one man in determined Opposition & hostility to the System" (Palmer 1977: 16). Despite the non-violent orientation of the anti-tithe campaign, clashes between peasants and tithe agents and their protecting forces frequently erupted. About 30 peasants and 13 police were killed in three major clashes between 1831 and 1834. Over 400 Irishmen were transported to Australia between 1831 and 1835 in connection with the "Tithe War" and the upsurge of rural violence. The tithe and agrarian agitation died down after 1833, after the government set up a special fund to pay the tithe and a stiff new Coercion Act was passed empowering officials to suspend habeas corpus in specified districts and to outlaw all meetings in such areas, even those called to petition parliament. In 1838 a permanent solution to the tithe dispute was found: the tithe was assessed on the landlord instead of on the tenant, so peasants paid it only indirectly through rent increases rather than directly to church agents.

In Great Britain, there was excitement in the early 1830s over demands for parliamentary reform, as well as severe agrarian disturbances and scattered outbursts of industrial unrest. The conservative Tory ministry of the Duke of Wellington resigned on November 16, 1830 upon losing a financial measure in the Commons, shortly after Wellington had aroused great anger by proclaiming that the existing parliamentary system "possesses the full and entire confidence of the people" (Willcox 1971: 207). An 18-month struggle for parliamentary reform followed, in which the new Whig ministry under Lord Grey (1830-4) pushed for a highly conservative reform measure, designed, as Grey put it, to "prevent the necessity for revolution" (Brock 1973: 336). The general fears of revolution, if reform were not implemented, were greatly heightened by an extraordinary outburst of rural violence that convulsed southeastern England between mid-1830 and mid-1831, peaking immediately after Wellington's resignation. The so-called Captain Swing riots aimed at higher wages and the destruction of threshing machines that threatened the jobs of agricultural laborers, who lived on the margins of existence even in good times. Altogether, there were almost 1,500 incidents reported during the Swing distrubances, including over 400 cases of machine-breaking, over 300 cases of arson and over 250 riots for higher wages and other demands. The Whig administration put down the disorders with stunning severity, especially since the only fatality during the disturbances was a single rioter shot by troops. Over 250 persons were sentenced to death, of whom 19 were actually executed, 481 were transported to Australia and 644 were jailed.

The Grey ministry presented its reform bill to the Commons in March 1831, as the Swing riots were petering out. The bill aimed at curbing the worst abuses of the old electoral system through the elimination or reduction of the representation of the rotten boroughs. It created new seats for the growing industrial towns and established a highly restrictive, but uniform, suffrage for all boroughs for the first time. Above all, the measure sought to block the emergence of a middle-class/lower-class coalition against the regime by co-opting the middle class. As the report of the Whig committee that formulated the bill stated, the measure sought to remove "all rational grounds for complaint from the minds of the intelligent and independent portion of the community" (Gash 1979: 147). Despite the highly conservative nature of the bill—as finally passed, it enfranchised about 3 per cent of the population of the United Kingdom, compared with about 2 per cent in 1830—when first introduced, it was defeated in the Commons. New elections in April 1831 were decisively won by reformers on the platform "the bill, the whole bill and nothing but the bill." Nonetheless, when reintroduced, the measure was defeated by the House of Lords in October 1831. Only the threat by King William IV (1831-7) to pack the Lords, and widespread fears of revolution, convinced the peers to pass the reform on June 4, 1832. The final measure not only enfranchised less than 15 per cent of the adult male population of the United Kingdom, but also maintained the open ballot and did nothing to curtail the corruption and bribery that were endemic in British and Irish elections. Gross disparities in the size of electoral constituencies remained, so that less than 20 per cent of the 800,000 voters balloted for 331 of the 658 members of the Commons.

During the period when the reform bill was under consideration, tens of thousands of people joined organizations and attended meetings to press for passage of the bill, such as the 200,000 who turned out for a meeting in Birmingham in May 1832. There was also considerable industrial unrest during the 1830-2 period, and in perhaps a score of cases industrial and political unrest combined to produce serious rioting, as at Bristol in October 1831. About a dozen people were killed and several hundred wounded before troops suppressed three days of rioting at Bristol, during which several government buildings were sacked or burned and prisoners were freed from jails. Four of the rioters were subsequently hanged and 26 were transported to Australia. In 1834, the Whigs, rechristened the Liberals, consolidated their 1832 triumph over the Conservatives (formerly the Tories) when an attempt by King William IV to appoint a Conservative ministry in defiance of a Whig parliamentary majority was rebuffed on appeal to the electorate, thereby establishing the principle that the crown would only appoint a ministry with a majority in the Commons. However, the working classes were bitterly disappointed that the "liberal" victories of 1832 and 1834 led to no change in their political impotence and economic misery. The 1832-4 liberal triumph opened the way to political influence for the rich businessmen, but otherwise left the British political system intact.

Legislation passed in the wake of the 1832 reform was

conservative in orientation and failed to address lower-class grievances. The municipal suffrage was expanded slightly in 1835, leaving the workers still disenfranchised, and while newspaper taxes were reduced in 1836 after a long and bitter struggle, the remaining taxes were still so high workers could not afford to buy newspapers (if they belonged to the literate half of the British population). In an attempt to cut down expenditures, the poor law was reformed in 1834, making the conditions of obtaining relief so unpleasant that workers were likely to turn to it only out of desperation.

Many workers disappointed with the 1832 reform bill and what followed turned to labor organization. Several attempts were made to build large-scale labor unions, the most comprehensive of which was the Grand National Consolidated Trade Union (GNCTU) under the presidency of the utopian reformer Robert Owen. The GNCTU sought to organize workers in all fields and to transform society through the use of the peaceful general strike along cooperative lines. The GNCTU grew enormously in a short period in 1834, attracting perhaps 500,000 members (although the lack of any dues structure makes the significance of this figure unclear). A series of hasty strikes, intense employer resistance, and the overbuilt and unwieldy nature of the GNCTU would probably have brought the organization down or led to a reshaping of its structure and objectives in any case, but the government dealt a death-blow to the movement in 1834 by prosecuting six agricultural laborers from Tolpuddle for administering "unlawful oaths." The prosecution was brought under an obscure law banning secret oath-taking passed during the Jacobin hysteria of the late 1790s. The Whig government decided to make an example of the six men, who had been in touch with GNCTU officials and had sought to organize agricultural workers. They were sentenced to transportation to Australia for seven years, despite the lack of any evidence linking them to violence or sedition of any kind. This gross miscarriage of justice led to mass worker demonstrations that may have been responsible for the pardoning of the "Tolpuddle Martyrs" in 1836, but it also led to the collapse of the GNCTU.

Working-class attention returned to political affairs in the late 1830s as the result of the failure of the GNCTU, intense anger over the poor law and the severe depression of the late 1830s. Following a series of riots against attempts to implement the poor law in 1837 in northern England, along with strikes and election riots in Glasgow, Manchester, and Birmingham, working-class grievances were gradually drawn together into a campaign for the so-called People's Charter, drafted in 1838 by the leading spirit of the London Working Men's Association, William Lovett. The charter called for universal male suffrage as well as other reforms designed to end electoral discrimination against the poor, including demands for salaries and elimination of the property requirement for members of the Commons, and introduction of the secret ballot. "Chartism" quickly developed into the largest mass movement in British history. Scores of monster demonstrations, often held by torchlight and accompanied by inflammatory rhetoric, attracted hundreds of thousands across Great

Britain in 1838 and 1839. In June 1839, a Chartist petition bearing almost 1.3 million signatures was introduced into the House of Commons, but it was quickly rejected, 235 to 46.

Chartism was always more a congerie of local organizations and grievances than a unified effort, and it was soon riven by divisions between those who favored peaceful agitation only and those who openly preached violence. The advocacy of violence seems to have been mostly bluster and there is little evidence of any serious attempts to plan revolutionary outbreaks, except among a few small bands of extremists. However, the constant talk of violence and evidence that some workers were purchasing or manufacturing weapons and ammunition and drilling in military fashion generated growing governmental alarm. In December 1838, the government banned further torchlight rallies. During the next six months, about 50 Chartists were arrested, often for seditious speech, but in a number of cases for violent offenses. In mid-July 1839, serious disturbances erupted in Birmingham, and for the next month there were scattered strikes and riots in several cities, followed by wide-scale arrests and trials of leading Chartists. On November 4, 1839 a band of over 2,000 coal and iron workers marched upon Newport, Monmouthshire, amidst widespread rumors of an imminent coordinated nationwide rebellion. Although the purpose of the Newport affair remains obscure to this day, it was quickly put down when troops fired on the marchers, killing about 15 and wounding about 50.

The riots of late 1839, the Newport "rising," and a few pathetic insurrectionary outbursts in January 1840 in the West Riding of Yorkshire triggered a general round-up of 500 or so Chartist leaders. By mid-1840 "almost every Chartist of any standing was in jail" (Derry 1963: 132). Many were convicted for acts of violence, but a number were given jail terms on press and speech charges. They included the drafter of the Charter, William Lovett, imprisoned for signing a document supporting popular resistance to government aggression; and the leading Chartist orator, Feargus O'Connor, given an 18-month sentence for seditious libel in his newspaper, the Northern Star, which reached the previously unheard-of circulation of 50,000 copies a week. Although severe and repressive measures were unquestionably used against the Chartists, they were far less harsh than those implemented against the Swing rioters ten years before. While 19 of the Swing rioters were executed and almost 500 were transported to Australia, the 1839-40 eruptions led to no executions and only a handful of transportation sentences.

Switzerland. The 1830 July revolution in France touched off a campaign of petitions and mass demonstrations--sometimes armed--in virtually all of the non-Landesgemeinde cantons, where two-thirds of the Swiss population lived. Demands were for expansion of the suffrage and civil liberties, open legislative sessions, and especially an end to economic and political discrimination against rural regions of the urban cantons. The heart of the movement was in the small towns; particularly impressive demonstrations were staged at Uster in Zurich canton (where 10,000 protesters gathered on November 22, 1830) and at Münsingen in Berne canton. Following considerable excitement, agitation, and in some cases, intimidation, ten cantons (Aargau, Thurgau, Zurich, Solothurn, Lucerne, Vaud, Glarus, St. Gallen, Fribourg, and Schaffhausen) bowed to most or all of the demands before any blood was shed. Open legislative sessions, freedom of speech, association, press, trade, and religion, and universal manhood suffrage were proclaimed in most of these so-called regenerated cantons.

Swiss politics during the 1834-8 period was dominated by foreign pressure to crack down on political refugees. Many Italians, Germans, and Poles fleeing the post-1830 reaction had found refuge and freedom to publish attacks upon their native governments in Switzerland. Mazzini's abortive attempt in early 1834 to launch an invasion of Sardinia from Switzerland led to a chorus of threatening demands from the conservative powers that activist refugees be expelled and their organizations dissolved. In mid-1834, the Swiss executive and diet declared that all refugees who menaced the peace of other states would be expelled. The expulsion decree was not completely enforced in all cantons, leading the conservative powers to threaten a blockade of Swiss frontiers in mid-1836. In August 1836 the Swiss diet again demanded the expulsion of activist refugees. While the cantons pondered the new decree, it was discovered that one "refugee," Auguste Conseil, whose expulsion the French had specifically demanded, was in fact a paid French agent. France broke diplomatic relations with Switzerland and sent troops to blockade the Swiss frontier after the diet had the audacity to appoint a committee to investigate the Conseil affair, whereupon the diet voted to apologize and submit to French demands in October 1836. In 1838, French-Swiss relations were again threatened when Louis Napoleon took refuge in Switzerland following his expulsion from France after he unsuccessfully attempted to stage a coup d'état in 1836. France demanded Louis Napoleon's expulsion and concentrated 25,000 troops on the Swiss border. The crisis ended when Louis Napoleon voluntarily left Switzerland, even as Swiss nationalists held protest meetings and prepared for battle.

The Low Countries. In Belgium the 1830 July revolution in France intensified the anti-Dutch agitation that had been building since 1815. On August 25, 1830, serious rioting erupted in Brussels. Reflecting both anti-Dutch sentiment and the anger and despair of the poor amidst terrible economic conditions, the rioting spread to other cities and featured attacks on symbols of Dutch rule and upon the houses and companies of rich Belgians. To control the lower classes, middle- and upper-class Belgian liberals and Catholics formed civic guards and a provisional government that declared Belgian independence on October 4, after 10,000 Dutch troops were forced to withdraw following four days of bloody fighting. In February 1831, a constituent assembly called by the provisional government and elected on a suffrage that enfranchised only 46,000 Belgians--less than the 60,000 entitled to vote for the former United Netherlands parliament and amounting to

1.1 per cent of the population--produced a constitution that was regarded as startlingly liberal elsewhere in Europe. Freedom of the press, speech, assembly, organization, and religion were established, as was the principle of parliamentary responsibility. However, trade unions and strikes remained illegal and the suffrage was kept at 1.1 per cent of the populace.

Dutch King William I refused to accept the June 1831 decision of a congress of European powers to sanction Belgian independence. The result was that Belgium and the rump Dutch Netherlands remained in a technical--and until 1832, physical--state of war. It paralyzed all other political activity in both countries until William suddenly announced in 1838 his willingness to accept a modified settlement concerning borders and division of the debt that had been offered by the European powers in October 1831.

Scandinavia. The 1830 European revolutions encouraged liberal tendencies and organization throughout Scandinavia. The grip of the Danish and Swedish monarchs and of the Norwegian bureaucrats, however, was only slightly eased in the 1830s. Given the general political apathy in Scandinavia during the Restoration, one historian has nonetheless aptly likened the impact of 1830 to "rain after a drought" (Hovde 1943: 518).

In Sweden, the 1830 revolutions gave encouragement to the liberal movement that had been growing slowly. A major liberal newspaper, Aftonbladet, was founded, and with its stinging attacks on royal autocracy, the paper became the leading arsenal in the liberal movement and the largest circulation newspaper in Sweden. Although King Charles John responded to the rising liberal tide with a vigorous program of press repression, Aftonbladet, edited by Lars Johan Hierta, evaded repeated withdrawals of its publishing license by changing its name to Second Aftonbladet, Third Aftonbladet, etc. After the Twenty-Third Aftonbladet appeared and a journalist's three-year jail term in 1838 sparked serious riots in Stockholm (which troops supressed at the cost of two lives), Charles John finally terminated his campaign against the opposition press. Between 1830 and 1838, when the king gave up the press battle, newspaper licenses had been revoked in 35 cases in Sweden and 23 press prosecutions were brought for libel or treason. Another tremendous liberal victory was recorded in Sweden in 1838 when the renowned conservative politician Eric Geijer announced his liberal conversion, creating "an intellectual and political earthquake" (Scott 1977: 385).

In Norway, the events of 1830 spurred political interest among the peasantry, who until then had generally accepted the dominant role of the urban bureaucratic-mercantile elements. A major catalyst for this interest was supplied by a peasant politician, John Neergaard. In 1830, Neergaard began distributing a 32-page booklet, the Olaboka (Ole's book), to the peasantry as he travelled around Norway agitating on their behalf. The Olaboka taught the peasants in simple language that only if they elected storting members from their own class would taxation and the oppressive power of the bureaucratic class diminish.

In the 1833 storting elections, peasant representation, which had averaged 23 of 96 members in the previous six elections, jumped to 45, becoming the largest single bloc. Although the peasants failed to crack bureaucratic domination of the government--no peasant served as a government minister until 1884 and none even served as a storting committee chairman until 1851--their concerns could no longer be ignored. The first significant result of the new peasant self-assertiveness was the 1837 law providing local self-government on the same relatively broad suffrage (about 9 per cent of the population) used for storting elections. Norwegian nationalist demands and the storting's abrupt dismissal of King Charles John's old proposals for constitutional revisions to increase his powers in Norway led the king to consider briefly once again a forcible constitutional coup in 1836. However, Swedish-Norwegian relations became less tense for about 20 years thereafter, at least partly because the Norwegian bureaucratic elite realized the king's support might prove useful against lower-class agitation.

In Denmark, the 1830 revolts spurred German nationalist agitation in Schleswig and Holstein, duchies that had belonged to the Danish crown since medieval times but had never become integrated into the Danish kingdom. Holstein was overwhelmingly German in language and culture and was a member of the German Confederation, while Schleswig was Danish in its northern half and German in the south, and did not belong to the confederation. The 1830 German nationalist agitation in the duchies centered around demands for the introduction of constitutional government and the tightening of ties between them, ultimately aimed at establishing German domination in Schleswig and making it a member of the confederation. The leader of the German nationalist movement in the duchies, Uwe Jens Lornsen, was dismissed from his minor official post, sentenced to a year in jail for activities prejudicial to the state, and eventually driven into exile. However, Danish King Frederick VI concluded that something had to be done to dampen the agitation and decided to establish consultative assemblies in the duchies. But realizing that he could not grant his German subjects more than he granted his Danish ones, he expanded the scheme to apply throughout his realm. This move, announced in 1831 and implemented in 1834, was greeted with a storm of approval, even though the four provincial assemblies (one each for Holstein, Schleswig, Jutland, and the Danish Islands) were purely consultative, met in secret, and were elected on a franchise that excluded over 97 per cent of the population.

The consultative assemblies--which marked the first major break in 170 years of purely absolutist rule in Denmark--and the new liberal newspaper Faedrelandet immediately launched a crusade for constitutionalism and political freedom. Soon, Frederick was considering new press regulations even more restrictive than the highly repressive 1799 law--which established the death penalty for advocating change in the government. As a result, almost 600 Danes, including over 100 officials and university professors, quickly signed a protest petition. Frederick's reply that "We alone know" what is good for the people furnished the opposition with a ready-made "symbol of inane autocracy" (Hovde 1943: 542) and led to the formation of the Society for the Proper Use of Freedom of the Press, which quickly attracted 5,000 members. Nonetheless, the king issued a new press law in 1837 that facilitated intensified harassment of Faedrelandet and the rest of the liberal press. Liberals were far more pleased by the royally decreed institution of self-government for Danish towns in 1837 (save Copenhagen, which had to wait until 1840) and for rural areas in 1841.

Iberia. The 1830 European revolutions led to an intensification of the reactionary nature of the regimes of Ferdinand VII in Spain and Miguel in Portugal, but also encouraged the liberal-constitutionalist oppositions. The liberal-constitutionalist forces triumphed by 1834 in both countries, but promptly split into bitter factions that kept Iberia embroiled in constant turmoil.

Two liberal risings in Portugal in 1831 and several attempted invasions of Spain by exile groups based in France and England in 1830-2 all failed, and were followed by the usual executions and jailings. In Portugal, Miguel's reign of terror reached its height in 1831, under the slogan "Death to the Liberals and Freemasons." However, the threat from the Portuguese left grew when Miguel's brother Pedro abdicated his Brazilian throne and returned to Europe in mid-1831 to lead his daughter Maria's cause against her uncle Miguel. Pedro openly recruited and equipped an army in England and France, whose governments were alienated by Miguel's arbitrary treatment of their citizens in Portugal and feared the growing influence of Austria, Russia, and Prussia in Portugal. Pedro sailed with 7,600 volunteers and mercenaries from France to the Azores and then to Oporto on the mainland, where he arrived in June 1832.

In Spain, justice minister Calomarde closed all universities from 1830 to 1832 to avoid meetings of "restless young people" (Livermore 1960: 365). Meanwhile, the right-wing opposition in Spain was becoming increasingly threatening. The October 1830 birth of a daughter, Isabel, to King Ferdinand's fourth wife threatened to deprive the ultra-reactionary forces of their expected triumph with the accession of Ferdinand's brother Carlos. Bitter disputes over the succession broke out between the partisans of Carlos and those of Isabel. Since Ferdinand and his wife, María Cristina, were determined that the crown go to their daughter, a bizarre coalition of convenience developed between the Isabeline forces and the constitutionalist forces that Ferdinand had persecuted for years. The coalition shared little more than a common opposition to the Carlists, gravitating together strictly under the principle "Support me and I will support you" (Carr 1966: 153). Although strict censorship was maintained and the king continued his absolute rule, minor concessions were made to the constitutionalists as the dynastic dispute intensified in 1832. The universities were reopened and a political amnesty allowed most of the 10,000 or so exiles of the 1820s to return to Spain.

The parallel succession conflicts in Spain and Portugal intensified during 1833-4 before the liberals triumphed. In Spain, Carlos, the absolutist pretender to the throne, was sent into exile in early 1833, a few months before Ferdinand died. María Cristina then became regent for three-year-old Isabel. In an attempt to conciliate the liberals, Cristina brought returning constitutionalist exiles into the government and issued a royal statute, or constitution, in April 1834. The royal statute established an upper legislative chamber, consisting of the high nobility and clergy together with royal appointees, and a lower legislative chamber elected by less than 0.2 per cent of the population. The legislature was empowered to approve taxes, but could not initiate legislation. The ministry was responsible to the crown alone, which retained an absolute veto. In protest, a major Carlist uprising broke out in northwestern Spain in 1834, backed by the local clergy, nobility and traditionalist peasantry. The Carlist forces were not defeated until 1839, after a bitter war marked by terrible atrocities.

In Portugal, the constitutionalist forces backing the claims of Maria captured Lisbon in July 1833. Pedro, acting as regent for Maria, repromulgated his 1826 constitutional charter (revoked by Miguel in 1828), which roughly paralleled the Spanish Royal Charter of 1834. In April 1834 the governments of Spain, Portugal, France and the United Kingdom signed the Quadruple Alliance to support the constitutionalist forces of Isabel and Maria against the claims of their absolutist uncles. This agreement, with subsequent British naval and financial backing and the entry of Spanish troops into Portugal in support of Maria, ended Miguelist hopes and also sealed the constitutionalists' victory in Spain.

The constitutionalist triumphs were consolidated in both Spain and Portugal by the confiscation and sale of huge amounts of church-owned land. Generally sold below its real value, it fell into the hands of a tiny fraction of the population. Thus, the sales did little to ease the catastrophic financial situations of the new regimes or the plight of the rural masses in either country. However, they did create a small but powerful new landowning bourgeois elite that became intensely loyal to the new regimes. Although remaining feudal dues and jurisdictions were abolished in both countries by 1836, nothing was done to reform tax and conscription systems and other forms of oppression that weighed upon the lower classes.

In both Spain and Portugal, the constitutionalist camps quickly became bitterly divided into two major factions. In each country, a conservative contitutionalist faction emerged dedicated mostly to "law and order" and the new political structure; simultaneously liberal-radical elements emerged that wanted to liberalize the 1834 royally decreed constitutions, expand the suffrage, adopt a stronger anti-clerical line and at least pay lip service to social reform. In both countries the power struggles of the early 1830s had rapidly politicized the urban middle and lower-middle classes, and it was especially to these groups that the liberal-radicals appealed. However, whenever these classes were aroused, causing enough disorder to win power for the liberal-radicals who had called upon them, the liberal-radicals suddenly shifted to the right in fear of what they had created. It became increasingly clear that, except among very small splinter groups on the left, the constitutionalist factions were more united than divided in their basic aims of power and patronage and their basic fear of radical social reform. The elaborate and flowery semantic debates of Iberian politics disguised the real issue between the factions, summed up in the Spanish phrase "Quítate tu para ponerme yo" ("You get out and let me in" [Brenan 1964: 20]).

In both Spain and Portugal, the liberal-radical constitutionalist factions came to power in 1836 by combined military and urban popular uprisings. The liberal constitutions of 1812 (Spain) and 1822 (Portugal) were forced upon Spanish Queen Regent María Cristina and Portuguese Queen Maria II (who ruled after the 1834 death of her father Pedro). Once in power, the liberal-radicals began their usual shift to the right. In 1837 in Spain and in 1838 in Portugal new constitutions were drawn up. They were compromises between the conservative 1834 royal documents and the earlier liberal constitutions. Both established two-house legislatures in which each house was elected by a highly restricted suffrage. In each the crown was empowered to appoint ministers, veto legislation, and dissolve the chambers. In Spain, about 2 per cent of the population was enfranchised, a figure ten times greater than in the 1834 charter and ten times smaller than in the 1812 constitution.

The compromise constitutions failed to stop the struggle for power and position. In Portugal, the liberal-radicals or "Septembrists" (they came to power in a September 1836 uprising) were beset by plots and scattered risings on behalf of, variously, Miguel, the 1822 constitution, and the 1834 charter. The continued disorder gradually shifted Portuguese politics to the right, and the "Septembrist" government became increasingly "Chartist" in orientation by 1840. In Spain, the conservative constitutionalists (Moderates) won control of the legislature in the 1840 elections and promptly set about trying to destroy the liberal-radicals (Progressives), attacking their urban lower- and middle-class political base by attempting to increase central control over muncipal governments and drastically decrease the liberal municipal suffrage. Since the local governments had considerable control over election lists and electoral supervision, the passage of a reactionary municipal law in mid-1840 and its ratification by the Queen Regent, despite the measure's clear violation of the spirit of the 1837 constitution, amounted to a Moderate coup d'état. Uprisings in a score of Spanish cities drove the Queen Regent into exile and brought to power a Progressive government under General Baldomero Espartero, a hero of the Carlist war.

The Balkans. In Serbia and Greece, political life in the 1830s centered around growing opposition, especially after 1835, to autocratic rule. The 1830s were marked in Bulgaria by slowly growing opposition to Turkish domination, and in the Danubian Principalities by similar resistance to Russian domination. In general, Balkan politics involved the activities of only a small clique of elites. The general population played almost no political role at all, save in occasional peasant uprisings, and the general economic backwardness of the Balkans blocked the rise of a middle class that might press for civil liberties. Thus, the Serbian and Greek opposition was led by local notables who had little interest in constitutionalism per se, but turned to demands for constitutional rule as a means of protecting themselves against arbitrary rule and gaining a chance to share governmental power and patronage. Similarly, in the principalities the opposition to Russian rule was organized by a small group of western-oriented students, intellectuals and lesser nobles.

In Greece, after a two-year search, the three protecting powers finally found a taker for the throne in May 1832, in Bavarian King Ludwig's 17-year old son Otto. From 1828 to 1831 the nominal ruler of Greece had been John Capodistrias, a Greek-born former Russian foreign minister, who had been elected president by a national assembly in 1827. Capodistrias's modernizing and authoritarian streaks led him to rule in an absolutist and highly centralist fashion that outraged local notables and military captains who had gained prominence during the revolution. The result was three separate revolts in 1830-31, the assassination of Capodistrias in October 1831, and civil war until Otto was chosen king in 1832. The 1832 settlement established boundaries for the new state that were restricted to the Morea and Rumely, thus excluding 75 per cent of the Greek population in the Near East. The settlement also provided that until Otto's twentieth birthday in 1835 power would be held by a three-man regency appointed by Ludwig, thus making Greece a Bavarian protectorate while also subject to the guarantee of France, Russia, and the United Kingdom, which provided financial loans to the new country. King Otto inherited a virtually bankrupt state that had been physically devastated by ten years of war and civil strife. He also inherited a country deeply divided by sectionalism, class cleavage, and three inchoate political parties, each of which looked to one of the three protecting powers for guidance and support. The parties were above all based on personal cliques and all sought mostly patronage and power for their leaders, most of whom had risen to prominence during the revolution and were determined not to be shunted aside.

Greek elites objected to numerous aspects of the policies pursued by the Bavarian regency (1832-5) and during Otto's personal and absolutist rule after he had attained his majority in 1835. First, the top posts in the king's entourage and the army were largely reserved for Bavarians, and until about 1838, the "Greek" army, which absorbed over 40 per cent of all state spending, consisted of 5000 Bavarian troops. Second, the regency, and the king afterwards, pursued a policy of rigid administrative centralization in violation of long traditions of strong local government in Greece. Third, the regency and Otto refused to promulgate a constitution or establish a legislature, thereby preserving all power to themselves and violating pledges made in 1832 by Bavaria and the protecting powers. Bavarian King Ludwig's hand was clearly involved in this policy; he advised his son Otto in 1835 that "a constitution is a lion's den from which no footsteps emerge"

(Petropulos 1968: 270). Fourth, the regency and Otto alienated all three parties by following alternative policies of ignoring all three, placating them all equally, or giving preference to one without really giving any substantive power. Fifth, the policy of Otto toward the Greek Orthodox church was objectionable to many Greeks. Otto, a Catholic, was made head of the Greek church, which was formally separated from the Constantinople patriarchate. This bizarre situation angered many of Otto's subjects, especially when hundreds of monasteries and nunneries in Greece were closed and their property confiscated. All of these policies alienated Greek elites, who, as in the case of the clergy, were deprived of their positions and property, or who, as in the case of secular elites, were deprived of their regional power bases, subjected to arbitrary royal decisions, and shut out of any possibility of wielding significant power in the central administration by the king's preference for absolutism and Bavarian advisers.

The rule of the regency and Otto was by no means brutal and rarely coercive, but the lack of any opportunity for Greek elites to obtain positions of power led to repeated uprisings, which generally ensued from a combination of local grievances, opposition to the king's church policy, demands for constitutionalism, and an end to "Bavarianism." There were two localized revolts in 1834, another in 1836, three in 1838-9 and a major abortive plot uncovered in 1839.

In Serbia, Prince Miloš, as a sop to the continuing complaints about his authoritarian rule, appointed a five-man cabinet in 1834, but it was powerless and entirely dependent upon him. A meeting of several thousand protestors at Kragujevac in January 1835 scared Miloš into granting a surprisingly liberal constitution, but he suspended it shortly thereafter under pressure from Austria, Turkey, and Russia. As a means of warding off growing interference from the other powers and asserting its own nominal sovereignty, Turkey sought to settle the constitutional issue by proclaiming a Serbian constitution on December 24, 1838. The 1838 document established a council of 17 senators, to be appointed by the prince but not removable unless it could be proved to Turkey that they had committed crimes against Serbian law. The council, or senate, was empowered to approve all laws and taxes, although the prince retained an absolute veto. The 1838 constitution also greatly strengthened the power and independence of the Serbian bureaucracy, which under Miloš had been subject to arbitrary treatment, firing and even corporal punishment. The next year was occupied by the inevitable power struggle between Miloš and the council, since the threat of an uprising had forced the prince to appoint his opponents to the senate. The senate steadily gained the upper hand and Miloš abdicated in June 1839 in favor of his son Milan, who died shortly after and was succeeded by Miloš's younger son, Michael, in early 1840. Meanwhile, the senate, in what amounted to a bloodless coup, resolved in 1839 that it, not the prince, would have the power to appoint future senators.

Unrest in Bulgaria during the 1830s reflected peasant resistance to continued Turkish misrule and oppression, and also a slow but steady rise in Bulgarian nationalism, which lagged behind nationalist aspirations elsewhere in the Balkans. This lag reflected the greater Bulgarian territorial proximity to Turkey, the entrenched Greek cultural domination, the relatively small Bulgarian merchant community, and the restricted contacts with western Europe. Minor clashes between bands of armed peasants and Turkish troops occurred almost every year, but in 1835, 1836, and 1837 there was a series of more serious peasant rebellions in northwestern Bulgaria.

Russian troops remained in occupation of the Danubian Principalities from 1829 until 1834 following the 1828-9 Russo-Turkish War. During this period there was considerable peasant unrest, and in 1831 a massive peasant uprising in Moldavia involving an estimated 60,000 insurgents was crushed by Russian cossacks. The four major leaders of the revolt were given ten-year terms in the salt mines, and others received 50 cudgel blows.

During the Russian occupation, the effective ruler of the principalities was the moderately progressive Russian Count Paul Kisselev. Kisselev more or less imposed constitutions, known as the Règlements Organiques (organic statutes) in Wallachia in 1831 and Moldavia in 1832. The Règlements, which were ratified by boyar councils, provided for the election of life-time princes in the two principalities by special assemblies representing the boyars and middle class. Ordinary legislation was to be enacted by assemblies of the highest-ranking clergy, sitting ex officio, and boyars, selected only by other boyars, with a majority chosen by the few dozen great boyars. The economic provisions of the Règlements further entrenched boyar domination of the principalities, clearly establishing their ownership of the land for the first time, reducing the land that the peasants could till by more than one-half and increasing the peasants' forced labor services in exchange for such usage. Although the peasants were technically confirmed in their personal freedom, severe restrictions were placed on their legal right to move, which amounted to a system of de facto quasi-serfdom. One peasant testified in 1848 that the Règlements Organiques:

> confined us on the landlord's estate as in a walled fortress with iron gates, so that there was no way by which we could get out; and even if we ran away, abandoning houses and orchards and vineyards, the work of our parents and our own, and they found our whereabout, they brought us back in chains, just as if we had been slaves, locking us up in their cellars or barns in winter time, with no fire and even throwing water over us that we should freeze, that our sufferings should frighten the others; so that many have remained crippled and cannot feed themselves today (Mitrany 1968: 40-41).

Even after withdrawal of Russian forces from the principalities in 1834, the real power remained in the hands of the Russian consuls in Bucharest (Wallachia) and Jassy (Moldavia). The post-1834 period in the principalities witnessed a slow but steady growth of opposition to the regime of the Règlements, supported by some of the lesser boyars and especially by Rumanian students and intellectuals educated in western Europe or exposed to western ideas. This opposition had a markedly romantic-nationalist focus, stressing the Latin-western heritage of Rumania's language and culture. It aimed at the creation of an independent and united Rumanian nation, opposed Russian domination, stood for constitutional government, and was at least theoretically dedicated to substantial social reform. A considerable amount of plotting and conspiratorial activities were carried on by this opposition, much of which remains obscure.

## The Revival of Political Dissent, 1840-1846

The period of political quiet that characterized the major regions of continental Europe between 1835 and 1839 ended after about 1840. Political dissent re-emerged in those regions, and increased in intensity in other areas, such as Scandinavia and the Balkans, where dissident activity had been growing even before 1840. Except in Iberia, where the theoretically liberal-radical governments that held power in 1840 gave way to highly conservative authoritarian regimes by 1843, the forces of dissent, liberalism, and nationalism gained strength everywhere in Europe between 1840 and 1846.

The marked increase in dissenting activity that characterized virtually all of Europe after about 1840 can be explained by a number of factors. Among them were the accelerated growth of urbanization, trade, industrialization, and population, which created larger middle and lower classes especially susceptible to politicization and political, social, and economic frustration. Industrialization markedly quickened after 1840, as the result of the sudden development of a great railroad boom, which resulted in the laying of 20,000 miles of track in 1840-50, compared with only 4,000 miles before then. Trade also increased significantly after 1840; thus, total international trade in the western world more than tripled between 1780 and 1840, but quadrupled between 1780 and 1850. The growth of mechanization, competition, international commerce, and merchant capitalism frequently destroyed formerly relatively stable local markets and had a severely adverse impact upon the status, prosperity, and independence of many urban artisans, and especially among rural cottage workers in the textile industry. The plight of the English handloom weavers, whose wages dropped by two-thirds between 1820 and 1845, was especially tragic. Rising population and land hunger also seems to have been particularly important in increasing rural unrest, especially in Scandinavia, Ireland, Russia, the Habsburg Empire, and southwestern Germany.

Another factor in stirring discontent was the change in political leadership between 1839 and 1844 in the Netherlands, Denmark, Sweden, and Prussia, resulting from the 1840 abdication of Dutch king William I and the deaths of the Danish, Swedish, and Prussian kings, each of whom had ruled 25 years or more. In each case the change in leadership created great hopes for liberalization, which were quickly frustrated, leaving behind considerably more anger than had existed under the old rulers.

The most important such monarchial change occurred in Prussia, where King Frederick William III died in 1840 after ruling for 43 years. Enormous hopes for political liberalization greeted the accession of King Frederick William IV (1840-58), which were massively fueled when the king began his reign by amnestying the Wachensturm prisoners of 1833 and others jailed for political offenses. He also appointed fired Göttingen professors to Prussian university posts, eased press controls, mended relations with the Catholic church, and eased Germanization pressures on the Polish minority in Poznania, which had become severe after the 1830 Polish revolt. However, it soon became apparent that Frederick William was imbued with a medieval-romantic view of paternalistic absolutism, and liberals became disillusioned as repression soon replaced reconciliation. The press liberalization, for example, lasted only a short time, with the Rhenish Gazette an early casualty. Edited by Karl Marx, it was suppressed in 1843.

Another major example was Denmark, where the death of King Frederick VI in 1839 after 31 years of rule and the accession of Christian VIII (1839-1848) was greeted with extravagant hopes of reform, largely generated by Christian's role as the liberal-nationalist king of Norway during its revolt against Swedish control in 1814. Christian was showered with petitions signed by thousands calling for constitutional government, but he ignored them. He responded similarly to the 1840 requests from the consultative assemblies for Jutland and the Danish Islands for constitutional government. In 1841, as liberal demands increased, the leading constitutionalist spokesman, Orla Lehmann, was jailed for three months for attempting to "spread hatred" (Birch 1938: 323) and transformed into a national martyr. Press prosecutions continued: during a six-month period in 1843, 10 per cent of the issues of the leading liberal newspaper Faedrelandet were confiscated.

Another factor in the rebirth of dissent after 1840 is that in some of the regimes repressive controls were either relaxed or became less efficient, with the result that it became easier to smuggle in banned materials and/or to publish critical accounts that probably would not have passed the censor in the post-1830 period. In a number of countries, certain widely circulated critical books had a major impact in fostering discontent among the urban middle and to a more limited extent, except perhaps in France, lower classes. In the Netherlands, for example, Jan Rudolf Thorbecke, a law professor at the University of Leyden, became the leader of a fledgling liberal movement overnight with the publication in 1839 of his Comment Upon the Constitution, which demanded reform. In the Habsburg Empire, a book published in 1842 and smuggled into the country, Austria and Its Future, created a sensation with its demands for constitutional government and decentralization, especially since it was obvious that the anonymous writer (Baron Victor von Andrian-Werberg) was a high-ranking state official. In Italy, two books published in 1843, Vicenzo Gioberti's On the Moral and Civic Primacy of the Italians and Cesare Balbo's On the Hope of Italy, made a tremendous impact upon middle-class opinion by their stirring nationalism and proposals for the formation of an Italian confederation under the presidency of the pope. France and Germany were both flooded with books and pamphlets on the "social question" (i.e., poverty, and especially urban squalor) during the post-1840 period. Among the most influential of these were two books published in France in 1840, Louis Blanc's Organization of Work and Pierre-Joseph Proudhon's What is Property? and one published in Leipzig in 1845, Friedrich Engel's The Condition of the Working Class in England in 1844. These books and most of the other materials on the "social question" published in France and Germany were passed by the censorship so long as they did not directly criticize the incumbent regimes or officials, even though they amounted to a general condemnation of the entire socio-economic structure.

There was a noticeable upsurge in working class unrest in the more advanced industrial regions in the post-1840 period. In Paris, a major strike wave in 1840, involving over 20,000 workers, was suppressed by military intervention and hundreds of arrests, trials, and sentences of transportation. Between 1844 and 1846 a series of strikes in the Loire mining region of France was suppressed by troops with considerable bloodshed. In Barcelona, the only advanced industrial center in Iberia, rebellions with strong class-conflict overtones erupted in 1841, 1842, and 1843. Industrial distress in Great Britain in 1842--in Manchester over 50 per cent of all workers were idle--led to an outbreak of severe rioting there that summer. At its height in August 1842, the "Plug Plug" riots paralyzed most of the northern and central industrial regions of England and affected industrial centers in Scotland and southern Wales. In Bohemia-Moravia, the most industrially advanced region of the Habsburg Empire, textile workers rioted in 1843-4, while in Prussian Silesia, about 5,000 desperate and starving linen handloom weavers, unable to compete against machine-made cotton fabrics, sacked the homes and factories of the wealthy in June 1844. The Silesian rising was put down by troops who killed 35 protesters, while about 40 survivors were given lashings and long jail terms.

In a number of regions, there were also signs of growing unrest among the peasantry in the post-1840 period. This was especially apparent in Russia, where, according to official statistics, there had been 41 peasant revolts in 1826-40, 44 during 1831-4, and 59 during 1835-9, but 101 in 1840-4. Nicholas's own secret police chief warned him as early as 1834:

> Every year the idea of freedom spreads and grows stronger among the peasants owned by the nobles. In 1834, there have been many examples of peasants' insubordination to their masters. And the enquiries show that nearly all these cases do not derive from ill-treatment or abuses but purely

from the idea of obtaining the right to freedom (Venturi
1966: 65).

Most of the Russian peasant disturbances were small and localized, but
there were major eruptions in 1842 (involving about 130,000 peasants)
in Kazan province and in 1843 in Perm and Orenburg provinces. The
usual response to such disorders was mass arrests, whippings,
conscription, and exile. Thus, over 4,000 were arrested after the 1843
riots. Elsewhere in Europe there were rural outbreaks in western
Wales in 1842-43, and in Slovenia and Transylvania in the Habsburg
Empire in 1845. There was also considerable unrest among peasants in
the Danubian Principalities, and in 1841, three separate uprisings in
Bulgaria. The Bulgarian 1841 uprising at Nish, on the Serbian frontier,
was especially serious, convulsing a large region. It was crushed with
great ferocity. Many Bulgarians were massacred by Turkish troops,
scores of villages were burned, and caravans of Bulgarian women and
children were sold into slavery. Thirty-one severed heads were
displayed on the bridge at the village of Nish. About 10,000 Bulgarians
fled into Serbia to escape the terror.

In Denmark, the 1840s were marked by the rapid growth of a
political peasants' movement that urged both democratic
constitutional reform and such class-based demands as the
transformation of leases into outright peasant ownership and
substitution of universal military service for a conscription system
that drew largely from the peasantry. In the fall of 1845, King
Christian, in the Bondecirkulaeret (Peasant circular), banned political
meetings in rural areas without official permission, thereby
stimulating a tidal wave of protest. This decree stimulated a marriage
of convenience between the peasant and urban constitutionalist
movements in 1846, resulting in the 1846 formation of the Society of
the Friends of the Peasants, which demanded rural and constitutional
reforms.

Growing lower-class urban and rural unrest was supplemented by
increasing middle-class discontent in many of the European countries
after 1840. In Great Britain, middle-class industrialists and reformers
organized a mass campaign to obtain repeal of the Corn Laws, which
artificially kept up the price of grain for the benefit of the landed
upper classes and forced businessmen to pay higher wages than they
wished to so that their workers could afford to eat. In Germany, Italy,
and the Habsburg Empire, middle-class discontent was
constitutionalist-nationalist in orientation. Although overtly political
organizations could not exist in these areas, liberals in the German,
Italian, and Habsburg lands increasingly met informally after 1840 or
used supposedly non-political cultural, literary, and scientific groups
as fronts for political and nationalist discussions. In the Habsburg
Empire, for reasons perhaps related to the conflict between Kolowrat
and Metternich in the State Conference, some of the extreme
repressive controls eased after 1840, and several societies of
businessmen, reformers and intellectuals were allowed to organize in

Vienna. Among them, the Concordia Society, the Legal-Political Reading Club, and the Lower Austrian Manufacturers Association became major liberal opposition centers. Thousands of copies of the newspaper Grenzboten, published in Leipzig, were smuggled into Austria and avidly read for their criticisms of the monarchy, and university students and professors circulated banned materials in classrooms and gathered in private homes to discuss ideas that could not be referred to publicly.

In Great Britain, France, and Sweden, a major focus of the rising post-1840 protest movement was parliamentary reform. In the 1840-1 Swedish riksdag session, liberals who controlled the peasants' and burghers' estates launched a major assault upon the government, demanding electoral reform and the establishment of parliamentary responsibility. The Swedish four-estate legislative system, which gave control of three of the four legislative houses to less than 5 per cent of the population, appeared increasingly anachronistic to the growing middle-class commercial and professional elements. Along with the rapidly increasing numbers of landless laborers and dwarf farmers, they did not fit into any of the traditional estates and were thus completely disenfranchised. Although no fundamental change was effected at the 1840-1 riksdag session, the opposition forced a minor administrative reorganization and the ouster of some of the most conservative ministers, thereby establishing the principle that the king at least had to consider public opinion when making cabinet appointments. In 1844, an extremely conservative proposal for electoral reform was rejected by the noble and clerical estates. The accession of Oscar I (1844-59) in 1844, after 34 years of Charles John's conservative rule, fostered hopes for reform, since Oscar had a reputation for being liberal. Although Oscar formally repudiated the 1812 law that authorized administrative suppression of newspapers and although he appointed more liberal ministers, reduced the interval between riksdag sessions from five to three years, and made a few conciliatory gestures to Norwegian nationalism, the basic political system of Sweden (and that of Norway, which stayed quiet during the 1840-5 period) remained unchanged.

Expansion of the suffrage was the major focus of the French middle-class opposition during the 1840s. The parliamentary opposition, known as the "dynastic left," also concentrated on attacking the gross corruption used in the drawing up of electoral lists and the use of official pressure during elections, as well as Prime Minister Guizot's use of jobbery and manipulation to control parliament. One common practice of Guizot was to encourage government employees to run for parliament, or to appoint elected members (who were unpaid) to government posts, thus creating large numbers of deputies who feared losing their paying jobs if they voted against the regime. By 1846, 184 of the 459 deputies held paying government posts. Although as early as 1837 150,000 Frenchmen had petitioned for suffrage extension, the legislature rejected such a reform measure in 1842.

In Great Britain, the drastic economic relapse of 1841-2 (after a brief recovery in 1840 from the 1837-9 depression), coupled with the release from jail of many Chartist leaders who had been imprisoned in 1839-40, revived the Chartist movement. Over 2 million people petitioned in May 1841 for release of the jailed leaders of the 1839 Newport "rising," and in May 1842 a petition with over 3.3 million signatures calling for universal male suffrage and the other Chartist demands was rejected by the Commons, 287-59. The involvement of some Chartist leaders in the spontaneous "Plug Plug" riots of mid-1842 gave the authorities an excuse to arrest large numbers of Chartists along with hundreds of rioters. About 80 persons were transported to Australia and over 250 were jailed in the "Plug Plug" riots. The arrests and rejection of the petition paralyzed the Chartist movement until it briefly flared up again during the 1848 revolutions.

The rising tide of post-1840 protest had strong nationalist overtones in Germany, Denmark, Italy, Switzerland, Ireland, the non-German lands of the Habsburg Empire, and the Danubian Principalities. German nationalism was stimulated by an 1840 crisis that threatened war with France, while nationalism in both Germany and Denmark was fostered by conflicting desires for domination over Schleswig-Holstein. In Italy, liberal-nationalist revolts, mostly under Mazzinian influence, erupted in 1841 and 1844 in the Kingdom of the Two Sicilies and in 1843 and 1845 in the Papal States. Although the revolts all failed and about a score of the rebels were executed, the uprisings attracted considerable attention and sympathy elsewhere in Europe.

In Switzerland, the period after 1839 saw a growing rift between the predominantly Protestant and urban cantons that had been "regenerated" in 1830 and the highly traditionalist and predominantly Catholic and rural Landesgemeinde cantons. Nationalist Swiss students and members of the middle class based in the regenerated cantons wanted a more centralized Switzerland, since they blamed the division of Switzerland into numerous virtually autonomous cantons for making the country an insignificant force in European politics and for paralyzing Swiss economic development through the multiplicity of tolls, currencies, and measures. These elements, known as the Radicals, also blamed the Catholic church for retarding Swiss cultural and educational development, and favored social reforms and an extension of civil liberties and universal suffrage to all cantons. Between 1839 and 1845, severe political conflict, sometimes verging on civil war, broke out between Radicals and conservative elements in about ten of the Swiss cantons.

In Ireland, Daniel O'Connell inaugurated a massive campaign in 1843 to bring about repeal of the 1800 Act of Union, which had eliminated the Irish parliament. Like his Catholic Emancipation Movement of the 1820s, O'Connell's "Repeal" movement was a socially conservative one, primarily designed to transfer power from the Anglo-Irish Protestant Ascendancy to the Irish Catholic middle class. "In social terms, O'Connellite Repeal meant, in essence, the old system under new and better management" (Tuathaigh 1972: 162). However, as in the case of the emancipation movement, Repeal attracted a near-millenarian fervor among the Irish peasantry that aroused deep distrust and fear among ruling circles in Ireland and Britain. O'Connell addressed hundreds of thousands of Irishmen at about 40 "monster meetings" in the summer and autumn of 1843--for example 500,000 at Cork in May and 300,000 at Kilkenny in June--called to agitate for an Irish parliament to solve the problems of Ireland. A final protest meeting scheduled for October 7 at Clontarf, near Dublin, was banned by the authorities. Although O'Connell capitulated and cancelled the meeting, he and six followers were arrested and convicted for sedition, fined and sentenced to a year in jail. The sentence was reversed on appeal in September 1844, after they had served most of it. The Clontarf affair, the jailings, O'Connell's advanced age, and exhaustion effectively ended the Repeal agitation.

In the Habsburg Empire, there was a significant rise in nationalist sentiment among the non-German groups during the 1840-5 period. In Hungary, the government's attempt to conciliate the diet in 1840 in order to obtain money and recruits by replacing unpopular officials and releasing the jailed nationalist leaders Kossuth and Wesselényi only strengthened the Magyar nationalist opposition. However, Magyar linguistic and cultural chauvinism rapidly alienated non-Magyar nationalities in Hungary, as was demonstrated in July 1845 at Agram (Zagreb) in Croatia, where Croat nationalists demonstrated and several of them were killed by troops. Meanwhile, in Bohemia, where the Czech majority had long been under German cultural and linguistic domination, the post-1840 period saw a strong rise in Czech nationalism. In the Danubian Principalities, conspiratorial Rumanian nationalist agitation against Russian domination continued despite arrests that disrupted groups in Wallachia in 1840 and Moldavia in 1846. In Wallachia, continued conflict between Prince Alexander Ghica and the boyar assembly led Russia and Turkey to depose Ghica in 1842. His replacement, George Bibescu, also clashed with the assembly and, with Russian encouragement, dissolved it in 1844 and ruled by decree for the next two years. In Moldavia, a considerable stir was caused in 1843 when Michael Kogălniceanu, a history professor at Mihilena Academy in Jassy, was suspended and exiled for his stirring demands for social reform. Subsequently, all higher courses at the academy were ended due to boyar opposition to providing higher education for the lower classes.

In the Low Countries, the ending of the long state of war between Belgium and the Netherlands in 1839 allowed normal politics to resume after a decade. In the Netherlands, where political activity had been virtually moribund under the authoritarian-paternalistic rule of King William I since 1815, the king was bitterly attacked for keeping the country on a war footing for years and ruining the nation's finances only to accept the same settlement that had been offered in 1831. In 1840 William abdicated, viewing the criticism as an intolerable affront, after the lower chamber of the Dutch parliament rejected his budget, 50-1, and passed several minor constitutional amendments increasing parliamentary control over the budget and the cabinet. William's son, William II (1840-49) was at first viewed as possibly more liberal, but the new king refused to support moderate electoral reforms proposed by the liberal leader Thorbecke and his followers, leading to their rejection by the legislature in 1845. Two radical journalists, Eillert Meeter and Adriaan van Bevervoorde, who demanded social reforms in the Netherlands, were repeatedly prosecuted during the 1840s, although eventually William II adopted the tactic of bribing them into moderation.

In Belgium, the disappearance of the Dutch military threat in 1839 and the subsequent collapse of the vocal Orangist (pro-Dutch) element led to the gradual disintegration of the Catholic-liberal alliance, held together previously mostly by fear of the Dutch. While Belgium was governed by a Catholic-liberal coalition between 1830 and 1847, Catholic interests, supported by King Leopold I (1831-65), had generally been dominant. In 1846, after a uniformly Catholic cabinet was formed despite strong liberal showings in the 1845 elections, liberals began organizing a distinct grouping, the Belgian Liberal party. The new party demanded complete separation of church and state and expansion of the franchise, as well as some window dressing calls for social reform. That the liberals came to power in the 1847 elections made little difference to the vast majority of the population. The liberals in Belgium, as in other European countries, were basically concerned with increasing the political power of the middle class. They had little interest in aiding the lower classes, who were disenfranchised and too demoralized, illiterate, and preoccupied with survival to wield any political clout.

In Serbia, the 1840-2 period was occupied by a power struggle between the senate and other forces that favored the 1838 constitution, and Prince Michael Obrenović, who sought to restore the autocratic rule enjoyed by his father Miloš, who had abdicated in 1839. In September 1842 a constitutionalist uprising forced Michael to flee to Austria. A general purge of pro-Michael forces followed, replete with jailings, beatings, tortures, and murders conducted without a semblance of legality. The senate, now clearly the dominant force in Serbia, convened a national assembly in September 1842 to ratify its choice as new prince, Alexander Karageorgević, son of the leader of the 1804 rebellion whom Miloš had had murdered in 1817. In October 1844, the "Hussar Rebellion," a pro-Obrenović rising launched by Serbian exiles in the Habsburg Empire, was put down with great cruelty, including another wave of executions, beatings, and tortures.

In Greece, opposition to the King Otto's rule mounted steadily after 1840. Greek unrest was heightened by the 1842 revolution in nearby Serbia and the action of the protecting powers in 1843 in refusing to grant further loans unless Otto accepted a commission to supervise Greek finances. This action, together with the king's failure to gain territory for Greece during an 1839-41 crisis threatening the territorial integrity of Turkey, was perceived by Greek elites as a national humiliation and a clear sign that the protecting powers had lost any remaining enthusiasm for Otto. On September 14, 1843 military units in Athens staged a bloodless coup with the backing of leaders of all three parties, demanding that Otto grant a constitution. Otto capitulated and also sent his remaining Bavarian advisers packing. A constituent assembly subsequently promulgated a constitution in March 1844 (largely drafted by France, Bavaria, and the United Kingdom) that established a lower legislative chamber elected by what amounted to universal male suffrage and an upper house appointed by the king. The king was empowered to appoint and dismiss ministers, veto legislation, dissolve the lower chamber and call new elections at his discretion.

These and other constitutional provisions created the potential for continued royal dominance. Otto was quick to take advantage of them, and continued to rule almost as autocratically as before. From 1844 until 1847 Otto ruled through Prime Minister John Kolettis, leader of the French party, who perfected a system of parliamentary dictatorship based on patronage, corruption, and outright coercion. Kolettis's technique, termed by one historian a "favlokratia" or "government by villains" (Kofas 1980: 9), included the widespread employment of brigands bands to terrorize the electorate, in return for which they received political protection for crimes and murders carried out in the course of normal business. Kolettis also relied upon massive annulment of "incorrect" election results, as in 1844, when 42 of 53 opposition mandates were disallowed. British Foreign Secretary Lord Palmerston, who hated Kolettis for favoring French interests in Greece, called him

> the chief and leader of all the robbers and scamps of Greece. ... Otto loves him as a second self, because he is as despotic as Otto himself; and as long as a majority can be had for Kolettis in the chamber, by corruption and intimidation, by the personal influence of the king and by money from France, Kolettis will remain minister (Kofas 1980: 17).

In Iberia, the 1840s witnessed a continuation of the power struggles of the 1830s. In 1840, liberal-radical parties held power in both Spain and Portugal, but by 1843 conservative and authoritarian regimes triumphed in both countries. In Portugal, the "Septembrist" government collapsed in the face of a bloodless "Chartist" coup in 1842, led by the supposedly Septembrist minister of finance, Costa Cabral. Cabral gagged the Portuguese press, which had been relatively free since 1834, repeatedly packed the upper house with new peers, and reduced the franchise for the lower house to 36,000 Portuguese (about 1 per cent of the population). Cabral encouraged economic development and reformed the administrative, tax and education systems, but also made sure he was justly rewarded for such efforts by rigging the elections so severely the opposition was virtually eliminated. Cabral's authoritarianism and tax increases, and especially his decree banning the traditional practice of burying bodies within churches triggered a peasant uprising in April 1846 that was joined by other opponents of his dictatorship, including Septembrists and Miguelists. In May 1846 Cabral fled Portugal and Queen Maria II handed over the government to the moderate Duke of Palmela. However, in October 1846, shortly before scheduled elections, Maria restored Cabralist leaders to the military and civil service, cancelled the elections, banned the opposition press and forced out Palmela in favor of the more conservative Duke of Saldanha. This "ambush of October 6" sparked a resurgence of civil war. The so-called patuleia ("rabble") of Oporto established a Septembrist junta in that city and risings in other parts of the country seemed about to topple the regime when Maria obtained British and Spanish military intervention to preserve her throne.

In Spain, General Espartero, who came to power at the head of a Progressive government as a result of the 1840 revolution, quickly alienated most of his original supporters. Popular rebellions broke out in Barcelona in 1841 and 1842, with the latter suppressed by a massive bombardment of the city and a wave of arrests that greatly discredited the regime. Middle-class Progressives, alarmed at the strength of radical groups displayed in Barcelona and in a number of municipal elections, began moving into the opposition Moderate party. In 1843, when Espartero dissolved a newly elected legislature that refused to support his policies, revolts broke out throughout Spain, backed by a coalition of Moderates who feared lower-class upheavals and left-wing Progressives angered by Espartero's conservative social policies. After a brief power struggle between the anti-Espartero factions, a Moderate (i.e., highly conservative) government under General Ramon Narváez emerged. Even Metternich was befuddled by the constant chaos in Spain, noting in April 1843 that after closely following Spanish affairs for 35 years he could only conclude that "the action most in keeping with reason is the one that is the least likely to happen" (Sauvigny 1962: 255).

Narváez ruled Spain with an iron hand almost continuously from May 1844 until January 1851. His governments were based on an extremely narrow but powerful coalition of wealthy landowners and industrialists. Revolts against Narváez in 1843-44 at Barcelona, Alicante, and Cartagena were followed by scores of arrests and at least 400 executions (on his death bed, when asked if he forgave his enemies, Narváez is reported to have replied, "I have no enemies. I have had them all shot" [Clissold 1969: 101]). All workers' societies were banned in 1844 and in that year a new rural police force, the Civil Guard, was created to stamp out brigandage and suppress peasant risings. Under the Moderate constitution of 1845, the power of the crown was increased and the upper house was made appointive rather than elective. The 1846 suffrage law reduced the franchise from about 600,000 to about 97,000 (0.6 per cent of the population). Electoral corruption became a fine art under Narváez, setting a pattern that was to last in Spain into the twentieth century and leaving violent upheaval as the only means of governmental change.

## On the Eve of Revolution, 1846-1847

The mounting political unrest apparent almost everywhere in Europe after 1840 greatly intensified after 1845. The major reason for this startling rise in discontent was the catastrophic economic crisis that struck Europe after 1845, touched off by three successive years (1845-7) of partial or total failure of the potato and grain harvests over most of central and western Europe. For the entire region, the price of potatoes and grains nearly doubled between 1845 and 1847. The agricultural crisis set off a major industrial-commercial depression by 1847, since the vast majority of Europeans had no money left to purchase other goods after buying food. Throughout the affected areas, millions of people suffered malnutrition and disease, lost their jobs and/or were forced to turn to relief. Between 1845 and 1847 the relief rolls in Belgium rose from 530,000 to 691,000; in Paris they climbed from 835,000 to 1,185,000. In Cologne and other cities of western Germany, one-third of the population was on relief by 1847. In Manchester, 300,000 were unemployed by that year, while in the French industrial town of Roubaix, 8,000 of 13,000 workers lacked employment.

The worst conditions were in Ireland, where 3 million people were fed from soup kitchens in 1847, one million died of disease and starvation and another million fled the country. Conditions were also especially horrible in Belgian Flanders, Prussian Silesia (where an estimated 50,000 died of disease and starvation), and Austrian Galicia (where about 230,000 perished). In Belgian Flanders many so-called window smashers deliberately committed petty crimes to gain regular meals in a jail cell. One window smasher declared, "If I had 10 francs, I would hire a lawyer to have my whole family jailed for half a year, so that they could leave prison fat and well-fed" (Mokyr 1976: 245).

Food riots were extremely widespread in 1846-7. At their peak in the spring of 1847, disorders broke out in over a dozen German cities, in many Dutch towns, and in Brussels, Vienna, Genoa, and parts of Scotland, southwest England, the Romagna, Lombardy, and Tuscany. Since rising middle-class political opposition accompanied the massive increase in lower-class unrest, it was widely predicted by 1847 that Europe was on the verge of a massive explosion. The American consul in Amsterdam wrote in 1847:

> All well-informed people express the belief that the present crisis is so deeply interwoven in the events of the present period that "it" is but the commencement of that great Revolution, which they consider sooner or later is to dissolve the present constitution of things (Hobsbawm 1962: 357).

The "spectre of communism" that Marx referred to in the first sentence of the Communist Manifesto, published in early 1848, was indeed haunting the conservative rulers of Europe. Metternich complained to his wife, "Ich bin so lebensmüde" (I am so tired of life) and noted the rising tide of opposition in Austria:

> I am no prophet and I know not what will happen; but I am an old practitioner, and I know how to discriminate between curable and fatal diseases. This one is fatal; here we hold as long as we can, but I despair for the issue (Ward 1970: 111).

Meanwhile, in Vienna the most popular hit of the day on the stage was about an old and faithful house servant who had outlived his usefulness. "All Vienna knew that the servant represented Metternich, long identified with the House of Habsburg" (Hammen 1969: 186).

The rising tension engendered by the economic problems of the 1845-57 period were exacerbated by a series of political conflicts that affected a number of European countries, notably the Habsburg Empire, Denmark, Germany, Switzerland, France, and Italy. In the Habsburg Empire, long-standing attempts by Polish revolutionaries to stir up a general uprising against the Austrian administration in Galicia ended up sparking a bloody peasant uprising against the Polish nobility instead in February 1846, during which about 2,000 members of the Polish landowning class were slaughtered. Plans for a simultaneous rising in Prussian Poland were foiled by mass arrests, but in Cracow an insurrection briefly succeeded until it was crushed by Austrian and Russian troops in early March, following which Austria formally annexed the tiny republic in violation of the 1815 Vienna treaty. Western liberals were outraged by the events in Prussia--where 250 Poles were prosecuted and 11 sentenced to death in a sensational trial--and especially by those in Galicia and Cracow, where the Austrians were execrated for violating the Vienna treaty and for allegedly deliberately encouraging the Galician peasantry to turn against their masters as a means of confounding the Polish rising. Far more damaging to the Habsburg regime than western public opinion--which never meant much to Metternich--was the massive peasant unrest inspired throughout the monarchy by the Galician uprising. Over 50,000 troops were required to force Galician peasants to resume labor services, and by 1847 peasants in many parts of the monarchy were enforcing their demands for an end to feudal dues and services by "practising go-slow, work to rule and sit-down strikes with a virtuosity from which a twentieth century trade union leader could learn much" (Macartney 1977: 289). Even the long-dormant provincial diets, especially those in Lower Austria and Bohemia, were stirring by 1847 and joined the Hungarian diet--captured by a liberal majority in the 1847 elections--in demands for major social, financial and constitutional reforms.

In Denmark, King Christian VIII signalled a major change of direction towards what became known as the "national liberal" movement in mid-1846. Christian repealed his 1845 ban on rural political meetings, ceased prosecuting the liberal press, and indicated in an "open letter" of July 8 that Schleswig would henceforth be regarded an an integral part of the Danish kingdom, thus accepting the so-called Edjder Program of the Danish national liberals, named for the Ejder River boundary between Schleswig and Holstein. In 1847 the National Liberal triumph was formalized in the consultative assembly elections.

In Germany, the excitement caused by the Schleswig-Holstein and economic issues was increased by growing middle-class agitation for constitutional reform in the state diets in 1846-7. In Baden, liberals triumphed in the 1846 elections and forced an easing of the censorship and police systems. Opposition deputies pressed vigorously for reform in the diets in Württemberg, Saxony, Hesse-Darmstadt, Nassau, and elsewhere. In Bavaria, the reactionary Abel ministry was forced out in 1847, and liberal opposition to King Ludwig I was facilitated by the king's senile passion for the young dancer Lola Montez. (It is reported that when the Archbishop of Munich remonstrated with Ludwig about Miss Montez, the king replied, "You stick to your stola and let me stick to my Lola" [Pinson 1954: 54].) German public attention focussed on Prussia--where communist reading groups had been broken up by the police in 1846--in April 1847, when King Frederick William IV summoned a "united diet" (vereinigter Landtag), consisting of all the provincial diets, to obtain financing for a railroad. Hopes rose that the united diet would be a prelude to a Prussian constitution and a genuine national legislature. However, the king refused even to promise that the united diet would be regularly convened. He also rejected any consideration of a constitution, declaring, "Never will I permit a written sheet of paper to come between God in heaven and this land" (Snell 1976: 75). In June 1847 the united diet rejected the railroad bill, 360-179, and was promptly dissolved by the king.

In Switzerland, the conflict between the Radicals and conservatives continued to intensify after 1845. In December 1845 seven conservative Catholic cantons (Lucerne, Uri, Schwyz, Unterwalden, Zug, Fribourg, and Valais) formed a defensive alliance, the Sonderbund, in possible violation of a provision of the 1815 agreement forming the Swiss confederation that banned the formation of "alliances between individual cantons prejudicial to the Confederation as a whole" (Gilliard 1955: 107). Radicals made rapid gains in other Swiss cantons in 1845-47, gaining power by coups in Geneva, Lausanne and Vaud, and by elections in St. Gallen, Zurich, Berne, and Solothurn. By mid-1847, the Radicals controlled a majority of votes in the Swiss diet. Civil war erupted in Switzerland on November 4, 1847 when the Sonderbund cantons seceded from the diet after rejecting that body's demand of July 20 that the Sonderbund dissolve. The Swiss civil war aroused enormous European interest, since it was universally regarded as a microcosm of the general European struggle between liberalism and conservatism. King Frederick William IV of Prussia declared that a liberal triumph in Switzerland would "infect Germany, Italy, and France" and cause "torrents of blood" to flow in Germany (Ward 1970: 101; Langer 1969: 136). France, Austria and Prussia tried to organize diplomatic intervention to save the Sonderbund—France, Austria and Sardinia also lent some military aid--but British opposition delayed delivery of notes from the conservative powers until after the Sounderbund had already been defeated in late November. Metternich declared in despair that "the powers are faced with radicalism in control" and referred to the Sonderbund defeat as a "harbinger of revolt in Germany" (Ward 1970:

102). In contrast, jubilant celebrations were held by liberals in southwestern Germany, France, Rome, Florence, and Leghorn, and over 5,000 Europeans sent congratulatory messages to the Swiss diet.

In France, the "dynastic left" parliamentary opposition organized a series of "political banquets" in 1847 to demand electoral reform. The "banquet campaign" designed to avoid restrictions on political meetings, was modelled on the legal agitation of the Anti-Corn Law League in the United Kingdom, which had finally obtained repeal of the Corn Laws in 1846 amidst the harvest crisis of that year. About 50 banquets were held in 28 French departments between July and December 1847. King Louis Philippe further antagonized his opponents when he referred to "agitation which is fomenting blind and hostile passions" in an address to the legislature on December 28, 1847 (Baughman 1959: 12). In this excited atmosphere, the students of Paris, who had been angered by previous political firings from teaching positions of the Polish nationalist Adam Mickiewicz in 1844 and the eminent historian Edgar Quinet in 1845, were greatly antagonized when the popular historian Jules Michelet's course at the Collège de France was cancelled for political reasons on January 2, 1848. Hundreds of students protested infringements on academic freedom on January 6 and February 3. The government banned another "political banquet" scheduled for February 22, and the sponsoring deputies, frightened by newspaper calls for a grand popular procession to precede the banquet, cancelled their plans. Nonetheless, a large crowd gathered in Paris on the morning of February 22. Although revolution had already broken out in Italy by then, the revolt that followed in Paris triggered a wave of revolutionary activity in Europe never equalled before or since.

In Italy, the liberal-nationalist cause was given tremendous impetus in June 1846 by the election of Pope Pius IX (1846-78) by the college of cardinals. A month after his election, Pius issued an amnesty for political prisoners that freed more than 1,000 detainees and allowed hundreds of exiles to return. The amnesty was followed by a series of reforms, including the building of railroads and telegraphs, gas lighting for Roman streets and improvements in the penal and educational systems. In March 1847, clerical press censorship was replaced with a much laxer system of lay censorship. In July 1847, partly in response to complaints about the Centurions, a popular civic guard was authorized, and in October a consultative assembly of laymen was established, marking the first step toward breaking the clerical monopoly on political power. Metternich was appalled and astounded, complaining, "A liberal Pope! That's really something new" (Sigman 1973: 199). But in Italy, Pius became a national hero, the subject of hymns of praise; handkerchiefs and medallions featured his portrait, which sold by the thousands. "Viva Pio Nono" became a universal slogan throughout the peninsula. Huge crowds, sometimes numbering 40,000, gathered daily in Rome to receive his blessings and cheer his reforms.

Demonstrations, invariably invoking Pius's name, mounted in the other Italian states, demanding changes in emulation of his reforms.

The December 1846 funeral of Count Federico Confalonieri, one of the most famous of the "Spielberg Martyrs" jailed in 1820 for Carbonari activities in Lombardy, attracted enormous crowds in Milan. The visit of Richard Cobden, the British anti-Corn Law activist, to Italy in mid-1847 was greeted with banquets in many cities, with each one understood to be a demonstration for political freedom. The ninth Italian scientific congress at Venice in September 1847 was permeated with a climate of barely suppressed nationalism. At one of the panels, Pius was constantly quoted, although to cry "Viva Pio Nono" was by then illegal in Lombardy-Venetia, while at another panel constant references were made to the disgusting <u>patate</u> crop (an Italian word meaning both "potato" and "German"). There were bloody clashes between police and demonstrators in 1847 in Parma, Lucca, Milan, Turin, and Naples. In response to the mounting excitement and mass demonstrations, press censorship was eased in 1847 in Tuscany and Sardinia, and a civic guard was authorized in Lucca and Tuscany. On September 12, 1847, 100,000 people attended a reception to urge further reforms upon Duke Leopold II of Tuscany. That same month risings erupted in the Kingdom of the Two Sicilies, followed by the normal jailings and executions. In early October, Duke Charles Louis of Lucca (1824-47) abdicated his throne in response to growing demonstrations. In late 1847, major movements developed in Venetia for press freedom and meaningful home rule, and in Milan for a boycott on smoking to protest the Austrian tobacco tax. Public outrage mounted dramatically in Lombardy after Austrian soldiers in Milan brutally attacked unarmed tobacco boycotters with swords and bayonets on January 3, 1848, killing five and seriously wounding 60 others.

In response to the rising Italian ferment, Austrian troops were stationed in Modena and Parma after the deaths of their rulers in January 1846 and December 1847, respectively. In mid-1847 the Austrian garrison at the fortress of Ferrara in the Papal States was reinforced, and Austrian troops began patrolling the town of Ferrara instead of confining themselves to the fortress as before. Pope Pius publicly protested this action, and Italians and European liberals reacted to it with outrage, viewing the Austrian action as an attempt to intimidate the Pope into reversing his course. After five months of diplomatic warfare, Austria backed down in December 1847, an action widely regarded as a stunning defeat for Metternich coming on the heels of his November setback in Switzerland.

The first revolutionary outbreak of 1848 came in Sicily, where a rebellion began in Palermo on January 12, demanding restoration of the 1812 constitution and autonomy from Naples. The Palermo rising triggered a widespread agrarian rebellion among the Sicilian peasantry, featuring the usual burning of property records and attacks on the property of the rich. On the Neapolitan mainland liberals seeking to take advantage of the Sicilian uprising demanded a constitution. On January 29, following a demonstration by 20,000 Neapolitans, King Ferdinand II (1830-59) granted a constitution for his entire realm, while also withdrawing his troops from all of Sicily except the Messina citadel. The events in Naples triggered great excitement and demands for similar concessions elsewhere in Italy. Constitutions were conceded in Sardinia (February 9), Tuscany (February 17) and the Papal States (March 15): one study notes it was "raining constitutions" (Berkeley and Berkeley 1940: 67). In Venetia, public opinion was outraged by the arrest of the leaders of the home rule movement, Daniel Manin and Nicolo Tomasseo, on January 18. Government proclamations in Venice were smeared with excrement, and huge crowds paraded past the jail where Manin and Tomasseo were held; people took off their hats and bowed as they walked in front of the prison cells. On February 25, martial law was declared throughout Lombardy-Venetia; it became treasonous to wear certain colors or badges, to sing certain songs, and even to applaud or hiss specified passages at the theatres. A few days later, news arrived that revolution had broken out in Paris on the night of February 23.

## The Revolutionary Wave of 1848-1849

An entire library could easily be constructed of books about the 1848-49 European revolutions, and no more than the barest summary of salient events relevant to the topic of political repression can be attempted in this work. Between January and June 1848, revolutionary outbursts or threatening demonstrations and riots occurred in every European country, except Portugal and Switzerland, both exhausted by recent civil wars, and those areas of extreme southeastern Europe, such as Serbia, Bulgaria, and Macedonia, which were largely cut off from developments elsewhere in the Continent by distance and economic and political backwardness.

The major centers of serious revolutionary outbreaks--counting all of the German and Italian states and the various Austrian provinces where uprisings occurred, it has been estimated that about 50 separate revolutions erupted--were France, Germany, Italy, the Austrian Empire, and Wallachia. In all of these areas, governments were either overthrown or at least profoundly reshaped. Elsewhere in Europe, the 1848 unrest was generally far less serious. In Belgium, the Netherlands, Denmark, Norway, Sweden, Moldavia, and Great Britain, disturbances were largely confined to desultory rioting and/or peaceful demonstrations. In the first three of these countries, significant constitutional reform--combined in the Belgian case with stiff repressive measures--averted more serious disorders. Rioting in the Norwegian capital, Christiania, on March 11-14, petered out without much effect, while more serious disturbances in Stockholm March 18-20 were put down when troops shot 30 people to death. In Moldavia, a mass reform demonstration was held on March 27, but plans for a revolutionary attempt were headed off by over 300 arrests.

In Great Britain, the European revolutions revived the Chartist movement, which promptly collapsed again following a mass demonstration for suffrage reform in London on April 10. Massive security precautions were taken for the demonstration, and the nearly 200,000 citizens sworn in as special constables, together with thousands of troops and police, far outnumbered the demonstrators. Police forbade the protestors to march to the House of Commons as planned. The cancellation of the march by Chartist leaders and the subsequent announcement by parliamentary officials that many of the claimed five million signatures on a Chartist petition were faked discredited the entire movement. Attempted insurrections by a few hotheads in the spring and early summer of 1848 were easily squelched, and resulted only in 16 sentences of transportation and about 100 jail terms.

In Ireland, Greece, and Spain, minor revolutionary uprisings in 1848 were quickly put down to the accompaniment, especially in Spain, of harsh repressive measures. In Ireland and Spain constitutional guarantees were suspended before any serious disorders occurred. In Spain, Narváez ruled without parliament for nine months, and had 13 people executed and about 2,000 people exiled to the Canary Islands and Fernando Po following three trivial outbursts. His tough actions made him a hero to European conservatives and led one observer to note, "He drew a line in the Pyrenees, and like God to the waters, he said to the revolution, 'Thou shalt not pass' " (Headrick 1976: 198). In Russia, 70 separate peasant disorders were recorded in 1848, an extraordinarily high number, but nothing significant was achieved, perhaps because martial law was proclaimed throughout the western provinces of Russia.

The 1848 outbreaks reflected a combination of social unrest that resulted especially from the 1846-8 economic troubles and political unrest that resulted from absolutist or highly restricted forms of government, repressive police controls, and restrictions upon freedom of speech and association. In those regions of Europe divided into small states and/or under the domination of non-native ethnic groups, such as Italy, Germany, Hungary, the Danubian Principalities, and the Austrian Slavic provinces, nationalist desires also played a major role in the revolts. Roughly speaking, economic distress impacted most upon the lower and lower-middle classes, and political and nationalistic motives especially inspired the middle and upper-middle classes, while issues related to political repression attracted support from almost all segments of the population (save the ruling elites). Everywhere demands for constitutional government (where it did not exist), dismissal of repressive ministries, expansion of the suffrage, liberation of political prisoners, and freedom of the press, association, and assembly were among the grievances most strongly voiced by protesters. These demands also brought about the first concessions offered by trembling governments or new regimes.

Although the Sicilian revolution of January 12, 1848 had great significance for Italy, it was the Paris revolution of February 23-24 that shook the political structure of Europe. The abdication of King Louis Philippe on February 24, followed by the granting of universal manhood suffrage and freedom of the press and assembly by a provisional republican government, triggered a wave of unrest in the

German states. In virtually all of the German states, there were peaceful demonstrations for political reform during the first two weeks in March, some of which reached major dimensions, such as the remonstrance of 10,000 people for universal male suffrage and civil liberties in Leipzig (Saxony) on March 1.

In the two dominant German states, Austria and Prussia, revolutionary uprisings broke out on March 13 and March 18 respectively, after troops opened fire on demonstrators in Vienna and Berlin. In Vienna, the major demands were for Metternich's dismissal, freedom of the press and constitutional government. By March 15, all three demands were granted by the feeble-minded Emperor Ferdinand, who at one point summarized the first response of most European rulers to the 1848 uprisings when he told his advisors, "Tell the people that I agree to everything" (Macartney 1969: 330). Prussian King Frederick William IV similarly capitulated on March 19 after about 230 civilians and 20 soldiers were killed in bitter fighting.

The news from Vienna triggered serious unrest in the non-German provinces of the Habsburg Empire. Mass meetings were held in Prague on March 11 and in Budapest on March 15. The Hungarian diet, meeting at Pressburg (Pozsony, Bratislava), voted on March 15 to demand a separate Hungarian ministry responsible to it. This demand was granted by Vienna on March 17 and followed by creation of a "responsible ministry" for the western half of the monarchy also on March 20. Meanwhile, anti-Austrian uprisings broke out in Milan and Venice, on March 18 and 22 respectively. Austrian forces in Venice capitulated quickly, but it took five days of bloody street fighting in Milan, which cost the lives of almost 500 rebels, before General Radetzky's troops withdrew from that city. At about the same time, the withdrawal of Austrian troops from Parma and Modena to aid Radetzky at Milan was followed by uprisings in those tiny states and the flight of their ruling dukes. The final successful uprising of 1848 came in June, when the government of Wallachia was overthrown by a popular revolt that featured a mixture of demands regarding civil liberties and social reforms.

The most significant and common gains made in Europe in 1848 involved the expansion of popular liberties and participation in government. Constitutional government was granted in the Austrian Empire, Wallachia, throughout Germany and Italy (in those states where it had not existed before) and in Denmark. Existing constitutions were significantly liberalized in France, Belgium, the Netherlands, and many German states, while the victors in the 1847 Swiss civil war consolidated their gains in the liberal Swiss constitution of 1848. Except in the Netherlands, wherever constitutions were liberalized, the suffrage was expanded, often sigificantly. Thus, in France the franchise jumped from about 250,000 to over 8 million after universal manhood suffrage was proclaimed on March 4. In Hamburg the electoral rolls increased from 1,500 to 30,000, and in Belgium voters increased from 55,000 to almost 80,000. In many areas where constitutions were introduced for the first time strikingly liberal franchises were introduced. Thus, in Denmark, under the 1849 constitution over 15 per cent of the population was enfranchised and in Austria and Prussia universal male suffrage was used to elect constituent assemblies. On the other hand, in Sardinia the royally decreed constitution of 1848 limited the suffrage to about 2 per cent of the population.

Constitutional demands were accompanied in most countries affected by the 1848 disorders with other concessions to popular demands for an easing of political repression. Thus, political prisoners were freed in general amnesties in France, Austria, and Prussia. In Berlin, mobs freed the Polish political prisoners jailed for their involvement in the 1846 conspiracy, then paraded them through the streets and before the royal palace. King Frederick William IV appeared on the balcony there and "bared his head in respect for those whom his courts had condemned to death or life imprisonment a year earlier" (Fejto 1973: 367). The newly freed French political prisoners were recruited for the Paris police force.

The other standard civil liberty demands granted in Denmark, France, the Netherlands, Wallachia, Austria, and most of the German and Italian states were freedom of the press, assembly, and association. These concessions led to an explosion of newspapers, political clubs, petitions, meetings and--in the more economically developed areas--trade unions. The spirit of the times was captured by a goldsmith named Bisky, who noted while addressing an outdoor assembly of thousands in Berlin on March 26, "Until now we were the big zero in the state. Finally we have a chance to speak up" (Marquardt 1974: 202).

In Paris, an estimated 450 newpapers--many of which were ephemeral--sprang up in the aftermath of the February revolution, and the combined daily press run of Parisian newspapers skyrocketed from 50,000 to 400,000. In Vienna, Rome, and Venice the granting of press freedom led to the emergence of about 100 new newspapers each. Tens of thousands of Europeans joined politically oriented clubs and scores of thousands attended political meetings and demonstrations once restrictions on assembly and association were lifted. Meetings and demonstrations in Berlin, Vienna, Budapest, Paris, Rome, and elsewhere frequently attracted crowds of 10,000 or more during the 1848 revolutions and their aftermath. In Germany, the Frankfurt National Assembly, popularly elected to draft a new constitution for the German confederation, received almost 10,000 petitions that called for various reforms during the year it met in 1848-9, one of which was signed by 120,000 people. In the small German state of Mecklenburg, 50,000 people signed petitions calling for the end of feudal vestiges. Paris was the center of the political club movement, with over 400 such groups formed in the immediate aftermath of the revolution. The novelist George Sand later recounted that when she found herself locked out of her Paris apartment one evening in March 1848 all three locksmiths she tried to summons could not be reached as each was attending a club meeting! The most popular Parisian clubs regularly attracted audiences of up to 5,000 for their meetings. Political clubs were also popular in Rome, Vienna, Prague, and other cities. They were especially popular in Germany, where the largest such group, the liberal middle-class Zentralmärzverein, attracted almost 500,000 members belonging to over 1,000 affiliated branches within a few months of its organization in late 1848.

In Germany and France, and to a lesser extent in other countries, the revolutionary ferment of 1848 was also reflected in significant trade union organization. In Paris, an estimated 300 workers' associations attracted about 50,000 members. National trade unions were formed by German printers, tailors, and cigar makers, and regional and national workers' congresses were held throughout Germany. The most ambitious attempt to form a national German workers' organization, the Verbrüderung, attracted an estimated 20,000 members. Printers organized the first nationwide strike in German history, and it is estimated that altogether more strikes occurred in the spring of 1848 in Germany than had occurred in the previous 50 years.

Wherever revolutions succeeded in bringing about an easing of political repression, frenzied and jubilant popular demonstrations followed. Thus, after Sardinian King Charles Albert announced that he would grant a constitution, a parade was held in Turin on February 27, 1848 to celebrate:

> In all, some 50,000 men marched in a procession that took five hours to pass before the king. ... Every city of Piedmont was represented, every guild, every profession and division of laborers and peasants. ... In the arcades along the way no one could move, so great was the crowd, and at every window and balcony were cheering people (Martin 1969: 286).

There were similar scenes after constitutions and freedom of the press were granted in the Habsburg Empire and the German states:

> Total strangers embraced one another and joined in singing ... the Viennese were drunk with freedom. ... In their intoxication the inhabitants of the capital wined and dined, danced and sang, marched and paraded with a joy that had rarely been seen even in the fun-loving Vienna (Rath 1957: 86, 90).

> The announcement [of Metternich's fall and the granting of a constitution] loosed a wave of merriment and wild enthusiasm such as Prague had probably never witnessed before. ... Thousands milled about in the streets; strangers embraced. . . . Within hours, the term "constitution," hitherto proscribed, became a magic word. ... Special "constitutional hats," low and wide-brimmed, were introduced and promoted vigorously. One enterprising merchant began to sell "constitutional parasols"; another peddled "constitutional rolls" (Pech 1969: 66).

In the smallest [German] provincial town, there were illuminations, festive parades by the riflemen's associations, banquets of local notables and embracing in the streets (Stadelman 1976: 76).

The mood of the March Days [in Germany] was summed up by the Russian revolutionary Bakunin: "It seemed as if the entire world was turned upside down. The improbable became commonplace, the impossible possible; people found themselves in such a state of mind that if someone had said, 'God has been driven from heaven and a republic has been proclaimed there,' everyone would have believed it and no one would have been surprised" (Noyes 1966: 57).

By late 1849, the impossible had become impossible again over much of Europe. Beginning with the suppression of an uprising in Cracow (annexed to Austria in 1846) in April 1848, and ending with the suppression of the revolution in Hungary by Austrian and Russian troops in October 1849, the revolutions in Germany, the Habsburg Empire, Wallachia, and Italy were crushed by military force, and the forces of social reform in France were dealt a stunning blow by the brutal suppression of a workers' uprising there in June 1848. Austrian troops crushed the revolts in northern Italy and the Habsburg Empire, while Russian and Turkish troops suppressed the Wallachian revolt, Russia helped put down the Hungarian revolution and Prussian troops suppressed rebels not only in Prussia but also in Saxony, Baden, and the Bavarian Palatinate in the spring of 1849.

In many cases, the military suppression of the 1848 revolutions was accompanied and followed by extremely harsh repression. Everywhere leftist newspapers and political organizations were suppressed and revolutionary activists were subjected to stiff reprisals. In the Two Sicilies, an estimated 15,000 to 30,000 people were jailed for their activities in 1848. In Paris, about 3,000 suspected participants in the June 1848 workers' rebellion were slaughtered in cold blood after the collapse of the rising; another 12,000 were arrested; and about 4,300 were ultimately jailed or deported to Algerian labor camps. After the suppression by Prussian troops of the May 1849 Baden revolt, 27 insurgents were executed, 1,000 received jail terms or other punishments and 10,000 fled to Switzerland to avoid reprisals. About 9,000 people were tried after the Dresden (Saxony) revolt of May 1849; four years later trials were still proceeding. In Lombardy-Venetia, Austrian authorities sentenced an estimated 4,000 people and executed another 960 for political offenses after they regained control. Liberal Europe was scandalized in August 1849 when Austrian troops flogged 17 Milanese who had hissed the display of the imperial colors and then billed the city of Milan for the ice, vinegar, and rods used in the flogging, as well as for the services of the jailers.

Following the suppression of the Hungarian revolution, which had evolved into a struggle for complete independence from Austria under the leadership of Louis Kossuth, about 150 people, including 13 prominent generals, were executed, and another 1,500 to 2,000 were given long jail terms, including many sentences of 10 to 20 years in chains. Almost 50,000 members of the Hungarian army were forcibly conscripted into Austrian regiments, while among the civilian population "prominent individuals, among them several ladies of high society, were whipped in public for nationalist sympathies; public gatherings and theater performances were banned; the display of national colors, the wearing of national costumes, and even the sporting of Kossuth-style beards became punishable offenses" (Janos 1982: 88). About 2,000 to 5,000 insurgents were killed (compared with about 1,200 troops) during the suppression of the Viennese revolution in October 1848, and many were summarily executed after the rebels surrendered. Twenty-five Viennese were officially tried and executed, and about 2,400 were jailed, of whom over 450 received long sentences. In the aftermath of a conspiracy uncovered in Prague in May 1849, 28 death sentences were handed out (all of which were commuted to jail terms) and another 51 suspects were sentenced to a total of 474 years in jail. Throughout the Austrian Empire, suspected rebels—even those who were acquitted or not even formally charged with illegal activities—were drafted into the army as punishment. Thus, the Austrian military command in Bohemia publicly announced on April 24, 1849 that because "often there is not sufficient evidence" for "legal" prosecutions in political cases, suspects in such cases would be drafted and "minor physical defects" could be overlooked (Pech 1969: 226).

Although ultimately the 1848 revolutions in the major European countries failed because they were crushed by military force, other factors were involved in their collapse. In all of the revolutionary countries splits developed between middle-class elements, which were content with constitutional and civil liberty reforms and an opportunity to hold governmental office, and working class elements, which wanted to go beyond these changes to significant social reforms. Lower-class radicalism, and, especially in Paris, Berlin, and Vienna, constant, usually low-level turmoil in the streets deeply frightened middle-class liberals and led to internal factionalization within the revolutionary coalitions or to middle-class defections from the revolution altogether. In the Habsburg Empire, and to a considerably lesser extent in Germany, conflicts between different nationality groups also severely weakened the 1848 revolutions. These conflicts were critical only in Hungary, where Magyar chauvinism led non-Magyar nationalities—the Croats, Slovaks, Serbs and Rumanians—to revolt against the Hungarian regimes and/or to actively aid Habsburg forces in suppressing the revolution.

Another factor that weakened the revolutionary governments of 1848 was, ironically, that they generally respected the civil liberties of their opponents and made no real effort to retaliate against officials of the former regimes. These officials were not killed, not jailed, and to a large extent not even dismissed from their positions. Thus, most of the revolutionary governments of 1848 never even tried to gain effective control of the civil service or—with disastrous consequences for them--even the armed forces. It was symptomatic of the general "gentleness" of the 1848 revolutions that no attempt was made in Austria to oust Emperor Ferdinand save by reactionary forces who succeeded in forcing him to abdicate so his conciliatory promises could be more easily ignored. Similarly, in the German states the existing monarch was forced out only in Bavaria, and there largely because of his love life rather than his politics. Especially in France and Prussia, conservative forces were given a freedom of organization and expression in 1848 that they had never dreamed of allowing their own opponents. The only country in which the actions of the revolutionary regime in 1848 were characterized by real savagery was Hungary, which faced both invasion from Austria and internal insurrections by the non-Magyar nationalities. Especially in the case of the Serbs and Rumanians, the insurrections often involved terroristic attacks and atrocities directed against Magyars. Altogether, an estimated 5,000 Serbs and Rumanians were executed by Magyar troops and officials in 1848 (not counting those killed in battle), mostly without benefit of any judicial procedure.

The 1848 revolutions were not complete failures. Constitutional government, albeit of a highly conservative nature, survived 1848 in Prussia and Sardinia, in each of which there had been complete absolutism before. Feudal dues and services were finally abolished as a result of 1848 in the Habsburg Empire and those regions of Germany where they were lingering, so that after 1848 such remnants existed only in Russia and the Danubian Principalities. Universal male suffrage outlasted the revolution in France, although election rigging rendered this somewhat nugatory until after 1860. The 1848 revolutions allowed Switzerland to adopt a strikingly liberal constitution without outside interference, led to a moderate expansion of the suffrage in Belgium, fostered a moderate democratization of the Dutch constitution and sparked a dramatic democratic breakthrough in Denmark. Finally, in many ways the 1848 revolutions established a political and social agenda that was to dominate European politics for the next 70 years.

Chapter 5

# The Age of Repression and Reconstruction, 1850-1870

*The Economic and Social Structure of Europe, 1850-1870*

The European continent enjoyed enormous and unprecedented economic growth during the 1850-70 period. However, the benefits of the great industrial and agricultural boom that marked the era were reaped primarily by the landed aristocracy and the rapidly emerging but relatively small class of industrial, commercial and financial entrepreneurs. The great bulk of the European population continued to live in or near a state of poverty and economic insecurity. Politically, the period was marked by a growing amalgamation between the traditional landed nobility and the rising bourgeoisie, who together tacitly agreed to share political and economic power while banding together against the threat posed by the lower classes.

The agricultural sector enjoyed high prices and significant modernization of techniques during the 1850-70 era. However, the agricultural boom was overshadowed by the staggering industrial growth of the period, which was symbolized by the great exhibitions in London in 1851 and 1862 and in Paris in 1855 and 1867. Especially affected by the industrial boom were Great Britain, Belgium, France, and Germany, as well as a few isolated regions or industrial sectors of other countries, such as Austrian Bohemia, Spanish Catalonia (whose textile industry made Spain the world's fourth largest cotton manufacturer), the Swedish iron industry and the Norwegian merchant marine. In Iberia, Scandinavia, the Habsburg Empire, the Netherlands, Switzerland, and the Russian Empire, the era saw major strides in the development of industrial infrastructures, such as road, railway, and telegraph networks, and the emergence of banking and credit institutions. The development of both heavy industry (such as steel, iron, and coal) and light industry (such as textiles) in these regions, however, lagged far behind the more advanced countries. The Balkans, and large areas in many other countries, such as northern Scandinavia, southern Italy and Spain, and vast stretches of the Russian Empire, were almost entirely unaffected by industrialization or other signs of modernization during the period. In Serbia, for example, in the late 1860s, there were no doctors in 7 of the 17 provinces. Even those countries significantly affected by industrialization were by no means completely transformed during the 1850-70 period. In France, for example, in the 1860s, 60 per cent of the industrial work force was employed in workshops with less than 10 employees, and 70 per cent of the population lived in rural areas.

European railway track increased from 14,500 to 63,300 miles during the 1850-70 period, while telegraph lines jumped from 2,000 to 11,000 miles. In the United Kingdom, production of coal and pig iron doubled between 1850 and 1870, while exports and imports nearly tripled. French coal and pig iron production tripled, while railway mileage and the number of industrial machines quintupled. The development of railway networks and steamships reduced the time required to go around the world from almost a year in 1848 to under three months in 1872, while the development of the telegraph made communications between major European cities instantaneous (in 1848, the most rapid communication service in Europe, that of the Rothschild bank, took five days to transmit news from Paris to Vienna).

The development of railroads and telegraphs increased the ease with which regimes could assemble and deploy troops, while the invention of new military technology, such as the breech-loading gun, the grooved-bore rifle, the machine gun, and improved artillery increased infantry firepower 60-fold between 1840 and 1870. Once dispatched to the scene of unrest loyal troops could thereafter easily put down all but the most serious of disorders. A high level of spending on military and police forces was characteristic of most European regimes in the post-1848 period, reflecting both fears of lower-class upheavals and heightened international tensions, which after 30 years of general peace between 1815 and 1848 led to five major wars among European powers between 1854 and 1870. Around 1870, Italy and Prussia both spent about ten times as much on the military as on education; Austria spent twice as much on the police alone as on the school system.

The 1850-70 economic boom was accompanied and to some extent fueled by rapid population and urban growth. The European population grew by more than 10 per cent during the period, increasing from about 265 to about 295 million, and the largest cities shared disproportionately in this expansion. The proportion of the population living in cities of over 100,000 almost doubled, rising from about 4 to about 7 per cent of the total. Some of the great cities grew at staggering levels. London jumped from 2.7 to 3.9 million between 1850 and 1870. Berlin grew from 419,000 to 826,000 and Vienna shot up from 444,000 to 834,000. Despite the rapid and unprecedented industrial and urban growth of the period, Europe remained primarily rural and agricultural throughout the era. Only in the Low Countries, France, and Great Britain did over 15 per cent of the population live in towns of 20,000 or more in 1870. More than 25 per cent of the labor force was employed in industry in that year only in those same countries, plus Germany and Switzerland (see Table 5.1).

The general economic prosperity of the times failed to improve the living standards of the mass of the population to any significant

Table 5.1:  European Historical Statistics, 1850 and 1870

| | % Population Enfranchised | | % Labor Force in Agriculture | | % Labor Force in Industry | | % in Towns 20,000+ | | % Adults Literate | | Life Expectancy[c] | | Mortality Rate (per thousand) | | Infant Mortality (per thousand) | |
|---|---|---|---|---|---|---|---|---|---|---|---|---|---|---|---|---|
| | 1850 | 1870 | 1850 | 1870 | 1850 | 1870 | 1850 | 1870 | 1850 | 1870 | 1850 | 1870 | 1850 | 1870 | 1850 | 1870 |
| Austria | 0 | 5.9 | 70 | 65 | 18 | 19 | 4 | 7 | 40 | 50 | | 30 | 33 | 32 | 248 | 256 |
| Belgium | 1.8 | 2.2 | 51 | 44 | 25 | 37 | 15 | 18 | 50 | 60 | 38 | 40 | 24 | 23 | 155 | 153 |
| Denmark | 15 | 15 | 49 | 48 | 22 | 24 | 9 | 10 | 85 | 90 | 42 | 44 | 21 | 19 | 140 | 136 |
| Finland | 6 | 6 | | 75 | | 10 | 0 | 1 | 70 | 75 | | 40 | 26 | 27 | | 200 |
| France | 20 | 26 | 52 | 50 | 27 | 26 | 10 | 19 | 55 | 69 | 39 | 39 | 23 | 24 | 166 | 173 |
| Germany | | - | | 50 | | 35 | 7 | 13 | 80 | 87 | 32 | 35 | 27 | 27 | 294 | 284 |
| Greece | 23 | 23 | 74 | 75 | 10 | 10 | 3 | 5 | 10 | 20 | | 35 | | 21 | | |
| Hungary | 0 | 6.5 | 75 | 70 | 10 | 10 | 5 | 6 | 25 | 36 | | | | 37 | 252 | |
| Italy | - | 2.0 | 62 | 61 | 17 | 23 | 11 | 11 | 20 | 31 | | 35 | | 31 | | 215 |
| Neth. | 2.5 | 2.9 | 44 | 37 | 24 | 29 | 22 | 24 | 70 | 75 | 35 | 38 | 26 | 25 | 188 | 200 |
| Norway | 8 | 7.5 | | 60 | | 23 | 4 | 6 | 85 | 90 | 45 | 48 | 18 | 18 | 110 | 107 |
| Portugal | 0.7 | 9 | | 65 | | 16 | 11 | 9 | 15 | 20 | | | | | | |
| Rumania | 0 | 15 | | | | | 9 | 10 | 10 | 15 | | | | 29 | | 207 |
| Russia[a] | 0 | 0 | | | | | 4 | 6 | 5 | 15 | | 25 | | 37 | | 270 |
| Serbia | 0 | 20 | | | | | 0 | 2 | 5 | 7 | | | | 32 | | |
| Spain | 1.1 | 24 | 70 | 70 | 15 | 15 | 10 | 13 | 20 | 35 | | 29 | | 31 | | 180 |
| Sweden | 6 | 5.8 | 80 | 72 | 10 | 15 | 3 | 6 | 90 | 95 | 41 | 44 | 21 | 19 | 152 | 135 |
| Switz. | 22 | 22 | | 50 | | 37 | 5 | 8 | 85 | 90 | | 40 | 23 | 23 | | 193 |
| U.K.[b] | 4 | 8 | 22 | 15 | 51 | 52 | 35 | 42 | 55 | 70 | 40 | 41 | 22 | 22 | 153 | 151 |

[a] Data for European Russia only
[b] Most non-electoral data for England and Wales only
[c] Life expectancy data is for males
Sources: Mackie and Rose 1974; Mitchell 1975:16-47, 51-64; Flora 1973:242-5; Dublin 1949:346-8.

extent save in Great Britain, where workers were on average about 10 per cent better off in 1870 compared to 1850. Average living standards also increased markedly in Ireland, but this was largely because the poorest 25 per cent of the population had been eliminated by death and emigration as a result of the Great Famine. In general, economic conditions remained exceptionally bad where they had been dire before 1850: in Russia, Hungary, and the Slavic regions of the Habsburg Empire, the Balkans, eastern Germany and the southern regions of Italy and Spain. Continuing population increases caused economic stagnation or even deterioration wherever industrial development was not advanced enough to create alternatives to agricultural employment. Thus, in Sweden, 48 per cent of the agricultural population in 1870 lacked enough land to support themselves, compared with less than one-third in 1815. In Hungary, about 40 per cent of the five million serfs freed of feudal obligations after 1848 were given no land to farm, and most of the others obtained only dwarf plots, creating a vast class of dependent agricultural laborers condemned to working for others at semi-starvation wages. Similar conditions existed in eastern Germany, Rumania, and the southern parts of Spain and Italy. Although the Russian serfs were freed in 1861, the terms of the emancipation left most of them as poverty-stricken as before.

Living conditions in urban areas, even in the more advanced and healthier countries, were also extremely poor during the 1850-70 period. The mortality rate in Stockholm in 1851-60 was twice that in Swedish rural areas. In Copenhagen, 36 percent of all children died before the age of two, while a study of 400 working class families in the Norwegian capital found an average of four persons living in each room in 1858. An estimated 30,000 prostitutes walked the streets of Paris, and in 1868 alone over 35,000 beggars and vagrants were arrested in the "city of light." In St. Petersburg, over 34,000 were arrested in 1869 for drunkenness. Because of urban crowding and the inability of many cities to keep pace with population growth in housing and sanitation facilities, the towns were especially vulnerable to epidemics. The worst such disasters in the 1850-70 period were the cholera epidemic of 1853-8, which killed almost 200,000 people in France, Portugal, and the United Kingdom alone, and another outbreak of the same disease in 1865-7, which carried off over 750,000 Europeans, including 240,000 Spaniards, 225,000 Germans and Austrians, 140,000 Italians, 90,000 Russians, and 50,000 Belgians and Dutch.

Average European life expectancy in 1870 was between 35 and 40, virtually unchanged since 1850, although figures varied widely from country to country. Thus, the average Spaniard and Russian lived less than 30 years, yet Scandinavians survived on the average for about 45 years (see Table 5.1). As in 1850, between 15 and 20 per cent of all European babies born alive in 1870 died before the age of one, varying from under 15 per cent in Scandinavia to over 25 per cent in Austria, Germany, and Russia. Over five million Europeans "voted with their feet" to show their dissatisfaction with life on the Continent by emigrating during the 1850-70 period. Most emigrants left from the

United Kingdom, Germany, Sweden, and Norway. While economic conditions were probably the primary factor in motivating emigration, many also left in hopes of finding a home where there were greater political freedoms and less class discrimination. Thus, one Swede wrote from the United States in 1852:

> I have missed Sweden but little. I long realized the oppression of her less fortunate citizens ... the undue power of higher classes, the disregard and harshness with which they used it to oppress the poor--a free land where all men have equal rights--this is what I sought (Anderson 1955: 383).

One important area where mass conditions unquestionably improved during the period was education. Between 1840 and 1880 the number of European children attending schools rose 145 per cent, far outstripping the 33 per cent population rise. Only Russia and the Balkans were not significantly affected by the general expansion of educational facilities and marked rise in literacy rates, although the Habsburg Empire, Iberia and Italy also lagged well behind other countries (see Table 5.1). To a large extent, educational expansion reflected the growing recognition by European governments that a literate citizenry was necessary for economic development and general national strength. Intensive efforts continued in most countries to control educational content so that pupils were taught only "correct" ideas, and some conservative politicians still feared extending any educational opportunities to the lower classes. Thus, the reactionary Spanish Prime Minister Juan Bravo Murillo (1851-2) declared in response to a proposal to provide schools for the poor, "You want me to authorize a school at which 600 working men are to attend? Not in my time. Here we don't want men who think, but oxen who work" (Brenan 1964: 56). Everywhere, only elementary schools were tuition free and publicly supported (in southern and eastern Europe even these did not exist); attendance at secondary schools and universities, which was necessary to obtain high-level positions in the civil service and the professions, was beyond the economic means of the vast majority of the population.

Politically the 1850-70 period saw a significant geographical expansion of the coalition between the traditional ruling classes and the rising bourgeoisie that had been evident even before 1848 in Iberia, Belgium, France, Switzerland, and Great Britain. This coalition was still tentative in many areas of Europe at the end of the period, and often had more the characteristics of a marriage of convenience than of true love. The traditional aristocracy and the rising industrial-commercial elites were drawn together by common fear of the lower classes and of a recurrence of 1848. The increasing realization of the old ruling elements that national economic and military strength was highly dependent on the skills of the bourgeoisie also fostered the coalition, as did the bourgeoisie's desire to gain social prestige, to share political power, and to obtain policies favorable to business interests and expansion. The 1848 revolts convinced the traditional elites that alienating the middle class would only lead to another dreaded liberal-lower-class coalition against them. For the bourgeoisie, the growing tendency to look to the old elites for support reflected not only fear of the lower classes, but also the pragmatic realization that the alternative of revolutionary plots and uprisings was increasingly unrealistic, since popular revolts could not overcome loyal armies. "When gatherings of enthusiastic middle class representatives had finished talking [in 1848] it was the professional armies of Russia, Prussia and Austria which had settled the fate of Europe" (Thomson 1966: 234).

In concrete terms, the pro-business policies adopted by many European governments during the 1850-70 period included such measures as lowering barriers to internal migration, trade and freedom of occupation, establishing state-sponsored credit institutions, and providing legal protection for joint-stock companies, tax concessions and sometimes direct subsidies to business operations, especially in connection with railroad construction. Although in a few states, such as Belgium, Switzerland, and France, the bourgeoisie tended to fill positions of both economic and political power, the more common pattern was for the nobility to continue to hold high political offices while inclining more and more toward pro-business policies. In the United Kingdom, for example, half of the members of the House of Commons in 1860 were tied to the nobility by heredity or marriage, and 31 families supplied 110 legislators to that body, equivalent to the total representation of Ireland. In Prussia in 1860, 60 per cent or more of all army officers, provincial governors, and ambassadors were aristocrats. The nobility continued to control huge landholdings in much of Europe, including the United Kingdom, Germany, the Habsburg Empire, Rumania, and Russia. Half of England was owned by 7,400 people in 1871, half of Hungary was owned by less than 20,000 landlords, and in Austrian Galicia 160 large landowners controlled about 20 per cent of the province.

Thus, a sort of power-sharing with separate spheres of influence developed, in which the old nobility held on to much of their land and formal political power, while providing commercial-industrial elites with a favorable business climate. The bourgeoisie in return concentrated most of their energies on economic activities, provided political support for the old elites and took no actions that would threaten the aristocracy's fundamental interests. To a limited but growing extent during the 1850-70 era, the marriage of convenience between the old and new elites was cemented by increasing social and economic interaction between the aristocracy and the commercial elements, which took such forms as intermarriage, joint ownership and service on the boards of directors of corporations, and growing state dependence on the financial community for the purchase of government bonds.

The aristocratic-bourgeois alliance advanced especially during the late 1860s. In 1866-7, constitutional revisions in Denmark, Sweden, Germany, Rumania, Austria, and Hungary marked crucial turning points in the evolution of the business-nobility coalitions, as had earlier constitutional settlements in 1848 in Sardinia (the core of the future united Italy) and the Netherlands, and the aftermath of 1830 in the United Kingdom, Belgium, Switzerland, France, and Iberia. In all of these regions (as well as in Norway ever since its 1815 settlement with Sweden), by 1870 the rising upper middle classes had won their basic demands in the civil liberties arena: constitutional government, a suffrage broad enough to encompass them, and a ban on prior censorship of the press (see Tables 1.1 and 2.1). Of all of the independent countries of Europe (with the exception of tiny Montenegro) only Russia lacked these features in 1870.

Although by 1870 the basic civil liberties demands of the upper middle classes had been satisfied, and even in Russia the government increasingly adopted policies that fostered economic growth and favored business interests, the lower classes in almost all of Europe continued to be systematically excluded from political power and denied channels whereby they might peacefully voice their grievances. Except in Switzerland, the vast majority of the adult male population was either legally still barred from voting in 1870 (see Table 1.1) or denied significant influence by electoral corruption (or, in the case of Denmark, by the absence of parliamentary responsibility by the government to the popularly-elected legislative chamber). While except in Russia prior censorship of the press had been abolished by 1870, all of the major countries except the United Kingdom still retained and used extensive discretionary authority to prosecute or hinder the radical and working-class press. Until very late in the 1850-70 period, trade unions and strikes continued to be illegal in most countries, while even after 1870 they were banned in several countries and subjected to severe administrative harassment in many others (see Table 2.2).

As during the pre-1850 period, day to day politics and public affairs during the following 20 years generally concerned only a small fraction of the population everywhere in Europe. The rural lower classes that constituted a majority of the European citizenry and the urban workers were too preoccupied with the daily struggle to survive to devote their energies to the decisions of kings and to parliamentary debates that rarely seemed to have any clear relevance to their concerns, especially since in most countries the majority of the population still could not vote. Although there were very sharp but brief economic downturns in 1857 and 1866, nothing like the economic disaster of 1846-8 occurred in the two decades after 1850 to mobilize lower-class discontent and focus it on the political arena. On the other hand, the gradual spread of literacy, schooling, and newspapers did combine to make "public opinion" more of a daily force to be reckoned with than ever before. This was especially true after the 1859-60 victories of Italian nationalism, which gave a tremendous boost to liberal, nationalist, and "underdog" hopes all over Europe. Several developments reflected a growing articulateness and organizational strength of the lower classes in the more advanced European societies by 1870: the formation of the First International (a group that sought to coordinate activities of working-class movements throughout Europe) in 1864; the 1867 electoral reform in the United Kingdom; the Spanish revolution of 1868; increased labor activity and the lifting of restrictions on trade unions in 1864-70 in France, Austria, Germany, Spain, and Belgium. As before 1850, organized working-class activities and discontent during the 1850-70 period were mostly evident among the relatively educated and independent skilled tradesmen and craftsmen who were increasingly affected by mechanization and the growth of trade and population, all of which frequently put downward pressure on wages and threatened their former ability to control prices and working conditions.

## A Decade of Reaction, 1850-1858

The decade following the suppression of the 1848-9 revolutions was one of dark reaction in all of the major countries of continental Europe, with the exception of the significant thaw in Russia after the death of Czar Nicholas I in 1855. Most of the minor European countries, as well as the United Kingdom, were also affected by the general mood of conservatism, and perhaps exhaustion, that prevailed in Europe in the 1850s, although political controls in these states were generally not nearly so harsh as in the major European regions. In short, the 1850s demonstrated something like a Newtonian law of politics, since generally the states that experienced the most severe upheavals in 1848 afterwards experienced the most severe reactions, while the regions that were relatively undisturbed in 1848 generally escaped severe repression afterwards.

### The Major Regions of the Continent, 1850-1858

The post-1848 regimes in Germany, the Habsburg Empire, France, Russia and Italy were dominated by restored absolutist or highly conservative constitutional monarchial rule, the secret police, strict press censorship, and tight restrictions or complete prohibition of political and working-class assembly and association. One historian's characterization of the regime in the Habsburg Empire as the "second enlarged edition of the Metternich system" (Jaszi 1966: 100) applies equally well to these other countries. As in 1815, the post-1848 regimes were dominated by a fear of recurring revolution, and all major aspects of policy were oriented towards preventing such an eventuality. Thus, the 1850s saw a general revival of a Restoration-style throne-altar alliance against subversion. A number of countries signed agreements (concordats) with the Catholic church that gave that body great power over the education systems, press, and other areas of society. Such concordats were signed in Tuscany in 1851, Austria in 1855, Naples and Württemberg in 1857, and Baden in 1859. The French Loi Falloux of 1850 and the regime of Prussian Minister of Education Karl von Raumer in the 1850s led to the establishment of similar clerical domination of the schools in those countries. The school systems in all of these areas reflected the dictum of the bishop of Barcelona: "Religion is the only guarantee of order" (Kiernan 1966: 127).

Most German states, with the notable exception of Bavaria, competed with each other to wipe out the constitutional gains of 1848, which Prussian King Frederick William termed the "democratic filth of the year of shame" (Pinson 1954: 111). In Saxony, Württemberg and Hesse-Darmstadt in 1850, and in most of the other states during the immediate post-1848 period, legislative assemblies elected under the liberal franchises of 1848 were dissolved, and the 1848 constitutions were abolished by royal decrees. In Prussia, where Frederick William had forcibly dissolved the 1848 constituent assembly in December 1848 and subsequently promulgated a constitution, his own provisions for universal and equal male suffrage were scrapped in May 1849 when the assembly elected under such provisions displeased him. Frederick William dissolved the chamber and decreed a new electoral law establishing the famous three-class voting system, which allowed the wealthiest 15 to 20 per cent of the voters to dominate elections completely. Prussian police pressure during elections in the 1850s was notorious, as were the rigid press controls and extensive spy apparatus organized during the reactionary ministry of Baron Otto von Manteuffel (1850-58) by interior minister Count Ferdinand von Westphalen, Karl Marx's brother-in-law. While Manteuffel's authoritarian ministry made minor concessions to the lower classes, especially the artisans, in an attempt to reconcile the poor to the crown, Westphalen's police did not scruple to use forged evidence in political trials, most notably in the notorious 1852 Cologne trial that destroyed Marx's Communist League and led to long jail terms for seven leaders of the group.

Efforts to coordinate the post-1848 reaction in Germany were undertaken by the restored Confederation diet. In 1852, the diet established a commission, popularly known as the "Reaction Committee" to pressure the states to revoke any remaining liberal left-overs. In 1853-4 the diet banned throughout Germany all workers' organizations "which pursue political, socialistic or communistic purposes" (Laidler 1968: 224), barred women and minors from joining associations, required the deposit of high caution bonds by all German newspapers and barred press criticism of public officials.

In the Habsburg Monarchy, where the new Emperor, Franz Joseph (1848-1916) had dissolved the Austrian Constituent Assembly in March 1849 and promulgated his own constitution (following the Prussian example), the decreed constitution, which included generous provisions for civil liberties, was never put in effect. It was finally abolished in December 1851, under the inspiration of Louis Napoleon Bonaparte's coup overthrowing the French constitutional regime earlier that month. Although equality before the law and the 1848 abolition of feudal dues and services was retained, popular representation at all levels was eliminated (save for powerless communal councils) and the empire reverted to complete absolutism for a decade. Franz Joseph, who invariably appeared in military uniform and decorated his audience chamber with pictures of the repression of the 1848 revolt in

Vienna, wrote to his mother, "We have thrown all constitutions overboard and there is now only one master in Austria" (Tapie 1971: 287). The Habsburg regime in the 1850s, known as the "Bach system" for Minister of the Interior Alexander Bach (1849-59), was to an extraordinary degree based on the police, the military and military police known as the gendarmerie, who were paid premiums depending upon the harshness of jail terms resulting from their arrests. Military rule or martial law was maintained in Vienna and Prague until September 1853, in Galicia and the Hungarian lands (including Croatia and Transylvania) until May 1854, and in Lombardy-Venetia until 1857. A swarm of police spies kept tabs on all suspected dissidents and prominent individuals, including Bach himself.

With the quasi-exception of Lombardy-Venetia, the entire monarchy was subjected to a highly centralized bureaucratic rule that swept aside traditional geographic boundaries and historic rights. German was made the only official language throughout the empire, and non-German nationalities were subjected to arbitrary command by imported officials known as "Bach's hussars," who knew nothing of their languages or customs. Even nationalities such as the Croats, who fought for Franz Joseph against the revolt of the Hungarians, received this treatment. A popular joke of the times bitterly commented that "the Croats got for reward what the Hungarians got for punishment" (Ignotus 1972: 67), and a Hungarian writer remarked that "all nationalities now received equal rights to become Germans" (Kosary 1969: 143). Although the Bach regime was strict everywhere, this was especially the case in Vienna, where severe military control was maintained until 1853; people were shot solely for possession of arms as late as the spring of 1849; and troops occupied the "Aula," the great university assembly hall that had been a major center of the 1848 revolution, until 1857. In Bohemia, where a rebellion in Prague had been bombarded into submission in June 1848 and a revolutionary conspiracy was squelched by harsh measures in May 1849, virtually all prominent radicals and liberals of 1848 were jailed, driven into silence or kept under surveillance by police chief Sacher Masoch. The great Czech journalist Karel Havliček was forced to close down two newspapers and was sentenced to administrative exile in the Tyrol even though acquitted by a jury for press offenses. In Hungary, which was arbitrarily divided into five administrative districts and deprived of any recognition of its national existence, hundreds were arrested for such offenses as singing seditious songs, wearing forbidden colors or making remarks that offended the police or one of "Bach's hussars." As late as 1852, death sentences were still being meted out for offenses of 1848 in Hungary, and Hungarians were still being flogged for political offenses. Perhaps the best summary of the regime was offered by a socialist veteran of 1848, who described the Bach system as a "standing army of soldiers, a sitting army of officials, a kneeling army of priests and a creeping army of denunciators" (Kimball 1964: 28).

In France, the period between the brutal suppression of the June 1848 workers' uprising in Paris and Louis Napoleon Bonaparte's

December 1851 coup d'état overthrowing the republican government was one of steadily growing reaction and repression, fed by panicky conservatives' fear of the "red spectre" posed by the lower classes. Controls on the press and freedom of association were drastically tightened after the "June Days" of 1848 and a state of siege was maintained for four months. Political controls continued to be stringent after the adoption of a new constitution in November 1848, which provided for universal male suffrage elections both for a unicameral legislative assembly and a president of the republic. In December 1848, Napoleon's nephew Louis Napoleon Bonaparte was overwhelmingly elected president, largely on the basis of his name and his chameleon-like ability to appear all things to all men.

Conservatives' fears were fed by the May 1849 legislative elections, which resulted in a conservative majority of 500 out of 760 members, but also returned about 180 radical republicans, generally known as Montagnards or Democratic-Socialists. A new excuse for repression was provided in June 1849 by an attempted uprising in Lyon--during which 200 rebels were killed and 1,200 arrested--and a simultaneous demonstration in Paris in protest against the dispatch of troops to help suppress the revolutionary republican government in Rome. Over 30 legislative deputies implicated in the protests were stripped of their seats, all political clubs were outlawed and the press was placed under new harsh restrictions, including a ban on publication of any "erroneous or inaccurate facts likely to disturb the peace" (Merriman 1978: 31). Nonetheless, in the March 1850 by-elections, Montagnards were elected in 21 of the 30 elections held to replace the deputies purged in 1849. Amidst a new wave of conservative panic, in mid-1850 a suffrage law was enacted that reduced the voting rolls by almost one-third--over one-half in Paris--and press controls were further intensified. Despite massive repression in 1851, including over 330 newspaper prosecutions, the political firings of about 1,500 teachers, dismissals of hundreds of locally elected mayors, and the dissolutions of hundreds of organizations and elected municipal councils, the Montagnards were only forced underground and not destroyed. Even though repression became so intense that simply wearing red ties and bonnets, singing opposition songs or crying, "Vive la République sociale" could lead to jail terms, the Montagnards were able to survive by meeting secretly or in the guise of social clubs or café conversation.

While the "red hysteria" continued to grow, Louis Napoleon and the legislative assembly became increasingly embroiled in a power struggle. After the Assembly rejected Louis's demand that the 1848 constitution be amended so he could run again for president, Louis effected a military coup on the night of December 1/2, 1851. Hundreds of legislators and opposition figures were arrested and the assembly was occupied by troops and dissolved. Although massive troop concentrations and preventive arrests blocked any serious resistance to the coup in the major cities, there was enormous opposition, involving an estimated 100,000 people, among Montagnards in about 30 departments of southern and central France. The opposition was put down with great harshness. A state of siege was imposed for about four months in half of France, about 500 civilians were killed in battle and a minimum of 27,000 people were arrested in a massive crackdown that completely destroyed the Montagnard network. Of those arrested, 9,600 were sentenced to deportation to Algeria, 1,500 were expelled from France and 8,000 were sentenced to police surveillance or "internment" in France away from their homes. Although about 3,500 of the deportation sentences were soon overturned and many other penalties were quashed during the next few years, by the time of a general amnesty in 1859 1,200 deportees were still in Algeria.

Although the state of siege was ended in March 1852, harsh repressive controls continued under the new regime, which in December 1852 was transformed into the Second French Empire, headed by Louis, restyled Emperor Napoleon III. All political societies were outlawed, the "Marseillaise" was forbidden as a republican song, and all newspapers were subjected to administrative warnings and suppression without recourse to the courts. Many newspapers were forced to close and those that remained were kept under such close supervision that one opposition legislator commented, "There is but one journalist in France and that journalist is the Emperor" (Kulstein 1969: 42). Until 1864, strikes were illegal, and until 1868 trade unions and unauthorized public assemblies were not tolerated. Between 1852 and 1860, over 700 prosecutions arising from strikes were initiated, leading to about 4,000 fines or jail sentences. An extensive secret police network kept tabs on public opinion, and education was rigidly and centrally supervised, especially during the reign of Fortoul as minister of education (1851-6). The teaching of philosophy was banned, instructors were told to shave off any "anarchical beards," and an estimated 3,000-4,000 teachers, including such well-known figures as the historian Jules Michelet, the former prime minister François Guizot, and the philosopher and former education minister Victor Cousin, were purged from their positions. Elective mayors were replaced by appointed officials, and massive purges of other local officials were conducted. In November 1858, for example, almost 400 French communes were without municipal councils because they had been suspended or dissolved by the government.

Under the decreed constitution of 1852, Louis appointed an upper legislative house, while the lower chamber was elected by universal male suffrage. Intense administrative pressure was used during elections until after 1860, and the lower chamber was almost emasculated by strict controls on its powers and procedures: it could meet only three months a year and lacked the right to initiate legislation, question ministers (who were responsible only to the president), publish accounts of its proceedings, or even choose its presiding officer. Louis Napoleon commented that the lower house--which one contemporary termed un parlement anonyme ("faceless parliament")--would not waste its time "in vain interpellations, in frivolous accusations, and in passionate struggles, the only object of which was to overthrow ministers in order to take their place" (Bury 1964: 38).

Italy during the 1850s, except Sardinia, endured a revival, in even more repressive garb, of the post-1820 and post-1830 reactions. Lombardy-Venetia remained under Austrian military rule until 1857, while Austrian troops propping up the rulers they had restored remained in Tuscany and Modena until 1855, in Parma until 1857 and in the northern and eastern portions of the Papal States until 1859. French troops occupied Rome, with a brief interruption in the 1860s, until 1870. The Austrian regime in Lombardy-Venetia was extremely harsh. After a secret organization that had been selling bonds to support Mazzinian conspiracies was uncovered in Lombardy in 1852, 100 were jailed and 10 (the "martyrs of Belfiore") were executed at Fort Belfiore near Mantua. Grand Duke Leopold II of Tuscany (1824-59), a relatively popular figure before 1848, became hated in the 1850s for retaining 10,000 Austrian troops in his realm, imposing strict press controls, wearing an Austrian uniform and revoking the 1848 constitution in violation of his promises. Modena's Duke Francis V (1846-59) took after his father, filling the jails with liberals and the streets with spies. In Parma, Duke Charles III (1849-54) closed the universities, personally caned passersby who failed to raise their hats to him, and had 300 people publicly whipped during the first five months of his reign for such offenses as possessing liberal pamphlets. In the Papal States, Pope Pius IX revoked most of his 1846-48 reforms and reverted to virtually absolute and clerical-dominated rule. Men were jailed for "appearing inclined to novelty" and "being too loquacious," and, in Perugia, even shoes and ribbons decorated with revolutionary colors were forbidden by the Austrians (King 1912: 376).

The regime in the Kingdom of the Two Sicilies became a European-wide scandal following an 1851 visit there by the the British politician William Gladstone that resulted in the publication of his Two Letters to Lord Aberdeen on the State Prosecutions of the Neapolitan Government. It described the regime there as based on "incessant, systematic, deliberate violation of the law." One striking sentence in Gladstone's work became famous: "I have seen and heard the strong and too true expression used, E la negazione di Dio eretta a sistema di governo--'This is the negation of God erected into a system of government' " (Hibbert 1970: 177). King Ferdinand, oblivious to the uproar, proceeded to a new series of political prosecutions, including the deportation of 100 bakers who struck at Palermo in 1851 and a trial of 300 liberals compromised in the 1848 revolution. An estimated 40,000 persons are believed to have suffered altogether from various political prosecutions, with hundreds jailed or exiled without trials or even charges. In the city of Naples, power during the 1850s fell increasingly into the hands of the Camorra, or organized crime. The British minister at Naples later wrote:

There was no class, high or low, that had not its representatives among the members of the Society, which

> was a vast organized association for the extortion of
> blackmail in every conceivable shape and form. ... No one
> thought of refusing to pay, for the consequences of a refusal
> were too well known, anyone rash enough to demur being apt
> to be found soon after mysteriously stabbed by some
> unknown individual, whom the police were careful never to
> discover (Hibbert 1970: 182).

In 1856, as the stench of the Ferdnandine regime grew more putrid,
Britain and France broke diplomatic relations with Naples.

The only ray of hope for Italian nationalists in the 1850s emanated
from Sardinia, which alone survived 1848 with an intact constitution
and freedom of the press. Sardinia gave refuge to an estimated
100,000 exiles from the other Italian states, and while by modern
standards it was hardly a democratic country, by comparison with the
rest of Italy it shone as a beacon of enlightenment and justice. The
1848 constitution restricted the suffrage for the lower house to about
2 per cent of the population and established an appointed upper house.
The dominant political figure of the 1850s, Count Camillo di Cavour
(prime minister 1852-61), although basically devoted to
constitutionalism, was extremely conservative on social issues, and not
above rigging elections, bribing and occasionally suppressing
newspapers, harassing republicans and clericals, and ruling by decree
during critical periods. The extremely narrow electoral base of the
regime made politics the concern of a narrow elite of aristocrats,
landowners, merchants, and industrialists who had little concern for
the interests of the lower classes. Political life consisted of a shifting
coalition of centrist factions with few real ideological differences.

The post-1848 period in Russia, until the death of Nicholas I in
1855, was a period of extreme reaction, even by the standards of
Nicholine rule. After 1848, all Russians living abroad were ordered to
return to the country, foreign travel to Russia was limited and the
censorship was drastically tightened. By 1850 there were at least 10
separate censorship authorities in Russia, leading one liberal censor to
complain, "If one adds up all the officials in charge of censorship, their
number would exceed the number of books published in a year"
(Riasonovsky 1969: 222). Phrases such as the "forces of nature" were
deleted from a physics textbook; Roman emperors "perished" rather
than "were killed"; and, after 1851, all musical scores had to be
submitted to censorship to detect possible cipher messages concealed
in the notation. Poets who confessed that their mistresses held
sovereign sway in their hearts were rebuked with the message that "no
law-abiding citizen ought to put anything above God and the Emperor"
(McManners 1969: 175). The exiled Russian intellectual Alexander
Herzen described the Nicholine regime as

> a living pyramid of crimes, abuses and bribery, built up of
> policemen, scoundrels, heartless German officials
> everlastingly greedy, ignorant judges everlastingly drunk,
> aristocrats everlastingly base: all this is held together by a

community of interest in plunder and gain, and supported by 600,000 animated machines with bayonets (Crankshaw 1976: 225).

Despite the severe nature of repressive controls in Germany, the Habsburg Empire, France, Italy, and Russia during the 1850s, scattered resistance activities did occur. One of the most common resistance techniques was political funerals, such as those held for the French republican politician and astronomer François Arago (1853), the Hungarian poet Mihály Vörösmarty (1855), the Czech journalist Karel Havlíček (1856), and the Italian patriot Emilio Dandalo (1859). In Hungary and Lombardy-Venetia social boycotts of Austrian officials and affairs sponsored by them were widespread. In Hungary the policy of "passive resistance" included not only refusal to associate with Austrians socially, but also refusal to accept any form of public office and widespread resistance to tax collections. The Hungarian gentry also expressed their opposition to the Bach regime by wearing traditional national dress and listening endlessly to the Magyar national dance, the csárdás, or to Franz Liszt's Hungarian Rhapsody no. 15, with its "Rákóczi March," named for a leader of an early eighteenth-century uprising against the Habsburgs. Magyar women wore necklaces made of coins minted in 1848 and bracelets engraved with the initials of revolutionary heroes. Throughout Italy, support for a united state under the leadership of Sardinia was expressed by slogans hailing opera composer Giuseppe Verdi, whose initials were used in wall graffiti to convey the message "V̲ittorio E̲mmanuelle R̲e D'Italia" (Victor Emmanuel [the ruler of Sardinia] K̲ing of Italy̲). Audiences attending Verdi's operas in Lombardy-Venetia often turned to boxes occupied by Austrian officers and chanted, "Viva Verdi!" while shaking their fists. In France, large quantities of material highly critical of Emperor Napoleon III were smuggled into France from the community of 10,000 or so French exiles living in England, Belgium, and Switzerland. The most notable exile, Victor Hugo, became something of a national hero. His bitter published attacks on the emperor were smuggled into France in hollowed-out lumps of coal, in hermetically sealed boxes dropped off the Brittany coast, and even occasionally in plaster busts of Napoleon III!

In some cases, opposition to the reactionary regimes of the 1850s took violent forms. Over 130 peasant disorders were recorded between 1850 and 1855 in Russia. A revolutionary conspiracy in Hungary was broken up in 1852 by mass arrests and followed by 25 executions and many jail sentences. In Italy, plotting by Mazzini and his disciples led to the usual fiascos. The most serious Mazzinian rising fizzled out in Milan in February 1853, shortly after the execution of five of the "martyrs of Belfiore." About 50 of an expected several hundred conspirators appeared and were quickly subdued, although not before 10 Austrians were killed and 54 wounded. Sixteen executions and hundreds of arrests followed. The families of those executed were billed for the rope used to hang their sons. Milan was cut off from the outside world for a month, with no one allowed to leave or enter without a permit, and a stage of siege was maintained for over a year. In mid-1857, a band of 22 men under the command of Carlo Pisacane, a Neapolitan aristocrat and one of the first Italian socialists, succeeded in freeing a thousand prisoners from the island prison of Ponza in the Two Sicilies before they were literally hacked to pieces by peasants who mistook them for brigands.

In March 1854, the tyrannical Duke Charles III of Parma was assassinated, but a subsequent attempted rising in Parma was crushed by 3,000 Austrian troops, three executions, and a state of siege that was maintained for a year. Napoleon III was the target of several assassination attempts, as was Frederick William IV of Prussia in May 1850 and Emperor Franz Joseph of Austria in February 1853. The attempt on Franz Joseph, by a Hungarian tailor, led to a general intensification of repression throughout the empire, and especially in Hungary, where almost 400 people were arrested in Pest alone, charged with condoning the attempt or "suspicious behavior" (Szabad 1977: 65). The would-be assassin was executed, and 18 of his co-workers were condemned to hard labor, imprisonment, or deportation. The most sensational attempt on Napoleon III, the bomb thrown by the Italian revolutionary Felice Orsini on January 14, 1858, killed eight people and wounded about 150. Orsini was executed, and a sweeping Law of Public Safety was immediately passed authorizing administrative imprisonment, expulsion, or transportation to Algeria of past political offenders, and, in the case of those without past political offenses, judicial prosecution of persons seeking to trouble the "public peace" or incite "hatred or mistrust of the Emperor's government" (Payne 1966: 277). Two thousand arrests and over 400 deportations followed.


## The United Kingdom and the Minor Continental States, 1850-1858

In most of the minor European continental states, as well as in the United Kingdom, repression did not reach the dimensions of that in the major European countries during the 1850s. However, the general mood throughout the Continent was deeply conservative.

Political conditions were extraordinarily quiet in the United Kingdom in the 1850s. British Chartism had collapsed in 1848, while the Repeal movement and its more radical spin-off, the Young Ireland movement, which was involved in a few weak revolutionary attempts in Ireland in 1848-9, had disintegrated with the death of O'Connell in 1847 and the failure of the 1848-9 risings. Although a few minor reforms were passed by parliament in the 1850s, notably elimination of the newspaper stamp tax, there was no organized working-class political movement and no sense of need for further social and political reforms, even though only 4 per cent of the population was enfranchised and millions of citizens lived on or below the margins of subsistence. Industrial and landed elites controlled both parties. Lord Palmerston, the Whig prime minister in 1855-8 and 1859-65, reflected the dominant mood when he was asked in 1864 what his legislative program would be: "Oh, there is really nothing to be done. We cannot go on adding to the Statute Book ad infinitum" (Arnstein 1971: 81).

In Norway, the 1848 revolutions in other European countries had inspired a lower-class movement of urban workers and rural landless laborers and dwarf farmers under the leadership of Marcus Thrane, the son of a bank director. The Thrane movement spread with incredible rapidity, reaching a peak membership of about 30,000 in about 300 local chapters by 1851. The foremost demand of the movement, expressed in a reform petition with 13,000 signatures presented to Swedish King Oscar I, was for universal suffrage. The continued growth of the movement inspired growing alarm among the ruling Norwegian bureaucrats by 1851. Thrane was arrested for blasphemy, and when this charge was thrown out of court, some minor disturbances involving members of the movement, which Thrane disavowed, were used as a pretext to re-arrest him, along with almost 150 other members in mid-1851. The young playwright Henrik Ibsen, who wrote for Thrane's newspaper, barely escaped arrest. After being detained for three years, Thrane and another leader were given four-year jail terms in 1854, and 130 others were fined or jailed for offenses "against the security of the state" and "against the public authorities" (Bull 1956: 30). Thrane's newspaper closed down in 1856 after repeated prosecutions. When Thrane emerged from jail in 1858, his movement was in ruins and he emigrated to the United States. The Thrane movement was totally crushed by the repression, and no other organized movement of Norwegian workers re-emerged until 20 years later.

In Sweden, King Oscar I, who had shown signs of moderate liberalism upon his accession to the throne in 1844, was deeply frightened by the 1848 riots in Stockholm, and became increasingly conservative thereafter. In 1851, he made known his opposition to an electoral reform plan introduced by his own government, thereby contributing to its rejection by all except the burgher estate in the riksdag. At about the same time, Oscar also reconstituted his cabinet along conservative lines and, with the help of the Stockholm police, muzzled two radical-socialist newspapers by buying them out. Throughout the 1850s Oscar personally dominated government policy, especially in foreign policy, relying for support largely on the high nobility who dominated the civil service.

In Denmark, 1848-9 had seen the acceptance of constitutionalism by the new king, Frederick VII (1848-63), the adoption of a liberal constitution providing for extensive civil liberties and election of both legislative chambers by quasi-universal manhood suffrage, and war with Prussia and other German states over the future of Schleswig-Holstein. The Schleswig-Holstein conflict was temporarily settled in 1851-2 when the European powers recognized the integrity of the Danish monarchy and the right to succession to the duchies by the next heir to the Danish crown. Denmark agreed to accept a personal union only with the duchies (i.e., the Danish constitution of June 1849 would not apply to them) and to provide special rights of self-government for the duchies in local matters. The settlement was a clear defeat for the German nationalists, but also discredited the Danish National Liberals who had supported the "Ejder Program" of integrating Schleswig into the Danish kingdom. As a result, King

Frederick turned to a conservative ministry headed by the reactionary prime minister Anders Örsted in 1852.

In 1854, Örsted proclaimed a constitution for the common concerns of the <u>helstat</u> (the kingdom and duchies together) by royal decree, leading to bitter opposition in the parliament (riksdag). The king replied by ousting opposition leaders from their seats and dissolving the riksdag. When the 1854 elections returned an opposition majority, Örsted was forced out. A new National Liberal cabinet obtained riksdag approval of a new <u>helstat</u> constitution, which established a national council (rigsråd) to handle defense, finance, and foreign policy, while leaving local matters to the riksdag (for Jutland and the islands) and the provincial assemblies of Schleswig and Holstein. The new <u>helstat</u> constitution aroused severe opposition in the duchies, where members of the provincial assemblies complained they had not been consulted, and in the German Confederation, where it was regarded as violating Holstein's special status as a confederation member. German pressure forced the National Liberal ministry of C. C. Hall to suspend the <u>helstat</u> constitution in Holstein in 1858. Opposition continued, however, in Holstein, where Danish officials sought to impose their language in German-speaking areas and to suppress German nationalist agitation by banning anti-Danish propaganda, public meetings and the importation of foreign publications.

In the Low Countries, constitutional reforms in 1848 survived the post-revolutionary reaction, but did not change the fundamentally conservative character of the regimes. In Belgium, where the Liberal party came to power in the 1847 elections, the suffrage had been expanded from 1.1 to 1.8 per cent of the population. In the Netherlands, the 1848 constitutional reform, sponsored by a deeply frightened King William II and largely drafted by the liberal leader Jan Thorbecke, replaced the formerly royally appointed upper legislative chamber with a body elected by the provincial estates and made the lower chamber, formerly elected by the provincial estates, directly elected. The 1848 constitution also generally strengthened the power of the Dutch parliament and granted freedom of the press, assembly and association. However, the basically conservative character of the Dutch (as well as the Belgian) liberals was demonstrated in 1850 when Thorbecke's ministry sponsored an electoral law that enfranchised only 2.5 per cent of the population for the direct elections for the lower chamber, compared to the approximately 3 per cent previously enfranchised in the former indirect elections for that body. In both Belgium and the Netherlands, the narrow suffrage allowed the major parties to ignore social issues and the yawning gulf between rich and poor. Taxation and conscription systems that bore unfairly on the poor were maintained; the plight of the lower class was ignored in parliamentary debates; and political controversy in both countries centered on whether state-supported or subsidized schools should be secular or religious in orientation. The totally unrepresentative character of parliamentary life in the Low Countries is clearly indicated by the fact that in 1850, 70 percent of the Dutch parliament held law degrees, at a time when less than 0.1 per cent of the Dutch population attended a university. Eighty-one of the 100 ministers who served in the Netherlands between 1848 and 1877 came from noble or merchant patrician families. Trade union activity remained illegal in both countries, and despite the freedom of press guarantees in the 1831 Belgian and 1848 Dutch constitutions, the few radical journalists sometimes faced severe persecution (in Belgium, this was partly due to pressure from Napoleon III, who resented criticism of him by French exiles and others in the Belgian press). Thus, in 1851 the radical Dutch journalist Eillert Meeter was forced into exile by a five-year jail term, and in 1854 journalist Jan de Vries was sent to jail for three years for attacking the monarchy.

In Switzerland, the extremely liberal 1848 constitution, with provisions for universal male suffrage in national and cantonal elections, guarantees of freedom of the press and association, and elimination of the death penalty, survived intact in the 1850s and made the country unquestionably the most democratic in Europe. However, the flood of about 15,000 French, German, Austrian, and Italian refugees into Switzerland during the 1848-52 period exposed the tiny country to a new round of threats and warnings from the conservative powers. Although the saber rattling was never translated into military action against Switzerland, partly because of mutual mistrust among the conservative powers, the Swiss may have warded off stronger action by themselves taking harsh measures against the refugees. Thus, in response to strong pressure from Napoleon III, many French refugees were expelled in February 1852. Other refugees were removed from border regions and expelled if they protested against such treatment. By early 1851, the British government was complaining that French pressures on Switzerland were compelling too many refugees to leave there for the United Kingdom; the British also sent a note to the Swiss asking their help to prevent the "further congregation of men of this kind in England" (Imlah 1966: 67).

In Iberia during the 1850s, authoritarian conservative forces continued to control the government of Spain, despite a briefly successful moderately liberal revolution in 1854-6, while in Portugal the highly authoritarian government in power in 1850 yielded to a more moderately conservative regime in 1851. In Portugal, Queen Maria II gave power back to Costa Cabral--whose dictatorship had led to rebellion in 1846--in June 1849, after British and Spanish military intervention in 1847 had saved her throne. Although Cabral began his rule with an amnesty, he soon resumed his old ways, "baking" new peers to control the upper house, clamping down on the press with a strict censorship law in February 1850 (known as the "lei de rolhas" or "law of the corks"), and in general steadily alienating all sectors of Portuguese opinion. In 1851, the Chartist leader Saldanha led a successful military coup against Cabral, which reflected the consensus among the small Portuguese upper and middle classes that a more broadly based system of government than the Cabralist regime was needed to end the fratricidal civil wars that had wracked and wrecked the country ever since 1820. At the beginning of his five-year rule,

Saldanha laid the legal basis for the subsequent system of "rotativism" that endured until about 1900 by expanding the suffrage, freeing the press, and slightly increasing the powers of the legislature. After 1850, the two major Portuguese parties, representing the heirs of the Chartist and Septembrist movements of 1835-50, tacitly agreed to "rotate" in power. They took turns ruling the country, with the aid of massive election rigging and the support of King Peter V (1853-61) and his successors. Assured of a chance to hold power every few years without the need to resort to violence, the parties lost any significant ideological differences and saw no need to try to appeal to the lower classes for support.

In Spain, an increasingly important factor after 1850 was the completely irresponsible and selfish nature of Queen Isabel II and her domineering mother María Cristina. Isabel's unwillingness to let the liberal opposition (Progressives) gain power led inevitably to conspiracies and uprisings, since the narrow suffrage, rigged elections and the tightly controlled press provided no legal alternatives. Criticism from the legislature was generally followed by dissolution and either rule by decree or new, rigged elections. Growing criticism of the system was fostered by a series of financial scandals involving the royal family, a cholera outbreak and economic downturn in 1853-4 and threatened famine in Galicia. Parliament was suspended twice in 1853, and in early 1854 a minor military mutiny at Saragossa was followed by a wave of arrests and press confiscations and declaration of a nationwide state of emergency. In late June, several of the more liberal Moderate (i.e. conservative) generals, led by Leopoldo O'Donnell, organized a military rising outside Madrid aimed at a slight broadening of the regime to avoid a general lower-class uprising, perhaps under the inspiration of Saldanha's 1851 coup in Portugal. When the rising failed to gain popular support, O'Donnell issued a manifesto at Manzanares on July 6 promising liberalized press and suffrage laws, and reestablishment of the national militia and municipal autonomy--both abolished by the Moderates after 1843. The Manzanares manifesto, which endorsed almost all of the key Progressive demands, triggered popular uprisings in numerous Spanish provincial centers. Queen Isabel issued a statement apologizing for a series of "deplorable misunderstandings" (Kiernan 1966: 79) and turned in desperation to General Espartero, the Progressive hero of 1840, who had quickly alienated his support once in power but had been transformed into a vague symbol of radical reform in his retirement.

Once in power, a government that largely owed its support to the lower and middle classes concentrated almost exclusively on fostering the interests of the upper and upper-middle classes. Despite some symbolic concessions, including an end to censorship and a ban on the death penalty for political offenses, the fundamental demands of the lower classes--an easing of food prices, reform of the class-biased tax and conscription systems and agrarian reform--were rejected, as were proposals for free primary education and freedom of assembly and association. The stillborn 1855 constitution and accompanying laws enfranchised less than 7 per cent of the population and continued severe press restrictions. When the government ordered all unions dissolved in Barcelona, 50,000 workers walked out in an extraordinary ten-day general strike, carrying banners reading "Association or Death" (Payne 1970: 15). Continued industrial unrest in Barcelona in early 1856 and a series of food riots in mid-1856 were met with a series of executions, including nine at Palencia, although no one had been killed in the disorders there.

By mid-1856, a rising tide of anti-red hysteria was sweeping Spain, much like the red fear of 1849-51 in France. Increasing factionalization within the government led Isabel to turn from Espartero to O'Donnell in mid-July, signalling the end to any possibility of significant reform. Futile uprisings in protest of O'Donnell's accession to power broke out in Madrid and Barcelona. They were harshly put down, with about 800 rebels and 100 government troops killed altogether. A state of seige was maintained until November, the constituent assembly, which had voted no confidence in O'Donnell, was dissolved, and the conservative 1845 constitution was repromulgated. Isabel turned to Narváez in October 1856, who responded with his usual election-rigging (with an electorate shrunken back down to 1 per cent of the population) and press crackdown, along with a further suppression of the Catalan labor movement. Narváez was given a new chance to show his repressive mettle in mid-1857 when a quasi-republican rising of about 200 artisans and day laborers erupted at El Arahal near Seville, complete with the burning of land records and attacks on landowners' houses. Fifty of the perpetrators were executed, many more were sent to penal settlements and mass arrests were effected in Madrid with studied brutality.

In July 1858 Isabel tapped O'Donnell once more in an attempt to appease growing discontent. O'Donnell governed for five years (the so-called long ministry of 1858-63) under the "Liberal Union" banner, a general coalition of the propertied classes in defense of the status quo, which included the more liberal Moderates and the more conservative Progressives. Although no fundamental change occurred, there was a general easing of tension as press controls were relaxed; the domestic economy was fueled by a great railroad boom; and public opinion was diverted by foreign adventures in Morocco, Vietnam, Mexico, the Dominican Republic, and Peru (which led to a 115 per cent increase in military spending betwen 1857 and 1860). Election rigging was conducted by the "Great Elector," Interior Minister Posada Herrara, with a certain amount of taste and tact that allowed dissidents to gain some representation. It was a sign of the times that in 1861 when 600 rebels under republican leadership seized the town of Loja, near Granada, and were soon joined by 10,000 armed peasants, "only" six executions followed, along with 400 sentences of transportation to penal colonies in Spanish Africa.

In the Balkans, the authoritarian rule of Turkey in Bulgaria and of King Otto in Greece continued during the 1850s. In the Danubian Principalities, the Russian yoke was cast off and autonomy gained as the result of the Russian defeat in the Crimean War. A power struggle in Serbia betwen the senate and the prince led to the restoration to power of former dictator Milos Obrenovic in 1858.

There was considerable unrest in Bulgaria during the 1850s. However, peasant uprisings, provoked by oppressive taxes and the gross corruption and extortion of Turkish landlords and officials and spurred by hopes of Russian liberation during the Crimean War, were all betrayed or easily suppressed. The most serious revolt erupted in 1850 in northwestern Bulgaria, where about 15,000 poorly armed peasants were crushed by Turkish troops. About 700 rebels were killed, compared with 15 Turks. Turkish troops burned down the entire village of Belogradchik and slaughtered over 2,000 civilians after suppressing the uprising.

In Greece, King Otto reverted to a thinly disguised absolute monarchy after the death of his favorite John Kolettis in 1847, ruling through a series of puppet prime ministers who manipulated elections. Otto attempted to take advantage of Turkish involvement during the Crimean War in 1854. He supported uprisings in Turkish-controlled Greek ethnic areas north of the Greek frontier, but this only triggered an occupation of Piraeus, the port of Athens, by French and British troops determined to uphold Turkish territorial integrity. The British and French also imposed a ministry against Otto's wishes and forced him to renounce his irredentist tactics. The occupation, which lasted from 1854 to 1857, gained the king considerable popularity.

In Serbia, the 1850s were marked by a power struggle between the self-perpetuating and dominant oligarchs in the senate and Prince Alexander Karageorgević. The infighting had little impact and aroused little interest among the peasants who constituted 90 per cent of the Serbian population, since they had little affection for either the senate or the prince. Serbia was essentially governed during the period by a senate-controlled central bureaucracy consisting largely of Austrian-born and -trained Serbs who regarded the peasants with patronizing disdain and conducted themselves as a separate and privileged caste. The peasants were burdened with heavy taxes to support a system that provided no significant benefits to them, despite their desperate need for cheap credit and improved transportation facilities. Bribery and corruption were pervasive and the heavy-handed police force summarily imposed fines, jail terms, and corporal punishment. The peasants were joined in their discontent by a small group of western-oriented liberals who wanted a popularly elected legislature and guarantees of civil liberties, and also by partisans of the Obrenović dynasty that had been deposed in 1842. The struggle between the prince and senate reached a climax in late 1857 when an alleged plot to kill Alexander hatched by senate members was uncovered. Four senators were jailed, and six others were forced to retire, while a general purge of Alexander's opponents was effected, claiming many innocent victims. The uproar caused by these events—including the brutal treatment of jailed suspects—led to Turkish intervention that forced Alexander to allow the jailed senators to go into exile and to restore the purged senators. In order to resolve the resulting impasse, a popular assembly, sponsored by a coalition of young liberals and Obrenović partisans, was convoked in 1858. The assembly voted to depose Alexander and restore Miloš Obrenović as prince.

In the Danubian Principalities, the defeat of Russia in the Crimean War and the Treaty of Paris in 1856 led to an end of the Russian protectorate. Although nominal Turkish suzerainty was recognized in the Paris treaty, this provision was effectively nullified by a joint guarantee of the European powers for an "independent and national administration" in the Principalities and a call for elections of assemblies to "express the wishes of the population regarding the definitive organization of the Principalities" (Seton-Watson 1934: 244-45). The Moldavian elections, held in July 1857 under Turkish supervision and Austrian military occupation, were marked by notorious and open fraud and coercion designed to prevent the victory of elements favoring a Wallachian-Moldavian union, which was feared for a variety of reasons by Turkey, Austria, and the United Kingdom. Unionist newspapers, organizations and meetings were outlawed, and numerous arrests, threats and beatings were carried out. The limited electoral lists, composed largely of property owners, were so massively purged that only about 10 per cent of the electorate was able to vote. The fraudulent vote led France, Russia, Prussia, and Sardinia, all pro-Unionist countries, to withdraw their ambassadors from Turkey. This pressure and open talk of war in France forced Turkey to agree to new Moldavian elections, which, conducted along with the Wallachian elections in September 1857, chose assemblies that overwhelmingly voted for a united, autonomous state under Turkish suzerainty, with constitutional government and a foreign prince. In August 1858, the European powers, meeting at Paris, established a confusing and ultimately unworkable regime, with separate administrations for the "United Principalities of Moldavia and Wallachia" together with a "central commission" to decide matters of concern to both provinces. Formal Turkish suzerainty and a collective guarantee of the powers was maintained. The electorate for the separate legislatures, which were each to choose their own life-time prince, was so restricted that less than 5,000 qualified to vote in a population of about four million.

## *The Revival of Dissent and the Reconstruction of Europe, 1859-1870*

The decade after 1858 in Europe was characterized by a mood very different from that of the 1850s. Political activity increased in tempo as political dissent reemerged, especially among the middle classes, and, often in direct response to this development, governments in a number of European countries restructured themselves to attempt to accommodate the middle classes without significantly altering the fundamental character of the regimes. Altogether, considerable governmental restructuring of one kind or another occurred during the 1860s in Germany, the Habsburg Empire, France, Sweden, Denmark, Greece, Serbia, Rumania, Spain, the Netherlands, the United Kingdom, Italy, and Russia. In western and central Europe, the general trend of these reforms was to create or consolidate a political structure in which power was shared by the traditional landed nobility and the rising upper-middle-class business community.

The revival of European dissent that was evident in many countries by the late 1850s, and especially after 1858, resulted from a number of factors. One was the defeat of Russia in the Crimean War of 1854-6, which ever since its crushing of the 1830 Polish revolt and the 1848 Hungarian and Rumanian uprisings had been "branded indelibly in the eyes of liberal Europe with the mark of the beast" (Crankshaw 1976: 104) and was universally regarded by European liberals as the "supreme enemy" (Seton-Watson 1967: 316). The Russian defeat encouraged European liberals; in addition, the failure of Austria to support Russia in the Crimean War irretrievably split the alliance of Austria, Prussia, and Russia, which had held firm since 1815. After 1855, Russia, under its new czar, Alexander II (1855-81), turned its attention to internal modernization, and its failure to support Austria proved decisive in the ouster of Habsburg influence from Italy and Germany after 1858. A second factor in the revival of dissent in the late 1850s was probably the Europe-wide financial and economic crash of 1857-9. It broke a general economic boom of the previous five years and shook the general complacency of the middle classes, and it also stirred a limited amount of working class unrest.

A third factor in fostering dissent in the late 1850s was the general and gradual loosening of repressive controls in Europe after about 1854. In the Habsburg Empire, military rule ended in 1853-4 (except in Lombardy-Venetia, where it terminated in 1857), and beginning as early as 1852 political amnesties were granted, culminating with a broad amnesty on the occasion of the emperor's marriage in 1854 and a general amnesty in 1857. In France, Emperor Napoleon III granted a general amnesty in 1859, which included the victims of the draconic Law on General Security of 1858, passed after the Orsini bombing. Many of the German states passed general amnesties between 1859 and 1863, including Prussia in 1862 and Würtemberg in 1863. The atmosphere in Germany changed markedly in 1858 when Prussian King Frederick William IV became mentally incapable and his brother, Prince William, became regent (and king as William I, 1861-88). Although William was a divine-right monarchist, he had a reputation for liberalism that was enhanced by his dismissal of the reactionary ministers Manteuffel and Westphalen, his appointment of a moderately liberal cabinet and his order that the police stop manipulating the elections. The most remarkable change in regime orientation before 1859 unquestionably came in Russia, where Czar Alexander II, who was basically conservative, realized after the Crimean War fiasco that major reforms were needed both to avoid internal upheaval and to strengthen the country against foreign foes. Shortly after his accession in 1855, Alexander relaxed restrictions on the press, education, and foreign travel. He also issued a general political amnesty that allowed prisoners exiled to Siberia (including the Decembrists) to return to European Russia and indicated his intention to abolish serfdom.

Unquestionably the single most important contributor to the rebirth of opposition activity in the late 1850s was the defeat of Austria by France and Sardinia in a brief 1859 war. While the Russian defeat in the Crimean War, the 1857-9 economic downturn, and the easing of repressive controls after 1854, especially in Russia and Prussia, were important factors, the defeat of Austria totally transformed the situation in Italy and greatly encouraged opposition forces throughout Europe. The Austrian defeat led directly to Sardinian annexation of Lombardy and indirectly in 1859-60 to subsequent revolts that ousted the Austrian-backed regimes in Parma, Tuscany, and Modena. There were also popular uprisings in the Papal States and the Kingdom of the Two Sicilies, aided by Sardinian military intervention (and, in the case of the Two Sicilies, aided also by an invasion of a volunteer army under the direction of Giuseppe Garibaldi). All of Italy, save for Venetia (under Austrian control) and Rome (under French occupation and Papal control) was annexed to Sardinia by 1860, after a series of manipulated plebiscites that showed popular support of 95 per cent or more for such action in the various former Italian states. During the plebiscites, opposition newspapers were suppressed and voting was conducted by open ballot and supervised by officials who had already sworn allegiance to Sardinian King Victor Emmanuel. In Sicily, the plebiscite results showed 432,053 to 667 for unity with Sardinia to form a new Italian state, even though many of the peasants either had no idea of what "Italia" meant or thought it was the name of Garibaldi's mistress or wife.

The great victories of 1859-60 for Italian nationalism stirred enormous hopes among nationalists throughout Europe, especially those in Germany, Denmark, Greece, Poland, Hungary, Bohemia, Norway, and the Danubian Principalities. The loss of Lombardy undermined what little support existed for the "Bach system" in the Habsburg Empire, while Emperor Napoleon's support for Sardinia, which led ultimately to annexation of most of the Papal States, deeply alienated French Catholics. French liberals were equally angered by the Emperor's decision to terminate the 1859 war with Austria—without consulting his ally Sardinia—before Venetia as well as Lombardy had been conquered, in violation of his pre-war promise to Sardinia. Thus, the 1859 Austro-Sardinian war revived liberal and nationalist hopes almost everywhere in Europe and drastically altered the mood of the Continent.

The Major Regions of the Continent, 1859-1870

The major European continental regimes were all characterized by policies of conservative reconstruction (or in the case of Italy, construction) during the 1859-70 period. These policies generally failed to address or appease the grievances of the lower classes. However, through parliamentary reforms and/or the easing of press and trade union controls in France, Germany, and the Habsburg Empire, they did create limited channels for the peaceful venting of working-class complaints, previously almost completely impossible. In Russia, the abolition of serfdom in 1861 failed to modify the autocratic and repressive nature of the regime. After 1867 it was the only one in Europe that operated without a constitution or an elected national legislature. The extension of the 1848 Sardinian constitution to formerly absolutist regions of Italy marked an expansion of civil liberties in theory, but in practice the highly restricted nature of the Italian suffrage (as in Austria-Hungary, Prussia, and almost all of the other German states) kept control in the hands of the wealthy. Especially in Italy and Russia, and to a somewhat lesser extent in France, Germany, and the Habsburg realm, organized political discontent continued to be frequently met with severe repression during the 1859-69 period, although dissent was certainly more tolerated than in the 1850s.

Italy. The events of 1859-60 created a new European power in Italy. The 1848 Sardinian constitution was extended to the rest of the peninsula, and in general a policy of "Piedmontization" was pursued. This policy imposed a highly centralized administrative system that placed the peninsula under the control of Sardinian officials, who clearly regarded southern Italians in particular as being inferior and uncivilized. Application of the Sardinian suffrage law throughout Italy kept political control in the hands of 500,000 voters (2 per cent of the population). The Sardinian system of the 1850s, marked by considerable electoral pressure and the manipulation of politics by shifting factions of mercantile, professional, and landed elites mostly concerned about power and patronage, obsessed with balancing the budget and lacking serious concern for the lower classes, intensified after Cavour's death in 1861. Taxation and conscription bore inequitably upon the lower classes, but never became the subject of concern in parliament, whose ability to concentrate on any subject was hampered by rapid ministerial changes. Partly because of semi-consitutional meddling by King Victor Emmanuel, who sometimes dismissed prime ministers without reference to parliament, there were 10 different governments between 1860 and 1869.

The government's failure to address the real problems of Italy was especially apparent with regard to the poverty-stricken south. The "Piedmontization" policy aggravated the problems of the poor there. There was a massive increase in taxation, and the domestic handicraft industry, which overnight lost tariff protection it had long enjoyed, was destroyed. Confiscated ecclesiastical lands in the south were snapped up by the traditional landed elites, who continued to enjoy a brutal semi-feudal domination over the peasantry, reinforced by gangs of armed thugs and retainers who were forerunners of the modern Mafia.

By 1861, a large scale outbreak of brigandage, which took on the dimensions of a separatist rebellion against Sardinia, was convulsing the former Two Sicilies. A parliamentary report read in secret session

to the legislature in 1863 termed the revolt a "savage protest against
centuries of injustice by men reduced to the utmost poverty" (Smith
1969: 74). Over 120,000 troops, almost half of the Italian army, was
dispatched to suppress the 1861 revolt. Both sides conducted
themselves with incredible savagery. Captured soldiers were
crucified, mutilated, or burned alive, while troops shot alleged
brigands on suspicion, deported thousands of peasants, and sacked and
burned entire villages accused of sheltering bandits. By 1863, after
one and a half years of fighting, 1,038 men had been summarily shot
for possession of arms; almost 2,800 had been jailed; and 2,413 had been
killed fighting. One Piedmontese general in Sicily ordered the
shooting of "anyone who by word or act insults the coat of arms of
Savoy [Sardinia], the portrait of the king or the national flag of Italy"
(Binkley 1963: 223). The 1863 Pica law authorized confinement for up
to a year under house arrest for "any vagabond or unemployed person,
or anyone suspected of belonging to the camorra [organized crime] or
harboring brigands" (Martin 1969: 572). The withdrawal of troops from
Sicily during the Austro-Prussian War coupled with a cholera epidemic,
a food shortage, rising prices, and a general economic crisis, triggered
another uprising there in 1866. Dozens of armed bands, representing a
wide variety of groups with grievances against the government, seized
Palermo for a week. The city was finally shelled into submission by
the navy and then occupied by 40,000 troops. Thousands of jailings and
hundreds of deportations followed.

Elsewhere in Italy, protest and dissent also often met harsh
repression. Thus, 35 professors were fired from the University of
Bologna for refusing to swear loyalty to the new Italy, and over 70
cardinals and bishops were jailed for opposing the government's
anti-clerical policies. By 1866, over 38,000 ecclesiastical bodies
housing tens of thousands of members of religious orders had been
suppressed, partly to raise money from confiscated property and partly
to punish the Church for its opposition to Italian unity and the
annexation of most of the Papal States in 1860. Rioting in Turin in
September 1864 in protest of the transfer of the Italian capital to
Florence was put down by troops who killed almost 200 people and
wounded hundreds more.

The major Italian political issue in the 1860s for the 2 per cent of
the population that could vote concerned the "leftovers" of 1859-60:
how to obtain control of Venetia and Rome. The ruling Right
(conservative) party, a loose union of conservative liberals under
largely northern Italian leadership, was inclined toward a cautious and
diplomatic approach. The opposition Left party, also known as the
Party of Action, included many southern politicians, Mazzinians,
monarchist ex-republicans and followers of Garibaldi, and was bent
upon immediate annexation of Rome and Venetia, by force if
necessary. It was also, theoretically, more inclined toward social
reform. The Italo-Prussian alliance during the 1866 Austro-Prussian
War gained Venetia, but the Roman question remained a constant
thorn in the government's side. In 1862 and again in 1867 the Right
government at first encouraged and then discouraged Garibaldi from

launching an armed attack upon Rome. In both cases, Garibaldi continued his efforts despite the government's wishes, with resultant fiascos, and in both instances the government lashed out with a wave of dissolutions of workers groups and democratic societies associated with Garibaldi and the Party of Action. For two years after the 1867 fiasco, in which Garibaldi's forces were beaten by French and Papal troops, Italy was ruled by General Luigi Menabrea (1867-69) in a highly authoritarian fashion.

Germany. The Italian events of 1859 gave German nationalists enormous encouragement. In September 1859 liberals from a number of German states formed the Nationalverein (National Union) to agitate for German unification. Although many German states severely harassed or entirely outlawed the group, it quickly became the leading voice of German nationalism, attracting 25,000 members by October 1862. Among the thinly disguised manifestations of German nationalism that were common in the wake of the Italian victory were the celebrations held across Germany on the centenary of Schiller's birth in November 1959--13,000 marched in Hamburg alone parading behind banners reading "Freedom, Truth and Law"--the Nuremburg "Sängerfest" (Song festival) of 1861, the July 1862 parade of 10,000 armed men before the Frankfurt meeting hall of the Confederation diet during a hunting festival, and the 1863 celebrations marking the fiftieth anniversary of the Battle of Leipzig. In Baden, a reform ministry came to power in 1860, and liberals won a majority in the lower house of the Hesse-Darmstadt diet in 1862. Similar gains were registered by liberals in Prussia, Bavaria, Württemberg and elsewhere.

German attention was focussed on Prussia in 1862, where conflict between King William I and the Prussian Landtag (lower chamber), under overwhelming liberal domination as a result of the 1861 elections, was growing. In 1860, the king had proposed an increase in the size of the army and the period of military service, along with a reduction in the size and importance of the national guard, which German liberals viewed as a guarantee of civilian influence in the military. Although the liberal Landtag majority was not fundamentally opposed to army reform, the king was completely unwilling to compromise, viewing all proposed modifications as a threat to his authority. In March 1862, William dissolved the Landtag, but the subsequent elections were disastrous for him, despite the use of severe electoral pressure. When the Landtag refused to pass an army financial measure in September 1863, William appointed the ultra-reactionary aristocrat Otto von Bismarck prime minister, a clear sign that he would not yield.

Bismarck withdrew the proposed budget from consideration and began a five-year period of rule without a budget approved by parliament, in clear violation of the Prussian constitution. The Landtag was again dissolved and despite the most extreme administrative pressure, a massive opposition victory was registered in the October 1863 elections. Meanwhile, liberal civil servants were fired, transferred, or otherwise penalized, and tough measures were taken against Prussian Poles who supported or participated in the 1863 revolt in Russian Poland. Almost 2,000 Prussian Poles were tried in 1864, with many sentenced to jail terms.

After 1863, Bismarck was able to divert public attention increasingly away from his violation of the constitution and to harness Prussian nationalist sentiment by adopting an aggressive foreign policy. In late 1863, Bismarck was presented with a golden opportunity for such diversion as a result of developments in Denmark. National Liberal pressure there on Prime Minister C. C. Hall to implement the Ejder Program led him to present a new helstat constitution, which encompassed the Danish kingdom and Schleswig only, to the Danish rigsråd. (Holstein had been granted a separate constitution in recognition of its special status as a member of the German Confederation.) The passage of this constitution and its approval by the new Danish king, Christian IX (1863-1906), were widely viewed as violating the Danish pledges of 1851-52 by uniting Schleswig with Denmark proper. The result, in 1864, was an Austro-Prussian invasion and a devastating defeat for Denmark, which lost all of both Schleswig and Holstein, including Danish-speaking northern Schleswig.

Subsequently, Austria and Prussia quarrelled over how to divide the spoils, and war between the two powers broke out in 1866. Bismarck was thus provided with more nationalistic divisionary material. The liberal opposition in Prussia was drastically weakened in the Landtag election of July 3, 1866, held on the very day of the climactic Prussian victory over Austria at Königgratz (Sadowa). As a result of the Austrian defeat, Prussia annexed all of Schleswig-Holstein along with four minor German states that had sided with Austria, and signed a compact with the remaining German states located north of the Main River, thus forming a new German union clearly under her domination. Amidst a wave of hosannas for Bismarck and nationalist jubilation, on September 3, 1866, most of the liberals in the Landtag joined conservatives to pass 230-75 a budget bill for 1866 that retroactively approved all government expenditures since passage of the last budget in 1861. "The theft of the cause of national unity was the most persuasive act of all in reconciling the German liberals to authoritarian rule" (Pflanze 1971: 12). The liberals had chosen to sell their constitutional principles for a nationalist pottage. It was a fateful day in German history, dealing a death blow to democratic hopes there for decades. Socialist leader Wilhelm Liebknecht wrote sardonically of Bismarck, "The stigma of violation of the constitution has been washed from his brow and in its place the halo of glory rings his laureled head" (Craig 1980: 10).

A new political organization, the North German Confederation, was created in 1867 to govern relations between Prussia and the 21 states north of the Main. It lasted only a few years before it was subsumed in a united Germany, but the confederation provided a blueprint for the structure of the German Empire of 1871. It created a constitutional framework dominated by Prussia, which itself remained under authoritarian and quasi-feudal rule safeguarded by the three-class voting system of 1849.

France. French Catholics and liberals who were alienated by Napoleon III's Italian policy were joined in their dissatisfaction by businessmen and large landowners angered by the emperor's abandonment in 1860 of France's traditionally protectionist tariff policy. Deserted by his long-time supporters--the Catholic conservatives and wealthy industrialists and landowners--the emperor tried to shore up the regime by placating the liberal middle-class opposition and the urban working class. The powers of the legislative chambers were gradually and modestly increased, beginning in 1860 with permission to hold public sessions and present an annual address to the emperor. Press controls were slightly eased in 1860-1, and in 1864 the right to strike, although hedged with restrictions, was granted. These and other concessions, including the 1859 general amnesty to celebrate the defeat of Austria in that year's war, amounted to a sort of creeping democraticization by executive fiat. However, they merely whetted the appetite of the working class and growing middle-class parliamentary opposition.

The regime was further undermined by the 1866 Austro-Prussian War, which created a strong Prussian-dominated German state on the eastern French border, and by the humiliating collapse of Napoleon's imperialistic adventures in Mexico in 1867. The emperor tried to appease the growing opposition by further concessions. He drastically eased regulations on press and assembly--including trade unions--in 1868, and he granted new powers to the legislature after 1866, such as the right of interpellation, of legislative inititative, and of electing officers. The culminating constitutional reform, approved overwhelmingly in a May 1870 plebiscite, established a system of ministerial responsibility to parliament. As before, the main effect of the reforms was simply to encourage dissent. The easing of election pressure, which had led to a doubling of the opposition vote in 1863 over the 10 per cent or so garnered in 1852 and 1857, resulted in the casting of about 3 million opposition votes (40 per cent) in 1869. Over 150 new papers sprang up within a year of the 1868 press liberalization, including Henri Rochefort's La Lanterne, which sold 120,000 copies of its first number, containing the famous opening sentence, "The Empire contains 36 million subjects, not counting the subjects of discontent" (Bury 1954: 108). When the emperor's dissolute cousin Prince Pierre Bonaparte killed a journalist in a brawl, 100,000 people turned out for the funeral on January 11, 1870. The handwriting was clearly already on the wall even before the French debacle in the 1870 war with Prussia brought the Second Empire crumbling down.

The Habsburg Empire. The "Bach System" in the Habsburg Empire was seriously undermined by the country's growing isolation in Europe in the wake of the Crimean War, the economic crash of 1857, the loss of Lombardy in the 1859 war with Sardinia, and heavy defense expenditures that caused severe financial problems and fostered growing demands from the rising German liberal bourgeoisie for greater civil liberties and controls over spending. Franz Joseph's promise of "modernizing" improvements at the end of the Italian war in mid-1859, followed by the dismissals of Bach and the hated police minister, Baron Johann von Kempen, only spurred rising discontent, especially in Hungary. Tax strikes and nationalist-oriented demonstrations, balls, and commemorative ceremonies increased in strength and militancy among the Magyars. Violent demonstrations in Pest in the summer of 1860 were answered with mass arrests.

Following two abortive constitutional reforms announced in August 1859 and March 1860, Franz Joseph proclaimed in the "permanent and irrevocable" (Macartney 1969: 506) "October Diploma" of October 1860 that substantial power would be granted to reconstituted provincial diets (Landtage), that Hungary would be restored to pre-1848 status, and that the Reichsrat, a central legislature elected by the Landtage, would be given authority over matters common to the entire empire. The October Diploma was quickly rejected by the German liberals, who feared that decentralization would weaken the influence of German and business interests. The Hungarian nationalists also denounced the Diploma, rejecting the concept of giving a central legislature any power over Hungarian affairs and demanding a return to the autonomy briefly granted in 1848. Hungary was convulsed anew with demonstrations and riots. Troops were dispatched to many areas in Hungary and at least seven people were killed.

Faced with contradictory demands from the German centralist liberals and the Hungarian nationalists, Franz Joseph decided to support the former. In the "February Patent" of 1861, the Reichsrat's power was considerably strengthened. Although the Landtage continued to elect Reichsrat members, their powers were trimmed and their electoral base was changed from the medieval estates system of the October Diploma to a complicated four-class scheme that disenfranchised 95 per of the population and vastly overrepresented great landlords and the disproportionately Germanic urban bourgeoisie. Thus, the Germans dominated the provincial Landtage in Carniola and Bohemia, even though Slavic groups constituted 90 and 60 per cent of the population of those provinces, respectively. In the Reichsrat, the great landlords, about 0.02 per cent of the population, were guaranteed about 30 per cent of the seats.

The February Patent was greeted with universal indignation among the nationalities, especially in Hungary, where demonstrations and conscription strikes increased. The newly elected Hungarian and Croatian diets both rejected the Patent and boycotted the Reichsrat, whereupon Franz Joseph dissolved them both, placed the two regions under absolutist rule and imposed a massive crackdown on the Hungarian and Croatian press that yielded about 500 imprisonments within eight months. Czech deputies from Bohemia and Moravia withdrew from the Reichsrat in 1863-4 to protest the biased Landtage electoral laws, while Poles from Galicia did likewise to protest dissolution of the Galician diet and imposition of martial law there in response to the 1863 insurrection in Russian Poland.

In 1865, the rump Reichsrat was suspended; martial law was ended in Galicia and Hungary; and the Hungarian and Croatian diets were reconvened when Franz Joseph decided he needed to bolster his domestic support amidst tensions leading up to the 1866 war with Prussia. Negotiations with moderate elements in Hungary, who were willing to settle for less than complete independence and viewed Austrian financial and political support as attractive because of signs of growing agrarian lower-class unrest, were stepped up after Austria's disastrous defeat in the war, since Franz Joseph sought to strengthen the monarchy in preparation for a hoped-for recovery of the Habsburg position in Germany.

In early 1867 an agreement, known as the Ausgleich, or constitutional compromise, was reached with Hungarian representatives. The Habsburg Empire was divided into two parts, with Franz Joseph serving as emperor of the western part (Austria, in popular, if technically inaccurate, parlance) and king of the eastern part (Hungary, including Croatia and Transylvania). Matters concerning foreign policy, defense and finance for the entire monarchy were to be decided by delegations from the Austrian Reichsrat and the Hungarian diet, and a common army, postal system, and currency were established. In other respects, Hungary and Austria were completely separated, with their own constitutions, legislatures, and ministries for domestic affairs. The real significance of the Ausgleich was control. In the monarchy, Slavic groups as a whole outnumbered Germans or Magyars; by dividing the realm in two the Germans were allowed to control Austria and the Magyars' Hungary, thus allowing each to dominate the other nationalities in their halves while ending the continuing struggle for power between them. As the first Austrian prime minister after the Ausgleich, Baron Friedrich von Beust (1867) told the first Hungarian prime minister, Julius Andrassy (1867-71), "You look after your mob and we will look after ours. As for the Slavs, we will squeeze them against the wall" (Beuer 1947: 40).

Although Franz Joseph retained significant power, especially in Austria, the Ausgleich marked a sharp departure from decades of absolutist-authoritarian rule in the monarchy. In both countries, two chamber parliaments were established, with upper houses dominated by the nobility and lower houses elected by about 6 per cent of the population. In Austria the complicated four-class voting system of 1861 was retained, which allowed the nobility to control about 30 per cent of the seats in the lower house, while in Hungary the nobility and middle classes were enfranchised. The emperor was given a dominant position with regard to military and foreign affairs, and was empowered, in both countries, to block proposed legislation, convene and dissolve parliament, and appoint ministries. No formal system of parliamentary responsibility was provided in either half of the monarchy. In Austria, the general confusion of nationalities, parties, and interests, combined with a looser constitutional scheme (including the power to rule by decree when the legislature was not in session) allowed the emperor to work his will, with or without a parliamentary majority. However, in Hungary, the ruling classes were agreed on the need to resist the non-Magyar nationalities, the lower classes and attempts by the king to expand royal power, and it was extremely difficult for Franz Joseph to govern with a hostile diet. Thus, constitutional government was in a sense always healthier in Hungary than Austria, although this more effective parliamentary control was mostly used to repress more efficiently the lower classes and the nationalities.

The first years of the post-Ausgleich regimes were politically fluid, marked by a mixture of reform and repression. A pro-Ausgleich majority in Austria was produced for the 1867 Reichsrat only through considerable pressure on the Landtage and dissolution of several of them, and left Franz Joseph highly dependent on the German centralist liberals, who favored not only the Ausgleich but also a curbing of monarchial powers. The liberal majority in the Reichsrat produced a set of constitutional guarantees, including freedom of assembly and association, which went far beyond similar measures in Hungary. However, both countries outlawed prior press censorship in 1867--though leaving plenty of loopholes, which were fully used in later years to harass opposition newspapers--and established compulsory primary education and formal equality for all nationalities.

The promised national equality was soon violated in practice, especially in Hungary. In Austrian Bohemia and Moravia, the Czechs were deeply angered as they saw the Hungarians given complete domestic autonomy while they continued to lack even control of their own Landtage. An extraordinary and unprecedented wave of protest demonstrations, known as tábory, attracted about one million participants in the Czech lands in 1868-9. Although the tábory were completely peaceful, Prague and its surroundings were placed under a state of emergency from October 1868 until April 1869, and hundreds of Czechs, including journalists and political leaders, were given jail terms. Within an 18-month period in 1868-9 Czech editors alone were sentenced to a total of 73 years and fined almost 50,000 gulden (about $24,000). Czech deputies from Bohemia and Moravia boycotted the Reichsrat, and by the end of 1869 most of the other nationalities also withdrew to protest German centralist domination.

Opposition to the Ausgleich in Hungarian Croatia was met with dissolution of the Croatian diet (sabor) by Franz Joseph, reduction of the Croatian suffrage by Hungarian decree, and rigged elections that finally produced a tame sabor. In 1868 the sabor reached a settlement with Hungary, known as the nagodba. The nagodba amounted to an enforced Ausgleich between Hungary and Croatia, allowing the Croats considerable domestic autonomy, but giving Budapest ultimate control over finances, trade, communications and foreign policy, and giving the Hungarian ministry the crucial power to appoint the Croat prime minister (ban), who was not responsible to the sabor.

The Russian Empire. In Russia, and especially in Russian Poland, Alexander II's liberalizing reforms stimulated unrest and hopes for further concessions that he had no intention of granting. Thus, the czar's public announcement in 1857 that he was planning to end serfdom triggered an enormous wave of anticipatory peasant unrest. About 500 peasant disturbances were recorded during the six years prior to the ending of serfdom in March 1861. The 1856-61 period also was marked by signs of unrest, including several strikes, among St. Petersburg workers, and ferment in the newly-augmented university community. Emancipation of the serfs was finally proclaimed by Alexander in March 1861, after the issue was studied for nearly five years. The details of the resulting land settlement were extremely complicated and varied from area to area. In short, the serfs did not get enough land, and they had to pay too much for what they got. Further, most of the freed serfs did not receive clear title to their land; instead, it was entrusted to peasant communes that were collectively responsible for redemption payments and taxes. Since no peasant owing redemption payments could leave his commune without its permission, most of the peasantry still lacked even personal freedom. When the terms of the emancipation settlement became known, a massive wave of violent protest convulsed rural Russia. Disturbances erupted on 1,200 estates, and Penza and Tambov provinces verged on open insurrection. Troops were called out in 500 instances. They put down the disorders with floggings, arrests, and deportations. The worst incident was the notorious massacre at Bezdna in Kazan province, in which over 100 peasants were slaughtered.

The peasant disturbances, which reached their height in the spring of 1861, were soon followed by demonstrations at the universities of St. Petersburg, Moscow, and Kazan by students protesting a sudden crackdown on unauthorized meetings and organizations and a drastic curb on admission of poor students to the universities. Over 600 peaceful student demonstrators were briefly arrested and in many cases severely beaten in St. Petersburg and Moscow in the fall of 1861. The University of St. Petersburg was closed for two years. Czarist authorities were further agitated when, beginning in late 1861 and continuing through 1862, a series of anonymous radical pamphlets, some of which openly called for revolution, were circulated in the major cities. Nerves were further set on edge in mid-1862 when a series of mysterious fires devastated St. Petersburg and a number of towns along the Volga River. These developments triggered a wave of arrests of radical writers and other suspects in 1861-2, along with the suspension of two radical journals, closure of reading rooms and the chess club in St. Petersburg, and the suppression of 300 workers' Sunday Schools in which educated Russians had volunteered to tutor members of the urban lower classes.

The severe unrest convulsing Poland in the early 1860s added to the nervousness in St. Petersburg. Polish nationalist sentiment had been inflamed by the events in Italy and several concessions made by Alexander, including an end to 24 years of military rule after the death of Marshal Paskevich in 1856 and the 1857 authorization for the formation of an Agricultural Society, which soon became the focus of

Polish public life. Despite the czar's warning to Polish nobles in May 1856, not to engage in "daydreams" (point de rêveries [Leslie 1963: 48]), the effect of his concessions, as in Russia proper, was to stimulate hopes and demands that he had no intention of conceding. Polish hopes grew for a restoration of autonomy or, among segments of the growing urban middle and working classes and intelligentsia, for a reestablishment of complete independence. Beginning in 1858 nationalist demonstrations were staged in Warsaw, usually in connection with funerals or memorial services for Polish patriots or with the celebrations of Polish anniversaries. On February 27, 1861, five demonstrators were killed when Russian troops fired on a Warsaw crowd, and on April 8, 1861 as many as 200 may have been killed when troops fired on a crowd protesting the dissolution of the Agricultural Society, which had criticized the terms of the emancipation decree. Although genuine attempts were made at reconciliation by czarist authorities in mid-1861, the Warsaw slaughters opened an unbridgeable gap between Polish public opinion and the Russian regime. It was widened when the Catholic church began to lead the nationalist movement. On October 15, 1861 Russian authorities arrested 3,000 people and forcibly cleared Warsaw churches that had been the site of all-day demonstrations commemorating the death of Polish patriot Tadeusz Kósciuszko. A severe regime of martial law was then instituted by General N. O. Sukhozanet.

Although Sukhozanet was recalled in the spring of 1862 and new conciliatory gestures were made, any sympathy they might have gained were lost when six Poles were executed in 1862 for attempts on the life of czarist officials. Throughout 1862, revolutionary underground movements were organized, and open rebellion erupted in Poland in January 1863 when it became known that an effort would be made to smash the underground by drafting leading Warsaw militants. The resulting conflict lasted well over a year before Russian troops crushed guerrilla resistance. Horrifying atrocities were committed by both sides.

As after the 1830 rebellion, the ultimate outcome of the Polish rising was massive repression and stepped-up russification. About 400 people were executed after some type of judicial procedure, while many others were summarily executed. About 3,400 were jailed, 7,000 were dispatched to penal army units and almost 19,000 received long terms of Siberian exile. Count M. N. Muravyov became notorious throughout Europe as the "hangman of Vilna" for his mass executions, deportations, and ruthless russification policies in his capacity of governor-general of Lithuania, where considerable support for the Polish rising was manifested. All remaining separate administrative organs for Poland were abolished. The "Kingdom of Poland" was renamed "Vistula Land," and completely incorporated into the Russian administration. Russian was made the official language, the education system was completely russified and the Catholic church came under severe administrative pressure.

In Finland, which by contrast to Poland remained relatively quiet despite the inspiration provided by events in Italy, Czar Alexander decided to reward "good behavior" and respond to some mild agitation for a convening of the Finnish diet by personally visiting Helsingfors in 1863 to convoke the diet. It was the first Finnish diet to meet in 54 years. He also signed a manifesto making Finnish co-equal with Swedish as an official language in all matters affecting Finnish speakers.

In Russia proper, the repressive wave of 1861-2 restored calm to the country, and Alexander returned to his reform campaign in 1863-5. University autonomy was greatly increased, lower education was expanded, prior censorship was lifted for some publications, and the notoriously archaic Russian judicial system was significantly modernized. ("The old court!" remarked one observer. "At the mere recollection of it one's hair stands on end and one's flesh begins to creep" [Riasanovsky 1969: 417]). Elective governmental organs (zemtvos) were instituted for rural Russia at the district and provincial level, although they were chosen on a class basis that gave the nobility (about 1 per cent of the population) over 40 per cent of the district zemtvos seats and about 75 per cent of the provincial zemtvos seats.

On April 4, 1866, the surface political calm in Russia was broken by an attempt on the czar's life. The perpetrator, Dmitri Karakazov, was an unbalanced member of a secret terrorist cell known as "Hell." The Karakazov affair triggered a new wave of arrests and reaction. Known in Russian history as the "white terror" of 1866-8, this crackdown marked a key turning point in Alexander's reign. The investigation of the Karakazov attempt was directed by Muravyov, the "hangman of Vilna," who ordered wholesale arrests of anyone suspected of having a "subversive turn of mind" (Ulam 1977: 9). Several hundred radicals were arrested, Karakazov was executed, and about 35 others received jail terms or sentences of exile. The two leading radical journals were suppressed, zemtvos powers were restricted, and reactionaries were named to key positions.


## The United Kingdom and the Minor Continental States, 1859-1870

As in the major European continental regimes, the general trend of the 1859-70 period in the United Kingdom and the minor continental states was that of conservative reconstruction. The poor continued to be excluded from politics in these regions also, except to some extent in Switzerland, Denmark, and Spain (after 1868). However, the general tone of political life was, save in the Balkans and Spain before 1868, far less repressive than it was in the major continental regimes (as it had been before 1860). In the United Kingdom and Switzerland, constitutional reforms considerably expanded democratic procedures during the decade. In Sweden, the archaic system of parliamentary estates was finally jettisoned in 1866 but was replaced by a highly conservative system that entrusted power to wealthy landowners and businessmen. The same elements triumphed in the Danish constitutional reform of 1866, which significantly reduced the suffrage for the upper legislative house. In the Netherlands, parliamentary responsibility was won in 1868, although the highly restrictive suffrage remained intact, as it did in Belgium, where trade unions were legalized in 1866. There were no significant developments in Portugal's system of rigged "rotativism," but in Spain, Queen Isabel's irresponsible and arbitrary rule triggered a revolt in 1868. This popular uprising overthrew the Bourbon monarchy and established a highly democratic regime, in theory. In practice, however, it failed to establish a political system that was able to foster either democratic or stable rule or gather widespread support. Although the Balkans were marked by much turmoil and surface political change in the 1860s, including revolutions in Serbia, Greece, and Rumania, beneath the surface the royal families and political cliques continued to manipulate politics and ignore mass concerns, as they always had.

The United Kingdom. In the United Kingdom, the mid-1860s were marked by a great upsurge of middle- and working-class interest in electoral reform. When the Italian revolutionary hero Garibaldi visited London in 1864, 30,000 mostly working-class Englishmen turned out to greet him, a clear sign of their re-awakening political interest. When a modest electoral reform proposal was turned down by the Commons in mid-1866, working-class anger was displayed in a series of massive suffrage demonstrations. In July, serious rioting erupted when the government tried to ban a demonstration at Hyde Park, London. In the last few months of 1866, mass demonstrations at Birmingham, Leeds, Manchester, and Glasgow attracted over 100,000 marchers each. A Conservative cabinet dominated by Benjamin Disraeli introduced a new reform bill in early 1867. Disraeli's bill was greatly liberalized in the Commons through a combination of party competition for working-class votes, fear of additional demonstrations and general confusion over the intricacies of the franchise. Together with companion measures for Scotland and Ireland passed in 1868, the 1867 England-Wales reform bill increased the suffrage for the United Kingdom from 1.4 to 2.5 million (from 4 to 8 per cent of the population). Although the upper crust of the urban working class was enfranchised, the vast majority of adult males were still excluded, especially in rural areas, where the suffrage was only marginally extended.

Although politics in Great Britain quieted down after passage of the 1867 reform bill, Irish unrest simultaneously heated up. The collapse of the Independent Irish party, a parliamentary-oriented Irish nationalist group, in the early 1850s damaged the cause of legal, non-violent reform in Ireland and fostered the growth of the revolutionary Fenian movement, formally known as the Irish Republican Brotherhood. The Fenians formed a secret society dedicated to revolution in Ireland and the establishment of an independent, non-sectarian Irish republic. The organization claimed a membership of 80,000 in England and Ireland by 1865. In 1861, when the body of Terence MacManus, a Fenian veteran of the Irish revolts of 1848, was shipped from the United States to Ireland, hundreds of thousands turned out for burial ceremonies, although all Catholic churches in Dublin were barred by Archbishop Paul Cullen from serving as a site for funeral services.

Although Fenianism was supposed to be a secret movement, it was riddled with government spies, including one agent who infiltrated its newspaper, Irish People. By 1865, Fenian plans for revolution were an open secret. In September 1865, the Irish People was raided and closed down and its staff was arrested, along with the leader of Fenianism in Ireland, James Stephens. In 1866, habeas corpus was suspended in Ireland and more Fenian leaders were arrested. The arrests and suspension of habeas corpus stampeded the movement's remnants into planning hasty, ill-prepared and poorly equipped risings. In February and March 1867, about 5,000 Fenians revolted in six Irish countries, but were easily put down by British troops. Twelve Fenians were killed, many were jailed and over 60 were transported to Australia. A side-event had greater impact in Ireland than the revolt itself. In September 1867, Manchester Fenians accidentally shot and killed a policeman as they were freeing two leaders who had been jailed after the rising. Despite the lack of evidence tying any individual to the fatal shot, three members of the Fenian rescue party were publicly executed in Manchester on November 23, 1867.

The hanging of the "Manchester Martyrs" swept Irish public opinion into extraordinary fervor. Huge funeral demonstrations and parades were held in many cities in Ireland and in Irish communities in Great Britain. The trial speech of one of the "martyrs," William P. Allen, inspired the song "God Save Ireland," which became the national anthem, and November 23, the "feast of the martyrs," replaced St. Patrick's Day as the national feast day. As the 1860s ended, the Fenians increasingly became Irish popular heroes and demands for amnesty for those jailed in 1866-7 became a major rallying cry. Over one million people attended 38 amnesty meetings in the Irish provinces of Munster and Leinster alone in 1869; one such meeting at Cabra near Dublin attracted 200,000 people in October.

Scandinavia. The 1859 events in Italy greatly spurred nationalism in Norway. The attempt of the new Swedish king, Charles XV (1859-72), to appease Norwegian sentiment ended up both in alienating Norwegians and in weakening monarchial power in Sweden. After 1858 the Norwegians enjoyed a growing romanticist linguistic-historical national revival. Charles sought to conciliate them by supporting an 1859 storting bill to abolish the position of stattholder, or Swedish royal viceroy, in Norway, long regarded by Norwegians as a symbol of their inferiority to Sweden. The Swedish ministry, which had long been smarting under the previous king's increasingly autocratic style and domination of foreign policy, seized upon this issue to establish their power over the king and proclaimed that any change in the Norwegian constitution must also be approved by the Swedish riksdag. They threatened to resign unless the king accepted this position. Charles capitulated and, breaking his promise to Norway, vetoed the storting stattholder bill. This affair was a critical turning-point both in embittering the Norwegians and greatly weakening the king's authority in Sweden. Although Norway was quiet during the 1860s and the bureaucracy continued to dominate politics, the romanticist national revival continued to grow and movements developed among the farmers and urban liberals to challenge the entrenched elite.

In Sweden, King Charles continued to lose his power, as his desire to aid Denmark in the 1864 war over Schleswig-Holstein was overridden by the cabinet and he was forced by threat of cabinet resignation to accept a proposal to replace the four-chamber parliament with a two-chamber house fashioned along modern lines. In order to convince the riksdag to pass the reform, Prime Minister Louis de Geer (1858-70) included provisions that restricted membership in the upper house to the wealthiest 6,000 Swedes and limited the lower-house franchise to about 5.5 per cent of the population--a decline from the 6 per cent who were entitled to vote for the existing four estates! Even this highly conservative bill passed only under the pressure of public meetings held throughout Sweden, a petition signed by 60,000 Swedes and the pressure of crowds who gathered outside the Riddarhus (estate of the nobility) during the critical vote in December 1865. Collectively, the new chambers proved to be even more conservative than the old estates. The upper house of 125 members, which was controlled by an electorate of less than 1 per cent of the population, included 64 members who formerly sat in the Riddarhus, plus representatives of the wealthiest industrialists and civil servants, while 107 of the 190 members of the lower house had formerly served in the old Estates. Sweden was ruled by an amalgamation of the old high nobility and the industrial plutocracy for the next forty years.

In Denmark the catastrophic loss of Schleswig-Holstein--about one-third of the land and population of the Danish monarchy--severely discredited the reigning National Liberals and led to a resurgance by the aristocratic great landholders, who had generally withdrawn from politics after passage of the liberal June 1849 constitution. With the aid of conservative factions in the National Liberal and farmers' parties, the great landowners secured passage of a new constitution in 1866 that retained the quasi-universal manhood suffrage for the lower legislative house (Folketing) established in the 1849 constitution but changed the suffrage for the previously similarly elected upper house (Landsting). In the new Landsting, the king appointed about 20 per cent of the members and the others were indirectly chosen by electoral colleges, half chosen by all Folketing voters and the other half by the wealthiest taxpayers only. This highly conservative revision of the 1849 constitution gave control of the Landsting to about 1,000 wealthy landowners and the richest 20 per cent of the urban population. It ensured that the make-up of the two chambers would drastically differ. However, no provision was made for resolving disputes between the two bodies, and ministerial responsibility to the Folketing was not established. The conservatively inclined Christian IX's first ministry under the 1866 constitution was based solely on the Landsting, headed by Count C.E. Frijs, the largest landowner in Denmark. His ministry was based on a coalition of the great landowners and conservative National Liberals and was directed against the small farmers and urban middle-class liberals and radicals.

The Low Countries and Switzerland. In the Netherlands, parliamentary responsibility became a major issue in the mid-1860s. Although it had seemingly been established in the 1848 constitution, the lack of highly organized Dutch political parties had given the conservatively inclined King William III (1849-90) considerable discretion in naming ministries, which he used between 1852 and 1862 to block liberal leader Jan Thorbecke from power. After Thorbecke's second ministry (1862-66) ended as a result of internal splits in the liberal party, serious clashes developed between a new conservative ministry and the liberal majority that still controlled parliament. William III dissolved parliament twice in two years, but in the 1868 election he was overwhelmingly rebuffed in a clear referendum on the issue of parliamentary responsibility. When the new parliament refused to approve a budget proposal, William and the cabinet gave way and parliamentary responsibility was finally established in Dutch politics. The continuing restriction of the suffrage in the Netherlands, as in neighboring Belgium, to less than 3 per cent of the population, insured that the events of 1868 had little impact outside the halls of parliament.

Belgium was generally quiet during the 1860s, with the major issue among the enfranchised population continuing to be whether or not the government should support religious education. In Switzerland also the 1860s were generally quiet, but there were further democratic advances in what was already the most democratic European nation. Several cantons adopted during the decade the referendum, a device that gave the entire voting population the right to approve or disapprove of cantonal legislation. The referendum, unique in Europe, was adopted in response to the feeling, especially in Zurich canton, that Swiss politics had come under the domination of professional politicians and rich businessmen.

Iberia. Portugal was quiet during the 1860s. The two major parties, the Regenerators (heirs to the Chartists) and the Historicals (heirs to the Septembrists) continued to "rotate" in power and to lose any significant differences between them. Between 1865 and 1868 Portugal was ruled by a coalition of the parties, known as the Fusão (Fusion). The regime was characterized by no recognition of social issues, poor management, waste, corruption, and a skyrocketing of the government debt.

In contrast to the quiet in Portugal, the regime of Queen Isabel in Spain rapidly deteriorated after O'Donnell's Liberal Union government fell in 1863, victim to internal splits and hostility from Isabel's increasingly reactionary and clergy-dominated camarilla. The 1863-8 period saw rapid ministerial turnovers, a major growth in republican strength and a narrowing of support for the regime to a hard core of reactionary clerical-conservative forces. A series of military plots emerged in 1865-6, including a mutiny of non-commissioned officers in

Madrid in June 1866, which was suppressed with 68 executions. General Narváez, called upon to serve as prime minister for the seventh time in July 1866, ruled for nine months without parliament, suppressed a new military plot in 1867, and adopted his usual program of executions, jailings, press repression, and firings of dissident professors. The death of Narváez in April 1868 and a severe economic depression in 1866-8, including a collapse of the railway boom, a crisis in the cotton textile industry, and the highest wheat prices in the century, weakened what was left of the regime. The end finally came in September 1868 when a military rising led by General Juan Prim sparked popular uprisings in Madrid and other cities. Isabel fled to France with her current lover, declaring, "I thought I had struck deeper roots in this land" (Atkinson 1960: 291).

Prim and the other military leaders of the rising sought only moderate reforms, so that, as Prim put it in 1865, property could be saved from the "tremendous social revolution which threatened it and which was fomented by reactionary governments" (Carr 1966: 257). However, a provisional government under Liberal Unionist General Francisco Serrano accepted the demands of the popular revolutionary junta in Madrid for press freedom and the convening of a constituent assembly to be elected by universal male suffrage to determine the future of Spain. The 1869 constitutional assembly confirmed the provisional government's establishment of universal male suffrage and provided extensive civil liberties, including freedom of the press and assembly and the right to form trade unions. However, it soon became apparent that while almost all elements in Spain agreed on opposition to Isabel, they could agree on little else. Factionalism and violent uprisings, led by Carlists and republicans (to protest the constituent assembly's decision to retain a monarchy), soon became so serious that constitutional guarantees were suspended and resort was made to the usual election rigging techniques. Even finding a king--Prim noted that locating a democratic king in Europe was "like looking for an atheist in Heaven" (Atkinson 1960: 299)--proved extemely difficult. The search ended up touching off the Franco-Prussian War of 1870 before Amadeo, the second son of King Victor Emmanuel of Italy, was chosen by a 191-120 vote in late 1870.

The Balkans. In the Danubian Principalities (known as Rumania after 1861), Serbia, and Greece, political affairs in the 1860s generally revolved around the machinations of the ruling princes and kings and small groups of politicians who vied for royal favor and fought among themselves. Although the Balkans were overwhelmingly poor and rural, the crying needs of the masses for cheap credit, marketing facilities and technical assistance were ignored by the tiny band of political leaders who struggled for power, patronage, and corrupt sources of wealth. Although, during the 1860s, Greece (1864), Rumania (1866), and Serbia (1869) all adopted seemingly liberal and democratic constitutions following revolutions, these documents were largely facades behind which rigged elections, royal families, and cliques of politicians continued to determine the course of events, and the masses remained in a state of ignorance, poverty, and powerlessness.

The assemblies elected in Wallachia and Moldavia in 1857 soon confounded the intention of the European powers to block a union of the two principalities. In early 1859, both chose the same person as prince. He was Alexander Cuza, a boyar of second rank known for his strong unionist stand. The European powers were too divided and preoccupied at that time with the threatened war between Austria and Sardinia to devote much attention to the Cuza affair, finally accepting the election as a <u>fait accompli</u> in September 1859. The absurdity of maintaining two separate administrations with a common prince convinced the powers in late 1861 to agree to a complete administrative union of the principalities, thereafter known as Rumania (this union was originally to be limited to Cuza's lifetime but became permanent when the powers allowed its continuation after Cuza was overthrown in 1866).

Cuza was hampered from the time of his election by opposition from the conservative great boyars who controlled the legislative assemblies (united in one body after 1861). They resented his reformist and authoritarian tendencies, and regarded him as an upstart lesser boyar, especially since his election had been somewhat of a fluke, resulting from a division among anti-unionist forces in Moldavia and pressure from threatening pro-unionist mobs in Wallachia. Cuza was also plagued by severe economic difficulties in the early 1860s that fostered unrest and demands for radical expansion of the suffrage--limited to 0.1 per cent of the population--from the commercial and urban middle and lower middle classes. Uprisings by merchants and craftsmen in 1860 and by peasants in 1862 were put down with considerable brutality.

Cuza responded to criticism from the left with a harsh 1862 press law. He abandoned his attempts to conciliate the conservative boyar-controlled assembly after it rejected a proposed agrarian reform in April 1864 and censured liberal Prime Minister Michael Kogălniceanu for attempting to "equalize society" (Bobango 1979: 165). Convinced that no progress could be made unless the suffrage was expanded, Cuza used troops to dissolve parliament in May 1864, and, in what amounted to a <u>coup d'état</u>, hastily staged a plebiscite in which all male adults voted on the subject of a new constitution and widened franchise. The plebiscite, held with opposition groups prevented from expressing their views, passed by 682,621 to 1,307. The suffrage was greatly expanded--although a majority of adult males were still excluded from voting--a pliable and largely appointed senate (upper house) was established and the power of the legislative assembly was reduced. Suppression of the opposition press and the rigged elections of November 1864 completed the transformation of Cuza into a semi-legal dictator. A flurry of reforms followed the 1864 <u>coup</u>, of which the most significant were the establishment of free and compulsory education, the imposition of a highly centralized administrative system, and a sweeping agrarian reform law intended to end all feudal dues and restrictions imposed on the peasantry and to create a land of independent small farmers.

The boyars hated Cuza for his coup and reforms, while his support among liberals declined after he fired Kogălniceanu in 1865. The peasantry was angered by a severe drought in 1864-5 and the government's failure to implement the spirit of the agrarian reform, while all segments of the population were alienated by Cuza's scandalous personal life. In August 1865, a popular uprising in Bucharest was forcibly suppressed with 20 deaths and hundreds of arrests. In February 1866 a conspiracy involving prominent liberal and conservative leaders won military backing and overthrew Cuza in a bloodless coup. A provisional government selected to replace Cuza Prince Charles of the German line of Hohenzollern-Simaringen (who reportedly had never heard of Rumania but accepted after consulting an atlas and declaring, "That is a country with a future" [Stavrianos 1963: 356]).

Soon a new Rumanian constitution was adopted with extensive guarantees of civil liberties. Although parliamentary responsibility was provided for, considerable power was reserved to the prince, including an absolute veto over legislation and the right to appoint ministries and dissolve parliament. A complicated voting system was established in which only the very wealthy could vote for the upper chamber, while all taxpayers elected the lower chamber on a class-weighted basis that gave control to about 5 per cent of the electorate. This system ensured that the great landlords and wealthy merchants would dominate politics. This was quickly indicated by passage in 1866 of a reactionary agrarian law that continued the process of reversing the intent of Cuza's 1864 reform, which had been sabotaged from the beginning by landowners who controlled local administration. The boyars were able to keep over half the total land, while the peasantry obtained land of low quality that amounted to less they had farmed for their own needs before the 1864 reform. In order to survive, the peasants were forced to lease additional land from the boyars at exorbitant rents or in return for labor, placing them in the same dependent and semi-feudal situation as before. The phoniness of the democratic promises of the 1866 constitution and the strong powers of the prince were demonstrated in the 1868 elections, when Prince Charles, annoyed with liberal leaders who had helped bring him to power, supervised rigged elections that virtually eliminated them from parliament.

In Greece, King Otto's popularity, which had grown in the 1850s because of his association with the Greek irredentist cause and his resistance to the Anglo-French occupation of 1854-7, suffered a sharp decline when he openly sympathized with the cause of the Austrian emperor, his fellow German, in 1859. Since Greek nationalists strongly identified with the Italian cause, Otto's stance was regarded as a betrayal. The contrast between Italy's victories and the failures of Greek irredentism and between west European support for Italian nationalism and opposition to Greek expansion was increasingly blamed on Otto's ineptness and alienation of the western powers.

By the early 1860s, the Greek press, freed from prior censorship under the 1844 constitution, was in full cry against the monarchy. Otto's prime minister, Anthanasios Miaoulis (1857-62), was nicknamed the "Minister of Blood" for his initiation of a wave of press prosecutions--and in some cases physical terrorism directed against journalists--which imprisoned many writers. A general uprising backed by both military and popular forces finally forced Otto to abdicate in October 1862. A constitutional assembly convened in February 1863 accepted the European powers' choice of Prince William George of Denmark, second son of the Danish king, to serve as the new king (as George I [1863-1913]). The new constitution gave considerable although strictly defined powers to the monarch, including the right to appoint ministers and dissolve parliament, but clearly intended to end the irresponsible quasi-absolutism of the previous 20 years. Constitutional rights and liberties were strengthened, and the principle of popular sovereignty was firmly stated, transforming Greece into what became known as a vasilevomeni dimokratia ("crowned democracy").

During the early years of George's reign the king in fact exercised considerably more influence than was intended under the 1864 constitution. However, to a large degree this was due to the irresponsible behavior of the leading politicians, who, after the demise of the old French-, Russian-, and English-oriented parties after the Crimean War, led parties based almost entirely upon personal allegiances. The major strategy of each political faction was to oppose any other group that held power, in hopes of being called to power by the king; then rigged elections could be held and the civil service purged wholesale and then restocked--sometimes down to the level of elementary school teachers--with patronage appointments. The lack of any political grouping based on principle made it impossible for any leader to gain majority support in the parliament, with the result that in the first 20 years of George's rule, there were 39 different ministries and nine elections (there were 11 ministries between 1865 and 1869 alone). Faced with this situation, the king frequently resorted to minority or extra-parliamentary governments. "It became customary for a minority government to dissolve the chamber and use the apparatus of the state, including the armed forces and brigand bands, to press the electorate to increase its strength at new elections" (Campbell and Sherrard 1968: 100).

In Serbia, the restoration of the former dictator Miloš Obrenović to the throne in 1858 (and after his death in 1860, his son Michael, who had been previously deposed in 1842) essentially led to a revival of princely absolutism. Miloš summed up his unchanged political philosophy by declaring, "No one is going to tell me what to do" (Dedijer 1974: 334). Although the 1858 popular assembly that deposed Alexander Karageorgević had established that an assembly would meet annually with control over taxation and the right to initiate legislation, this body was whittled down in 1859 to a purely advisory group meeting only every three years. Police pressure produced pliable majorities in the assembly. Freedom of speech and press was almost completely suppressed. The leader of the liberal opposition, Vladimir Jovanović, was barred from his elected assembly seat and forced into exile, from which he published an influential opposition newspaper that was smuggled into the country. In 1863, police uncovered a supposed plot against Prince Michael's life. Thirty-five alleged conspirators were arrested with great haste, but the government was unable to make a convincing case in court. When the defendants were all acquitted by the Supreme Court, Michael had five court members (including three former justice ministers) charged with malfeasance and tried by a specially appointed tribunal that gave them two- to three-year jail terms. Virtually the only opposition forum was the Society of Serbian Letters, which was temporarily shut down by the government in 1864 after attempts were made to elect as honorary members leading European liberals such as Garibaldi. Dissident teachers were purged, most notably Djuro Daničić, a leading philosopher and intellectual, who was transferred from his position as professor of medieval Serbian literature to a job in the postal administration in 1865.

Michael sought to divert growing discontent--reflected in liberal successes in 25 per cent of the 1867 assembly elections--by constructing an elaborate system of Balkan alliances to oust Turkey from southeastern Europe, but these plans collapsed when he was assassinated on June 9, 1868. The assassination was followed by a military coup and the convocation, under strong military pressure, of a national assembly that elected Michael's cousin Milan Obrenović prince under a regency until he reached his majority in 1873. Sixteen persons were executed for alleged complicity in the assassination, which was blamed on Karageorgević plotting, although the investigation was carefully controlled to avoid implicating many prominent Serbians. A constitutional assembly in 1869 approved a new document that had many liberal trappings but retained ultimate power in princely hands. A regular legislature (skupština), elected on a broad franchise approaching universal male suffrage, was established for the first time since the winning of autonomy. However, the prince was empowered to convene and dismiss the skupština at will, appoint one-fourth of its membership, have an absolute veto, and rule by decree when it was not in session. The skupština soon became known as the "Chamber of Echoes" (Stavrianos 1958: 258).

In Bulgaria, there was a major increase in nationalist sentiment during the 1860s. The most significant movement was more anti-Greek than anti-Turkish, directed at the establishment of a Bulgarian church independent of the Greek Orthodox patriarchate at Constantinople and staffed by Bulgarian clergy. Public pressure, in some cases accompanied by rioting, effectively ousted Greek clergy from Bulgarian churches by the late 1860s. In March 1870 the Turkish government granted the Bulgarian desire for an autonomous church, partly to damp unrest in Bulgaria and partly to embroil the Greeks and Bulgarians with each other to divert their attention away from anti-Turkish machinations.

The Rise of the Working Class

Aside from widespread governmental restructuring, a marked aspect of European development in the 1860s was the growth of an organized working-class movement in the more advanced countries. One explanation for this development was the general ferment in Europe in the 1860s that helped politicize the lower classes in the more urban and industrial societies and energized the middle classes, which were able to play a more direct political role because they were enfranchised in almost all countries by the end of the decade. Another factor was the European industrial depression of 1866, which was severe enough to alarm many workers but not long-lasting enough to destroy embryonic labor groups. Still another factor was a loosening of restrictions on labor unions in many of the more industrial areas. Unions were either explicitly legalized or tolerated in Belgium (1866), France (1868), Spain (1869), Germany (1869), and Austria (1870), and had long enjoyed a semi-legal status in the United Kingdom.

A final factor was the encouragement given to the development of working class movements by the formation of the First International in 1864, an organization composed of representatives of labor movements in different countries, which by 1870 had come under Marxist socialist influence and included delegates from Britain, France, Germany, Belgium, Switzerland, Italy and the Habsburg Monarchy. The First International was to a large extent a paper organization, with no power to order national labor movements to do anything and usually with such little money it could not even afford to pay rent for an office or a salary to its general secretary. Nonetheless, the International helped boost the morale of the European labor movement, provided publicity, sometimes helped raise financial assistance during major strikes (such as the Paris bronze workers strike of 1867 and the 1868 Geneva building workers strike), and in some cases successfully discouraged workers from crossing national boundaries to replace strikers.

The strongest labor movement to emerge by 1870 was in Great Britain, where in 1869 a national trade union congress was attended by delegates representing 250,000 union members, almost exclusively organized in the highly skilled trades. An estimated 70,000 Parisians belonged to trade unions by 1870 and an estimated 90,000 Frenchmen struck in that year--as many as had struck in the four-year period from 1865 through 1868. In Germany, two socialistic political organizations had about 25,000 members by 1869, and at least 35,000 workers were organized in labor groups. Over 170 strikes erupted in Germany between January 1869 and July 1870, compared with only 107 strikes during the entire 1850s. There were also bursts of strikes in the very late 1860s in Austria, Belgium, the Netherlands and Italy. In Spain, about 40,000 workers were organized by 1870, following the lifting of restrictions on trade unions after the 1868 revolution.

By the late 1860s, the increased working-class activity was stirring nervous reactions and growing repression in many European countries. In Italy, a two-day general strike in Bologna in April 1868 was broken by arrests and the dissolution of workers and political organizations. Severe rioting in many Italian areas in December 1868-January 1869, protesting a new tax on basic foodstuffs, was suppressed by troops who killed 257 people, wounded 1,100, and arrested almost 3,800. Belgian troops shot many strikers and arrested many others, including the leading members of the Belgian section of the International, following major outbursts of strikes among coal miners in 1867 and 1869. Dutch authorities announced in 1869 that illegal but hitherto tolerated strikes would thereafter be suppressed. French troops killed 27 strikers and wounded 30 others in two 1869 clashes, and leaders of the French International were prosecuted and jailed three times in 1868-70. In Hungary, an organization of landless rural workers led by Janos Asatalos, which peacefully demanded democratic and social reforms, was destroyed by scores of arrests in 1868. All meeting halls of the movement were closed, and their publications were confiscated. In Austria, there were harsh reprisals after about 20,000 workers demonstrated in Vienna on December 13, 1869 to demand universal suffrage, freedom of the press, and removal of remaining restrictions on trade unions. Although the government quickly legalized unions and strikes, it also had 15 leaders of the demonstration sentenced to long jail terms for high treason and dissolved all existing labor organizations.

A major explanation of the rising tide of anti-labor repression in Europe in the 1868-70 period was the grossly exaggerated picture many governments developed of the strength of and threat posed by the First International. Since the organization was openly socialist and included delegates from many different European countries, conservative European politicians conjured up images of a vast international revolutionary conspiracy something akin to Metternich's nightmares concerning the Restoration secret societies. Thus, during the July 1870 high treason trial of the leaders of the December 1869 Vienna demonstration, the public prosecutor spoke of the International as a "shadow government, a second government in the state, forming a dangerous opposition all the more serious because this second power, this second government draws its strength and sustenance not from one state alone, but from the whole world" (Braunthal, I, 1967: 106). All the fears of European conservatives were reinforced and vastly magnified by the 1871 Paris Commune.

Chapter 6

# The Age of Repression and Reform, 1870-1914

## *The Economic and Social Structure of Europe, 1870-1914*

European society between 1870 and 1914 was at the crossroads or transition between the ancien regime of 1789, dominated by the landed aristocracy and absolute monarchy, and today's regime of modern capitalism, dominated (at least outside the Soviet sphere among the developed countries) by the industrial and financial bourgeoisie and the professional classes and politicians. The amalgamation between the landed aristocracy and the rising industrial bourgeoisie that was clearly forming between 1850 and 1870 was considerably consolidated during the 1870-1914 period, and an overwhelming percentage of the Continent's wealth and political power was controlled by these two small fractions of the population.

Around 1900, less than 1 per cent of the population owned more than 40 per cent of the land in Austria, Hungary, and Rumania; less than 4 per cent owned 25 per cent or more of the land in Denmark, England, Germany, France, and partitioned Poland. Although exact data are not available for the pre-1914 period for some of the other countries, it is estimated that around 1900 the Russian nobility, about 1 per cent of the population, owned 25 per cent of the land (excluding that held by the czar and the government), that 10 per cent of landowners in Italy held 85 per cent of that country and that 1 per cent of the landowners in southern and central Spain controlled over 40 per cent of the territory in those regions. In human terms, around 1900 approximately 5,000 landlords each owned about half of Rumania and the United Kingdom; 324 owners controlled 20 per cent of Hungary; and about 300 landlords held approximately 25 per cent of the Austrian provinces of Galicia, Bohemia, Moravia, and Silesia. Studies of total wealth (as opposed to land ownership only) indicate that around 1910 the richest 1.5 per cent of the Swedish population owned 55 per cent of the country's private wealth, that 5 per cent of the population of Great Britain controlled over 60 per cent of the national income, that 7 per cent of the Hungarian population received over one-third of the national income, and that 2 per cent of all persons who died in France left 50 per cent of all wealth that was passed on to heirs.

Table 6.1: European Historical Statistics, 1870 and 1910

| | % Population Enfranchised | | % Labor Force in Agriculture | | % Labor Force in Industry | | % in Towns 20,000+ | | % Adults Literate | | Life Expectancy[c] | | Mortality Rate (per thousand) | | Infant Mortality (per thousand) | |
|---|---|---|---|---|---|---|---|---|---|---|---|---|---|---|---|---|
| | 1870 | 1910 | 1870 | 1910 | 1870 | 1910 | 1870 | 1910 | 1870 | 1910 | 1870 | 1910 | 1870 | 1910 | 1870 | 1910 |
| Austria | 5.9 | 21 | 65 | 53 | 19 | 23 | 7 | 14 | 50 | 83 | 30 | 41 | 32 | 22 | 256 | 180 |
| Belgium | 2.2 | 22 | 44 | 23 | 37 | 46 | 18 | 25 | 60 | 87 | 40 | 47 | 23 | 15 | 153 | 137 |
| Bulgaria | – | 23 | 85 | 82 | 5 | 8 | | 6 | | 38 | | 44 | | 23 | | 152 |
| Denmark | 15 | 17 | 42 | 40 | 24 | 28 | 10 | 21 | 90 | 95 | 44 | 55 | 19 | 13 | 126 | 105 |
| Finland | 6 | 45 | 75 | 70 | 10 | 12 | 1 | 9 | 85 | 99 | 40 | 44 | 27 | 18 | 200 | 114 |
| France | 26 | 29 | 50 | 43 | 26 | 30 | 19 | 26 | 69 | 88 | 39 | 48 | 24 | 19 | 173 | 129 |
| Germany | – | 2 | 50 | 38 | 35 | 43 | 13 | 35 | 87 | 95 | 35 | 47 | 27 | 17 | 284 | 170 |
| Greece | 23 | 23 | 75 | 66 | 10 | 13 | 5 | 13 | 20 | 40 | 35 | | 31 | | | |
| Hungary | 6.5 | 6.2 | 70 | 63 | 10 | 17 | 6 | 13 | 36 | 69 | | 46 | 37 | 24 | | 212 |
| Italy | 2.0 | 8.3 | 61 | 55 | 23 | 27 | 11 | 28 | 31 | 60 | 35 | 46 | 31 | 21 | 215 | 153 |
| Neth. | 2.9 | 14 | 37 | 28 | 29 | 33 | 24 | 34 | 75 | 90 | 38 | 53 | 25 | 14 | 200 | 111 |
| Norway | 7.5 | 33 | 60 | 47 | 23 | 25 | 6 | 18 | 90 | 95 | 48 | 55 | 18 | 14 | 107 | 70 |
| Portugal | 9 | 12 | 65 | 57 | 16 | 21 | 9 | 12 | 20 | 31 | | | | 21 | | 150 |
| Rumania | 15 | 16 | | 80 | | 8 | 10 | 11 | 15 | 35 | | | 29 | 27 | 207 | 209 |
| Russia[a] | 0 | 15 | | 75 | | 10 | 6 | 10 | 15 | 45 | 25 | | 37 | 30 | 270 | 250 |
| Serbia | 20 | 23 | 85 | 80 | 5 | 10 | 2 | 4 | | 20 | | | 32 | 23 | | 152 |
| Spain | 24 | 24 | 70 | 66 | 10 | 15 | 12 | 17 | 35 | 48 | 29 | 41 | 31 | 24 | 180 | 159 |
| Sweden | 5.6 | 19 | 61 | 51 | 17 | 32 | 6 | 15 | 95 | 98 | 44 | 55 | 19 | 14 | 135 | 77 |
| Switz. | 22 | 22 | 50 | 27 | 37 | 46 | 8 | 20 | 90 | 98 | 40 | 50 | 23 | 15 | 193 | 107 |
| U.K.[b] | 8 | 18 | 15 | 10 | 52 | 56 | 42 | 62 | 70 | 95 | 41 | 51 | 22 | 15 | 151 | 115 |

[a] Data for European Russia only  [b] Most non-electoral data for England and Wales only
[c] Life expectancy data is for males
Sources: Mackie and Rose 1974; Mitchell 1975:16-47, 51-64; Flora 1973:242-5; Dublin 1949: 346-8.

# REPRESSION AND REFORM, 1870-1914

While the wealthy bankers, merchants, and industrialists gained increasing political power almost everywhere in Europe after 1870, the nobility continued to exercise an influence vastly disproportionate to their size in most countries. This was especially the case in the United Kingdom, Germany, the Habsburg Empire, Sweden and Russia. In Prussia around 1910, the nobility virtually monopolized the upper legislative house, held 25 per cent of lower legislative seats, and occupied 55 per cent of all army ranks of colonel and above, 11 out of 12 provincial administrative headships, 23 out of 27 regional administrative headships, 60 per cent of all prefectures, 80 per cent of ambassadorships and 9 out of 11 cabinet positions. In the United Kingdom, the nobility held almost half of all cabinet seats between 1886 and 1916, monopolized the upper legislative house, and held 10 per cent of all seats in the House of Commons. In Hungary, between 1875 and 1918, the nobility held about 75 per cent of all cabinet posts and positions as chief county administrative officers, all the seats in the upper legislative house, and 50 per cent of the seats in the lower legislative house. In Austria, until 1896 the nobility was guaranteed 25 per cent of lower legislative mandates and around 1905 filled 50 per cent of the generalships in the army and the highest positions in the civil service. In Russia, largely because of class-biased suffrage rules, the nobility, about 1 per cent of the population, held half of all seats in the lower legislative house after 1907 and well over half of all seats in district and provincial assemblies. In St. Petersburg, it was common to see signs posted in the more fashionable public gardens banning "dogs, common people and enlisted men" (Tannenbaum 1977: 49).

In most European countries--Prussia, Hungary, and Russia were somewhat exceptional--the nobility and upper middle classes tended to blend together increasingly after 1870. Many nobles whose wealth was based on land were severely hurt by the worldwide 1873-97 agricultural depression. In central and eastern Europe many never recovered from the loss of feudal dues and services resulting from the abolition of serfdom. Subsequently, the nobility increasingly intermarried and joined in commercial ventures with the high bourgeoisie. In effect, they offered the prestige of their names in exchange for the more tangible rewards of wealth.

> Politically, nobles and wealthy burghers generally held the same conservative views, and shared the same suspicions of social and political reform. Marriages between scions of great noble houses and daughters of rich industrialists and bankers multiplied, especially in the last decades of the nineteenth and first years of the twentieth century. ... The style of life and the self-assurance of the great capitalists differed hardly at all from that of the high nobility and many were themselves ennobled. In a sense there was an interpenetration of high nobility and high bourgeoisie, in which nobles became bourgeoisified and bourgeois became feudalized (Blum 1978: 422).

The rising power of the industrial and commercial bourgeoisie after 1870 reflected the ever-increasing pace of industrial and urban development, which in comparison with previous periods reached staggering dimensions between 1870 and 1914, fostering massive urbanization and the rise of a large urban industrial working class (which was, however, still primarily based in small factories and workshops). European manufacturing output quadrupled between 1870 and 1910. During this same period, the number of European cities housing over 100,000 people increased from about 70 to over 180, and their total population jumped from about 20 million to about 60 million, or from about 7 to about 14 per cent of the total European population. The percentage of the population living in cities of 20,000 or more also doubled, jumping from about 15 to about 30 per cent of the Continent's inhabitants during the era.

The rapid pace of industrialization and urbanization during the 1870-1914 period was accompanied by significant increases in the literacy rate throughout Europe, although, as before, the countries of northwestern Europe remained far more educated than the regions of southern and eastern Europe (see Table 6.1). Except in Iberia, the Balkans, and Russia, elementary school instruction was made both free and compulsory by around 1870. To some extent, the provision of such facilities reflected altruistic motives of middle class liberals. However, to a greater extent their establishment reflected the feelings of middle- and upper-class elites that strong countries could be built only by at least minimally educated and literate citizens (the development of mechanized industry and advanced weaponry generally required basic literacy) and that state-controlled education could develop patriotism, refute subversive ideas circulating among the lower classes, and tame signs of savagery among the most deprived elements of the population. Thus, Adolph Thiers, a leading French politician, who served as president of France in 1871-3, defined the purpose of education as teaching that "suffering is necessary in all estates, ... and that, when the poor have a fever, it is not the rich who have sent it to them" (Price 1972: 254). Around 1900, an English school inspector asserted that "if it were not for her 500 elementary schools, London would be overrun by a horde of young savages" (Tannenbaum 1977: 29). Despite the perceived advantages that an educated populace could provide for a state, some conservative observers remained doubtful and feared that education would only create expectations among the lower classes that could threaten the established order. Thus, Russian Finance Minister Sergei Witte lamented, "Education foments social revolution, but popular ignorance loses wars" (McClelland 1979: 116-17).

Everywhere, compulsory elementary school education was used (along with the universal military service also introduced in most European countries around 1870) to inculcate patriotic and nationalistic feelings. Regional loyalties, dialects, and festivals were deliberately shunned in favor of material stressing the national language, history, and holidays. Especially in Russia and Hungary, the schools were also used to destroy systematically the culture of ethnic minorities. Thus, one Magyar political writer observed that the Hungarian schools were like a "huge machine, at one end of which Slovak youth are thrown in by the hundreds and at the other end of which they come out as Magyars" (Seton-Watson 1934: 400).

Even after free elementary education was provided in most countries, the children of the lower classes were left disadvantaged. They could still not afford the secondary and college education that the upper and middle classes could purchase and that was necessary more than ever after 1870 to obtain positions of high status, pay, and power in societies that were undergoing rapid modernization. Thus, as late as 1914, fewer than 3 per cent of children between the ages of 14 and 18 in the most advanced countries of Europe were enrolled in secondary schools of any kind, and less than 1 per cent of the university age population in any country were attending an institution of higher education. The effect of such denial of free education on lower-class mobility was rarely recognized as explicitly as in an 1887 decree by Russian Minister of Education Ivan Delianov, which instructed the state-supported secondary schools that (almost uniquely) existed in Russia to refuse to admit "children of coachmen, menials, cooks, washerwomen, small shopkeepers and the like" since it was "completely unwarranted for the children of such people to leave their position in life" (Alston 1969: 129).

Despite the massive and unprecedented industrialization and urbanization of the 1870-1914 period, about 60 per cent of all Europeans continued to make their living from agriculture, and about 70 per cent lived in rural areas or small towns at the end of the era. Further, while modernization affected all of the European countries, its impact was extremely uneven across the Continent. Data reflecting such indices of modernization as urbanization, labor force in industry, literacy, life expectancy, and infant mortality demonstrate clearly that by the end of the era the most developed countries were in northwestern Europe and the least developed nations were in southern and eastern Europe (see Table 6.1). Thus, in countries such as the United Kingdom, France, and Switzerland, literacy rates and the percentage of the labor force employed in industry were twice those in the Balkans, Iberia, Hungary, and Russia, and urbanization and mortality rates also showed sharp divergences. The Balkans remained the most backwards area of Europe: Serbia and Bulgaria each had only about 16,000 factory workers in 1910, for example, and in that year fewer than half of all Serbian army recruits had ever heard of King Peter, the monarch since 1903. The countries of central Europe—Germany, Italy, and Austria—were in between the most and least developed areas of Europe both in geography and in indicators of modernization. (Germany was among the most industrialized, urbanized, and literate countries, but showed health-related indices generally well below northwestern European levels; further, there was a glaring contrast between western Germany, one of the major European industrial centers, and eastern Germany, which remained dominated by enormous semi-feudal agrarian estates, their Junker landlords and masses of wretched landless agricultural laborers.)

Although conditions of the majority of the European population could not be described as good anywhere, they were unquestionably best in northwestern Europe by 1914. During the 1873-96 period, when industrial and agricultural prices declined throughout Europe, wages remained relatively stable for industrial workers, and real wages consequently increased for them by 30 per cent or more during these years in northwestern Europe. Although high inflation—over 35 per cent between 1895 and 1914—led to real wage stagnation or declines in this region between 1900 and 1914, over the entire 1870-1914 period gains in living standards were substantial for the overall population. Thus, in France, savings banks deposits increased tenfold, and meat consumption per capita jumped over 25 per cent between 1870 and 1914. Yet, even at the end of the period, numerous studies indicate that even in such relatively wealthy regions as England at least one-third of the population lived in dire poverty and most workers had to spend over half of their income on food alone (compared with about 75 per cent 50 years before, however). In 1917, a medical survey of males in the United Kingdom discovered that only one-third were in satisfactory health, while over two-thirds suffered marked or partial disabilities.

In southern and eastern Europe, although the population lived longer in 1914 than they did in 1870, they did not live much better. These areas were overwhelmingly rural and agricultural, and most of the farmers lacked enough land to support themselves (largely because of inefficient agricultural techniques and resultant poor crop yields) or were completely landless. In Hungary and southern parts of Italy and Spain, millions of completely landless peasants worked at starvation wages for the landlords and were often completely unemployed for four or more months of the year. In southern Spain, "inquiry after inquiry revealed wages which would not cover the day laborer's minimum expenditure on food" (Carr 1966: 417). In Russia, where population in the European regions increased by an astounding 90 per cent between 1860 and 1910, the proportion of the peasantry lacking enough land to support themselves jumped from under 30 to over 50 per cent during the same period. As Russian Minister of Finance Count Sergei Witte wrote to Czar Nicholas II in 1898, "Your majesty has 130 million subjects. Of them barely more than half live, the rest vegetate" (Kochan 1966: 45).

A root cause of the extremely poor conditions in southern and eastern Europe was the continued rapid rate of European population growth during the 1870-1914 period. Although the entire Continent was affected by the rise in population from about 290 to about 450 million during the period, residents of overcrowded rural areas in northwestern Europe could often find employment in urban industry, while in southern and eastern European there was usually no alternative to subdividing an already inadequate family plot or hiring out as a landless laborer.

Emigration figures clearly reflect growing land hunger and unemployment in southern, central, and eastern Europe, especially after 1890. Altogether, an astounding 35 million Europeans left for overseas between 1870 and 1914. About 75 per cent of the 10 million who left before 1890 departed from northwestern Europe, while about 65 per cent of the 25 million who emigrated during the following 25 years came from southern, central, and eastern Europe. Economic conditions in these regions would unquestionably have become far worse save for this massive emigration, which greatly reduced land hunger and downward pressure on wages. Especially in southern Italy, migration virtually denuded entire villages. Thus, in September 1902, when Prime Minister Giuseppe Zanardelli made one of the very rare trips of Italian politicians to the neglected south, he was greeted by the mayor of Moliterno in Basilicata on behalf of the town's 8,000 citizens, "3,000 of whom are in America and the over 5,000 who are preparing to follow them" (Seton-Watson 1967: 310). Large-scale emigration during the period from the United Kingdom, Scandinavia, and Germany played a significant role in the improvement in conditions there also. For example, the number of landless laborers and dwarf farmers in Norway declined by over two-thirds between 1855 and 1910, a period in which about 700,000 Norwegians (almost one-third of the 1900 population of 2.2 million) left the country.

Everywhere, although especially in southern, central and eastern Europe, urban conditions, and especially urban housing conditions, were deplorable for a substantial percentage of the population. Many of the rapidly growing European cities could not keep up with the demand for housing, and the result was often exorbitant rents and overcrowded and unsanitary accommodations. Around 1900, studies found that half or more of all working class families living in Budapest, Helsinki, Athens, Berlin, Chemnitz, Breslau, and Dresden inhabited one-room dwellings, and that, if "overcrowding" were defined as living in dwellings in which more than two persons occupied a room, over 25 per cent of the total population of Berlin, Vienna, Moscow, St. Petersburg, Budapest, Sofia, Bucharest, Breslau, and Chemnitz endured such conditions. In Budapest, nearly 10 per cent of the population lived ten or more to a room in 1910, while in Berlin 600,000 people were housed more than five to a room in 1912. After a major uprising in Barcelona in 1909, the civil governor, referring to the city's "morbid social conditions," noted that "in Barcelona there is no need to prepare a revolution; it is always ready made" (Carr 1966: 484).

The poor paid a heavy price for their terrible living conditions. In Berlin, the mortality rate in 1885 for persons inhabiting one-room apartments was 30 times that of persons living in four-room apartments, 22 times that of three-room apartment dwellers and seven times that of persons in two-room apartments. Mortality rates in the worst proletarian districts in Paris and Vienna in the late nineteenth century were four times as high as those in the richest areas of those cities. In Belgium, average life expectancy for the poor around 1900 was about 18, but about 54 for the wealthy. In Denmark, the infant mortality rate around the turn of the century was three times higher among children of the working class than among those of government officials, and mortality rates among those between the ages of 15 and

36 on poor relief were ten times higher than those for the comparable population at large. In central Europe, rates of tuberculosis contraction were two or three times higher among the workers than among the prosperous classes, and rates of measles, diphtheria, typhus, and cholera were 30 to 60 times higher among the poor. The poor were even distinguished by their short stature: "The average European worker was at least three inches shorter than the average bourgeois" (Tannenbaum 1977:158).

## General Patterns of Repression and Reform, 1870-1914

The 1870-1914 period, and especially the years after 1880, saw a marked increase in lower-class organization in comparison with the 1850-70 era. Although the industrial working class constituted less than 30 per cent of the European labor force as late as 1914, its rapid growth--in Sweden, for example, from 182,000 to 350,000 between 1873 and 1914 and even in Russia from 700,000 to 3.4 million between 1865 and 1914--and concentration in urban centers led to a rising tide of working-class organization and demands for reform. Except in the most economically backwards regions of Europe, such as the Balkans, trade unions and socialist parties were formed everywhere by 1900. They steadily grew in strength except in such countries as Russia, Italy, Spain, and Hungary where periodic waves of repression decimated them. Particularly after 1890, unions and socialist parties for the first time began to make significant inroads beyond the skilled trades and crafts, penetrating unskilled and semi-skilled workers, including those in heavy industry and large factories. Everywhere working-class groups demanded social reform but above all stressed the need for the introduction of universal male suffrage and freedom of organization wherever such were lacking. There was also a rising tide of rural discontent during the period in the Balkans and other regions, such as southern Spain, Russia, Hungary and Austrian Galicia where economic and social conditions were especially poor.

During the 1815-70 period, most European countries tended to go through phases of repression and relative toleration at about the same time. Thus, repression increased simultaneously in many countries in response to the 1820, 1830, and 1848 revolutions, while repressive pressure eased generally during the early 1840s and late 1850s, as the memory of past revolutionary outbursts eased. After 1870, this pattern of common response across Europe greatly diminished as differing degrees of modernization increasingly distinguished different regions of the Continent. For the most part, the least highly developed regions of southern and eastern Europe (Iberia, the Balkans, Hungary, and Russia) clung to repressive regimens after 1870, while the most developed northwestern European countries (the United Kingdom, France, Switzerland, Scandinavia, and the Low Countries) became increasingly reformist in orientation and the "in between" countries of central Europe (Germany, Italy, and Austria) responded to dissent with a mixture of reform and repression. Nonetheless, there were some common patterns that can be identified in the response of European governments to developments during the 1870-1914 period. For example, all of the regimes made at least some symbolic efforts during these 45 years to appease some working-class demands and thus avoid severe continuing social unrest. Thus, in every European country except Hungary and Portugal, universal or quasi-universal male suffrage was effected by 1914, although it was vitiated by class-weighted voting schemes, gross gerrymandering, election rigging and/or the lack of parliamentary responsibility in almost all of the countries of southern, central, and eastern Europe. In most of the countries some easing of controls on the press, assembly and trade union activities also occurred after 1870 (see Tables 1.1, 2.1 and 2.2). Although socialist parties were effectively outlawed for long periods after 1870 in Germany, Italy, Austria, France, Hungary, and Russia, by 1910 socialists were allowed to function openly at least to some extent almost everywhere. Despite such liberalization, it should be added, in southern, central, and eastern Europe, unions and socialist groups and opposition newspapers continued to be subjected to often-severe persecution and administrative harassment.

Advances in suffrage and civil liberties were accompanied, except in the southern and eastern European lands of Russia, Hungary, Iberia, and the Balkans, by significant social welfare reforms after 1870. By 1914, although mass living conditions remained extremely poor almost everywhere in Europe, all of the countries of central and northwestern Europe had introduced reasonably effective laws providing social insurance and regulating some of the worst abuses in the factories concerning the employment of women and children. The average work week for urban industrial employees declined from about 90 hours in 1850 to about 65 hours in 1914, although in southern and eastern Europe, work weeks of 80 hours or more were still known on the eve of World War I. One worker in Bialystok (Russian Poland) declared after a 12-hour day had been won there, "Before that I hardly knew my own children; I would leave for work when they were still asleep and when I returned from work they were asleep again; only on Saturday did I have time to hold my child" (Mendelsohn 1970: 86).

While the overall pattern of responses of European governments to dissent increasingly diverged by geographic region after 1870, some traces of common patterns across the Continent during particular time periods in response to well-publicized political developments can still be found. By far the most spectacular such incident from the standpoint of generating conservative fears and repressive reactions across Europe was the Paris Commune of 1871, which fostered a dread of lower-class radicalism that to a considerable extent colored politics in many European countries until about 1890. The Commune was a side effect of the Franco-Prussian War of 1870, which in turn resulted from a dispute over the throne vacancy created by the 1868 revolution in Spain. French disasters in the war triggered a bloodless revolution in Paris in September 1870 that overthrew the regime of Napoleon III. Subsequently, a major split developed between Paris and the French provinces over continuation of the war against Prussia. French elections in February 1871 produced a monarchist-dominated National Assembly that was determined to end the war despite strong republican sentiment in Paris for prolonging the struggle. The assembly's endorsement of a peace settlement, its decision to sit at Versailles rather than in Paris and its passage of several poorly conceived laws that created financial havoc in Paris deepened the split. On March 18, 1871 insurrection erupted in Paris. An elected muncipal government, known as the Commune of Paris, was established in Paris after Adolph Theirs, the head of the Versailles government, withdrew all his forces from the city. Partly because many wealthy Parisians had fled during the war-time Prussian siege and subsequent events, the Commune was dominated by an assortment of working-class and lower-middle-class delegates. Although the general tenor of the Commune was strongly republican, anti-clerical and in support of social reform, it was not dominated by any particular ideology, was not particularly radical, and, contrary to later mythology, was not strongly influenced by Marxism or controlled by members of the International.

The Commune was too rent by internal divisions and too preoccupied by ludicrously inadequate attempts to organize defenses against the inevitable attack from Versailles to accomplish much. By the time it was crushed in late May, the Commune's most radical actions were the continuation of the wartime moratorium on rents and bills and abolition of factory fines and night work in bakeries. Extremist elements, not really representative of the Commune as a whole, came to the fore only as the Versailles forces, aided by the German release of 40,000 French prisoners of war, tightened their noose around Paris in April. It was only after captured Commune soldiers were executed that hostages were taken, and only after the Versailles forces began mass executions of prisoners during the final offensive of May 22-28 that 56 hostages were shot by Communards, and many of Paris's finest buildings, including the Tuileries, the Palace of Justice, the Ministry of Foreign Affairs and the City Hall, were set aflame.

As horrible as the carnage attributable to the Commune was, it paled in comparison to the atrocities of the Versailles troops. Theirs's forces lost about 900, while about 25,000 Parisians were killed, the vast majority of whom were slaughtered in cold blood. More people were killed during the semaine sanglante ("bloody week") than died throughout France during the 18 months of the famous Reign of Terror of the 1789 revolution (March 1793-July 1794). At the prison of La Roquette alone, 1,900 were shot in two days.

> Many were shot for having watches as probable "officials" of the Commune. The wearing of a pair of army boots was sufficient to lead to arrest and often execution, or a discolored right shoulder from a rifle butt or simply blackened hands. ... [One Versaillese official] had 111

prisoners shot for having white hair, on the grounds that they were of an age to have taken part in the 1848 revolution (Edwards 1971: 344).

The streets of Paris were filled with dead bodies, and the waters of the Seine were fouled with blood for weeks. At the Trocadero there was a stack of 1,100 corpses, while the yard of the Ecole Polytechnique was piled with bodies three yards high in a 100-yard long line. Theirs telegraphed his prefects, "The ground is paved with their corpses; this terrible spectacle will be a lesson to them" (Jellinek 1965: 369). The stench in Paris became so bad that birds fell dead in the streets, and a huge funeral pyre at Buttes-Chaumont filled the skies of eastern Paris with a cloud of foul smoke that hung over the area for days.

In addition to summary executions, the suppression of the Commune was accompanied by mass arrests, estimated at about 40,000 to 50,000. After ad hoc prisons established at Versailles became so crowded that many prisoners went mad, 28,000 were dispatched by boat to coastal fortresses and islands off the west coast of France, where conditions were still so bad that almost 1,200 perished while being detained. Over 30,000 of those arrested were eventually freed, after being held for months, either without any trial or after hearings before military tribunals. Twenty-six Communards were executed after trials, while another 14,000 (including 3,400 sentenced in absentia) were convicted. Over 4,500 were given long jail terms and 5,000 were sentenced to deportation in the hellish colony of New Caledonia. Many of the prisoners sent to New Caledonia died during the five month voyage. Thus, of the 650 sent on the ship Semiramis, 34 were dead and 60 seriously ill upon arrival, while 300 of the 588 prisoners on the Orne had scurvy when the ship docked at Melbourne en route.

Although the Commune's atrocities were relatively trivial compared to those of the Versailles forces, the reports carried by the European press about the events in Paris concentrated almost exclusively on the shooting of hostages and the burning of public buildings by the Communards. The European press and conservative politicians quickly decided that the International had somehow been to blame for the Commune, a charge that was quite false but that gained credibility since some Commune leaders had belonged to the International and many members of the International, notably the organization's hitherto relatively obscure secretary, Karl Marx, both embraced the Commune and claimed responsibility for it. Since the 1870-1 period was also marked by an unusual wave of strikes that affected many of the European countries, by the spring of 1871, "All Europe seemed to see the work of the Commune and the International in every disorder" (McClellan 1979: 171). In 1871-2, Germany, Spain, and France all appealed for concerted European action against the International. A French diplomatic note of June 6, 1871 termed the International a "germ" and an "agent of destruction aimed at all nations," which must be destroyed. Bismark's newspaper mouthpiece, the Norddeutsche Allgemeine Zeitung, termed establishment of a European alliance against the International "the only possible means of saving the state, church, culture, in a word, everything which makes up the life of European states." The Spanish government branded the International a group that "flies in the face of all human tradition, strikes God from the mind, denies family and the principle of heredity, and rejects alike the sublime principles of nationality and civilization." As late as 1878, several years after the International had disintegrated amidst widespread repression and internal factionalism, Pope Piux IX termed the group a "criminal organization" that sought to destroy the "basis of authority in this world" (Braunthal, I, 1967: 158-62; McClellan 1979: 180).

The various appeals for joint action against the International were blocked by British resistance, although the German, Austrian, and Hungarian governments issued a symbolic declaration in November 1872 denouncing the International's tendencies as "in complete contrast with, and antagonistic to, the principles of bourgeois society" and therefore to be "vigorously repelled" (Braunthal, I, 1967: 160-61). Fears of the Commune and the International were also clearly reflected in the agreement by the Emperors of Austria, Germany and Russia at Berlin in 1873, in what became known as the "league of the Three Emperors" (Dreikaiserbund), to work together, for among other things, the "repression of revolutionary movement in Europe" (Lipson 1962: 279).

These symbolic declarations of 1872-3 were supplemented by campaigns of police harassment and prosecution of labor and socialist activities in many European countries in the 1870s. Both the International and left-wing organizations in many countries fell victim to the triple burden imposed by this campaign of repression, the severe economic depression of the mid-1870s and the bitter internal disputes between followers of socialist Karl Marx and those of anarchist Michael Bakunin. However, fears generated by the Commune and the International lingered on and helped shape the highly conservative course of politics in many countries, especially in Germany, Austria, Hungary, Spain, Italy, France, Russia, and Denmark for 20 years or more after 1870. Almost everywhere in Europe, the political mood was extremely conservative during the 1870s. Although "liberal" parties representing largely upper-middle-class interests held power for part or all of the decade in a number of countries, including Italy, Belgium, the Netherlands, the United Kingdom, Austria, Hungary, Serbia, and Rumania, these groups defined "liberalism" almost solely in terms of elimination of governmental restrictions on business and were for the most part as socially conservative and repressive as their officially "conservative" opponents had been before them. Although with a few exceptions, such as in Spain after 1874, France until 1879, and Russia, repressive political controls in the 1870s were not as severe as in the 1850s, the general mood of the period was not dissimilar to that following the 1848 revolution. The formal existence of constitutional guarantees and freedom of the press from prior censorship in all countries save Russia, and of trade union freedom in some countries helped to ensure that the 1870s reaction never became extreme in most countries. But the period was almost completely devoid of progress in civil liberties (only Portugal, for example, expanded the suffrage during the 1870s, while Spain and Hungary reduced it) or social legislation.

Just as the fears provoked by the Commune were dying down around 1880, they were revived by the assassination of Czar Alexander II of Russia in 1881, other terrorist incidents in 1881-7 in Ireland, Spain, France, Germany, Austria and Poland, and the emergence of a tiny but highly vocal anarchist movement that openly advocated violence. Fears of anarchist terrorism were considerably stimulated by an 1881 meeting of anarchists in London shortly after the assassination of Alexander. They claimed to represent groups with a total membership of 50,000. The London Congress, which was thoroughly infiltrated by police agents, issued a militant declaration endorsing the use of "propaganda by the deed" (i.e., terrorism) and urged all affiliated organizations to study the "technical and chemical sciences" and to exert every effort "to arouse the spirit of revolt in those sections of the popular masses who still harbor illusions about the effectiveness of legal methods" (Nomad 1966: 75-76). Although the Congress, which was attended by only 45 delegates, resolved to form an Anarchist International, most of its affiliated organizations existed only on paper, and a proposed 1882 congress never met. The so-called "Black International" was "long to remain a terrifying spectre in the minds of governments, but it was no more than a spectre" (Woodcock 1962: 260).

Although the terrorist incidents of the 1880s revived the fears invoked by the memory of the Commune, they did not have anything like the Commune's impact. However, with a few notable exceptions, such as Norway and Switzerland, the dominant tone of European political life continued to be conservative, and in many countries (especially Russia, Germany, Spain, Denmark, Austria, and Hungary), highly repressive during the 1880s, there was far greater progress in the area of civil liberties and social legislation than there had been during the preceding decade. Thus, during the 1880s, the national franchise was extended in Austria (1882), Italy (1882), Norway (1884), the United Kingdom (1884), and the Netherlands (1887). The local suffrage was also expanded in a number of countries, including Belgium (1883), France (1884), Great Britain (1888), and Italy (1889). Restrictions on trade unions and freedom of the press were significantly eased in France and Spain, and comprehensive social insurance programs were enacted during the 1880s in Austria and Germany.

During the 1890s, conservatives' fears were stoked by such developments as the formation of the Second International; the inauguration of widespread May Day strikes in 1890; and, in France, Spain, and Italy, an outburst of violent incidents, including another round of terrorist attacks. The Second International, organized at a conference in Paris in 1889--the 100th anniversary of the French Revolution--was, as its name suggests, designed to replace the First

International. Like the First International, it was mostly a propaganda organization and had no real power to direct or compel action by affiliated European workers' movements. Further, by any reasonable analysis, despite the frequent use of militant language, the Second International and almost all of its affiliated organizations were essentially reformist in orientation, stressing above all universal male suffrage where this did not exist and quite willing to use legal-parliamentarian approaches wherever possible. However, by raising the spectre of an internationally coordinated, subversive workers' movement, the Second International revived memories of the secret societies of the Restoration, the alleged revolutionary plotting of the First International and the terrorist machinations of the non-existent "Black International." Conservatives' fears were especially focussed on the strikes and demonstrations sponsored by the Second International each year on May Day to demand an eight-hour work day and other reforms. Particularly during the first May Day celebrations in the early 1890s, many European governments feared the outbreak of revolution and took extreme precautions or repressive measures. Thus, during the first great--and entirely peaceful--May Day demonstration in Vienna in 1890, according to contemporary newspaper accounts:

> The soldiers are in readiness, the gates of the houses are being locked, victuals are being prepared in the houses just as before a siege, businesses are deserted, women and children do not venture upon the streets, on all minds weighs the impression of a heavy anxiety (Jenks 1960: 171).

Despite the May Day demonstrations and other developments during the 1890s that caused unease among conservatives, the decade in general witnessed a continuation of the trend apparent in the 1880s for many governments to respond to political and social unrest with reform as well as, or in some cases, a substitute for repression. Although there was still a great deal of repression in the 1890s, especially in Italy, Russia, Germany, Spain, and Hungary, the overall tone of European life was considerably less harsh and restrictive than in the previous decade. In Austria and Germany, for example, socialist parties and trade unions were allowed to function openly after 1890, after years of being forced underground. In Italy, which had one of the worst civil liberties records of any European state in the 1890s, the decade ended with a substantial rebuff to the forces of repression. In France, although a series of terrorist incidents triggered harsh repressive measures in 1892-4, jury acquittals in a major political case in 1894 and the ultimate outcome of the notorious Dreyfus case were major victories for civil liberties. Even in Russia, there was a slight easing of the pervasive atmosphere of repression with the death of Czar Alexander III in 1894. The decade also saw significant suffrage reforms in Spain (1890), Belgium (1893), the Netherlands (1896), Austria (1896), and Norway (1898), important social legislation in, among other countries, the Netherlands and Denmark, and even significant tax reforms that slightly shifted the burden off the backs of the poor in Germany, Italy, Austria, Norway, Spain, and the United Kingdom. The general change in the European atmosphere since the days of the 1870s was particularly evident in the great reform encyclical Rerum Novarum issued in 1891 by Pope Leo XIII (1878-1903). Only 13 years after Pope Pius IX's denunciation of the First International, Leo criticized the exploitation of workers by capitalists, endorsed the formation of Christian trade unions, and called for intervention by the state to aid the poor and thus dampen the tendency towards class conflict. Although Rerum Novarum upheld the principle of capitalism and termed class division and suffering inevitable, it also declared, "It is shameful to treat men like chattels to make money by," and asserted that "everyone has the right to procure what is necessary to live" (Hayes 1963: 144).

The period between 1900 and 1914 witnessed a marked increase in the general level of political conflict in Europe. Although the 1875-1900 period had been almost completely devoid of revolutionary upheavals or massive opposition violence (except in Italy during the 1890s), every major country in Europe and some of the minor ones were seriously threatened by internal strife and/or the rise of working-class unions and political parties during the following 15 years. Successful revolutions after 1900 brought down governments in Serbia (1903), Greece (1909), and Portugal (1910); serious nation-wide revolutionary outbursts threatened the regimes in Russia (1905) and Rumania (1907). More limited but threatening outbreaks of civil disorder convulsed regions of Spain (1902-1905, 1909) and Italy (1914), while mass strikes and demonstrations for suffrage reform and social justice rocked Russia (1902-1903 and 1912-14), Sweden (1902), Belgium (1902, 1912-13), the Netherlands (1903), Austria (1905), Germany (1905-1906, 1908, 1910), France (1906-1908), Bulgaria (1900, 1906-1907), and Great Britain (1910-14). On the eve of World War I, social tensions were severely threatening the stability of the regimes in Russia, Austria, Spain, Italy, Germany, and the United Kingdom. There is little doubt that officials in some of these countries, notably Austria and the United Kingdom, at least subconsciously welcomed the outbreak of war as a means of diverting internal tensions away from what threatened to become civil wars at home.

The marked rise in social tensions after 1900 can be explained by a number of factors. One is simply the continued growth of industrialization, urbanization, and literacy in Europe, which created a larger working class and one that was both more exposed to and more capable of responding to political agitation. Another factor is unquestionably the considerable improvement in mass living conditions (and the state of civil liberties) that was evident by 1900 in many countries of Europe, compared with 1850. By 1900, with the notable exception of Russia, prior press censorship had been abolished throughout the Continent. Trade unions and socialist parties could function almost everywhere, and they enjoyed a remarkable growth during the 1900-1914 period, providing an institutionalized source of working-class agitation and organization that had previously been lacking in most countries. Further, since in most countries outside of southern and eastern Europe workers had more leisure time and enjoyed better health as hours of work declined and real wages increased after 1870, they had more opportunity and energy to devote to organized activity aimed at bettering their lot. Probably another contributing factor to the rise in unrest after 1900 was the end of the so-called long depression of 1873-97, which relieved workers of fears of unemployment if they lost their jobs during labor strife, combined with the aggravation caused by the stagnation or decline in real wages after 1900. Finally, the factor of contagion must be noted. The Russian Revolution of 1905, for example, directly inspired mass suffrage demonstrations in Austria and Germany in 1905-1906, the separation of Norway from Sweden in 1905 inspired Magyar nationalists in Hungary, and the Turkish revolution of 1908 provided an example for the Greek military in 1909.

Probably more fundamental than any of the factors discussed thus far in fostering post-1900 unrest was simply the increasingly anachronistic nature of the regimes in those areas of Europe most disturbed during the 1900-1914 period: Russia, the Balkans, Iberia, Germany, and the Habsburg Empire. In all of these regions extremely undemocratic and narrowly based regimes had been able to survive with relatively little difficulty before 1900 to a large extent because mass politicization was extremely retarded. Thus, the traditional aristocracy in Russia, amalgamations of the old nobility and the new rich upper-middle classes in Germany, Iberia, and the Habsburg realm, and professional bureaucratic-political cliques allied with the crown (and in the case of Rumania with the landed nobility) in the Balkans had been able to rule relatively unchallenged, even though governmental benefits went almost exclusively to the ruling groups and governmental burdens fell almost exclusively on the lower classes. Before about 1900, the masses in these regions were, on the whole, too poor, ignorant, disorganized, and repressed to seek to challenge the power structures. While 1900 was not, of course, a magical date that transformed European politics, the emergence of a far stronger, more organized and more militant lower-class challenge to the status quo thereafter suggests the year was an important turning point. Where regimes could or would not adjust to and accommodate the emergence of these new social forces, the result was severe and continuing turmoil. There was also significant social unrest between 1900 and 1914 in some regions of northwestern Europe, such as France, Sweden, the United Kingdom, and the Low Countries, where the regimes demonstrated considerably more flexibility than did those of southern, central, and eastern Europe both before and after 1900 in responding to the demands of emerging contenders for power. But on the whole, the unrest in these areas was considerably less severe than elsewhere. And not coincidentally, within northwestern Europe social tensions were the highest in Belgium, which had been the least responsive to lower class demands and the most repressive in the region, while the least disturbed country was Switzerland, the most democratic and least repressive nation of Europe.

Despite the marked increase in working-class organization and opposition activity that marked the fifteen years after 1900, the general tendency towards reform that marked the 1890s continued to manifest itself. Thus, there were significant suffrage reforms in Austria (1906), Finland (1905), Italy (1912), and Sweden (1907-1909). National elections and constitutional government were finally introduced in Russia in 1905, although continued czarist repression soon reduced these to insignificance. Significant social reforms were enacted during the 1900-1914 period in a number of countries, including Belgium, Greece, Italy, Norway, Sweden, and the United Kingdom, and at least symbolic reforms were enacted in other countries, such as Rumania and Spain. On the other hand, as social tensions continued to increase, signs of a new wave of repression were apparent in a number of countries, particularly Germany, Austria, Hungary, and Russia, on the eve of World War I.

*Regional Differentiation, Repression and Reform, 1870-1914*

While, as the foregoing discussion indicates, some common themes relevant to political repression in Europe can be traced on a Continent-wide basis for the 1870-1914 period, unquestionably the most significant trend of the era with regard to repression was not commonality but differentiation by geographic region. By 1914, all of the countries of northwestern Europe were functioning democracies, while almost all of the countries of southern and eastern Europe were fundamentally authoritarian in their basic political characteristics. The central European countries of Germany, Italy and Austria were characterized by a mixture of democratic and authoritarian elements.

Growing Reformism in Northwestern Europe

Although repression by no means disappeared from the repertoire of governmental behavior in northwestern Europe after 1870, the predominant response in this region to lower-class discontent, especially after about 1880, was measures of conciliation and reform. Thus, all of these nations in the 1870-1914 period adopted reasonably effective factory health, safety, and hours legislation, child and female labor laws and partial or comprehensive systems of old age, disability, accident, and health insurance. By 1870, universal male suffrage already existed for lower legislative chambers in France, Switzerland, and Denmark; significant suffrage reforms were passed in all of the other countries of the region between 1884 and 1909. By 1914, all of the northwestern countries enjoyed reasonably or completely free elections, universal or quasi-universal male suffrage for lower legislative houses (although drastically distorted in Belgium by plural voting) and, except in Sweden, parliamentary responsibility based on the lower chamber. By 1890, all of these nations also had more or less complete freedom of the press, allowed socialist parties and trade unions to function subject only to sporadic harassment, and allowed virtually complete freedom of association and assembly. In sum, by 1914, stable democratic government, or a close facsimile thereof, existed throughout northwestern Europe.

A number of factors coalesced to encourage democratization and reformism rather than repression in response to working-class discontent in northwestern Europe in the post-1870 period. One important factor was that, with the notable exception of France, the northwestern countries were already the most democratic regimes on the Continent by 1870. In that year only the Low Countries had a severely restricted suffrage, and only France severely restricted freedom of the press, association, and assembly, for example (although the Danish, Swedish, and Dutch socialists still suffered considerable harassment until about 1890). The relatively democratic nature of northwestern European politics by 1870 fostered further democratization since lower-class grievances could not be easily hushed up and, especially as suffrages were further broadened and parliamentary responsibility became widespread, the lower classes began to wield growing political power. Relative tolerance of dissent combined with the advanced economic development of the region facilitated the emergence of strong socialist and trade union movements whose agitation for democratic and social reforms caused ruling circles considerable concern about the potential for serious unrest unless concessions were granted. Throughout the region, significant reforms usually followed highly organized and prolonged working-class agitation. On the other hand, partly because of the availability of peaceful channels for dissent, working-class movements in northwestern Europe, except France and Belgium, were notably non-violent and moderate in their tactics after 1850, which decreased the likelihood of a knee-jerk repressive response to their grievances by conservative elites. This moderation also partly reflected the marked improvement in mass living conditions in northwestern Europe after 1870--which incidentally provided workers with additional leisure time and energy to devote to organizing in behalf of their interests.

Wherever working-class movements succeeded in gaining concessions that increased their strength and political power, the gains were soon parlayed into additional victories that further consolidated their position. Thus, social reforms and modifications of discriminatory tax and conscription systems closely followed expansion of the suffrage (and in Denmark, the introduction of parliamentary responsibility) during the 1870-1914 period in the Low Countries, Scandinavia, and the United Kingdom. The relative wealth of the societies of northwestern Europe also facilitated reform by making it possible for ruling elites to make economic concessions that did not seriously threaten their own welfare.

The United Kingdom. Politics was generally calm and modestly reformist in Great Britain during the 40 years after the 1867-8 suffrage expansion, but frequently tumultuous in Ireland. Among the further reforms enacted by parliament in the immediate post-1867 period were a secret ballot law in 1872, the unambiguous legalization of trade unions and peaceful picketing in 1871-5, the opening of almost all governmental offices to civil service competition, slum clearance legislation, and pure food and drug laws. In 1884 the suffrage was further expanded from about 9 to about 16 per cent of the population of the United Kingdom (although the poorest one-third or so of the adult male population was still disenfranchised), and in 1888 elected local government was finally established in rural Great Britain. The pace of reform slowed down notably during the generally calm period of political domination by the Conservative party between 1885 and 1905. However, the political realities of a broad suffrage combined with free elections (especially after passage of the 1883 corrupt practices law) and the sense of noblesse oblige felt by the aristocrats who dominated the Conservatives led them to compete to some extent with the more business-oriented Liberal party for lower- and middle-class support.

There was a brief flurry of excitement in Great Britain 1886-7 when high unemployment led to a series of protest rallies in London. A February 1886 rally ended up in minor rioting, leading to the sedition prosecutions and acquittals of several radicals, including Henry Hyndman, founder of the first British socialist group. A number of other demonstrations followed in 1886-7, including a huge rally of 50,000 people on November 13, 1887 ("Bloody Sunday"), dispersed with considerable violence when police and troops enforced a ban on rallies at Trafalgar Square. Another well-publicized flaw in the British civil liberties record was the repeated barring from parliament of the atheist politician Charles Bradlaugh, who refused to take the prescribed oath. Bradlaugh was finally seated in 1886 after being elected by his Northampton constituents six times.

The turmoil in Ireland in the last quarter of the nineteenth century contrasted sharply with the general calm in Great Britain. Ireland quieted down briefly after the Fenian agitation of the late 1860s, perhaps partly in response to some minor reform legislation passed by parliament in 1869-70, including disestablishment of the Anglican Church in Ireland. However, a series of harvest failures after 1877, combined with downward pressure on agricultural prices resulting from foreign competition, a shortage of credit, and a declining demand for migratory labor caused severe distress and a massive increase in evictions of tenant farmers, which mounted from 463 in 1877 to 3,465 in 1881. As evictions jumped, so did the number of agrarian "outrages," such as cattle maiming, hayrick burning, intimidation, and physical assaults—including 32 murders and attempted murders during the last months of 1881 alone. Altogether "outrages" skyrocketed from 863 in 1879 to 4,439 in 1881, by which time rural Ireland was in a state of virtual insurrection. In some cases mobs of hundreds or even thousands of persons violently resisted eviction attempts. Much of the inspiration for the Irish discontent was provided by the Irish National Land League, formed in October 1879 and presided over by Irish parliamentary leader Charles Parnell.

Although the Land League disavowed the use of violence, its slogan "The land of Ireland for the people of Ireland"--referring to the fact that about half of the island was owned by about 800 mostly Anglo-Protestant landlords--and organizational activities unquestionably encouraged what became known as the "Irish Land War."

The British government responded to the Irish disorders with a combination of repression and concessions. In 1881 a Coercion Act was passed that suspended the right of habeas corpus in Ireland and authorized detention without trial of anyone reasonably suspected of intimidation, violence, or incitement to violence. Under this measure, 955 people were interned, of whom only 40 per cent were accused of violent acts, as opposed to "non-violent intimidation," illegal meetings, threatening letters, seditious speeches and the like. Also in 1881, parliament passed a major agrarian reform measure for Ireland, which in effect established "dual ownership" of land between landlords and tenants, including provisions for the establishment of rent levels by impartial bodies and strict regulations limiting evictions save for non-payment of rent and other narrowly defined situations. The major flaw of the Land Act was that it did not apply to about 130,000 tenants in arrears on their rents.

Parnell was jailed in October 1881 under the Coercion Act for his violent attacks on the inadequacies of the Land Act, and the Land League was outlawed when he issued a manifesto from his jail cell urging a general rent strike. Both Parnell and the British government were alarmed at the subsequent sharp rise in agrarian disorders (3,498 between October 1881 and April 1882). Parnell, who was a social conservative and feared losing control of the land movement to radicals, agreed in April 1882 to the "Kilmainham Treaty" (named for his jail), in which he promised to discourage agitation and support constitutionalism. He in turn was promised by Liberal Prime Minister Gladstone (1880-5) that coercion would be discontinued and rent arrears eliminated so all tenants could qualify under the 1881 Land Act. However, four days after Parnell was released from jail under the Kilmainham Treaty in May 1882, the newly appointed chief secretary for Ireland, Lord Frederick Cavendish, and his chief aide were assassinated in Dublin by members of a secret society unaffiliated with the Land League. Public outrage over the Cavendish murder led Gladstone to introduce a new coercion bill in 1882. The bill led to three years of what amounted to martial law in Ireland, but the liberal leader carried out his Kilmainham pledge in the 1882 Arrears Act, which paid the rent for the 130,000 tenants in arrears. Amidst the strict controls of the Coercion Act, improved economic conditions, and a general reduction of about 20 per cent in rents under the 1881 Land Act, Ireland quieted down for a few years after 1882, with agrarian offenses dropping from 3,433 to 762 between 1882 and 1884.

The lifting of coercion in Ireland in 1885, a new economic decline, and perhaps the defeat of an Irish Home Rule bill by the House of Commons in June 1886 triggered a new upsurge in agrarian disorders, with 1,310 agrarian crimes (including a high percentage of threatening letters) recorded between January 1886 and March 1887. The Land

League, outlawed in 1881 but resurrected by Parnell in late 1882 as the Irish National League, expanded markedly, with over 1,200 branches by January 1886. Shortly after strongly anti-Home Rule Conservatives won the July 1886 parliamentary elections, the National League initiated the "plan of campaign," which called for the refusal to pay more than what tenants considered fair rents. The Conservative government of Lord Salisbury (1886-92) responded to the renewed Irish turmoil with a combination of repression and reform reminiscent of Gladstone's policy at the beginning of the decade. The 1885 Ashbourne Act (passed during a previous brief Salisbury ministry), which provided low interest loans to Irish tenants for the purchase of their farms, was considerably liberalized and re-funded in 1888 and 1891. Measures were also taken to support public works, industry, agriculture, and technical education in Ireland. At the same time, the Plan of Campaign was declared illegal, and a harsh new Crimes Act was passed in 1887. It outlawed boycotting, conspiracies against rent collection, and resistance to eviction, as well as incitement to such behavior. By 1890, the Crimes Act, economic recovery, and government-backed landlord cooperative measures succeeded in defeating the National League and the Plan of Campaign. Altogether, 1,614 persons were convicted under the Crimes Act. Over 30 members of parliament belonging to Parnell's party were prosecuted or jailed for speeches in which they promoted the Plan of Campaign, and in a number of cases public meetings in Ireland deemed to have illegal purposes were banned.

In Great Britain, a series of anti-labor court decisions and rising prices after 1895 led to a resurgence of reform demands and swept a Liberal ministry into power in the January 1906 elections after 20 years of almost continuous Conservative rule. The Liberals immediately embarked upon a general program of social reform in response to the rising tide of working-class discontent. The 1906 Trades Disputes Act once again clearly established the legality of peaceful picketing that had been threatened by court decisions. It also reversed the 1901 Taff Vale decision of the House of Lords (in its capacity as Supreme Court) that had threatened to destroy the entire labor movement by stipulating that unions could be held financially accountable for damages caused by actions of their individual members. In 1909, Liberal Chancellor of the Exchequer David Lloyd George presented to parliament a budget that included various provisions to fund increased military spending and the Liberal program of social legislation that would have slightly dented the fortunes of the very rich. The House of Lords, which had repeatedly blocked or amended reform legislation ever since the Liberals came to power in 1906, rejected the budget, 350 to 75, after it had passed the Commons, 379 to 149, in defiance of 50 years of constitutional practice dictating that the Lords pass revenue bills without change. Prime Minister Henry Asquith (1908-16) obtained a dissolution of the Commons from King Edward VII (1901-10), which led to an election in January 1910. The main issues of the election were the budget and reduction of the power of the Lords. During the campaign, Lloyd George, referring to the qualifications of the Lords, noted, "They need not be sound, either in body or in mind. They only require a certificate of birth, just to prove they are the first of the litter. You would not choose a spaniel on these principles" (Arnstein 1971: 188). Although the Liberals lost strength in the elections, a clear endorsement was obtained for their position.

The Lords passed the budget in 1910, but a parliament bill for a drastic reduction of their power was rejected by them after it passed the Commons. This led to another dissolution and a secret promise by the new king, George V (1910-36), to create enough new Lords to pass the bill if the Liberal position was again endorsed by the voters, as it was in the December 1910 elections. On August 10, 1911 the House of Lords, under the threat of the creation of up to 400 new peers, passed the parliament bill, 131-114. The bill provided that the Lords could henceforth delay revenue bills by only a month, even if they refused to pass them, and that all other legislation would take effect if passed three times within a two-year period by the Commons, regardless of the Lords' action.

Meanwhile, trade union membership in the United Kingdom jumped from 1.7 to 2.7 million between 1910 and 1914, and the strike rate in 1911-15 doubled that of 1906-10, while the number of strikers and man-days lost to strikes tripled. Clashes between strikers and government forces were common during these disputes. Five workers were killed altogether during the 1910 Welsh miners' strike, the 1911 Liverpool dock strike and the 1913 Dublin transport strike, a total higher than the sum of all workers killed in labor strife in the United Kingdom since the "plug plug" riots of 1842. Several prominent labor leaders, including the syndicalist Tom Mann and the Irish labor agitator James Larkin were jailed for sedition (although Larkin was quickly freed from his seven-month term due to an enormous public outcry). Also during the 1910-14 period, extremist suffragettes resorted to such tactics as disrupting meetings, destroying mail, bombings, arson, slashing paintings in public galleries, and cutting telephone wires to press their demands for enfranchising women.

A resurgence of the Irish crisis after 1910 proved even more threatening to the peace of the United Kingdom than did the labor and suffragette violence of the 1910-14 period. After the collapse of the Land League and the Plan of Campaign agitation of the 1879-90 period, Irish discontent had become greatly muted for about 20 years. Laws passed in 1903 and 1909 under both Conservative and Liberal governments expanded funding and liberalized the terms for peasant farm purchases, with the result that by 1922 about 200,000 peasants had been enabled to buy about half the land of Ireland and the agrarian problem had been virtually resolved. However, Irish nationalism grew markedly after 1910 and demands for Home Rule increased. In 1912, the Asquith government, which was partly dependent upon Irish party support for its majority, introduced a moderate Irish Home Rule bill, which under the 1911 parliament bill was bound to come into effect in 1914 despite the overwhelming opposition in the House of Lords. The prospect of the bill's passage aroused hysterical opposition among Irish

Protestants and a considerable sector of the Conservative party. By mid-1914, Ireland was on the verge of civil war and elements within the British army were on the verge of mutiny at the prospect of enforcing Home Rule in Ireland. Only the outbreak of World War I in August postponed the ultimate violent resolution of the Irish situation.

The Low Countries. The dominant political issue in the Low Countries after 1885 was suffrage reform. Between 1870 and 1885 politics was quiet in both Belgium and the Netherlands. Trade union activities petered out amidst economic difficulties, and the disenfranchisement of 97 per cent of the population in both countries made it easy for political elites to ignore social issues and continue to confine their squabbling primarily to the question of state subsidies for religious education. The Commune seems to have had little effect on Dutch politics, but in Belgium the traditional policy of accepting political refugees was significantly modified. Some of the leading Communards were banned entirely from Belgium, and others were forbidden to engage in political activity while in the country. When the French author Victor Hugo, himself a refugee since the 1851 Napoleonic coup in France, protested the Belgian policy, he was expelled from the country in May 1871. Intense surveillance of labor and political meetings was maintained in Belgium throughout the 1870s.

Although working class agitation for suffrage reform began in both Belgium and the Netherlands in the early 1880s, it was not until serious riots rocked the two countries in 1886 that the ruling elites woke up to the fact that the lower classes had serious complaints. In Belgium, violent riots, involving tens of thousands of workers, erupted in the second half of March 1886 throughout much of the country, especially in the Liège and Borinage industrial districts. Widespread looting and destruction of factories and the houses of the rich marked the disorders. The riots originally had little political content. However, as they continued, an extraordinary 260,000 copies of a pamphlet that called for universal suffrage, The Catechism of the People by Alfred Defuisseaux, were sold, and the disorders were generally interpreted as an elemental working-class demand for social and political reform. In Amsterdam, extremely serious riots, known as the Eel Revolt (Palingoproer), broke out in July 1886, when police tried to prevent the illegal practice of palingtrekken, a brutal lower-class sport in which live eels were pulled apart. As in Belgium, the riots originally had no political import, but as they developed they showed "the extent of popular hatred for a police force that for years had been brutally chasing socialists and putting down demonstrations" (Kossmann 1978: 316). The 1886 riots were put down with great severity. In Belgium, martial law was declared, about a dozen were killed and another dozen were seriously wounded by troops. About 25 were killed and 100 wounded by troops and police in Amsterdam. Only a few of the several hundred arrested in Amsterdam were eventually sentenced (and they were shortly pardoned), but in Belgium scores of those arrested, including Defuisseaux, were given jail terms ranging up to 20 years of solitary confinement, or even life imprisonment.

The disturbances of 1886 sent a real shock wave through Dutch and Belgian society and brought the social and suffrage questions to the fore for the first time. Parliamentary committees were established in both countries in 1886 to report on the conditions of the poor, and in each case they issued devastating reports about the previously ignored squalor of the lower classes. Minor ameliorative legislation was passed in the next few years, such as the new restrictions on child and female labor that passed in both countries in 1889. In the Netherlands, the 1886 riots also led directly to expansion of the suffrage from about 3 to about 6 per cent of the population in 1887. Nevertheless, both governments remained highly conservative in orientation. In January 1887 the Dutch socialist leader Domela Niewenhuis was sent to jail for a year for criticizing the king in his newspaper. While he was in jail (before being pardoned in August 1887 as the result of widespread public protests), on February 19, 1887, king William III's seventieth birthday, the "Orange Fury" (Oranjefurie) erupted, with mobs manhandling well-known socialists and wrecking their offices and homes "while the police stood by or even lent a helping hand" (De Jong 1971: 70). In Belgium, the authorities remained adamant until 1893 over suffrage reform, even as the letters SU for suffrage universel "obtained an almost magic function and represented for the illiterate Belgian workers what the ichthys sign had been for the early Christians and the cross for the crusaders" (Kossmann 1978: 318). Huge strikes and demonstrations, attracting scores of thousands demanding suffrage reform, rocked Belgium every year between 1886 and 1892. In May 1892, a general strike involving hundreds of thousands of Belgian workers was called off after 10 days when parliament promised to call a constituent assembly to revise the suffrage. Yet another general strike for suffrage reform erupted in April 1893 to protest the constituent assembly's rejection of universal and equal male suffrage. At least 200,000 workers struck, and the rioting that ensued was severely repressed by troops who killed 20 demonstrators, arresting and wounding many others. On April 18, 1893, at the height of the strike, the constituent assembly adopted a scheme for universal male suffrage that gave extra votes to the wealthy and well educated, thus allowing about 30 per cent of the electorate to cast a majority of the votes.

Although Dutch suffrage agitation was far more sedate than that in Belgium, in 1896 the Dutch parliament again expanded the suffrage, this time from about 6 to about 11 per cent of the population. In both countries, the suffrage reforms of the 1890s were followed by modest social reforms, although in general Dutch governments yielded to lower-class demands earlier and with considerably more grace. The Dutch liberal ministry of Nicolaas Pierson (1897-1901) became known as the "Cabinet of Social Justice" for its reform measures, which included provisions for accident insurance, slum clearance, tax reform, and compulsory elementary education as well as an end to the practice of allowing the wealthy to buy substitutes for the draft. Compulsory elementary eduction and an end to purchases of draft exemption were effected in Belgium only ten years later.

By 1902, the Belgian plural voting scheme was arousing renewed demands for universal and equal male suffrage. In April 1902, an estimated 300,000 Belgian workers struck and demonstrated, with considerable violence, on behalf of suffrage reform. About 60,000 troops were mobilized and many workers were killed or wounded. However, the Belgian parliament remained adamant and rejected reform. The victory of the conservative Catholic party in the 1912 elections led to another outburst of rioting and the killing of several more demonstrators. Thousands of meetings to demand suffrage reform were held throughout Belgium when parliament met in November 1912. Rank-and-file pressure virtually forced the socialist leadership to schedule a general strike for April 1913 after a suffrage reform bill was defeated again in the legislature in Feburary 1913. About 400,000 workers struck on April 13, including 120,000 of 132,000 miners and almost the entire work force in the key industrial provinces of Hainaut and Liège. The strike was completely peaceful. It was called off after ten days when the parliament made a vague gesture in the direction of reform, although universal and equal male suffrage was effected in Belgium only in 1919.

In the Netherlands, militant elements in the labor movement organized in the syndicalist-oriented National Labor Secretariat (NAS in Dutch) suffered a crushing defeat in 1903. When the conservative government of Abraham Kuyper (1901-1905) introduced a bill to ban strikes in public services, including railroads, shortly after a railroad strike forced employers to recognize unions in January 1903, the NAS called a general strike in protest. Although 60,000 workers responded to the strike call on April 6, the movement collapsed by April 9 because of poor organization, the failure of moderate unions to support it, and the government's intimidation: 5,000 soldiers were placed in Amsterdam, all railroad stations were occupied by troops, and final passage of the strike bill was scheduled for April 11, with harsh penalties to take effect immediately. Tens of thousands of railroad workers were fired or penalized by their employers after the strike disintegrated, and the NAS virtually collapsed. It was replaced by the far more moderate Netherlands Federation of Trade Unions as the dominant labor movement.

Agitation for further suffrage reform grew in the Netherlands in the immediate pre-World War I period. In 1910, 1911, and 1912, suffrage demonstrations attracted thousands of people on the day the Dutch parliament convened (known as "Red Tuesday"), and over 300,000 Dutch citizens signed petitions in 1910-11 for suffrage reform. Universal and equal male suffrage was finally adopted in the Netherlands in 1917.

Switzerland. Switzerland was both the most democratic and the most tranquil country in Europe during the 1870-1914 period. In 1874, the referendum, which had been adopted in a number of cantons in the 1860s to give the entire electorate the right to vote on proposed cantonal legislation, was extended to the national level in an important constitutional revision (which itself was approved by popular vote, as was required for all constitutional amendments under the 1848 document). Among the first federal laws approved by national legislative referendum were a comprehensive factory regulation bill in 1877, which decreed eleven hours as the maximum working day in Switzerland and barred children from factory work, and an 1879 measure that abolished capital punishment. In 1891, a constitutional amendment allowed 50,000 citizens to force the national government to submit proposed constitutional amendments to a popular vote (a device known as the initiative) even if the regime opposed them. Both the referendum and initiative were unique in Europe and gave the Swiss electorate far more opportunity to enforce their views than the usual casting of ballots only on election day. In many of the cantons, the legislative referendum was extended during the post-1870 period to cover all bills passed by cantonal assemblies rather than only those that generated a specified level of organized popular opposition. The general spirit of Swiss democracy was also reflected in the widespread adoption of proportional representation after 1890, which guaranteed minority parties the right to obtain legislative seats.

Throughout the 1870-1914 period, the Swiss press and elections were among the freest in Europe; the small but growing trade unions and socialist party were almost completely unhindered in their functioning; and political calm was the norm. However, there were a few scattered and relatively insignificant cases of repression and bloodshed. For example, a number of Swiss cantons banned display of the red flag in the aftermath of the 1871 Paris Commune. In 1877, authorities in Berne canton tried to block a march commemorating the Commune under the banner of the red flag, leading to serious fighting, jail terms for 30 demonstrators, and the expulsion from Berne of a number of protesters. In 1886 and again in 1912, attempts by authorities in Zurich to restrict labor picketing led to strife. In the first instance one man was killed during a clash with police--a truly exceptional occurrence in Swiss history after 1848--and in the latter, troops were called out in response to a peaceful general strike of 20,000 workers.

The refugee problem caused Switzerland more difficulties during the 1870-90 period. Foreign pressure, especially from France and Germany, was influential in leading to the closure of a couple of anarchist newspapers edited by refugees, and in a number of cases anarchist and socialist exiles were expelled from Switzerland when it appeared their continued presence would cause conflict with foreign governments. Thus, in 1888 German pressure led to the expulsion of the editors of the German socialist newspaper Sozialdemokrat, which had been published in Switzerland and smuggled across the border. Serious conflict with Germany was barely averted in 1889 when Swiss officials arrested and expelled a Prussian police official named Wohlgemuth who was attempting to hire Swiss informants.

Scandinavia. In Denmark and Sweden, the dominant political issues after 1870 were suffrage reform and parliamentary responsibility, while in Norway the primary development was a growing nationalist movement that led to complete independence from Sweden in 1905. Fears aroused by the Commune seem to have played a significant role in keeping Danish politicians on a highly conservative and often authoritarian course between 1870 and 1900. The Danish section of the International, which had about 4,000 members in 1871, ran into severe repression after it sponsored a mass meeting in Copenhagen in May 1872 in support of a bricklayers' strike and mild social reforms. The meeting was barred by the authorities and forcibly broken up by mounted soldiers in the "Battle on the Common." Three leaders of the Danish International, including its chairman, Louis Pio, were arrested and given three- and five-year jail terms. In 1873, the Danish Supreme Court outlawed the International, and an attempt to set up a new organization along the same lines that year led to another arrest and jail sentence. In 1875, the original three jailed leaders were pardoned and resumed their activities with the working-class movement. In 1877, one of them, Harold Brix, was sent to jail for six years for his journalistic efforts, and the other two, Pio and Poul Geleff, were apparently threatened by the police and then bribed into leaving the country. This turn of events was viewed as a betrayal by many workers, and together with poor economic conditions dealt a severe blow to the Danish labor movement, which thereafter took on a considerably more moderate tone.

Meanwhile, in the 1872 elections, the United Left (Venstre) party, a coalition of large and small farmers, won control of the lower house (Folketing) on a platform that called for social and tax reform, a return to the democratic constitution of 1849 with its provisions for quasi-universal male suffrage for both legislative chambers, and the introduction of parliamentary responsibility to the more popularly based Folketing. "Nothing above and nothing beside the Folketing" became a popular Venstre slogan (Oakley, 1972: 198). The Folketing soon became embroiled in conflict with the Conservative (Höjre) party, a coalition based on the old National Liberals and the great landowners that dominated the upper house (Landsting), over Höjre demands for refortification of Copenhagen, a project the Venstre regarded as a waste of money. Although two Höjre ministries were forced out, King Christian IX continued to appoint Höjre cabinets that lacked Folketing support. In 1875 the king turned to J.B.S. Estrup (prime minister 1875-94), a reactionary landowner who had been one of the chief drafters of the conservative 1866 constitution. Continued conflict over the Copenhagen fortification issue led Estrup to dissolve the Folketing repeatedly. Growing electoral victories for the Venstre followed, but support for Estrup from the king continued.

The Höjre won only 19 of 102 Folketing seats in the 1884 elections, but the king continued to support Estrup, and a complete deadlock ensued. From 1885 until 1894 Estrup essentially ruled by decree. Estrup subjected the socialist press and the embryonic trade unions to considerable harassment, further antagonizing the opposition. By 1885 there was open talk of revolution in some liberal-radical Danish circles, culminating in calls for the formation of rifle clubs and an unsuccessful attempt on Estrup's life in that year. Estrup thereupon issued new decree laws that imposed harsh fines and jail terms for oral or written incitement against the government and forbade the purchase and carrying of weapons. They also authorized the barring or dismissal of dissident teachers and established a special force of mounted gendarmes (the hated "Light Blues") to intimidate the opposition. Public meetings were kept under tight surveillance and the leader of the Venstre, Christian Berg, was sentenced to six months in jail when he had a policeman removed from the platform from which he was giving an address.

Estrup managed to retain quasi-dictatorial power until 1894 by agreeing in 1891 to support social welfare legislation backed by a segment of the Venstre. However, in 1894 he was forced to resign when moderate elements in both the Venstre and Höjre parties reached a compromise on Copenhagen's fortification and agreed to repeal the existing decree laws and end rule by decree. Nonetheless, King Christian IX continued to rely upon Höjre ministries, which were based on the less popularly elected upper house, and he refused to accept the principle of parliamentary responsibility to the more popularly elected and Venstre-dominated Folketing.

In 1901, Christian finally accepted the principle of parliamentary responsibility based on the Folketing and called the Venstre party to power after the Höjre was reduced to 8 out of 114 Folketing seats in the elections of that year. The suffrage for the Landsting became a major issue after 1907 because of the upper chamber's repeated delay or blockage of reform legislation. After the Landsting blocked a measure to reform itself, the three major Danish moderate and left-wing parties agreed in March 1914 on a plan of constitutional reform establishing universal adult suffrage for both legislative chambers. The constitutional reform was passed by the lower house in June 1914 by 102 votes to two, but a conservative boycott in the Landsting made it impossible to bring the reform to a vote there. The Landsting was thereupon dissolved and in the resulting election the Höjre finally lost control of that body. The outbreak of World War I delayed final approval of the new constitution until June 1915.

In Sweden, where the 1866 suffrage reform excluded 95 per cent of the populace from obtaining any significant political influence, conservative interests reigned, and there was little general public interest in government until a dispute over tariffs in the late 1880s aroused great controversy. The highly conservative orientation of the government was clearly demonstrated by the vigorous repression of the first important strike in Sweden's history, that of about 7,000 lumber workers who peacefully left their jobs in the Sundsvall lumber industry in 1879 to protest a large wage reduction. When the strikers ignored orders to return to work, King Oscar II responded to the governor's appeal for help with a telegram that became famous: "Calm all the right-minded and warn all disturbers, for patience must have a limit. Cannon boats and soldiers are on the way" (Scott 1977: 413). The troops broke the strike by forcibly escorting many workers back to the sawmills, evicting about 1,000 from their company-owned homes and jailing over 40 strikers on vagrancy and other charges.

In the 1880s, many Swedish socialists were fined and jailed for such offenses as lèse-majesté, blasphemy and libel, and the police frequently obstructed socialist meetings and demonstrations, which stressed above all the need for suffrage reform. One reason for the regime's nervousness was the radical tone of much early Socialist party rhetoric, which had far more bark than bite. Thus, in 1886 the socialist leader and future prime minister Hjalmar Branting (who was fined in 1887 and 1895 and jailed for three months in 1889 for his writings) declared, "Universal suffrage is the price with which the bourgeoisie can buy a settlement through administration in place of liquidation ordered by the court of the revolution" (Scott 1977: 405). A significant turning point came in 1889, when the government failed to gain legislative approval to outlaw agitation for measures "that imply a threat to the societal order or a danger to its existence" (Tingsten 1973: 51). After 1889, both the persecution of the socialists and the tone of the party's rhetoric were greatly moderated. However, growing demands by the socialists and others got nowhere until 1907. In 1893 and 1896 "People's Parliaments" were convened in Stockholm to agitate for suffrage reform. About 150,000 Swedes voted for delegates to the 1893 session, a figure 15 per cent higher than the highest voter turnout for any election to the Swedish lower legislative house. In 1899, a petition with 364,000 signatures calling for suffrage reform was presented to the king, but the ultra-conservative Swedish upper house continued to block any concessions, as it had since the early 1880s.

In May 1902, 120,000 Swedes struck peacefully for three days to demand suffrage reform, but reform bills backed by both Liberal and Conservative governments were defeated in 1902, 1904, 1905, and 1906, because of disagreement between the two legislative chambers. A conservative ministry under Arvid Lindman (1906-11) finally obtained passage of a suffrage reform bill in 1907-1909. Quasi-universal male suffrage was established for the lower house, doubling the electorate to almost 20 per cent of the population. The electorate for local elections, and thus indirectly the upper house, was left at about 15 per cent, but eligibility requirements to sit in that chamber were greatly reduced and the maximum number of plural votes any elector could cast was reduced from 5,000 in rural and 100 in urban areas to 40 in either instance.

Swedish politics remained unsettled because of demands for further suffrage reform, the disparate makeup of the two legislative chambers, and the failure of kings Oscar II and Gustav V (1907-50) to accept the principle of parliamentary responsibility based on the lower chamber. In 1914, Gustav forced Liberal Prime Minister Karl Staaf (1911-14) to resign by publicly supporting a program of increased defense expenditures that Staaf had rejected and refusing to promise not to make future political statements before informing his government. In 1917, Gustav finally accepted the principle of parliamentary responsibility to the lower house, and in 1918-21 universal and equal adult suffrage for both houses was finally enacted.

The dominant theme in Norwegian politics between 1870 and 1905 was the growth of nationalistic (i.e., anti-Swedish) feeling, which along with the relatively egalitarian nature of Norwegian society rallied the country together and greatly moderated class conflict. After 1869 the storting was almost completely controlled by a coalition of farmers and urban radicals and liberals united in the Left (Venstre) party by a desire to increase the storting's power and decrease Norwegian subordination to Sweden. After a struggle lasting several years, the storting forced Swedish King Oscar II to accept the principle of parliamentary responsibility by impeaching, convicting and removing from office eight members of the royally appointed Norwegian ministry in 1884. In July 1884, after much delay and apparently some consideration of a <u>coup,</u> Oscar bowed to the inevitable and asked Johan Sverdrup, leader of the Venstre party, to form a ministry. This landmark development in Norway finally broke the power of the entrenched bureaucratic class.

Norwegian-Swedish relations gradually drifted into another crisis after 1890 over Norwegian demands for an independent consular service to represent Norwegian foreign policy interests, especially those of the merchant marine, which was the third largest in the world in 1900 and far larger than Sweden's. Norway backed down in 1895 on this issue after the Swedish legislature threatened military measures. However, subsequently a Radical Left ministry under Johannes Steen (1897-1902) came to power in Norway and set about bolstering Norwegian unity and defenses by passing a bill for universal manhood suffrage and strengthening fortifications along the Swedish border. After long negotiations failed to resolve the consular issue, the storting unanimously declared Norwegian independence in mid-1905. Following a brief war scare and negotiations in which Norway agreed to demolish some of her frontier fortifications, Oscar renounced the Norwegian throne on October 26, 1905. Under strong British pressure, the Norwegians agreed to retain a monarchy as a sign of their respectability in a European world that still regarded republics as tainted with subversion.

In all three of the Scandinavian countries, significant democratic breakthroughs during the 1870-1914 period were followed almost immediately by the passing of important political and social reforms. Thus, in Denmark, the 1901 inauguration of parliamentary responsibility based on the lower chamber, known as the <u>systemskiftet</u> ("change of system") was greeted with joyful celebrations throughout the country and inaugurated a new era of democracy. A flurry of reforms followed the <u>systemskiftet,</u> including democratization of the local suffrage, introduction of an income tax and other tax reforms, modernization of the school system and introduction of state-subsidized unemployment insurance. In Sweden, the 1907-1909 suffrage law was also quickly followed by other reforms, including the first income tax, old age pensions and measures improving the safety of working conditions, modernizing the penal code, limiting working hours, and barring night work by women. In Norway the introduction of parliamentary responsibility in 1884 and a modest suffrage expansion in 1885 were followed within the next few years by numerous reforms, including bills for educational expansion, factory inspection, workmen's compensation, trial by jury and a progressive income tax. The adoption of universal male suffrage in 1898 and Norwegian independence in 1905 triggered another flurry of reforms, especially during the Liberal ministries of Gunnar Knudson (1908-10, 1913-20). They included universal adult suffrage (i.e., including women) for local elections in 1910 and for storting elections in 1913, and a variety of social welfare bills, including sickness insurance, factory inspection, and child labor laws.

France. French politics in the 1870s was occupied with repressing the remnants of the Commune and with struggles over what form of government to establish with the demise of Napoleon III. Until about 1880, civil liberties were either nonexistent or extremely tenuous in France. Forty departments remained under a state of siege until 1873, and Paris and other major radical centers were under military rule until 1876. Strict controls were imposed on the press and public assembly. Arrests and trials for offenses connected with the Commune--including subsequent verbal and printed support ·for it--continued for about five years; as late as December 1876, 400 new prisoners were dispatched to New Caledonia. Passage of the Dufaure Law of 1872 outlawed the International in France and generated another spate of arrests and trials that completed the decimation of socialist organizations. The entire complexion of Paris was changed by the repression of the Commune, as the city lost an estimated 50,000 workers and suffered a severe labor shortage for several years. Some key industries were almost destroyed, for example the shoe-making trade, which lost about half of its workers. The destruction of workers' organizations and the general atmosphere of fear was so intense that fewer French workers struck between 1871 and 1877 than in 1869-70 alone. Even an extremely moderate workers' group, the Circle of the Workers Syndical Union, which opposed strikes and stressed the development of worker-owned cooperatives, was disbanded by the government in 1872, partly because members had "smiled when they voted the article which forbade political and religious discussions" and partly because the group "might be dangerous in the future" (Bernstein 1965: 62). A socialist-oriented international student congress planned for Paris in 1876 was banned, as was an international labor congress scheduled there for September 1878. When attempts were made to convene the latter, the government arrested over 30 members of the organizing committee, including Jules Guesde, the leader of the embryonic French socialist movement, whose newspaper had been forced to close a few months earlier after a long period of harassment. Total French union membership by as late as 1880 is estimated at about 25,000, compared with about 70,000 in Paris alone in 1870.

On the political front, although monarchists held a clear majority in the National Assembly elected in 1871, they were bitterly divided between proponents of the Bourbon and Orléans dynasties. The monarchist factions became deadlocked when the Bourbonists refused to accept the Orléans pretender and the Bourbon pretender insisted on the impossible condition that the revolutionary tricolor flag be abandoned in favor of the white Bourbon standard. When the deadlock between the monarchist factions continued, the assembly finally established what became known as the Third Republic on January 30, 1875, by a vote of 353 to 352. Subsequently a two-house legislature was established, with the lower house elected by universal male suffrage and the upper house chosen by electoral colleges of officials and parliamentary deputies in a manner vastly overrepresenting rural France. Both houses voting together were empowered to elect a president who would serve for seven years, with the authority to appoint ministers and dissolve the lower house (chamber of deputies) with the consent of the upper (senate).

The 1876 elections for a new legislature produced an enormous republican majority in the chamber, but a slight monarchist senate majority. In May 1877, the reactionary French president, Marshal MacMahon (who had been chosen to replace Theirs in 1873 when monarchist forces in the assembly began to view Theirs as "soft" on republicanism), appointed a monarchist ministry that soon clashed with the chamber. With the senate's support, MacMahon dissolved the chamber and scheduled new elections for October 1877, which were held under conditions of administrative pressure and repression that were shocking even for France. Almost every prefect in the country was replaced; over 1,700 municipal councils were dissolved; and about 2,500 press prosecutions were brought within a period of six months. Nonetheless, a clear republican majority was returned and MacMahon was forced to appoint a republican ministry in December 1877, thus establishing the principle of parliamentary responsibility to the chamber and drastically curtailing the power of the French president. The power of dissolution was never used again during the remaining 63 years of the French Third Republic. Senatorial elections produced in January 1879 produced a republican majority in that body also. Shortly thereafter, MacMahon resigned as president and was replaced by the republican Jules Grévy.

The clear triumph of the republican cause by early 1879 led to a 20-year period of domination by the moderate wing of the republican movement, known as the "Opportunists," so called because "they claimed only to introduce reforms when they were opportune--which was seldom" (Brogan 1963: 178). Leon Gambetta, the leading Opportunist, once declared, "There is no social question" (McManners 1969: 320). Although the Opportunists favored an expansion of civil liberties, their major principles were negative--they were against the monarchy, the Catholic church, and lower-class radicalism. The major republican rival faction, the Radicals, were theoretically more inclined to at least verbal support of social reform, but in practice were distinguished from the Opportunists mostly by being more anti-monarchist, more anti-clerical, and, especially in the 1880s, more anti-German--i.e., determined to reclaim Alsace-Lorraine. Both republican groups paid little heed to the urban working class, with the result that the Socialist party began a period of slow but steady growth once severe repression eased after 1879.

Although social legislation made no progress in France in the 1880s, civil liberties and democratic procedures were expanded. Despite continuing repression of working-class movements in the late 1870s, a major campaign for amnesty for the Communards had been organized then, and "more than any other single fact created a class consciousness among the French working class and prepared the ground for the formation of an independent [socialist] party" (Stafford 1971: 153). In an attempt to appease the amnesty movement and hold off socialist gains, a partial amnesty was granted by the legislature in March 1879, which left 1,200 Communards still serving sentences or in exile, including over 500 still at New Caledonia. The partial amnesty only fueled a movement for a complete amnesty; returning Communards and the funerals of Communards who died attracted huge crowds, such as a burial service on September 28, 1879 attended by 20,000. In July 1880, a virtually complete Communard amnesty bill was finally passed, after the government had become convinced that continuing agitation was more threatening than the release of the remaining Communards would be. The committee report supporting passage of the bill suggested the amnesty would remove a "last cause for unrest" and contribute to "making concord reign among all those who are determined to support the government which France has freely chosen" (Joughin 1955: 447), which, translated, meant that given the hostility to the republic from the monarchist-clerical right the government was convinced that some symbolic concession was needed to shore up support on the left. Other democratic measures implemented during the 1880s included passage of a liberal press bill in 1881, legalization of trade unions in 1884, expansion of local self-government, and a modification of the composition of the senate.

The major energies of the Opportunists between 1880 and 1885 were devoted to weakening the power of the Catholic church, a program that not only had the virtue of weakening a strong anti-republican element, but also united republican factions and diverted the attention of the urban working class away from demands that might threaten property. Meanwhile, the fears inspired by the Commune were revived by a series of apparently anarchist-inspired bombings and assassination attempts between 1881 and 1884 in which two people were killed. In January 1883, 54 prominent anarchists, including all the leading militants of eastern France and the Russian exile anarchist theoretician Prince Peter Kropotkin (who had been expelled from Switzerland in 1881 under Russian diplomatic pressure following the assassination of Czar Alexander II), were tried at Lyon under the 1872 law barring membership in the International. Although no evidence was introduced linking any of the prisoners to acts of violence and even the prosecutor admitted the International no longer existed, the prisoners were found guilty. Kropotkin and six other prominent anarchists were given four- and five-year jail terms. The

Kropotkin affair caused great indignation among many European intellectuals. Respected journals published articles that he composed in jail, the French Academy of Sciences offered to send him any needed books, and scores of prominent Englishmen urged his release. Meanwhile, in March 1883, after police broke up a meeting of unemployed Parisians, about 500 of the demonstrators marched through the streets and distributed bread that had been pillaged from a few bakers' shops. Louise Michel, an immensely popular anarchist who had served time in New Caledonia for her Commune activities, was sentenced to six years in solitary confinement for her role in this trivial incident, and other prominent anarchists were given eight-year terms. By mid-1885, demands for the release of Kropotkin and the "red virgin" (Michel), and general social tensions amidst economic conditions that left 200,000 Parisians unemployed, reached major proportions in France. Despite strong Russian diplomatic pressure to keep Kropotkin in jail, he, Michel, and the other jailed anarchists were all freed by presidential pardons by January 1886.

Between 1886 and 1889 French politics was dominated by the Boulanger affair, in which a disparate coalition of nationalists, monarchists, and the poor rallied around the figure of General Georges Boulanger, a handsome army officer who captured the public imagination, in hopes that he would overthrow the regime and establish a sort of "Bonapartism, but without a Bonaparte" (Buy 1954: 180). Although in early 1889 a Boulangist coup appeared inevitable, the entire movement quickly collapsed when the general lost his nerve and fled to Belgium. After the diversion provided by anti-clericalism and Boulangism in the 1880s, French public attention was distracted again from the social issue in the early 1890s by another anarchist scare and by the notorious Panama Canal financial scandal, in which it was revealed that numerous politicians and journalists had been paid off to cover up the mismanagement that led to the collapse of the Panama Canal Company. The anarchist scare resulted from the explosions of about ten bombs in Paris between March 1892 and August 1894, which killed ten people, including five police and an anarchist who had planted three of the bombs. The climax of the French terrorist wave of 1892-4 was the June 24, 1894 assassination of French President Sadi Carnot by the Italian anarchist Santo Caserio. Caserio apparently acted to avenge the execution of Auguste Vaillant, who had thrown a bomb into the French chamber of deputies six months earlier. Caserio was in turn himself executed on August 15, 1894.

The 1892-94 terrorist attentats ("attacks") cast a deep shadow of fear over conservative French society. On December 11, 1893, two days after Vaillant's bomb, the French legislature (in what the left termed les lois scélérates, or the "scoundrel laws") made it illegal to print material that directly or indirectly incited terrorism, to apologize for such deeds, or to associate with intent to commit such acts. Massive police raids and arrests followed, anarchist clubs and discussion groups were suppressed, and two leading anarchist newspapers were closed down. After the Carnot assassination, additional anti-anarchist measures were taken, including the barring of propagation of anarchist ideas (left undefined) by "any means whatever" (Woodcock 1962: 314), including private letters and conversations. Many well-known non-violent anarchists, including the leading geographer Elisée Reclus and the artist Camille Pissarro, fled France to avoid prosecution. On August 6, 1894, the government began a mass trial of 30 leading anarchists that was designed to show the link between intellectuals, such as Jean Grave, editor of the suppressed anarchist newspaper La Révolte, and anarchist terrorists. The Procès des trente (Trial of the thirty) was a fiasco for the prosecution, which could show no ties between most of the accused and any illegal activities. Three petty burglars who had been thrown in to confuse the issue were convicted by a jury, but the other defendants were all acquitted. This prosecution marked the end of the great anarchist scare, although an even more crucial factor was that the anarchist movement in France had been scattered and the attentats came to an end. In January 1895, President Félix Faure issued a general political amnesty. Altogether jail terms of 322 years had been handed out, mostly for verbal and printed crimes, during the height of the scare.

Further distraction from the social issue was provided by the Dreyfus case, which dominated French politics in the late 1890s. The details of the case are impossibly complicated, but in short it involved the false conviction in 1894 and subsequent life-time deportation and detention on a prison island of Alfred Dreyfus, a member of the Army General Staff, on charges of espionage. The 1894 prosecution seems to have been carried out in good faith, although the fact that Dreyfus was Jewish focussed suspicion on him, and there were serious procedural irregularities involved in his court martial. The "Dreyfus Affair" did not really begin until late 1896, when an army intelligence officer uncovered conclusive evidence that Dreyfus was not guilty, supporting the long-standing claims of Dreyfus's family. This evidence gradually became known, but top army and governmental officials refused to re-open the case, arguing that Dreyfus was indeed guilty and that the entire affair was an attack upon the honor of France, and particularly that of the army, which was hypersensitive to such concerns after the fiasco of 1870. While growing segments of French liberal opinion began to view the entire affair as a gross miscarriage of justice, monarchists, reactionary Catholics, anti-semites and fanatic patriots saw the case as evidence of an international Jewish conspiracy to disrupt French society. In late 1898, the government was forced to re-open the case when it became known that a key piece of evidence had been forged by an overzealous army intelligence officer who subsequently committed suicide. By the time of Dreyfus's new court martial in mid-1899, the affair was attracting widespread attention throughout Europe, including a demonstration of 50,000 people on behalf of Dreyfus in London. After the August 1899 court martial reached the ludicrous conclusion that Dreyfus was guilty of espionage but with "extenuating circumstances," President Emile Loubet put an end to the farce by pardoning him. In 1906 a French court official quashed the 1899 court martial verdict.

The Dreyfus affair revealed that a substantial segment of the population was still bitterly authoritarian and anti-republican in spirit, but ultimately strengthened the regime and discredited such forces. Between 1900 and 1914 the republic was never again seriously menaced as a regime, but the now-dominant Radical party still failed to produce any real positive program, to concern itself with the plight of the lower classes, or in general to conduct itself significantly differently from the Opportunist party. Although some minor social legislation was passed, including a 10-hour work day (1900) and a six-day work week (1906), French social legislation and working conditions lagged far behind the other industrialized nations of northwestern Europe. Between 1900 and 1905 the Radicals concentrated on revenging themselves on the Catholic church for the clerical position in the Dreyfus Affair. During the fanatically anti-clerical ministry of Emile Combes (1902-1905), scores of unauthorized teaching congregations were dissolved, leading thousands of their members to flee the country, and at least 12,000 schools conducted by such groups were closed.

Between 1906 and 1910, French public attention was dominated by a series of militant and occasionally violent strikes organized by the General Confederation of Labor (CGT in French), which had been formed in 1902 in an attempt to unite all French labor organizations. The first major CGT action, a nationwide general strike on May 1, 1906 to demand an eight-hour day, was partly triggered by the March 1906 mine disaster at Courrières, which killed over 1,100. As the strike date approached, troops were brought into Paris, the city was placed under a state of seige and many middle-class Parisians fled the city in a state of panic. Others hoarded enough food to withstand a long siege and "then had to serve the accumulated macaroni and ham for weeks to protesting families" (Wohl 1966: 26). On the eve of the strike, the government announced the discovery of a supposed plot by syndicalists, anarchists, monarchists and right-wing Catholics to overthrow the government. Although everyone knew this "plot" did not exist, it provided an excuse for the government to arrest the CGT leadership (along with some monarchists) and to launch widespread raids in the Paris area. Despite these measures, over 200,000 workers struck and about 25 per cent won some reduction in work hours. During the next two years, Prime Minister Georges Clemenceau (1906-1909), who publicly termed himself "France's number one cop" (Sedgwick, 1968: 83), responded to a series of CGT strikes with great vigor and considerable brutality, with the result that 19 workers were killed and about 700 were injured. Jail terms totaling 104 years were handed out. CGT leaders who responded to the casualties with posters referring to a "Gouvernement d'Assassins!" and calling for a "Réponse aux Massacres!" were arrested on charges such as "insults to the army" (Levine 1914: 185).

The 1906-10 period of militant labor strife climaxed with a general strike of railroad workers in October 1910, which featured considerable violence and sabotage. Prime Minister Aristide Briand (1909-11), a former socialist who had once vigorously advocated the use of the syndicalist general strike, crushed the walkout by arresting the leadership and drafting strikers, thus placing them under military discipline. After the 1910 strike, CGT adopted a distinctly less militant character, although nonetheless there were numerous arrests of CGT leaders in 1912 for anti-military propaganda. French politicians were rescued from facing the "social question" after 1910 by the growing threat of war in Europe.

## Intransigence in Southern and Eastern Europe

While northwestern Europe gradually, and sometime unsteadily, moved towards greater democratization and emphasis on reform rather than repression after 1870, the economically backwards countries of southern and eastern Europe (Russia, Iberia, Hungary, and the Balkans) responded to rising lower-class discontent mostly with intransigence and repression. The political system in most of these countries was open, as late as 1914, to only a tiny fraction of the population, as rigged elections and/or highly restricted electoral systems remained in place (except in Serbia and Greece) throughout the 1870-1914 period. Spanish social and literary critic Ortega y Gasset's description of Spanish political life around 1900 accurately portrayed conditions in most of the countries of southern and eastern Europe: he referred to "phantom parties that defend ghostly ideas, and, assisted by the shades of newspapers, run ministries of hallucination" (Meaker 1974: 3-4).

Aside from restrictions on the electoral process, trade unions and socialist groups were subjected to severe harassment throughout the 1870-1914 era in Iberia, Hungary and Russia (in the Balkans economic development was too retarded to provide a basis for significant urban working class movements before 1914). In Hungary and Russia, freedom of association and the press were constantly severely restricted before 1914, while such freedoms were extremely tenuous or subjected to frequent suspension in the Balkans and Iberia (except in Greece and in Serbia after 1903). Although living and working conditions in southern and eastern Europe were exceptionally bad, as late as 1914 social legislation was either totally lacking or completely inadequate.

Although developments in industry, education and health in southern and eastern Europe lagged far behind the rest of the Continent, progress in all of these areas did occur after 1870. For example, manufacturing output doubled in Spain and increased six times in Russia between 1870 and 1914. Even in the Balkans, exports tripled between 1886-90 and 1911, and by 1910 Rumania emerged as the world's fourth largest wheat exporter. Although literacy rates in southern and eastern Europe were laughable compared to northwestern Europe, there was also dramatic progress in this area, resulting, for example, in a doubling of the literacy rate in Greece, Hungary and Rumania, and a tripling of the rate in Russia between 1870 and 1910 (see Table 6.1). This economic and educational progress, combined with the extremely poor living conditions in southern and eastern Europe, created a growing number of politicized and discontented citizens after 1870. Around 1870, the phony (and, in the case of

Russia, non-existent) parliamentary regimes in these regions aroused relatively little opposition (except in Spain) from populations that were too ignorant, disorganized, isolated by agrarian locales and preoccupied with survival to organize effective resistance. By about 1890 and thereafter, however, the growth of a sizable urban industrial working class in Iberia, Hungary and Russia, and the growth of rural working-class organization and discontent in these regions and the Balkans created a situation that was bound to create severe difficulties unless significant adjustments were made by regimes that had remained virtually unchanged since 1870 or before. Since such adjustments were not made, the inevitable result was severe political turmoil and instability in these regions, especially after about 1890 (much as had occurred under similar conditions and for similar reasons in northwestern Europe between 1815 and 1850). In Hungary, for example, where severe peasant disturbances occurred during the 1890s following two decades of relative quiet, a peasant named Albert Szilagi who appeared before a government investigating committee declared:

> The rightful demands of the laborers increased because the people of the land study more, know more, see more. How can you blame us? We have learnt how to read and write. We would now like to wear better clothes, eat like human beings and send our children to schools (Janos 1982: 162-3).

In addition to the Hungarian outbreaks, all of the major uprisings and revolts that erupted in Europe after 1890 burst out in southern and eastern Europe. These included successful revolutions in Serbia (1903), Greece (1909), and Portugal (1910), as well as massive nationwide uprisings in Russia (1905) and Rumania (1907) and more localized but still severe disturbances in Spain (1901-1905, 1909), and Bulgaria (1900).

The answer to why the regimes in southern and eastern Europe remained rigid as discontent and its organized expression grew after 1870 is probably similar to the explanation of similar behavior among northwestern European elites in 1815-50. Since the lower classes were excluded from the suffrage and in general from access to the political system, it was easy to ignore their concerns most of the time. Pure greed, bad judgment and deeply rooted fear are also unquestionably major explanations of the behavior of the dominant groups. The social gulf between the ruling elites and the masses in these regions, as in northwestern Europe before 1850, was so great that the concept of sharing power with the average citizen undoubtedly struck many ruling elites as tantamount to handing over their fate to savages. Especially in Spain, Hungary, and Russia, the frequent resort to violence by opponents of the regimes fostered knee-jerk repressive reactions. Finally, the relative weakness of the opposition forces--at least in comparison to the organized working-class movements of northwestern Europe--which itself partly reflected the success of past repression as well as retarded economic development, made ruling elites conclude that repression was likely to be both effective and relatively non-costly.

The Russian Empire. Russia remained an extremely reactionary and repressive state throughout the 1870-1914 period. In 1900, it was the only country that maintained prior press censorship and lacked an elected national legislature. Even after concessions were made on these issues in the aftermath of a massive popular uprising in 1905 the regime continued to be little more than an extension of the czar's will, enforced, often with great brutality, by the police and the military.

In the 1870s, the increasingly conservative and repressive posture adopted by Czar Alexander II after the 1866 attempt on his life was reinforced by fears generated by the Paris Commune and rising signs of political discontent among the students, intellectuals, and the urban working classes. The decade was therefore marked by massive political arrests and a series of notorious trials. The most dramatic of these arose from the Populist (narodniki) movement of the mid-1870s, when several thousand young members of the intelligensia, mostly middle and upper class college students, "went to the people" to try to convince them of the need for dramatic reforms in Russia. Most of the narodniki donned peasant dress, went into rural areas, sought work as farm employees, teachers and doctors, and devoted their energies to radical, but peaceful propaganda. In general, the peasants reacted with hostility or incomprehension and in some cases reported the narodniki to the police, who in any case had little difficulty in spotting the obviously urban radicals. Between 1873 and 1877, over 1,600 narodniki were questioned by police. Of these, 525 were held for trial, 79 were administratively deported under 1870-1 decrees authorizing such punishment for strike leaders and suspected subversives and criminals, and the others were placed under police surveillance. Two groups that sought to organize urban workers were broken up with arrests in Odessa and Moscow in 1875-6, and in December 1876 a peaceful demonstration of a few hundred workers and intelligentsia at Kazan cathedral in St. Petersburg was brutally dispersed by police, and 32 arrests were made.

The year 1877 was one of political trials in Russia. In January, five persons were given 10-15 years at hard labor for the Kazan cathedral demonstration, and 10 others were sentenced to indefinite Siberian exile. "Society was dumbfounded at this display of official stupidity and savagery" (Ulam 1977: 255). Next the labor organizers arrested in 1875-6 were tried and given long jail terms in many cases. In October 1877, the climatic "Trial of the 193," involving the narodniki, was held. Many of the "193" had been jailed for three or four years by the time the trial began, a fact that added considerably to the general public sympathy for their plight. About half of the defendants were acquitted, but most of these were administratively exiled. Sentences for the others ranged from a few days in prison to 10 years at hard labor.

On January 24, 1878, the day after the sentences of the "193" were handed down, a new era in the Russian revolutionary movement was inaugurated when a young woman, Vera Zasulich, shot and wounded General Feodor Trepov, the brutal governor of St. Petersburg, in retaliation for his violent prison flogging of one of those jailed for the Kazan cathedral demonstration. The Zasulich attempt was not the first incident of revolutionary violence during the 1870s--two police spies were assassinated in 1876-7 and a few attempts to instigate peasant revolts had been broken up with the usual arrests--but it marked the beginning of the systematic use of terror against government officials, and also of a rising sense of panic among regime authorities. This hysteria was reinforced when a jury acquitted Zasulich, despite her obvious guilt, in March 1878. Subsequently, all cases of "resistance to the authorities, rebellion, assassination" or attempted assassination were taken away from juries and tried by military tribunals (Seton-Watson 1967: 423). The 1878-9 period witnessed a rash of rural, student, and labor protests, leading to hundreds of arrests, expulsions and terms of exile, along with the assassination of the Kiev police chief, the head of the Russian secret police, the governor of Kharkov province and three police spies.

On April 2, 1879, large portions of Russia were placed under the rule of military commanders who were given almost unlimited administrative powers. About 15 accused terrorists were executed following military trials during the rest of the year. For the next two years, the Russian government was kept in a state of hysteria by the activities of an organization known as the People's Will, which was formed in 1879 for the express purpose of assassinating the czar. The People's Will issued clandestine publications demanding revolution in Russia and made repeated attempts on Alexander's life, including the February 5, 1880 bombing of the royal palace in St. Petersburg, which killed 11 people. A little more than a year later, on March 1, 1881, the group succeeded in murdering the czar. Five members of the organization, which never had a hard core of more than 50, paid for the deed with their lives on April 3, 1881 in an execution carried out before a crowd of 100,000.

The reign of the new czar, Alexander III (1881-94), was one of unrelieved reaction in all aspects of Russian life. Alexander surrounded himself with notorious reactionaries, such as Konstantin Pobedonostsev, his ideological mentor and Procurator of the Holy Synod, who termed parliamentary government "the great lie of our time" and expressed a desire to "keep people from inventing things" (Seton-Watson 1967: 461; Riasonovsky 1969: 435). An August 1881 "provisional decree" authorized the declaration of states of emergency and assumption of sweeping powers of search, censorship, and administrative imprisonment and deportation when necessary to insure "order and social tranquillity" (Charques 1965: 30). This "provisional decree" was renewed repeatedly until the collapse of the czarist regime in 1917, and was in effect almost continually over large areas of Russia. Press controls were severely tightened after 1881, and in 1884 university autonomy was completely abolished and all forms of corporate student activity were outlawed.

In 1889, the office of land captain (zemsky nachalnik) was created in rural areas to replace formerly elected justices of the peace, and their occupants were given virtually omnipotent power over the villages, including the power to set aside court decisions, local elections and the decisions of local elected officials, as well as the authority to impose fines and short jail terms without trials. Since the land captain was appointed by the central government and was invariably a member of the local nobility, "for all practical purposes this was the restoration of the despotic power over the life and affairs of the peasantry which had been exercised by the landowners under serfdom" (Charques 1965: 32). In 1890 and 1892, respectively, suffrage laws for rural and urban government were revised, drastically reducing the franchise in the cities, and greatly limiting peasants' influence in the rural zemtvos.

During Alexander's reign, Russian courts sentenced over 20 people to death for political offenses, and well over 2,000 dissidents were given judicial or administrative sentences of jail or exile. Among those executed were five people, including Alexander Ulyanov, the brother of Lenin, hanged in May 1887 for an abortive plot against the czar's life. In Russian Poland, a socialist workers-oriented group, Proletariat, was destroyed by arrests and executions when it turned to terrorist tactics in 1884 after its peaceful attempts to organize were disrupted by mass arrests in Warsaw in late 1883 and early 1884, during which troops surrounded entire working class districts and conducted sweeping searches. Further police arrests of over 500 members in 1884-6 destroyed what was left of Proletariat and its terrorist arm, the "Fighting Squad," after two police agents had been assassinated, another suspected (but innocent) informer was killed and an additional police informant was twice wounded. Five Poles implicated in terrorist activity were hanged in 1886, about 25 other Proletariat members were given long jail terms and hard labor, and another 275 members were given other punishments, including many sentences of Siberian exile and jail.

By 1890, opposition activity in the Russian Empire had been almost completely suppressed. However, public anger over the massive famines and cholera epidemics of the early 1890s (which killed about 500,000 people), the death of Alexander III in 1894, the growth of a significant urban industrial working-class and middle-class intelligentsia and deteriorating rural conditions led to a massive and unprecedented upsurge in dissent during the first decade of the reign of the new czar, Alexander's son Nicholas II (1894-1917). Although Nicholas publicly referred to growing demands for representative government as "senseless dreams" (bezmyslennie mechtaniya) and pledged to uphold the principle of autocracy "as firmly and as unflinchingly as my late unforgettable father" (Crankshaw 1976: 311), the period after 1895, and especially after 1900 witnessed the growth of massive protest movement.

Huge strikes, involving tens of thousands of workers, convulsed the St. Petersburg textile industry in 1896-7, Rostov-on-Don in November 1902 and virtually all of the major industrial centers in southern Russia in July 1903. Poor harvests in the late 1890s led to sporadic peasant disorders, and a serious famine in 1901 was followed by massive peasant uprisings in March-April 1902 in Poltava and Kharkov provinces in the southern Ukraine. After 1895, significant middle-class opposition, based on zemtvos officials and employees, students, urban intellectuals, and members of the professions, staged increasingly frequent unauthorized demonstrations and used literary, cultural, and professional groups as "fronts" for the organization of anti-regime activity. This middle-class opposition demanded above all civil liberties and constitutional and representative government. In 1904 the liberal middle-class opposition formed an underground and illegal political movement, the Union of Liberation, that demanded the "establishment in Russia of a constitutional regime" with the "fundamentally essential" condition of "universal, equal, and direct suffrage and secret ballot," a demand soon known as the "four tailed" (četyrek hvostka) suffrage (Galai 1973: 190).

In Finland, which had been basically quiet and loyal to the Russian Empire ever since Russian rule began in 1809, public outrage exploded after Nicholas suddenly abrogated the country's long-respected autonomy in the so-called February Manifesto of 1899. The February Manifesto essentially reduced the Finnish diet to a purely advisory role on any matter pertaining to Finland that the czar ruled as also affecting the entire Russian Empire. Over 500,000 Finns, about 40 per cent of the population, signed petitions protesting the manifesto. The Finnish plight attracted considerable international attention and sympathy. Thus, over 1,000 distinguished Europeans, including Herbert Spencer, Florence Nightingale, Anatole France, Emile Zola, and Henrik Ibsen, signed a petition entitled "Pro Finlandia" urging the czar to reverse his course, but Nicholas refused to receive the delegation that sought to present the document to him. Despite growing repression, Finnish resistance continued. In November 1899, for example, a giant press convention originally called to collect a pension fund for journalists was transformed into a Finnish nationalist celebration, at which composer Jean Sibelius's great work "Finlandia," dedicated to press freedom, was played for the first time. When an attempt was made to conscript Finns for the Russian army for the first time in 1902, a new protest petition gathered 500,000 signatures, and 60 per cent of those called up failed to respond. Russian Finance Minister Sergei Witte remarked to the new Finnish governor-general, Nicholas Bobrikov (1898-1904), "Muravyev [the so-called hangman of Vilna who brutally suppressed the 1863 Polish revolt] was appointed to put down an uprising, but you evidently have been appointed to create one" (Pogorelskin 1976: 235).

In Poland, political tensions were considerably aggravated by the 1899-1903 economic depression, which was intensified by the disruption of trade and loss of eastern markets arising from the 1904 Russo-Japanese War. Several hundred people were arrested after a February 1904 anti-war protest in Warsaw, and thereafter Poland was convulsed by continual riots and demonstrations. Hundreds were arrested and over 30 killed or injured during a clash between workers under the leadership of the increasingly insurrectionary-oriented

Polish Socialist party and troops and police in Warsaw on November 13, 1904.

The government's basic response to the rising tide of opposition after 1895 was massive repression. Troops were called out almost 2,000 times between 1895 and 1905 to suppress strikes and demonstrations and frequently dispersed them with great brutality, often wielding whips and sabres. Hundreds of strikers and peasants were killed and injured, and tens of thousands of peasants, strikers, students, and radicals were arrested, most of whom were engaged in peaceful activities. Socialist organizers were driven underground by such tactics as the arrest of over 500 people who tried to create a nationwide Marxist organization in 1898. The 1881 "Exceptional Measures" suspending normal judicial procedures were invoked over growing regions until by 1904 more than half of the Russian Empire, including most of the major cities, was affected. In Finland, Bobrikov abrogated all semblances of freedom of the press, speech, and assembly after 1899, and in 1903 he was given total dictatorial powers, which he used to further suppress Finnish freedoms and to administratively banish the leaders of the constitutionalist opposition. As tensions and repression increased during the pre-1905 period, small groups in Poland, Finland and Russia proper emerged devoted to revolutionary and terrorist tactics. Dozens of czarist officials were assassinated between 1901 and 1905, of whom the most prominent were interior ministers Sipyagin (April 2, 1902) and Plehve (July 15, 1904) and Finnish dictator Bobrikov (June 16, 1904).

The assassination of Plehve, which was greeted with open jubilation by many Russians, was followed by a brief easing of repressive controls, known as the "political spring" (pravitel'stvennaja vesna) of August-December 1904. However, the easing of controls on the press and public assembly, unaccompanied by any concessions to constitutionalism, only strengthened, emboldened, and angered the opposition. During the last few months of 1904, the Union of Liberation and other groups organized a series of about 40 "political banquets," based on the French banquet campaign of 1847-8, as a forum in major Russian cities for the issuance of their demands. "An orgy of speech-making on the theme of 'a constitution' [referred to in the press with the euphemism 'reform'] marked the closing weeks of the year" (Charques 1965: 109). The leading slogans of the day were, "Down with the autocracy!" "Long live the constitution!" and "We can't go on living like this!" (Tak bolshe zhit nelzia) (Charques 1965: 109; Galai 1973: 211). Although Nicholas signalled an end to the "political spring" by announcing a crackdown on illegal meetings and assemblies on December 12, the opposition continued to grow. About 50,000 workers in Baku struck in December for civil liberties and constitutional government as well as for improved living and working conditions, and in St. Petersburg about 150,000 workers out of an industrial labor force of 175,000 walked out to enforce similar demands in early January 1905.

The 1905 Russian revolution was touched off when about 200,000 marchers in St. Petersburg were fired on by troops on January 9 while peacefully demanding reforms. "Bloody Sunday," which left a minimum of 130 people dead and 300 wounded, was a catastrophe for the regime from which it never recovered, shaking the fundamental allegiance of millions of Russian peasants and workers to the throne. As Lenin noted, "The revolutionary education of the proletariat made more progress in one day than it could have made in months and years of drab, humdrum, wretched existence" (Kochan 1966: 80). The next year was filled with an enormous wave of strikes, demonstrations and frequently bloody clashes with the authorities--about 2500 died in battles in Odessa and Poland alone--which paralyzed the regime. Altogether 2.8 million workers struck in 1905, twice as many as that recorded for any other European country in any year before 1914. The urban strike movement reached its peak in October 1905, with what amounted to a nationwide general strike on the entire railroad system and in all major urban areas, including those in Finland, Poland, Georgia, the Ukraine, and the Baltic regions. In St. Petersburg, even the Maryinsky Theatre ballet dancers struck, while in the czarist imperial retreat city of Tsarkoe Selo, primary school children refused to say their morning prayers. Although the 1905 revolution was essentially urban-centered, there were also recurrent waves of peasant unrest, including strikes and attacks on nobles and their property, especially in the Baltic provinces, Georgia and the black-earth provinces of south-central Russia. The peasant disorders peaked in November-December, when almost 1,400 outbreaks were recorded. In the Baltic provinces, about 1,000 German landlords and Russian officials and soldiers were murdered, and entire districts were taken over by Lettish and Estonian peasants.

In many ways the 1905 revolution was a Russian counterpart to the 1848 European revolt, although it was far more bloody and prolonged and took place in a far more industrially developed society. As in 1848, the fundamental unifying demand of the revolutionary coalition was for constitutional government, a broad suffrage and civil liberties. As in 1848, the break-down in governmental authority was followed by a mass upsurge in political expression. Numerous trade unions were organized, and in St. Petersburg, Moscow, and about 50 other cities, "soviets" were formed to coordinate efforts among workers. The St. Petersburg and Moscow soviets together represented about 300,000 workers. Unions were also formed by numerous professional groups, such as lawyers, teachers, veterinarians, and journalists; in May, 14 of these groups formed the Union of Unions, with perhaps 100,000 affiliated members, to press demands for a constituent assembly. The All-Russian Peasant Union formed in May had over 200,000 members from 26 provinces six months later.

Under the impact of the October strikes, Czar Nicholas, fearing his throne was in jeopardy, conceded the major constitutional and civil liberties demands of the protestors. In the so-called October Manifesto (October 17, 1905), he promised freedom of religion, speech, assembly, and association and announced plans for a legislative body elected by universal male suffrage to approve all proposed laws. Shortly thereafter a restricted political amnesty was granted, and all remaining preliminary press censorship was abolished. In early November, Nicholas repealed the decrees applied to Finland under the February Manifesto, and agreed to accept a system of universal adult suffrage and complete civil liberties for Finland. Poland received no concessions to demands for autonomy, however, despite a lengthy general strike in Warsaw. Strikes for economic purposes were legalized throughout the empire in December 1905, and trade unions and other voluntary associations were legalized, subject to severe restrictions, in March 1906. As in 1848 in Europe, the granting of constitutional government and civil liberties was greeted in Russia with enormous popular enthusiasm:

> For about three days [after the October Manifesto], it appeared that all of urban Russia was holding jubilee. ... All over the country, crowds milled and marched, waving red banners, singing the Marseillaise, shouting their triumph and generally acting the part of conquerors (Harcave 1970: 199-200).

The revolution expired as an organized and mass protest movement by early 1906. One reason for this was sheer exhaustion. Another was that the October Manifesto and other concessions split the revolutionary coalition by satisfying most members of the liberal opposition, while failing to appease revolutionary groups like the Social Revolutionaries and Social Democrats (Marxists) who wanted an overthrow of the monarchy and regarded the Manifesto as a trick--in Trotsky's famous phrase, "A police whip wrapped in the parchment of a constitution" (Crankshaw 1976: 354). But the most important reason for the expiration of the revolution was undoubtedly the use of massive repression. Rural disorders were put down by thousands of troops who meted out mass beatings and shootings and tens of thousands of sentences of jail and Siberian exile. The most savage repression occurred in the Baltic provinces, where troops commanded by Major General Alexander Orlov executed over 2,000 rebels, burned hundreds of peasant homes, and carried out mass arrests and floggings. In mid-November, all members of the central body of the Peasant Union were arrested, and in early December the St. Petersburg Soviet was decapitated by the arrest of 250 leaders. Two weeks later, a last-gasp revolutionary uprising in Moscow, led by the Bolshevik faction of the Social Democrats, was crushed by three days of artillery bombardment that destroyed an entire quarter of the city. About 1,000 rebels were killed in the fighting and many others were summarily executed afterwards. Thousands of Moscovites were arrested and exiled to Siberia. In other urban areas, strikes and protests were put down by bombardments, the arrests of soviet and labor leaders, the closure of radical newspapers, the purging of dissident zemtvos and municipal officials and the imposition of tight restrictions on freedom of assembly. Altogether, it is estimated that the regime killed 15,000 people and arrested another 70,000 by April 1906.

Although the 1905 revolution was over as an organized mass protest movement by early 1906, for the next two years widespread terrorist attacks, amounting to guerrilla warfare, continued to plague czarist officials. Altogether, over 4,000 people, including the governors of two provinces, the governor-general of Warsaw and the military commandant of St. Petersburg, were killed by terrorist attacks in 1906-1907. Prime Minister Peter Stolypin's (1906-11) reply to the terror campaign was an equally ruthless repression. Over 3,200 people were executed after courts-martial between 1905 and 1908, including over 1,000 killed after trials by special summary tribunals between August 1906 and April 1907, with sentences carried out within 24 hours of verdicts. In Poland, over 40,000 people went through the Warsaw prisons alone between February 1905 and June 1907, of whom 258 were sentenced to death.

As the kramola ("sedition") in the streets was being beaten into submission, an electoral law was finalized in February 1906, establishing a highly complicated class-biased voting system for the promised national legislature (duma). In April 1906 Nicholas announced a set of Fundamental Laws that retained great powers for himself, including sole control of the army and foreign policy, an absolute veto, the right to dissolve the duma, and the right to issue emergency laws subject to later duma approval when that body was not in session. Ministers were made responsible only to the czar, and almost 40 per cent of the state budget was excluded from legislative purview.

Although the voting system was grossly biased in favor of the landowners and wealthier urban elements, the elections of April 1906 produced a duma overwhelmingly dominated by opposition forces that demanded parliamentary responsibility, suffrage reform, and other liberal measures. After three months, the duma was forcibly dissolved by troops. Despite massive governmental pressure, new elections in early 1907 produced a legislature even more hostile to the regime. Sixty-five Social Democrats were returned, every one of whom had previously been arrested, jailed, or exiled. The czar wrote to his mother shortly after the Second Duma convened, "One must let them do something manifestly stupid or mean and then--slap! And then they are gone" (Kochan 1966: 121). An excuse was soon found in the form of a document forged by a secret police agent supposedly showing socialist complicity in a plot to incite mutiny in the armed forces, and the duma was dissolved three months after it was elected. Shortly after, 30 socialist deputies from the duma were given long terms of convict labor in Siberia, and massive arrests of radicals were effected, along with a general crackdown on student activism and freedom of assembly and labor organization. Simultaneously with the Second Duma's dissolution, Stolypin issued a new electoral law in clear violation of the 1906 Fundamental Laws, which required legislative approval for such a measure. The new law drastically reduced the representation for non-Russian nationalities and drastically increased the voting weight of the 100,000 great landlords, so that this 1 per cent of the electorate was assured of about 50 per cent of the duma seats. Under this new electoral system, the czarist regime was finally able to obtain a conservative majority in the new 1907 elections and the Third Duma served out a full five-year term.

The 1907-11 period, known in Soviet historiography as the "years of repression and reaction" was generally quiet, as the radical opposition was effectively paralyzed by Stolypin's intense repression. Revolutionary leaders were dead, jailed, or in exile, and their organizations were shattered. Trade union membership in St. Petersburg and Moscow plummeted from 100,000 to 40,000 between 1907 and 1909. Only 46,000 Russians struck in 1910, compared with 2.8 million in 1905, 1.1 million in 1906 and 740,000 in 1907.

In Finland also, a new period of repression began in 1907. In July 1906 Czar Nicholas had ratified a new Organic Law passed by the Finnish diet, which established a system of universal adult suffrage (including women). This increased the Finnish suffrage from 126,000 to 1.3 million and theoretically transformed Finland into the most democratic country in Europe. However, after 1906 the czar repeatedly blocked progressive diet legislation and dissolved that body almost every year between 1907 and 1914, since the Finnish electors repeatedly chose a body dominated by Finnish nationalists, in which the socialists were the strongest single party. In June 1910, the czar signed a Russian duma law that reduced Finnish autonomy to meaninglessness by withdrawing a wide range of matters, including the press, the schools, public order, the post, railways and military service, from the jurisdiction of the Finnish diet. Dissident Finns were given savage sentences of administrative exile, purged from civil service positions, and jailed.

In Russia proper, Stolypin concentrated during the 1907-11 period on implementing his land reform program, decreed after dissolution of the First Duma. It left untouched the holdings of the great landlords but sought to increase incentives and productivity among the peasantry by ending the stranglehold of the commune over land usage in favor of consolidated and individually owned peasant plots. By 1915, about 50 per cent of all peasant households owned such plots, and, together with a series of good harvests and continuing repressive measures, the reform led to a decline of peasant outbreaks from 1,337 in 1907 to 196 in 1915.

A gradual relaxation of repression followed Stolypin's mysterious assassination in 1911. Censorship and controls on opposition party activities eased considerably, until by 1912 even revolutionary parties, such as the Bolsheviks, were able to publish legal daily newspapers. In 1913 an amnesty was granted to "literary political" offenders to celebrate the tercentenary of the Romanov dynasty. Political opposition to the regime revived dramatically after the events of April 4, 1912, when a crowd of 5,000 peaceful strikers at the Lena gold mine in Siberia was fired on by troops, with resultant casualties of about 200 deaths and an equal number injured. Public outrage was considerably compounded when Minister of the Interior A. A. Makarov told the duma that troops had no alternative but to shoot when confronted with a demonstrating mob. "So it has been and so it will be in the future" he declared (Phillips 1975: 12).

The Lena Gold Mine Massacre's impact was much like that of Bloody Sunday seven years before, triggering a massive strike movement that never ceased before the outbreak of World War I. In April-May 1912, about 500,000 workers struck in St. Petersburg and Moscow alone, a figure higher than the number of strikers throughout Russia during the entire previous four years. Strikes continued to increase, jumping from a total of 725,000 strikers throughout Russia in 1912 to 887,000 in 1913 and almost 1.5 million during the first half of 1914. In July 1914, on the eve of World War I, St. Petersburg exploded after police brutally attacked a demonstration of thousands of metal workers who had gathered to support striking Baku oil workers, killing two and wounding 50. Over 100,000 workers struck in protest; barricades were erected; and for a week the Russian capital was in the throes of vicious street fighting.

Iberia. In Spain, the 1868 revolution rapidly descended into chaos after 1870, and ultimately led to a reactionary restoration of the Bourbon monarchy in 1874. Thereafter, Spain adopted the system in effect in Portugal since the 1850s, in which two essentially identical parties that ignored the needs of the impoverished masses took turns governing, with the proper "rotation" and the exclusion of other forces guaranteed by systematic and massive election rigging. In Spain, the government newspaper even published the 1886 election returns before the balloting occurred! This system, known as the turno pacífico in Spain, and rotativism in Portugal, provided relatively stable government until about 1890, but rapidly broke down in both countries thereafter as modernization created new forces that could not be accommodated by the old system and foreign policy disasters discredited the regimes. In Portugal, the end result was a revolution that overthrew the monarchy in 1910, while in Spain the upshot was an escalating cycle of violence and repression that verged on civil war by 1914.

The Spanish chaos during the 1868-74 revolution perfectly illustrated the wisdom of the Duke of Wellington's comment of 50 years before that "Spain is the only country where two and two do not make four" (Payne 1967: 1). The election of Amadeo, son of the king of Italy, as the king of Spain in late 1870 alienated the republicans, the Carlists, the Bourbon legitimists and clerical elements of the revolution who disliked the anti-clericalism of the Italian government. When even those who had supported his candidacy grew increasingly divided, Amadeo abdicated in February 1873, declaring privately, "I don't understand anything: we are in a cage of madmen" (Herr 1974: 107). After Amadeo's abdication, the federal republic that was then established was soon confronted by simultaneous 1873 risings of the Carlists in northeastern Spain and of extreme federalist republicans, dissastisfied with the pace of decentralization and lusting for control of local power and patronage, in southern and eastern Spain. The federalist or "cantonalist" revolts forced the government to suspend civil liberties and rely heavily upon the conservative army leadership, which suppressed the revolts quickly (save for Cartagena, which held out for five months) and with considerable harshness. About 15,000 Spaniards were arrested and 1,400 were deported to the Philippines. Most of the cantonalist risings had no connection with the Spanish International, which had an estimated membership of 60,000 members in 1874 despite being outlawed in 1872. However, the entire cantonalist movement became tarred with the brush of social radicalism as the result of an insurrection organized by the Spanish International at Alcoy in July 1873 after police fired on an unarmed crowd during a general strike of paper workers. The Alcoy revolt was accompanied by some gruesome atrocities, which were not particularly unusual in Spain but were grossly exaggerated and enormously publicized by the Spanish press.

In early 1874, after the cortes, angered by the harshness of the repression of the cantonalist revolts, voted no confidence in the government, soldiers forcibly dispersed the legislature and transformed the republic into a thinly disguised military dictatorship. The International was again outlawed, about 500 of its leaders were jailed, its meeting halls were closed and virtually all International sections, trade unions, and even workers' discussion groups were dissolved. In late 1874, another military coup restored the Bourbon monarchy under Alfonso XII (1874-85).

Political leadership under the restored dynasty was assumed by Antonio Cánovas del Castillo, head of the Conservative party, which was heir to the old Moderates and more conservative Liberal Unionists. In an atmosphere marked by fears of Spanish republican radicalism, the Commune and the International, Cánovas called elections for a constituent cortes in 1876 under the universal male suffrage rules of the 1869 constitution (to maintain a semblance of legality and continuity). Extreme intimidation, mob violence and fraud were employed by Interior Minister Francisco Romero Robledo to force anti-dynastic candidates to withdraw, and parties and newspapers that did not support the principle of a Bourbon constitutional monarchy were not allowed to function. A docile majority of 365 out of 557 seats for Cánovas was produced, although even so it was deemed necessary to cancel or reverse 42 elections. While the constituent cortes met, a massive purge of thousands of local officials and judges was instituted; trade unions and strikes were outlawed; and the Catholic Church was given virtually unlimited control over Spanish education. The cortes drafted what proved to be a slightly liberalized version of the 1845 constitution, reflecting Cánovas's desire to broaden the base of the Isabelline regime without jeopardizing the essential interests of the wealthy landowners and businessmen. After the 1876 constitution went into effect, relentless pressure was maintained for the rest of the decade against clandestine trade unions and sections of the International. After an assassination attempt on King Alfonso XII in October 1878, there was a massive wave of arrests of trade union militants and Internationalists.

After 1876, Spain gradually adopted the turno pacífico, with Cánovas (prime minister 1876-81, 1884-85, 1895-97) taking turns governing with the Liberal party of Práxedes Mateo Sagasta (prime minister 1881-3, 1885-90, 1892-5), which included the heirs of the more reformist Liberal Unionists and the more conservative Progressives. While the Liberals were tinged with anti-clericalism and more favorable toward civil liberties, both parties had no interest in the problems of the lower classes and reflected coalitions of the Spanish ruling classes, namely, the big landowners, industrialists and bankers, the Church, the military and the professional politicians and civil service.

As in Portugal, the system was ultimately based on a network of local political bosses, or caciques, who were given carte blanche by the central government to manipulate local taxation, patronage, public works, and even conscription in return for producing the proper election results. The power of the caciques in their localities was so great that one contemporary writer remarked, "Not even the leaves on the tree die without the permission of the caciques" (Kern 1973: 45). Descriptions of Portuguese rotativism and the Spanish turno pacífico are literally interchangeable:

The [Portuguese] parties were simply groups of clients depending upon a boss or leader and eagerly coveting public jobs. Elections were "made" by the government, which always won them by means of a network of local authorities. Consequently, instead of the king choosing the prime minister based on popular voting, it was the king who had to dissolve the House of Deputies, in order that the government might have a majority in the next House, which it "made." Premierships changed from one to the other party, whenever the ruling party, or an agreement between the two, or even the king thought it convenient. Reasons varied greatly from case to case: often a simple fatigue of governing brought about the change; at other times, it was the fear of some responsibility, a parliamentary debate in either house of Parliament, a press campaign cleverly oriented, personal matters affecting any cabinet member, or the like (Oliveira Marques 1976: 52).

There was in fact little of substance in the conflict between the two [Spanish] parties. Each in opposition flagellated the other for the alleged abuses and betrayals of principle, each in office pursued identical tactics and a scarcely distinguishable policy. In part this rested on a genuine concern never again to split the nation or incite to arms. But it conveyed also with time the impression of cynical abandonment of principle in favor of a tacit agreement to alternate in power at decent intervals and to share less the responsibilities than the spoils of office (Atkinson 1960: 306).

In Portugal, <u>rotativism</u> functioned smoothly in the two decades after 1870 amidst a political scene free of serious opposition and marked by general complacency. In 1871, the year of the Paris Commune, there was a brief red scare in Portugal, which led the government to suppress a series of lectures given in Lisbon by a young intellectual, Antero de Quental, on the state of Portuguese society. However, for the most part Portuguese politics proceeded calmly for 20 years after 1870, usually under the direction of Regenerator party leader Fontes Pereira de Melo (prime minister 1871-7, 1878-9, 1881-6), known for his policy of public works and railroad expansion ("Fontismo"). The Portuguese political leadership was so confident that in 1878 the suffrage was expanded from 9 to about 14 per cent, making it one of the broadest in Europe, and in 1885 the upper legislative chamber was slightly democratized.

In Spain, politics was slightly more turbulent between 1875 and 1890, but the regime was never seriously threatened. A wave of rural violence, including food riots, brigandage, crop burnings, and murders in the 1881-3 period among the brutally impoverished peasants of Andalusia, especially in the provinces of Cadiz and Seville, aroused much conern. It is not clear whether these disorders resulted from the activities of the highly militant Andalusian wing of the Workers Federation of the Spanish Region, which claimed a membership of almost 60,000 shortly after trade unions were tolerated in Spain again in 1881, or were the response of a desperate rural working class to severe droughts and crop failures in 1881-2, which led to massive unemployment and price increases of almost 100 per cent for wheat in western Andalusia. The murder of a tavern owner and his wife near the town of Jerez de la Frontera, near Cadiz, in December 1882, was followed by the announced police discovery of a secret terrorist organization, the Black Hand (la Mano Negra). Although the very existence of the Black Hand remains disputed by historians to this day, its alleged discovery touched off massive arrests of Federation members in southern Spain. Over 5,300 were jailed in the cities of Cadiz and Jerez alone in February-March 1883. "No proof was necessary: suspicion by a landlord, a magistrate or a Civil Guard, or the merest suggestion from anybody else was enough evidence for a <u>journalero</u> [day worker] or any politically minded person to be imprisoned" (Lida 1969: 316). Harassment of the remnants of the Federation in the south continued throughout 1883, reaching its peak during an agricultural workers' strike at Jerez in the early summer. Troops were sent to Jerez to harvest the crops and break the strike; a curfew was imposed subjecting anyone found in rural areas after 10 p.m. to arrest; and the civil governor issued a decree that amounted to a call for extermination of the Federation:

> Any damage or fire thought ... accidental will be presumed ... the work of individuals discovered in the immediate area; or, if no one is found, of those individuals who compose the local junta of the nearest branch of the International or the Workers Federation (Waggoner 1972: 184).

While the Jerez strike was being crushed, the trials of the alleged Black Hand members were held. They were basically inconclusive, revealing police torture and the determination of judges to jail leading Federation members "whether guilty or not of the crimes attributed to them" (Carr 1966: 443). About 300 were given jail terms and nine were executed. The combined impact of the Black Hand trials, the crushing of the Jerez strike, and some futile strikes in Catalonia led to the rapid collapse of the Federation, which could not withstand the mass arrests and desertions that resulted despite its disavowal of all connection with terrorism. By late 1883, only 3,000 of the formerly 30,000 Andalusian members remained.

Some minor concessions were made in Spain in the 1880s to uphold a democratic façade, but as in the case of the Portuguese reforms of 1878 and 1885 they in no way changed the basic nature of the system, which continued to be protected by caciquismo and election rigging. Thus, even while Sagasta brutally suppressed the alleged Black Hand disorders during his first ministry in 1881-3, press restrictions were relaxed considerably and trade unions were granted de facto toleration (although the latter was effectively eliminated in practice during the mid-1880s). During Sagasta's second ministry in 1885-90, unions were formally legalized and in 1890 universal male suffrage was re-established for local and national elections.

In both Spain and Portugal, the relatively stable systems of the pre-1890 period unravelled after that date. In both countries, this disintegration reflected growing discontent among the lower and middle classes over economic grievances and the rigidity and corruption of the political system; it also reflected an increasing sense, reinforced by foreign policy disasters of 1890 in Portugal and 1898 in Spain, that the Iberian countries had become fourth-rate powers because of incompetent leadership. In both countries the political systems were completely unable to accommodate the rapid growth of new forces, including republican, socialist, trade union and, in Spain, regionalist elements. As these movements grew, the Iberian political elites carried on as before, pausing only to apply increasing force and chicanery to rig elections in rural areas (it became increasingly difficult to fake elections in the politicized cities), and growing more disconnected from social realities. The Iberian political crisis was greatly intensified by the fragmentation of each country's two major political parties after 1900. The Spanish system never recovered from the assassination of Cánovas in 1897 and the death of Sagasta in 1903, while the two major Portuguese parties split into five factions between 1901 and 1910.

Serious disintegration began earlier and proceeded more rapidly and completely in Portugal than in Spain. Three events that occurred in rapid succession in 1889-92 gravely undermined the Portuguese regime: the successful 1889 republican uprising in Portugal's former colony, Brazil; Portugal's humiliating surrender in 1890 to Britain over conflicting territorial claims in Africa; and a severe financial crisis in 1890-2 that pushed the country to the verge of bankruptcy. Although rotativism continued to function until 1906, the entire political system became the target of growing public cynicism after 1890 as the two rotating parties, the Regenerators and the Progressives (formerly the Historicals) "neither regenerated nor made progress" (Benton 1977: 31) and did nothing to disprove the feeling that they were corrupt and useless organizations whose only purpose was to dip into the public treasury when their turn came to "rotate" in power. The growing discontent of the urban middle and lower classes was tapped with ever-increasing effectiveness by the moderate and middle class-led republican movement, which skillfully painted the monarchy as the prime source of evil in Portuguese political life, thereby diverting lower-class discontent away from more class-based issues. Portugal gradually became what King Carlos I (1889-1908) termed a "monarchy without monarchists" (Wheeler 1978: 31).

From 1890 to 1893, the hollowness of the two-party system was demonstrated when both joined together to form a crisis coalition government. When a pure Regenerator party government in 1893 was unable to solve the nation's financial problems, Prime Minister Hintze Rebeiro (1893-7) postponed the 1894 election, dissolved the cortes and ruled by decree under emergency powers. The 1895 elections were held under special provisions that barred minority parties, leading even the Progressives to abstain. The new cortes reduced the suffrage by 50 per cent and repealed the 1885 reform that had ended hereditary seats and introduced elections for the upper legislative chamber. In 1897, following an attempt on King Carlos's life, which may have involved an agent provocateur, a royal decree authorized the banishment after trial by a secret court to the Portuguese East Indies of any individual suspected of anarchistic ideas and practices. Sixty-six opponents of the regime were quickly deported under this provision.

Despite the growing repression, republicans continued to gain strength, and scores of illegal strikes were organized by a burgeoning trade union movement, including a virtual general strike at Oporto in 1903. Meanwhile, factionalism within the two major parties became so great after 1900 that Joao Franco, the leader of a Regenerator splinter group called to power by King Carlos in 1906, was unable to obtain a legislative majority even after conducting elections. He dissolved the legislature in 1907 but failed to call new elections, instead ruling by decree. Franco also suppressed almost the entire Lisbon press, eliminated trial by jury and normal constitutional protections in political cases, closed Coimbra University after a pro-republican strike was organized there, and dissolved the Lisbon municipal government and other dissident local elective bodies.

Republican opposition to the Franco dictatorship, organized in secret societies, such as the Carbonária, led to plans for an uprising on January 28, 1908, which were uncovered by police, along with weapons stockpiles in various locations around Lisbon. A wave of arrests, including those of four republican legislators, followed the abortive revolt. Martial law was imposed in Lisbon and on January 31 Franco issued a decree authorizing deportation to Timor of persons indicted for political offenses. On February 1, King Carlos and the heir to the throne, Prince Luis Filipe, were assassinated in Lisbon after republican conspirators were unable to carry out their original plans to kill Franco. The new king, Manuel II (1908-10), made a genuine attempt to conciliate the opposition by dismissing Franco, repealing the repressive decrees of 1907-1908 and releasing many jailed politicians and journalists. However, the king continued to rely on ministries controlled by the old politicians, and the legislative elections of 1908 and 1910 were rigged by the usual methods in rural areas. The republican cause continued to gain strength, as was dramatically indicated when republicans won control of Lisbon in the November 1908 city elections and when a record 14 republicans were elected in 1910 legislative elections.

Republican revolutionary plotting was speeded up by a wave of rural violence and agitation and a series of urban strikes that swept the country between August and October 1910, threatening a general social upheaval that might prove far more radical than the moderate reforms favored by the middle class republicans. On October 4 an uprising led by military elements succeeded in overthrowing the regime, largely because of widespread outbreaks of popular support in Lisbon and elsewhere and the general irresolution of the loyalist military forces.

Although the republican regime that was subsequently established amnestied political prisoners and restored press freedom, it was gravely weakened by its almost exclusively urban middle class base. The politicians who dominated the new regime had no serious interest in social reform and little agreement over anything other than opposition to the monarchy and the Catholic church and the desire to gain control of power and patronage. The clergy and Catholic faithful were soon antagonized by harsh anti-clerical laws, which included the abolition of all Catholic orders, the nationalization of all Church property and even the outlawing of wearing religious dress in public. The monarchists, alienated by the abolition of the crown, constantly plotted against the regime. Monarchist-backed risings were uncovered or suppressed in 1911, 1912, and 1913. Scores of real or imagined monarchists were arrested and held under poor conditions, which were considerably exaggerated and widely publicized abroad, thereby blackening Portugal's reputation and leading to enormous agitation against the republic in Great Britain.

The Portuguese left was deeply angered by the regime's labor policies. Although strikes were legalized in 1910, nothing was done to improve wages and working conditions, which steadily deteriorated, leading to a jump in emigration from 40,000 in 1910 to 60,000 or more annually in 1911-13. About 200 strikes, many under syndicalist influence, erupted in 1910-12, including major rural walk-outs in the southern Alentejo region in 1911-12 and a 1912 general strike in Lisbon. Many of the strikes were put down with great ferocity by landowners, businessmen, troops, police, and unofficial republican vigilante groups. Workers' organizations were forcibly dissolved, and strikers were beaten and arrested; the strikers retaliated with increasing vandalism, sabotage, and bomb throwing. The 1912 Lisbon general strike, a response to repression of the Alentejo strikes, was met with a state of siege, the closure of workers' headquarters and about 600 arrests. The government of Alfonso Costa (1913-14), the leader of the most radical republican faction, which came to power in opposition to the Alentejo repression, was responsible for the reactionary 1913 electoral law, which cut the suffrage in half. He also oversaw the ruthless repression of street demonstrations, closure of the syndicalist union and the jailing of scores of workers.

In Spain sensational incidents of often violent repression and opposition to the regime dominated the 1890s. Massive labor demonstrations in Andalusia on May Day in 1890 and 1891 led to waves of arrests, and a general strike in Barcelona on May Day 1891 led to violent clashes with the police and the imposition of martial law. In January 1892, about 500 peasants under anarchist leadership seized control of the Spanish Andalusian town of Jerez de la Frontera, killing two or three shopkeepers in the process. The Jerez rising was quickly suppressed, leading to over 600 arrests, beatings, military trials, many jail terms, and four executions. In revenge for the executions, a bomb attempt was made on the life of the leading Conservative General Martínez Campos in Barcelona in September 1893, which left the target relatively unscathed but killed six bystanders. In revenge for the execution of the bomb thrower, a young anarchist named Paulino Pallás, his friend Santiago Salvador threw a bomb into the Barcelona Teatro Liceo on November 7, 1893, as local society attended the opening of the opera season. Twenty-two people were killed and 50 wounded. A massive wave of repression ensued, during which all Barcelona workers' centers were closed and thousands of people were arrested and in many cases tortured at the Montjuich prison fortress. Six persons were executed, five of whom had no connection with the bombing. Altogether, an estimated 20,000 Spaniards were held for at least brief periods under preventive arrest during 1892-3 in response to the Jerez rising and the Barcelona bombings.

After the Teatro Liceo explosion, the Spanish legislature decreed the death penalty for those committing crimes with explosives and provided life imprisonment for those advocating violence through speech, press, or even pictures. Nonetheless, on June 7, 1896, a bomb was thrown into a parade in Barcelona, killing 12 and wounding 54. Another massive wave of arrests followed, accompanied by new police tortures at Montjuich. Although responsibility for the bombing was never established, several prisoners died from the savage tortures, five were executed, about 20 got long jail terms and another 60 were acquitted but then re-arrested and given administrative exile in the deadly African colony of Rio d'Oro. On August 8, 1897, an Italian anarchist, Michele Angiollilo, avenged the Montjuich horrors by assassinating Spanish Prime Minister Cánovas. He was in turn executed.

Somewhat obscured by the terrorist incidents of the 1890s was a significant rise of more moderate opposition forces to the Spanish regime that could not be accommodated within the existing system, including Catalan regionalism and the development of republican, socialist, and trade union organizations. Muncipal elections had to be massively annulled and then suspended in 1893, 1895 and 1896 when early returns showed strong support for groups opposed to the restoration system, and in the 1891 and 1893 cortes elections republicans won over 30 seats, mostly from the cities, where election rigging was becoming increasingly difficult in the face of a more aroused and articulate public opinion. The growing Spanish crisis was greatly intensified by the disastrous defeat by the United States in 1898. Middle-class shopkeepers and businessmen increasingly joined the rising opposition tide thereafter, demanding a general democratic "regeneration" of Spanish politics and society.

Spain endured almost constant crisis and violence after 1900, with hardly a year going by without martial law being imposed somewhere in the country. The first major social conflicts of the new century were a series of strikes in Barcelona in 1901-1903, including a week-long general strike of 80,000 workers in February 1902, and enormous, mostly rural, strikes in Andalusia in 1902-1905. In each case the government responded with massive repression, including hundreds of arrests and the closure of scores of unions, workers centers, and newspapers. Amidst the continuing repression, a genuine attempt at conservative reform was attempted by Prime Minister Francisco Silvela (1899-1900, 1902-1903), one of the few Spanish political leaders who wanted an end to electoral corruption and a modernization of the tax and economic systems. However, the entrenched interests blocked any meaningful reform, leading Silvela to resign from politics after the failure of his second ministry, declaring, "You see before you a man who has lost faith and hope" (Carr 1966: 480).

A resumption of terrorist bombings after 1904 considerably added to Spanish political tensions. In 1906, an assassination attempt on King Alfonso XIII (1886-1931) killed 23 people and seriously injured over 100. Barcelona was plagued with a series of mysterious bombings that continued even after the arrest and execution of the police informant and bomb perpetrator Juan Rull. Conservative Prime Minister Antonio Maura's (1907-1909) proposal in early 1908 to give the government sweeping administrative power to suppress the anarchist movement and expel and jail all those who wrote or spoke on behalf of anarchistic ideas aroused a storm of opposition. In opposing the bill, the Liberals, for the first time since 1875, agreed to work with republicans and other groups outside the system. Maura was forced to withdraw the bill and to restore constitutional government in Barcelona, which had been suspended when the measure was proposed.

Maura, who deeply antagonized broad segments of Spanish society by his authoritarian manner, was brought down in the aftermath of a major uprising in Barcelona in July 1909 in protest of the calling up of Catalan reserves to support the army's blundering adventures in Morocco. Bitterness among the Barcelona working class had been inflamed by the continued operation of a conscription system that bore only on the poor, a decade-long depression in the Catalan textile industry and the apparent pointlessness of the Moroccan war, which was generally believed to serve only the mineral interests of the large capitalists and perhaps also the financial interests of the Jesuits. Even the conservative newspaper La Correspondencia de Espana, declared on July 12 that there was no purpose to the conflict, "unless it be to spend a hundred million or more pesetas that are badly needed at home and could serve no purpose in Morocco at all" (Payne 1967: 107). Another factor in whipping up working-class anger in Catalonia was the vicious and demagogic anti-clerical agitation of the republicans under Alexander Lerroux, who sought to attract support from the poor while diverting their anger away from the middle class, a goal made relatively easy by decades of blind adherence to reactionary causes by the Catholic heirachy. During the "Tragic Week" (Semana Trágica) about 30,000 protesters controlled the streets of Barcelona, raised barricades, burned and sacked about 80 Catholic churches, monasteries and welfare institutions and murdered several clerics. After taking no significant action for three days, troops and police put down the rioting with great severity, killing 104 civilians and wounding 300, and suffering 8 deaths and 124 injuries themselves. In the aftermath of the Tragic Week, martial law was maintained throughout Spain until late September and in Catalonia until early November. Almost all private secular schools in Catalonia were closed, and local unions, opposition papers and left-wing political clubs were suppressed. About 2,000 people were arrested, of whom five were executed, 59 received life jail terms, and over 400 were handed shorter jail terms or other punishments. One of those executed, after a farcical trial, was the well-known anarchist theoretician and educator Francisco Ferrar, founder of the violently anti-clerical Escuela Moderna ("modern school") in Barcelona. Although Ferrar undoubtedly favored a revolutionary overthrow of the Spanish government and his prior activities helped fuel the climate that led to the Tragic Week, he was not in Barcelona during the largely spontaneous disturbances and his execution amounted to a judicial murder. (Recently uncovered evidence does suggest Ferrar was the "master mind behind the 1905 and 1906 attempts on the life of Alfonso XIII" [Maura 1968: 142].) Ferrar's execution on October 13, 1909 sparked massive protest demonstrations across Europe--15,000 turned out in Paris--and a chorus of demands from the Liberals and republicans for Maura's resignation. Although Maura retained a parliamentary majority, Alfonso XIII forced him out in mid-October.

The new Liberal prime minister, Segismundo Moret, ended martial law in Catalonia and granted a general amnesty to the imprisoned rebels of the Tragic Week before giving way in February 1910 to the reformist Liberal José Canalejas. Canalejas eased the tax burden on the poor and ended the discriminatory draft system in favor of universal military service, but by 1910 divisions in Spanish society were beyond repair. A national anarcho-syndicalist union, the National Confederation of Labor (CNT in Spanish), attracted delegates representing 30,000 workers to its first congress in September 1911. The congress immediately called a general strike in Bilbao to support local strikers and protest the continuing Moroccan

war.  The general strike gained the reluctant support of the Spanish
socialists and soon spread over much of Spain.  Canalejas responded by
imposing martial law throughout the country, closing CNT and
socialist meeting halls, suppressing the anarchist press, and imposing
partial censorship on the rest of the print media.  Scores of labor
militants throughout Spain, including 500 in Barcelona alone, were
arrested.  Strike leaders were given heavy sentences, and five
anarchists were given the death penalty (later commuted to life
imprisonment) for their role in a full-scale insurrection at Cullera,
near Valencia.  The CNT was declared illegal by a Barcelona judge in
October 1911, forcing it underground for three years.  In 1912
Canalejas broke a railroad strike by drafting 12,000 workers and
placing them under military discipline.  In November 1912, he was
assassinated by an anarchist, sparking a new general crackdown.

After the assassination of Canalejas, the disintegration of the
Spanish political system rapidly intensified.  Both the Liberals and
Conservatives split in two, and in the elections of early 1914 a
government failed to win a majority in the elections it administered
for the first time since 1840.

Hungary.  Hungarian politics, protected throughout the 1870-1914
period by a franchise that excluded about 95 per cent of the
population, usually focused on sterile and ultimately phony debates on
the so-called Issue of Public Law (a közjogi kérdés)--the relationship
between Hungary and the Habsburg Monarchy.  Although supposedly
what was at issue were disagreements between the dominant party
that defended the 1867 Ausgleich (known at first as the Party of 1867
and later as the Liberal party) and opposition parties that demanded
greater or even complete independence from Austria, in fact the
opposition groups essentially consisted of "an embittered political
counter-class of 'outs' whose members shared the fundamental
philosophical premises of the 'ins,' but who wanted to get their share
of the spoils of the state, and hoped to accomplish this by changing the
terms of the Compromise of 1867" (Janos 1982: 134).  One striking
indicator of the lack of any real difference between the parties was
that during the 30 years of unbroken Liberal party rule between 1875
and 1905, a total of at least 250 parliamentary deputies defected from
the Liberals to the opposition and subsequently returned!

After 1870, the ruling Party of 1867 rapidly lost popular support,
resulting from growing opposition to the Ausgleich, internal
factionalization, a series of bad harvests, scandals and budget deficits,
and the disastrous 1873 financial crash, which threatened the
government with bankruptcy and brought it to the brink of total
collapse.  These events, combined with the fears created by the Paris
Commune, the emergence of several rapidly suppressed socialist and
workers' groups, and continuing unrest in Croatia seemed to pose the
possibility of a general lower-class upheaval.  Faced with this
increasingly critical situation, the Party of 1867 opened negotiations
with the leading anti-Ausgleich group, known as the Left Center.  The
latter realized after the notoriously corrupt 1872 elections that it

could never gain power in a constitutional manner, knew that any attempt to implement its program would only lead to Austrian military intervention, and feared that its continuing opposition would encourage the lower classes and ethnic minorities. The falseness of the Hungarian political debate was clearly and suddenly exposed in early 1875 when the two parties agreed to merge, accept the Ausgleich, and rule as the Liberal party. Although a majority of the population--if one includes the ignored and oppressed lower classes and ethnic minorities--unquestionably opposed the regime, as most probably did a majority of the voting population, Liberal party Prime Minister Kálmán Tisza (1875-90) and his successors were able to maintain power through a system of institutionalized and massive electoral corruption, based on the restricted franchise, the open ballot, gerrymandering, and bizarre, intricate, and often forceful methods of bribery and intimidation. As part of the negotiations leading up to the 1875 merger, the franchise was reduced in 1874 from about 6.5 to about 5.1 per cent of the population, and the domination of the Liberal party was further assured by a massive gerrymander effected in 1877.

While the interests of the landowners and businessmen were tended by the Liberal party, the needs of the urban and rural masses for social justice were ignored and demands of the ethnic minorities for fair treatment were summarily and sometimes brutally rejected. Although non-Magyars composed about 45 per cent of the population of Hungary (excluding Croatia) and formed the majority in many counties, they were never appointed to a single top county administrative position and, partly because of discriminatory suffrage laws, never gained a majority in a single county legislature. In the Hungarian diet, excluding the Croatian seats, non-Magyars held only about 10 of the over 400 seats.

Although the 1868 nationalities law promised public education in the native tongue of ethnic groups, the schools were almost totally Magyar in language, and Magyar was the only language used in the courts and the postal, telegraph, and railway service. Even danger notices were in Magyar only. After the Liberal party came to power, efforts by the nationalities to organize their own institutions and gain concessions often met severe reprisals, especially in the case of the 25 per cent of the population that was Slovakian or Rumanian. Privately financed Slovakian secondary schools were shut down, while the Rumanian national flag and Rumanian songs were outlawed. Scores of Rumanian children were expelled from school for using their native tongues there or speaking it "ostentatiously" in the streets. Slovakian and Rumanian nationalists, including journalists, were frequently given savage prison terms, as in the case of a Slovak leader who was jailed for noting that the "non-Magyar peasant stood like an ox, dumb before the courts of his native land" (Seton-Watson 1934: 398). A journalist was jailed for a year in 1888 for writing such comments as, "From day to day there are increasing signs that the Rumanians are awakening and understand the patriot's voice" (Seton-Watson 1972: 442).

In Croatia, there was an extremely serious and violent revolt in

1883, reflecting festering dissatisfaction with the 1868 Nagodba and its frequent violation by Hungary and intense rural distress resulting from declining farm prices and an enormous increase in the tax load, amounting to 118 per cent in the 1868-78 period alone. Thousands of peasants, mostly armed with farm implements, seized and held important provincial centers in Croatia for about a month before troops put down the revolt, killing 34 and arresting over 1,000. The Croat constitution was suspended and a new ban, Károlyi Khuen-Hédérváry (1883-1903) was appointed. For the next 20 years, Khuen-Hédérváry ruled Croatia with an iron hand, under the slogan, "Work, Order and Law." The press was severely restricted and the Sabor controlled by reducing the suffrage to 45,000 in a population of 2.5 million, using Hungarian-style electoral corruption, expelling dissidents and setting Serbs and Croats against each other. "Behind the fair facade of constitutionalism, Khuen-Hédérváry exercised the powers of an Oriental despot" (May 1968: 266).

Although Kálmán Tisza's 15-year authoritarian reign as Hungarian prime minister ended in 1890, as he grew tired of the continued demands by Magyar nationalists for revision of the Ausgleich, his resignation led to no fundamental changes in the regime. Thus, in 1894 Rumanians living in Transylvania were prosecuted for "incitement against the Magyar nationality" for having brought an appeal for redress of grievances to Emperor Franz Joseph in 1892 (which he had refused to read). Fourteen Rumanians were sentenced to a total of 32 years in jail and the Rumanian National Committee was ordered dissolved. The prosecution became a European cause célèbre and a great blow to Hungarian stature in the eyes of European public opinion: the Hungarian prosecutor told one of the accused at the end of the trial, "You are the condemned, but we are the vanquished" (Seton-Watson 1934: 415).

Socialist and trade union movements, which had been weakened during the pre-1890 period by governmental harassment (including stiff anti-anarchist legislation in the 1880s), internal squabbling, and the small size of the industrial work force, continued to suffer considerable persecution after 1890, although they were usually able to carry on some activities. Peasant demonstrations in central Hungary in 1891 and 1894 were put down with considerable bloodshed and the imposition of martial law. During the brutal ministry of Baron Dezsö Banffy (1895-9), freedom of speech and assembly were harshly curbed. During the 1896 elections, opposition candidates were jailed and 32 people were killed and over 70 wounded as a result of disorders and military repression.

Large-scale harvest strikes in the summer of 1897, involving tens of thousands of workers, were met with martial law, mass arrests and bloodshed, and press prosecutions. The leader of the movement, the socialist István Varkonyi, was jailed in early 1898, and his organization collapsed when his newspaper was suppressed; all delegates to a scheduled national congress were arrested; and all travel across the country was banned. During the 1897-8 disturbances, an estimated 51 workers were killed, 114 were wounded and sentences of over 170 years in jail were handed out for political agitation. In 1898 the Hungarian diet completely outlawed all agrarian unions and strikes.

Although there was some easing of repression during the administration of Kálmán Szell (1899-1903)--for example national trade unions for industrial workers were allowed to form for the first time--Szell was forced out by Franz Joseph in June 1903 amidst a new debate on the question of "public law." Franz Joseph acted because Magyar nationalist obstruction in the Hungarian diet prevented Szell from gaining passage of a bill to expand the number of Hungarian army recruits to the common Habsburg army. The nationalists demanded concessions from Franz Joseph concerning organization of the army, notably the institution of Magyar rather than German as the language of command for Hungarian regiments, which the Emperor was not willing to make.

Szell was replaced by Croatian Ban Khuen-Hédérváry, whose departure from Croatia was accompanied by violent riots there by Serbs and Croats to protest Magyar oppression, as well as a peasant uprising against the great Croatian landlords. Martial law, which had been repeatedly invoked by Khuen-Hédérváry during his final years as ban, was reimposed after his departure; hundreds were arrested, and 10 people were reportedly killed by troops. In Budapest, Khuen-Hedervary had no more luck with the diet than had Szell. In November 1903, Franz Joseph turned to Kálmán Tisza's eldest son, István, with the understanding that Tisza would gain passage of an army expansion bill in return for concessions on many army issues, save for the retention of German as the sole language of command. Tisza soon showed he was a true Magyar in suppressing lower-class unrest. In 1904, he smashed a railroad strike by using troops and conscripting workers and placing them under military discipline; May 1905 harvest strikes were crushed by the arrest of over 5,000 workers, who were jailed in stables and pigsties when the prisons overflowed. However, Tisza was unable to overcome Magyar nationalist obstruction in the diet on the army issue, as deputies turned the parliamentary chamber into a shambles by wrecking ministerial benches and ripping woodwork from the walls.

In desperation, Tisza dissolved parliament and resorted to the truly extreme measure of allowing free elections in Hungary for the first time since 1867. "He decided to break the opposition by given them responsibility" (Stone 1967: 171). Although a broad and internally divided coalition of forces opposed to the Liberal party won the elections, Franz Joseph refused to accept their demands on the army language and other questions and, in violation of Hungarian constitutional practice, appointed a non-parliamentary ministry of obscure civil servants headed by Baron Geza Ferjérváry. Ferjérváry openly appealed to the lower classes and nationalities for support against the coalition. Restrictions on freedom of assembly and association were lifted and the socialists and trade unions were openly encouraged. Thus, in September 1905, the socialists organized without opposition from Ferjérváry a 24-hour general strike in Budapest that featured a demonstration of 100,000 for universal male suffrage.

Socialist party membership jumped from 53,000 to 130,000 between 1904 and 1906. An unprecedented wave of almost 1,500 strikes erupted in Hungary in 1905-1907, and a socialist agricultural union, which Ferjérváry authorized despite the 1898 law banning agrarian unions, recruited over 70,000 members within a year. On October 28, 1905 Ferjérváry played his trump card by endorsing universal male suffrage, thereby posing to the Magyar elite (among whom belonged most leaders of the coalition) the mortal threat of placing decisive power in the hands of the lower classes and nationalities. Meanwhile, Croat and Serb politicians in Croatia and Austrian-ruled Dalmatia and Istria sought to take advantage of the Hungarian confusion by burying their differences and drafting and endorsing the Fiume resolutions in late 1905. These resolutions offered support to the Magyar coalition as a counter to Ferjervary's courting of the lower classes, in return for democratic concessions in Croatia and loyal observance of the 1868 Nagodba. The coalition indicated support for the Fiume resolutions.

In February 1906, Franz Joseph, who had previously prorogued the coalition-controlled diet, used troops to dissolve that body forcibly. At this point, the coalition, thoroughly frightened by the rise of lower-class and Serbo-Croatian agitation, and especially by the prospect of suffrage reform, decided to settle with the emperor. In secret with the coalition, Franz Joseph agreed to appoint a coalition-based ministry under Alexander Wekerle (1906-10), and in return the coalition agreed to abandon its demand on the army language question, to increase military recruits, to collect taxes that had not been paid over the past year, and to expand the suffrage significantly.

Once in office the Wekerle coalition ministry violated its private promises to Franz Joseph to enact suffrage reform, its public promise to liberalize the Croatian regime and its campaign pledge to secure the use of Magyar for the command of Hungarian troops. The ministry was further characterized by extreme discrimination against the socialists and Slovak and Rumanian minorities. The 1898 ban on agricultural strikes and unions was stiffened in 1907, and the agricultural workers' union was reduced from 72,000 to 12,000 within a six-month period by severe persecution, including jail terms totalling over 18 years handed out to 700 laborers. Sentences totalling over 5 years were handed out to socialist journalists in 1907, while in 1906-1908 about 100 Slovaks and Rumanians, including several parliamentary deputies, were sentenced to a total of over 65 years in prison for various political offenses, including poems and newspaper articles. The October 1907 massacre at Csernova, in which troops who had been stoned by a crowd of protesting Slovak peasants killed 16 and wounded over 60, attracted widespread European indignation.

Little changed in Hungary after the Wekerle coalition ministry unravelled in early 1910 and the old Liberal party, reconstituted as the Party of Work, resumed power by the usual methods of electoral corruption under Khuen-Hédérváry (1910-12) and István Tisza (1912-17). Thus, according to socialist tallies, they suffered almost 1,000 indictments and jail sentences totalling 256 years in the immediate pre-war period. In 1914, 32 Hungarian Ruthenians were fined and sentenced to a total of almost 400 years in jail on charges of plotting to unite Ruthenian-populated lands with Russia.

Despite the severe repression, socialists were able to mobilize many thousands of protesters repeatedly for street demonstrations and solidarity strikes to demand suffrage expansion and other reforms. "This they did regularly between 1906 and 1913, when on at least a dozen occasions they shut down public utilities and means of public transportation and turned the streets of Budapest into a bloody battleground between themselves and the police" (Janos 1971: 42). Thus, in 1907, 200,000 turned out for a suffrage demonstration, and on May 23, 1912 ("Bloody Thursday") a huge suffrage protest and general strike led to severe rioting after troops fired on demonstrators, killing six and wounding over 200. In March 1913, the diet passed an absurdly inadequate suffrage bill, which extended the vote from about 6 to about 8 per cent of the population, leaving Hungary with the most restrictive franchise in Europe.

In Croatia, there was continual disorder and severe repression between 1906 and 1913. Huge demonstrations were held to protest the coalition's violation of its promises, and in the 1908 elections to the Sabor, Ban Baron Paul Rauch (1908-10) was unable to arrange the election of a single deputy who favored Hungarian governmental policies. For the next two years, all pretense of constitutionalism in Croatia was dispensed with, as Rauch indefinitely prorogued the Sabor, ruled by decree, censored the press and restricted freedom of assembly. Rauch's policy culminated in the notorious Agram (Zagreb) treason trial of March 1909, which was designed to curb the growing spirit of Serbo-Croatian cooperation and to tar the opposition with the charge of being the pawns of Serbian irredentists. Fifty-three Serbs and Croats were charged with conspiring to unite Croatia and Bosnia with Serbia, and 31 were convicted and given jail terms totalling 184 years. However, the scandalously unreliable nature of the evidence offered against them and the obvious bias of the court severely discredited Hungarian justice in the eyes of European public opinion, and the defendants were all freed on appeal.

A brief attempt was made to conciliate Croatia in 1910 when Khuen-Hédérváry appointed Nikola Tomásić as ban (1910-12). The Sabor was reconvened after two years of rule by decree and the Croatian franchise was increased from 45,000 to 190,000. However, after the October 1910 elections returned an opposition majority, Tomásić dissolved the Sabor and conducted new elections in December 1911 under conditions of extreme coercion. Newspapers were repeatedly confiscated; almost all opposition meetings were barred; and widespread arrests of opposition candidates and voters were made. However, Tomásić was able to win only 23 of the 88 Sabor seats and handed in his resignation. The new ban, Edward von Cuvaj (1912-13) dissolved the diet before it could even meet, confiscated 200 newspapers within a month, closed the University of Agram, and suspended the Croatian constitution in March 1912, following massive protest strikes by school children in Croatia, Dalmatia, and Bosnia.

Two attempts were made to assassinate Cuvaj, one of which wounded him severely.

Under István Tisza, Hungarian-Croatian relations were considerably eased when the liberal Baron Ivan Skerlecz replaced Cuvaj. Constitutional government was restored in Croatia in October 1913, and other concessions were made. In the December 1913 elections the Serbo-Croat coalition won control of the Sabor and thereafter became the government party.

<u>The Balkans.</u> The Balkans lacked a hereditary nobility (except in Rumania). They had only a small non-agricultural mercantile-industrial element during the 1870-1914 period because of economic retardation, which continued even after the emergence of independent states, following the long centuries of Turkish rule. Political power was held instead by squabbling urban-based professional politicians and ruling princes and kings who were concerned almost exclusively with political power and patronage and were almost totally ignorant of and unconcerned with the crying needs of the rural masses for credit and technical assistance. Except in Serbia after 1903 and in Greece after about 1880, the Balkan political systems were all based on rigged elections, and ultimately "real power lay in the police and the army" (Jelavich and Jelavich 1977: 170).

While the peasantry provided military conscripts and heavy taxes to support oversized armies, the bloated urban civil service, and overbuilt capital cities, they got virtually nothing back from the government. In Serbia, for example, less than 1 per cent of the state budget was devoted to agriculture in 1900, while in Bulgaria the military consumed more money in 1894 than spending for the ministries of education, interior, justice, commerce, and agriculture combined. A Bulgarian novelist writing in 1892 captured the general sense of peasant discontent resulting from such policies:

> The peasant has but the vaguest idea of our transition from servitude [Turkish control] to independent life; for him it matters little whether he pays tax to Akhmed or Ivan. In fact, Ivan is often more distasteful to him than Akhmed, for Akhmed could be more easily fooled or bribed; Akhmed did not take his son off as a soldier whereas Ivan does; Akhmed was naive and spoke Turkish, while Ivan is to all appearances a Christian like him, speaks Bulgarian, yet exacts more from him than did Akhmed. The meanings of state, rights and duties for the peasant adds up to tax-payment and sending his son off as a soldier (Stavrianos 1963: 208).

A popular Bulgarian saying was "Ot turkso, polosho" (Things were better under the Turks [Bell 1977: 4]).

The European-wide agricultural depression of 1873-96, rapid population growth and governmental neglect led to a deterioration of rural conditions everywhere in the Balkans after 1870. By 1900, about half of the rural families in Serbia and Bulgaria lacked enough land to support themselves. Conditions were unquestionably the worst in Rumania, where the system generally known as neoiobăgia ("neo-serfdom") was characterized by the peasant saying, "May God never lay upon a man as much as he can bear" (Mitrany 1968: 81). In Rumania, about 85 per cent of the peasantry was landless or held insufficient land to support themselves by 1905, while the population increase of 54 per cent between 1862 and 1905 allowed landlords to force wages down and to increase rents by an average of about 150 per cent.

The Rumanian political system remained extraordinarily rigid during the 1870-1914 period despite a rising tide of peasant protest that culminated in a massive uprising and bloodbath in 1907. The two major Rumanian parties, the Liberals and Conservatives, both of whom were based on the well-to-do landlords and merchants, established after 1870 a system of rotation in power essentially identical to that used in Spain in Portugal. The system was based on the highly discriminatory suffrage system of 1866 (which was imperceptibly modified in 1884), systematic election rigging, the existence of two parties whose differences were minimal compared to their tacit agreement to ignore the peasantry and uphold the status quo, and the cooperation of Prince Charles I (1866-1914, king after 1881). Since Charles was empowered to dissolve parliament and appoint new ministries that could always count on rigging the subsequent elections, he retained "in his own hand the power to drive each successive drove from the trough of office when its appetite seemed to him sufficiently appeased" (Seton-Watson 1934: 385).

Peasant discontent with this system, expressed in localized uprisings in 1888, 1889, 1894, 1900 and 1904, finally erupted on a mass scale in March 1907. Scores of thousands of peasants seized land, attacked the houses of the landlords and estate managers throughout the country, and in a number of cases murdered their oppressors. About 120,000 troops put the rebellion down by killing an estimated 10,000 peasants and razing entire villages to the ground. Many other peasants were arrested, as were several leading intellectuals who expressed sympathy for them, including the great historian Nicholas Iorga. Another thousand people were expelled from the country, among them Christian Rakovsky, a leader of the tiny Rumanian socialist movement, who was born in Bulgaria but had lived in Rumania since the age of seven. Although legislation designed to improve rural conditions was passed in the aftermath of the revolt, as had been the case with previous such measures it proved inadequate in conception or was sabotaged in execution, "fated to disappear without a trace in the quicksand of Rumania's public life" (Mitrany 1968: 89).

Bulgaria gained autonomy from Turkey as the result of the Russo-Turkish War of 1877-8 and the Berlin peace conference of 1878 (which also established the complete independence of the previously autonomous Turkish realms of Serbia and Rumania). The Russo-Turkish War followed an uprising in Bulgaria in mid-1876, which had been put down by the Turks after heavy fighting and followed by massive reprisals, including the sacking and burning of hundreds of villages and the slaughter of over 10,000 Bulgarians in cold blood. The so-called Bulgarian Horrors led to Russian intervention after Turkey refused to accept Russian demands for reform. They also stirred intense indignation throughout Europe, including scores of protest meetings in Britain and denunciations from many prominent writers and politicians, including William Gladstone, Victor Hugo, Leo Tolstoy, and Garibaldi.

In 1879, a Bulgarian constituent assembly, meeting at Turnovo--partly elected and partly appointed by a temporary Russian administration authorized by the Berlin Congress--adopted a constitution that was markedly more democratic than a draft prepared by Russian officials. Complete freedom of the press, assembly and association were established, as was a one-house legislature elected by universal male suffrage. A prince, to be elected by a special assembly, was empowered to convene and dissolve the legislature and appoint ministers who would be jointly responsible to the legislature and himself. The first prince, Alexander of Battenburg, of the royal house of the German state of Hesse-Darmstadt, nephew of Czar Alexander II of Russia, was in fact imposed by the great powers.

The 1879-81 period was characterized by a power struggle between Alexander, with support from the conservative faction that had been outvoted in the constituent assembly, and the dominant Liberal party. Alexander appointed a Conservative ministry after his 1879 arrival in Bulgaria. He dissolved the legislature and appointed another Conservative government after the Liberals won an overwhelming victory in the fall 1879 elections. When the elections of January 1880 returned an increased Liberal victory, Alexander, fearing intervention from the west European powers, was forced to appoint a Liberal government when Czar Alexander refused his repeated pleas for approval to suspend the constitution.

A change in Russian attitudes after the 1881 assassination of Alexander II allowed Prince Alexander to effect a coup d'état, suspending the 1879 constitution and dissolving the legislature in May 1881. Amidst the arrest of Liberal leaders and suppression of the opposition press, rigged elections were held for a new constituent assembly that empowered Alexander to rule by decree for seven years. Subsequently the universal male suffrage of 1879 was drastically reduced and a new cabinet was established, based on a coalition of Conservative politicians and Russian military officers who had dominated the Bulgarian army since 1878. Much to their dismay, Alexander and the Conservatives discovered that they had merely changed Liberal domination for Russian domination. In the fall of 1883, the Conservatives and Prince Alexander reached agreement with the Liberals to restore the 1879 constitution and establish a unity government to end Russian domination. The Russian generals resigned and after a short period of coalition government the May 1884 elections returned Petko Karavelov (1884-7) to power. Leader of the left-wing Liberals, he had been prime minister at the time of the 1881 coup.

The new Russian czar, Alexander III, was deeply offended by the events of 1883 and was even more outraged when in 1885, following an anti-Turkish uprising in the ethnically Bulgarian but Turkish-controlled region of Eastern Rumelia, Bulgaria annexed that territory. Czar Alexander could not accept the existence of an enlarged, non-Russian dominated Bulgaria. In mid-1886, pro-Russian Bulgarian army officers, acting with Russian knowledge and assistance, arrested Prince Alexander at gunpoint, forced him to abdicate and escorted him from the country. The pro-Russian regime that was then established was quickly overthrown by a popular revolt organized by Stefan Stambolov, a leader of the 1876 uprising and president of the legislature. Prince Alexander returned to Bulgaria, but abdicated again when Czar Alexander made clear his unremitting hostility.

From 1887 until 1894 Bulgaria was effectively ruled by Stambolov, who was easily able to dominate the new prince, Ferdinand of Saxe-Coburg. Ferdinand was inexperienced, almost totally ignorant of Bulgaria, and weakened by the refusal of the European powers to recognize him and by Czar Alexander's almost psychopathic hostility. Stambolov's rule was marked by repeated plots of Russian agents and their accomplices to overthrow the regime, including plans to assassinate both himself and Ferdinand, reminiscent of the People's Will campaign against Czar Alexander II a few years before. Stambolov's response to the Russian plots and other signs of opposition to his government, both violent and non-violent, was brutal and ruthless repression. At least 14 persons implicated in Russian-inspired plots were executed, while hundreds of other suspects in plots and other political opponents were arrested, beaten, tortured and/or fired from posts. Elections were grossly fraudulent, with troops and bands of hired thugs "encouraging" opposition voters not to show up.

Prince Ferdinand, who increasingly resented Stambolov's domination, engineered the latter's ouster in May 1894. Stambolov was subsequently subjected to a campaign of unmerciful government harassment and was murdered in July 1895 under circumstances that suggested, to some, Ferdinand's involvement. However, the general level of political violence and repression seems to have declined after Ferdinand took over, although the level of corruption probably increased. Political prisoners were amnestied and the Socialist party, forced to operate clandestinely under Stambolov, was allowed to function openly. For the rest of Ferdinand's reign, until 1918, Bulgarian political power rested almost totally in his hands, as he encouraged party factionalism, played political leaders against each other and made all dependent upon his power to appoint ministries and allow them to rig elections.

Opposition to the Bulgarian system of artificial politics, vast corruption, and neglect of the peasantry grew considerably after the 1890s. In 1900, imposition of a tithe on agricultural produce in Bulgaria following a series of catastrophic harvests provoked intense indignation among the peasantry, as did the illegal removal of locally elected officials who opposed the measure. Huge protest demonstrations were held throughout the country, especially in northeastern Bulgaria. After peasants forcibly resisted attempts to arrest protest leaders in late April, a large area of northeastern Bulgaria was placed under martial law, and over 500 peasants were arrested. The most violent clashes in the 1900 tithe protests came at Shabla-Durankulak, near Dobrich in northeastern Bulgaria, on June 1, 1900. Thousands of peasants resisted arrest attempts against a local mayor and efforts to collect the tithe. After several soldiers were killed by a volley from the peasant lines, the troops went on a five-hour rampage, killing 90 peasants, wounding over 400 and arresting hundreds more.

Although the tithe was repealed in 1901, the so-called Second Stambolovist Regime of 1903-1908 in Bulgaria provoked another upsurge of protest, reflecting opposition to widespread corruption, increased press and police controls, harassment of unions and opposition parties and a doubling of indirect taxes. Partly under the influence of the 1905 Russian revolution and partly in protest against the harsh policies of the regime, a wave of about 270 strikes erupted in Bulgaria in 1905-1907. In December 1906-January 1907, a 42-day railway strike took place, to which the government responded by evicting numerous workers' families from state-owned houses in mid-winter and conscripting into the army all railway workers of military age. Opposition to the regime climaxed in January 1907, when thousands of Sofia University students and striking railwaymen hissed Prince Ferdinand at the opening of the newly completed National Theatre in Sofia. The government responded by closing the university, firing several professors, expelling, jailing, and drafting many students, and tightening restrictions on civil liberties. In March 1907 Prime Minister Dmitar Petkov (1906-1907) was assassinated in apparent retaliation.

Ferdinand switched to a new party and policy in early 1908, leading to a reopening of Sofia University and a return of the expelled students of 1907, along with an easing of press censorship. However, the usual election rigging continued and Ferdinand continued to bolster his own power, taking advantage of the 1908 revolution in Turkey to declare Bulgaria's complete independence and grant himself the title of czar. Bulgaria's disastrous defeat in the Second Balkan War of 1913 greatly rejuvenated the opposition to Ferdinand. In the 1913 elections the administering party failed to win a majority for the first time in Ferdinand's reign. Ferdinand refused to appoint a new ministry and dissolved the opposition-controlled legislature when it refused to approve his budget. Despite the use of extraordinary pressure in the March 1914 elections, including the kidnapping of opposition candidates and the annulment of some results, the government was able to gain only a slim majority of seats.

In Serbia, although there was a great deal of superficial political change between 1870 and 1903, below the surface the regime remained essentially a police state controlled by the Obrenović dynasty, usually with the cooperation of palace political cliques. Theoretically liberal constitutions adopted in 1869, 1889, and 1901, as well as seemingly democratic laws concerning the press, assembly and association passed in the 1880s made little difference in practice, since most elections were rigged and civil liberties were often suspended when the government felt endangered. The first Serbian socialist writer, Svetozar Markovic, had his newspaper suppressed in 1872 after he defended the Commune, and was arrested in 1874 for criticizing the government in another paper. He was given an 18-month jail term (reduced to 9 months on appeal) after a widely publicized trial in 1874 that attracted hundreds of spectators. Markovic fled into exile in 1875 upon his release when the government made it·clear he would otherwise be prosecuted again for his continued journalistic endeavors.

Prince Milan Obrenović (1868-89, king after 1882) and his son and successor Alexander Obrenović (1889-1903) devoted most of their energies to their scandalous personal lives and attempting to block from power the peasant-based Radical party, which in the early 1880s developed into the first mass political party in Serbian history. In 1883, for example, after the Radicals won an overwhelming Skupština majority, King Milan refused to appoint a Radical ministry. When he subsequently issued a decree confiscating all private arms (whose possession was a long-standing Serbian tradition), a wide area in northeastern Serbia exploded in the so-called Timok Rebellion. The revolt took a week to crush, and led to 90 death sentences (of which 20 were carried out) and over 600 jail terms. In the 1886 elections, massive police pressure and the annulment of 24 mandates was required to block the Radicals from a legislative majority. In June 1899, an assassination attempt against Milan, who remained a power behind the throne even after his abdication in 1889, was used by King Alexander as an excuse for a general proscription of the Radicals, who were the only effective political force left in Serbia because of Alexander's highly repressive policies. Martial law was maintained in Belgrade for six weeks, and Radicals were subjected to courts-martial and administrative exile. About a dozen top Radical leaders, including the future prime minister Nikola Pašić, were given long jail terms despite the lack of any evidence tying them to the assassination attempt.

Although Milan abdicated in 1889 in frustration after losing the support of even the palace politicians, and a highly liberal constitution was adopted in that year, Alexander's policies were more arbitrary and authoritarian than his father's, especially after a military coup was effected by Alexander in 1893 with Milan's help. Public meetings, political parties and press freedom were abolished or subjected to crippling restrictions, and repeated purges of the civil service were effected as Alexander's political moods shifted. In 1894, he revoked the 1889 constitution in favor of the more restrictive 1869 document, then promulgated a more liberal constitution in 1901, which he suspended for 45 minutes (!) in 1903 in order to dismiss parliament and impose new restrictions on civil liberties.

Opposition to Alexander mushroomed after his July 1900 marriage to a woman of extremely bad reputation. Protest meetings in Belgrade were brutally dispersed in March 1902 and March 1903, and the elections of May 1903 were held under such extreme conditions of police terror that most politicians boycotted them. Finally, on the night of June 10/11 1903 a group of army officers stormed the royal palace and murdered the king and queen. A provisional government including conspirators and leaders of the political parties was formed, and the Skupština elected as king Peter Karageorgević, son of Prince Alexander Karageorgević, who had been deposed in 1858. Subsequently, Serbia enjoyed free elections, parliamentary government, a free press and other civil liberties. King Peter (1903-31), who had translated John Stuart Mill's On Liberty into Serbo-Croatian, ruled as a genuine constitutional monarch, in marked contrast to past Serbian rulers.

The major flaw in the new Serbian democracy was the government's inability to cleanse the army of conspiratorial elements that had brought the new regime to power and were willing to act on their own to further Serbian irredentism violently. One such group, the Black Hand, furnished pistols and bombs to Serbian irredentist groups in Austrian-controlled Bosnia-Herzegovina that were used in the June 1914 assassination at Sarajevo, which touched off World War I. Although the Black Hand effectively operated as a state within a state, Prime Minister Pašić (1906-1908, 1909-11, 1912-19), "feared this secret organization and dared not oppose it too openly for fear the same thing might happen to him" as to King Alexander (Stavrianos 1958: 551).

Greece, especially after 1875, was by far the least repressive of the Balkan states, except for Serbia after 1903. Yet the Greek government displayed only a little more energy or concern for popular needs than elsewhere in the Balkans. There was a rising tide of agitation in Greece in the early 1870s against King George's repeated resort to minority or extra-parliamentary governments and what was viewed as the king's role in perpetuating the Greek system of political paralysis and corruption. A young Greek politican, Charilaos Tricoupis, attracted great public attention and became a liberal hero when he was jailed in the summer of 1874 after publishing a newspaper article that attacked the king's policies. In 1875, amidst rising anti-dynastic agitation, King George called on Tricoupis to form a government, accepting Tricoupis's conditions that fair elections be held and that only majority parties henceforth be called upon to govern. The first fair elections in modern Greek history resulted in a defeat for Tricoupis but the theoretical principal of parliamentary responsibility was thus established. Although electoral corruption declined thereafter, the lack of coherent parties continued to make establishing and maintaining a majority government difficult. The result was that Greece had 13 different ministries between 1875 and 1882.

Between 1882 and 1897 a quasi-two-party system developed, with Tricoupis and Theodor Deliyannis alternating in power after free elections. Tricoupis's party favored concentrating on the internal modernization and economic development of Greece, while Deliyannis stressed demagogic agitation of Greek irredentist causes. The Tricoupis-Deliyannis system did not break completely with the former regime, since personal loyalties still played a major role and switching back and forth between the parties was common. Sometimes the ideological differences between the parties was mostly for public consumption: Deliyannis once defined his philosophy as being "against everything Tricoupis is for" (Dakin 1972: 141). To the extent the ideological differences were real, the two politicians tended to checkmate each other. Greece did not have the resources to support irredentism, while the continued high military expenditures that resulted from Deliyannis's agitation drained away resources desperately needed for the internal development that Tricoupis favored.

Tricoupis was able to make some progress in developing Greece's railways and merchant marine, and especially in curbing brigandage, cleaning up Greek elections and curbing the former practice of wholesale purges of the civil service with each change in the government. Repressive incidents were relatively rare, at least partly because there was virtually no radical opposition. However, journalists such as the satirical poet George Souris were occasionally prosecuted for criticizing the king, and the tiny socialist party suffered harassment, as in the 1894 martyrdom of socialist leader Kallergis, who was imprisoned for organizing a large May Day demonstration in Athens.

Greek politics plunged into severe crisis as a result of the sound defeat by Turkey in 1897. The war stemmed from Deliyannis's hope to exploit an anti-Turkish revolt in Crete in favor of union with Greece. This fiasco and the Greek failure to make irredentist gains in Crete and Macedonia fostered a growing sense, especially among the middle classes, students, and elements of the military, that only a major reform of political life could create a nation strong in domestic and foreign affairs. This belief intensified as Greek politics after Tricoupis's death in 1896 returned to the pre-1882 pattern of multiple parties, characterized by personalistic leadership, demagoguery, corruption and an almost exclusive focus on patronage. This system produced eight elections and 11 ministries between 1897 and 1909. A British observer noted in 1902, "No difference of principle divides one party from the other; ... the difference is of men, not measures--the sweets of office versus the cold shades of opposition" (Papacosma 1977: 17).

A severe economic depression in 1908 and the example of the modernizing revolution effected in that year by the Turkish military greatly intensified discontent, especially among Greek army elements who had grievances related to pay, promotions, and the dominant role of members of the royal family in military affairs. On August 28, 1909, 5,500 soldiers organized in the Military League demonstrated near Athens for reforms. The military demands, which were supported a month later by a popular demonstration of 50,000 people in Athens, brought about the resignation of the government of Demetrios Rallis (1908-09) and led to a one-year period of thinly disguised military rule. Under pressure from the Military league, the Greek parliament passed a series of mild reforms. That the military did not favor any drastic reshaping of Greek society was demonstrated in March 1910, when five peasants were killed and 35 wounded by troops during unarmed protests demanding land reform.

By early 1910, amidst growing popular disillusionment and internal divisions, the Military League leaders began searching for a way to return power to civilian politicians. They turned for guidance to Eleutherios Venizelos, a Greek nationalist politician from Crete, in tacit recognition that they lacked the expertise needed to direct political affairs. The league agreed to dissolve when King George accepted Venizelos's proposal to elect a national assembly that would revise the constitution. Between 1910 and 1912 the assembly passed a series of moderately reformist laws and constitutional amendments, including the establishment of free, compulsory elementary education, factory health, safety and hours legislation, expansion of civil liberties guarantees and numerous social reforms, including a progressive income tax, improved security of civil service tenure and land reform in Thessaly, which was dominated by large estates.

Although Venizelos's reforms were progressive he was far more opportunistic than principled. A new generation of middle-class bourgeois politicians emerged under Venizelos, but his regime failed to really break the old Greek pattern of clientele, patronage, and personalistic-based politics. Thus, the considerable expansion of the state apparatus under his supervision and improved security of civil service tenure "meant in practice the disbursement of valuable patronage and the establishment of an apparently permanent public service very largely Venizelist in its loyalties" (Campbell and Sherrard 1968: 116). On the whole, his reforms were designed mostly to fend off demands for more fundamental change.

Those who failed to show the proper appreciation faced severe reprisals. Attempts by the tiny Greek socialist movement to organize met persecution and jailing. In response to a series of militant strikes, in some cases featuring clashes with police and troops, which shook Greece between 1911 and 1916, the government inaugurated a large-scale persecution of trade union activists, including the jailing and ill-treatment of many, police shootings of strikers, and the sacking of trade union offices.

Reform and Repression in Central Europe, 1870-1914
Both geographically and politically, Italy, Germany, and Austria constituted a transition zone between the relatively democratic countries of northwestern Europe and the politically repressive regimes of southern and eastern Europe. In addition Austria and Italy were economically "in between" the industrially advanced northwestern European region and the economically backwards lands of southern and eastern Europe. Germany, on the other hand, was the leading continental European industrial power. By 1914, Germany, Italy, and Austria had adopted social welfare legislation comparable to that in northwestern Europe, but repressive political controls maintained by these regimes were far more restrictive and long-lived than in the northwest (although, especially after 1900, not nearly so

strict as those in southern and eastern Europe). Thus, the three-class voting system was maintained in Prussia until 1918 and until after 1905 Austria and Italy maintained extremely restrictive electoral systems. Parliamentary responsibility was never established before World War I in Austria or Germany, and election rigging was a feature of Italian balloting throughout the 1870-1914 period. In Austria and Germany controls of the press were far harsher than those in northwestern Europe throughout the period, and in Germany this was also the case with regard to freedom of association. Yet, there was a general trend towards an easing of repression. In particular, the expiration of laws and cancellation of states of emergency that for years had made socialist and trade union activity illegal were major reforms in Germany in 1890, in Austria in 1891, and in Italy in 1900. In Austria in 1896 and 1907 and in Italy in 1912, there were also significant electoral reforms.

Ruling elites in central Europe seem to have responded to rising lower-class unrest after 1870 with a mixture of reform and repression mostly out of fear: fear that without repression a lower-class takeover or uprising was inevitable, and fear that without some reforms repression alone could no longer hold back the tide. In each country governmental fears were stoked by radical rhetoric, and, in Austria and Italy, sporadic violence, by lower-class militants during the 1870-1900 period, but in each there was a considerable easing of such militancy after trade unions and socialists were allowed to openly function. Although, except in Germany, this lessened militancy fostered further relaxation of repressive controls after 1900, in none of the central European countries did working class groups have a fair chance of gaining significant governmental power or influence before 1914.

Italy. The completion of Italian unity with the annexation of Rome in September 1870, after the withdrawal of French forces during the war with Prussia, was followed by a growing sense of popular disillusionment, expressed in the popular saying, "Si stava meglio quando si stava peggio" (We were better off when things were worse)(Hughes 1967: 3). While before 1870 the major difference between the conservative or Destra (right) party and the Party of Action or Sinistra (left) had focussed on varying approaches to the Roman question, after that date the two groups became increasingly indistinguishable. This is not surprising, since only 2 per cent of the population could vote and both parties were based on the upper and upper middle classes. It was said, with considerable truth, that the Italian government stood for the rule "over 30 millions, by 3,000, for the benefit of 300,000" (Hughes 1965: 53).

In theory, the Sinistra was more anti-clerical and more supportive of the poor and the problems of southern Italy than the Destra; in practice the Sinistra's real objection to the Destra after 1870 was that the Destra had held power continually since 1860 and intended to keep it, while the Sinistra was willing to side with all discontented elements in hopes of alleviating its own discontent, namely, that it was out of power. The Sinistra's task was made considerably easier by poor economic conditions in Italy in the early 1870s, a general feeling that Destra rule was lacking in excitement and romance, and the grievances of the southerners and the rural and urban poor, who endured terrible conditions and responded with widespread peasant revolts in 1871 and even more widespread rioting in 1873-4. A significant factor leading to the growing unpopularity of the Destra was its harsh attitude toward civil liberties. Prime ministers Giovanni Lanza (1869-73) and Marco Minghetti (1873-76) generally acted upon the principle "prevenire, non reprimere" (prevention, not repression), which meant heading off disorder by restricting freedom of assembly and association and making preventive arrests.

Repressive measures were enforced especially harshly in Sicily, where separatist and pro-Bourbon sentiment was widespread and terrorist and Mafia activities were carried out under the protection of local elites and with the cloaks of a climate of fear and a conspiracy of silence. The government resorted there to thousands of arbitrary arrests and jailings without trial of Bourbonists, clericals, republicans, Internationalists, and anyone else deemed unreliable. In 1875 Minghetti gained parliamentary sanction for an exceptional law that legalized many of these practices, including such tactics as the use of preventive arrest, house arrest, limitations upon movement, and administrative deportation.

On the Italian mainland, the major target of preventive repression was the International, whose Italian membership grew from about 5,000 to 30,000 between 1871 and 1874 amidst deteriorating economic conditions and a burst of enthusiasm for the vaguely understood Commune. The Italian International was subjected to intense police surveillance and sporadic persecution during the 1871-3 period, although its members were solely involved in propaganda, organizing and strike activities at that time. Thus, in June 1871, the International section in Florence was dissolved by the police on the grounds that it was too sympathetic to the Paris Commune, "the declared enemy of every government and the subverter of all social order"; a few months later the key Naples section suffered a similar fate when the interior minister termed the group a "permanent offense to the laws and fundamental institutions of the nation, as well as an obvious danger to public order" (Hostetter 1958: 157, 173).

The government was severely discredited in 1874 when a group of prominent republicans meeting at the Villa Ruffi near Rimini were arrested. They had to be released after being held for five months since there was no case against them. A few days after the Villa Ruffi arrests, a group within the International (which had been driven underground by widespread arrests and dissolutions in 1873) led a revolt at Bologna, which quickly fell apart when less than 200 of an expected 3,000 conspirators showed up and were quickly dispersed by troops. In the aftermath of the Bologna fiasco, the International in Italy was crippled by suppression of its press, dissolution of surviving sections and the arrest of several hundred members. Similar measures were invoked against several republican groups. Yet the government was so discredited by the economic situation, the Villa Ruffi arrests, and the general post-1870 dissillusionment that despite intense administrative pressure the Sinistra made striking gains in the November 1874 elections. Further, all of the Internationalists involved in the Bologna rising were acquitted in a series of trials in 1875-6.

In March 1876, the Destra government fell as the result of an internal split, and, for the first time, King Victor Emmanuel II asked a leader of the Sinistra, Agostino Depretis (prime minister 1876-8, 1878-9, 1881-7) to form a ministry. Although the Sinistra had strongly criticized the Destra for civil liberties abuses, the November 1876 elections, conducted by Sinistra Interior Minister Giovanni Nicotera, surpassed all records for administrative pressure. After obtaining the desired majority (380 of 510 seats), Nicotera pursued a policy of harsh repression against radical and clerical elements, including severe limitations on public assemblies, suppression of some newspapers and the bribery of others, and the deportation of labor agitators to penal colonies. Although a strong faction within the International attempted to return to open and peaceful methods in the aftermath of the 1875-6 acquittals, another small group decided to return to the insurrectionary path and organized a new uprising at San Lupo, near Benevento, on April 8, 1877. The 26 anarchists who showed up were driven into the nearby hills and captured after a few days by police and troops who were well aware of their plans. The San Lupo rising was followed by the outlawing of the Italian International, wholesale dissolution of its sections, closure of socialist meeting halls, arrests of its leaders and confiscation or banning of socialist newspapers, measures that were applied to both the insurrectionist and legalitarian wings of the organization. However, after Nicotera was replaced in December 1877, when it was revealed he had been tapping private telegraph messages, a new ministry under Benedetto Cairoli announced a policy of "Repression, not prevention," and all those arrested at San Lupo were either acquitted or released under a political amnesty granted by the new king, Humbert I (1878-1900).

The new tolerant policy was soon discredited by a series of terrorist incidents in November 1878. On November 17, a man tried to kill the king in Naples, and within a few days bombs were thrown into a monarchist parade in Florence, killing four people, and into a crowd in Pisa. Although only the Pisa bombing was linked with an Internationalist--the Florence bomb may have been thrown by an agent provocateur--public opinion blamed the International for all three incidents. Cairoli was forced out and a new Depretis ministry returned to the previous approach. This time the International was totally destroyed by a new wave of arrests, trials, dissolutions and administratively imposed sanctions.

During Depretis's almost continuous rule between 1878 and 1887 and the following Sinistra ministry of Francesco Crispi (1887-1891), the differences between the Destra and Sinistra continued to erode. What became known as trasformismo, a system that was to dominate Italian politics until World War I, developed. Under trasformismo the artificiality of the two-party system was recognized by the open invitation of Depretis and Crispi to Destra members to join the government, with the understanding that patronage and spending policies would be adjusted to reward the "transformed deputy." The common fear of the Destra and Sinistra of the extreme clericals on the right and the republicans and working class radicals on the left was far more powerful than any remaining differences between them. Thus, they "laid aside their internal quarrels and joined in parcelling out power and jobbery" (Smith 1959: 111).

Trasformismo both reflected and systematically reinforced the elimination of issues, especially those relevant to the needs of the poor and the south, from Italian political life. The line between the government and opposition became increasingly blurred, and since the government always won elections through administrative manipulation and trasformismo buy-offs, no deputy could ever hope to gain influence except by joining the system. Although when out of power the Sinistra had indicated it would be attentive to the problems of the south and poor, once in office the Sinistra continued the Destra practice of forming alliances with local elites and turning a blind eye, especially in the south, to continuing corruption and exploitation of the poor. In short, the coming to power of the left after 1876 made little difference to most Italians and merely reinforced the general image of parliament as a squalid setting for what the opposition deputy Felice Cavallotti termed a politics of "acrobatics, optical tricks, petty transactions and 'transformations' " (Salomone 1960: 15).

The Depretis and Crispi regimes did institute some modest reforms, notably enlargement of the parliamentary suffrage in 1882 from about 2 to about 7 per cent of the population, an expansion of the municipal franchise in 1889, and education, public health, penal and legal reforms, including a theoretical legalization of the right to strike in 1889. But in general the attitude of the regime continued to be conservative and frequently highly repressive. Continued election-rigging, exclusion of the poor from the suffrage, and the voluntary abstention from politics of many Catholics who opposed the anti-clericalism of the regime made the suffrage expansion relatively insignificant, while unions and left-wing political organizations faced continuing discrimination and persecution. Thus, agricultural workers' strikes in the Polesine in 1880 and in the Po Valley in 1885 were both crushed by mass arrests. In the latter case the arrest of thousands of strikers and the use of troops to gather the harvest succeeded in smashing the agricultural labor movement for many years. Anarchist leaders Errico Malatesta and Francesco Merlino were given three years for conspiracy in 1884 for their propaganda activities and attempts to reorganize the International, and 58 Florentines who merely signed a manifesto supporting them were given jail terms of 30 months each (later reduced on appeal). The Italian Workers' Party, an urban working-class group that reached a membership of 30,000 within three years of its formation in 1882, also came under attack from the government after it supported the Po Valley strikes and backed socialist parliamentary candidates. In 1886 the party was dissolved for fomenting strikes, its paper was suppressed, and the leadership was given jail terms ranging from 2 to 18 months.

In the 1890s, repression of opposition groups in Italy reached dimensions unmatched in any other major European country except Russia. In 1892-3, a Sicilian labor movement, the Fasci dei Lavoratori, rapidly spread throughout the island, apparently spurred by enormous economic distress caused by sharp drops in the price of agricultural exports and the continued gross exploitation of the peasantry and workers by local businessmen, landlords and officials. Between March and December 1893, the Fasci membership jumped from 200,000 to 300,000, major successes were made in local elections and widespread strikes gained significant concessions. Although Fasci leaders urged non-violence, a wave of land seizures and attacks on communal and tax offices in dozens of rural Sicilian towns erupted between October 1893 and early 1894, at least partly in response to increasing repression, which included the arrests of Fasci organizers, bans on meetings, and agent-provocateur activity designed to discredit the movement. Police and troops responded to the violence with extreme measures, killing 92 demonstrators and wounding hundreds more by the end of 1893.

Prime Minister Giovanni Giolitti resigned in November 1893, under fire for refusing to take even harsher measures against the Fasci and for his role in a bank scandal. Crispi returned to power. Declaring absurdly that a Russian-French-Vatican-Sicilian separatist plot was behind the disorders, he imposed martial law in Sicily in January 1894, and also at Massa-Carrara, where marble workers had struck and had attacked police and tax-collection buildings in support of the Fasci. Hundreds were arrested and tried by military tribunals at Massa-Carrara. The 50,000 troops sent to Sicily maintained martial law until August, carrying out mass arrests and deporting 1,000 to penal islands without trials. All workers groups were dissolved, and freedom of the press, meeting, and association was suspended.

In July 1894, in the atmosphere created by bomb explosions in Rome, an attempt on Crispi's life, and the recent assassination of French President Sadi Carnot, Crispi pushed two stringent laws through parliament. Effective until December 1895, the laws provided heavy penalties for "incitement to class hatred" in the press, gave the police extended powers of preventive arrest and detention, and authorized three-year jail terms for anyone found demonstrating a "clear intention to commit overt acts against the social structure" (Seton-Watson 1967: 167; Thayer 1964: 70). Although Crispi had promised the law would be used only against criminal and anarchist agents, in October 1894, a time of general tranquillity in Italy, he declared the Socialist party and about 250 other "subversive" organizations dissolved, many of which were trade unions and workers' associations or moderate political groups without strong ties to the socialists. The socialist press was suppressed and socialist deputies were arrested once parliament was adjourned and they lost their immunity. Although Crispi obtained a strong majority in the May 1895 elections--held after a massive purge of electoral rolls that reduced the suffrage by over 30 per cent--the socialists returned 15 deputies, including three jailed leaders of the Fasci, compared to only five legislators in 1892. Crispi was finally forced to resign in 1896 as a result of his disastrous colonial adventures in Ethiopia, where 6,000 Italians were killed at Adowa on March 1.

The Adowa disaster intensified the general feeling that Crispi's repressive tactics had gone too far. When Antonio di Rudinì became prime minister (1896-8), his first actions, including a general political amnesty in March 1896, were conciliatory, but he soon shifted in a repressive direction in response to growing conservative pressure. Socialist clubs and newspapers, along with trade unions, were again harassed or suppressed, especially after major left-wing gains in the March 1897 elections, and strikes were forcibly beaten down. The right-wing pressure on Rudinì reflected the left's electoral gains, as well as a record number of strikes in 1896-7 and growing peasant outbreaks. Beginning in the fall of 1897, a wave of strikes, land seizures, demonstrations and bread riots spread up the Italian peninsula from south to north, frequently leading to bloody clashes with police, the imposition of martial law, and widescale, arbitrary arrests. At the height of the disorders in April-May 1898, military government replaced civilian rule in 30 of Italy's 59 provinces. The most serious trouble erupted in Milan, shortly after the Italian police killed the son of an opposition member of parliament in Pavia on May 5. Three Milanese workers were arrested on May 6 for distributing handbills that protested the Pavia incident. When workers gathered to protest the arrests, police and soldiers opened fire on the crowd, killing two, wounding 14 others, and taking the life of a policeman who was in the line of fire. After mounted police brutally dispersed protest demonstrations on May 7, barricades went up in Milan and troops "shot down the unarmed populace without mercy" (Whyte 1965: 206), resulting in an official toll of 80 civilians killed and 450 wounded, compared with two deaths and 50 injuries among the forces of order. During the disturbances, one republican member of parliament was arrested when found carrying a map of Milan's street car lines, which was viewed as evidence of conspiratorial plotting; a monastery was bombed and stormed and the resident Capuchin monks and their mendicant guests fleeing amidst the cannon fire were detained on suspicion of being disguised revolutionaries.

After suppressing the Milan disorders, the government began a massive wave of indiscriminate repression, insisting that what had in fact been spontaneous disorders resulted from a vast socialist plot to overthrow the regime. Thousands of political dissidents of all stripes, including "every opposition figure of any standing" (Hughes 1967: 61) from socialists to Catholic priests, were arrested. Over 100 newspapers and universities all over Italy were shut down, as were hundreds of trade unions and philanthropic groups and over 3,000 Catholic organizations. Almost 700 people were convicted and sentenced to a total of 1,400 years in jail and given fines that totaled 34,000 liras. Among them was Filippo Turato, a socialist member of parliament who had tried to head off mob violence in Milan but was sentenced to 12 years in jail for "stirring up class hatred" in a speech delivered two months before the riots. King Humbert added to the growing revulsion against the government by congratulating General Fiorenzo Bava-Beccaris, the "butcher of Milan," and honoring him with the Grand Cross of the Order of Savoy for his "great services to the State in the suppression of the revolution" (Whyte 1965: 207).

Rudinì resigned in June 1898 in the face of obvious parliamentary and public disapproval of the repression. He was replaced with General Luigi Pelloux (1898-1900). Like Rudinì, Pelloux began his ministry with conciliatory gestures, but then shifted to a repressive policy. The repressive measures against Catholic priests were cancelled; martial law in the provinces where it had been imposed ended in August 1898; and after 400,000 Italians petitioned for the release of those jailed, a partial amnesty was issued in January 1899, freeing 2,700 people, most of whom had not yet been tried. In Februrary 1899, however, Pelloux asked parliament to pass a harsh coercion bill, which would have given the regime wide power to deport administratively and arrest and to suppress public meetings, dissident organizations, and newspapers. A bitter parliamentary battle ensued in which a broad coalition of parliamentary left groups, including socialists, radical monarchists, and republicans, resorted to obstruction to prevent passage of the bill. When Pelloux's attempt to enact the bill by royal decree was declared unconstitutional by the high court of appeal and parliamentary obstruction continued, he decided to call new elections in mid-1900, which returned a slim legislative majority for the government, but a minority of popular votes. Everyone recognized that the election was a crushing moral defeat for Pelloux and the policy of reaction. The government resigned on June 18, 1900. A general amnesty was granted, and even the assassination of King Humbert on July 29 by an anarchist failed to trigger a new round of repression.

For the next 15 years, Italian politics was dominated by Giovanni Giolitti, interior minister under Giuseppe Zanardelli (1901-03) and thereafter almost continuously prime minister (1903-1905, 1906-1909, 1911-14). Giolitti's approach amounted to a sort of super-trasformismo, in which the techniques of absorbing opposition politicians into an amorphous centrist liberalism were applied on a far broader and grander scale than under Depretis or Crispi. In particular, Giolitti deliberately attempted to bring both the major left (socialist) and right (Catholic) oppositions into the pale of political respectability for the first time. Giolitti's approach reflected a politics of principle no more than past masters of trasformismo, but rather a common sense recognition that the continued exclusion of Catholics and, especially, the rapidly growing and politicized lower classes posed a serious threat to the stability of Italian society.

The great achievement of Giolittism between 1900 and 1910 was the considerable easing of class conflict, at least in comparison with the stormy 1890s. Although one major reason for this amelioration was the enormous Italian economic progress during this decade--per capita income increased about 30 per cent between 1896-1900 and

1911-15—others included the enactment of a considerable body of social legislation, Giolitti's open tolerance of the Socialist party, and his policy of using troops and police only to maintain public order rather than to break strikes, as had been common practice before 1900. Although a strong minority segment of the labor and socialist movements beteen 1900 and 1910 continued to adhere to a militant class conflict philosophy, their general tendency during the period was clearly in the direction of reformism.

Italy was by no means a country of complete social tranquillity during the 1900-1910 period. The remaining militants within the socialist and labor movements were invigorated by repeated incidents, especially in the south, in which workers were wounded or killed by police and troops. As a result of these so-called proletarian massacres, an estimated 40 workers were killed and over 202 wounded between June 1901 and September 1904. After two peasants were killed and seven wounded at Cerignola (Apulia) in May 1904 and additional "massacres" occurred at Castelluzzo (Sicily) and Buggerrù (Sardinia) in September of that year, a protest general strike, reluctantly supported even by reformist socialists, paralyzed Milan from September 16 to 20 and spread to other major cities throughout Italy. Subsequent "massacres" triggered general strikes in Turin in May 1906 and in Milan in October 1907.

One major flaw in Giolitti's system was his continuation of the traditional trasformismo approach of accepting the support of southern elites and ignoring their gross exploitation of the lower classes and their use of massive electoral corruption to maintain their power. This reflected his conviction that the problems of the south and the power of southern elites were so entrenched that there could be no change. Consequently, his governments always relied on a core of 200 or so southern deputies who ruled almost half the country with methods that Giolitti realized would be intolerable elsewhere in Italy. Giolitti defended these practices, declaring, "A tailor who has to cut a suit for a hunchback is obliged to make a hunchback suit" (Seton-Watson 1967: 254). Another major flaw in Giolitti's approach was that by trying to please every major faction in the country he ended up antagonizing everyone by a policy that one critic termed, repairing "day by day the leaks of the moment" and appeasing "whoever shouts loudest" (Seton-Watson 1967: 253). The climax to his policy of super-trasformismo came in 1911-12, when Giolitti almost simultaneously inaugurated a pointless colonial war in Libya to appease the right-wing nationalists and obtained parliamentary approval of universal manhood suffrage to appease the left. The Libyan War deeply antagonized the left and shifted the balance in the Socialist party towards a quasi-revolutionary posture, while the suffrage expansion deeply frightened conservatives and nationalists, and greatly spurred previous tendencies towards proto-fascist vigilante activities on the right.

An economic downturn in 1912-13 and new "proletarian massacres" furnished considerable ammunition for left-wing militants. More industrial workers struck in 1913 than had in any previous year in

Italian history, including a long and bitter syndicalist-led strike in Ferrara province and two general strikes in Milan. In May 1914, Prime Minister Antonio Salandra (1914-16)--it was Giolitti's habit to resign during periods of trouble to demonstrate his indispensability--banned all anti-military demonstrations scheduled throughout Italy for June 7. Police, seeking to prevent the scheduled demonstration at Ancona, shot and killed three people and wounded 10, setting off "Red Week." A nation-wide general strike called for June 9 by the Socialist party and the moderate-dominated General Confederation of Labor (CGL in Italian) sparked spontaneous riots throughout much of the country. The most serious disorders occurred in Emilia-Romagna and the Marches in east-central Italy. Rioters there attacked churches and landlords' villas, looted stores, destroyed telegraph wires and railroad lines, hoisted the red flag over town halls in Bologna and elsewhere and announced the reduction of prices and taxes and the establishment of local "republics." Although the disorders petered out in most places when the CGL called off the strike almost immediately, it took 100,000 troops and 10 days to restore order completely. In the June 1914 municipal elections, socialists gained control of many important towns, including Bologna and Milan. Nationalist right-wing extremists simultaneously began forming "volunteers for the defense of order" in several cities, a prelude to Mussolini's post-war fascist movement.

Germany. The Prussian defeat of France in 1870 led to the creation of the German Empire under Prussian leadership and domination in January 1871. The new empire included all of the German states except for the Habsburg lands and had a constitutional structure based on the 1867 North German Confederation. The lower legislative house (Reichstag) was elected by universal male suffrage and had wide power over legislation and budget, but the imperial chancellor and ministers were responsible to the German emperor alone. The upper house (Bundesrat) consisted of representatives of the 25 federal states (which retained considerable powers over local affairs, including education, police, taxation, and health services). The Bundesrat had to initiate and approve all Reichstag legislation. Prussia had an absolute veto over all constitutional changes through its representation in the Bundesrat, and could block other legislation through its influence over the smaller states. The Prussian king served automatically as German emperor and controlled the armed forces and foreign policy, including the power to declare war and make peace. Partly because the Reichstag was always divided into many parties, none of which commanded a majority, and partly because of the German constitutional structure, the new state remained until 1918 a pseudo-democracy in which real power was retained by the Prussian king and officials to whom he was willing to delegate power. The conservative character of the Prussian state government and bureaucracy, which set the tone of German political life, was guaranteed by retention of the 1849 three-class suffrage system that gave control of the Prussian lower house to 15 per cent of the electorate. Both Prussian policy and German policy were dominated by the concerns of an amalgamation of traditional feudal-agrarian (Junker) and big business interests throughout the 1870-1914 period.

For two decades after 1870, the dominant German political figure continued to be Otto von Bismarck (Prussian prime minister, 1862-90; and German chancellor, 1871-90). In both his domestic and foreign policies, Bismarck was obsessed with potential threats to the new empire. In domestic affairs, this led to thousands of press prosecutions under the formally liberal 1874 press law, and to a series of repressive asaults against Catholics, Poles, socialists and trade unions, all of whom were viewed by Bismarck as threats to the unity of an ethnically German, predominantly Protestant, and politically conservative regime.

The anti-Catholic struggle of the 1870s, known as the Kulturkampf ("battle over culture"), included measures such as the expulsion of all Jesuits from Germany, the banning of teaching by members of religious orders in the Prussian schools and strict limits on clerical discussions of public affairs. The Kulturkampf aroused intense resistance from German Catholics, and by 1876 it had led to the jailing or exile of all Prussian bishops as well as 1,800 parish priests. In Prussian Poland, 100 bishops, priests, and deacons were jailed. The Kulturkampf was accompanied there by intense Germanization measures, such as the imposition of German as the language of elementary school instruction. Despite the intense pressure, support for the Catholic Center party increased during the 1870s, and after 1878 Bismarck largely abandoned the Kulturkampf, instead bringing the Center party into a consolidated conservative business-Junker alliance. However, measures against the Poles intensified. In 1886, 30,000 Polish non-citizen inhabitants of Prussia were summarily expelled from the country, and 100 million marks were appropriated to buy land owned by Poles so it could be transferred to German ownership. In 1887 Polish was abolished as a subject for study in the schools of Prussian Poland.

Bismarck's war against the socialists and their trade unions was deeply influenced by his fear of the forces represented by the Paris Commune and was pursued with far greater ruthlessness and persistence than was the Kulturkampf. Two socialist-oriented groups, the Socialist Democratic Workers party, sometimes known as the Eisenach party, and the General German Workers' Association (ADAV in German) were the targets of such severe persecution during the 1871-6 period that they were forced to merge for self-protection in 1875 into what eventually became the Social Democratic party (SDP). The two leading members of the Eisenach party, August Bebel and William Liebknecht, were given two-year jail terms for high treason in 1872 for criticizing the German annexation of Alsace-Lorraine, and almost every other prominent member of their organization was jailed (Bebel was elected to the Reichstag in 1871 while in prison awaiting trial). In 1874, mass sentences were handed out to Berlin members of both socialist groups, culminating with the outlawing of the central ADAV office in Berlin and the closure of many local branches. Despite the continuing harassment, including suspension of the newly formed SPD throughout Prussia in 1876, the German socialist movement gained strength, obtaining 9 per cent of the vote and twelve Reichstag seats in 1877, compared with 3 per cent and one seat in 1871. By 1877, the SPD had about 40,000 members, was publishing over 40 papers with a circulation of 150,000 and had organized about 30 national trade unions with an estimated membership of about 50,000.

In 1878, Bismarck took advantage of the general hysteria generated by two attempts upon the life of Emperor William I--the second of which seriously injured the monarch--to hold new Reichstag elections that strengthened the conservative parties and produced a majority willing to strike harshly at the SPD, which had had no connection with the assassination attempts. Amidst a climate in which over 500 people were convicted for lèse-majesté during the three months after the second attempt on June 2--one women got an 18-month sentence for declaring, "The Kaiser (Emperor) is not poor, he can afford to care for himself" (Carlson 1972: 143)--the Reichstag enacted the so-called anti-socialist law in October 1878. The measure, which was originally effective for three years, but was subsequently renewed four times (1880, 1884, 1886, 1888) before expiring in 1890, outlawed all societies, meetings and publications that aimed "at the overthrow of the existing political or social order through social democratic, socialistic or communistic endeavors" (Lidtke 1966: 339). The law also authorized the government to impose a "minor state of siege" in areas where the public safety was "menaced" by such activities, thereby authorizing suspension of freedom of assembly and the administrative expulsion of socialist "agitators." Although the SPD had never endeavored to "overthrow the existing order," save by legal-parliamentary means, between 1878 and 1890, the party was outlawed and driven underground. During that period, about 1,500 socialists were condemned to a total of 1,600 years in jail, 900 people (including many men with families) were expelled from their homes, 352 political associations were dissolved, and 1,299 different publications, including 104 newspapers and periodicals, were banned. Among the many German socialists forced to live in exile as a result of the law were Eduard Bernstein, the founder of "revisionist" socialism, who edited Sozialdemokrat, the party newspaper, from exile in Switzerland and London before returning to Germany after expiration of the law; and the electrical engineering genius Charles Proteus Steinmetz, who after 1889 lived in the United States, where he invented numerous devices for the General Electric Company, taught at Union College in Schenectady, New York, wrote many scientific books and papers, and served as president of the Schenectady board of education.

Despite the intense pressure, the SPD was able to survive and even to grow. Thousands of copies of Sozialdemokrat were smuggled into the country from abroad and clandestine meetings and front groups such as cultural, recreational, and scientific organizations were used to carry on party business. The anti-socialist law did not prohibit SPD members from running for office in Reichstag elections, and temporary groups focussing on electoral activities were tolerated and became a major center of SPD activities. The SPD percentage of the vote in the 1887 Reichstage election was slightly higher than it had been in 1877, the year before the passage of the anti-socialist law. Amidst the continuing repression, an extensive program of social welfare insurance, including accident and health coverage, was shepherded through the Reichstag by Bismarck in an attempt to wean workers away from the socialists. While these programs were inadequate in many ways and failed to stop the growth of the SPD, they provided levels of protection for German workers well above those established almost anywhere else in Europe.

The dismissal of Bismarck as imperial chancellor and Prussian prime minister by the new emperor, William II (1888-1918), in 1890, marked the end of an era, but it led to no fundamental revision of the regime's orientation or hostility to socialism. Ultimately, William II dismissed Bismarck because he was determined to rule Germany himself and escape from Bismarck's domineering shadow. The immediate excuse for the action was William's desire at the beginning of his reign to make some concessions to the working class, and his refusal to accept Bismarck's suggestions of a constitutional coup (Staatssreich) in early 1890 that would abolish universal suffrage for the Reichstag after that body refused to extend again the expiring anti-socialist law. William II was just as devoted to the concept of divine right monarchy as previous kings of the Prussian Hohenzollern dynasty, and reverted to the usual stance of unremitting hostility to the lower classes when he felt his early gestures were not rewarded with the hoped-for enthusiasm. Workers remembered for a long time his address to military recruits at Potsdam in November 1891:

> During the present subversive activities of the socialists, it can happen that I will order you to shoot at your own relatives, brothers, even parents--which may God forbid--but nonetheless you will have to obey my command without demur (Hall 1977: 121).

With the lapse of the anti-socialist law, the SPD and socialist trade unions were able to function openly. This was reflected in a quadrupling of the SPD popular vote and an increase in their share of Reichstag seats from 3 to 20 per cent of the total between 1887 and 1903, and a jump in socialist union membership from 100,000 to 900,000 during the same period. However, the party and its unions were still subjected to considerable harassment and repression. Between 1890 and 1912, SPD members were sentenced to a total of 164 years of hard labor and 1,244 years imprisonment and were fined over 550,000 marks for speeches, publications, and other purely political offenses, including thousands of convictions for criticizing William II. Throughout the 1890s the threat of resurrected anti-socialist legislation hung over the SPD, and there was frequent talk in government circles about the need for a coup to eliminate the party and universal Reichstag suffrage. As late as 1906 SPD headquarters in Berlin burned all incoming letters, made no copies of outgoing ones and operated without either a telephone or a typewriter to thwart surveillance and police raids. Until 1914, SPD members were, as before 1890, effectively banned from civil service and academic positions. Local notices proclaiming military boycotts on businesses often read, "out of bounds to military personnel, since frequented by prostitutes, pimps and Social Democrats" (Hall 1977: 119-20).

The failure to reapportion the Reichstag after 1870 and discriminatory suffrage systems in many German states, as well as the continued harassment and persecution of the SPD, deprived the party of fair representation in many German legislative bodies. Although the relatively liberal state suffrage systems in Baden, Bavaria, and Württemberg were further democratized in 1904-1906, suffrage laws were changed in a reactionary direction designed to curb rising socialist power in Saxony (1896), Brunswick (1899), Lubeck (1904), Hamburg (1906), Hesse (1909) and some of the Thuringian states. The 1896 suffrage law in Saxony, for example, reduced SPD representation in the state diet from 15 to one out of 82 seats, although socialists controlled 22 out of the 23 Saxon Reichstag seats, which were elected by equal and universal male suffrage. The Prussian three-class system remained intact, as did the traditional estates system in Mecklenburg in which the great landlords alone were represented and no elections at all were conducted. Even the conservative historian Heinrich von Treitschke described the Mecklenburg system as one "no civilized nation could regard without a blush of shame" (Craig 1980: 66).

Although state suffrage discimination systems in Germany had always been a political issue to some extent, the 1905 Russian revolution and the reactionary suffrage laws passed in the post-1895 period combined to make suffrage perhaps the leading focus of domestic political controversy between 1905 and 1914. In 1905-1906 and again in 1908 and 1910 massive suffrage demonstrations attracted hundreds of thousands of protesters.

Despite the continuous legal guerrilla warfare (Nadelstich-politik) waged against them, both the socialists and their unions registered strong gains during the immediate pre-war period. SPD membership jumped from 500,000 to 1.1 million and membership in socialist unions increased from 1.3 to 2.6 million between 1905 and 1914. In 1912, the SPD became the largest Reichstag grouping, and between 1910 and 1914 socialists won over 20 per cent of municipal council seats in Germany's six largest cities, despite widespread discriminatory suffrage systems.

These gains aroused a growing sense of alarm in German conservative circles and stepped up repression in the 1912-14 period. Thus, in the first six months of 1913 alone, convictions were obtained against 104 SPD journalists leading to sentences totalling 40 years in jail and almost 11,000 marks in fines. During a short but violent coal strike in the Ruhr valley in March 1912, over 1,500 strikers were prosecuted. Prison sentences were handed out that exceeded the total imposed on the entire labor movement during any year of the preceding decade. "To call 'Pfui' and ironically tip hats to the strike-breakers were offenses that brought prison sentences" (Schorske 1965: 278). Also in 1912, unions were classified for the first time as political associations, thereby subjecting them to police surveillance and barring persons under age 18 from joining, although about 15 per cent of the work force was composed of such youths.

Along with the socialists, Prussian Poles continued to suffer from discrimination and oppression during the post-1900 period, which was marked by an intensified drive to Germanize the administration and educational and cultural institutions in ethnic Polish areas. The Polish cause received considerable European sympathy in 1901 when resistance by Wreschen (Września) schoolchildren to the enforced exclusive use of German in religious instruction was suppressed by floggings and other reprisals. Scores of parents who supported the Wreschen children were jailed. In 1904, the German government was again embarassed before European public opinion when a Polish peasant, Michal Drzymala, ignored a law that prohibited construction of houses that would contravene the spirit of Germanization. He lived in a circus wagon on his property. In 1906 a year-long general school boycott by Polish children in Poznań province who refused to attend German-language religious instruction was forcibly terminated by the authorities.

Throughout the 1890-1914 period, William II retained ultimate power in Germany, including control of the military and foreign policy and sole power to appoint ministries that were not responsible to the Reichstag. The legislature made no serious attempt to gain control over these areas, largely as a result of the timidity of the middle-class parties that feared that weakening the power of the emperor would open the way for the SPD to triumph. This timidity was clearly demonstrated in 1913, after military officials arrested and detained 28 civilians in the town of Zabern (Saverne) in total disregard of the 1911 statute that had finally established constitutional rule in Alsace-Lorraine. The officers involved were cleared by the courts and the government defended the army's actions before the Reichstag. Although there were howls of protest in that body and the legislators actually voted no confidence in the government by a vote of 293 to 54, no effort was made to press the matter or to use it to try to bring about parliamentary responsibility or any other real change in the conduct of political affairs.

Austria. Austrian political life after the 1867 Ausgleich centered around two major types of controversies: 1) struggles by the lower classes and emerging trade unions and socialist movement for an expansion of the suffrage and civil liberties; and 2) growing agitation by the non-German nationalities for greater power, influence and linguistic concessions, especially among the Czechs of Bohemia and Moravia, whose demands for unity and autonomy were viewed by the large German minority there and by German speakers elsewhere in Austria as an intolerable threat. After 1890, civil liberties and the suffrage were significantly expanded, although restrictions on the press and association continued to be more severe than in northwestern Europe and the lack of parliamentary responsibility and the proliferation of parties left great powers in the hands of Emperor Franz Joseph. But the nationality problem was aggravated by political liberalization. Suffrage expansion and lessened repression after 1890 contributed to mass politicization of the Czechs as well as that of other previously weak and unorganized groups, such as the Galician Ruthenes, the Carniolan Slovenes, and the Istrian and Dalmatian Serbo-Croats. By 1914, Austria was completely paralyzed by nationality conflicts.

Although Franz Joseph alternated between German liberal anti-clerical centralist and relatively pro-Slavic clerical conservative decentralist ministries between 1870 and 1890, strong repressive controls directed against opposition newspapers and the emerging trade union and socialist movements remained constant. Thus, the German liberal ministry of Prince Adolf von Auersperg (1871-79) brought over 1,100 press prosecutions in 1877-8, while the clerical conservative ministry of Count Edward von Taaffe (1879-83) confiscated newspapers in 635 instances in 1880. Although trade unions and strikes were formally legalized in 1870, in practice labor organizations that fomented strikes or displayed other forms of militant behavior were dissolved or subjected to severe harassment. Because of government repression and the severe economic depression of the 1873-9 period, a trade union movement that enrolled an estimated 83,000 members in 1873 almost completely disintegrated within a few years. Efforts by socialists to organize also faced severe reprisals, such as the well-publicized trial of Galician socialists in 1880 (which ended in acquittals) and long jail terms for persons convicted of smuggling or printing radical literature in the early 1880s.

Partly because of such measures, a small number of Austrian radicals embraced the anarchist concept of terrorist "propaganda of the deed," and between 1882 and 1884 they carried out several pointless murders. In response to these incidents, Austrian police reacted to any signs of radicalism with severe measures. Such tactics led in a number of cases to rioting in 1882-3, as workers protested police brutality and such actions as the dissolution of the Vienna shoemakers' union and confiscation of its treasury on the grounds of distribution of illegal literature. Hundreds of workers were arrested and many were given 15-month jail terms during the crackdown on radicals and the clashes with protesters.

In January 1884, following the brutal murder of a Viennese money changer and his two small children, the Taaffe government, with the subsequent approval of the Reichsrat, suspended civil liberties, including freedom of assembly and jury trial, in Vienna and its environs. These measures were repeatedly renewed until the Reichsrat forced their termination in 1891, although the terrorist incidents ended after the execution of two anarchists in the autumn of 1884. Although the Reichsrat defeated, in 1886 (and again in 1891), the government's attempt to outlaw socialism entirely, it did approve in that year a bill that suspended jury trials throughout Austria for offenses "inspired by anarchistic activities aiming at the violent overthrow of the existing political and social order" (Kenner 1956: 24). The suspension of civil liberties in Vienna between 1884 and 1891 was accompanied by the suppression or dissolution of many unions, political clubs and newspapers, the administrative expulsion of 300 workers from the area, and large numbers of arrests. For all practical purposes, it was impossible for socialist groups and unions to function openly in Austria throughout the 1880s. As in Germany, the harsh anti-socialist repression of the decade was accompanied by passage of an extensive social welfare insurance program designed to show workers that the state was concerned about them and that they need not turn to radicalism.

The expiration of the exceptional measures in 1891 was followed by a rapid growth of socialist and labor organizations--Socialist party membership, for example, jumped from 16,000 to almost 50,000 between 1888 and 1891. The early 1890s also saw the emergence of a mass movement for further liberalization of the suffrage, which had been marginally expanded from about 6 to about 7 per cent of the population in an 1882 reform that retained the four-class voting system of 1861 that allowed less than 2 per cent of the population to elect two-thirds of the Reichsrat. Following massive public demonstrations in 1893-4, Prime Minister Count Casimir Badeni (1895-97) obtained passage of a measure in 1896 that extended the suffrage to virtually all adult males, but retained a class voting system so that while 20 per cent of the population was enfranchised, 2 per cent could elect a legislative majority.

A significant easing of controls on the press, speech, and assembly during the administration of Ernest Koerber (1900-1905)--the first commoner to serve as prime minister--and the influence of the 1905 Russian Revolution fostered another mass suffrage reform movement in 1905. On November 28, 1905, 250,000 paraded in a huge silent suffrage demonstration in Vienna, and great remonstrances were held in other cities, including marches of 90,000 in Prague and 40,000 in Trieste. Under this pressure, Prime Minister Baron Paul von Gautsch (1905-1906) introduced a bill for universal and equal male suffrage in February 1906; it became law in January 1907. Although the Germans were vastly overrepresented in the nationality-based electoral districts that were drawn up, with corresponding underrepresentation for the Slavs, the reform marked a considerable democratic advance. However, as it turned out, the nationality conflicts in Austria were only aggravated by the bill, and by 1907 they were too bitter to allow increasing democratization to facilitate a peaceful or rational solution.

The most intractable of the nationality problems was the struggle between Czechs and Germans for domination of Bohemia-Moravia. As early as 1871, Franz Joseph had discovered that any attempt to conciliate the Czechs would meet severe resistance from other quarters, but that failure to meet their demands generated intense anger among the Czech majority in the provinces. Mass demonstrations in Bohemia-Moravia in 1870-1 demanding concessions after the Prussian victory over France in 1870--following which Franz

Joseph abandoned his dreams of challenging Prussian supremacy in Germany and temporarily devalued the importance of German-Austrian support—led the emperor to dump his German centralist ministry in early 1871 and assign to his new prime minister, the clerical conservative Count Charles Hohenwart, the task of appeasing the Czechs. Hohenwart proclaimed a general amnesty in Bohemia-Moravia and then obtained a legislative majority for himself in the Reichsrat by dissolving that body and a number of provincial diets and using the usual imperial pressure and electoral manipulation. Franz Joseph then issued a rescript in September 1871 that seemed to hold out the promise of a settlement with the Czechs like the 1867 Ausgleich with Hungary. A storm of disapproval immediately erupted from Germans in Bohemia and elsewhere, coupled with disapproving pressure from Germany and from Hungary, where Magyar leaders feared that their own nationalities would be encouraged by the concessions to the Czechs. Faced with these pressures and a minor uprising in Croatia that aimed at formation of a southern Slav state, the emperor suddenly reversed himself, rescinding the rescript and forcing Hohenwart out. A new German liberal centralist ministry under Prince Adolf von Auersperg gained a Reichsrat majority by the usual means.

Franz Joseph's about-face led to great anger in Bohemia. General Alexander Koller, who had headed the Prague martial law regime of 1868-9, was re-installed as governor of Bohemia, and a state of emergency was imposed for over two years. Civil liberties were suspended; the Czech press was subjected to relentless prosecution; 700 political activists were jailed; all associations advocating resistance were dissolved; and freedom of assembly was rigidly curtailed.

While the Czechs remained deeply alienated, the Polish nobility in Galicia was won over by a series of concessions. These included the designation of Polish as the official provincial language and a de facto arrangement that gave the Polish upper-class autonomy in Galicia and free rein to continue their traditional exploitation of the Polish, and especially the Ruthenian, lower classes, in return for their support of the government in Vienna. This arrangement continued until the end of the monarchy, although it required increasing measures of force and the frequent use of troops and prosecutions to keep down the Ruthenes. Since there was no German element in Galicia as there was in the Czech lands, this agreement posed no threat to the German Austrians.

When Franz Joseph tired again of the German liberal centralists in 1879—largely because of the Auersperg ministry's opposition to the Austrian occupation of Bosnia-Herzegovina, with its large Slavic element, in the aftermath of the Russo-Turkish War of 1877-8—he decided to renew his efforts to conciliate the Czechs. The Taaffe regime of 1879-93, known as the Iron Ring, was based on a coalition of all the decentralist and anti-German-liberal forces, i.e., the Slavs, the German clerical conservatives and the local aristocracies. Taaffe lacked any systematic or coherent program, instead resorting to what he termed a policy of <u>forwürsteln</u> ("muddling through") and "keeping all the nations of Austria in a state of equal, well-tempered dissatisfaction" (Skilling 1970: 263). The Czechs were brought back into the Reichsrat by a series of minor concessions, including the establishment of a Czech University at Prague, the revision of the Bohemian Landtag franchise so that it yielded a Czech majority, and the establishment of Czech as an official language for "external purposes" (interactions between citizens and the bureaucracy but not for internal bureaucratic communications) in Bohemia and Moravia. However, Taaffe's refusal to grant the basic Czech demands of administrative union and autonomy of the "Czech crownlands" (Moravia, Bohemia, and Silesia) and his severe repression of the Czech nationalist press led to growing scorn for what a rapidly emerging militant group known as the "Young Czechs" called the "policy of crumbs. Taaffe's policies and those of the moderate "Old Czechs" were decisively repudiated in the 1889 Bohemian diet elections and the Bohemian Reichsrat elections of 1891.

In the early 1890s, Bohemia-Moravia became the locus of mass demonstrations for suffrage reform and nationalist concessions, with historical anniversaries, such as the 477th anniversary of John Hus's martyrdom on July 6, 1892, used as excuses for highly politicized commemorations. Following outbreaks of vandalism in Prague in August-September 1893, including the destruction of German signs and imperial emblems, a night of window-smashing and other relatively trivial disorders, a state of emergency was declared there and in five adjacent districts; it remained in effect from September 1893 until October 1895. During these 26 months, freedom of assembly and trial by jury were suspended; 17 political associations, including the Young Czechs, were suppressed; eight newspapers were shut and the rest were subjected to prior censorship; 179 persons were prosecuted, and a total of 278 years in jail terms were handed out. In the most notorious trial arising from these events, 68 members of a left-wing organization, Omladina, were convicted of subversion on the basis of largely fabricated evidence and given 96 years in prison sentences. In March 1895, Bohemian Governor Count Franz Thun issued decrees requiring all schools to fly the imperial colors and banning the display of Czech colors and insignia. He told complaining teachers, "If you do not obey orders, I shall break your necks" (Garver 1978: 24).

Another attempt was made to solve the Czech problem during the Badeni ministry of 1895-7. The state of emergency in Prague was lifted and a number of political prisoners, including the Omladina victims, were freed in 1895. In 1897 Badeni issued rules requiring all civil servants in Bohemia and Moravia to be fluent in both Czech and German as of mid-1901, thus threatening the jobs of German civil servants, few of whom spoke Czech, even though the majority of the population in the two provinces was Czech. The Badeni language ordinances marked the beginning of the end of constitutional rule in Austria. Germans in Bohemia, Vienna, and elsewhere staged massive demonstrations and riots and obstructed the functioning of the Reichsrat and some of the provincial diets. Although minor Czech disturbances in 1893 had been answered with martial law, the severe German disturbances of 1897 led to the dismissal of Badeni. Badeni's fall sparked four days of severe anti-German riots by the Czechs, which led to another installment of martial law in Prague and the wounding of almost 300 people by troops and police.

Violent nationality conflicts increased significantly in Austria after 1897, often sparking severe disorders in the Reichsrat as well as in the streets. The Reichsrat was repeatedly paralyzed by disorders and obstruction and Franz Joseph and his ministers increasingly resorted to rule by decree. When a statue of Athena, the goddess of wisdom, was constructed outside the Reichsrat building in 1902, the joke circulated that they "must build her outside, since she is unwelcome inside" (Florence 1971: 68). The situation worsened after the 1907 suffrage reform, as it became almost impossible to find a stable parliamentary majority or avoid obstruction by the 30 or so mostly ethnically oriented parties that gained legislative seats.

There were new riots and another period of martial law in Prague in 1899 when German pressure forced total repeal of the Badeni ordinances; the pattern was repeated again in December 1908. Meanwhile, the Ruthenian peasants, who had long been treated as virtual serfs by the Polish landlords of Galicia, revolted in 1898 and again in 1902, with 120,000 agricultural workers striking in the latter year. In April 1908 the violently anti-Ruthene governor of Galicia was assassinated by a Ruthenian student who sought to avenge the death of a compatriot at the hands of the police. Italians and Germans in the Tyrol fought in 1904, and there was severe rioting between Germans and Slovenes in Carniola in 1908 and between Italians and Slovenes in Trieste in early 1914. Ater 1900, nationality conflicts not only frequently paralyzed the Reichsrat but also periodically obstructed proceedings in the provincial diets in Bohemia, Styria, Carniola, Galicia, Istria, and the Tyrol. Prime Minister Karl Stürgkh (1911-16) finally dissolved the Bohemian diet, which had been paralyzed by German filibustering since 1908, in 1913, and replaced it by an appointed committee. Before the outbreak of World War I in August 1914, the Reichsrat and all of the provincial diets were also dissolved. "Francis Joseph's long reign, which had been inaugurated with the dictatorial rule of [the Bach system], closed with the authoritarianism of Stürgkh" (May 1968: 434).

# Part Three

# Summary and Conclusions

# Political Repression in Nineteenth-Century Europe

## *The Impact of Political Repression in Nineteenth-Century Europe*

The fundamental conclusion of this study is that the use of and the struggle against political repression is one of the great themes of nineteenth-century European history. Nineteenth-century political repression and the fight against it helped to shape fundamental aspects of European political development both in the short and long term, in some cases leaving historical legacies that continue to affect European politics and society even today.

Political repression was especially pervasive and significant in affecting the nineteenth-century development of Russia, Spain, France, Italy, Germany, the Habsburg Empire, Portugal, Serbia, and Rumania; it was less frequent or intense but still significant in shaping events in the United Kingdom, Belgium, the Netherlands, Greece, and Bulgaria; and it was markedly less pervasive and significant for the development of Switzerland and Scandinavia (although at times it was of considerable importance in Sweden and Denmark). Especially in the first group of countries, suffrage restrictions and the limitations on freedom of the press, association, assembly, and the right to form trade unions and to strike that prevailed for most or all of the 1815-1914 period had a major impact. These restrictions systematically excluded the masses of the population from any possibility of peacefully voicing their grievances or gaining significant institutionalized economic, social, or political power. This systematic exclusion, which prevailed in most European countries until after 1860 and in the most repressive regimes until and beyond 1914, is absolutely crucial to an understanding of one of the most fundamental aspects of nineteenth-century European history--the "benign neglect" displayed by ruling elites towards the most pressing economic and political concerns of the mass of the population. The institutionalized exclusion of the masses from political power or expression of their grievances also helps to explain the frequent resort to violence by the lower classes in many European countries, especially before 1850. It is also a critical element in triggering such civil-liberties-related issues as suffrage reform and freedom of the press as key political demands of the lower and middle classes and in the grossly class-biased nature of governmental taxation, spending, conscription, and tariff policies in many of the regimes.

Perhaps the single most significant and effective technique of political repression was the class-biased suffrage, which as late as 1880, excluded more than 90 per cent of the population (or, put another way, more than 60 per cent of adult males) from the franchise in Austria, Belgium, Finland, Hungary, Italy, the Netherlands, Norway, Russia, Spain, Sweden, and the United Kingdom (see Table 1.1). Further, in most countries with a more liberal suffrage system in 1880, elections were either systematically rigged (e.g., Bulgaria, Portugal, Rumania, Serbia) or the lack of parliamentary responsibility greatly reduced the significance of a broad franchise (e.g., Denmark, Germany). The highly systematized, institutionalized, day-to-day, and non-violent nature of most class-biased suffrage systems made them both extraordinarily effective instruments of political repression and extremely easy to underestimate in historical retrospect. Most political scientists and historians are well aware that such systems were widespread in nineteenth-century Europe. However, they generally tend to point this out once or twice in passing, even in lengthy studies dealing with European politics and social history (because the discrimination was so institutionalized and was rarely manifested in spectacular incidents), without analyzing the impact that suffrage restrictions had on the basic nature of European political development during the era. Such suffrage restrictions along with gross and massive electoral corruption were in fact an absolutely fundamental aspect of European politics, economics, and society in the nineteenth century and continually shaped the most fundamental aspects of European development. Nothing is more striking in an examination of nineteenth-century European politics than the failure of most European governments--at least until the very late part of the century, by which time the suffrage had been extended in many countries--to concern themselves in any serious way with the major problems that impacted upon the mass of the population, such as gross maldistribution of wealth and land, malnutrition and abominable housing and working conditions. To a considerable extent, this failure reflected the fact that suffrage restrictions limited the political arena to a tiny and privileged minority who either had little concern for such problems since they were not affected by them or feared that solving them would mean a diminuation of their own wealth and power. In explaining why Hungarian legislators as late as 1900 paid no attention to the wishes of the poor, Count Albert Apponyi, a prominent Hungarian conservative politician, offered considerable insight into the general nature of politics in many countries of nineteenth-century Europe when he pointed out, "Not a single member's election depended on the ballots of workers" (Kosary 1969: 1974).

Thus, in Spain, Portugal and Rumania, where the rural masses lived in conditions of brutalized poverty and ignorance, suffrage restrictions and institutionalized election-rigging allowed so-called "liberal" and "conservative" parties to take turns running the country while not even pretending to have serious differences or to pay attention to the conditions of the majority of the population. Although poverty and illiteracy in Belgium and the Netherlands were among the worst in western Europe, the fact that less than 5 per cent of the population in those two countries could vote before 1885 made it easy for the major parties to concern themselves mostly with questions related to government funding of religious schools. In Hungary and Italy, where less than 10 per cent of the population could vote as late as 1910, although the major parties in the post-1860 period claimed to differ from each other, when opposition parties came to power (in Italy in 1876 and in Hungary in 1906) their policies turned out to be almost identical to those of the parties formerly in office. In Bulgaria, Serbia (until 1903), and Greece (until about 1880), election rigging and the dominant powers of the ruling princes and kings created systems of urban-based professional politicians and palace cliques that had little interest in or knowledge of the problems of the poverty-stricken rural masses who formed the overwhelming majority of the Balkan population. In Germany, Sweden, Austria, and Denmark (until 1901), suffrage restrictions and the lack of parliamentary responsibility insulated politicians from the need to pay much attention to the needs and concerns of their constituents. In Russia, until 1905 the czar and his advisers were sheltered from hearing the political demands of the population by the lack of any elections or legislative assembly, and even after then the suffrage system and restricted powers of the duma reduced parliamentary government to a farce.

In most countries where free elections existed and the suffrage was significantly broadened in the post-1880 period, the political influence and impact of the working classes grew dramatically. Thus, in Austria, the socialists, who had been totally excluded from the Reichsrat under the pre-1896 electoral system that enfranchised 7 per cent of the population, returned 10 parliamentary deputies under the five-class voting system of 1896 and 87 deputies under the system of universal and equal male suffrage inaugurated in 1907. In Belgium, the socialists received a grand total of 167 votes and returned no deputies in 1892 under a suffrage system that disenfranchised 98 per cent of the population, but gained 240,000 votes and elected 28 deputies in 1894 under the system of universal male plural voting established in 1893. When universal and equal male suffrage was instituted in Belgium in 1919, socialist representation jumped overnight from 34 to 70. After the anti-socialist law in Germany expired in January 1890, thus removing numerous restrictions on party activities, socialist ballots leaped from 760,000 in the 1887 elections to 1.4 million in the elections of February 1890. Socialist representation in the lower house of the Swedish legislature jumped from 35 in 1911 to 64 in 1912 after a major franchise extension. A similar reform for elections to the Swedish upper chamber in 1918 was followed by an increase in socialist representation there from 17 in 1918 to 52 in 1919.

Where free elections existed, expansion of the suffrage and/or the adoption of parliamentary responsibility was often followed not only by increased working-class representation in parliamentary bodies but also by a considerable increase in legislative attention and enactments directed towards the social needs of the general population. Thus, in the United Kingdom, the reform of 1867, which increased the suffrage from 4 to 8 per cent of the population, was followed by a series of reform bills in the next ten years, including the passage of a secret ballot law, unambiguous legalization of trade unions and peaceful picketing, the opening of almost all government jobs to civil service competitive examination, and slum clearance, public health, and food and drug laws. Similar flurries of reform legislation followed political democratization in the Low Countries and Scandinavia. In the Netherlands, for example, after the 1896 suffrage reform that increased the franchise from 6 to 12 per cent of the Dutch population, the "Cabinet of Social Justice" (1897-1901), enacted a series of important measures, including abolition of the purchase of draft exemptions and the introduction of compulsory elementary education.

In the regimes of southern and eastern Europe where suffrage restrictions and election rigging as well as other forms of political repression remained prominent until 1914, social legislation lagged far behind, as is suggested by the abominable health and literacy statistics of those countries (see Table 6.1). Almost without exception, the most repressive regimes over the entire period of the nineteenth century (i.e., Russia, the Hapsburg Empire, the Iberian countries, and the Balkans) produced populations on the eve of World War I that were the most illiterate, had the shortest life-spans, and lived and worked under the worst conditions. Certainly political repression alone cannot explain the persistence of terrible social and economic conditions, but it was precisely the repressive governments that most blocked the demands of the masses from being heard by the politicians and least had to worry about being voted out if they ignored such demands. Also, it was precisely in these regimes that there is the clearest evidence that political elites deliberately sought to keep the masses in a condition of ignorance and servitude in order to stifle challenges to the status quo. The statement of Friedrich von Gentz, Metternich's secretary, to British reformer Robert Owen, deserves recall: "We do not desire to have the masses well off and independent. How could we rule over them?" (Artz 1963: 239). Instead of focussing their attention on mass concerns, wherever political repression insulated their regimes European politicians focussed almost exclusively on patronage, power, and corruption (as in Italy, Iberia, and the Balkans) or on sterile ideological debates (as in the disputes over "the question of public law" in Hungary and the political struggles over anti-clericalism and church-state relations in the Low Countries before 1885).

While suffrage restrictions were the single most important and effective form of political repression in nineteenth-century Europe, other types of repression also significantly aided in maintaining the status quo. For example, although restrictions on trade unions and strikes could never be completely enforced in the more industrialized countries, they unquestionably greatly weakened the ability of the working classes to organize for economic purposes. This can be clearly seen by examining data on the growth of trade union movements after they were legalized. In France, it is estimated that in 1884, the year trade unions were legalized, there were about 70 semi-clandestine unions with 70,000 members. Ten years later, almost 2,200 unions with over 400,000 members existed in France. In Germany, membership in socialist unions jumped from 140,000 to 680,000 between 1889 and 1899, following the 1890 expiration of the anti-socialist law. In Italy, where strikes and unions were effectively illegal until 1900, the average number of strikes per year jumped from 611 to over 900 between 1895-9 and 1900-1904, while union membership leaped from under 150,000 to almost 700,000 between 1900 and 1904. In Russia, almost 250,000 workers joined unions within a year of their legalization in 1906, although a new wave of repression soon reduced them to insignificant numbers.

While about 10 million Europeans had joined unions by 1914, it should be noted that most workers did not join even after they could do so legally. Thus, it is estimated that on the eve of World War I only 25 per cent of all wage earners in Great Britain and Germany were unionized and that only about 10 per cent were unionized in France and Italy. Unfortunately, it is almost impossible to draw significant conclusions from these data since, while many workers undoubtedly did not join unions out of apathy or acceptance of their situation, many others chose not to join out of fear of reprisal from their employers or governments or because they could not afford to pay the dues. Failure to join a union cannot be automatically interpreted as a reflection of satisfaction with jobs and/or politics. Many unorganized German workers, for example, took part in the strike wave of 1905 and the revolution of 1918. Similar behavior by unorganized workers in Italy, France, Russia, Spain, and elsewhere after 1914 suggests to one labor historian that "their earlier inaction was less the consequence of an acceptance of the prevailing social and political order but was rather the result of economic and political controls excercised by employers and the state, not only through overtly repressive institutions but also through company-provided housing, employer monopoly of the labour market, etc." (Geary 1981: 126).

Along with suffrage and labor organization restrictions, limitations on the press also had a major impact in hindering the growth of opposition movements in nineteenth-century Europe. For example, after press regulations were lifted in France during the 1848 revolution, hundreds of new papers sprang up in Paris alone, and the combined daily press run for all Paris newspapers rose from 50,000 to 400,000. When press controls were greatly eased in France in 1881, after 30 years of severe controls following the 1848 revolution, the number of provincial dailies increased from 114 to 280 between 1880 and 1885. In the Habsburg Empire, the number of periodicals doubled with the collapse of press controls during the 1848 revolutions, then returned to below pre-1848 levels during the reactionary period of the 1850s. When press controls eased in the empire afterwards, the number of newspapers and magazines published skyrocketed, reaching

1,378 by 1882 and 5,534 after the abolition of stamp taxes and caution deposits in the 1890s, compared to 128 in 1856. The sudden explosion of political clubs and meetings throughout Europe in 1848 and their rapid disappearance in the post-1848 reaction offers additional evidence as to the effectiveness of nineteenth-century political repression.

The conclusions advanced thus far suggest that political repression significantly delayed the emergence of opposition (including middle-class) movements, greatly facilitated governmental neglect of popular needs, and in general played a major role in shoring up the societal status quo. These conclusions are all based essentially on historical retrospective, but it is important to note also that nineteenth-century Europeans themselves recognized the great significance that political repression played in their lives. It would be misleading to suggest that the majority of the nineteenth-century European population was in a constant ferment over civil liberties violations; a majority of any population is rarely engrossed with political issues except under truly extraordinary circumstances. Even during the 1848 upheaval in Germany, it is reported that workers heckled one speaker at a rally with the cry, "Was geht uns Pressfrieheit an? Fressfreiheit ist es, was wir verlangen" (What do we care about freedom of the press? Freedom to eat is what we want) (Conze and Groh 1971: 157). Nonetheless, political repression was an issue of great importance to key segments of the European population. Most mass movements and revolutionary upheavals in nineteenth-century Europe expressed demands for an end to various forms of political repression. In a number of cases, as in the 1848 revolutions and the 1905 Russian Revolution such demands were the central issues that sparked violence and cemented otherwise disparate groups, such as professors, journalists, artisans, and factory workers, into an opposition coalition.

During the 1815-1870 period, the middle class made demands for constitutional government, freedom of the press, and an expanded suffrage their major political platform. After 1870, the rising urban industrial proletariat focussed on demands for universal male suffrage. In virtually every country where universal male suffrage had not been achieved, this demand became the major political goal and organizing tool of socialist parties. Demands for such reform became either the single most important or one of the most important continuing domestic political issues in Austria, Belgium, Germany (in state elections), Hungary, the Netherlands, Italy, Russia, and Sweden between 1880 and 1914. In Belgium, there were four general strikes, some of impressive dimensions, over the suffrage issue, and massive demonstrations were organized for suffrage reform in most of these other countries.

The majority of the revolutionary outbreaks in Europe during the 1815-1914 period focussed upon civil liberties demands. Thus, the 1820-1 revolts in Iberia and Italy all demanded constitutional government. The 1830 July revolution in France was directly touched off when King Charles X attempted to nullify the elections of that year by dissolving the parliament, reducing the suffrage, and censoring the press. The 1830 outbreaks in Germany, Switzerland, and Italy all included constitutional government, expansion of the suffrage, and/or freedom of the press as their prime objectives. Also in 1830 press repression was the key factor in the outbreak in Belgium, while constitutional violations were a key factor in Poland. The immediate cause of the February 1848 revolution in France was the government's attempt to ban an opposition political banquet and the subsequent slaughter of peaceful demonstrators on February 23. In Austria and Prussia also, the 1848 revolts were sparked by troops firing on demonstrators who were demanding civil liberties and constitutional government. Throughout Italy, Germany, and the Habsburg Empire the key demands of the revolutionary coalitions in 1848 were constitutional government, freedom of the press, liberation of political prisoners, and a widened suffrage. The Spanish revolution of 1868 was largely directed against the autocratic and repressive rule of Queen Isabel, while the European demands of 1848 were repeated almost verbatim in the 1905 Russian revolution.

Aside from the role that demands for civil liberties played in mass movements and popular revolts in the nineteenth century, another indication that political repression was a major irritant to many Europeans was the extensive clandestine resistance that repressive governmental policies met in many countries. Thus, underground political organizations and trade unions existed in all European countries that had a social base to support them, and where this base was highly developed, as in France, there were scores of secret opposition groups and thousands of strikes during the 1815-1880 period when such tactics were usually illegal. Probably the most highly developed form of resistance to political repression was the massive smuggling of books and periodicals and the widespread technical evasion of censorship regulations. Resistance to political repression sometimes took on highly creative forms, such as the boycotting of symbols or persons associated with repression, the booing or applause for politically tinged dialogue in plays and operas and the organization of politicized funerals, memorial services, and historical commemorations.

Hatred of political repression also often influenced the views of liberal Europeans towards foreign policy questions. Thus, during the 1815-70 period, western liberals universally execrated the Russians, the Austrians, and the Turks because of their repressive policies. They also automatically exalted the Poles, the Italians, and the Balkan peoples, since they were seen as the prime victims of those reactionary regimes. The liberal forces in the 1847 Sonderbund war in Switzerland also attracted immense sympathy among western liberals. Sometimes the identification of western liberals with the alleged victims of repression bordered on the ludicrous. Their general view that the Greeks who revolted against Turkey in 1821 were the reincarnation of Athenian democrats, fighting above all for civil liberties and western-style constitutionalism, was truly absurd, and if they viewed the Polish aristocrats who spearheaded the 1830 revolution as paeans of democratic and social virtue, this certainly was not the view of the Polish peasantry, as the landlords were to learn in 1846 in Galicia.

After 1870, the Turks, Russians and Austrians remained the subject of western liberal execration, but as the influence of democratic doctrines spread and news coverage improved, civil liberties abuses in any country could become the target of international campaigns of opprobrium. Thus, the "Bulgarian horrors" of 1876; the Spanish tortures of anarchists, the Dreyfus case in France, and the Hungarian persecution of Rumanian nationalists in the 1890s; and the Bloody Sunday massacre in Russia, the Russian suppression of Finnish nationalism, the Spanish judicial murder of the anarchist educator Francisco Ferrar, and the Hungarian trials of Serbo-Croat nationalists in the 1900-14 period all became the targets of European-wide expressions of outrage.

Thus far, the impact of political repression in nineteenth-century Europe has been discussed in terms of relatively short-term effects--the creation of political grievances, the hindrance of the emergence of working-class movements and the insulation of repressive regimes from the need to be responsive to their citizens. Political repression also had broader and longer-term impacts of even greater significance, although it is much more difficult to document such results precisely. For example, by around 1900, when significant mass politicization had occurred even among the more backwards European regimes, it is likely that some European governments depended for their very survival upon the continued existence of political repression. It seems probable that if truly free elections had been held around 1900 in which significant choices had been offered to a universal adult electorate, the governments of Russia, Spain, Hungary, Portugal, Italy, Rumania, Serbia, Bulgaria, and perhaps several others would have been drastically changed. The impact of such a development obviously belongs to the realm of historical "might have beens," which become almost impossible to fathom, but unquestionably it would have been extremely significant.

Another long-term impact of political repression in nineteenth-century Europe was in molding the basic pattern of governmental and opposition attitudes and behaviors in shapes that persisted well beyond 1914 in many instances. For example, it is impossible to understand the present-day alienation of large segments of the Spanish, Italian, and French working classes and their attraction to communism without knowing how the governments in those countries treated labor in the past--in France, stories of the 1848 June Days and the 1871 Commune are still remembered and retold. On a more general level, the nature of the political system in each country profoundly affected the form that political opposition took. In short, those countries that were consistently the most repressive, brutal, and obstinate in dealing with the consequences of modernization and developing working-class dissidence reaped the harvest by producing oppositions that were just as rigid, brutal, and obstinate--i.e., the Spanish anarchists and the Russian Social Revolutionaries and

Bolsheviks. As one historian has noted, the Russian socialist opposition, while preaching constitutionalism and democracy as an ideal, was "compelled by circumstances to adopt every device of conspiracy and terrorism" (Thompson 1966: 402). On the other hand, those countries that were consistently the most reasonable and responsive in dealing with the inevitable demands for growing popular participation in public life that came with modernization, such as Switzerland, Scandinavia, and Great Britain (at least after 1850) produced the most reasonable and moderate opposition groups. Even Karl Marx conceded in a speech in Amsterdam in 1872 that where democratic avenues were open, there was no need to resort to violence: "We do not deny that there exist countries like America, England, and if I knew your institutions better, I would add Holland, where the worker may be able to obtain their ends by peaceful means" (Nomad 1961: 138). Conversely, even moderate socialists warned that, if civil liberties continued to be denied or were taken away, the working classes might be forced to resort to violence. Thus, August Bebel, the moderate leader of the German socialists, warned in 1895 when the Reichstag was considering a reimposition of the expired anti-socialist law of 1878-90: "If those who are duty-bound to respect and uphold the law violate it in a brutal and forcible manner then the people will be released from their contractual obligations towards the government and they may act as they deem appropriate" (Maehl 1980: 287).

Those countries that fell into the category between the most repressive and the least repressive regimes tended to produce schizophrenic working-class oppositions, torn between moderate and militant wings (e.g., France, Italy and Germany). The militant segments of these oppositions, clearly influenced by recent history, argued around 1900 for a revolutionary strategy at least partly on the grounds that the regimes would never allow them to come to power through democratic means. The moderate segments argued for a peaceful approach, implicitly and sometimes explicitly contending that channels were open enough to allow for a democratic conquest of power. Significantly, key statements of the moderate or "revisionist" socialist approach were made in Germany by Georg Vollmar (1891) and in France by Alexander Millerand (1896), shortly after an easing of repressive controls in those countries. Clearly in Germany, and probably also in other countries, such as France, Austria, and Italy, that eased away from formerly draconian regimes after 1880, the moderates also greatly feared that a radical approach would lead to a return to the harsh repression of the past and destroy the socialist and trade union parties that had rapidly grown up. The impact of past repression on a moderate, such as the German socialist leader Bebel, can be clearly grasped in a speech he gave in 1903, recalling the days of the anti-socialist laws, which had expired 13 years previously:

> Blows simply rained down on us and everything was broken up. ... Hundreds and hundreds of our comrades became unemployed and we were driven from our homes like mangy

dogs. ... When I recall how we were made to report at the
police station, had our measurements taken and were
treated generally like criminals, photographed and then
given three days to clear out--this was an experience I shall
remember as long as I live (Braunthal, I, 1967: 259).

Oppositions in the "in between" regimes often espoused revolutionary
goals while acting in essentially reformist ways (e.g. the German
socialists) or used militant tactics in support of reformist ends (e.g.,
the Belgian socialists). It was in such countries that socialist
statesmen were prone to make statements like that of the German
Kaul Kautsky, who declared, "Social democracy is a revolutionary
party, but not a party which makes revolutions" (Hall 1977: 20) and the
Italian Filippo Turati, who announced, "I am a reformist because I am
a revolutionary and a revolutionary because I am a reformist"
(Seton-Watson 1967: 267).

Certainly political repression <u>alone</u> cannot explain the behavior of
working-class organizations in nineteenth-century Europe, but it did
play a major role. One recent study of European labor protest in the
nineteenth century strongly supports this contention, concluding that
"the major determinant of the forms of political action adopted by the
different national labour movements was the role of the state and of
the social groups it claimed to represent" and that political repression
was "the most direct mechanism whereby the state impinged on the
structure and aims of labour protest" (Geary 1981: 60, 64).
Exceptionally strong evidence that supports this argument was
provided by developments in Germany. In the southern states of
Baden, Württemberg, and Bavaria, where universal male suffrage
existed at the state level after 1890 and civil liberties were
comparatively well respected, socialists cooperated with bourgeois
parties in parliament and electoral arrangements. However, in
Prussia, Saxony and other northern German states where
discriminatory state suffrage systems and repressive civil liberties
controls remained in effect, the posture of German socialists remained
far more defiant and militant and such cooperative endeavors were
shunned and denounced. "The South German Social Democrats even
horrified their North German comrades by allowing members of the
party who had been elected vice-presidents of their land [state]
parliaments to participate in the customary New Year's reception at
the court dressed in tailcoats!" (Holborn 1969: 361). Similarly strong
evidence is provided by the Habsburg Empire, where the Austrian
government and the Austrian socialists both became increasingly
moderate in their attitudes towards each other after 1890, while in
Hungary the regime and the socialists remained in a state of extreme
mutual hostility until 1914. One historian notes that the Austrian
Socialists turned "almost overnight from a mainly extra-parliamentary
crusade into a parliamentary party" (Cole, III, 1960: 544) after the
granting of universal male suffrage there.

A final and extremely major long-term impact of political
repression in nineteenth-century Europe was in blocking the formation

of democratic habits and attitudes among both the ruling and ruled elements of the more repressive countries. One of the major explanations of the widespread development of post-World War I totalitarian or authoritarian governments that dominated all of southern, eastern, and central Europe (Spain, Portugal, Italy, Germany, Austria, Hungary, Greece, Russia, Bulgaria, Yugoslavia, Rumania) save only Czechoslavakia is ultimately that no tradition of political democracy had developed in these regions before the war. Only where democratic habits had been reasonably well-established before World War I (i.e., in Great Britain, France, Switzerland, Scandinavia, and the Low Countries) did they persist after the war. In other words, to a significant extent, post-World War I totalitarianism and authoritarianism was simply a modernized and more encompassing version of much of nineteenth-century Europe. Except in Russia, the repressive regimes of the post-1918 period tended basically to represent an updated version of late nineteenth-century European politics: a more ruthless and determined version of the repressive upper-class/middle-class coalition united against the by then even more mobilized lower class. This argument provides a corrective to the analyses so frequently made that tend to attribute interwar fascism almost solely to the disruptions caused by World War I and the great depression and to ignore the pre-1914 background.

The phony nature of the parliamentary regimes in the pre-World War I period in southern, eastern, and central Europe not only shaped and prefigured such attitudes and behavior by political elites after the war, but also greatly contributed to the growth of anti-parliamentary movements among the masses and their lack of strong support for democratic politics. Since the only experience of the masses in such countries as Portugal, Italy, Russia, and Germany before World War I with "parliamentary" regimes was with grossly distorted versions of such, it is hardly surprising that they generally rejected the concept of parliamentary democracy.

Even today, the boundary between the reasonably stable and democratic regimes of northwestern Europe and those European regimes that are either highly repressive (e.g., eastern Europe) or at most shaky democracies (e.g., Greece, Spain, Portugal, Italy) is not much different from that of 1914. Indeed, it is interesting to note that all of the constitutional regimes in Europe as early as 1815--the United Kingdom, France, the united Netherlands, the Swiss cantons, Norway, and Sweden--were located in northwestern Europe, and that feudalism and its remnants died out first there. The long-term results of the 1830 and 1848 revolutions widened further the gap between the relatively more democratic region of northwestern Europe and the rest of the Continent, so that by 1870 these differences were very marked. As historian David Thomson has noted, "Deviant paths, once followed in history, seldom end at the same destination" (1966: 427).

The clear connection between economic development and political democratization in nineteenth-century Europe supports the argument frequently advanced by political scientists that a certain level of prosperity and the existence of a significant middle class are key facilitators for democratic development. But this connection is clearly not automatic, since Germany was more economically developed yet less democratically advanced than a number of the northwestern European countries by the beginning of World War I. Ultimately, explanations for democratic development must be largely sought in deep-rooted historical traditions and processes, such as the long tradition of authoritarian rule and paternalistic-hierarchical politics in Germany versus the ingrained traditions stressing the rule of law and, at least relatively, respect for the lower classes characteristic of Scandinavian history.

## Trends in Nineteenth-Century European Political Repression

There were at least two major trends over time concerning the intensity of political repression in nineteenth-century Europe. The first was that repression tended to go through cyclical variations on a virtually European-wide basis, at least until about 1880. In other words, repressive levels tended to increase and decrease in a cyclical fashion, and the peaks and valleys tended to occur at about the same time in many different countries. Thus, peaks of repression occurred in many countries immediately after the revolutionary outbreaks of 1830 and 1848 and the Paris Commune of 1871, while the periods after the immediate revolutionary scares died down, such as approximately 1840-5 and 1859-68, were times of relative easing of repressive tension in most countries (and a subsequent growth of opposition). Quite clearly, these variations in levels of repression were directly related to the fears of the European ruling classes. Revolutionary outbreaks almost anywhere in Europe (and especially in France!) during the half-century following the defeat of Napoleon generated fears throughout the Continent of another general upheaval and thus led to widespread crackdowns. When these fears eased—often because repression had been quite successful in intimidating, jailing, or exiling dissenters—controls did also. None of this is particularly surprising, except the <u>extent</u> to which so many governments acted simultaneously in harmony. Even though transportation and communications were far less advanced in the nineteenth century than they are today, the near-simultaneous outbreaks of revolution in many countries in 1820, 1830, and 1848 and the almost identical responses of most governments to them suggest that to a much greater degree than at present there was a general feeling among both governmental and opposition forces in the nineteenth century of a general struggle between the forces of "order" and "liberty" that transcended national boundaries. This sense, and along with it the tendency of governments throughout Europe to react similarly on civil liberties questions in response to contemporary events, disintegrated rapidly after 1880, reflecting especially the increasing split between the more repressively inclined and more industrially backward (except for Germany) countries of southern, central, and eastern Europe, and the more democratically inclined and industrially developed nations of northwestern Europe.

A second major trend concerning the intensity of political repression is that there was a significant decline in the reliance of governments upon repression as a sole or major response to opposition movements after about 1860, and even more so after about 1890. This decline is particularly evident for the countries of northwestern Europe, but even in most of the other nations a decline in the general level or repression by 1914 is clear (e.g. the end of serfdom and the institution of an elected legislature in Russia and the tolerance of socialist and labor groups by 1900 in Germany, Austria, and Italy). The tendency towards lessened reliance upon repression after 1860 reflected, again especially in northwestern Europe but also to a significant extent in other countries, changes in the behavior of both the authorities and the opposition forces. In short, the authorities deliberately decided to adopt more ameliorative policies as an alternative form of social control, and the opposition became considerably less militant and provocative of repression. These two developments, of course, interacted with and encouraged each other.

The authorities decided to adopt more ameliorative policies for two major reasons: one was precisely that opposition forces became far less inclined to militant behavior (for reasons to be discussed shortly) and therefore repression seemed less needed; the other was that ruling elites increasingly realized that repression was simply not going to solve the problem of lower-class unrest, especially since the very modernization processes (primarily the spread of literacy, urbanization, and industrialization) that all countries encouraged to some degree after 1850 for reasons of national strength, survival, and prestige were creating and mobilizing dissenting groups. To follow a policy that was bound to foster the growth of the organized lower-class opposition groups and then to respond to that growth with a policy only of repression increasingly struck many European elites as a futile policy that threatened to create endless social turmoil. These elites realized that, if they were to maintain the bulk of their wealth, power, and prestige, the only choice open was either a substitution of mild reform for repression in an attempt to wean the masses away from radicalism or a continuing state of psychological and in some cases physical civil war that would prove increasingly costly and destabilizing. Even the extremely conservative Hungarian Prime Minister István Tisza urged some minimal reforms in his country, noting that "the rise of the working class is an inevitable concomitant of industrialization" and that a "class raised to decent human standards (would) be less dangerous than a morally and materially frustrated mass of humanity that had nothing to lose" (Janos 1982: 164). Thus, European elites increasingly adopted the policy advocated in 1799 by Prussian chancellor Heinrich von Goldbeck with regard to land reform: "It is better to give up something voluntarily than to be forced to sacrifice everything" (Blum 1978: 361). Those states that rejected this policy, such as Spain, Russia and Hungary, chose paths that led only to bitter hatred and civil wars.

In studying European history during the 1815-1914 period, one repeatedly runs across references to the fear of revolution in the immediate background of major reforms, confirming the hypothesis that in at least some cases elites quite deliberately chose a path of amelioration rather than one of repression and possible serious violence. Thus, in the United Kingdom in 1832 (the electoral reform), in Hungary in 1848 and in Russia in 1861 (the abolition of serfdom), in the Netherlands in 1848 and in Russia in 1905 (the constitutional reforms), in Germany in 1890 (the expiration of the anti-socialist laws) and in Italy in 1900 (the resignation of Prime Minister Pelloux despite a slim electoral victory), there is evidence of conscious decisions by elites that reform was preferable to the prospect of ever increasing doses of repression and civil chaos. Quite frequently, conservative European political leaders openly admitted that reform was necessary at least partly to quiet and tame the lower classes and thus to bolster the existing regimes. The French political leader Guizot espoused the cause of extending primary education to the lower classes since, "The less enlightened the multitude, the more amenable it is to being misled and subverted" and the more likely the masses would improve their living standards and "create sources of wealth for the state" (Vaughan and Archer 1971: 129).

Even in Russia, although the reforms were never significant enough, peace was the clear motivation behind the two most important reforms of the century--the emancipation of the serfs in 1861 and the granting of constitutional government in 1905. Thus, in announcing his intention to abolish serfdom, Czar Alexander II told a group of Moscow nobles in March 1856, "It is better to abolish serfdom from above than to await the time when its abolition would begin from below" (Collins 1964: 387). Other European statesmen made essentially identical comments in urging the need for reform. In supporting the adoption of social insurance programs in Germany during the 1880s, Emperor William II declared, "A remedy cannot be sought merely in the repression of socialist excesses. There must be at the same time a positive advancement of the welfare of the working classes" (Rich 1970: 177). Bismarck added that the adoption of such reforms to help the poor reflected not only a "duty of humanity and Christianity" but was also a "conservative policy which has as its goal to encourage the view among the unpropertied classes of the population that the state is not only a necessary institution but also a beneficent one" (Hayes 1963: 27). Bismarck conceded that without lower-class agitation there would have been no reform, noting in 1884, "If there had been no Social Democracy and if many people had not feared it even the modest progress which we have now achieved in the field of social reform would not have been made" (Maehl 1980: 222). Italian Prime Minister Giolitti told his parliament in 1901:

If you wish to defend our present institutions, you will have to persuade these new classes that they have more to gain from these institutions than from utopian dreams of violent change. ... It depends on us whether they will turn out to be a conservative force, a new element in the greatness and prosperity of the country, or a revolutionary force for its ruin (Smith 1969: 215).

Greek Prime Minister Venizelos used an identical argument to urge his parliament to adopt ameliorative reforms in 1911, declaring that his purpose was to "forestall dangerous outbreaks from the working classes by timely attention to their fair demands" (Jecchinis 1967: 28). When Austrian Prime Minister Gautsch introduced a suffrage reform bill in 1906 after massive demonstrations demanding reform, socialist leader Victor Adler noted wryly, in an echo of Czar Alexander's statement of 50 years before, "We believe that he has been overcome by the holy spirit, but we suspect that this time by way of exception instead of coming down from above, the holy spirit has come up from below" (McGrath 1974: 234).

The adoption of a more reformist approach did not mean a complete end to the use of repression, even in the more liberal states of northwestern Europe, but it usually did lead to focussing repression much more carefully on only the most extreme and militant groups, instead of on virtually all dissidents, as before, and gradually implementing reform as the predominant response to the more moderate dissidents. In effect, an attempt was made to "buy off" the masses while still striking out at the most radical groups (e.g. the CGT in France and the NAS in the Netherlands), and in many countries this resulted in a noticeable decrease in the general level of repression.

The shift to a more reformist response to dissent was greatly facilitated, at least in the northwestern and central European countries where it was most marked, by a lessened militancy and violence on the part of opposition forces after 1850. Although there was clearly great dissatisfaction with the status quo evidenced among the lower classes in some of these countries, notably Britain, France, Germany, Austria, and Italy, as late as the eve of World War I, there were serious outbreaks of popular violence in this region between 1850 and 1914 only in Belgium, Italy and, during 1870-1, in France. On the other hand, in southern and eastern Europe, where the ruling elites continued to stress repression over reform, serious outbreaks occurred in virtually every country between 1850 and 1914, and militancy increased among the lower classes during the pre-World War I period. The general decline in lower-class militancy in northwestern and central Europe can be explained by a number of factors, all of which reinforced each other. One such factor was unquestionably the general tendency towards expansion of the suffrage and lessened restrictions on the press, association, and trade unions, which greatly increased the avenues available for peaceful protest. "Wherever parliamentary institutions, however imperfect, and wider electorates, however defective, were firmly established, they had a moderating and civilizing effect, taming revolutionary fervor as much as they tempered arbitrary government" (Thomson 1966: 363). After socialist organizations were tolerated in France after 1880, in Austria and Germany after 1890 and in Italy after 1900, for example, party rhetoric and behavior considerably moderated, while before those dates continued severe prosecution had driven socialist groups in the directions of conspiratorial plotting and in some cases open advocacy of violence. By 1911, for example, Italian Prime Minister Giovanni Giolitti could boast in parliament, "The results have shown that my system, semi-revolutionary in appearance, was the only one really conservative....the Socialist Party has greatly moderated its program, Karl Marx has been relegated to the attic" (Salomone 1960: 59, 107).

Another factor in moderating working-class militancy outside of southern and eastern Europe was the marked increase in European living standards and working conditions after 1870, which at least partly resulted from the adoption of social welfare legislation (see Table 6.1). In northwestern and central Europe, there were substantial increases in average real wages in the 1870-1914 period and improvements averaging about 25 per cent in such measures of well-being as life expectancy and infant mortality rates. These developments unquestionably sapped working-class militancy, as one former Chartist noted to his dismay during a visit to Lancashire in 1870:

> In our old Chartist days, it is true, Lancashire working men were in rags by the thousands; and many of them often lacked food. But their intelligence was demonstrated wherever you went. You would see them in groups discussing the great doctrines of political justice. ... Now you will see no such groups in Lancashire. But you will hear well-dressed working men talking, ... of "Co-ops" and their shares in them or in building societies. And you will see others, like idiots, leading small greyhound dogs (Mosse 1974: 26).

A third factor leading to an end to the revolutionary outbursts of the 1820-48 era was the development of military and other technologies that made the likelihood of successful popular uprisings increasingly remote. The development of telegraph and railroad networks and new inventions in military technology, such as the machine gun and more powerful artillery, made it much easier after 1850 for governments to mobilize, concentrate and use troops in an overwhelming fashion. Even Friedrich Engels, Marx's long-time compatriot, conceded in 1895 that in an age of railways and modern military technology revolutionary enthusiasts could not hope to succeed on the barricades.

A fourth factor in sapping working-class militancy after 1850 was the development of massive emigration from Europe. The emigration of about 40 million Europeans in the 1850-1915 period not only helped decrease population pressure and thereby raise living standards but also offered an "escape hatch" for Europeans who were frustrated with conditions of social and political oppression in their homelands. To a disproportionate degree, moreover, the emigration drained Europe of the most vigorous elements of its population, those who would be most likely to participate in militant protests. Thus, while slightly under 50 percent of the European population was male and about 40 per cent of the population was between the ages of 15 and 40, over 60 per cent of emigrants were male and about 75 per cent were in the 15-40 age group.

A final contributing reason to the decline of working-class militancy after 1850--and one that is extremely difficult to demonstrate with any degree of exactness--was the diversion of working-class frustrations and anxieties away from class conflict and into such diversionary channels as chauvinistic nationalism, pro-imperialism, anti-semitism, and anti-clericalism. To what degree attempts were made by ruling elites to direct working-class frustrations deliberately into these "safer" channels is difficult to determine, although there is little doubt that such efforts were quite consciously made in some cases. For example, middle- and lower-middle-class republican parties in France, Spain, and Portugal deliberately focussed working-class resentment on the Catholic church and away from issues threatening to property. Thus, one historian has noted that in France after 1870, anti-clericalism was the "only device which the republicans could use to evoke the memories of 1789 without having to put their hands into their pockets to pay for social reforms" (McManners 1969: 320). Comparable parties in Germany and Austria and the czarist government in Russia used anti-semitism for the same purpose. Russian Interior Minister Plehve, for example, is reported to have told a group of Jewish leaders who protested the role of the Russian government in organizing anti-Jewish riots (pograms), "If you will put a stop to the revolution, I will end the pograms" (Salisbury 1978: 103).

There is also some evidence that elites deliberately whipped up nationalistic sentiment and sponsored adventures abroad during the great age of European imperialism (1870-1914) to divert public attention away from issues of social justice at home. Thus, Plehve is reported to have told Czar Nicholas II shortly before the outbreak of the 1904 Russo-Japanese War, "What we need to hold Russia back from revolution is a small, victorious war" (Charques 1965: 87). Along similar lines, German Admiral Alfred von Tirpitz argued that the nationalistic and economic gains to be made by following an imperialistic policy would produce a "powerful palliative against both educated and uneducated social democrats" and German foreign minister Bernhard von Bulow wrote, "Only a successful foreign policy can help to reconcile, pacify, rally, unite" (Wehler 1970: 152; Anderson 1972: 48). The economic benefits of imperialism were described by the British colonialist Cecil Rhodes to a friend:

> Yesterday I attended a meeting of the unemployed in London and having listened to the wild speeches which were nothing more or less than a scream for bread I returned home more than ever convinced of the importance of

imperialism ... the great idea in my mind is the solution of the social problem. By this I mean that in order to save the 40 million inhabitants of the United Kingdom from a murderous civil war the colonial politicians must open up new areas to absorb the excess population and create new markets for the products of the mines and factories. ... If you wish to avoid civil war than you must become an imperialist (Gollwitzer 1969:136).

It should be noted that if imperialistic policies were designed to dampen and divert domestic unrest, they sometimes proved to be dramatic failures that severely discredited a number of European governments, as in Italy in 1896, Greece in 1897, Spain in 1898, and Russia in 1905.


## An Afterthought

The lessons of nineteenth-century Europe suggest that political repression is, from a non-judgmental standpoint, an apparently "normal" aspect of the political modernization process. The key modernizing processes of expanding education, industrialization, and urbanization all tend to mobilize segments of national populations that are formerly too isolated, ignorant, or complacent to seek to advance their positions through organized and continuing means. This mobilizing process leads to repressive reactions on the part of traditional and rising elites who feel threatened by challenges to their power. Even in the most modernized region of Europe in the nineteenth century, significant democratization occurred only when ruling elites felt that the costs of maintaining severe repression were too high and when, in the period after 1850, dramatic advances in living standards and the availability of emigration as an escape valve moderated the attitudes of opposition groups. In the less advanced regions of Europe, such as Italy, Iberia, Russia, and the Balkans, democratization was delayed until after World War II or has not yet developed because of the weakness of opposition forces, continued advances in military technology, and slow economic development. These factors combined to lower the cost of maintaining repression and reduce both the incentives and the resources to substitute reform for repression. Unfortunately, the pattern of highly prolonged repression characteristic of the modernization process in the southern and eastern regions of Europe seems much more likely to be duplicated in the contemporary Third World than the relatively brief period of severe repression that marked the modernization of northwestern Europe. Modern forms of communications, transportation, and military technology--much of it provided by the most "advanced" and "progressive" countries of the world--make the cost of maintaining repression in the Third World today far less than it was in nineteenth-century Europe. Further, there is no "new world" to take in the population surplus of the developing world today as there was in nineteenth-century Europe, and no wave of technologically induced prosperity seems about to wash over the Third World, at least partly because the world economic structure has condemned developing countries to a seemingly permanent status as the provider of raw materials and low-wage labor for the developed world. That the means of repression is now highly efficient and that Third World elites cannot "buy off" the masses without a major redistribution of wealth that they are not likely to foster combine to suggest that the human rights question will be with us for a long time to come. But then, it has been already.

# References

The following references include only materials quoted directly in the text or which were of considerable importance as sources. The references are numbered in order and listed alphabetically by author. At the end of the list, the sources are classified by number according to their subject matter.

1. Abendroth, W. (1972) A Short History of the European Working Class, NLB, London
2. Alston, P.L. (1969) Education and the State in Tsarist Russia, Stanford University Press, Stanford, Calif.
3. Amann, P.H. (1975) Revolution and Mass Democracy: The Paris Club Movement in 1848, Princeton University Press, Princeton, N.J.
4. Aminzade, R. (1981) Class, Politics and Early Industrial Capitalism: A Study of Mid-19th Century Toulouse, France, State University of New York Press
5. Anderson, E.N. and P.R. (1967) Political Institutions and Social Change in Continental Europe in the Nineteenth Century, University of California Press, Berkeley and Los Angeles
6. Anderson, I. (1955) A History of Sweden, Weidenfeld and Nicolson, London
7. Anderson, M.S. (1966) Europe in the Eighteenth Century, 1713-1783, Holt, Rinehart and Winston, New York
8. ____ (1968) Eighteenth-Century Europe, 1713-1789, Oxford University Press, New York
9. ____ (1972) The Ascendancy of Europe: Aspects of European History, 1815-1914, Rowman and Littlefield, Totowa, N.J.
10. Arnstein, W.L. (1971) Britain Yesterday and Today: 1830 to the Present, D.C. Heath, Lexington, Mass.
11. Artz, F.B. (1929) "The Electoral System in France During the Bourbon Restoration, 1815-30," Journal of Modern History, I, 205-18
12. ____ (1963) Reaction and Revolution, 1814-1832, Harper & Row, New York

13. Aspinall, A. (1949) Politics and the Press c. 1780–1850, Home & Van Thal, London

14. Atkinson, W.C. (1960) A History of Spain and Portugal, Penguin, Baltimore

15. Aya, R. (1975) The Missed Revolution: The Fate of Rural Rebels in Sicily and Southern Spain, 1840–1950, Center for Anthropology/Sociology, University of Amsterdam, Amsterdam

16. Balmuth, D. (1979) Censorship in Russia, 1865–1905, University Press of America, Washington, D.C.

17. Bassow, W. (1954) "The Pre-Revolutionary Pravda and Tsarist Censorship," American Slavic & East European Review, 13, 47–65

18. Bater, J.H. (1976) St. Petersburg: Industrialization and Change, McGill-Queen's University Press, Montreal

19. Baughman, J.J. (1959) "The French Banquet Campaign of 1847–48," Journal of Modern History, 31, 1–15

20. Bazillion, R.J. (1978) "Saxon Liberalism and the German Question in the Wake of the 1848 Revolution," Canadian Journal of History, 13, 61–84

21. Beck, E.R. (1979) A Time of Triumph and of Sorrow: Spanish Politics During the Reign of Alfonso XII, 1874–1885, Southern Illinois University, Carbondale

22. Beik, P.H. (1965) Louis Philippe and the July Monarchy, Van Nostrand, Princeton, N.J.

23. Bell, J.D. (1977) Peasants in Power: Alexander Stamboliski and the Bulgarian Agrarian National Union, 1899–1923, Princeton University Press, Princeton, N.J.

24. Bendix, R. (1969) Nation-Building and Citizenship, Anchor, Garden City, N.Y.

25. Benton, R.E. (1977) The Downfall of a King: Dom Manuel II of Portugal, University Press of America, Washington, D.C.

26. Berkeley, G.F.-H. & J. (1932–1940), Italy in the Making, 3 vols., Cambridge University Press, Cambridge

27. Berlin, I. (1959) Karl Marx, Oxford University Press, London

28. Bernstein, S. (1955) Essays in Political and Intellectual History, Paine-Whitman, New York

29. ____ (1965) The Beginnings of Marxian Socialism in France, Russell & Russell, New York

30. Beuer, G. (1947) New Czechoslovakia and Her Historical Background, Lawrence & Wishart, London

31. Bezucha, R.J., ed. (1972) Modern European Social History, D.C. Heath, Lexington, Mass.

32. ____ (1974) The Lyon Uprising of 1834: Social and Political Conflict in the Early July Monarchy, Harvard University Press, Cambridge, Mass.

33. Binkley, R.C. (1963) Realism and Nationalism, 1852–1871, Harper & Row, New York

34. Birch, J.H.S. (1938) Denmark in History, John Murray, London

35. Black, C.E. (1943) The Establishment of Constitutional Government in Bulgaria, Princeton University Press, Princeton, N.J.

36. Blanning, T.C.W. (1970) Joseph II and Enlightened Depotism, Longman, London
37. Blewitt, N. (1965) "The Franchise in the United Kingdom, 1885–1918," Past and Present, 34, 27–52
38. Blit, L. (1971) Origins of Polish Socialism: The History and Ideas of the First Polish Socialist Party, Cambridge University Press, Cambridge
39. Blum, J. (1978) The End of the Old Order in Rural Europe, Princeton University Press, Princeton, N.J.
40. Bobango, G.J. (1979) The Emergence of the Romanian National State, Columbia University Press, New York
41. Bonjour, E., H.S. Offler and G.R. Potter (1952) A Short History of Switzerland, Oxford University Press, London
42. Bookchin, M. (1977) The Spanish Anarchists: The Heroic Years, 1868–1936, Free Life, New York
43. Boyd, C.P. (1979) Praetorian Politics in Liberal Spain, University of North Carolina Press, Chapel Hill
44. Bramstedt, E.K. (1945) Dictatorship and Political Police, Oxford University Press, New York
45. Braunthal J. (1967) History of the International, 1864–1914, Praeger, New York
46. Brenan, G. (1964) The Spanish Labyrinth: An Account of the Social and Political Background to the Spanish Civil War, Cambridge University Press, Cambridge
47. Broeker, G. (1970) Rural Disorder and Police Reform in Ireland, 1812–1836, University of Toronto Press, Toronto
48. Breunig, C. (1970) The Age of Revolution and Reaction, 1789–1850, Norton, New York
49. Brock, M. (1973) The Great Reform Act, Hutchinson University Library, London
50. Brogan, D.W. (1963) The French Nation: From Napoleon to Petain, 1814–1940, Harper & Row, New York
51. Bruun, G. (1960) Nineteenth Century European Civilization, Oxford University Press, London
52. Bull, E. (1956) The Norwegian Trade Union Movement, International Confederation of Free Trade Unions, Brussels
53. Burtsev, V. (1927) "Police Provocation in Russia," Slavonic and East European Review, 6, 247–60
54. Bury, J.P.T. (1954) France 1814–1940, Methuen, London
55. ___ (1964) Napoleon III and the Second Empire, Harper & Row, New York
56. Campbell, J. and P. Sherrard (1968) Modern Greece, Praeger, New York
57. Campbell, P. (1958) French Electoral Systems and Elections Since 1789, Archon, Hamden, Conn.
58. Carlson, A.R. (1972) Anarchism in Germany: The Early Movement, Scarecrow, Metuchen, N.J.
59. Carr, R. (1966) Spain, 1808–1939, Oxford University Press, London
60. ___ (1980) Modern Spain, 1875–1980, Oxford University Press, London

61. Caute, D. (1966) The Left in Europe Since 1789, McGraw-Hill, New York
62. Charques, R. (1965) The Twilight of Imperial Russia, Oxford University Press, London
63. Chevigny, P. (1972), Cops and Rebels: A Study of Provocation, Curtis, New York
64. Clark, S. (1979) Social Origins of the Irish Land War, Princeton University Press, Princeton, N.J.
65. Clogg, R. (1980) A Short History of Modern Greece, Cambridge University Press, Cambridge
66. Cobban, A. (1965), A History of Modern France, Vols. 2–3, Penguin, Baltimore
67. Collins, I. (1959) The Government and the Newspaper Press in France, 1814–1881, Oxford University Press, London
68. ____ (1964) The Age of Progress: A Survey of European History from 1789–1870, Edward Arnold, London
69. Cole, G.D.H. (1960–62) A History of Socialist Thought, Vols. 1–3, MacMillan, London
70. Craig, G. (1964) The Politics of the Prussian Army, 1640–1945, Oxford University Press, London
71. ____ (1980) Germany 1866–1945, Oxford University Press, London
72. Crankshaw, E. (1976) The Shadow of the Winter Palace: Russia's Drift to Revolution, 1825–1917, Viking, New York
73. Curtis, L.P. (1963) Coercion and Conciliation in Ireland, 1880–1892, Princeton University Press, Princeton, N.J.
74. Dakin, D. (1972) The Unification of Greece, 1770–1923, St. Martin's, New York
75. Dawson, W.H. (1914) Municipal Life and Government in Germany, Longman, London
76. Deak, I. (1979) The Lawful Revolution: Louis Kossuth and the Hungarians 1848–1849, Columbia University Press, New York
77. Dedijer, V., et al (1974) History of Yugoslavia, McGraw-Hill, New York
78. de Jong, R. (1971) "Ferdinand Domela Nieuwenhuis: Anarchist and Messiah," Delta, pp. 65–78
79. de Meeus, A. (1962) History of the Belgians, Praeger, New York
80. Derfler, L. (1966) The Third French Republic, Van Nostrand, Princeton, N.J.
81. Derry, J.W. (1963) A Short History of 19th Century England, Mentor, New York
82. Derry, T.K. (1973) A History of Modern Norway, 1814–1972, Oxford University Press, London
83. ____ (1979) A History of Scandinavia, University of Minnesota Press, Minneapolis
84. Dill, M. (1961) Germany: A Modern History, University of Michigan Press, Ann Arbor
85. Dontas, D.N. (1966) Greece and the Great Powers, 1863–1875, Institute for Balkan Studies, Thessaloniki
86. Dowe, D. (1978) "The Workingmen's Choral Movement in Germany Before the First World War," Journal of Contemporary

History, 13, 269–96

87. Doyle, W. (1978) The Old European Order, 1660–1800, Oxford University Press, London

88. Dragnich, A.N. (1974) Serbia, Nikola Pašić, and Yugoslavia, Rugers University Press, New Brunswick, N.J.

89. ___ (1978) The Development of Parliamentary Government in Serbia, Columbia University Press, New York

90. Droz, J. (1967) Europe Between Revolutions, 1815–1848, Harper & Row, New York

91. Dublin, L.I., A.J. Lotka and M. Spiegelman (1949) Length of Life: A Study of the Life Table, Ronald, New York

92. Dupeux, G. (1976) French Society 1789–1970, Methuen, London

93. Duveau, G. (1968) 1848: The Making of a Revolution, Vintage, New York

94. Dziewanowski, M.K. (1976) The Communist Party of Poland: An Outline of History, Harvard University Press, Cambridge, Mass.

95. Edwards, S. (1971) The Paris Commune: 1871, Quadrangle, New York

96. Eidelberg, P.G. (1974) The Great Rumanian Peasant Revolution of 1907, E.J. Brill, Leiden

97. Emerson, D.E. (1968) Metternich and the Political Police: Security and Subversion in the Habsburg Monarchy (1815–1830), Martinus Nijhoff, The Hague

98. Emmons, T. (1977) "Russia's Banquet Campaign," California Slavic Studies, 10, 45–87

99. Evans, R.J. (1979) " 'Red Wednesday' in Hamburg: Social Democrats, police and Lumpenproletariat in the suffrage disturbances of 17 January 1906," Social History, 4, 1–31

100. Evans, S.G. (1960) Short History of Bulgaria, Lawrence & Wishart, London

101. Eyck, E. (1958) Bismarck and the German Empire, Norton, New York

102. Eyck, F.G. (1959) The Benelux Countries: A Historical Survey, Van Nostrand, Princeton, N.J.

103. Fasel, G. (1970) Europe in Upheaval: The Revolutions of 1848, Rand McNally, Chicago

104. Fejto, F., ed. (1973) The Opening of an Era: 1848, Grosset & Dunlap, New York

105. Fetscher, E.B. (1980) "Censorship and the Editorial: Baden's New Press Law of 1840 and the Seeblätter at Konstanz," German Studies Review, 3, 377–94

106. Flora, P. (1973) "Historical Processes of Social Mobilization: Urbanization and Literacy, 1850–1965," in S.N. Eisenstadt and S. Rokkan (eds.), Building States and Nations, Sage, Beverly Hills, Calif.

107. Florence, R. (1971) Fritz: The Story of an Assassin, Dial Press, New York

108. Ford, F.L. (1970) Europe 1780–1830, Longman, London

109. Forstenzer, T.R. (1981) French Provincial Police and the Fall of the Second Republic, Princeton University Press, Princeton, N.J.

110. Fried, R. (1963) The Italian Prefects, Yale University Press, New Haven, Conn.

111. Gallaher, J. (1980), The Students of Paris and the Revolution of 1848, Southern Illinois University Press, Carbondale

112. Galai, S. (1973) The Liberation Movement in Russia, 1900–05, Cambridge University Press, Cambridge

113. Galenson, W. (1949) Labor in Norway, Harvard University Press, Cambridge, Mass.

114. ____ (1952a) Comparative Labor Movements, Prentice–Hall, New York

115. ____ (1952b) The Danish System of Labor Relations, Harvard University Press, Cambridge, Mass.

116. Garver, B.M. (1978) The Young Czech Party 1874–1901, Yale University Press, New Haven, Conn.

117. Gash, N. (1979) Aristocracy and People: Britain 1815–1865, Harvard University Press, Cambridge, Mass.

118. Gay, P. (1970) The Dilemma of Democratic Socialism: Eduard Bernstein's Challenge to Marx, Collier, New York

119. Gazi, S. (1973) A History of Croatia, Philosophical Library, New York

120. Geary, D. (1981) European Labour Protest, 1848–1939, St. Martin's, New York

121. Gilbert, Felix (1970) The End of the European Era, 1890 to the Present, Norton, New York

122. Gilliard, C. (1955) A History of Switzerland, Greenwood, Westport, Conn.

123. Gillis, J.R. (1977) The Development of European Society, 1770–1870, Houghton Mifflin, Boston

124. Ginsborg, P. (1979) Daniele Manin and the Venetian Revolution of 1848–49, Cambridge University Press, Cambridge

125. Georgescu–Buzau, G. (1965) The 1848 Revolution in the Rumanian Lands, Meridiane, Bucharest

126. Goldstein, R.J. (1968) Political Repression in Modern America: From 1870 to the Present, Schenkman, Cambridge, Mass.

127. Gollwitzer, H. (1969) Europe in the Age of Imperialism, 1880–1914, Harcourt, Brace & World, New York

128. Grebing, H. (1969) The History of the German Labour Movement, Oswald Wolff, London

129. Grenville, J.A.S. (1976) Europe Reshaped 1848–1878, Fontana, London

130. Gualtieri, H.L. (1946) The Labor Movement in Italy, Vanni, New York

131. Gulick, C.A. (1948) Austria from Habsburg to Hitler: Labor's Workshop of Democracy, University of California Press, Berkeley and Los Angeles

132. Hall, A. (1974a) "By Other Means: The Legal Struggle Against the SPD in Wilhelmine Germany, 1890–1900," Historical Journal, 17, 265–86

133. ____ (1974b) "The Kaiser, the Wilhelmine State and Lèse-majesté," German Life and Letters, pp. 101–15

134. ___ (1976) "The War of Words: Anti-Socialist Offensives and Counter-propaganda in Wilhelmine Germany, 1890–1914," Journal of Contemporary History, 11, 11–42

135. ___ (1977) Scandal, Sensation and Social Democracy: The SPD Press and Wilhelmine Germany, Cambridge University Press, Cambridge

136. Hales, E.E.Y. (1954) Pio Nono: A Study in European Politics and Religion in the Nineteenth Century, P.J. Kenedy, New York

137. ___ (1966) Revolution and Papacy, 1769–1846, University of Notre Dame Press, Notre Dame, Indiana

138 Hamerow, T.S. (1966) Restoration, Revolution, Reaction: Economics and Politics in Germany, 1815–1871, Princeton University Press, Princeton, N.J.

139. ___ (1969) The Social Foundations of German Unification, 1858–1871: Ideas and Institutions, Princeton University Press, Princeton, N.J.

140. ___ (1974) The Social Foundations of German Unification, 1858–1871: Struggles and Accomplishments, Princeton University Press, Princeton, N.J.

141. Hammen, O.J. (1969) The Red '48ers: Karl Marx and Friedrich Engels, Scribner's, New York

142. Hanchett, W. (1976) "Tsarist Statutory Regulations of Municipal Government in the Nineteenth Century," in M.F. Hammond (ed.), The City in Russian History, University Press of Kentucky, Lexington

143. Harcave, S. (1970) The Russian Revolution of 1905, Collier, New York

144. Harrison, J. (1978) An Economic History of Modern Spain, Holmes & Meier, New York

145. Hastad, E. (1957) The Parliament of Sweden, Hansard Society, London

146. Hayes, C.J.H. (1963) A Generation of Materialism, 1871–1900, Harper & Row, New York

147. Headrick, D.R. (1976) "Spain and the Revolutions of 1848," European Studies Review, 6, 197–223

148. Hearder, H. (1963) A Short History of Italy, Cambrdige University Press, Cambridge

149. ___ (1970) Europe in the Nineteenth Century, 1830–1880, Longman, London

150. Helmreich, J.E. (1976) Belgium and Europe: A Study in Small Power Diplomacy, Mouton, The Hague

151. Hemmins, F.W.J. (1971) Culture and Society in France, 1848–1898, Batsford, London

152. Henderson, W.O. (1969) The Industrialization of Europe, 1780–1914, Harcourt, Brace & World, New York

153. Hennessy, C.A.M. (1962) The Federal Republic in Spain: Pi y Margall and the Federal Republican Movement, 1868–1874, Oxford University Press, London

154. Hennock, E.P. (1973) Fit and Proper Persons: Ideal and Reality in Ninetenth Century Urban Government, Edward Arnold, London

155. Herr, R. (1974) An Historical Essay on Modern Spain, University of California Press, Berkeley and Los Angeles
156. Hibbert, C. (1970) Garibaldi and His Enemies, New American Library, New York
157. Hilton-Young, W. (1949) The Italian Left: A Short History of Political Socialism in Italy, Longman, London
158. Hobsbawm, E.J. (1962) The Age of Revolution, 1789–1848, Mentor, New York
159. ____ (1979) The Age of Capital, 1848–1875, Mentor, New York
160. Hodgson, J.H. (1967) Communism in Finland, Princeton University Press, Princeton, N.J.
161. Hohenberg, J. (1971) Free Press, Free People: The Best Cause, Columbia University Press, New York
162. Holborn, H. (1969) A History of Modern Germany, 1840–1945, Knopf, New York
163. Holt, E. (1971) The Making of Italy, 1815–1870, Atheneum, New York
164. Homan, G.D. (1966) "Constitutional Reform in the Netherlands in 1848," Historian, 28, 405–25
165. Horowitz, D.L. (1963) The Italian Labor Movement, Harvard University Press, Cambridge, Mass.
166. Hosking, G.A. (1973) The Russian Constitutional Experiment: Government and Duma, 1907–1914, Cambridge University Press, Cambridge
167. Hostetter, R. (1958) The Italian Socialist Movement: Origins (1860–1882), Van Nostrand, Princeton, N.J.
168. Hovde, B.J. (1943) The Scandinavian Countries, 1720–1865: The Rise of the Middle Classes, 2 vols., Chapman & Grimes, Boston
169. Hubbard, W.H. (1970) "Politics and Society in the Central European City: Graz, Austria, 1861–1918," Canadian Journal of History, 5, 25–45
170. Hughes, H.S. (1965) The United States and Italy, Norton, New York
171. Hughes, S. (1967) The Fall and Rise of Modern Italy, Minerva, New York
172. Ignotus, P. (1972) Hungary, Praeger, New York
173. Imlah, A.G. (1966) Britain and Switzerland, 1845–1860, Archon, Hamden, Conn.
174. Ingraham, B.L. (1979) Political Crime in Europe, University of California Press, Berkeley and Los Angeles
175 Jackson, J. (1962) Marx, Proudhon and European Socialism, Collier, New York
176. Janos, A.C. (1971) "The Decline of Oligarchy: Bureaucratic and Mass Politics in the Age of Dualism (1867–1918)," in A.C. Janos and W.B. Slottman (eds.), Revolution in Perspective: Essays on the Hungarian Soviet Republic of 1919, University of California Press, Berkeley and Los Angeles
177. ____ (1982) The Politics of Backwardness in Hungary, 1825–1945, Princeton University Press, Princeton, N.J.
178. Jaszi, O. (1966) The Dissolution of the Habsburg Monarchy,

University of Chicago Press, Chicago

179. Jecchinis, C. (1967) Trade Unionism in Greece, Roosevelt University, Chicago

180. Jelavich, C. and B. (1977) The Establishment of the Balkan National States, 1804–1920, University of Washington Press, Seattle

181. Jellinek, F. (1965) The Paris Commune of 1871, Grosset & Dunlap, New York

182. Jenks, W.A. (1950) The Austrian Electoral Reform of 1907, Columbia University Press, New York

183. _____ (1960) Vienna and the Young Hitler, Columbia University Press, New York

184. _____ (1965) Austria Under the Iron Ring, 1879–1893, University Press of Virginia, Charlottesville

185. _____ (1978) Francis Joseph and the Italians, 1849–1859, University Press of Virginia, Charlottesville

186. Johnson, R.J. (1972) "Zagranichnaia Agentura: The Tsarist Political Police in Europe," Journal of Contemporary History, 7, 221–42

187. Joll, J. (1966a) The Anarchists, Grosset & Dunlap, New York

188. _____ (1966b) The Second International, 1889–1914, Harper & Row, New York

189. _____ (1976) Europe Since 1870, Penguin, Baltimore

190. Jones, W.G. (1970) Denmark, Praeger, New York

191. Joughin, J.T. (1955) The History of the Amnesty of 1880: The Paris Commune in French Politics, 1871–1880, 2 vols., Johns Hopkins University Press, Baltimore

192. Jutikkala, E. (1962) A History of Finland, Praeger, New York

193. Kann, R.A. (1974) A History of the Habsburg Empire, 1526–1918, University of California Press, Berkeley and Los Angeles

194. Kaplan, F.L. (1977) The Czech and Slovak Press: The First 100 Years, Association for Education in Journalism, Lexington, Kentucky

195. Kaplan, T. (1977) Anarchists of Andalusia, 1868–1903, Princeton University Press, Princeton, N.J.

196. Kendall, W. (1975) The Labour Movement in Europe, Allen Lane, London

197. Kenner, F. (1956) Trade Unions in Austria, International Confederation of Free Trade Unions, Brussels

198. Keith–Lucas, B. (1952) The English Local Government Franchise, Oxford University Press, London

199. Kent, S. (1937) Electoral Procedure Under Louis Philippe, Yale University Press, New Haven, Conn.

200. Kern, R.W. (1973) "Spanish Caciquismo," in Kern (ed.), The Caciques, University of New Mexico Press, Albuquerque

201. _____ (1974) Liberals, Reformers and Caciques in Restoration Spain, 1875–1909, University of New Mexico, Albuquerque

202. Kieniewicz, S. (1947) "The Free State of Cracow, 1815–1846," Slavonic and East European Review, 26, 64–89

203. _____ et al. (1968) History of Poland, Polish Scientific Publishers,

Warsaw

204. Kiernan, V.G. (1966) <u>The Revolution of 1854 in Spanish History</u>, Oxford University Press, London

205. Kimball, A. (1973) "Harassment of Russian Revolutionaries Abroad," <u>Oxford Slavonic Papers</u>, <u>6</u>, 48–65

206. Kimball, S.B. (1964) <u>Czech Nationalism: A Study of the National Theatre Movement, 1845–1880</u>, University of Illinois Press, Urbana

207. King, B. (1912) <u>A History of Italian Unity</u>, Vol. I, Nisbet, London

208. Kirby, D.G. (1979) <u>Finland in the Twentieth Century</u>, Hurst, London

209. Kirchheimer, O. (1968) <u>Political Justice</u>, Princeton University Press, Princeton, N.J.

210. Knapp, V.J. (1976) <u>Europe in the Era of Social Transformation</u>, Prentice–Hall, Englewood Cliffs, N.J.

211. Knoellinger, C.E. (1960) <u>Labor in Finland</u>, Harvard University Press, Cambridge, Mass.

212. Kochan, L. (1963) <u>The Making of Modern Russia</u>, Penguin, New York

213. ____ (1966) <u>Russia in Revolution, 1890–1918</u>, New American Library, New York

214. Kocik, A. (1961) <u>The Danish Trade Union Movement</u>, International Confederation of Free Trade Unions, Brussels

215. Kofas, J.V. (1980) <u>International and Domestic Politics In Greece During the Crimean War</u>, Columbia University Press, 1980

216. Kosary, D. and S. Vardy (1969) <u>History of the Hungarian Nation</u>, Danielson, Astor Park, Fla.

217. Kossev, D.H. Hristov and D. Angelov (1963) <u>A Short History of Bulgaria</u>, Foreign Languages Press, Sofia

218. Kossmann, E.H. (1978) <u>The Low Countries, 1780–1940</u>, Oxford University Press, London

219. Kousoulas, D.G. (1974) <u>Modern Greece</u>, Scribner's, New York

220. Kovrig, B. (1979) <u>Communism in Hungary</u>, Hoover Institution Press, Stanford, Calif.

221. Kulstein, D.I. (1969) <u>Napoleon III and the Working Class</u>, Calif. State Colleges, Los Angeles

222. Lafferty, W. (1971) <u>Economic Development and the Response of Labor in Scandinavia</u>, Universitetsforlaget, Oslo

223. Laidler, H.W. (1968) <u>History of Socialism</u>, Crowell, New York

224. Landauer, C. (1959) <u>European Socialism</u>, Vol. I, University of California Press, Berkeley and Los Angeles

225. Langer, W.L. (1969) <u>Political and Social Upheaval, 1832–1852</u>, Harper & Row, New York

226. Larson, K. (1948) <u>A History of Norway</u>, Princeton University Press, Princeton, N.J.

227. Lees, A. (1974) <u>Revolution and Reflection: Intellectual Change in Germany during the 1850s</u>, Martinus Nijhoff, The Hague

228. Leslie, R.F. (1956) <u>Polish Politics and the Revolution of November 1830</u>, University of London Press, London

229. ____ (1963) <u>Reform and Insurrection in Russian Poland</u>,

1856–1865, University of London Press, London
230. _____ (1964) The Age of Transformation, 1789–1871, Harper & Row, New York
231. _____ (1980) The History of Poland Since 1863, Cambridge University Press, Cambridge
232. Levine, I.R. (1973) The New Worker in Soviet Russia, Macmillan, New York
233. Levine, L. (1914) Syndicalism in France, Columbia University Press, New York
234. Liang, H. (1980) "International Cooperation of Political Police in Europe, 1815–1914," Mitteilugen des Österreichischen Staatsarchivs, 33, 193–217
235. Lida, C.E. (1969) "Agrarian Anarchism in Andalusia," International Review of Social History, 14, 315–52
236. Lidtke, V.L. (1966) The Outlawed Party: Social Democracy in Germany, 1878–1890, Princeton University Press, Princeton, N.J.
237. Lipson, E. (1962) Europe in the Nineteenth Century, Collier, New York
238. Lis, C. and H. Soly (1979) Poverty and Capitalism in Pre-Industrial Europe, Humanities, Atlantic Highlands, N.J.
239. Livermore, H.V. (1960) A History of Spain, Grove, New York
240. _____ (1969) A New History of Portugal, Cambridge University Press, Cambridge
241. _____ (1973) Portugal: A Short History, Edinburgh University Press, Edinburgh
242. Lorwin, V.R. (1954) The French Labor Movement, Harvard University Press, Cambridge, Mass.
243. Lougee, R.W. (1972) Midcentury Revolution, 1848: Society and Revolution in France and Germany, D.C. Heath, Lexington, Mass.
244. Lüdtke, A. (1979) "The Role of State Violence in the Period of Transition to Industrial Capitalism: The Example of Prussia from 1815 to 1848," Social History, 4, 175–221
245. Macartney, C.A. (1962) Hungary: A Short History, Aldine, Chicago
246. _____ (1969) The Habsburg Empire, 1790–1918, Macmillan, New York
247. _____ (1977) "1848 in the Habsburg Monarchy," European Studies Review, 7, 285–309
248. _____ (1978) The House of Austria: The Later Phase, 1790–1918, Edinburgh University Press, Edinburgh
249. MacDonagh, O. (1968) Ireland, Prentice-Hall, Englewood Cliffs, N.J.
250. MacDermott, M. (1962) A History of Bulgaria, 1393–1885, Allen and Unwin, London
251. Mackie, T.T. and R. Rose (1974) The International Almanac of Electoral History, Macmillan, New York
252 Maehl, W. (1980) August Bebel: Shadow Emperor of the German Workers, American Philosophical Society, Philadelphia
253. Mallinson, V. Belgium, Praeger, New York
254. Margadant, T. (1979) French Peasants in Revolt: The

Insurrection of 1851, Princeton University Press, Princeton, N.J.

255. Marichal, C. (1977) Spain (1834–1844): A New Society, Tamesis, London

256. Marlow, J. (1971) The Peterloo Massacre, Panther, London

257. Marquardt, F.D. (1974) "A Working Class in Berlin in the 1840s?" in H.U. Wehler (ed.), Sozialgeschichte Heute, Vanderhoeck and Ruprecht, Göttingen

258. Martin, G. (1969) The Red Shirt & the Cross of Savoy: The Story of Italy's Risorgimento, Dodd, Mead, New York

259. Martin, W. (1971) Switzerland: From Roman Times to the Present, Praeger, New York

260. Mather, F.C. (1959) Public Order in the Age of the Chartists, Manchester University Press, Manchester

261. Maura, J.R. (1968) "Terrorism in Barcelona and Its Impact on Spanish Politics, 1904–1909," Past and Present, 41, 130–83

262. May, A.J. (1963) The Age of Metternich, 1814–1848, Holt, Rinehart and Winston, New York

263. ____ (1968) The Hapsburg Monarchy 1867–1914, Norton, New York

264. Mayer, A.J. (1971) Dynamics of Counterrevolution in Europe, 1870–1956, Harper & Row, New York

265. ____ (1981) The Persistence of the Old Regime, Pantheon, New York

266. McCaffrey, L.J. (1968) The Irish Question, 1800–1922, University of Kentucky Press, Lexington

267. ____ (1979) Ireland: From Colony to Nation State, Prentice-Hall, Englewood Cliffs, N.J.

268. McClellan, W.D. (1964) Svetozar Marković and the Origins of Balkan Socialism, Princeton University Press, Princeton, N.J.

269. ____ (1979) Revolutionary Exiles: The Russians in the First International and the Paris Commune, Frank Cass, London

270. McClelland, C. (1980) State, University and Society in Germany, 1700–1914, Cambridge University Press, Cambridge

271. McClelland, J. (1979) Autocrats and Academics: Education, Culture and Society in Tsarist Russia, University of Chicago Press, Chicago

272. McConagha, W.A. (1942) Development of the Labor Movement in Great Britain, France and Germany, University of North Carolina, Chapel Hill

273. McGrath, W.J. (1974) Dionysian Art and Populist Politics in Austria, Yale University Press, New Haven, Conn.

274. McGrew, R.E. (1960) "The First Cholera Epidemic and Social History," Bulletin of the History of Medicine, 34, 61–73

275. ____ (1965) Russia and the Cholera, 1823–1832, University of Wisconsin Press, Madison

276. McManners, J. (1969) European History, 1789–1914, Harper & Row, New York

277. Meaker, G.H. (1974) The Revolutionary Left in Spain, 1914–1923, Stanford University Press, Stanford, Calif.

278. Mendelsohn, E. (1970) Class Struggle in the Pale: The Formation of the Jewish Workers' Movement in Tsarist Russia, Cambridge

University Press, Cambridge

279. Merriman, J.M. (1978) The Agony of the Republic: The Repression of the Left in Revolutionary France, 1848-1851, Yale University Press, New Haven, Conn.

280. Mertens, C. (1925) The Trade Union Movement in Belgium, International Federation of Trade Unions, Amsterdam

281. Miller, K.E. (1968) Government and Politics in Denmark, Houghton Mifflin, Boston

282. Mitchell, B.R. (1975) European Historical Statistics, 1750-1970, Columbia University Press, New York

283. Mitchell, H. and P.N. Stearns (1971) Workers and Protest: The European Labor Movement, The Working Classes and the Origins of Social Democracy, 1890-1914, Peacock, Itasca, Ill.

284. Mitrany, D. (1968) The Land & the Peasant in Rumania, Greenwood, New York

285. Mokyr, J. (1976) Industrialization in the Low Countries, 1795-1850, Yale University Press, New Haven, Conn.

286. Monas, S. (1961) The Third Section: Police and Society in Russia under Nicholas I, Harvard University Press, Cambridge, Mass.

287. Moody, J.N. (1978) French Education Since Napoleon, Syracuse University Press, Syracuse, N.Y.

288. Moore, B. (1966) Social Origins of Dictatorship and Democracy, Beacon, Boston

289. Morgan, R. (1965) The German Social Democrats and the First International, 1864-1872, Cambridge University Press, Cambridge

290. Moss, B.H. (1976) The Origins of the French Labor Movement, University of California Press, Berkeley and Los Angeles

291. Mosse, W.E. (1962) Alexander II and the Modernization of Russia, Collier, New York

292. ____ (1974) Liberal Europe: The Age of Bourgeois Realism, 1848-1875, Harcourt Brace Jovanovich, New York

293. Munro, W.B. (1913) The Government of European Cities, Macmillan, New York

294. Musulin, S. (1975) Vienna in the Age of Metternich, Westview, Boulder, Colo.

295. Naimark, N. (1979) The History of the "Proletariat": The Emergence of Marxism in the Kingdom of Poland, 1870-1887, Columbia University Press, New York

296. Namier, L. (1964) 1848: The Revolution of the Intellectuals, Anchor, Garden City, N.Y.

297. Neufeld, M.F. (1961) Italy, School for Awakening Countries: The Italian Labor Movement in its Political, Social and Economic Setting from 1800 to 1960, Cornell University Press, Ithaca, N.Y.

298. Newman, E. (1974) Restoration Radical: Robert Blum and the Challenge of German Democracy, 1807-48, Branden, Boston

299. Noland, A. (1956) The Founding of the French Socialist Party (1893-1905), Harvard University Press, Cambridge, Mass.

300. Nomad, M. (1961) Apostles of Revolution, Collier, New York

301. Norman, E. (1973) A History of Modern Ireland, Penguin, Baltimore

302. Nowell, C.E. (1952) A History of Portugal, Van Nostrand, New York

303. Noyes, P.H. (1966) Organization and Revolution: Working Class Associations in the German Revolutions of 1848-1849, Princeton University Press, Princeton, N.J.

304. Oakley, S. (1972) A Short History of Denmark, Praeger, New York

305. Oliveira Marques, A.H. (1976) History of Portugal, Columbia University Press, New York

306. Olson, K.E. (1966) The History Makers: The Press of Europe from its Beginnings through 1965, Louisiana State University Press, Baton Rouge

307. Österud, O. (1977) Agrarian Structure and Peasant Politics in Scandinavia, Universitetsforlaget, Oslo

308. Otetea, A., ed. (1970) The History of the Romanian People, Twayne, New York

309. Packe, M.S.J. (1957) The Bombs of Orsini, Secker and Warburg, London

310. Palmer, R.R. (1969-70) The Age of the Democratic Revolution, 2 vols., Princeton University Press, Princeton, N.J.

311. Palmer, S.H. (1977) "Rebellion, Emancipation, Starvation: The Dilemma of Peaceful Protest in Ireland, 1798-1848," in B.K. Lackner and K.R. Philp, The Walter Prescott Webb Memorial Lectures: Essays on Modern European Revolutionary History, University of Texas Press, Austin, pp. 3-38

312. Pamlényi, E. (1975) A History of Hungary, Collet's, London

313. Papacosma, S.V. (1977) The Military in Greek Politics: The 1909 Coup D'Etat, Kent State University Press, Kent, Ohio

314. Passant, E.J. (1962) A Short History of Germany 1815-1945, Cambridge University Press, Cambridge

315. Payne, S.G. (1967) Politics and the Military in Modern Spain, Stanford University Press, Palo Alto, Calif.

316. ____ (1970) The Spanish Revolution, Norton, New York

317. ____ (1973) A History of Spain and Portugal, 2 vols., University of Wisconsin Press, Madison

318. Payne, H.C. (1963) "The Exiled Revolutionaries and the French Political Police in the 1850s," American Historical Review, 68, 954-73

319. ____ (1966) The Police State of Louis Napoleon Bonaparte, 1851-1860, University of Washington Press, Seattle

320. Pech, S.Z. (1969) The Czech Revolution of 1848, University of North Carolina Press, Chapel Hill, N.C.

321. Pelling, H. (1976) A History of British Trade Unionism, Penguin, Baltimore

322. Penn, V. (1938) "Philhellinism in Europe," Slavonic Review, 16, 638-53

323. Petropulos, J.A. (1968) Politics and Statecraft in the Kingdom of Greece, 1833-1843, Princeton University Press, Princeton, N.J.

324. Petrovich, M.B. (1976) A History of Modern Siberia, 1804-1918, 2 vols., Harcourt Brace Jovanovich, New York

325. Phillips, G.W. (1976) "Urban Proletarian Politics in Tsarist

Russia," Comparative Urban Research, 3, 11–20

326. Pinkney, D. (1972) The French Revolution of 1830, Princeton University Press, Princeton, N.J.

327. Pinson, K.S. (1954) Modern Germany: Its History and Civilization, Macmillan, New York

328. Pogorelskin, A.E. (1976) "The Politics of Frustration: The Governor-Generalship of N.I. Bobrikov in Finland, 1898–1904," Journal of Baltic Studies, 7, 231–46

329. Polisensky, J. (1980) Aristocrats and the Crowd in the Revolutionary Year 1848: A Contribution to the History of Revolution and Counter-Revolution in Austria, State University of New York Press, Albany

330. Popperwell, R.G. (1972) Norway, Westview, Boulder, Colo.

331. Porter, B. (1979) The Refugee Question in Mid-Victorian Politics, Cambridge University Press, Cambridge

332. Post, J.D. (1977) The Last Great Subsistence Crisis in the West, Johns Hopkins University Press, Baltimore

333. Price, R. (1971) "Conservative Reactions to Social Disorder: The Paris Commune of 1871," Journal of European Studies, 1, 341–52

334. ____ (1972) The French Second Republic: A Social History, Cornell University Press, Ithaca, N.Y.

335. ____, ed. (1975) Revolution and Reaction: 1848 and the Second French Republic, Croom Helm, London

336. Puntila, L.A. (1975) The Political History of Finland, 1809–1966, Heinemann, London

337. Rader, D.L. (1973) The Journalists and the July Revolution in France, Martinus Nijhoff, The Hague

338. Rath, R.J. (1944) "Training for Citizenship in the Austrian Elementary Schools During the Reign of Francis I," Journal of Central European Affairs, 4, 147–64

339. ____ (1957) The Viennese Revolution of 1848, University of Texas Press, Austin

340. Reichard, R.W. (1953) "The German Working Class and the Russian Revolution of 1905," Journal of Central European Affairs, 13, 136–53

341. ____ (1969) Crippled from Birth: German Social Democracy, 1844–1870, Iowa State University Press, Ames

342. Reichert, R.W. (1963) "Anti-Bonapartist Elections to the Academie Française during the Second Empire," Journal of Modern History, 35, 33–46

343. Resnick, D.P. (1966) The White Terror and the Political Reaction after Waterloo, Harvard University Press, Cambridge, Mass.

344 Reynolds, J. (1954) The Catholic Emancipation Crisis in Ireland, 1823–1829, Yale University Press, New Haven, Conn.

345. Riasanovsky, N. (1959) Nicholas I and Official Nationality in Russia, 1825–1855, University of California Press, Berkeley and Los Angeles

346. ____ (1969) A History of Russia, Oxford University Press, London

347. Rich, Norman (1970) The Age of Nationalism and Reform, 1850–1890, Norton, New York

348. Rice, E.F. (1970) The Foundations of Early Modern Europe, 1460–1559, Norton, New York

349. Ridley, F.F. (1970) Revolutionary Syndicalism in France, Cambridge University Press, Cambridge

350. Ringer, F.K. (1979) Education and Society in Modern Europe, Indiana University Press, Bloomington

351. Robbins, J.J. (1942) The Government of Labor Relations in Sweden, University of North Carolina Press, Chapel Hill

352. Roberts, H.L. (1951) Rumania: Political Problems of an Agrarian State, Yale University Press, New Haven, Conn.

353. Roberts, J.M. (1972) Europe, 1880–1945, Longman, London

354. ____ (1976) Revolution and Improvement: The Western World, 1775–1847, University of California Press, Berkeley and Los Angeles

355. Robertson, P. (1960) Revolutions of 1848: A Social History, Harper & Row, New York

356. Robinson, H. (1948) The British Post Office: A History, Princeton University Press, Princeton, N.J.

357. Rohr, D.G. (1963) The Origins of Social Liberalism in Germany, University of Chicago Press, Chicago

358. Rokkan S. and J. Meyriat, eds. (1969) International Guide to Electoral Statistics, Vol. I, Mouton, The Hague

359. Rokkan, S. (1967) "Geography, Religion and Social Class: Cross–cutting Cleavages in Norwegian Politics," in S.M. Lipset and S. Rokkan (eds.) Party Systems and Voter Alignments, Free Press, New York

360. ____ (1970) Citizens, Elections, Parties, David McKay, New York

361. Romani, G.T. (1950) The Neapolitan Revolution of 1820–1821, Northwestern University Press, Evanston, Ill.

362. Romein, J. (1978) The Watershed of Two Eras: Europe in 1900, Wesleyan University Press, Middletown, Conn.

363. Roth, G. (1963) The Social Democrats in Imperial Germany, Bedminster Press, Totowa, N.J.

364. Rothschild, J. (1959) The Communist Party of Bulgaria: Origins and Development, Columbia University Press, New York

365. Rudé, G. (1964) The Crowd in History, 1730–1848, Wiley, New York

366. ____ (1966) Revolutionary Europe, 1783–1815, Harper & Row, New York

367. ____ (1978) Protest and Punishment: The Story of the Social and Political Prisoners Transported to Australia, 1788–1868, Oxford University Press, London

368. Rustow, D.A. (1955) The Politics of Compromise: A Study of Parties and Cabinet Government in Sweden, Princeton University Press, Princeton, N.J.

369. Ruud, C.A. (1979) "Limits on the 'Freed' Press of 18th– and 19th–Century Europe," Journalism Quarterly, 56, 521–30

370. Sablinsky, W. (1976) The Road to Bloody Sunday, Father Gapon and the St. Petersburg Massacre of 1905, Princeton University Press, Princeton, N.J.

371. Sagarra, E. (1977) <u>A Social History of Germany, 1648–1914,</u> Holmes & Meier, New York

372. St. Clair, W. (1972) <u>That Greece Might Still Be Free: The Philhellenes in the War of Independence,</u> Oxford University Press, London

373. Salisbury, H. (1978) <u>Black Night, White Snow: Russia's Revolutions, 1905–1917,</u> Doubleday, New York

374. Salomone, A.W. (1960) <u>Italy in the Giolittian Era: Italian Democracy in the Making, 1900–1914,</u> University of Pennsylvania Press, Philadelphia

375. Sauvigny, G. (1962) <u>Metternich and His Times,</u> Darton, Longman & Todd, London

376. _____ (1966) <u>The Bourbon Restoration,</u> University of Pennsylvania Press, Philadelphia

377. Schneiderman, J. (1976) <u>Sergei Zubatov and Revolutionary Marxism: The Struggle for the Working Class in Tsarist Russia,</u> Cornell University Press, Ithaca, N.Y.

378. Schorske, C.E. (1965) <u>German Social Democracy, 1905–1917,</u> Wiley, New York

379. Schulte, H.F. (1968) <u>The Spanish Press, 1470–1966,</u> University of Illinois Press, Urbana

380. Scobbie, I. (1972) <u>Sweden,</u> Praeger, New York

381. Scott, F.D. (1977) <u>Sweden: The Nation's History,</u> University of Minnesota Press, Minneapolis

382. Sedgwick, A. (1968) <u>The Third French Republic, 1870–1914,</u> Crowell, New York

383. Sewell, W. (1980) <u>Work and Revolution in France: The Language of Labor from the Old Regime to 1848,</u> Cambridge University Press, Cambridge

384. Seton-Watson, C. (1967) <u>Italy from Liberalism to Fascism, 1870–1925,</u> Methuen, London

385. Seton-Watson, H. (1967) <u>The Russian Empire, 1801–1917,</u> Oxford University Press, London

386. Seton-Watson, R.W. (1911) <u>Corruption and Reform in Hungary: A Study in Electoral Practice,</u> Constable, London

387. _____ (1912) <u>Absolutism in Croatia,</u> Constable, London

388. _____ (1934) <u>A History of the Roumanians,</u> Cambridge University Press, Cambridge

389. _____ (1965) <u>A History of the Czechs and Slovaks,</u> Archon, Hamden, Conn.

390. _____ (1972) <u>Racial Problems in Hungary,</u> Fertig, New York

391. Sheehan, J.J. (1978) <u>German Liberalism in the Nineteenth Century,</u> University of Chicago Press, Chicago

392. Shorter, E. and C. Tilly (1974) <u>Strikes in France, 1830–1968,</u> Cambridge University Press, Cambridge, Mass.

393. Sigmann, J. (1973) <u>1848: .The Romantic and Democratic Revolutions in Europe,</u> Harper & Row, New York

394. Simon, W.M. (1955) <u>The Failure of the Prussian Reform Movement, 1807–1819,</u> Cornell University Press, Ithaca, N.Y.

395. Skilling, H.G. (1970) "The Politics of the Czech Eighties," in P.

Brock and H.G. Skilling (eds.) The Czech Renascence of the Nineteenth Century, University of Toronto Press, Toronto

396. Smith, A. (1979) The Newspaper: An International History, Thames & Hudson, London

397. Smith, F.B. (1966) The Making of the Second Reform Bill, Melbourne University Press, Melbourne

398. ____ (1970) "British Post Office Espionage," Historical Studies, 14, 189–203

399. Smith, D.M. (1968) A History of Sicily: Modern Sicily After 1715, Viking, New York

400. ____ (1959) Italy: A Modern History, University of Michigan Press, Ann Arbor

401. Snell, J.L. (1976) The Democratic Movement in Germany, 1789–1914, University of North Carolina Press, Chapel Hill

402. Spencer, P. (1956) "Censorship by Imprisonment in France, 1830–1870," Romanic Review, 47, 27–38

403. Spring, D., ed., (1977) European Landed Elites in the Nineteenth Century, Johns Hopkins University Press, Baltimore

404. Squire, P.S. (1968) The Third Department: The Establishment and Practices of the Political Police in the Russia of Nicholas, Cambridge University Press, Cambridge

405. Stadelmann, R. (1975) Social and Political History of the German 1848 Revolution, Ohio University Press, Athens

406. Stafford, D. (1971) From Anarchism to Reformism: A Study of the Political Activities of Paul Brousse, 1870–90, University of Toronto Press, Toronto

407. Stavrianos, L.S. (1958) The Balkans Since 1453, Holt, Rinehart & Winston, New York

408. ____ (1963) "The Influence of the West on the Balkans," in C. and B. Jelavich (eds.), The Balkans in Transition, University of California Press, Berkeley and Los Angeles

409. Stearns, P.N. (1971) Revolutionary Syndicalism and French Labor, Rutgers University Press, New Brunswick, N.J.

410. ____ (1974) 1848: The Revolutionary Tide in Europe, Norton, New York

411. ____ (1975) European Society in Upheaval: Social History Since 1750, Macmillan, New York

412. Steinby, T. (1971) In Quest of Freedom: Finland's Press, 1771–1971, Government Printing Office, Helsinki

413. Stewart, J.H. (1968) The Restoration Era in France, 1814–1830, Van Nostrand, Princeton, N.J.

414. Stokes, G. (1975) Legitimacy Through Liberalism: Vladimir Jovanović and the Transformation of Serbian Politics, University of Washington Press, Seattle

415. Stone, N. (1967) "Constitutional Crisis in Hungary, 1903–1906," Slavonic Review, 45, 163–82

416. Szabad, G. (1977) "Hungarian Political Trends Between the Revolution and the Compromise," Studia Historica, 128, 11–167

417. Talmon, J.L. (1967) Romanticism and Revolt, Europe 1815–1848, Harcourt, Brace & World, New York

418. Tamason, C.A. (1980) "From Mortuary to Cemetary: Funeral Riots and Demonstrations in Lille, 1779–1870," Social Science History, 4, 15–31

419. Tannenbaum, E.R. (1977) 1900: The Generation Before the Great War, Anchor, Garden City, N.Y.

420. Tapic, V.L. (1971) The Rise and Fall of the Habsburg Monarchy, Praeger, New York

421. Taylor, A.J.P. (1962) The Course of German History, Capricorn, New York

422. ____ (1971) The Struggle for Mastery in Europe, 1848–1918, Oxford University Press, London

423. ____ (1976) The Habsburg Monarchy, 1809–1918, University of Chicago Press, Chicago

424. Thayer, J.A. (1964) Italy and the Great War, University of Wisconsin Press, Madison

425. Thomis, M.I. and P. Holt (1977) Threats of Revolution in Britain, 1789–1848, Archon, Hamden, Conn.

426. Thomson, D. (1950) England in the Nineteenth Century, Penguin, Baltimore

427. ____ (1966) Europe Since Napoleon, Penguin, Baltimore

428. Thomson, S.H. (1953) Czechoslovakia in European History, Princeton University Press, Princeton, N.J.

429. Thompson, J.M. (1967) Louis Napoleon and the Second Empire, Norton, New York

430. Thorsen, S. (1953) Newspapers in Denmark, Det Danske Selskab, Copenhagen

431. Thurer, G. (1971) Free and Swiss: The Story of Switzerland, University of Miami Press, Coral Gables, Fla.

432. Thurston, R.W. (1980) "Police and People in Moscow, 1906–1914," Russian Review, 39, 320–38

433. Tilly, C. (1969) "Collective Violence in European Perspective," in H. Graham and T. Gurr (eds.), Violence in America, Bantam, New York

434. Tilly, C., L. Tilly and R. Tilly (1975) The Rebellious Century, Harvard University Press, Cambridge, Mass.

435. Tingsten, H. (1973) The Swedish Social Democrats, Bedminster, Totowa, N.J.

436. Tobias, H.J. (1972) The Jewish Bund in Russia from Its Origins to 1905, Stanford University Press, Stanford, Calif.

437. Tokés, R. (1967) Bela Kun and the Hungarian Soviet Republic, Praeger, New York

438. Tuathaigh, G. (1972) Ireland Before the Famine, 1798–1848, Gill and Macmillan, Dublin

439. Tuchman, B.W. (1967) The Proud Tower: A Portrait of the World Before the War, 1890–1914, Bantam, New York

440. Turin, S.P. (1935) From Peter the Great to Lenin: A History of the Russian Labor Movement, King & Son, London

441. Ulam, A.B. (1977) In the Name of the People: Prophets and Conspirators in Prerevolutionary Russia, Viking, New York

442. Ullman, J.C. (1968) The Tragic Week: A Study of

Anti-Clericalism in Spain, 1875–1912, Harvard University Press, Cambridge, Mass.

443. Valentin, V. (1940) 1848: Chapters in German History, Allen & Unwin, London

444. Venturi, F. (1966) Roots of Revolution: A History of the Populist and Socialist Movements in Nineteenth Century Russia, Grosset & Dunlap, New York

445. Verney, D. V. (1957) Parliamentary Reform in Sweden, 1866–1921, Oxford University Press, London

446. Vicens Vives, J. (1969) An Economic History of Spain, Princeton University Press, Princeton, N.J.

447. Vlekke, B.H.M. (1945) Evolution of the Dutch Nation, Roy, New York

448. Waggoner, G.A. (1972) "The Black Hand Mystery: Rural Unrest and Social Violence in Southern Spain, 1881–1883," in R. Bezucha (ed.), Modern European Social History, Heath, Lexington, Mass.

449. Wåhlin, V. (1980) "The Growth of Bourgeois and Popular Movements in Denmark, ca. 1830–1870," Scandinavian Journal of History, 5, 151–83

450. Waldman, M. (1973) "Repression of the Communards," Canadian Journal of History, 8, 225–46

451. Walker, B.M. (1973) "The Irish Electorate, 1868–1915," Irish Historical Studies, 18, 359–405

452. Walkin, J. (1954a) "The Attitude of the Tsarist Government toward the Labor Problem," American Slavic and East European Review, 13, 163–84

453. _____ (1954b) "Government Controls Over the Press in Russia, 1905–1914," Russian Review, 13, 203–209

454. Wandycz, P.S. (1974) The Lands of Partitioned Poland, 1795–1918, University of Washington Press, Seattle

455. Wangermann, E. (1973) The Austrian Achievement, 1700–1800. Harcourt Brace Jovanovich, New York

456. Ward, D. (1970) 1848: The Fall of Metternich and the Year of Revolution, Weybright and Talley, New York

457. Ward, J.T. (1973) Chartism, Barnes & Noble, New York

458. Webb, R.K. (1969) Modern England: From the Eighteenth Century to the Present, Dodd, Mead, New York

459. Weckerle, E. (1947) The Trade Unions in Switzerland, Swiss Federation of Trade Unions

460. Wedderburn, K.W. (1965) The Worker and the Law, Penguin, Baltimore

461. Wehler, H. (1970) "Bismarck's Imperialism 1862–1890," Past and Present, 48, 119–54

462. Weisser, H. (1975) British Working Class Movements and Europe, 1815–1848, Manchester University Press, Manchester

463. Weisser, M.R. (1981) Crime and Punishment in Early Modern Europe, Humanities Press, New York

464. Werner, G.S. (1977) Bavaria in the German Confederation, 1820–1848, Fairleigh Dickinson Press, Rutherford, N.J.

465. Western, J.R. (1967) The End of European Primacy, 1871–1945,

Harper & Row, New York

466. Wheeler, D.L. (1978) Republican Portugal: A Political History, 1910-1926, University of Wisconsin Press, Madison
467. Whitridge, A. (1949) Men in Crisis: The Revolutions of 1848, Scribner's, New York
468. Whyte, A.J. (1965) The Evolution of Modern Italy, Norton, New York
469. Whyte, J.H. (1965) "Landlord Influence at Elections in Ireland, 1760-1885," English Historical Review, pp. 740-60
470. Wicks, M. (1968) The Italian Exiles in London, 1816-1848, Books for Libraries, Freeport, N.Y.
471. Wickwar, W.H. (1928) The Struggle for Freedom of the Press, 1819-1832, Allen and Unwin, London
472. Wiener, J.H. (1969) The War of the Unstamped: The Movement to Repeal the British Newspaper Tax, 1830-1836, Cornell University Press, Ithaca, N.Y.
473. Willcox, W.B. (1971) The Age of Aristocracy, 1688-1830, Heath, Lexington, Mass.
474. Williams, R.C. (1972) Culture in Exile: Russian Emigrés in Germany, 1881-1941, Cornell University Press, Ithaca, N.Y.
475. Williams, R.L. (1969) The French Revolution of 1870-1871, Norton, New York
476. Windmuller, J.P. (1969) Labor Relations in the Netherlands, Cornell University Press, Ithaca, N.Y.
477. Wohl, R. (1966) French Communism in the Making, 1914-1924, Stanford University Press, Stanford, Calif.
478. Wolfe, B.D. (1964) Three Who Made a Revolution, Delta, New York
479. Wood, A. (1964) Europe, 1815-1945, McKay, New York
480. Woodbridge, G. (1970) The Reform Bill of 1832, Crowell, New York
481. Woodcock, G. (1962) Anarchism, World, Cleveland
482. ____ (1972) Pierre-Joseph Proudhon, Shocken, New York
483. Woodhouse, C. (1974) "The Defense Question and Danish Politics, 1864-1914," Scandinavian Studies, 3, 201-28
484. Wuorinen, J.H. (1965) A History of Finland, Columbia University Press, New York
485. Yarmolinsky, A. (1962) Road to Revolution: A Century of Russian Radicalism, Collier, New York
486. Zacek, J.F. (1970) "Metternich's Censors: The Case of Palacký," in P. Brock and H.G. Skilling (eds.) The Czech Renascense of the Nineteenth Century, University of Toronto Press, Toronto
487. Zelnik, R.E. (1971) Labor and Society in Tsarist Russia: The Factory Workers of St. Petersburg, 1855-1870, Stanford University Press, Stanford, Calif.
488. Zuckerman, F.S. (1977) "Vladimir Burtsev and the Tsarist Political Police in Conflict, 1907-1914," Journal of Contemporary History, 12, 193-219

REFERENCES ORGANIZED BY SUBJECT

## European Histories

General Social and Political Histories of Nineteenth-Century Europe,
5, 9, 31, 39, 51, 68, 123, 152, 210, 237, 276, 288, 403, 411, 427,
479
Studies of Europe, 1815-1850: 7, 8, 12, 36, 39, 48, 87, 90, 108, 149,
158, 225, 230, 262, 310, 322, 332, 354, 366, 417, 463
Studies of Europe, 1850-1870: 33, 129, 149, 159, 230, 292, 347
Studies of Europe, 1870-1914: 121, 127, 146, 189, 264, 265, 333, 347,
353, 362, 419, 440 465

## Topical Studies

1848: 3, 76, 93, 103, 104, 124, 125, 141, 147, 164, 243, 248, 296, 303,
320, 329, 335, 339, 355, 393, 405, 410, 443, 456, 467
Education: 2, 111, 270, 271, 287, 338, 350
Freedom of Assembly and Association: 5, 19, 24, 86, 98, 342, 418, 449
Freedom of the Press: 5, 13, 16, 17, 67, 105, 133, 134, 135, 161, 194,
306, 337, 369, 379, 396, 402, 412, 453, 471, 472
Police and Military: 70, 245, 256, 260, 313, 315, 432, 433
Political Prisoners and Exiles: 174, 205, 209, 269, 331, 367, 402, 470,
474
Secret Police: 44, 53, 63, 97, 186, 234, 286, 318, 319, 356, 398, 404, 488
Statistics: 91, 106, 251, 282, 358
Suffrage Restrictions: 5, 11, 24, 37, 48, 57, 75, 99, 142, 154, 182, 198,
199, 293, 358, 360, 368, 386, 397, 445, 451, 469, 480
Trade Union and Socialist History and Restrictions: 1, 4, 27, 28, 29,
32, 42, 45, 52, 58, 61, 69, 113, 114, 118, 128, 130, 131, 157, 165,
167, 175, 176, 179, 187, 188, 195, 196, 197, 214, 220, 222, 223,
224, 232, 233, 236, 242, 252, 272, 278, 280, 283, 289, 290, 297,
299, 300, 303, 321, 340, 341, 349, 351, 363, 364, 365, 377, 378,
387, 392, 409, 433, 434, 435, 436, 444, 452, 459, 460, 462, 476,
477, 481, 482, 487

## Country and Regional Studies

Balkans: 23, 35, 40, 56, 65, 74, 77, 85, 88, 89, 96, 100, 125, 179, 180,
200, 215, 217, 219, 268, 284, 352, 364, 372, 388, 407, 408, 414
France: 4, 22, 29, 32, 50, 54, 55, 57, 66, 67, 92, 95, 109, 111, 151, 181,
191, 199, 221, 233, 242, 254, 279, 287, 290, 299, 319, 326, 334,
335, 337, 342, 343, 349, 376, 382, 383, 392, 402, 406, 409, 413,
429, 450, 475, 477
Germany: 20, 58, 70, 71, 75, 84, 99, 101, 128, 132, 133, 134, 135, 138,
139, 140, 162, 227, 236, 244, 252, 257, 270, 289, 298, 303, 314,
327, 340, 341, 357, 363, 371, 378, 391, 394, 401, 405, 421, 461, 464
Habsburg Empire: 30, 76, 97, 107, 116, 131, 169, 178, 182, 183, 184,
193, 194, 197, 206, 246, 247, 248, 263, 273, 294, 320, 329, 338,
339, 375, 389, 395, 420, 423, 428, 455, 486

Hungary: 172, 177, 216, 220, 245, 312, 386, 387, 390, 415, 416, 437
Iberia: 14, 15, 21, 25, 42, 43, 46, 59, 60, 114, 147, 153, 155, 195, 200,
    201, 204, 235, 239, 240, 241, 255, 261, 277, 302, 305, 315, 316, 317,
    379, 442, 446, 448, 466
Italy: 15, 26, 110, 124, 130 136, 137, 148, 156, 157, 163, 165, 167, 170,
    171, 185, 207, 258, 297, 309, 361, 374, 384, 399, 400, 424, 468
Low Countries: 78, 79, 102, 120, 150, 218, 253, 280, 285, 447, 476
Russian Empire: 18, 38, 53, 62, 72, 94, 98, 112, 142, 143, 160, 166,
    192, 202, 203, 208, 211, 212, 213, 228, 229, 231, 232, 271, 275,
    278, 286, 291, 295, 325, 328, 336, 345, 346, 349, 370, 373, 377,
    385, 404, 412, 432, 436, 441, 444, 452, 453, 454, 478, 484, 485,
    487, 488
Scandinavia: 6, 34, 52, 82, 83, 113, 115, 145, 168, 190, 214, 222, 226,
    281, 304, 307, 330, 351, 359, 368, 380, 381, 430, 435, 445, 449,
    483,
Switzerland: 41, 122, 173, 259, 431, 459,
United Kingdom: 10, 47, 64, 73, 81, 117, 198, 249. 256, 260, 266, 267,
    301, 311, 321, 331, 344, 367, 397, 425, 426, 438, 451, 457, 458,
    460, 462, 469, 471, 472, 473, 480

# Index

Readers interested in material concerning particular countries are advised to consult topical entries (i.e., Suffrage discrimination in nineteenth-century Europe), which in many cases have material under subheadings for specific countries, as well as country entries (i.e., Belgium, Hungary).

Academic freedom in nineteenth-century Europe. See Education, political controls on, in nineteenth-century Europe; Firings of teachers for political reasons in nineteenth-century Europe

Adler, Victor, 43, 85, 347

Agents provocateurs, in nineteenth-century Europe: in Belgium, 72; in Germany, 73; in Hungary, 155; in Italy, 314, 316; in Lombardy, 72; in Portugal, 292; in Russia, 73-74; in Spain, 72, 295; in United Kingdom, 114, 115, 116; problems in studying, 72; see also Secret police in nineteenth-century Europe

Agriculture and rural conditions in nineteenth-century Europe, 17, 91, 92, 94-95, 97-99, 170, 180, 193, 194, 195, 196, 241, 244-45; see also Rural unrest and uprisings in nineteenth-century Europe

Akarp Law in Sweden (1899), 60

Alexander, Prince of Bulgaria, 305, 306

Alexander I, Czar of Russia, 123, 129, 130-31, 135

Alexander II, Czar of Russia, 216, 225-28, 252, 272, 278-79, 305-06

Alexander III, Czar of Russia, 279-80, 305-06

Alexander Karageorgević, Prince of Serbia, 177, 214-15, 236

Alexander Obrenović, King of Serbia, 22, 308-09

Alfonso XIII, King of Spain, 288, 295, 296

Algeria, 80, 190, 204, 208

Amadeo, King of Spain, 233, 287

Amnesties, political, in nineteenth-century Europe: in Austria, 328; in France, 188, 204, 216, 222, 272, 273, 274; in Germany, 216; in Habsburg Empire, 154, 188, 216; in Italy, 314, 318; in

Papal States, 151, 183; in
Portugal, 211, 293; in
Prussia, 171, 188, 216; in
Russia, 216, 283, 286; in
Russian Poland, 153; in
Spain, 164, 296
Amsterdam, 65, 180, 264
Anarchists: in Austria, 326–37; in
France, 272–73; in Spain,
295–96; in 1880s, 252; see
also Anti-anarchist laws
Anti-anarchist laws in nine-
teenth-century Europe: in
Austria, 50, 59, 326–27; in
France, 273–74; in Hungary,
299; in Spain, 295; see also
Anarchists
Anti-clericalism in nineteenth-
century Europe: diverting
working-class unrest, 349; in
France, 147, 272, 275, 249;
in Italy, 219; in Portugal,
293, 349; in Spain, 296, 349;
see also Clerical influence
Anti-semitism, in nineteenth-
century Austria, Germany,
and Russia, as diverting
working-class unrest, 349
Anti-Socialist Law (Germany,
1878–90), 46, 49, 50, 52–53,
60, 62, 71, 322–23, 341
Arakchevyev, Alexis, 129–30
Arrests, trials and punishments of
political dissidents in
nineteenth-century Europe:
for press offenses, 38,
42–43; for trade union
activities, 58–61; in Austria,
59, 88, 239, 326, 327; in
Baden, 190; in Bavaria, 149;
in Belgium, 60–61, 239, 262;
in Bohemia, 191, 202, 225,
328, 329; in Bulgaria, 305,
306, 307; in Croatia, 302; in
Danubian Principalities, 185;
in Denmark, 142, 171, 266,
267; in Finland, 286; in
France, 38, 58, 61, 80, 88,
112, 147, 172, 198, 203, 208,
239, 250, 270, 272, 273, 274,

275, 276; in Germany, 38,
60, 64, 88, 123, 149, 321, 322;
in Habsburg Empire, 155, 191,
223, 239; in Hungary, 23,
149, 154, 191, 202, 208, 239,
298, 299, 300, 301, 302; in
Ireland, 118, 157, 176, 230,
259, 260; in Italy, 22, 122,
151, 219, 238, 313, 314, 316,
317; in Lombardy-Venetia,
80, 124, 151, 185, 190, 207; in
Modena, 124, 205; in
Norway, 143, 209; in Papal
States, 122, 124, 125, 152; in
Portugal, 128, 164, 292, 293;
in Prussia, 149, 150, 172, 181,
201, 221; in Russia, 74, 79,
80, 129, 131, 173, 226, 228,
278, 279, 280, 282, 284, 285;
in Russian Poland, 153, 181,
227, 280, 281; in Rumania
304; in Sardinia, 124; in
Saxony, 190; in Serbia, 177,
214, 237, 308; in Spain, 81,
126, 128, 164, 179, 186, 213,
288, 290, 294, 295, 296, 297;
in Sweden, 59, 88, 162, 268;
in Tuscany, 151; in Two
Sicilies, 81, 151, 184, 190, 205,
219; in United Kingdom, 58,
80, 88, 114, 115, 116, 157, 158,
159, 160, 175, 186, 258, 260,
261; see also Political
prisoners in nineteenth-
century Europe
Assassinations and assassination
attempts and plots in
nineteenth-century Europe:
in Austria, 333; in Bulgaria,
306, 307; in Cracow, 145; in
Croatia, 302; in Denmark,
267; in Finland, 282; in
France, 73, 83, 112, 148, 208,
272, 273; in Habsburg
Empire, 208; in Germany,
73, 123, 322; in Greece, 167;
in Ireland, 259; in Italy, 314,
315, 318; in Modena, 124; in
Papal States, 125; in Parma,
282; in Portugal, 292; in

Prussia, 208; in Russia, 73, 79, 228, 252, 279, 282, 285, 286; in Russian Poland, 227, 282; in Serbia, 214, 237, 308; in Spain, 294, 295, 296, 297; in United Kingdom, 116

Assembly and association, restrictions of and regulations on, in nineteenth–century Europe: as a political issue, 47–48, 102, 107, 186; in 1815, 105; in Austria, 47–50, 200, 225, 253, 312, 326, 327; in Belgium, 47, 162; in Bohemia, 50, 52–55, 328, 329; in Bulgaria, 47–50, 305; in Danubian Principalities, 48; in Denmark, 48–49, 51, 173, 181, 257, 267; in Finland, 282; in France, 47–48, 50, 52–53, 55, 147–48, 183, 200, 203–04, 222, 270, 273; in Germany, 47–53, 200, 201, 253, 312, 322–23; in Greece, 47–48, 310, 311; in Hungary, 47–48, 53–54, 239, 299, 300; in Iberia, 47; in Ireland, 51, 76, 176, 259, 260; in Italy, 47–49, 51, 54, 200, 220, 253, 312, 313, 314, 316, 317; in Lombardy–Venetia, 54, 184–85; in Low Countries, 47; in Netherlands, 48–49, 210, 257; in Norway 143; in Portugal, 48; in Prussia, 47, 321–22; in Rumania, 47–48; in Russia, 47–52, 200, 278, 281, 282, 283, 284, 287; in Sardinia, 48, 52; in Scandinavia, 47; in Serbia, 47–48, 50, 52, 237, 307–308; in Sweden, 49, 268; in Spain, 48, 50, 53, 212, 288, 296; in Switzerland, 47–48, 52, 141, 160, 211, 265; in Two Sicilies, 48; in United Kingdom, 47, 53, 114, 160, 258; techniques used to evade, 50–55, 173–74, 183, 281, 282, 322–23;

techniques used to implement, 47–50; see also Political banquets, as means of evading restrictions on assembly and association in nineteenth–century Europe, Political funerals, as means of evading restrictions on assembly and association in nineteenth–century Europe

Athens, 177, 214, 245

Auersperg, Prince Adolf von, 326, 328

Ausgleich, 224, 297, 298, 299, 215

Austria in the nineteenth century: overall impact of political repression upon, 334, 335, 338, 341–42, 343; economic and social background, 1870–1914, 241, 242, 244; political developments, 1870–1914, 247, 248, 251, 252, 253, 254, 255, 256, 297, 311, 312, 325–30; see also Habsburg Empire (for material for the period before 1870)

Austro–Sardinian War of 1859, 217, 223

Bach, Alexander, 202, 207, 217, 222, 223

Baden, 102, 123, 148, 150, 182, 200, 220, 324, 342

Badeni, Casimir Count, 327, 329–30

Bakunin, Michael, 85, 189, 251

Balkans in the nineteenth century: 91, 93, 98, 99, 100, 193, 196, 197, 243, 244, 247, 303–04, see also Bulgaria, Greece, Rumania, Serbia

Barcelona, 68, 81, 92, 172, 179, 213, 245, 294, 295

Bavaria, 102, 123, 148–49, 151, 167–68, 178, 182, 192, 201, 220, 324, 342

Bebel, August, 86–87, 88, 321, 341–42

Belgium in the nineteenth

century: economic and social background, 1815–1870, 94, 193, 196, 197, 198, 199, 200; economic and social background, 1870–1914, 241, 245; overall impact of political repression in, 333, 334, 335, 338; political developments, 1815–1830, 103, 109, 139–40; political developments, 1830–1839, 156, 161–62; political developments, 1840–1849, 177, 180, 185, 187, 192; political developments, 1850–1858, 207, 210–11; political developments, 1859–1870, 229, 232; political developments, 1870–1914, 251, 252, 253, 255, 256, 257, 262, 264

Béranger, Pierre, 87, 113

Berlin, 30–32, 46, 51, 66, 67 187, 188, 191, 194, 245

Berne, 141, 150, 160, 182, 265

Berry, Duke of, 112, 146

Birmingham, 30, 46, 115, 158, 159, 160

Bismarck, Otto von, 17, 220–22, 250, 321–23, 346

"Black Hand" in Spain, 290–91

"Bloody Sunday" in Russia (January 9, 1905), 64–67, 282–83, 287, 340

Bobrikov, Nicholas, 281, 282

Bohemia, 99, 138, 172, 176, 181, 191, 193, 202, 223, 225, 240, 325, 327, 328, 329, 330

Bologna, 238, 313, 320

Bolzano, Bernard, 76, 137

Branting, Hjalmar, 43, 268

Breslau, 30, 57, 245

Brunswick, 148, 324

Brussels, 161, 180

Bucharest, 169, 245

Budapest, 19, 53, 187, 188, 245

Bulgaria in the nineteenth century: economic and social background, 1870–1914, 241, 244; overall impact of political repression in, 333, 334, 340, 343; political developments, 1815–50, 134, 156, 168–69, 173; political developments, 1850–1870, 213, 214, 237; political developments, 1870–1914, 254, 277, 303–307

"Bulgarian horrors" of 1876, 304–305, 340

Burschenschaften, 122–24, 137, 148, 149

Cabra, Costa, 178–79, 211

Caciques (in Iberia), 21, 289

Calomarde, Francisco, 128, 164

Canalejas, José, 296–97

Cánovas de Castillo, Antonio, 288, 291

Carbonari, Italian, 107, 113, 121–22, 124, 125, 150, 151, 121–22, 184

Carlile, Richard, 43, 116

Carlists, 128, 164–65, 287

Carlos I, King of Portugal, 292, 293

Carlos, pretender to the throne of Spain, 164–65

Carlsbad Decrees in Germany (1819), 34, 45, 123, 124, 149

Carniola, 97, 223, 326, 330

Catalonia, 193, 294–96

Catherine the Great, Empress of Russia, 37, 98

Catholic Association, in Ireland, 51, 118

Catholic Emancipation Movement in Ireland, 118–19

Cato Street Conspiracy, in United Kingdom (1820), 116

Cavour, Count Camillo di, 121, 206

Centurions, Papal States, 125, 152, 183

Charbonnerie Française, 113

Charles Albert, King of Sardinia, 151, 189

Charles I, King of Rumania, 235, 304

Charles III, Duke of Parma, 205, 208

Charles IV, King of Spain, 125
Charles X, King of France, 8, 25, 34, 104, 113, 145, 146,
Charles XIV John, King of Sweden, 44, 88, 104, 142, 143, 162-63, 174
Charles XV, King of Sweden, 230-31
Chartist movement in Great Britain, 17, 159-60, 175, 185-86, 208
Cholera outbreaks in nineteenth-century Europe, 92-93, 152-54, 196, 219, 280
Christian VIII, King of Denmark, 171, 173, 181
Christian IX, King of Denmark, 221, 231, 266, 267
Christiania (Oslo), 143, 185, 196
Clerical influence in nineteenth-century Europe: during the Restoration (1815-30), 96, 108-09; during the post-1848 reaction, 200; in Belgium, 177; in Balkans, 134; in France, 108, 111, 113; in Germany, 108; in Greece, 168; in the Habsburg Monarchy, 108; in Iberia, 108, 125; in Italy, 108; in Switzerland, 175; see also Anti-clericalism in nineteenth-century Europe
Cobbett, William, 43-44
Coercion and Insurrection Acts in Ireland, 117-18, 157, 259, 260
Cologne, 29-30, 32, 66-67, 180
Communications in nineteenth-century Europe, 93, 194
Congress of Verona, 127, 141
Congress of Vienna, 107, 108, 110, 119, 120, 131, 181
Conservatives in nineteenth-century Europe: acceptance of moderate reform after 1870, 345-47; attitudes toward suffrage, 3, 5-8; attitudes toward the press, 34, 36; attitudes toward trade unions, 55; general

political views, 107-108; fears of working-class organization, 239, 250-53
Constitutionalism, demands for, as political issue in nineteenth-century Europe: 36, 107, 186, 199, 338-40; in Danubian Principalities, 170; in Denmark, 163, 171; in Germany, 120, 148, 173, 182, 187; in Greece, 167, 178; in Italy, 150, 173; in Portugal, 126; in Prussia, 182; in Serbia, 167, 168; in Spain, 126; in Two Sicilies, 184
Copenhagen, 27, 30-31, 33, 142, 196, 267-68
Cousin, Victor, 75, 204
Cracow, Republic of, 110, 145, 181, 190
Crimean War, 214, 215, 216, 217, 222, 236
Crispi, Francesco, 6, 314-15, 316, 318
Croatia, 176, 191, 202, 223, 224, 225, 297, 298-99, 300, 301-303, 328
Cuza, Alexander, 234
Czechs. See Bohemia, Moravia
Dahlmann, Friedrich, 75-76
Daničić, Djuro, 76, 237
Danubian Principalities in nineteenth-century Europe: economic and social background, 1815-50, 97-98, 100, 101; in 1848, 186-88, 190; political developments in 1815-30, 110, 134-36; political developments in 1830-9, 156, 167, 169-70; political developments in 1840-6, 173, 175-76; political developments in 1850-8 213-14, 215; see also Rumania (for material concerning events after 1858)
Daumier, Honoré, 43, 147
Deaths of protesters and rebels, resulting from clashes with authorities in nineteenth-

century Europe: in Austria, 23, 65; in Belgium, 67–68, 262, 263, 264; in Bulgaria, 65, 173, 214, 304–305, 307; in Croatia, 65, 176, 299, 300; in France, 64, 65, 66, 67–68, 106, 147, 203, 204, 241, 275; in Germany, 64, 66, 67–68; in Greece, 65, 311; in Habsburg Empire, 65, 66; in Hungary, 23, 65, 67–68, 154, 223, 299, 301, 302; in Ireland, 67–68, 157, 230; in Italy, 65, 66, 67, 219, 238, 316, 317, 319, 320; in Lombardy, 184, 187; in Netherlands, 65, 262; in Portugal, 128; in Prussia, 65, 66, 67, 172; in Rumania, 234, 304; in Russia, 64, 65, 66, 67, 68, 131, 153, 187, 226, 282; in Russian Poland, 65, 227, 281; in Serbia, 132; in Spain, 67–68, 213, 296; in Sweden, 65, 162, 185; in Switzerland, 265; in United Kingdom, 106, 115, 157, 160, 261; see also Massacres in nineteenth–century Europe

Decembrist revolt, in Russia (1825), 130–31

Deliyannis, Theodor, 309–310

Denmark in the nineteenth century: economic and social background, 1815–50, 101, 102; economic and social background, 1850–70, 195, 198, 199; economic and social background, 1870–1914, 240, 241, 245; overall impact of political repression upon, 333, 335; political developments, 1815–1830, 104, 141–42; political developments, 1830–9, 156, 163–64; political developments, 1840–6, 170–71, 173, 175; political developments, 1847–9, 181, 187; political developments,

1850–8, 209–10; political developments, 1859–70, 216, 217, 221, 228, 231–32; political developments, 1870–1914, 251, 252, 253, 257, 265–67, 269

Depretis, Agostino, 314, 315, 318

Djak's Rebellion in Serbia (1825), 133

Dreyfus affair in France 253, 274, 340

Dufaure Law of 1872 in France, 270

Edgar Quinet, 75–77

Education, expansion and funding of, in nineteenth–century Europe: 194, 197, 243–44; literacy data, 91, 96, 195, 197, 241, 243–44, 254

Education, political controls imposed upon, in nineteenth–century Europe: 74–79, 96, 108, 200–01, 243–44; in Austria, 74, 78, 137, 154; in Bulgaria, 307; in Denmark, 75; in Germany 74–76, 123, 150; in Hungary, 298; in Portugal, 128; in Prussia, 74, 78; in Spain, 164; in Russia 74–75, 78–79, 130, 226; in Russian Poland, 131; in Switzerland, 75; see also Firings of teachers for political reasons in nineteenth–century Europe

Edward VII, King of the United Kingdom, 260

Elections in nineteenth–century Europe. See Suffrage discrimination in nineteenth–century Europe

Emigration in nineteenth–century Europe, 196–97, 245; and lessened working–class militancy, 348–49

Ernst Augustus, King of Hanover, 75, 150

Espartero, Baldomero, 166, 179

Essen, 31–2

Estrup, Jacob, 3, 266–67

Executions of political dissidents and rebels in nineteenth-century Europe: in Baden, 190; in Bulgaria 306; in Denmark, 142; in France, 68, 105, 111, 112, 113, 190, 208, 249–40; in Habsburg Empire, 69, 191, 202, 208; in Hungary, 154, 191, 192, 202, 207; in Ireland, 118, 230; in Italy, 175, 219; in Lombardy, 69, 190, 205, 207; in Modena, 124; in Papal States, 125; in Parma, 208; in Portugal, 105, 126, 128, 164; in Russia, 131, 279, 280, 284, 285; in Russian Poland, 227, 280; in Sardinia, 124, 151; in Serbia, 132, 133, 177, 308; in Spain, 105, 128, 164, 179, 186, 213, 233, 291, 294, 296, 340; in Switzerland, 105; in Two Sicilies, 124, 184; in United Kingdom, 114–16, 157, 158, 230

Exiles (political) in nineteenth-century Europe: circumstances leading to flight, 81–82; conditions of their lives, 83–85; diplomatic crises arising from, 82–83, 141, 161, 211, 265; from Bulgaria, 173; from Danubian Principalities, 81; from France, 81–82, 207, 211; from Germany, 81–82, 123, 161, 190, 211, 322; from Habsburg Monarchy, 81–82; from Italy, 81, 151, 161, 206, 211; from Netherlands, 211; from Russia, 84, 85; from Russian Poland, 81–82, 84, 148, 152, 161; from Serbia, 177; from Spain, 128, 164; in Belgium, 81–83; in Switzerland, 81–82, 85, 141, 161, 190, 211, 265; in United Kingdom, 81, 83–84

February Manifesto in Finland, 281, 284

Fenians (Irish Revolutionary Brotherhood) in Ireland, 229–30, 258

Ferdinand, Czar of Bulgaria, 20, 22, 306–307

Ferdinand, Emperor of Austria, 155, 187, 192

Ferdinand I, King of Two Sicilies, 48, 121, 122, 124

Ferdinand II, King of Two Sicilies, 184, 205

Ferdinand VII, King of Spain, 125, 126, 128, 164, 165

Férjérvary, Baron Geza, 300, 301

Ferrar, Francisco, 296, 340

Finland in the nineteenth century: social and political developments, 1815–1870, 130, 132, 195, 227–28; overall impact of political repression in, 334; social and political developments, 1870–1914, 241, 256, 281, 282, 284, 286, 340

Firings of teachers for political reasons in nineteenth-century Europe: in Austria 76, 77, 137; in Baden 76, 77; in Danubian Principalities, 76, 176; in Denmark, 77; in Finland, 76; in France 75, 76, 77, 183, 203; in Germany, 123, 150; in Hanover, 75, 76, 78; in Italy, 75, 77, 219; in Prussia, 78; in Russia, 77; in Russian Poland, 76; in Saxony, 77; in Serbia 75, 77; in Spain 77, 78; in Switzerland, 75; in Württemberg, 76, 123; see also Education, political controls imposed upon in nineteenth-century Europe

France in the nineteenth century: economic and social background, 1815–50, 92, 93, 95, 98, 101; economic and social backbround, 1850–70, 193, 194, 196, 197, 198, 199, 200; economic and social background, 1870–1914, 241,

244, 245, 247; overall impact of political repression in, 333, 337, 340–41, 343; political developments, 1815–30, 103, 105, 106, 109, 110, 111, 113, 120, 122, 130, 136; political developments, 1830–9, 145–48, 150–51, 161, 165, 167; political developments, 1840–6, 172, 178, 174; political developments, 1847–9, 180, 183, 186–90, 192; political developments, 1850–8, 200, 202–205, 206, 207, 208, 211, 214; political developments, 1859–1870, 215, 216, 217, 218, 220, 222, 240; political developments, 1870–1914, 248–50, 251, 252, 254, 255, 257, 265, 270–76

Franchise in nineteenth–century Europe. See Suffrage discrimination in nineteenth–century Europe

Francis I, Emperor of Austria, 70, 74, 103, 108, 137–39, 153, 154–5

Francis I, King of the Two Sicilies, 124

Francis IV, Duke of Modena, 121, 150–51

Francis V, Duke of Modena, 205

Franco–Prussian War, xiv, 248–49, 312, 320, 327

Frankfurt, 103, 120, 194, 220

Franz Joseph, Emperor of Austria, 25, 54–55, 201–202, 208, 223–25, 299, 300, 301, 326, 327, 328, 330

Frederick VI, King of Denmark, 96, 141–42, 163, 171

Frederick VII, King of Denmark, 209–10

Frederick William III, King of Prussia, 120, 123, 124, 171, 176–77

Frederick William IV, King of Prussia, 11, 67, 171, 182, 187, 188, 201, 208, 216

French Revolution, 37, 57, 69, 113, 249

Galicia (Austrian), 15, 23, 33, 65, 138, 155, 180–81, 198, 202, 223–24, 240, 247, 326, 328, 330; discrimination against Ruthenians in, 23, 326, 328, 330

Garibaldi, Giuseppe, 217, 219, 220, 229, 237, 305

Gautsch, Baron Paul von, 327, 347

Gentz, Friedrich, 36, 71, 96, 124

George I, King of Greece, 88, 236, 309

George IV, King of United Kingdom, 119

George V, King of United Kingdom, 261

German Confederation. See Germany

Germany in the nineteenth century: economic and social background, 1815–50, 93, 94, 95, 97, 98, 101, 102; economic and social background, 1850–70, 193, 194, 196, 197, 198, 200; economic and social background, 1870–1914, 240, 241, 242, 244, 245; overall impact of political repression upon, 333, 335, 338, 341–42, 343, 344; political developments, 1815–30, 102, 107, 109, 110, 119–20, 122–24, 130, 137, 141; political developments, 1830–9, 148–50; political developments, 1840–6, 170–73, 175; political developments, 1847–9, 180, 182, 186–192; political developments, 1850–8, 200, 201, 207, 210; political developments, 1859–70, 216, 217, 218, 220–22; political developments, 1870–1914, 247, 248, 250, 251, 252, 253, 254, 255, 256, 265, 311, 312, 320–25, 345, 346, 347; see

also Baden, Bavaria,
Hanover, Hesse,
Hesse-Cassel,
Hesse-Darmstadt,
Mecklenberg, Nassau,
Prussia, Saxony,
Saxe-Weimar, Württemberg
Gervinus, George, 75–77
Giolitti, Giovanni, 22, 316, 318–20,
346, 347
Gladstone, William, 205, 259,
260, 305
Glasgow, 116, 159, 229
Greece in the nineteenth century:
overall impact of political
repression upon, 333, 335,
343; revolution of 1821,
110–11, 136, 339; social and
political developments,
1820–50, 134–36, 156, 166–68,
177–78, 186; social and
political developments,
1850–70, 195, 213, 214, 216,
217, 229, 233, 235–36; social
and political developments,
1870–1914, 254, 255, 256,
276, 277, 309–11
Gregory XVI (Pope), 145, 151, 152
Grey, Lord, 157–58
Guizot, François, 3, 6, 174, 204,
346
Gustav V, King of Sweden, 268–69
Habsburg Empire, in the
nineteenth century:
economic and social
background, 1815–50, 97, 101;
economic and social
background, 1850–70, 193,
196, 197, 198; overall impact
of political repression in,
333, 337; political
developments, 1815–30, 102,
103, 109, 110, 119–20, 121, 122,
123, 124, 137–39, 141; political
developments, 1830–9, 15,
154–55; political
developments, 1840–6, 170,
171–76; political
developments, 1847–9,
180–81, 186–92; political

developments, 1850–8, 200,
201, 202, 205, 207, 208;
political developments,
1859–70, 216, 217, 218,
222–25; see also Austria,
Hungary (for material
concerning period after 1870)
Hambacher Fest in Bavarian
Palatinate (1832), 149
Hamburg, 64, 103, 187, 220, 324
Hanover, 30, 75, 102, 148, 150
Havlíček, Karl, 44, 53, 88, 202,
207
Heine, Heinrich, 38, 82, 120, 146
Herzen, Alexander, 84, 154, 206
Hesse, 324
Hesse-Cassel, 148, 150
Hesse-Darmstadt, 122, 182, 201,
220
Housing conditions in nineteenth-
century Europe, 99–100,
246–47
Hierta, Lars Johan, 44, 162
Hugo, Victor, 38, 82, 110, 207,
262, 305
Humbert I, King of Italy, 314, 318
Hungary in the nineteenth
century: discrimination
against non-Magyars, 19,
298–99, 301, 302, 340;
economic and social
background, 1815–50, 93, 94,
95, 97, 99, 101; economic and
social background, 1850–70,
195, 196, 198; economic and
social background, 1870–1914,
240, 241, 242, 243, 244, 245;
overall impact of political
repression in, 334, 338, 340,
342, 343; political
developments, 1815–30, 103,
106, 137–39; political
developments, 1830–9,
154–55; political
developments, 1840–9, 176,
181, 186, 187, 190–92; political
developments, 1850–8, 202,
207, 208; political
developments, 1859–70, 217,
223–25; political

developments, 1870–1914,
240, 241, 242, 243, 244, 245,
247, 248, 251, 252, 253, 255,
256, 276, 277, 297–303, 328;
see also Austria, Habsburg
Empire
Hunt, Henry, 53, 115
Iberia, 93, 107, 109, 110, 187, 193,
197, 199, 243, 244, 247, 248,
255; see also Portugal; Spain
Ibsen, Henrik, 209, 281
Imperialism, as a factor in diverting working–class unrest in
nineteenth–century Europe,
349–50
Industrialization and industrial
conditions in nineteenth–
century Europe, 91, 95–96,
100, 170, 193–94, 195, 241,
243–44, 247, 254
Infant mortality in nineteenth–
century Europe, 92, 195, 196,
241, 244, 246
International, First, 199–200, 226,
228–29, 250–51, 253–54, 270,
272, 288, 313, 315
International, Second, 252–53
Ireland in the nineteenth century:
economic and social back-
ground, 94, 99, 101, 116–17,
196; political developments,
1815–30, 109, 114, 116–19;
political developments,
1830–49, 156–57, 170, 175–76,
180, 186; political
developments, 1850–70,
229–230; political
developments, 1870–1914,
252, 257, 258–62
Irish National Land League,
258–59, 261
Irish Revolutionary Brotherhood.
See Fenians
Isabel II, Queen of Spain, 78, 164,
212–13, 229, 232–33
Italy in the nineteenth century:
economic and social
background, 1815–50, 93, 98,
99, 101; economic and social
background, 1850–70, 193,

194, 195, 196, 197; economic
and social background,
1870–1914, 240, 241, 244, 245,
246; overall impact of
political repression upon,
333, 334, 335, 338, 340–41,
343; political developments,
1815–30, 102, 106, 109, 110,
119–24, 141; political
developments, 1830–46,
150–52, 172–73, 175; political
developments, 1847–9,
183–84, 186, 188, 189, 190, 192;
political developments,
1850–8, 200, 205–206, 207,
208; political developments,
1859–70, 216, 217, 218,
218–220, 227, 235, 238;
political developments,
1870–1914, 247, 248, 251, 252,
253, 254, 256, 287, 311,
312–20; trends in political
repression concerning, 346,
347, 350; see also (for period
before 1860) Lombardy,
Lombardy–Venetia, Lucca,
Modena, Papal States,
Parma, Sardinia, Two
Sicilies, Venetia
Jerez de la Frontera, 290, 294
John VI, King of Portugal, 126, 127
Jovanović, Vladimir, 46, 236
July Ordinances in France (1830),
113, 145
June Days in France (1848), 202,
340
Khuen-Héderváry, Karolyi, 299,
300, 301, 302
Kingdom of the Two Sicilies.
See Sicily; Two Sicilies,
Kingdom of the
Kogălniceanu, Michael, 76, 176,
234–35
Kolettis, John, 22, 178, 218
Kossuth, Louis, 43, 82–83, 155,
176, 190
Kotzebue, August von, 123, 129
Kropotkin, Prince Peter, 43, 72,
85, 272, 273
La Rochelle, Four Sergeants of,

Labor, and laboring classes in nineteenth–century Europe. See Trade unions in nineteenth–century Europe; Agriculture and rural conditions in nineteenth–century Europe; Urbanization and urban conditions in nineteenth–century Europe

Labor force structure in nineteenth–century Europe, 194, 195, 241, 244, 247

Lavrov, Peter, 85, 87

Law on Associations in France (1834), 147–48

Law of Public Safety in France (1858), 208

Legislative dissolutions in nineteenth–century Europe: in Austria, 25; in Bulgaria, 25, 305, 307; in Croatia, 25, 302; in Danubian Principalities, 176; in Denmark, 25, 210, 266–67; in Finland, 25, 286; in France, 25, 113, 203; in Germany, 201; in Greece, 25, 216; in Hapsburg Empire, 24, 201, 224; in Hungary, 24, 301; in Netherlands, 25, 232; in Portugal, 25, 292; in Prussia, 24, 25, 201, 220; in Rumania, 25, 234; in Russia, 24, 25, 285; in Saxony, 25; in Sardinia, 25; in Spain, 25, 179, 213, 221; in Württemberg, 25

Leipzig, 30–31, 32, 187

Lena Gold Mine Massacre in Russia (April 4, 1912), 65, 67, 286

Lenin, V. I., 46, 74, 87

Leo XII (Pope), 124

Leo XIII (Pope), 254

Leopold I of Belgium, 82–83, 177

Leopold II, Duke of Tuscany, 184, 205

Liberals in nineteenth–century Europe: general attitudes relevant to political repression, 107, 177, 339; views on freedom of assembly and association, 47–48, 102, 107, 186; views on constitutional reform, 36; views on the press, 36, 107; views on suffrage, 3, 6, 36; see also Middle classes

Liebknecht, William, 87, 221, 321

Life expectancy in nineteenth–century Europe, 92, 195, 196, 241, 244, 246

Literacy in nineteenth–century Europe. See education, expansion and funding of, in nineteenth–century Europe

List, Friedrich, 76, 123

Liverpool, Lord, 34, 114, 117

Lloyd George, David, 260–61

Lombardy, 61, 119, 180, 217, 222; see also Lombardy–Venetia

Lombardy–Venetia, 119, 121, 124, 151, 184, 185, 202, 205, 207; see also Lombardy, Venetia

London, 83, 84, 93, 100, 106, 114, 115, 193, 194, 229

Louis XVIII, King of France, 111–13, 128

Louis Philippe, King of France, 83, 146, 147, 183, 186

Lovett, William, 159, 160

Low Countries, 98, 194, 247, 255, 257, 336; see also Belgium, Netherlands, United Netherlands

Lower classes, conditions of, in nineteenth–century Europe. See Agriculture and rural conditions; Urbanization and urban conditions

Lucca, 120, 184

Ludwig I, King of Bavaria, 148, 151, 167, 182

Lyon, 46, 54, 57, 66, 147, 272

Mail, surveillance of, in nineteenth–century Europe: in

Austria, 137; in France,
71–73; in Germany, 71; in
United Kingdom, 71
Malatesta, Errico 85, 315
Manchester, 46, 92, 100, 115,
159, 172, 180, 229, 230
"Manchester Martyrs," 230
Manteuffel, Baron Otto von, 201,
216
Manuel II, King of Portugal, 293
María Cristina of Spain, 164,
165, 166, 128, 212
Maria I, Queen of Portugal,
125–26
Maria II (Maria de Gloria),
Queen of Portugal, 127, 164,
166, 179, 211
Marx, Karl, 43, 82–84, 86, 171,
172, 180, 201, 250, 251, 341,
347
Massacres, in nineteenth–century
Europe, in Austrian Galicia,
181; in Bulgaria, 173, 214; in
France 68, 147, 190, 249–50;
in Greece, 136; in Serbia,
132–33; in Russia, 226; in
Rumania xii, 304; see also
"Bloody Sunday" in Russia;
"Bulgarian Horrors" of 1876;
Lena Goldmines Massacre in
Russia; June Days in France;
Peterloo Massacre in United
Kingdom
Maura, Antonio, 295–96
Mazzini, Giuseppe, 46, 71, 82,
151, 161, 175, 205, 207, 219
Mecklenberg, 103, 188
Metternich, Klemens von, 34, 36,
43, 70–71, 83, 108, 119, 120,
122, 123, 124, 129, 141, 145,
149, 150, 155, 173, 179, 180,
181, 182, 183, 184, 187, 189,
200, 239
Michael Obrenović, King of
Serbia, 168, 177, 236, 237
Michelet, Jules, 75, 77, 183,
204
Mickiewicz, Adam, 81, 183
Middle classes in nineteenth–
century Europe, coalition

with upper classes, 193,
197–99, 216, 240, 242;
discontent and demands for
political reforms, 101–02,
107, 109, 144, 172, 186, 191,
199; living conditions, 101–02,
215–16; see also Liberals in
nineteenth–century Europe
Miguel, King of Portugal,
127, 164–65
Milan, 54, 65, 66, 184, 320
Milan Obrenović, King of
Serbia, 22, 87, 187, 207,
208, 237, 308
Military technology in nineteenth–century Europe,
effect of, in dampening
working class militancy,
348; new developments in, 194
Miloš Obrenović, Prince of
Serbia, 133–34, 168, 177, 214,
215, 236
Modena, 119, 121, 124, 150, 184,
187, 205, 217
Moravia, 97, 223, 225, 240, 325,
329
Mortality rates in nineteenth–
century Europe, 92, 195, 196,
241, 244, 246
Moscow, 30–32, 53, 80, 93, 226,
245, 283, 284, 286, 287
Muravyov, Count M. N. 227, 228,
281
Naples, 97, 121, 124, 151, 184,
185, 200, 205, 313
Napoleon I, 34, 42, 106, 111,
119, 120, 126–27, 142, 344
Napoleon III, 41–42, 52–53, 55,
58, 71, 73, 80, 82–83, 85, 86,
87, 88, 142, 148, 161, 201–05,
207, 208, 211, 216, 217, 222,
248, 270
Narváez, Ramon, 36, 179, 213,
233
Nassau, 18, 182
Netherlands in the nineteenth
century: economic and
social background, 1815–50,
91, 95, 100; economic and
social background, 1850–70,

193, 195, 196, 199; economic
and social background,
1870–1914, 241; overall
impact of political
repression upon, 333, 334,
335, 336, 338, 343; political
developments, 1815–30, 103,
109, 139–40; political
developments, 1830–46,
161–62, 170–71, 176–77;
political developments,
1847–9, 180, 187; political
developments, 1850–70,
210–11, 216, 228–29, 232;
political developments,
1870–1914, 251, 252, 253,
262–64; trends in political
repression concerning, 347
New Caledonia, 80, 250, 270,
272, 273
New Catholic Association in
Ireland, 118–19
Newport rising in United
Kingdom (1839), 160, 175
Nicholas I, Czar of Russia,
40, 71, 96, 152–54, 172, 200,
206
Nicholas II, Czar of Russia,
245, 280, 282–86, 349
Niuwenhuis, Domela, 43, 263
Nobility, European, in the nineteenth century, 26, 100, 101,
103, 105, 197–98, 242; in
Austria, 101, 198, 242; in
Denmark, 101; in Germany,
198, 242; in Hungary, 101,
139, 198, 242; in Prussia, 101,
198, 242; in Spain, 101; in
Sweden, 101, 242; in the
United Kingdom, 101, 104,
198, 242
North German Confederation,
18, 221–22, 320
Norway in the nineteenth
century: economic and
social background 1815–50,
94, 100; economic and social
background, 1850–70, 193,
195, 197, 199; economic and
social background, 1870–1914,

244, 245; overall impact of
political repression in, 334,
343; political developments,
1815–39, 103, 109, 139–40,
161–62; political
developments, 1840–9,
170–71, 176–77, 180, 187;
political developments,
1850–70, 210–11, 216, 228–29,
232; political developments,
1870–1914, 244, 245, 252,
253, 254, 255, 256, 265–66,
269–70
O'Connell, Daniel, 51, 86, 118,
175–76, 208
O'Connor, Feargus, 160
O'Donnell, Leopoldo, 212, 213,
232
Orsini, Felice, 83, 85, 208,
216
Oscar I, King of Sweden, 174,
209
Oscar II, King of Sweden, 267,
268
Otto, King of Greece, 167–68,
177, 213, 214, 235–36
Ottoman Turkey, 82, 91, 98–99,
102, 110, 132–37, 168, 176, 177,
213, 214, 237, 255, 304, 306,
307, 310, 339
Owen, Robert, 96, 159, 336
Palmerston, Lord, 83, 178, 208
Papal States, 119, 120, 121,
124–25, 150–51, 152, 175, 184,
185, 205, 217, 219, 220
Paris, 39, 42, 53, 65, 66, 80, 92,
99, 100, 106, 146–47, 148, 172,
180, 181, 188, 189, 190, 191,
193, 194, 196, 202, 245,
248–50, 252, 270
Paris Commune of 1871, developments in France, xii, xiv,
68, 72, 80, 239, 248–50, 270,
340, 344
Paris Commune of 1871, fears
inspired by: in Austria, 251;
in Belgium, 262; in Denmark
251, 266; in Europe
generally, 248, 250–52; in
Germany, 250, 251, 252, 321;

in Hungary, 251, 297; in
Italy, 251, 313; in Portugal,
290; in Russia, 251, 278; in
Serbia, 308; in Spain 250,
251, 288; in Switzerland, 265
Parma, 119, 120, 150, 184, 187,
205, 208, 217
Parnell, Charles, 258–60
Pašić, Nicholas, 43, 308, 309
Paul I, Czar of Russia, 37, 129
Pedro, King of Portugal,
164–66
Peter Karageorgević, King of
Serbia, 244, 309
Peterloo Massacre in United
Kingdom (August 16, 1819),
53, 115, 144
Phanariot Greeks, 134–36
Philhellenism, 110–11, 136
Philike Hetairia, 107, 134–35
Pica law of 1863 in Italy,
219
Piedmont. See Sardinia
Pius VII (Pope), 121
Pius IX (Pope), 152, 183–84, 205,
251, 254
Plehve, V. K., 43, 73, 282, 349
Plug Plug riots in United
Kingdom (1842), 172, 175
Poland, 98, 99, 240, 252, 284,
285; see also Poles; Russian
Poland
Poles: in Austria, 131, 181; in Ger-
many, 131, 171, 181, 221, 321,
325; see also Poland,
Russian Poland
Political banquets, as means of
evading restrictions on
assembly and association in
nineteenth–century Europe:
in France 51, 183; in
Germany, 149; in Italy, 184;
in Russia, 51, 282
Political funerals, as means of
evading restrictions on
assembly and associations in
nineteenth–century Europe:
in Bohemia, 53, 207; in
France, 53–54, 207, 222,
272; in Germany, 53; in

Hungary, 53, 207; in Ireland,
229, 230; in Italy, 207; in
Lombardy, 184; in Russia, 53;
in Russian Poland, 227; in
Spain, 53; in United
Kingdom, 53; techniques
used, 53–54
Political prisoners in nineteenth–
century Europe, 80–88;
books written by, 80, 87;
conditions of, 80–81, 86–87;
escapes from jail of, 85; in
France, 80; in Russia, 80; in
United Kingdom, 80; in
Spain, 81; in Two Sicilies, 81;
see also Arrests, trials and
punishments of political
dissidents in
nineteenth–century Europe
Political repression, definition
of, xii–xiii
Political repression in nineteenth–
century Europe: as affected
by regional differentiation
of Europe, 244–48, 256–57,
276–78, 311–12, 344–45, 347;
as contemporary political
issue, 333, 338–40; as factor
in explaining exclusion of
masses from political
power, 333, 334, 337–38; as
factor in explaining neglect
of social reforms, 333–35; as
factor in explaining resort
to violence by opposition
groups, 333; as factor in
international relations,
339–40; as factor in survival
of regimes, 340; as factor in
weakening opposition
movements, 335, 337–38; as
issue in revolutionary
outbreaks, 338–39; as
shaping attitudes of elites
and oppositions, 340–43;
explanation for cyclical
peaks and valleys of, 344–45;
in comparison with
contemporary third world,
xii, xv, 350–51; long–term

diminishing of and explanations for, 345–50; resistance to, 339; trends concerning increases and decreases of, 344–51

Population and population growth in nineteenth–century Europe, 94–95, 170, 194, 245

Portugal in the nineteenth century: economic and social background 1815–70, 101, 195, 196; economic and social background, 1870–1914, 241, 248; overall significance of political repression in, 333, 334–35, 340, 343; political developments, 1815–30, 102, 105, 109, 125–28; political developments, 1830–49, 164–66, 178–79; political developments, 1850–70, 211–12, 229, 232; political developments, 1870–1914, 248, 252, 254, 277, 287, 289–94, 304

Prague, 30, 55, 187, 188, 189, 191, 202, 225, 327, 328, 329, 330

Press and Aliens Conclusum in Switzerland (1823), 141

Press, regulation and repression of, in nineteenth–century Europe: "Aesopian language" used to evade, 43–44; as a political issue 36, 102, 107, 199, 338–40; caution money requirements, 35, 41; clandestine publishing to evade, 43, 46; conservatives' attitudes towards, 34, 36; evasion of, by technicalities, 44–46; impact of, on journalists and newspapers, 37, 39–43, 337–38; in 1815, 105; in 1850–1870, 199; in Austria, 35–43, 105, 200, 223, 225, 326, 327; in Baden, 148, 182; in Bavaria, 148–49; in Balkans, 276; in Belgium, 35, 51, 162, 211; in Bohemia–Moravia, 44, 202, 225, 328, 329; in Cracow, 145; in Croatia, 223, 299, 320; in Denmark, 35, 105, 163–64, 171, 181, 210, 266, 267; in Finland, 282; in France, 25, 34, 35–42, 45–46, 111, 112, 113, 147, 148, 200, 203, 204, 222, 252, 257, 270, 271; in Germany, 34–39, 41, 45–46, 105, 123, 148, 149, 150, 200, 201, 321, 324; in Greece, 235–36, 276, 309, 310; in Hapsburg Empire, 188, 223; in Hungary, 35, 37, 39, 41, 223, 225, 236, 298, 299; in Italy, 35, 200; in Ireland, 236; in Lombardy–Venetia, 54–55, 188; in Netherlands, 35, 41–42, 105, 140, 177, 211, 216; in Norway, 35, 37, 209; in Papal States, 103, 183, 188; in Portugal, 35, 178, 179, 211, 292, 293; in Prussia, 35, 38, 171; in Rumania, 35, 234; in Russia, 35, 37–41, 105, 129, 130, 154, 199, 200, 206, 216, 226, 228, 276, 279, 283, 284, 286; in Russian Poland, 131; in Sardinia, 35, 184, 206; in Serbia, 35, 44, 46, 236, 276, 307, 308, 309; in Spain, 35–38, 40–41, 105, 126, 164, 212, 213, 233, 252, 291, 295, 297; in Sweden, 35, 37, 44, 88, 105, 142, 162, 174, 209, 268; in Switzerland, 35, 141, 160, 211, 265; in Tuscany, 184, 205; in United Kingdom, 35–37, 41–42, 46–47, 114, 116, 154, 160, 199, 208; liberals' attitudes towards, 36, 107; licensing requirements to effect, 36–38; press taxes to effect, 35, 41, 45–46; prior censorship as technique to implement, 35–8;

prosecutions and arrests of journalists to implement, 39; protests against, 36, 40; punitive (post–publication) censorship as technique to implement, 37–39; requirement to name "responsible editor" as technique to implement, 45; resistance to and evasion of, 43–47, 173, 207; variety and nature of regulations to implement, 37, 39–40, 45

Proudhon, Pierre–Joseph, 43, 86, 172

Prussia in the nineteenth century: economic and social background, 1815–1914, 96, 97, 194, 198, 242; political developments, 1815–30, 102, 103, 109, 110, 120, 122, 123–24, 141; political developments, 1830–46, 145, 149, 150, 170–72; political developments, 1846–9, 180, 182; political developments, 1850–69, 201, 209, 215, 216, 218, 220–22, 224; political developments, 1870–1914, 248–49, 320, 321, 322, 324, 328

Prussian Silesia, 16, 65, 67, 172, 99, 101, 172

Purges of governmental employees for political reasons in nineteenth–century Europe: in Bulgaria, 306; in France, 112, 204, 271; in Greece, 236; in Portugal, 292; in Prussia, 221; in Serbia, 214; in Spain, 288; in Two Sicilies, 124; see also Firings of teachers for political reasons in nineteenth–century Europe

Quinet, Edgar, 75–77, 183

Repeal movement in Ireland, 175–76, 208

Revolutions of 1820, 21, 81, 247; in Danubian Principalities, 134–35; in Greece, 110,

134–136; in Iberia, 113, 126–27, 338; in Italy, 109, 112, 122, 338; in Spain, 122

Revolutions of 1830, 8, 34, 81, 144–70, 247, 344; in Belgium, 144–45, 161–62, 339; in France, 113, 144–48, 161, 338; in Germany, 144–45, 148–49, 338; in Iberia, 144, 156, 164; in Italy, 144–45, 149–51, 339; in Russian Poland, 144–45, 148–49, 152–54, 339–40; in Scandinavia, 156, 162–64; in Switzerland, 141, 144, 156, 160–61, 338; in United Kingdom, 144, 156–58

Revolutions of 1848, 48, 50–51, 75, 81, 96, 102, 180–85, 247, 347; arrests and jailings as a result of, 190–91; causes of, 180–86; economic crisis of 1845–7 leading to, 180; celebration of civil liberties gains during, 188; civil liberties gains made during, 187–8; executions following, 190–91; expansion of suffrage during, 187–88; freeing of political prisoners during, 188; growth of press during, 188; growth of political activity during, 188; growth of trade unions during, 188; in Austria, 188, 339; in Baden, 190; in Bavaria, 190; in Belgium, 187, 192; in Danubian Principalities, 186, 187, 188, 190, 192; in Denmark, 187, 188, 192; in France, 186, 187, 188, 189, 190, 192, 339; in Germany, 186, 187, 188, 189, 190, 191, 339; in Greece, 186; in Habsburg Empire, 186, 187, 188, 189, 190, 191, 192, 339; in Hungary, 186, 187, 188, 190, 191; in Ireland, 186; in Italy, 186, 187, 188, 190, 339; in Lombardy–Venetia, 187, 190; in Modena, 187; in

the Netherlands, 187, 188,
192; in Parma, 187; in
Prussia, 187, 188, 190, 192,
339; in Sardinia, 188, 189,
192; in Saxony, 190; in Spain,
186; in Switzerland, 187, 192;
in Two Sicilies, 190; in
United Kingdom, 186;
liberalization of assembly
and association restrictions
during, 188; liberalization of
constitutions during, 187;
liberalization of press
restrictions during, 188;
long-term gains made by,
191–92; reasons for failure
of, 191; suppression of, 190–91
Rochefort, Henri, 88, 222
Rome, 150, 183, 188, 205, 217,
219–20, 312
Rudinì, Antonio di, 317–18
Rull, Juan, 72, 295
Rumania in the nineteenth
century: economic and
social background, 1850–1914,
195, 196, 198, 240, 241;
overall impact of political
repression in, 333, 334–35,
340, 343; political
developments, 1859–70, 216,
217, 229, 233–35; political
developments, 1870–1914,
251, 254, 255, 256, 276, 277,
304–305; see also Danubian
Principalities (for material
concerning events before
1859)
Rural unrest and uprisings in
nineteenth-century Europe:
in Balkans, 99, 132, 303–04;
in Bulgaria, 173, 214, 306–07;
in Croatia, 298; in Denmark,
173; in Greece, 311; in
Habsburg Empire, 99, 173,
181; in Hungary, 299–300, 301;
in Ireland, 99, 117, 159, 258,
260; in Italy, 99; in Norway,
142, 162–63; in Portugal,
293–94; in Rumania, xii, 304;
in Russia, 99, 172–73, 207,

226, 280–81, 283; in Sicily,
184; in Spain, 99, 213, 290,
294, 295; in United
Kingdom, 157–58, 173; see
also Agriculture and rural
conditions in
nineteenth-century Europe
Russia in the nineteenth century:
economic and social
background, 1815–50, 93, 97,
98, 99, 101; economic and
social background, 1850–70,
193, 196, 197, 198, 199;
economic and social
background, 1870–1914, 240,
241, 242, 243, 244, 245;
overall significance of
political repression in, 333,
334, 335, 338, 340–41, 343;
political developments,
1815–30, 103, 109, 110, 122,
128–32, 133, 136, 141; political
developments, 1830–49, 141,
145, 167, 168, 169, 170,
172–73, 176, 181; political
developments, 1850–69, 200,
206, 207, 217, 218, 225–28;
political developments,
1870–1914, 247, 248, 251, 252,
253, 255, 256, 272, 276, 277,
278–87
Russian Poland, 130, 131–32, 152–
53, 225–27, 248, 281–82, 283
Russian revolution of 1905, 50–51,
78, 282–86, 324
Russo–Turkish War of 1877–8,
304–305, 328
Sagasta, Praxedes Mateo, 288,
291
St. Petersburg, 30–33, 45, 64–67,
80, 99, 129, 130, 153, 196,
226, 242, 245, 279, 280, 282,
283, 284, 285, 286, 287
Saldanha, Duke of, 179, 211, 212
Salisbury, Marquis of, 8, 260
Sanfedesti. See Centurions
Sardinia (Piedmont) in the
nineteenth century:
political developments,
1815–40, 82–83, 109, 121, 122,

124, 151, 161; political
developments, 1840–60, 182,
185, 188, 189, 205–207, 215,
217, 222, 234
Saxe-Weimar, 120, 122
Saxony, 94, 99, 102, 148, 150,
182, 187, 190, 201, 324, 342
Scandinavia, 93, 98, 109, 193,
245, 247, 257; overall
impact of political
repression in the
nineteenth–century, 333,
336, 341, 343, 344; see also
Denmark, Norway, Sweden
Schleswig–Holstein, 163, 175,
181, 209–10, 221, 231
Secret societies in nineteenth-
century Europe: in France,
113; in Ireland, 117; in
Portugal, 107, 126, 292; in
Russia, 130; in Spain, 107,
126; see also Carbonari,
Italian; Philike Hetairia
Secret police in nineteenth-
century Europe: tactics
used by, 69–74; in Austria,
69–71, 137, 200, 202; in
France, 200; in Germany,
200; in Italy, 124, 152, 200; in
Modena, 205; in Russia, 69,
71–74, 154, 200; in Spain, 126;
in Sweden, 142; see also
Agents provocateurs in
nineteenth–century Europe;
Mail, surveillance of the, in
nineteenth–century Europe
September Laws in France (1835),
148
Serbia in the nineteenth
century: economic and
social background, 91, 93,
193, 195, 241, 244; overall
impact of political
repression upon, 333, 334,
340; political developments,
1815–50, 110, 132–34, 136, 156,
166–68, 177; political
developments, 1850–70,
214–15, 216, 229, 233, 236–37;
political developments,

1870–1914, 241, 251, 276, 277,
303, 304, 307–309
Serfdom in nineteenth–century
Europe, 97–99; in Austria,
97; in Hungary, 197; in
Poland, 98; in Russia, 97–98,
196
Siberia, 80, 85, 87, 217, 227, 278,
284, 285
Sicily, 93, 97, 121, 185, 217, 219,
313, 316, 319; see also Two
Sicilies
Six Acts in Germany (1832), 149
Six Acts in United Kingdom
(1819), 115
Social reform in nineteenth-
century Europe: and
lessened working–class
militancy, 345–48; and
relationship to suffrage
reform, 334–336; as growing
trend after 1870, 248,
252–54, 256; as result of
fear of revolution, 346; as
tactic to dampen
working–class unrest,
345–48; in Austria, 311, 327;
in Belgium, 263; in France,
275; in Germany, 311, 323; in
Greece, 311; in Ireland, 259,
261; in Italy, 311, 315; in
Netherlands, 263; in
northwestern Europe,
256–57; in Spain, 296
Socialists in nineteenth-
century Europe: 241, 247,
248, 251, 254, 257; and
repression of freedom of
assembly and association,
47, 48, 49, 50, 51, 52, 53;
and repression of freedom
of the press, 36, 39, 43, 45,
46; and suffrage
discrimination, 335, 338; in
Austria, 326, 327; in
Denmark, 257, 266; in
France, 270, 272; in
Germany, 12, 19, 46, 49,
238, 321–25; in Hungary,
299, 301–3; in Italy, 319–20;

in Netherlands, 257, 263; in
Russia, 282, 284, 285, 286;
in Sweden, 251, 268; see also
Anti-Socialist law in
Germany; International,
First; International, Second
Sonderbund War in Switzerland,
182-83
Spain in the nineteenth century:
economic and social back-
ground, 1815-50, 93, 98, 99,
101; economic and social
background, 1850-70, 193,
195, 196; economic and social
background, 240, 241, 245;
overall impact of political
repression in, 333, 334-35,
340, 343; political
developments, 1815-30, 102,
105, 106, 109, 125-28;
political developments,
1830-49, 156, 164-66, 172,
178-79, 186, 189; political
developments, 1850-69,
211-13, 216, 228, 229, 232-33;
political developments,
1870-1914, 247, 250, 251, 276,
277, 287-91, 294-97
Stockholm, 28, 65, 92, 162, 185,
196
Stolypin, Peter, 73, 285, 286
Strikes, in nineteenth-century
Europe: in 1848, 189; in 1860s,
238; in 1870-1, 250; in
Austria, 57, 238; in Belgium,
60-61, 68, 238, 239; in
Bohemia-Moravia, 162; in
Bulgaria, 60; in Denmark,
266; in France, 57, 58, 60,
61, 62, 68, 146, 147, 172, 270,
275-76; in Germany, 57, 61,
62, 68, 189, 238; in Greece,
61, 311; in Hungary, 60,
300-01; in Italy, 60, 61, 62,
68, 238, 319-20; in
Netherlands, 238, 264; in
Portugal, 61-62, 292-94; in
Prussia, 172; in Russia, 52,
57, 67, 226, 280-82, 283,
286, 287; in Spain, 60, 62,

172, 238, 290, 291, 295; in
Sweden, 59, 61, 267; in
United Kingdom, 61, 62, 115,
159, 172, 261; see also Trade
unions and strikes,
repression and regulation of
in nineteenth-century Europe
Suffrage discrimination in nineteenth-century Europe:
against women, 6; as factor
in explaining exclusion of
masses from power and
neglect of social reform,
334-36; as factor in slowing
growth of working-class
political movements; class
voting systems, 7, 10-13,
31-33; conservative support
for, 3, 5-8; electoral
corruption and fraud, 19-24;
electoral coups d'état,
24-25; for local elections,
29-33; for lower legislative
chambers, 8-25; for upper
legislative chambers, 25-29;
gerrymandering, 18-19, 22;
high minimum age
requirements for voting,
16-17; high age requirements
to serve in legislatures,
17-18, 28; in 1815, 105; in
1850-70 period, 195, 199; in
Austria, 4-6, 11-12, 15, 18-20,
24-25, 26, 29, 32-33, 188,
218, 223, 224, 252, 253, 256,
312, 325, 327, 328, 336; in
Baden, 123, 324; in Balkans,
20, 25, 31, 233, 303, 336; in
Bavaria, 123, 324; in
Belgium, 4-6, 8, 13, 15-17,
26-31, 161-62, 187, 210, 232,
252, 253; in Bulgaria, 4, 20,
22, 24-25, 26, 29, 306, 307,
334; in Croatia, 24-25, 225,
299, 302; in Danubian
Principalities, 215; in
Denmark, 4, 15-17, 25,
26-28, 30-33, 163, 188, 209,
228, 231, 256, 267; in
Finland, 4, 6, 11-13, 15, 25,

26, 256, 284, 286; in France, 4, 8, 11, 13, 15, 17–18, 20, 24–25, 26–28, 105, 111, 112, 113, 145, 146, 174, 187, 203, 204, 252, 256, 271; in Germany, 4, 12, 16–19, 26, 31–33, 105, 218, 320, 324; in Greece, 4, 18, 20, 22, 25, 26, 29–31, 178, 214, 236, 309; in Hamburg, 187, 324; in Hungary, 4, 6, 9–10, 13, 15–24, 26, 31, 33, 225, 252, 258, 297, 298, 301, 302, 336; in Iberia, 20, 25, 31, 336; in Ireland, 15, 119; in Italy, 4, 6, 8–9, 13, 16–18, 20, 22–25, 26, 29–31, 218, 252, 256, 312, 314–16, 319; in Low Countries, 20, 25, 257, 262, 336; in Mecklenburg, 324; in Nassau, 18; in Netherlands, 5, 6, 9, 13, 15–18, 25, 26, 29–31, 210, 232, 252, 253, 263–64; in Norway, 5, 6, 9, 15–18, 26, 29–31, 104, 105, 252, 269, 270; in Portugal, 4, 13, 15, 18, 20, 22, 24–25, 26, 29, 31, 127, 166, 178, 212, 252, 290, 292, 294, 334; in Prussia, 7, 11–12, 15–16, 20, 24–25, 31–33, 188, 201, 218, 220, 222, 312, 320, 324; in Rumania, 5, 11–13, 15–16, 18, 20, 22, 24–25, 26–29, 31, 234, 235, 304, 334; in Russian Poland, 131; in Russia, 5, 6, 7, 10–13, 15–16, 20, 24–25, 26, 29, 31–33, 228, 242, 256, 278, 280, 283, 285, 336; in Sardinia (Piedmont), 25, 28, 188, 206; in Saxony, 25, 324; in Scandinavia, 18, 20, 25; in Serbia, 5, 15–18, 20, 22, 24–25, 237, 309, 334; in Spain, 5, 6, 9, 13–4, 16–18, 20–22, 24–25, 26, 30–31, 126, 165, 166, 179, 212, 213, 233, 252, 253, 288; in Sweden, 5, 6, 11–13, 15–18, 26–28, 30–31, 105, 209, 225, 231, 267, 268,

269; in Switzerland, 4, 15, 20, 26, 29, 103, 105, 140–41, 161, 211, 256; in United Kingdom, 4, 6, 10–11, 13, 15–20, 25, 26, 28–29, 101, 105, 158, 159, 200, 208, 229, 252, 258; in United Netherlands, 105; in Württemberg, 25, 324; indirect voting, 13, 15; lack of payment for legislators, 17, 28; liberals' views towards, 3, 6; open balloting, 15–16, 258; plural voting systems, 10–11, 27–28, 31; ; restrictions on eligibility of service, 17–18, 28; statistical data concerning, 4–5, 195, 240; wealth restrictions to implement, 3–13, 26–27, 31–33; see also Legislative dissolutions in nineteenth-century Europe; Suffrage reform, agitation for in nineteenth-century Europe

Suffrage reform, agitation for, in nineteenth-century Europe: 247, 338–40; in Austria, 254, 255, 312, 327, 329, 338; in Belgium, 177, 254, 262–64; 338; in Denmark, 265–67; in France, 174, 183; in Germany, 254, 255, 324, 338; in Hungary, 300, 302, 338; in Italy, 338; in Norway, 209; in Netherlands, 254, 262–64, 338; in Portugal, 165; in Russia, 254, 281, 282–83, 338; in Spain, 165; in Sweden, 174, 231, 254, 265, 267–68, 338; in Switzerland, 160, 175; in United Kingdom, 114–15, 119, 157–60, 174–75, 185–86, 229; see also Suffrage discrimination in nineteenth-century Europe

Sweden in the nineteenth century: economic and

social background, 1815–50, 94, 98, 101; economic and social background, 1850–70, 195, 196, 197, 198, 199; economic and social background, 1870–1914, 241, 242; overall significance of political repression in, 333, 334, 335, 338, 343; political background, 1815–50, 103, 104, 132, 142, 156, 162, 174; political background, 1850–1869, 209, 216, 228, 231; political background, 1870–1914, 265–66, 267–70

"Swing riots" in United Kingdom (1830–31), 157–58

Switzerland in the nineteenth century: economic and social background, 1815–50, 93, 98, 100, 101; economic and social background, 1850–1914, 193, 194, 195, 198, 241, 244; overall impact of political repression in, 333, 338, 341, 343; political developments, 1815–30, 103, 105, 107, 109, 110, 140–41; political developments, 1830–49, 151, 156, 160–61, 175, 182–83, 184, 187; political developments, 1850–70, 211, 228, 232; political developments, 1870–1914, 247, 252, 255, 264–65, 272

Taaffe, Count Edward von, 326, 328

Ten Articles in Germany (1832), 149

Terrorism in nineteenth-century Europe: in 1880s, 252; in 1890s, 252; in Austria, 326; in France, 272, 273–74; in Italy, 314; in Portugal, 293; in Russia, 279, 282, 285; in Russian Poland, 280; in Spain, 290, 294, 295

Thiers, Adolph, 243, 249, 271

Thorbecke, Jan Rudolf, 171, 177, 210, 232

Thrane, Marcus, 209

Timok Rebellion in Serbia (1883), 308

Tisza, István, 300, 301, 303

Tisza, Kálmán, 298, 299, 300

"Tithe War" (1830–3) in Ireland, 156–57

"Tolpuddle martyrs" in United Kingdom, 159

Toulouse, 30, 57–58, 62

Trade, in nineteenth-century Europe, 93, 170

Trade unions, in nineteenth-century Europe, 55–63, 188, 237–39, 247, 254, 257; see also International, First; International, Second; Strikes in nineteenth-century Europe; Trade unions and strikes, repression and regulation of, in nineteenth-century Europe

Trade unions and strikes, repression and regulation of, in nineteenth-century Europe, 55–63, 105, 217, 238; as political issue, 55, 57, 247; impact of, 62, 337; in Austria, 55–56, 58, 200, 238, 239, 312, 326; in Balkans, 56; in Bulgaria, 307; in Belgium, 56–58, 60, 62, 200, 229, 238; in Denmark, 56, 60, 63, 266; in France, 55–58, 61–63, 146, 147, 189, 200, 204, 222, 238, 239, 252, 270, 275–76, 337; in Germany, 55–56, 58–63, 189, 200, 238, 312, 324, 337; in Greece, 56, 60, 311; in Hungary, 55–56, 58, 276, 299, 300, 301; in Italy, 55–56, 62, 312, 314, 315, 316, 319, 337; in Low Countries, 55, 211; in Netherlands, 56–58, 239, 264; in Norway, 56, 209; in Portugal, 55–57, 60, 293–94; in Prussia, 60; in Russia, 55–57, 60, 62–63, 278, 282, 283, 284, 286, 337; in Saxony, 58; in

Scandinavia, 55; in Spain, 55–58, 60, 179, 200, 213, 233, 238, 252, 290, 291, 294, 295, 296, 297; in Sweden, 56, 58, 60, 267; in Switzerland, 55–56, 265; in Two Sicilies, 205; in United Kingdom, 55–56, 58, 61, 63, 114, 116, 159, 199, 200, 238, 258, 260; resistance to, 62–3; techniques used to implement, 55–63; see also Strikes, in nineteenth–century Europe

Transportation, in nineteenth–century Europe, 93, 170, 180, 194

Transylvania, 19, 155, 173, 202, 224

Travel, restrictions on, for political reasons in nineteenth–century Europe: in Austria, 154; in Germany, 150; in Russia, 154, 206, 216

Trepov, Feodor, 85, 279

Trials, of political dissidents in nineteenth–century Europe. See Arrests, trials and punishments of political dissidents in nineteenth–century Europe

Tricoupis, Charilaos, 88, 309–310

Trotsky, Leon, 85, 87

Turati, Filippo, 317, 342

Turin, 65, 184, 189, 219

Turkey. See Ottoman Turkey

Tuscany, 119, 120, 151, 180, 184, 185, 200, 205, 217

Two Sicilies, Kingdom of the 109, 119, 120, 121, 122, 124, 152, 175, 184, 186, 205–206, 208, 217, 218; see also Sicily

United Kingdom of Great Britain and Ireland in the nineteenth century: economic and social background, 1815–50, 91, 93, 94, 95, 98, 100; economic and social background, 1850–70, 193, 194, 195, 196, 197, 198, 199; economic and

social background, 1870–1914, 240, 241, 244, 245; overall impact of political repression in, 333, 334, 336, 341, 343; political developments, 1815–30, 103, 104, 105, 106, 107, 109, 110, 113–19, 122, 136; political developments, 1830–49, 151, 156–60, 165, 167, 172–75, 178, 179, 183; political developments, 1850–70, 200, 207, 208, 211, 216, 228, 229–30; political developments, 1870–1914, 247, 251, 252, 254, 255, 256, 257–62; see also Ireland

United Netherlands, 103, 139–40

Upper classes in nineteenth–century Europe: coalition with middle classes, 193, 197–99, 216, 240, 242; conditions of, 240, 242; see also Nobility, European in the nineteenth century

Uprisings and insurrections in nineteenth–century Europe: in Austrian Galicia, 181; in France (1816) 112, (1817) 112, (1821–22) 113, (1831) 144–47, (1832) 147, (1834) 147, (1836, 1840) 148, (1849) 203, (1851) 203; in Germany (1833) 149; in Greece (1830–1) 167, (1834, 1836, 1838–9) 168, (1843) 177, (1862) 236; in Hungary (1831) 154; in Ireland (1813–16) 116–17, (1823) 117, (1867) 230; in Italy (1841, 1843, 1844, 1845) 175, (1861, 1866) 218–19, (1874) 313, (1877) 314;; in Milan (1853) 207; in Papal States (1817) 121; in Piedmont (1833, 1834) 151; in Portugal (1817) 126, (1823) 127, (1826) 127, (1831) 164, (1834) 164, (1836) 166, (1846) 178–79, (1910) 293; in Russia (1825) 130–31; in Russian Poland

(1863) 53, 221, 224, 327; in
Rumania (1865, 1866) 235; in
Serbia (1800–15) 132–33, (1821,
1825) 133, (1842) 177, (1844)
177; in Spain (1814, 1815, 1816,
1817) 126, (1822–23) 127,
(1830–32) 164, (1836) 166,
(1840) 166, (1841, 1842, 1843)
172, 179, (1854) 212, (1857,
1861) 213, (1865–6) 232–33,
(1868–1875) 50; 229, 233, 258,
339, (1909) 295–96, (1911) 297;
in Two Sicilies (1828) 124,
(1847) 184; in Switzerland
(1845–47) 182; in United
Kingdom (1817) 115, (1820) 116,
(1839) 160, (1840) 160; see
also Revolutions of 1820;
Revolutions of 1830;
Revolutions of 1848; Rural
unrest and uprisings in
nineteenth–century Europe;
Russian Revolution of 1905
Urbanization, and urban conditions, in nineteenth–century
Europe, 17, 91–92, 95, 99–100,
170, 194–95, 196, 241, 243,
245–47, 254, 255
Venetia, 217, 219
Venice, 54, 119, 184, 187, 188
Venizelos, Eleutherios, 311, 347
Victor Emmanuel I, King of
Sardinia, 121
Victor Emmanuel II, King of
Sardinia and Italy, 25, 207,
217, 218, 233, 314
Victoria, Queen of England,
82–83, 117
Vienna, 23, 30–33, 57, 65, 66, 70
99, 180, 181, 187, 188, 189, 191,
194, 202, 245, 253, 327, 329
Violence in nineteenth-
century Europe. See
Assassinations and
assassination plots in
nineteenth–century Europe;
Deaths of protesters and
rebels resulting from
clashes with authorities in
nineteenth–century Europe;

Executions of political
dissidents and rebels in
nineteenth–century Europe;
Rural unrest and uprisings in
nineteenth–century Europe;
Uprisings and insurrections
in nineteenth–century Europe
Vladimeriscu, Tudor, 135
Voting in nineteenth–century
Europe. See Suffrage
discrimination in
nineteenth–century Europe
Wachensturm uprising in
Germany, 1833, 149, 171
Warsaw, 152, 227, 280, 281,
284, 285, 292
Wartburg Castle meeting of
1819 in Germany, 122
Wellington, Duke of, 119, 157,
287
Wesselényi, Baron Miklos, 155,
176
Westphalen, Count Ferdinand
von, 201, 216
William I, King of Prussia and
Germany, 25, 216, 220, 322
William II, King of Prussia and
Germany, 75, 78, 87, 323,
325, 346
William I, King of the Nether-
lands, 103, 139–40, 142, 162,
170
William II, King of the Nether-
lands, 177, 210
William III, King of the
Netherlands, 232, 263
Witte, Sergei, 243, 245, 281
Working classes and working-
class organizations in
nineteenth–century Europe.
See Trade unions in
nineteenth–century Europe;
Agriculture and rural
conditions in nineteenth–
century Europe;
Urbanization and urban
conditions in nineteenth–
century Europe
Württemberg, 103, 123, 148, 149,
150, 182, 200, 201, 216, 220,

324, 342
Zasulich, Vera, 85, 279
Zurich, 140–41, 150, 160, 161,
    182, 232, 265

## ABOUT THE AUTHOR

ROBERT JUSTIN GOLDSTEIN is associate professor of political science at Oakland University, Rochester, Michigan. He was an undergraduate at the University of Illinois (Champaign-Urbana) and received the master's and Ph.D. degrees from the University of Chicago. He previously taught at San Diego State University. His first book, Political Repression in Modern America: From 1870 to the Present (Boston: Schenkman / G. K. Hall), was published in 1978. Professor Goldstein's work has appeared in a wide variety of scholarly and journalistic publications, including American Studies, Columbia Human Rights Law Review, Comparative Social Research, Journalism Monographs, The Nation, and The Progressive.